D1217823

LIVES IN TRANSIT
A Collection of Recent
Russian Women's Writing

Edited by Helena Goscilo

Ardis

Ardis Publishers
15 Monarch Bay Plaza, #394
Dana Point, CA 92629

Library of Congress Cataloging in Publication Data

Lives in transit : a collection of recent Russian women's writing /
  edited by Helena Goscilo.
      p.   cm.
  ISBN 0-87501-100-4 (alk. paper) : ISBN 679-76297-3
  (pbk. : alk. paper) :
  1. Russian literature—Women authors—Translations into English.
  2. Russian literature—20th century—Translations into English.
  I. Goscilo, Helena, 1945-
  PG3213.L58   1995
  891.708'09287–dc20   93-22986
                                                                CIP

To Isis,

my favorite Siberian—
ultimate snow queen,
connoisseur of beer,
source of intense joy

CONTENTS

Preface

When still only a gleam in my anthologizing eye, this collection was envisioned as a complement to and "update of" *Balancing Acts* (Indiana UP, 1989; Dell, 1991). Intent on introducing previously untranslated or little-known women writers to Western readers, I earmarked for inclusion names chiefly from among the younger generation— Svetlana Vasilenko, Irina Polianskaia, Valeria Narbikova. It rapidly grew clear, however, that among older, established writers a sea change of sorts had occurred during glasnost: a few had branched out in unexpected thematic directions (e.g., Viktoria Tokareva) or had modulated from implication to explicitness (e.g., Galina Shcherbakova), so that their more recent fiction reflected a new stage in their literary development. Furthermore, a number of texts that might not instantly fire readers' admiration on stylistic grounds impressed me as having cultural value by virtue of the dialogue they opened up with earlier statements of and solutions to gendered dilemmas (notably, Liubov' Iunina's "Woman in a One-Room Apartment" as a riposte to Natalia Baranskaia's "Kiss"). The additional element of serendipity finally, and inevitably, led me to reconceive the shape of the project: it now spans several generations of writers, consists of texts primarily from the 1980s (the pieces by Marina Tsvetaeva and Iunina constitute the two exceptions), and focuses on what the West deems typically "women's" concerns.

A modest number of lyrics supplement the fiction for the sake of pleasure and pragmatism: some of the best Russian poetry today is authored by women (hence the pleasure), and since so little of it becomes transformed into English, the opportunity to acquaint readers of contemporary prose by Russian women with a sampling of their verses proved irresistible (here the pragmatism). Of the six poets represented in this volume, Elena Ignatova and Zoia Ezrokhi make their English-version debut by the rhyming grace of Walter Arndt.

As always, the anthology expanded in the process of assembly, which partially, if paradoxically, explains why several writers tentatively slated for inclusion at some stage of the project ultimately disappeared from it: Nina Gorlanova, Nina Iskrenko, Valeria Narbikova, Irina Povolotskaia, Elena Tarasova. Since other anthologies of Russian women's writing in translation reportedly being compiled right now doubtless will take these authors into account, their omission here will not prove critical in the long run.

***

To all of the participants in this project—the authors of the original texts, the translators, and the Ardis staff—I extend gratitude, as well as rueful apologies for the sundry delays occasioned in part by *my* life in transit. Special thanks go to those translators who grappled stoically with brutally complex texts and discovered ingenious solutions to seemingly insurmountable problems and conundrums, notably Walter Arndt, Helen Burlingame, and Elisabeth Jezierski. To Mark Altshuller I am indebted on a number of fronts: for cheerfully placing his linguistic expertise at my disposal, for drawing my attention to Alla Kalinina's fiction, and for his readiness—out of friendship and collegiality—to read and discuss texts that are fundamentally alien to his temperament and convictions.

In the initial stages of editing, Alexander Zholkovsky bailed me out of more than one tricky spot, combining invaluable disquisitions on nuances of contemporary Russian with vivid illustrations of Russian sexism. Brittain Smith helped with xeroxing and other practical matters during a research trip to Russia (1990) undertaken to interview some of the writers represented in the collection. As usual, Vladimir Padunov and Nancy Condee contributed in numerous ways that challenge definition. And Bozenna Goscilo's impeccable sense of style saved me from my most lurid instincts.

Finally, I am happy to acknowledge two institutions whose material support has underwritten work on various aspects of this collection: (1) IREX, which awarded me three short-term research grants in 1988, 1990, and 1992, during which I conducted interviews in Moscow and St. Petersburg with most of the writers included in this volume; and (2) the National Humanities Center in Research Triangle Park, NC, where, with the aid of a National Endowment to the Humanities fellowship, I spent 1990-91 as a resident scholar, enjoying the hospitality of the Center's staff.

***

Footnotes to the stories, provided so as to clarify references that may be puzzling to the hypothetical "general reader," have been confined to a minimum. Julie Barnes, John Beebe, Helen Burlingame, Arlene Forman, Isabel Heaman, Elisabeth Jezierski, and Teresa Polowy supplied most of the footnotes to their translations; I appended the rest.

Information about the authors contained in the appendix cites English titles in the main body of the text, but gives only Russian sources in the bibliography, since the overwhelming majority of the authors' works have not been translated and thus would be inaccessible to readers without Russian. By the same logic, documentation in Russian follows the Library of Congress system of transliteration, whereas elsewhere all Russian words, names, etc., are transliterated according to a simplified system for the sake of readability.

Introduction

Squaring the Circle

> "[T]here is the heterosexist, patriarchal culture, which has driven women into marriage and motherhood through every possible pressure—economic, religious, medical, and legal—and which has literally colonized the bodies of women."
>
> *Adrienne Rich*

> "The body [...] is a powerful symbolic form, a surface on which the central rules, hierarchies, and even metaphysical commitments of a culture are inscribed and thus reinforced through the concrete language of the body. [...] The body is [...] also a *practical*, direct locus of social control."
>
> *Susan R. Bordo*

I

For Russian women's culture, the 1990s ushered in the best of times—and the worst of times. Indeed, this decade may well be remembered not only for the disintegration of the Soviet empire, but also for the potential re-vision of gender in a country programatically and pragmatically committed to sexist ideology and praxis. Almost as revolutionary in its own way as the sudden proliferation of youthful Moscow millionaires, luxury goods, and neologisms from American business-speak is the emergence, especially in Moscow, of miscellaneous institutions, publications, and personalities that reflect an increased gender consciousness. Some may be called feminist, others "gender cognizant"; some engage in political activism, others watch from the sidelines; some hyperbolically credit a grasp of gender politics with the potential for resolving Russia's ills, whereas others, more cautiously, restrict themselves to scholarly investigations of what currently holds the West in intellectual thrall. Virtually all, however, register gender as a significant political, social, and cultural category, even if the majority acknowledge it more as an internationally recognized mode of cultural analysis than as a felt way of life—"something you write," not "something you do."

Gender awareness and incipient feminism (for to speak of full-blown feminism in Russia is, at best, premature)[1] not only have infiltrated segments of Russian society, but also have started becoming institutionalized on a small scale. Notably, the assiduous efforts of a group of feminists headed by Anastasia Posadskaia[2] culminated in the creation of Moscow's Gender Center under the aegis of the Academy of Sciences. Since its inception in April/May 1990 the Center has organized two massive meetings of the "Independent Women's Forum" in Dubna (1991 and 1992); it has brought out a number of feminist publications;[3] its members, especially Posadskaia, Olga Voronina, and Tatiana Klimenkova, regularly participate in gender conferences abroad,[4] as well as granting interviews to foreign journalists, contributing to anthologies of women's criticism,[5] and seeking foreign publishers for their own research.[6] The lesser known Moscow Women's Center called Gaia, registered in June 1990, has finally got off to a belated start with aid from the West. Meanwhile, in April 1993 the Petersburg Center for Gender Issues came into formal existence under the vigorous leadership of Olga Lipovskaia, editor of *Women's Reading* (Zhenskoe chtenie). Although the recently conceived Advanced Women's Courses at the Russian State Humanities University (RGGU) are still forging their academic profile, a few of its faculty members and students have succeeded in finding an international forum for their scholarship:[7] Olga Vainshtein has written on the semiotics of women's fashion;[8] Natalia Kamenetskaia and other pioneering women artists who collaborated on *Idioma*—the excellent Russian issue of *Heresies* devoted to Russian women's art (No. 26)—are the moving spirit behind the first in a planned seven-year series of international conferences titled "Signs of the Times" in Moscow (1993). The series is designed to reassess traditional critico-theoretical modes of thought in light of recent developments (including gender awareness) and to spotlight women's creativity within contemporary cultural production. Furthermore, Moscow University plans to introduce a women's studies course into its curriculum, while the First Legal University for Women, which opened in Moscow in 1993, offers Russian-American classes in the basics of accounting, advertising, and marketing. Even such hierarchical bastions of traditional Russian values as Pushkinskii Dom have orchestrated conferences specifically around women's literature (December 1993).[9]

The prospects in politics, however, continue to look bleak, for women's political involvement verges on nil, as does the meaningful representation of women's interests within existent structures. Yet the recent registration (September 1993) of Russia's first official women's political party, the Party of Political Equality, may augur well for the future. Partly because its spokeswoman, Elena Lukashenko, has been associated for some time with Alexander Rutskoi's retrograde group and, moreover, has maintained that the party will accept male members, journalists understandably doubt that the party will favor a radical feminist agenda. Nonetheless, the newly constituted party has declared provision for women's special needs as its overriding goal.[10] And the respectable showing of the electoral association called Women of Russia in the recent elections may spur female political leaders to agitate more boldly for women's rights in the future and Russian society to take their constituency more seriously.[11]

By contrast to the dearth of female input into politics, the plethora of women's nonacademic organizations that have materialized in the last few years is remarkable. The most vital of these groups include the club Transfiguration (Preobrazhenie), headed by Diana Medman, which has just published the first issue of its journal, *Transfiguration: A Russian Feminist Journal* (Preobrazhenie: Russkii feministicheskii zhurnal) and *What Women Want...* (Chego Khochet Zhenshchina, 1993), a volume of the top fifteen stories from the competition in women's short fiction sponsored by Transfiguration last year (1992); SAFO (Free Association of Feminist Organizations [Svobodnaia Assosiatsiia Feministskikh Organizatsii, 1990]), headed by Nastasia Filippova, which grew out of a combined conference-*cum*-art exhibition (1990); a group called NEZHDI (Independent Women's Democratic Initiative [Nezavisimaia Zhenskaia Demokraticheskaia Initsiativa]), which attempts to educate women in the politics of employment and gender discrimination.[12] The Moscow association "Missiia" formed in 1989 and set as its practical agenda the integration of women into business and politics—an admirable goal that so far has yielded scant results. And, finally, late 1992 saw the birth of Nadezhda Radio, a broadcast station run by women for women, supported by the Women's Union of

Russia (1991)[13] and financed by an anonymous commercial enterprise that, together with the radio station, has founded a joint-stock association.[14]

New women's magazines, journals, and newsletters, such as *Business Woman* (Delovaia zhenshchina, 1990), *Moscow Woman* (Moskvichka), *Elle*, and *Natali*, have established a readership sufficiently loyal to ensure their economic health. Similarly, sections of long-established magazines and journals, such as the weekly *Ogonek* and the elite Academy of Sciences publication *Social Sciences and the Contemporary World* (Obshchestvennye nauki i sovremennost'), now contain, respectively, a woman's section and serious investigations of gender-related problems.[15] In addition, some high quality scholarly journals, such as the *New Literary Review* (Novoe literaturnoe obozrenie), plan to devote entire issues to feminism, while *Foreign Literature* (Inostrannaia literatura, 1992) semi-regularly carries items on gender. The third volume of the literary magazine *Glas*, called "The Woman's View," contains exclusively female prose and poetry.[16]

These are merely samples of phenomena that only wishful thinking, however, could call widespread. Indeed, reports confirm that the overwhelming mass of Russians respond hostilely to these novelties.[17] In that sense Russian majority opinion accords with American, for despite two decades of feminist activity and scholarship in the United States, middle America in the mass does not take kindly to restructuring gender along de-misogynizing lines. Confusion joins the hostility, for the speed and indiscriminate nature of publishing in Russia today often lead to the juxtaposition of porn and titillating materials, on the one hand, with sober commentary on sexism and gender, on the other. Consequently, readers resistant to change and accustomed to the misogyny cemented into Russian thought or those incapable of differentiating between genres often mistake soft porn FOR feminism. Such a confusion comes easily to a society that for decades has equated the "liberated woman" (*emantsipantka*) with aggressively "shocking" and licentious behavior: incessant smoking and drinking, unbridled promiscuity, hatred of men, and/or "masculine behavior"—code words for suspected lesbianism. Despite the repeal in April 1993 of the law criminalizing homosexuality, the majority of Russians still stigmatize male homosexuality and lesbianism as dread perversions. The large-scale rejection of alternate sexual preference in a country of compulsory heterosexuality[18] manifested itself in the mixed reception, marred by abuse and occasional violence, of the gay/lesbian pride demonstrations ("Turn Red Squares into Pink Triangles") that took place in Moscow and Petersburg in June 1991, followed by the first International Gay and Lesbian Symposium and Film Festival (July 23-August 2, 1991). Yet the mere fact that such groups could convene and their participants not yield to threats and pressure is an encouraging index of Russia's increased, if far from extensive, tolerance for multiplicity.[19]

The cultural climate of the "new permissiveness" can absorb not only a brand of cultural production by women that formerly was anathemized, but also the overtly sexist obloquy by literary critics and journalists that it elicits. Under the unpredictable conditions of Russia's bumpy transition to a market economy, women's creativity gives every evidence of flourishing. In cinema the innovative tendencies are exemplified by the gynocentric films of Kira Muratova and Lana Gogoberidze; in art by the paintings and installations of Bella Matveeva, Maria Konstantinova, and Larisa Zvezdochetova; and in poetry and prose, by the texts of Zoia Ezrokhi, Nina Iskrenko, Liudmila Petrushevskaia, Svetlana Vasilenko, Nina Gorlanova, Marina Palei, Elena Tarasova, Valeria Narbikova, Larisa Vaneeva, and Nina Sadur.[20]

II

Today's complex economic and cultural circumstances in Russia have dislodged the insurmountable barriers to publication formerly confronting women. A number of related factors account for dramatic changes in the status not only of high culture in general (demotion) but also of women's writing in particular (promotion). A market approach to books, the desire or need to attract an audience of consumers able to purchase reading materials in foreign currency, and the recognition that extensive interaction with the West carries practical and intellectual benefits have tempered reflex Russian condescension toward women's literature. In visibility and recognition female authors have gained appreciable ground.

This year, Liudmila Ulitskaia and Valeria Narbikova originally numbered among the six finalists for the Booker award,[21] as did Liudmila Petrushevskaia last year. After a quarter-century of malign neglect, today Petrushevskaia is probably the most popular Russian writer (as well as the most *unpopular* among some), despite her unwavering focus on the female half of the world. Although Narbikova enjoyed only a brief honeymoon with enthusiasts of her pseudo-erotic prose, that enthusiasm indisputably stemmed from the titillation aroused by a *woman's* alleged frankness about sexual matters. And her ranking for the Booker suggests that among the "happy few" she still commands interest. Since money has no gender, some women have been able to take advantage of the opportunity, unprecedented in Soviet society, for authors to finance the production costs of their own books, e.g., Vaneeva's *Sorrow of the Flesh* (Skorb' ploti, 1990). And, finally, the enterprising experiment in non-Soviet collectivity by a post-Stalinist generation of women has resulted in three collections of contemporary women's writing: *The Woman Who Doesn't Remember Evil* (Ne pomniashchaia zla, 1990), compiled by Vaneeva, *The New Amazons* (Novye Amazonki, 1991), assembled by Vasilenko, and *Abstinents* (Abstinenki, 1991), edited by Olga Sokolova. Tellingly, the critical reception of this "new women's prose" recalls orthodox Soviet attacks against "dissident" writers in the heyday of stagnation. Against the background of the Soviet conventions that dictated the inelastic pseudo-norms for womanhood and women's fiction, these stories may well dismay and outrage the average Russian reader.

Anyone examining these texts closely can appreciate their shock value in the Soviet context, for they are premised on a revisionist concept of womanhood and a potentially subversive notion of female subjectivity. What earlier was repressed as unspeakable or unladylike now receives explicit, ironic, often emphatic articulation. What was taboo has become virtually *de rigueur*. To measure the distance traveled in a few short years one need only compare three texts that, *mutatis mutandis*, treat the same situational dilemma—a dilemma that briefly allured the Western media during the 1980s: the pitfalls and pleasures of a liaison between a middle-aged woman and a considerably younger man. The mere elaboration of such a *siuzhet* in the 1970s signaled the author's readiness to take risks; to posit an outcome or resolution that violated the straitlaced ideology of the Soviet family was unthinkable.

The earliest of the "older woman/younger man" scenarios came from Natalia Baranskaia, who during this era repeatedly if timorously broached substantial women's issues. While airing such problems as men's physical abuse ("A Lively Young Fox Terrier" [Molodoi, veselyi foks]), women's double burden (*A Week Like Any Other* [Nedelia kak nedelia]), and misogynistic stereotyping of single women ("Woman with an Umbrella" [Zhenshchina s zontikom]), Baranskaia shied away from pursuing the implications of these troubling symptoms to their logical conclusions. She preferred to deflect confrontation with the ubiquitous sexism of Russian society by ascribing women's wholly understandable outbursts of misery and desperation to their "irrational emotional nature." Unlike her Western readers, Baranskaia in *A Week Like Any Other* seems to share her heroine's bewilderment about what triggers her tearful attacks of frustration. In Baranskaia's "The Kiss" (wr. 1970s), which revived the immemorial older woman/young man quandary in contemporary literature, the highly educated linguist Nadezhda Mikhailovna argues herself out of temptation and categorically rejects the sexual/romantic option, escaping, significantly, into her socially sanctioned role of mother. Belonging to a less inhibited generation, Liubov Iunina in "A Woman in a One-Room Apartment" (pd. 1979) permits her equally intelligent, ambitious female protagonist to contemplate rebelling against the (internalized) social conventions that regulate women's sexual conduct. Whether Iunina's heroine succumbs to her youthful subordinate's pursuit remains an open question at the narrative's inconclusive end. By the late 1980s Liudmila Ulitskaia's cultured yet zestfully raunchy Gulia—presumably in her 50s or 60s—not only engineers the seduction of her close friend's son, but subsequently enjoys bragging about her adventure. Moreover, Ulitskaia invests the entire episode with earthy humor, unproblematically presenting Gulia's sexual energy as healthy appetite.

The authors' markedly differing attitudes regarding (1) women's sexuality, (2) appropriate behavior for women "of a certain age," and (3) the pressures to fulfill one's social and biological "obligations" via maternity reflect an evolution: from an acceptance of officially promoted, inhibitive family values, with their concomitant taboos (hyperbolized in the 1970s, during the publicized demographic crisis), to a more flexible perspective that accommodates multiple, individual options for women's sexual self-expression, including hedonism (a relatively recent development in Russian thinking).[22] Without claiming that Russia has taken a quantum leap from widespread prohibition to complete liberty in sexual matters, one can appreciate how the last decade has extended the boundaries of the permissible in its women's portrayal of their appetites— an extension charted by the three narratives under discussion. Ulitskaia's "Gulia," in fact, may be read as Russia's variant of Betty Friedan's ebullient challenge to the "age mystique" in *The Fountain of Age*.[23]

In general, women's literature during the 1980s and early 1990s has shifted emphases, broadened its purview, and flouted miscellaneous thematic and stylistic prohibitions. Recent Russian women's fiction reveals a keen interest in those concerns that the West deems typical for female writers: Disintegration of the family (Polianskaia's "Where Did the Streetcar Go?") and alternatives to standard family structures (Shcherbakova's "Uncle Khlor and Koriakin"); psychological hardships facing children of divorced parents (Rubina's "The Blackthorn"); awakening of female sexuality (Mass's "The Trap"); male violence (Vaneeva's "Venetian Mirrors") and rape (Nabatnikova's "The Bus Driver Astap"); birthing and abortion (Palei's "The Losers' Division" and Nabatnikova's "The Phone Call"); relations between the sexes as warfare (Sadur's "Wicked Girls" and Nabatnikova's "Phone Call"); men's fundamental incapacity for affection and fidelity, or, in its softer formulation, the mutual incomprehension of the sexes that inheres in insurmountable gender differences (Palei's "Rendezvous" and Sadur's "Worm-eaten Sonny").

Instead of observing Soviet cultural convention by sanctifying reproductive prowess and motherhood, recent women's prose has not shrunk from satirical or mixed portrayals of maternity. Nina Katerli's "Slowly the Old Woman..." limns the Soviet version of the quintessential "Jewish mother" immortalized by Philip Roth, Joseph Heller, and Woody Allen, with all of her pathos and intolerable busybodiness. Makarova's "Rush

Job" offers a less noxious variation on the same stereotype. Terminal haplessness is the chief trait of Vaneeva's dithering mother in "Venetian Mirrors," whose inability to cope with the most elementary childcare teeters on the absurd. Her antithesis is Rubina's divorcée Marina. Refracted through the affectionate but uncomprehending eyes of her son, Marina emerges as an appealing and multi-faceted character who, despite explosions of temper and the strain of overwork and emotional solitude, sustains profoundly loving bonds with the boy, in whom she struggles to implant sound values. A major accomplishment of the story is that through Rubina's deft layering the reader simultaneously sees Marina's spiritual generosity and warmth along with the warts in her temperament. Although the child's narrative viewpoint inevitably frames her within the role of "mother," her portrait cannot be contained within the parameters of that function alone. Instead of idealizing maternity, Rubina wisely humanizes it.

While paternity tends to be notable for its absence from women's prose (as well as from male prose and everyday Russian life), Shcherbakova's tongue-in-cheek "Uncle Khlor and Koriakin" makes it the basis of the reconstituted family. Given the wildly improbable scenario of two middle-aged Russian men vying for guardianship of a little girl, the story's charm resides not in verisimilitude, but in the fairy tale or fantastic element of this domestic utopia. Such a postmodernist *ménage à trois* is the stuff of situation comedies (e.g., the French film *Trois hommes et un couffin*). A skeptic whose other works consistently eschew facile solutions to problems, Shcherbakova undercuts the plausibility of the story's "happy ever after" ending by the exaggerated simplicity of its achievement. One responsible and loving father might tax the reader's credulity; two such fantasy figures signal a joke at the naive reader's expense.

Perhaps the single greatest innovation in this corpus is its discovery of the body as an authenticating locus of female experience and a source of powerful rhetoric. Russian critics with a penchant for neat taxonomies have sweepingly excoriated the "physiological tendency" in current Russian women's fiction on the shaky grounds of "bad taste," without, however, analyzing its diverse functions.[24] Any reader attuned to difference instantly notices how markedly those functions vary from author to author. For instance, Nabatnikova's "Bus Driver Astap" and Tokareva's "First Try" thematize woman's body. The former explores the volatile hypothesis of women's alleged complicity in their own rape. Nabatnikova complicates the fraught issue by pointedly casting a female athlete (whose very profession presumably demands physical "fitness" and "purity") as the rape victim, and the victim of *her* racism— a racism expressed on the "bodily level"—as her assailant. Whatever subtleties she introduces into the dynamics of their relationship, Nabatnikova, who refers to the rape as "shar[ing] in that mystery that nature had designed to serve the sacred cause of human renewal," ultimately resorts to the disreputable maneuver of sexualizing her protagonist's moral punishment for racial prejudice.

In kindred fashion, biology dispenses what Tokareva apparently considers just desserts to the protagonist of "First Try." After manipulating her way to success and recognition through sexual favors, Mara finally succumbs to terminal breast cancer, the pain and humiliations of the disease mortifying the sinful body that she pragmatically exchanged for sundry perquisites. Here again the female body becomes the visible site of a punitive restoration of "ethics." Whereas Nabatnikova sexualizes moral "justice," Tokareva moralizes bodily dissolution.[25] Both authors' methods of meting out retribution for "deviational misconduct" carry chilling implications, especially in the AIDS era.[26] And both stories unwittingly prompt what strikes me as an unanswerable question: If the gender-specific "semi-consensual rape" (!) and terminal breast cancer qualify as "just punishment" for, respectively, a woman's racism and "sleeping her way to the top," what would constitute an analogous moral redress for male transgressors? Castration and colon cancer?

By contrast, for writers such as Petrushevskaia, Ulitskaia, Nina Gorlanova, Marina Palei, Elena Tarasova and Svetlana Vasilenko the inordinate suffering undergone by women's bodies provides a rich rhetoric grounded in maximal palpability. The dehumanizing details that vividly document women's lived experience not only dispel the iconography of woman as Nurturing Mother and Madonna/Angel in the House, but simultaneously serve as a discursive mode of redefining gender inscription in their fiction.[27] Ulitskaia's "Chosen People," like Tarasova's "The Woman Who Doesn't Remember Evil," dissociates the female body from the teleology of procreation and from voyeuristic sexual desire—the traditional frameworks within which woman's physicality has been depicted and delectated. In "Going After Goat Antelopes" and "Shamara" Vasilenko implicates her female protagonists' frank sexual wants in an existentialist aura of post-nuclear apocalypse. She thereby infuses the lush, freely articulated sensuality of her profoundly thoughtful women with a cosmic vitality that seems to defy the destructive innovations of the modern technological age. In her talent for conveying with immediacy and self-assurance women's robust delight in bodily pleasures, while fully integrating it with their astute perceptiveness, Vasilenko has no rivals.

Palei and Sadur, by contrast, ironize and deconstruct age-old myths surrounding the female body. Reading like a fictional gloss on John Berger's revolutionary *Ways of Seeing* (1972), Palei's "Rendezvous" unmasks the euphemized relations between so-called male creativity and the female body/beloved/Muse as one-way traffic between a self-positing subjectivity and an instrumentalized object. Recognizing that such inequitable male-female power relations reduce woman to a mere reflection of male identity, Palei places readers outside this structure through a shift in viewpoint that invites them to objectify and ultimately satirize the self-validating male perspective.

Sadur likewise dismantles hardy gendered myths. Her quasi-folkloric cycle of stories titled *Touched* (Pronikshie), to which "Worm-eaten Sonny" and "Wicked Girls" belong, creates a credible world of primal psychic impulses and fantastic occurrences. In this mysterious universe of spells, incantations, magic potions, and enchanted objects, the question of human agency—so vital to the feminist enterprise—fades into virtual irrelevance. Within the vortex of seemingly uncontrollable, irrational forces, relations between the sexes invariably define themselves as violent battles, with the male as brutal antagonist or invader.[28]

Of all Sadur's narratives, "Worm-eaten Sonny" most colorfully revisions gender roles, through ironic reversal. Inverting the lapsarian myth, Sadur posits not apple-biting Eve, but flesh-obsessed Adam as the fatal cause and carrier of mortality. An insatiable consumer of everything around him, Man sucks dry the life juices of Woman, just as the worms inside his rotting brain feed off his gray cells. Its black humor notwithstanding, "Worm-eaten Sonny" shows manhood in a devastating light and is, as Sadur herself has remarked, a rather nasty story.[29] Perhaps its harsh image of masculinity, which recalls some of Fay Weldon's mordant male portraits, would have less impact were it not projected through the startling lexical combinations, clever paronomasia, and skillful instrumentation that comprise Sadur's highly original language.[30] Poetry and revilement tethered to an animistic world model make for a potent synthesis.

Like "Worm-eaten Sonny," Kalinina's "Sergusha" spotlights the male body, but in an appreciably different mode. Kalinina effects a paradigm shift by transferring the problem of obesity—a constant in feminist debates—to the domain of masculine vulnerability. In a sense she rewrites the myth of Pygmalion and Galatea. Although her Galatea

(Galia) obediently refashions her physical and professional self according to the perceived expectations of her brilliant Pygmalion (Sergusha), her awe at his intellectual superiority does not deter her from replacing the fat-jiggling Sergusha with the "body beautiful" Seriozha as a worthier romantic/sexual partner. By separating power and intelligence from sexual desirability in men, and above all by masculinizing fatness and treating it as in some way significant in a man's life, Kalinina works against gender stereotype.

Apart from its increased gender consciousness, its concentrated focus on the body, and its predilection for debunking myths, contemporary Russian women's prose also departs stylistically from female fiction of earlier decades. Above all, the dislocated, unstable, or unidentifiable viewpoint that Tatyana Tolstaya exploits to magnificent effect is favored by Palei, Sadur, Larisa Vaneeva, and Irina Polianskaia. This technique, which frequently takes the form of a constant, unsignalled oscillation between subjective reflection and flight of imagination or recollection, on the one hand, and external description of empirically verifiable phenomena, on the other (characteristic of the texts by Bella Ulanovskaia, Vaneeva, and Polianskaia anthologized here) makes for a less linear and transparent text. In Makarova's and Ulanovskaia's prose, that linearity is further disrupted by an elliptical narrative, whereby omissions create cryptic spaces and a jaggedness of plotline that in Vaneeva's case, for example, breeds mystification bordering on confusion. In short, partly owing to its modernist devices, recent women's prose has become a pleasurably more challenging read than in the past. Indeed, anyone unfamiliar with folkloric patterns, motifs, and conventions may find Sadur's stories opaque or, at the very least, enigmatic. Much of Ulanovskaia's "Albinos" reads like a cryptogram, encoded for aficionados of Russian culture and those initiated into various aspects of the author's personal and professional biography. Less than attentive readers may lose track of Vasilenko's artfully orchestrated clusters of repetitions, which, like Ariadne's thread, enable them to retrace their steps out of her verbal maze toward revelation and/or meaning.

Whereas Iunina, Tokareva, Mass, Kozhevnikova, Ulitskaia, Shcherbakova, Kalinina, Nabatnikova—and to a lesser degree Rubina and Katerli—adhere to a more traditional style, Ulanovskaia, Vasilenko, Sadur, Palei, and Vaneeva, like Tolstaya, Petrushevskaia, Narbikova, and Gorlanova, ambiguously distance themselves from traditions through irony, self-consciousness, and play. At stake here is not the superiority of detachment over advocacy, but the degree of narrative and rhetorical sophistication that leads one to reconceive those very categories. That contrast may be illustrated specifically by two parallel summative statements on gender difference. For instance, Kozhevnikova's bland observation that "because men are different [from women], they get distracted by business and force you to wait" pales beside the barbed originality of Sadur's savage metaphor: "Man has been bitten by the demon of betrayal... He's swallowed a scorpion." Wit and self-confident derision have supplanted conciliatory resignation. Among the stylistically more venturesome writers, anger, violence, and impatience prove valuable emotions, for they energize the narrative and find forms of expression whose freshness augurs a future for Russian women's fiction.

In her study of contemporary Anglophone feminist prose, Gayle Greene privileges the circle as metafictional structure and metaphor, arguing that it enables a critique of traditional narrative, suggests alternatives, and generates productive ambiguities.[31] Her words, not coincidentally, partially echo the authors' collective preface to the anthology titled *The Woman Who Doesn't Remember Evil*: "Yet one should recall that for a woman the closed circle of everyday life, the circle of hell, is also the circle of life, which presupposes the endlessness of the journey."[32] Circle as trope figures prominently, in fact, not only in the titles of stories by Tolstaya, Petrushevskaia, and T. Gorbulina (a tendency noted by Evgenia Shcheglova's bilious diatribe against the "new women's prose"), but also in Natalia Ivanova's review essay of recent Russian women's writing.[33] Whether circularity necessarily possesses all of the advantages Greene ascribes to it seems debatable to me. One thing, however, I am convinced of: When Russian women writers finally succeed in combatting the animus against gendered creativity that automatically equates everything female with second-rate, they will have squared the circle.

Pittsburgh, December 1993

Notes

1. Such experienced feminist activists as Olga Lipovskaia (the editor of *Women's Reading* [Zhenskoe chtenie] from St. Petersburg) and the economist Anastasia Posadskaia, now head of Moscow's Gender Center, frankly acknowledge that at this stage feminism in Russia is a fledgling movement that has attracted a tiny minority.

2. For a sensitive and thoughtful interview that documents Posadskaia's "route to feminism," see Anastasia Posadskaya, "Self-Portrait of a Russian Feminist," *New Left Review* 195 (1992): 3-19.

3. *Feminism: Perspectives for Social Knowledge* (Feminizm: Perspectivy sotsial'nogo znaniia), ed. Ol'ga Voronina, 1992, *Woman in a Changing World* (Zhenshchina v meniaiushchemsia mire), ed. Natal'ia Rimashevskaia, 1992, *Woman and Social Politics (Aspect of Gender)* (Zhenshchina i sotsial'naia politika [gendernyi aspekt], ed. Zoia Khotkina (1992).

4. For example, "Gender in Two Cultures" (New York, 1991), "Restructuring Gender" (Helsinki, 1992), "Women in Russia" (Bath, 1993).

5. For example, *Perestroika and Soviet Women*, ed. Mary Buckley (1992), *Women in the Face of Change*, ed. S. Rai et al. (1992).

6. For example, *Democracy Minus Woman Isn't Democracy*, a volume of essays edited by Anastasia Posadskaia, slated for publication by Verso in England, 1994.

7. Some American Slavists translate Vysshie zhenskie kursy literally—as Higher Women's Courses—but in the given instance such a rubric is a misnomer or a Briticism, since the courses are intended for advanced students.

8. Ol'ga Vainshtein, "Odezhda kak smysl: ideologemy sovremennoi mody," *Inostrannaia literatura* 7 (1993): 224-232.

9. For additional gender-based institutions that have arisen in the last few years, see "Women's Discussion Club," the Moscow/New York publication produced by Interlegal, an agency founded by lawyer Nina Beliaeva.

10. "RFE/RL Daily Report," No. 181, 21 September 1993, RFE/RL Research Institute, Munich.

11. For information on the elections, see the RFE/RL Daily Report, No. 238, 14 December 1993, from Radio Free Europe/Radio Liberty Inc.

12. For more information on the rise of recent women's groups, see Ol'ga Lipovskaia, "New Women's Organisations," *Perestroika and Soviet Women*, ed. Mary Buckley (Cambridge: Cambridge UP, 1992): 72-81. As the title indicates, given the accelerated pace of events in Russia today, this volume was already somewhat outdated by the time of publication. See also "Discussion Group Club."

13. On the structure, program, and activities of the Women's Union of Russia, see "Women's Discussion Club" (February 1993).

14. "Women's Discussion Club" (January 1993): np.

15. See, for example, *Obshchestvennye nauki i sovremennost'* 4 (1991): 125-145, and 1 (1993): 174-193.

16. The editors of *The New Literary Review* and *Glas* are both women, Irina Prokhorova and Natasha Perova, respectively. To my knowledge, until the 1990s only men occupied the post of edi-

tors-in-chief and dominated editorial boards of mainstream journals.

17. For a sampling of anti-feminist manifestations in the mass media, see the list provided by Elena Leonoff in *WEW* (May 1993): 28-29.

18. On this formulation, see Adrienne Rich, "Compulsory Heterosexuality and Lesbian Existence" (1980), in Adrienne Rich, *Blood, Bread, and Poetry: Selected Prose 1979-1985* (NY: W.W. Norton & Co., 1986) 23-75.

19. For reports on gay/lesbian activities in Moscow and Petersburg, see the publications of IGLHRC, the International Gay and Lesbian Human Rights Commission, headed by Julie Dorf in San Francisco.

20. For commentary on and examples of scurrilous harangues against the "new women's prose" masquerading as reviews, see *Skirted Issues: The Discreteness and Indiscretions of Russian Women's Prose*, ed. Helena Goscilo (*Russian Studies in Literature*) (M.E. Sharpe: Armonk, NY, 1992).

21. Narbikova's name was ultimately removed from the list, for her narrative, *Okolo ekolo*, was justifiably disqualified for having been published too early (1990-1991) to enter this year's competition.

22. On that development in American society, see Barbara Ehrenreich, Elizabeth Hess, Gloria Jacobs, *Re-Making Love: The Feminization of Sex* (Garden City, NY: Anchor/Doubleday, 1986).

23. Betty Friedan, *The Fountain of Age* (NY: Simon & Schuster, 1993).

24. For samples of such criticism and commentary on its "bad faith," see *Skirted Issues*.

25. The maimed female body as a site of moral retribution threatens to become a leit-motif in Tokareva's recent stories. For a startling instance of such displacedment onto female flesh, see Viktoria Tokareva, "I Am. You Are. He Is" [Ia est'. Ty est'. On est'], *Novyi mir* 9 (1991): 129-51.

26. On the political nature of disease metaphors, see Susan Sontag, *Illness as Metaphor* (NY: Vintage, 1977/1979) and *Aids and its Metaphors* (NY: Farrar, Straus & Giroux, 1988/1989).

27. For further analysis of this point, see Helena Goscilo, "Inscribing the Female Body in Women's Fiction: Cross-Gendered Passion à la Holbein," *Gender Restructuring in Russian Studies*, eds. Marianne Liljeströmm Eila Mäntysaari, Arja Rosenholm (Tampere: University of Tampere, 1993) 73-86.

28. Hence Sadur's use of German culture in depictions of the assaulting male, which exploits Russians' persistent association of destructive aggression with Nazism. "Wicked Girls" illustrates this device to perfection.

29. During a taped interview with me in Moscow, May 1993.

30. Sadur's puns are complex and witty: e.g., the conclusion of "Wicked Girls" plays on the Russian "Gori," which is the imperative form of "Burn," while also phonetically rendering the Russian pronunciation of "Harry." Similarly, in "Worm-eaten Sonny," the worms inside the male brain simultaneously "feed off" the gray cells and "squeal"—both meanings contained in the verb "pishchat," which Sadur highlights through prolonging the "i" in the Russian original.

31. Gayle Greene, *Changing the Story* (Bloomington: Indiana UP, 1991) 15-16.

32. Larisa Vaneeva, ed., *Ne pomniashchaia zla* (M. Moskovskii rabochii, 1990) 4.

33. On this, see *Skirted Issues* 19, 56. Shcheglova's own review is called "In Her Own Circle" (V svoem krugu).

LIVES IN TRANSIT

Prose

Gulia

Liudmila Ulitskaia

Gulia's nameday fell on Christmas Eve. As someone who from childhood had unconsciously, and, with the years, more and more consciously and vigorously, professed the universal and mysterious religion of the holiday, Gulia didn't let a single nameday of hers go by without celebrating. Even in exile, and when she was in the camps, she would organize something from what paltry means were at hand, would pull those crunching starched holiday granules out of the air, stick them together, and pass them around to whoever happened to be at her side at the time.

She observed her nameday, her birthday, and also her late mother's and sisters' birthdays, the wedding anniversary of her first marriage, as well as Easter, Whitsunday, all twelve fixed-day holidays,[1] and the majority of official occasions. She observed New Year twice—both Old Style and New, and also Christmas: at first just the Catholic one, which she justified by her grandmother's Polish background, and then the Orthodox one too. She didn't omit the 1st of May and the 8th of March, nor did she ignore the 7th of November. She adhered to established rituals as much as possible. So she liked to begin celebrating her birthday, which came at the beginning of summer, on June 3rd, from the morning on. If circumstances allowed, she would take off with one of her female friends for the Agricultural Exhibit or for the Botanical Gardens, would walk about for two hours or so, telling her friend incredibly scandalous stories from her early youth; then they'd go to the Prague restaurant, where they'd have as festive a fixed price dinner as one could buy for eight rubles in the old currency, subsequently a ruble thirty according to the new.

Then they would come to Gulia's apartment to relax, and after a rest, they'd drink coffee with a liqueur that had been stocked in advance, ice cream, and Grilliage candies—while their teeth could still handle them and until they disappeared for good from the stores.

When the quantity of liqueur consumed significantly exceeded the amount of coffee, Gulia would take the guitar down off the wall and, scrupulously observing his intonations and pronunciation, would give a rendition of Vertinsky,[2] passing in significant silence over certain steamy reminiscences.

This whole routine was called a "spree," and her favorite partner in these vegetarian orgies was Verusha—Vera Alexandrovna.

Her role changed many times in the course of life—she was an ecstatic admirer, confidante, rival and even patron in the various periods of their life, which was layered like a geological cross section. Vera Alexandrovna was a semi-relative, semi-shadow, the tissue paper of memory and the most compelling evidence Galia had of the reality of her own life...

Long before St. Evgeniia's day, which fell on Christmas Eve,[3] Vera Alexandrovna would start worrying about the fact that she wouldn't be able to get Gulia a nice gift that year and that the latter would be upset.

This time among some papers left to her by a late relative she found an old photograph that was supposed to confirm her mythical family relationship to Gulia. That relationship hinged on Gulia's mother's cousin, who was supposedly the second wife of Vera Alexandrovna's grandfather. The photograph in question showed the noble couple, and Vera Alexandrovna liked to think that she had discovered this most fragile evidence of a family relationship. Vera Alexandrovna added to the photograph, which comprised the spiritual part of the nameday gift, a small bottle of Yugoslav shampoo and a rather miserable box of candy. This candy especially worried her, and she even asked Shurik what he thought of the nondescript box. Shurik glanced at the box with exaggerated interest and said:

"It's wonderful, Mama, just wonderful! The way you've arranged it is just perfect. It's a very elegant gift."

Somewhat comforted, Vera Alexandrovna went to the kitchen to heat the hair tongs. While she was curling her fluffy yellowish-white hair, San Sanych spread shoe polish thickly on his hiking shoes—his favorite footwear, which combined great sturdiness with a low price. Both mother and son joined in the overture of Gulia's celebration, consisting of the smell of overheated tongs, singed hair, shoe polish, and innocuous cheap aftershave lotion.

On the little oval table covered by a splotchy teacloth stood a long dish with sochivo[4] and a bottle of fortified sweet red wine. A small Christmas tree stood in a large vase that was chipped at the top and for that reason had not been sold. The newspapers with Julietka's shit, which usually were spread evenly all over the room, were swept into a corner in honor of the occasion, and from time to time were taken out to the garbage dump.

During the final hours of Christmas Eve the guests couldn't have meat with their meal, but when it was close to eight and vespers at St. Ilia's Church were ending, Gulia would embrace the first day after Christmas, which meant serving meat appetizers, sometimes even hot ones. The two-hour fast was ending, and they could begin eating meat.

How wonderful it was to see them take their seats around the table. San Sanych gazed at them with affectionate admiration, at the wispy old ladies, the select, who had kept in shape the last twenty-five years by paying fines for each reference to sickness, bodily functions, and, God forbid, death. Literature, art, reminiscences of youth, social gossip—that was what their conversation always revolved around.

Now they were talking about hats: about how young women didn't know how to wear hats, which were an emblem of one's sex, evidence of talent or mediocrity, a sign of social belonging, and an index of one's intellectual level. Concretely, they were talking about Zinaida Gippius's hats. Then Gulia somehow made an easy transition to the superiority of "Swedish marriages" over *ménages à trois*... then moved along some winding path to Diaghilev, to ballet in general, and Maia Plisetskaia...

They talked and talked... The star of Christmas had long since been lost in the scattering of countless ordinary stars, and through the long room, from the triple-casement high window to the hall door that had been cut in, spoiling the aristocratic suite-like style of this formerly fine room, streamed a draft that chilled the old women's shoulders, with their worn shoulder blades.

The slushy, inauthentic winter, as if overcome by sudden shame, had greeted Christmas with a seasonal frost as if it had been ordered for the occasion. The lackluster wind from the window grew increasingly harsh. Gulia placed an old fur coat on the wide marble windowsill, but the heating, which was set at zero, couldn't cope with the rapid drop in temperature.

Throwing kerchiefs, scarves, and Gulia's robes over their shoulders, they started talking about the cold spells of '73 or '75—they were a little confused as to when—of '41, '24, and, God forbid!, '13.

They demolished everything that the Prague restaurant's kitchen could offer Gulia: stuffed goose, and Czech meat loaf, and vol-au-vint with some kind of nonsense inside it. They'd have drunk everything too, but out of long habit Gulia had kept hidden a small carafe of cognac and a half-bottle of Portuguese port that someone had brought as a gift and that Gulia considered not much better than the domestic Crimean.

When the conversation turned to weather, Julietka jumped down from the small couch and, her whole demeanor showing contempt for such a commonplace turn in the conversation, lay down on the velvet cushion.

In appearance Julietta and Gulia had nothing whatever in common. Julietka was a smooth-haired dachshund mix, while Gulia was a purebred borzoi of an old woman, with slender legs and nostrils like braces, and thin, finely arched eyebrows that were pencilled in like arcs. What they had in common lay deeper and was not perceptible to anyone inattentive. It expressed itself in their aristocratic disdain for trifles, in a lousy surface and an unusually solid inner core of character.

Gulia experienced a slight irritation at the same time as Julietka and was just about to suggest a hand of cards, but, unexpectedly, San Sanych, who until then had maintained a modest silence all evening as he gazed with affectionate admiration at these shabby, fragrant, frail, herculean ladies, old maids, old maenads, angels and witches—San Sanych quietly said:

"Gulia, you've got a terrible draft here. You need to seal the window. I'll come tomorrow after work around seven thirty and do it. Don't go out then, please."

"My precious!" screeched Gulia. "Shurik, you sweetheart! How nice it was of you, Verochka, to be seduced into having a child!"

And, jumping lightly from her armchair, she hopped over to San Sanych and, her renownedly magnificent bust encased in a corset resting against his shoulder, she kissed him on the balding back of his head. They started talking about children.

Gulia slept badly. She had stomach pains, and toward morning she had to get up twice to go to the toilet. Gulia blamed the port. Out of a sense of solidarity, Julietta also made a mess right there on the floor, since Gulia had forgotten to lay down the usual section of *The Literary Gazette* for her when she went to bed. This, however, rather endeared her to Gulia, for they both usually suffered from constipation, and since Julietta didn't drink port, her upset stomach could be explained exclusively by a profound spiritual bond.

Gulia was freezing, she couldn't get warm for a long time under two blankets and a fur coat, her stomach pains persisted, and she fell asleep only after heating a kettle of water and filling a hot water bottle.

Waking up past noon, she lay in bed for another hour—she never liked to get up right away—enjoying the pleasant feeling of lightness and emptiness in her stomach and happy to see a harsh winter sun. It was beastly cold in the room, there was a soft layer of hoarfrost on the windowsill. Gulia examined her room with lively interest; it had been a long time since she had seen it so brightly illuminated. The room had a high ceiling and lacked proportion—it was a third of a hall with three windows, the plaster made a graceful turn here, and when Gulia entered this room soon after returning from deportation and hastily married the imposing owner of the room, for a long time she looked for the spot to place the bed, for, having her own special relations with space, there was no way she could bring this fragment of plaster on the ceiling in line with her own body as it lay in bed... But about three months into this extravagant marriage, the owner of the room suddenly died, leaving Gulia his dusty, ramshackle antique inheritance.

The room was bright blue. Gulia had almost made it red, but Verusha had said that she wouldn't set foot in the house then, and Gulia had told the painters to paint it blue. It turned out wonderfully: Gulia lived as if against the backdrop of a theater set, the walls were so fantastically, so improbably blue, and all the things—the worn Karelian birch, the faded bronze frame of the darkened mirror, harmoniously lived up to this unnatural blue.

Unwashed dishes stood on the table as if arranged for a stilllife and Gulia smiled as she propped up her pillow at the head of the bark. She never had insomnia or night-mares, and would depart each evening on this bark, to sail in the heavens, remember-ing to whisper: "Glory to you, God, we've made it through another day. And please—no dreams, if possible..."

This time, however, toward morning she did have a dream, but it didn't surface right away and it cast a pall on Gulia's sunny mood. The dream had no plot. There was a feeling in it of some alien power, of a closed space. And the texture was vulgar, incredibly vulgar. Forget it, forget it, I don't want to remember! A smooth woolen cloth on the table... Captain Utenkov gently whispering the vilest profanity in her ear... And he went on... and on... The knave... Swine... Saved her. Go away! I don't want to!

But the dream had already broken through to the surface and she remembered it despite herself. She, Gulia, is standing in a study, on an immaculately clean carpet run-ner in large disgusting boots, and Captain Utenkov is savoring her aristocratic maiden name, and suddenly a heavy desire wells in her, pounding like a large fish's tail. And Utenkov becomes someone else, someone she loves, someone intimately close... he grows clearer and stops being Utenkov altogether... and all this goes on, without reach-ing any conclusion or resolution... What nonsense! Ugh, what nonsense! I've asked you before—please, no dreams...

Ah, yes! Shurik is coming to seal the window. How sweet he is. Yes, the window. I have to get up and tidy the place. It'd be nice to have a hot bath. I don't feel like clean-ing it, though. The neighbors are pigs. The bathtub's so incredibly dirty that it's disgust-ing just to stand in it, let alone take a bath...

And her morning got on its way. At three she drank some coffee. She answered the phone. Yesterday's guests called, and also someone for the neighbors. She read part of a French detective novel. It was boring. She heated up some sausage. Julietta didn't eat. She got another call, from Beatrice, a Jew from America who had settled in Russia, with whom she'd become friends in exile, who invited her over. "I'll go," decided Gulia. "To hell with the window! It's winter, so obviously it's cold. And so it should be. And who knows whether Shurik will actually come or not."

"Alright, Betka, I'll be over!" promised Gulia. As soon as she hung up, Shurik called, asking whether she had any wadding in the house.

"Maybe we should put it off?" Gulia wanted to renege.

"No way. You'll catch a cold. It's freezing there, and drafty too!"

So Gulia called Beatrice back, explaining that she'd come a little later.

San Sanych came at eight. Sensing that her visit was already falling through and her holiday, with a swish of its tail, was beginning to slip through her fingers, Gulia started to get angry: at Shurik, who has late, at herself, for having agreed to have the windows sealed, which she'd always done quite well without, and even at Beatrice, sweet, gentle Beatrice, with her crude male voice, Beatrice, whose naivete verged on idiocy.

"It's beastly cold, at least 20 below," announced San Sanych in a frozen voice as he took off his coat inside Gulia's room. No one ever took off his outer clothes by the coatrack in the hallway. They were convinced that if the coat weren't stolen, then the change would disappear from the pockets for sure.

"Terribly cold, as I said," continued San Sanych, taking hanks of tape out of his battered briefcase. "Put some tea on, will you. And a pan with water—the paste has to be boiled."

With a sense of doom Gulia went to the kitchen, realizing that she wouldn't be able to pay her visit today.

Shurik hastily drank some tea, then climbed onto the windowsill and pulled open the inner frame. The copper latches with long bolts running the entire length of the frame worked splendidly, though they were about a hundred years old, but the actual frames were rotten. The layer of cold air trapped between them instantly billowed and filled the room.

With a knife San Sanych started stuffing thin rolls of wadding into the gaps between the frames. Gulia sat in an armchair, with Julietta in her arms, and kept asking kindly what she could do to be useful.

San Sanych loved Gulia. He'd known her since childhood, but in snatches. She had been imprisoned three times, twice on account of her husbands, as she believed, and once, as she herself explained, for an excess of education. The last time was already after the war, during the brief period of her unmarried life. Usually she had one husband right after another, but this time she happened to be in a husbandless phase, and she got a job.

Apart from high school, Gulia had no other formal education, but she knew languages well, and by today's standards, even superbly. Gulia's mother was half-German and had grown up in France, so both those languages were spoken at home. Moreover, an Englishwoman had lived with them, a Miss Frost who, contrary to general opinion about the English, was unbelievably garrulous. She filled the entire house with her ceaseless birdlike twitter and only someone deaf could have avoided learning the language in her presence. During the last summer before the war, fourteen-year-old Gulia, who picked up languages easily, fell in love with an Italian singer, a teacher then living in Moscow, and in two months she easily learned Italian, delighting the honey-voiced teacher with the ease of her speech and the un-northern ardor of her ways.

She acquired Polish, owing to force of circumstance, when she was deported. During a visit Vera Alexandrovna accidently left behind an Agatha Christie mystery in Polish, and Gulia, who hadn't yet tasted the delights of that particular genre, sank her teeth into it and for many years didn't even bother looking at anything other than dear little Agatha, as she affectionately called her.

Gulia got a job as a reviewer and translator in a technical department somewhere and had been working there a little over a year when she got embroiled in an idiotic conflict. It grew and solidified until her boss wrote an official letter to the authories accusing her, with utter inconsistency, of cosmopolitanism, espionage, and simultaneously, of being apolitical. The charge, even for those times, was so absurd that after half a year, even before Stalin's death, Gulia was released.

In the intervals between her various deportations, Gulia contrived to live like a bird; instantly marrying anew, she celebrated her tumultuous love fest, laughed unrestrainedly, visited people non-stop, and "fluttered like a vivid butterfly," in the words of the careful Verusha, who was mortally terrified of life. But Gulia didn't change the colors of her frivolous exterior.

Shurik was born when Gulia, after her first stint in the camps, was living at Verusha's in Kaluga, and he proved to be the first and only child with whom Gulia became involved from the very start, when he was a baby. She somehow managed to overcome her revulsion at this damply-snotty period of existence, which aroused her squeamishness. In any event, she made an exception for Shurik.

Even when she left Verusha to join Pavel Arkadievich—it's difficult now to establish what number husband he was—she would visit Vera and Shurik all the years she spent with him until his death, in an unabating gaiety of spirit and body, and, contrary to her inner makeup, she almost came to really love him.

During these early years of Shurik's life Gulia would appear in festive silk, in a cloud of perfume and a wispy foam of frail curls, with pencilled eyebrows and eyes that were a true emerald green. The affectionate boy would hug her slippery silk-clad knees and swoon, his heart dilating. And Gulia's fingers, the red nails curving slightly inward, would ruffle the fine hair that he was fated to lose all too soon.

Then Gulia vanished—and Shurik missed her. When she returned for good, however, Shurik's heart was no longer capable of grand festive moments; and Gulia was no longer so silky. Besides, that year he turned sixteen, and found silk, honey, fur, ice, and other of the world's perfections in other vessels.

Gulia quickly got married again to a handsome old man with a famous last name. True, he himself wasn't the famous one, alas; he only happened to have the same name, but who'd dare ask that question?

Gulia lived to the full; she didn't miss a single opening of some new art exhibit, a show, premiere, benefit, or visiting artist. Her last husband died unnoticed and Gulia announced to her women friends that thereafter she would be a nun, though definitely uncloistered...

San Sanych, who by that time had lost a significant part of his hair, gained a lot of weight and, having acquired a far from repulsive resemblance to a potato, was then serving a totally different idol, but he didn't ever shirk any of Gulia's unceremonious demands—which he, however, never characterized as demands—to move some furniture, to drive her to the dacha or to escort her to the railroad station. San Sanych suffered, nonetheless, understanding that Gulia was old and that he was of insignificantly little help to her, so he was happy to seal the windows because it meant having the chance to do something useful for dear Gulia.

The triple-casement window was extravagantly, aristocratically tall: from the windowsill he could barely reach higher than half the frame with his hand, and the gaps proved bottomless; they ate up three packs of wadding, an entire pile of rags, torn into strips, and the end of the job still wasn't in sight.

Gulia, enraptured, was three hours into a story about her tender friendship with some Max, but San Sanych had no idea that she was talking about Voloshin.[5] Seeing that San Sanych had finished the inner frames, Gulia with a wink pulled out a small decanter of cognac and some forgettable appetizer.

"The guests polished off everything yesterday and I've not been out of the house today," Gulia explained the modesty of the offering. "But let's have a bite, my dear friend," she cooed. From an early age Gulia had liked the lively way alcohol accelerated the blood, and she pulled out some large green glasses. "It's crazy, of course, to drink cognac out of glasses like these, especially green ones, but the small ones, they're all dirty." And she waved her hand in the direction of the garbage table, as she called it, which stood beside the door with yesterday's unwashed dishes on it.

"You know, it occurred to me, to hell with this slavery! If I don't want to wash them, then I have the right not to, ultimately, don't I. You agree, pal?"

"Of course, Gulenka," replied San Sanych with a smile, his head cocked to the side, touched at the sight of her. He gazed at her with delight, and she sensed this and started to turn coy. "You're amazing. There are no longer people like you in our generation."

"What do you mean?" asked Gulia, who liked all kinds of compliments and was expecting to hear something pleasant. "A drop more, sweetie. That's it. That'll be enough."

"To your health! Gulia, you're a remarkable woman! You're the most wonderful of women! I'm not telling you anything new, but you're *ewig weiblich!* Helen, Margarita, and Beatrice[6] all rolled into one!" San Sanych spouted this inspired nonsense with sincere delight as he raised the murky green glass.

Gulia burst out laughing, holding her thin hand, with its concave pianist's wrist, to her forehead.

"It's been so long since I heard these noble names, that at first I was amazed that you'd included my dear Beatrice, Beatrice Abramovna, in such elevated company! Ah, I forgot to call her!" she remembered through her laughter.

"Come on, Gulia! Why don't you let a man take delight in you!"

"Don't I? Go ahead, please, as much as you want! What can be nicer for a lady than such delight... What, indeed...," and she dissolved in laughter again.

"Oh, Gulia, Gulia, how can one not love you? It's simply impossible not to!" blared San Sanych in a voice nasal with cold.

She sat in the wide armchair, the armrest of which was tied with an old belt from a robe. Her light blue, freshly-dyed hair curled in wisps of smoke around her little skull; as always, her eyebrows were pencilled in sharply, and beneath them her clever jeweled eyes were smiling.

San Sanych poured them both another round.

"Yes, Gulia, dear, I want to drink to the miracle of femininity, the miracle of your femininity!" San Sanych solemnly pronounced the toast and, bending down, kissed her hand.

Something stirred in her memory. Something intimate-beloved- familiar, which had become faintly visible in Capt. Utenkov's features—it was Shurik! Shurik!

But San Sanych, the fool, continued his speech-making. Softened by the cognac, he babbled about the silky knees that he'd loved so much in his childhood, about the soft gloves whose touch had so excited him, and even about the spyglass of which she'd once made him a gift...

With fingers weighed down by large unattractive rings Gulia unfastened the top three buttons of her purple blouse, gave a deep sigh, and quietly but distinctly said, "Shurik, I don't feel well..."

"My God! Gulenka, what's the matter?! Maybe I should call the doctor?!" San Sanych stopped short, sincerely alarmed that she wasn't feeling well.

"No, no, come on now, there's absolutely no need! It happens. It's vascular. It's the change in the weather. Help me onto the bed. That's it. Thank you, dear boy!" and, following her ingenious inspiration, Gulia drew the innocent, enraptured San Sanych, who suspected nothing and was already absolutely doomed, to her moored bark. "The pillow just a bit higher, please, and undo my corset, dear!" ordered Gulia in a languid voice. San Sanych obeyed. Two thin-skinned autumnal melons slowly tumbled out into San Sanych's hands.

"Perhaps I should get you some medicine? I'll get it right away..." babbled San Sanych in some confusion.

"Ah, what can medicine do now," said Gulia with grand condescension, and San Sanych finally realized that he'd been cornered...

The bark sailed off, and in that instant San Sanych felt that all the idiotic roundabout, vapid compliments that he'd babbled half an hour ago were the absolute sacred truth.

Her thick nails tapping, Julietka moved from her velvet cushion to the armchair, leaped onto it and settled down without taking her little black eyes from her owner's thin white legs.

At a quarter to six the lock in Gulia's room clicked as she escorted San Sanych to the door. They were the same height: long-legged Gulia and stocky San Sanych in his thick winter coat. She snagged herself on the coatrack and knocked down the broom that was propped up against the neighbor's door and, planting a kiss on his forehead, said in an unexpectedly loud, deep voice:

"Thank you, Shurik!"

"For what?" Shurik asked quietly.

"For everything!" the radiant Gulia introduced a tragic note.

Gulia didn't remove the two green glasses from the oval table for three days. Her women friends would visit her and she would seat them in the armchair, and, indicating the glasses, would say languidly:

"I must say that at our age these love games are too exhausting." She'd pause and continue casually, "I had a visit from a lover. A young one. I'm so tired I don't have the strength to wash out a pair of glasses."

And with her middle finger she would prop up her eyelid, which had started drooping of late, and she'd observe the expression on her friend's face closely—so as not to let slip by even this last drop of a holiday that had come so unexpectedly.

Translated by Helena Goscilo

From the author's manuscript

Notes

1. In the Orthodox Church, holidays divide into the twelve that occur on fixed days of the year and those whose dates change from year to year, depending on their temporal relationship to Easter.

2. Alexander Vertinsky, a popular singer of satirical songs who fell into disfavor with the Soviets and lived in Paris, was persona non grata in Russia until glasnost.

3. Gulia's nameday falls on 24 December, according to the Old Style, i.e., New Style, 6 January. The name Gulia is not normally used as a diminutive of Evgeniia. Throughout the story Ulitskaia uses a variety of affectionate diminutives for Gulia, for her dog Julieta, and for the other characters.

4. Sochivo—a traditional Christmas dish of sweet rice or wheat.

5. Maksimilian A. Voloshin (1877-1932), a poet who from 1917 lived in Koktebel, in the Crimea.

6. Helen of Troy, the object of Paris's desire, is the pretext for the war between the Greeks and the Trojans described in Homer's *Iliad* and Virgil's *Aeneid*. Margarita is the embodiment of the Eternal Feminine in Goethe's *Faust*, while Beatrice was the poetic inspiration and necessarily distant beloved of Dante.

First Try

Viktoria Tokareva

My address book is as overpopulated as a post-war communal apartment. A few pages have fallen out, and water spilled on one, washing out the ink. I need to redo the book and, at the same time, update it, carrying some of the people over into my future, and burying others deep in my memory.

Someone gave me a new address book, and one fine day I sat down to recopy it. The old one is a cipher of my life, coded in letters and numbers, names, and telephone numbers. It's a shame to part with it, but I must. Time, which knits the thread of narrative, insists upon it.

I open it to the first page: "A"—Alexandrova, Mara...

Her full name was Marla. But people aren't responsible for their names, they just get them. Her pregnant mother had been walking around the zoo and had read the name Marla on the tigress' cage. The tigress was young, supple, not worn out yet by captivity. Her wild, incomprehensible name fit her, and the romantic mother decided to give her future child the same name. If she had a boy, he'd be Marlin.

She had a girl. During the baby's first nursery years, the "l," which was an awkward and strange sound for the Russian ear, disappeared from her name, and from that time on, she was always called Mara. The name Marla Petrovna was listed only on her passport.

Her father was killed during the third year of the war. She and her mother had been evacuated to the Siberian countryside. The only thing that remained in Mara's memory from the period of evacuation was the big beige rear of a horse outside the window. A policeman rode the horse when he came to visit her mother, who was embroidering a shirt for him. She also remembered a red-headed doctor; her mother had embroidered a shirt for him too. Mara was always sick with something, and the doctor would come and treat her. Her mother would bend over her and beg, "Untie my hands!" Mara didn't understand what her mother wanted. Her hands weren't tied, and they waved around in all directions.

Then the war ended. Mara and her mother returned to Leningrad. From that period, she remembered the German prisoners; they were building a bathhouse. Children would come and watch in silence. The Germans had normal human faces and looked like ordinary people, just like everyone else. One chubby-faced man with round glasses cried all the time. Mara once brought him some bread and canned crab. After the war, those cans were piled high in pyramids on the store counters. Now they've all disappeared. Where? Perhaps the crab have crawled off to other shores? However, we're not concerned with the present now, but with the past. Mara was in grade school then and sang in the school choir:

> Stalin is our guiding light,
> Stalin is our youth's ideal.

Songs and glory crown our fight.
He inspires our battle zeal!

Her mother was busy with her own life. She had turned thirty. At that age, a woman needs a husband, and not just any husband, but one she loves. He must be found, and the search is a serious matter which consumes a person completely.

Mara was left to her own devices. One day she was standing in line for movie tickets and was short five kopecks. They wouldn't give her the ticket, and the movie had already started. Mara ran down the street heading for home and sobbing loudly. Passersby stopped, shocked by her despair.

There were also happy times. Once when she was at a Young Pioneer summer camp, she was chosen as a member of the council. She got to wear two stripes with a star above them on her sleeve. She was a big boss and even had her own group of sycophants, who kissed up to her. For the first time, Mara experienced the taste of power. There's nothing sweeter.

At home, they were never short of rats. Her mother would catch them in rat traps, and then, while they were still in the cage, drown them in a bucket of water. Mara remembered one rat's paws, with their five little clean pink toes, which clung to the cage wires as the rat scrambled about the cage to the top, trying to save itself from the inexorably rising water. Her mother didn't have sense enough to spare her daughter this sight.

Mara was a strong "C" student, but her friends were exclusively those with "A's." Proximity to this select group lent an aura of eliteness to Mara herself. This satisfied her power complex. It has to be said, though, that the "A" students were glad to be Mara's friends and they even had jealous scenes among themselves over the right to possess her heart.

Stalin died in the spring of '53. From morning until night the radio broadcast wonderful funeral music. This was a good time because in school they hardly did any work. The teachers cried real tears. Mara and Rita Nosikova decided on an impulse to go to the leader's funeral in Moscow, but Mara's mother wouldn't give her any money...

At that age time drags on forever, but passes quickly. Mara grew, and grew, and grew up. She met a handsome journalist named Zhenya Smolin at an officers' club party. He asked her to waltz with him. They spun around the ballroom. Her dress swirled around her. Centrifugal forces pulled them away from one another, but they clasped each other tightly with their young arms, looking into each other's eyes the whole time. It was madly exciting.

At eighteen, Mara married him.

It was a very hasty marriage, an express marriage. Right after the ceremony at the civilian registry office, they started to yell at each other, and then they continued to argue morning, noon, and night... They argued passionately and then would make up with the same passion. Their life consisted of arguments and embraces. They waged a continuous struggle for power. Mara discovered that she was pregnant and didn't know whether it was from the arguing or the embracing. Her stomach grew bigger in the fifth month, then suddenly seemed to shrink. It turns out that pregnancy can take this sort of pathological turn when the fetus, after growing to a certain point, begins to retrogress, shrinks, and dies. In an effort to protect the mother from infection, nature destroys the fetus. It's born after nine months, as if at full term, but it's tiny, dead and enclosed in its own sarcophagus. Amazing things happen in this world, and of course it had to happen to Mara, of all people. The doctors tried to find the cause, but Mara already knew what it was; her love, which had never fully matured, had begun to develop recessively and degenerated until it died.

After she got out of the hospital, Mara went south so she could dive into the salty, resilient sea, wash off her past life, then lie on the beach and close her eyes. And no one was to bother her. And she didn't need anything.

She was in this state when the quiet and taciturn Dima Palatnikov came and silently started courting her. Mara called him Dimychka. Dimychka was chronically quiet, but he understood everything, just like a dog. And like a dog, he exuded devotion and warmth. People are usually silent for two reasons: either because they're very intelligent or because they're hopelessly stupid. Mara tried to figure out what the case was with Dimychka. Sometimes he'd say something, express a complete idea or an observation. It wouldn't be at all stupid, but you could do without it. When Dimychka didn't like something, he'd close his eyes: "I don't see you, I don't hear you!" Apparently, this was something left over from childhood. Then he'd open his eyes, but his expression would remain unchanged. With eyes open or closed, he was the same. His eyes were inexpressive and in no way reflected the workings of his mind. And such a man, without eyes or words, was the only one who suited Mara's frayed nerves and cursed body.

Mara and Dimychka returned to Leningrad together. Dimychka was a traditionalist; once you had sex, you had to get married. And so they got married, obtained a cooperative apartment, and bought a car.

Dimychka was a doctor—an ear, nose, and throat specialist. What could he make? Financially, Mara bore the brunt of supporting the family. She discovered a hidden talent; she sewed and charged a lot for it. The price obviously didn't correspond to what she produced and even exceeded common sense. However, it all was based on a voluntary principle: if you don't want it, you don't have to pay for it. And if you do pay, then you're a fool. Mara made money off other people's stupidity.

There are always plenty of fools around, so money flowed in like a river. One thing was missing, however—prestige. This was during the sixties, when astronauts were popular. There were very few of them, but everyone talked about them, as with movie stars. But a dressmaker was something archaic and outdated, like a Chekhovian seamstress. If you said "dressmaker" to someone, they'd start to laugh. They'd also report you for making money on the side illegally. Mara asked her customers not to give her apartment number to the elevator operator who sat downstairs, her evil eye staring right through everyone. Mara stitched away on her sewing machine and jumped at every ring of the doorbell, like a member of an underground resistance group.

Today, at the end of the eighties, a lot has changed. Astronauts have multiplied in such numbers that you can't keep track of them. And talented clothes designers are as famous as movie stars. However, that's now. Then it was different...

Tired of jumping at the ring of the doorbell and humiliating herself, but at the same time having saved enough money for some valuables and a nice apartment, Mara quit sewing and went to work at a television station. Now, that's a place where people become faceless, like on the subway. Yet when someone asked, "What do you do?", you could answer, "I'm a director's assistant." Now, that's not like being a dressmaker. Although an assistant director is something like a waitress; people are always saying, "Give me this!" "Bring me that!" "Go away!"

It was during this period in her life that my path crossed with Mara's, and that was when her name was entered in my address book.

We met in Komarovo, near Leningrad. My husband and I had gone there on vacation to stay at the Theater Society's Union resort. It was the off-season, the hotel was empty, and the society was offering rooms to non-theater organizations. That included us, geologists.

On one of the days when my husband and I were taking a walk not far from the main building, a young woman wearing an expensive full-length fur coat approached us and asked whether we were staying in the hotel. As soon as we said yes, she started asking what the place was like, if she might see a room and if it was worth coming here. I didn't want to go back in, but I couldn't turn her down because she was wearing a real fur coat, while I had on some synthetic trash. And, besides, she was pushy. It was somehow understood that I should obey her. I meekly said, "Certainly," and took this stranger into my own hotel room, number 315. She inspected everything in the room, including the closets, which she opened without my permission. Meanwhile, she introduced herself: her name was Mara, and her husband was Dimychka.

Dimychka waited for his wife in silence, completely expressionless. Every so often he'd say, "Come on, Mara, let's go."

We went to see our guests off. Dimychka walked beside us as if he had nothing to do with any of this, but he exuded decency and calm. They made a nice couple, as in a vaudeville skit: the comedian and the straight man. Dimychka didn't speak, but Mara was constantly at it; she soared, she laughed loudly, flashing her beautiful white teeth and her golden-red hair. She was self-assertive. She asserted herself, her fur coat and her essence. She was simply expending useless energy into outer space. I guessed that she'd decided to latch onto us on the path out of boredom. She was bored with being alone with Dimychka and needed an audience. At the moment, the audience happened to be me, a poor little geologist living off of my salary—ordinary, mass-produced, thirteen to the dozen.

They left that evening after dinner. Mara promised to make me a skirt and demanded my friendship in exchange. I agreed. Mara had some sort of magnetic power; you didn't want to, but you did what she wanted. It's like sunflower seeds: they're awful, but you can't stop eating them.

After they left, I said,"They've invited us over to their place!"

"You'll have to go without me," said my husband brusquely.

Mara disgusted my husband, but she attracted me. Everything she did was "over the mark"—she overexcelled, overstepped the social norms that imprisoned me, shackled by "one shouldn't" and "one mustn't." I was elementary and unleavened, like Jewish matzo, which tastes good when you eat it with something spicy. Mara became that spicy something for me. So, drawn by the skirt, her promised friendship, and my need for "over the mark," I called Mara and went to Leningrad.

She opened the door. I started as if I'd been splashed with cold water. Mara was stark naked. Her breasts looked as shameless as church domes without crosses. I expected her to be embarrassed and rush around looking for a bathrobe, but Mara just stood there, calmly, almost arrogantly, as if she were wearing an evening dress.

"Why are you," I said in a flustered voice, "naked?"

"What's wrong?" Mara was surprised. "It's only a body. Is yours different from mine?"

She was right. My body was the same as hers, generally speaking. I gave in and stepped inside the room. Mara led the way into the apartment, with her naked rear end in full view.

"Are you taking a bath?" I guessed.

"I take fresh-air baths. The skin needs to breathe."

Mara sat down at her sewing machine and started to sew the skirt for me. She tied a stiff piece of fabric around her chin, the way they tie the jaws of the deceased before burial.

"What are you doing that for?" I asked.

"So that I don't get a second chin. My head's bent downward all the time."

Mara finished the job in forty minutes, threw me the skirt and named the price. It turned out to be ten rubles more than what we had agreed upon. You just don't do that. I felt ashamed for her, grew embarrassed and nodded my head slightly to say that it was all right. After paying her, I realized that I still had enough for a ticket back to Moscow, but not for sheets to sleep on. The conductor would probably be surprised.

"You'll have to sew a zipper in yourself," said Mara. "I don't have any black ones right now." That meant that she'd charged me an extra ten rubles for not sewing in the zipper.

The fresh-air bath session was over. Mara removed the cloth from around her head and slipped on a Japanese robe with dragons on it. The robe was made of the finest silver-gray, mother-of-pearl silk.

"Did you make that yourself?" I gasped in astonishment.

"Don't be stupid! This is a real kimono," declared Mara in offended tones. "It's imported!"

I got the picture: she sewed for others and, with the money she made, bought imported clothes for herself.

With her jaw free, Mara could eat and talk. She brewed some coffee and started telling me about her next-door neighbors in apartment number 50. Their names were Alexander and Sofia—Sasha and Sosha for short. Sosha was petite, fair, and colorless, as if she had been pulled out of hydrogen peroxide. But there was something about her that made your eyes want to linger and take a good look at her. And once you started looking, you discovered more and more... Pale northern women, like northern flowers, have much more charm to them than the blatantly gorgeous southern dahlias. Dahlias strike you at once, and all you can do is stand and reel. But you won't stand there for long. You'll get sick of looking at them. But with a forget-me-not, you stare and get drawn in... However, neither northern flowers nor Sosha was the point. The point was that Mara had fallen in love with Sasha and needed to tell someone about it. Otherwise her feelings would overwhelm her, she wouldn't be able to breathe.

Mara chose me as that person. I was someone safe, from another town, a chance acquaintance, like a taxi driver. She could confess to me, then get out and immediately forget about it. Instead of saying good-bye and leaving on time, I sat there like a spineless lump until two in the morning. Meanwhile, my dear husband was waiting in the dark and cold on the train platform in Komarovo, meeting the trains arriving from Leningrad one after another and not knowing what to think.

We spent the entire night sorting out her relationship with Sasha, and then the whole day trying to catch up on our sleep. An entire day of my vacation flew out the window. And all because of what? Because of Sasha and Sosha. Or rather, because of Mara. I established the pattern only later on: wherever Mara is, there disaster awaits me. If she called, it was always when I was in the middle of washing my hair. I'd run to the phone, explain that I couldn't talk, but then for some reason I'd talk to her anyway. Shampoo would run into my eyes, water down my back, and I'd end up catching cold and getting sick. If she called under normal circumstances, and I'd succeed in hanging up the receiver once the conversation was over, then for some reason my foot would catch on the phone cord as I'd be walking away from the phone, and I'd fall, breaking my knee and the telephone at the same time. I'd end up limping and cut off from the world. It was as if God were shaking his finger in front in my face and warning me not to get involved with her. But the devil would wink at me, and I couldn't do anything about it.

Our stay at Komarovo ended with my husband and my returning to Moscow on dusty mattresses without sheets, and with a zipperless skirt, the bitter aftertaste of an argument, and a ruined vacation.

Mara stayed in Leningrad. She worked at the television station, and made money on the side by sewing. Actually, it was the other way around. She earned a living on her sewing machine and made money on the side at the television station. But at home and at work, day and night, she constantly thought of Sasha. Dimychka wasn't any older than Sasha, but he seemed old. Even when he was three years old, he was an elderly man. There was a picture of him in a photo album as a three-year-old child with droopy cheeks and a pompous look on his face, like a dentist with an established practice. But, Sasha, even at forty, was still a three-year-old, as helpless as a genius, with everything in him crying out, "Love me!" Sosha was so lucky...

Out of the blue Dimychka took up "natural healing." He let urine settle in glass bottles as part of a new method of treatment: returning its own wastes back to the body. While right next door there was someone so clean after a swim, so spiritual after a symphony by Kalinnikov, and as alien as someone from another planet... All of the best things in life were passing Mara by. All that was left for her was the petty bustle of her television work, capricious customers and urine in three-liter bottles.

One day Mara was returning home when the same elevator operator, the one with the evil eye, called her over and told her in strict confidence that the wife who lived in apartment number 50 had left her husband for another man. This other man had shown up during the day in a yellow Zhiguli, and they'd carried out her clothes and linens in bundles, and in way of furniture, just a rocking-chair. This new man, obviously her lover, was dark-complexioned, had a moustache, and was very stylish. His summer shoes and jacket were monogrammed with his initials.

"Maybe he monograms them himself," suggested Mara, trying to distract the elevator operator from the change of expression on her face.

Sasha came by after the concert that evening, wearing a black suit with a bow tie, and asked when he should wash the potatoes, before or after peeling them. Mara said he should wash them twice, once before and once afterwards. Sasha stood there and didn't leave. Mara invited him in. She fried him some potatoes, while Sasha sat next to Dimychka, and neither of them said anything. Dimychka generally wasn't talkative, whereas Sasha just didn't want to talk to anyone, yet dreaded staying alone in his apartment. This is precisely what he wanted: simply to sit in silence with someone, and not just anyone, but with a lively, sensible person.

Mara fried the potatoes in boiling oil, the way they're cooked in restaurants. There wasn't any meat, so she fried some Georgian suluguni cheese, dipping it in egg and flour before frying it. She fed the men. Sasha had never eaten hot cheese before. He ate and cried, but the tears didn't flow from his eyes, they just filled in his heart. Mara loved Sasha, so her heart grew heavy from his tears. She also sat in silence.

That was at eleven o'clock at night. At four o'clock in the morning, Mara slipped out of their wide conjugal bed, away from the sleeping, wheezing Dimychka, put on her slippers and the robe with the dragon on it, went out on to the stair landing, and rang Sasha's doorbell.

She heard footsteps right away. Sasha wasn't sleeping. The door immediately swung open. Sasha hadn't locked it. He was waiting for Sosha, certain she would change her mind and come back. She needed a shock to put everything in its proper place. And now everything was in its proper place. Sosha had returned and was ringing the doorbell. He forgave her. He wouldn't say a single word of reproach to her, but would simply kneel in front of her. To hell with male pride. Pride means loving yourself; but he loved her, Sosha.

Sasha opened the door. His neighbor was standing on the doorstep. Someone else's woman, and besides, one he deeply disliked. Sasha couldn't stand her categorical manner and the way she laughed. She was an army sergeant, not a woman.

Sasha's face was like a thermometer measuring all of his feelings, and Mara saw it move from wild happiness at 100 degrees, to bewilderment and then down to zero and below. Mara understood everything.

"Excuse me," she said in a guilty tone, "but I was frightened. I thought you wanted to jump out of the window. All nonsense, of course... Excuse me, please."

Sasha realized that here was someone concerned about a fellow human being—she couldn't sleep, became alarmed, and ran over to see him. This meant he wasn't as alone in the world as he thought. Even if there was only one person who cared. Even if he didn't need her at all. He was grateful, in any event.

"Come in," invited Sasha.

"It's late, though," Mara objected weakly.

"No, it's early," Sasha corrected her and went off to make some coffee.

What else could he do with a female visitor who showed up at 4:00 a.m.?

Mara sat down at the table. She looked at Sasha's back and felt guilty. Of what? Of loving him, whereas he didn't love her. She had just read that in Sasha's face. Why was she any worse than Sosha, that colorless moth, that traitor? Here's how she was worse. Men should be tormented, not beguiled and flirted with. Mara followed her thoughts and didn't recognize herself. In principle, she'd been designed and produced by nature to be a consumer. She was ready to consume everything and anything, to shove it all into herself through all her orifices: eyes, ears, mouth and so forth. But with this man it was just the opposite: she wanted to share everything with him, to give up her last piece of bread to him, to give away her last shirt. She wanted simply to give him her body and soul as a gift, if only he'd take them—if only they'd be of use to him. It turned out that Mara had accumulated so many untapped feelings and words, and so much tenderness, intellect and energy, that a whole fertile layer had formed. If a seed were to fall into the rich soil, immediately a magical shrub of love would spring up, just like in a cartoon.

Her first husband, Zhenka Smolin, was also a consumer. His main question was, "Why do I have to?" He felt that he didn't owe anyone anything and that everyone owed him. Mara also felt that everyone owed her. That set one ego against the other. They fought until there was blood, and it resulted in two coffins: one for their souls, the other for their flesh. With Dimychka, Mara had recuperated from the previous devastating war. It wasn't love, however, but healing and survival. This was love, and her heart was prepared. But, Sasha the sower was saving his seed for another field.

Mara grew chilly and felt like complaining. But to whom? In order to complain, you need a person who's interested in you. Your mother, for instance. But her mother had forgotten how she herself had suffered. Now she just ridiculed everything that happened in life. And Dimychka? What could she say to him? That she loved Sasha and was living with Dimychka only because she feared loneliness?

Mara wilted and no longer looked like an army sergeant. Sasha poured them some coffee. He sat down beside her, and rested his head on her shoulder.

"Mara, do you know a good doctor? Take me to a doctor," he said.

"What's wrong with you?"

"I'm, well...I'm basically not a man."

"In what sense?" asked Mara, not understanding.

"The most literal. Sonya left me because of it."

"Maybe the problem's not you, but Sonya?"

Mara sensed people's souls through her skin. She was convinced that sexual energy, like any energy, has its own density and radius. Some men don't radiate anything. Anything at all. But other men emanate so much sexual energy that without a space suit, you'll get irradiated. She could feel Sasha's sexual energy, even through the concrete walls of her apartment.

"What does Sonya have to do with it?" Sasha lifted his head from Mara's shoulder. "You probably don't understand what I'm taking about."

"I understand perfectly well. Let's go." Mara stood up from the table.

"Where?" asked Sasha, not understanding.

"I'll show you."

Sasha obeyed. He followed Mara. They lay down on the wide Arab bed. Mara didn't believe that Sosha was right. She wanted to prove her wrong. And she did. She proved to Sasha not only that he was sound as a man, but, more importantly, that he was a prodigy of masculinity. He belonged to the select few. Only someone who's a biological wonder can sense life and its concentrated essence so subtly and powerfully. Men like Sasha no longer existed. Well, maybe there was another one like him somewhere in India or China. But there definitely wasn't anyone like him in the Soviet Union. In any case, Mara hadn't heard of one.

Sasha smiled blissfully, his body afloat. Mara propped herself on her elbow and looked at him. He was so completely hers, as if he'd grown inside of her, and she'd given birth to him, as if up until now they'd shared a common circulatory system.

"Would you like me to tell you how I love you?" asked Mara.

He gave a barely perceptible nod. He didn't have the strength to nod firmly. For a long time, Mara searched for words, but only the simplest and most banal ones came to mind.

"You're so good," she said. "You're the best. You're unique."

Sasha wanted to sleep, yet he didn't want to waste time sleeping. They talked until six in the morning. Like a true psychoanalyst, Mara forced Sasha to return to the scene of the accident and to recall how everything started.

And Sasha remembered. Two years ago, he and Sosha were vacationing by the sea. He went swimming during a storm and couldn't get back to the shore. All of a sudden he realized that he wasn't going to make it back, that he'd drown near the beach.

When he returned to their hotel room, he was staggering. He lay down on the bed, closed his eyes, and saw layers of muddy green water in front of him. Sosha's body and soul were in a completely different state. She reached for her husband, but she seemed like a wave to him, and he wanted to dive out of her. Sosha got insulted, and, in an unexpectedly rude voice, she said, "You're impotent."

Sasha tried right then and there to refute the accusation, but nothing worked. That evening he remembered that nothing had worked, got scared, and now fear, not fatigue, got in the way. As time went on his fear solidified and his mind was blocked. His brain sent out wrong signals, and a chance word turned into a diagnosis.

Sosha stopped believing in him. And he stopped believing in himself. Then he started thinking that his problem was apparent, that everyone saw what was wrong with him and snickered behind his back. Sasha started to play poorly in the orchestra, and the conductor lost interest in him. The competition was soon approaching. Sasha knew that everyone else would outperform him. Sonya had left him. The members of the orchestra would leave too. He was an empty, senseless, sexless shell. The whole city, the whole world was laughing behind his back. That night he went out onto the balcony, looked down and already saw himself flying, all twisted, with his arms and legs blowing back, then lying on the asphalt in a ridiculous splat. Sasha felt no pity for himself, just disgust. He didn't like himself, whether alive or dead. And if you don't like yourself, then how can you demand it of others. At that minute, the doorbell rang, someone else's wife entered and said, "You're the best. You're unique."

He kissed Mara's hand. How else can you thank someone for bringing you back to yourself? Live it up. You're the best. You're unique.

Mara had returned Sasha to the scene of the accident. She had removed the broken part in his brain, and life started running on all four wheels again.

In the morning, Mara returned to the sleeping, unsuspecting Dimychka. But Sasha couldn't sleep. He was beginning a new life.

There was a concert that evening. The conductor said that Sasha's B flat made the whole symphony. The other musicians noticed that Sasha's eyes were shooting stars, just like a May Day firework display. He'd grown younger, more fit, and handsome. Sasha, for his part, noticed what remarkable talents surrounded him, bringing metal and wood to life. After all, what is a trombone or a violin? They're just metal and wood. But when a person breathes his entire soul into them, they come alive. And vice versa. If a person stifles his soul, then he turns into wood or metal. That can really happen.

After the concert, Sasha didn't walk or plod home, as he used to, but cut through space. He rushed home, where Mara was waiting for him. She had discovered Sasha, like a continent, and intended to found her own state there. But Sasha wasn't looking so far ahead. He simply rejoiced and affirmed his sense of self. He affirmed and confirmed it.

A month passed in this way.

During this month, Sosha built a new nest with her husband Irakli. It's one thing to date a person, but it's another thing to live together in the same house. Irakli filled the house with guests, which was part of his national tradition, and Sosha quietly served things at the table, then cleared them off. That was also part of the tradition; a woman should know her place.

Irakli worked as a construction engineer and was writing his dissertation on the subject of "Eliminating the Consequences of an Atomic Explosion." Sosha thought that after an atomic explosion there'd be nobody left to eliminate the consequences. She didn't understand anything about it and didn't want to. As it was, that's all they ever harped on about day and night on television; it was awful. But in Sasha's music, she'd understood everything. In seven years of living together, she had learned to read the conductor's score and to distinguish the principal part from the secondary, she knew all the musicians in the orchestra and could follow their individual instruments as they blended. With her eyes closed, she could tell who was playing: "That's Fima, that's Dodik, that's Andrei... Now everyone together—Fima, Dodik, and Andrei."

That had been a good time.

Sosha felt nostalgic for her previous life, although she was completely happy with Irakli. She made Georgian khinkali instead of Russian pelmeni, and in the midst of it she'd think about how Sasha was hungry and neglected, while Irakli was surrounded by guests, khinkali and Sosha. She'd sigh and dial Sasha's number. But when she heard his voice, she'd hang up. What could she say to him?

Sasha knew who was calling, and whenever Mara would reach out to answer the phone, he'd fall on the receiver, like a kite from the sky. He was hiding Mara from Sosha.

One day he anxiously said to her, "Listen, get your hairpins, brooches and other stuff together. Sosha's coming over today."

"What for?" Mara was unpleasantly surprised.

"She wants to fix me lunch. She thinks I'm starving."

Mara gathered up her personal belongings and took them back home to Dimychka. She was living in two different homes; luckily it was only four steps from the first to the second one, much as in the war song, where death was only four steps away.

Dimychka didn't suspect anything. He was busy. People were flocking to him, since people have always believed in healers more than in bona fide doctors. It was actually more convenient for him when Mara was at the neighbor's house.

Sasha also liked the set-up. His work was pure joy, and Mara was pure joy. But the greatest joy of all was when Sosha would come to visit. She would come in the middle of the day, with a guilty expression, and move around quietly, sorting things out, cooking, and vacuuming. Sosha was a good person; Mara was passion incarnate. He desired her. But he loved Sosha. Those aren't the same things, it turns out. A wise man once said that the flesh is a horse, but the soul is a rider. If you only listen to the horse, it'll lead you to the barn; you should listen to the rider.[1]

Mara took her things home once, and then again. The third time, though, she left them out in plain view. Sosha didn't notice. So Mara called her at work at the Scientific Research Institute and set up a meeting with her in the Tauride Gardens. Sosha was surprised, but she came. She already had guessed what the impending conversation was about; Mara would fly in as the guardian angel of hearth and home and try to talk her into returning to Sasha. After all, Mara didn't know why she'd left. To a bystander, everything looks great, almost ideal, as it always does when you're not directly involved.

Mara was late. Sosha gazed mournfully at the palace that Potemkin had built as a place where he and Catherine the Great could be together. When it was finished, though, Catherine already had a new lover—she'd already used up Potemkin. Why could Catherine do that, but not Sosha? She's not a tsarina, of course, but, then, no one's building palaces for her, either. Just a one-room apartment in a new housing development.

Mara appeared and, while still approaching, said, "Don't come to see Sasha anymore. You left him, and that's an end to it."

"What business is that of yours?" Sosha asked in surprise.

"The most personal. He's mine." (Sosha gaped.) "Yes, mine," repeated Mara. "Body and soul, and you've got no business at his place. We can do just fine without your crummy soups!"

Dimychka had figured out that when cows are slaughtered, they must experience a deathly terror. This terror passes into their blood and through the blood into their muscles. And the whole human race is poisoned by this animal terror... It's the source of aggression, crime, sickness, and premature aging. People should eat the fruits of the sea and the forest instead. After all, eating live, intelligent creatures is tantamount to cannibalism.

What struck Sosha was not the part about the "crummy soups," but Sasha's double-dealing. A two-faced Janus. Well, all right, at least everything was clear now. She could stop torturing and tormenting herself, just peacefully divorce him and get legally married. And let Mara have Sasha.

"Here's to you!" cried Sosha, making a vulgar yet refined gesture with her pale, sensitive fingers.

"He's mine!" Mara repeated, ignoring the vulgar gesture.

"We'll see..."

That same evening Sosha returned to Sasha's, and the elevator operator saw her dragging the rocking chair into the elevator.

And that same evening Mara went over to Sasha's apartment and rang the doorbell. Sosha opened the door. She was wearing an apron. Evidently her Georgian had trained her to work round the clock.

"I left my malachite ring here," said Mara.

"Where?" asked Sosha.

"In the kitchen. Or maybe in the bedroom," said Mara, to indicate where she'd been.

Sosha didn't invite her in. She left, then came back.

"Your ring isn't here," she said. "You left it in someone else's bedroom." And she closed the door.

Her ring in fact was at home in her jewelry box. Mara knew that, but she just wanted to make waves by throwing a stone into their smooth family life. But she didn't have a big stone, just a little oval shaped piece of malachite. Sasha didn't consider himself guilty of anything. He hadn't invited Mara over. She had come on her own in the middle of the night. He hadn't seduced her, either. She herself had got him to lie down beside her. He hadn't promised her anything. Her hopes were her own. True, she did love him. But whereas she did, he didn't.

A week later, Sasha stepped into the open elevator, and there stood Mara. Had he known that she was inside, he'd have taken the stairs to the sixteenth floor. They rode up together in silence. Sasha tried to look past her, but Mara stared straight at him, her eyes seeking his. Then she asked him point blank, "So, that's how it is?"

"So it seems," Sasha answered. And that was all.

Six months later Sosha went back to Irakli. Mara didn't try to find out the reason. She didn't go back to Sasha, and he didn't ask her to, either. He was hoping to find a woman who'd unite body and soul in one, so that the horse and the rider would think alike and move in the same direction.

Mara's shuttle-style way of life ended. She settled down quietly alongside Dimychka and told everyone that things were great. That the family is the laboratory for stability, and her home is her castle. She thought up the part about the laboratory herself, but the English had coined the saying about the castle. But sometimes Mara would become hysterical in her castle for no reason at all. She'd throw dishes out of the window, and Dimychka would be horrified, because the cups and plates could hit someone on the head.

The public life of the country flowed on against the background of people's private lives. Nikita Sergeevich Khrushchev came to power, and the first thing he did was rescind Stalin. "Stalin—our guiding light, Stalin—our youth's ideal" turned out to be a tyrant and a murderer. The thaw touched everyone with its breath of spring. Solzhenitsyn's *One Day in the Life of Ivan Denisovich* was published. Everyone read it and understood that a new era had dawned.

Nikita Sergeevich was a regular person, and people didn't have to be afraid of him. They could even joke about his being a "cornball."[2] It all ended with him being removed from office. He was the first and so far the only head of state to be deposed during his lifetime and to die while on a pension. The sculptor whom Khrushchev had criticized in front of the entire country sculpted a monument of him, made of black and white stone.—Light and darkness, tragedy and farce.[3]

Then began the time that is now called the "period of stagnation." A new term appeared—"dissident," and those derived from it: "he went diss," "a bunch of dissidoes," etc... Stagnation was evident in politics and in the economy, but in Mara's life the seventies were a period of storm and stress.

Mara met Myrzik. He had a first name, a last name, and an occupation; he was an assistant cameraman. But Mara called him Myrzik, and it stuck.

They met at the television studio. One day, as they left work together, Mara was complaining that the station ate up all of her time and that she didn't have any left for her personal life.

"How old are you?" asked Myrzik in surprise.

"Thirty-seven," answered Mara.

"Well, what kind of personal life does a person have at thirty-seven?" Myrzik asked, in sincere surprise. "It's all over. The train's left, and the tracks have been dismantled."

Mara looked with astonishment at this idiot who'd come from Moscow on a business trip, while he examined Mara with the eyes of an orphaned waif. They both remarked later that it was this look that decided everything. Was it love at first sight, or, more precisely, at second sight? It was more complicated and simpler than that.

Mara's life with Sasha and Dimychka on the same floor was over. She had died there. She had to leave and go anywhere she could. She'd even thought of finding a worthwhile Jew and sailing off with him over the wide blue sea, as far away from home as possible. But no one worthwhile showed up, just Myrzik. Mara saw that he was a bit young for her, a bit weak, and generally just Myrzik. But she had to put an end to her old life.

When Mara announced to Dimychka that she was in love, he didn't understand what she wanted from him.

"I'm in love," Mara explained.

"Well, go on being in love. Who's stopping you?"

"I want to leave you."

"But why?"

"So that I can love him."

"And am I interfering with that?"

Mara lowered her head. At that moment, Dimychka seemed to her a bigger man than Myrzik. Myrzik wanted her all to himself, so that no one else could have her. But if Dimychka couldn't be everything for her, he was willing to step aside and watch over her from a distance. She, Mara, was pushing him out of her orbit. And he was afraid not for himself, but for her. Mara burst into tears.

Their conversation took place in a cafe. Myrzik was sitting at the next table, as if he were a stranger. From his position, he was watching to make sure that Dimychka didn't leave with Mara, that there weren't any slip-ups, and that he, Myrzik, would end up the winner.

Afterwards, Myrzik said to Mara, "Your head hung like a wounded bird's. I felt so sorry for you."

Mara wondered where he had seen a wounded bird. He had probably hurt it himself. An orphanage kid.

Mara and Myrzik moved to Moscow. Once they got settled in the capital, Mara remembered me and started coming over to the house with Myrzik. She took him around with her everywhere, as confirmation of her power as a woman and a living sign of esteem. Myrzik worshiped and deified Mara. Everything she said and did seemed brilliant to him and the only thing possible. He stared obliviously and couldn't take his eyes off her.

My husband and I had just had a baby girl, and we felt that the greatest rightness and truth in life was standing before us. But in the sudden flash of Mara and Myrzik's happiness, my life, which was draped in dirty diapers, seemed colorless. I felt that the plug had been pulled out of the rightness of my life, as if out of a rubber toy, and the rightness began to escape out of me with a hiss.

We sat in the kitchen drinking tea. Mara was showing Myrzik off to us. "Look at his hand." She grabbed his wrist and pulled his hand closer for our examination. His hand was like any other, but Mara roared with laughter, her large, bright teeth sparkling. "Look at his ear." She started to rake aside his Esenin-like curls. Myrzik tried to struggle free, while Mara roared with laughter. They simply exuded happiness. Myrzik's happiness was sunny, but Mara's was moonlike, it reflected his. But it was happiness, nonetheless.

Suddenly Mara pulled Myrzik from his seat, and they got ready to go home. Our baby was asleep. We went out to see them off. Mara drew me ahead and began trying to persuade me to leave my husband. It's so great when you leave your husband, she said. It revitalizes you, as if you've been reborn and are living anew.

I listened to Mara and thought about my own love. My husband and I had met on a geological expedition. We both were single, and everything happened naturally of its own accord. The tents were set up for groups of four people, so at night we went off to make out in the taiga. We spent a long time looking for a spot that wasn't swampy or covered with ants. We finally found a flat, firm area, spread out a raincoat, and immediately the headlights of a truck shone on us. It turned out we had chosen a spot on the road. I darted into the bushes like a goat and lost my bra. Some guys from our geology group found it in the morning, but they wouldn't give it back. And whenever I ran Komosmol meetings and appealed to their Komsomol honesty and conscience, the guys who were sitting in the back row would insidiously hold up my bra for me to see.

That was a good time but it was over. After ten years, our love had lost its zest and become routine, like putting on your working overalls. But I knew I wasn't going to start a new life, and my future looked long and lonely to me, like the steppe.

My husband was probably thinking the same thing. We walked back to the house in silence, like strangers. Our baby was awake and crying. To me she appeared to be mourning my life.

Well, that's Mara for you. She was like a candle—she shone for a while, smoked, and dripped wax... She'd stirred a yearning in me for fatal passions and the hot breath of life. But what was the point of it?

So Mara and Myrzik were living in Moscow in his one-room apartment in the Bibirevo district. Bibirevo was somewhere between Moscow and Kaluga. The identical apartment buildings were as depressing as a rainy summer.

Mara called a carpenter named Gena, who put up wood paneling in the sun porch, insulated the walls and ceiling, and installed a steam heater. The additional room that resulted was narrow and long, like part of a corridor, but it was a room, nonetheless. Mara put a little table in it, placed her Singer sewing machine on top of the table, and set up an ironing board along the wall. Now it was full steam ahead... That road was familiar and nice. She sewed only for those whom she liked inside and out. She threw herself into friendships, getting so close to her friends that you couldn't even fit a piece of paper between them. Then, just as quickly, she'd quarrel with them and push them away. She had a need for conflict. There was an infernal streak in her that would lash out. Say what you will, she was destined to live in hell.

After a year, Mara traded the apartment in Bibirevo for one on Kutuzov Avenue, bought a used Moskvich, and a Japanese Seiko camera. The camera was meant for Myrzik. Mara had decided to make a press photographer out of him, so that he could capture on film all the wonderful or ugly moments, depending on what the country wanted at a given time—a burning truck, a model worker or children going to school for the first time.

Mara tore down the walls in the new apartment and had the small area converted into a darkroom. She helped Myrzik not only develop his photos, but also choose his subjects. She turned out to be talented at that, as at everything else. Myrzik was asked to work for Novosti Publishers, propagandizing the Soviet way of life. Thanks to Mara he had an exhibit, and, also thanks to Mara, he got into fights with everyone. Myrzik was fired from his job.

Mara was like a strong medicine with side effects. On one hand, it cured you, but on the other hand, it caused weakness and vomiting. No one knew which was better.

At first Myrzik thought that things couldn't be any other way, but one day it suddenly became clear that they could indeed be different. He broke up with Mara and left her for another woman who was young, gentle, and pregnant with his child. She called him Leonid Nikolaevich, not Myrzik. With Mara he'd forgotten what his name really was.

If you went back to the beginning of their love, then his feelings for Mara had been incomparably stronger and more powerful than this new love. But, with Mara, there were no prospects for the future—just a new car, a summer home, a steam bath for the summer home. But, for whom? Myrzik had grown bored living just for himself. He wanted a son, so he could give him a happy childhood. Myrzik had grown up in an orphanage and knew what childhood was.

Mara tried to stop Myrzik by depriving him of his material well-being. But Myrzik managed somehow to hold onto it. How he succeeded in doing this was unbelievable. He took the Seiko camera for himself, and chased Mara out of the house, just like a fox after a hare. That's Myrzik for you.

He returned to work and conquered the world. Well, not the whole world, but the part that he could grasp mentally. Myrzik did just fine without Mara, he even prospered, and that upset her most of all.

At that crucial moment in her life, Mara began to show up at my house again, and she stayed with us for a few days. She didn't have anywhere to rest her head: literally, she didn't have anywhere to sleep. She knew half of Moscow, but no one needed her. They needed her when she was successful and happy, not robbed and driven out. She, in turn, didn't need famous people featured on magazine covers. She wanted to lean on us, ordinary and solid people. We were geologists—the earth was solidly under our feet, it wouldn't slip out from under them.

My husband went to spend the night with his parents, who lived just one floor below us. Mara slept in his place. Tragedy normally elevates a person, but Mara managed to remain unchanged even now. Because she had a cold, and garlic works as an antiseptic, Mara stuck some garlic up her nose. She started snoring because her nose was plugged up, and the strange sounds and smells kept me awake. I fell asleep towards morning, just when Mara woke up. She needed sympathy, and people can offer sympathy only if they're awake, not asleep.

So Mara shook me awake and informed me of what she had sacrificed for Myrzik's sake: Dimychka, her home, and the architecture of Leningrad... She asked me to remember what Myrzik had been when she met him—a wimp: "Bring me this! Bring me that! Go away!" And what did he become? As soon as he became something, he found out that he didn't need anyone who'd been privy to his previous life. She was such a fool to have trusted him. After all, it had been written all over his face. He used her, squeezed her dry like a lemon, and threw her away. Alone in a strange city.

"Go back home," I advised her. "Dimychka will be happy to have you back."

Mara stopped talking and began thinking it over. She would be returning to the sixteenth floor where yellow-eyed Sasha came and went, so near you could reach out and touch him, and yet so far. As if he were from another era. From the 21st century. Oh, Sasha, you twinkling star, where are your nightingales singing now? Before, she couldn't have ever imagined leaving her husband, house, and possessions. But after Sasha, she threw everything to the wind with no regrets. The worse it was, the better it was. So she ended up with Myrzik. She survived through him. But he also turned out to be strong medicine with side effects. He cured her, but he also crippled her. Now here she was, sitting in someone else's home with garlic up her nose. Some fate—to make a real man out of one, a press photographer out of the other, and to get what in return?

"I created them, and they betrayed me..."

"You created them for yourself, though, so that things would be good for you," I corrected her.

"What's the difference?" Mara didn't understand.

"You were selfish and self-centered. Self-centered people are like canned food; they lose their vitamins and aren't good for you."

"And what do you do that's unselfish?" Mara wondered. "Are you raising your child for some man who doesn't belong to you?"

At any reminder of my daughter, whatever the context, a wave of tenderness always washed over my face.

"She says 'free' instead of 'three,' and 'I'm firsty' instead of 'I'm thirsty.' I'll teach her how to speak correctly, and I'll toilet train her. I'll also prepare her for kindergarten, for being a member of a group. Then I'll ensure a bright future for her."

"But why should the future be bright, and not the present?" asked Mara. "When society can't offer anything here and now, it gives you a lot of pie in the sky. And you eat it up."

In other words, my generation is knee-deep in propaganda. And the older generation, which believed in Stalin—what were they wading in?

"You should emigrate," I advised. "Everyone there is like you."

"What do I need them for? And what do they need me for? I'm forty years old. There's only a demand for antiques at secondhand stores. It's all over. The train's left, and the tracks have been dismantled, as of blessed memory, Lionechka said."

"Who's Lionechka?" I couldn't remember.

"Myrzik."

Mara switched on the table lamp. I could tell that she wasn't sleeping, and I didn't sleep either. Mara had once again stirred something in me.

I thought about how, by the age of forty, she had already created a "bright present" for herself twice—first with Dimychka in Leningrad and then with Myrzik in Moscow. For five years, my husband and I hadn't been able to afford to have a child, and we didn't have any place to live. We lived at his parents', crowding and mooching off of them. Now it'll take us ten years to move from a one-room to a two-room apartment. You only start living like a human being when you're around fifty years old, and then, at fifty-five, you're written off and retired. Figure it out yourself...

When Mara's not around, I'm fine. As people say in telegrams, I am healthy, successful at work, and happy in my personal life. But as soon as Mara appears, I become a slave, entangled, dependent, and blinkered. And my one source of happiness is—that I'm not aware of *how* poorly I really live.

Then Mara disappears and again things are all right. Life's livable.

This time she disappeared to the Crimea. The sea had always come to her rescue. She washed away her tears with sea-water, went far off so she could sunbathe in the nude, lying on a rock like a lizard, its torn-off tail growing back.

Myrzik had said that the train had left and the tracks had been dismantled. That wasn't true, though. Myrzik had left, but the rails were still there, intact. That meant that a new train would be coming. Not just any old freight train, but a luxury express train heading for a long happy life. Of course, she could stop bustling about and sit and wait at the way station, counting on chance. But chance had thrown her Zhenka, Dimychka and Myrzik. Chance was blind. She needed to intervene in fate and prepare the chance herself.

Sasha and Myrzik were stalks bending in the wind. They needed support. At forty, though, you want someone strong that you can lean on. Who's holding the steering wheel these days? Some famous Washnscrub, Head of sinks and Boss of tubs.[4] But, where could you find this man? You couldn't just walk into his office. You had to get a special pass. The police would then compare the pass against your passport and memorize the number, series, housing registration, when it was issued, by whom. And who knows, maybe you'd go in and shoot Washnscrub, although Moscow's hardly Italy, and Washnscrub is 70, so who needs him anyway? The blood in his veins had already curdled thick like sour milk.

However, Mara had marked out her target, and she moved towards it, like a long-range ballistic missile. After soaking up the sunshine and completely restoring her torn-off tail, Mara returned to Moscow and yanked the "Seiko" from around Myrzik's neck so hard that she almost tore his head off with it. She got the necessary slip of paper and went into Washnscrub's office.

He already knew that someone was coming to take his photograph.

Mara sat down in front of him, her legs crossed, and began to examine his face. Washnscrub was an old, incorporeal, dried-up grasshopper. His glasses magnified his eyes. Something protruded on his back under his coat. It might have been a hump, or perhaps an oxygen pillow, or maybe flying equipment. He had an abstract, expressionless face.

"Could you take off your glasses?" Mara asked.

He took them off and laid them on the table. Mara snapped a few pictures, although she knew that something wasn't right.

"Look more animated," Mara requested.

But how do you do something when there's nothing with which to do it? Mara couldn't change his face, so she decided to change the perspective. First, she stood on a chair. Then she lay down on the floor. Then she squatted down. The buttons on her jacket came open and Washnscrub could see her evenly tanned beige breasts, which stuck out like two piglets.

Washnscrub had forgotten the last time he'd seen anything like them or whether he'd ever seen them before. Although he was the boss, he was nonetheless an ordinary man, and his reaction was also ordinary: it was one of surprise. He was so surprised that his stagnant blood stirred and started flowing in his veins. Washnscrub remembered that he was a man, whereas before he had only guessed it because of his name and patronymic. His face grew animated. The pictures turned out better than any he'd ever had taken before.

The billiard ball of fate had gone right into the pocket. If only nothing would interfere with it. Mara saw to it that nothing did. She bought the souls of two secretaries, thereby capturing the fortress gates. Then she took the fortress itself.

Mara trained Washnscrub to her way of being, and after a very short time, it seemed to him that she had always been there. It's the feeling you have for a nursing infant. It's strange to think that until recently, the child hadn't existed at all. Not anywhere. But once he's born, it seems as if he's always been there.

There was one big drawback in Washnscrub's life—his age. This was complicated by his indifference. You can't do anything, but you also don't want to. Mara swept away this indifference with her magnetic storm, the way clouds break up on the day of the opening ceremonies of the Olympics. Roused from his indifference, Washnscrub took energetic action, and four months later Mara was living in a separate two-room apartment in a brick apartment building located in a quiet downtown district, where Washnscrub was received as if he were at his own home.

Mara couldn't stand dirt, so she would meet him at the elevator with house-slippers and would put them on his feet. Then she would put him in the bathtub, where she could wash the whole day and his entire previous life off him. Washnscrub would lie in the soft suds and feel that finally, at seventy, he had found happiness. The only negative element was the thought of death. It would be hard to part with this sort of life, which had unexpectedly come to him in the twilight of his years. But he tried not to think about it. As Napoleon's mother had said, "May it last as long as possible," meaning her son's reign as emperor. But she still knitted him some wool socks, in case he got exiled to St. Helena.

After his bath, they'd sit down at the table. The table was of Karelian birch, and on the plates of dark-blue and white English china would be steamed veal cutlets, the ground meat whipped up in a mixer, with cream added. The crystal glasses would be filled with beet juice and a dash of lemon. Beets cleanse the blood and eliminate carcinogens. And Mara would be wearing her robe with the dragons on it, just like a Japanese geisha. The Japanese know how to live—dinner and the tea ceremony, followed by another sort of ceremony.

So at the end of his life Washnscrub had acquired a home and a woman. His wife was a government official, for whom official life had always been more important than the personal. Their home was run by their shrewd cleaning lady Valia. His son was fifty years old now and was a grandfather himself. To forget his loneliness, Washnscrub worked day and night and served his country in the sphere entrusted to him. And suddenly Mara appeared. She turned out to be no less important to him than his whole country. She was equally important. And sometimes even more.

For her part, Mara was grateful to Washnscrub. Gratitude is good soil. Even if you can't grow the magic shrub of love in it, you can at least grow a good tree with edible fruit.

Mara turned out to have a talent not only for sewing and photography, but also for affairs of state. She was something like the Marquise de Pompadour; and she pompadoured.

Her previous lovers, Sasha and Myrzik, had been her creations. She'd molded them and made them, admittedly for her own interests. She'd created them and used them, but they benefitted from it, too. Sasha had gained strength in body, spirit, and hope. Myrzik in his business and finances. But it was Washnscrub who created Mara. As a creator, Mara stagnated, but as a consumer, she flourished. She could use Washnscrub by the handful. She didn't have to go out looking.

Mara wanted to take part in some useful independent activities. She'd received a diploma in pedagogy through a correspondence program. Washnscrub arranged for her to study at an institute attached to the Academy of Pedagogical Science. Mara began to write her dissertation with the aim of someday heading a department, and eventually the whole institute. And later maybe even the entire academy. Why not? The train was moving. The tracks were clear. She was a virtuoso locomotive driver.

On the weekends, Washnscrub would leave for his country house with his family. This gave Mara a break from him. During the next such break, she invited me to come over to her apartment so that she could show off her new power to me, and so that I could walk around her apartment, oohing and aahing.

I was impressed most by the spacious hallways and the lamps hanging from the ceiling and the walls. They looked as though they came from the Tauride Palace. Potemkin had hung them there, and Mara had taken them for herself, since she was a present-day tsarina. The lamps had a dull bronze glow, and emanated an aura of age, mystery, and the talent of an unknown master craftsman. This was the rich home of a high-priced mistress.

I recalled my own apartment, where the ceiling was only two and one-half meters from the floor and lay practically on top of my head. I called my apartment the bunker. The only thing missing was a victrola playing the World War II song "To the Front, Young Woman!" I recalled my in-laws' apartment. They were Komsomol members in the 1920s who, in a spirit of self-sacrifice and selflessness had built this society—and where did they live? In a communal apartment in a single room that was partitioned off by screens. And they didn't complain. They knew that Moscow was suffocating from a housing shortage. There were people still living in basements. So they could put up with it. But Mara got everything right away, just because she had shown off her suntan at the right moment. So some would have a bright future, while others already had a bright present.

Mara noticed that I was feeling depressed and decided that I envied her. I, too, wanted to be the Marquise de Pompadour to Louis XV.

"You know what you lack?" Mara asked sympathetically.

"What?"

She tried to pick the right word, but there was only one that fit. There just wasn't any synonym for it.

"You're very decent," was how Mara phrased it, trying to get around the word she really wanted to use.

"I feel comfortable being that way," I said.

"You feel comfortable being that way because you hide your lack of initiative in life behind your decency."

"On the other hand, I don't hurt anyone."

"You don't hurt anyone, but you don't help anyone either. You simply don't exist."

I gasped for breath. Mara interpreted my pause as a period and decided that the subject had been exhausted. She moved on to the next one.

"My dissertation is almost finished. My defense is coming up."

It had taken my husband six years to fight his way through the barbed wire of his dissertation and reach his defense.

"What's it on?" I asked, hiding my true feelings under a show of interest.

"The sexual education of students in their senior year."

I kept a respectful silence. Mara was an expert on this question and there was no reason she shouldn't share her experience with the next generation. She informed me that she was currently working on a chapter entitled "The Culture of Intercourse." Intercourse was meant not in the sexual sense, but in the general sense of social interaction. Sexual education isn't taught at all in school. They count on the family to do it. But the family doesn't teach it either. The entire country is ignorant. Mara had gathered and summarized the experiences of other countries. She explained it all very interestingly. I was distracted from my bitterness at the inequalities in class that I'd been thinking about earlier. The hypnotic waves that Mara emanated washed over me. Like a fish, I swam toward her hook.

Without any sort of transition, Mara asked, "Would you like to trade your apartment for a two-room one? There are three of you, after all."

I was dumbfounded. That was my dream. My own space. My bright present.

"Could I really?" I asked, made timid by the mere hope of such a thing.

"He's in Peru right now," Mara said, talking about Washnscrub, "But when he comes back in a week, I'll have a talk with him."

So I had swallowed the bait, hook and all. Now Mara could yank at my lip and pull me around in any direction. And that's just what she did.

During the following week, Mara came over to my house several times. She did a good job of cleaning out my library. It was an exaggeration to call it a library, but my husband and I did have our favorite books.

Besides spiritual values, Mara also deprived our house of peace. My husband hated her, and became nervous and withdrawn when she was around. Mara didn't seem to notice, though, and would rush to give him a kiss. He would stiffen, waiting for her to finish hugging him, as disgusted as if he were being attacked by a slippery, loathsome, and dangerous crocodile. He didn't believe in the success of the venture for one second and despised my going along with it. I was afraid that Mara would notice, and then everything would fall through. She needed the devoted eyes of a dog, not those of a wolf, which look off into the forest no matter how much you feed the animal. I tried to keep Mara outdoors. We lived on the outskirts of Moscow, next to a wonderful virgin forest. At one time, there had been summer homes there.

It was spring. At the edge of the forest stood a lone, slender pussy willow. The buds were a tender yellow in hue, fuzzy, and as big as chicks. The pussy willow looked like a young girl who had gotten all dressed up before a dance.

Mara couldn't stand it when beauty existed for its own sake. She decided to take part of this beauty home and put it in a vase. Let beauty serve her. I assumed that she would break off one or two branches, maybe even three. It would hurt the tree, of course, but it could cover its wounds with sap and bandage itself with bark. It would recover.

What Mara did is still fresh in my mind to this day. She didn't just snap off a branch, but instead pulled it down toward her, peeling away a long strip of bark from the tree. Then she did the same thing to a second, third, and fourth branch. She destroyed a whole layer of the poor tree and skinned it alive, leaving it bare. We walked away, and I glanced back. The pussy willow looked as if it had walked out of the Gestapo headquarters. It stood there, torn to shreds and defiled, deprived of its plant consciousness.

I should have turned around and left then. To hell with her, the apartment, and the extra room. But I knew that if I didn't try to get us the apartment, no one else would. So I had to put up with it, and I did. I only asked her, "Why did you do that?"

"I treat everyone the way I've been treated," Mara replied.

First there had been Zhenka Smolin, then the polite and spiritual Sasha. Then there was Myrzik, the orphanage boy, and now old man Washnscrub, who could be her grandfather, and whose love for her resembled incest. If they had treated her *like that* then why couldn't she do the same to others—to people, trees and everything that came her way?

As we walked away, I could feel behind me the pussy willow following me with its eyes and thinking, "How could you!" I was thinking the same thing about myself. "How could you!"

A week went by, and Washnscrub returned. I didn't hear anything from Mara. I waited. I wasn't just waiting, but living under the pressure of high expectation. I was exhausted, every nerve twanging. The only thing that could bring me relief was knowing something definite. I called Mara. Feeling as if I were parachuting into a black abyss, I asked, "Is he back?"

"He is," Mara replied calmly and with dignity.

"Have you talked to him?"

"Yes, I have."

She didn't say anything, as if she didn't understand why I was calling.

"Well, what did he say?" I asked, unable to contain myself.

"Nothing," Mara answered calmly with the same dignity. "He said to me, 'I'm sick of all your endless favors. First you expect me to find a hospital bed for your Tatar Usmanov, then you want me to arrange a place for your idiot friend Artamonova. Leave me alone! Let me die in peace!' And it's true—he can only stretch himself so far," Mara ended in a confiding tone.

I didn't know who this Tatar Usmanov was, but I was the Artamonova idiot. I slammed down the receiver and went out of my mind for half the day. My husband rejoiced. I had been taught a lesson: if you don't respect a person, don't ask him for any favors. If you ask, you lower your moral standards and yourself, and then you get what you deserve. It's your own fault. And that's the way it should be. Life is logical.

I'd learned my lesson, and from it I made the far-reaching conclusion that I shouldn't associate with Mara. Never again. Not for any reason. When she called, I would hang up. If she called back, I didn't get up to answer. I was afraid to some extent. I knew that if I answered I'd say "yes" to her. Then she would pull me out of my burrow by that "yes," bombard me with her hypnotic waves, suck me in with her electromagnet, and, just like a rabbit, I'd crawl into her maw again.

Let her live her own life, and I'll live mine. The poet Voznesensky once wrote, "We were learning not how to survive, but how to push speedometers to the limit." But I'm not pushing anything. I live by the proverb, "The quieter you go, the further you get." The only question is, further from *what*?

Five years passed.

Nothing was happening in our country. Scared by the Prague spring, Brezhnev tried to fix it so that nothing would change and everything would remain the same. No fresh currents flowed. Life gradually turned into a swamp and was covered by duckweed.

Nothing was happening in my personal life either. We lived in our one-room apartment, as before. There was always activity in our co-op building, though. Someone died, someone got divorced, someone left for other shores. Apartments were vacated, but not for us. You had to give a bribe to the chairman of the co-op to get one of them, but we didn't know how much to give him or how to do it. We were afraid of offending him.

I didn't associate with Mara, but echoes of her life did reach me.

Mara was working in some prestigious institution that was part of the Academy of Sciences. It was her training ground, where she could do whatever she wanted. She fired people, made appointments to positions, and had the power to push through or hold up other people's dissertations. An incessant battle raged, with the horses and men all getting entangled.

Mara had to be fired, but first they had to render her harmless. Kartseva, the lab director, took on this feat. She was sure that Washnscrub had no idea that Mara was making free use of his name everywhere, which left him vulnerable. Kartseva called Washnscrub on his private line, introduced herself, opened his eyes to the truth and hung up feeling that justice had been restored.

What happened next was like a fairy tale with an unhappy ending. Within a week, Kartseva's laboratory ceased to exist. And as soon as the laboratory was gone, so was her job and the 360-ruble-a-month salary that came with it. Her little red book containing her building pass became invalid, and the security guard refused to let her into the Academy. Mara roared with laughter, her beautiful white teeth sparkling.

Where did Professor Kartseva, a Communist, disappear to? Did she fight or did she just give up, realizing the futility of resisting? Did she hold it against Mara, or did she feel respect for a force like that? No one knows. They say she became a janitor, so that she would never have to deal with the state machinery again. In the winter she cleared away the snow. In the fall she swept away the leaves. That's all.

The victim had eliminated herself. Her co-workers subsided and shut themselves in their offices, as if they were burrows. Sycophants sprang up, like cornflowers in a field. Mara got a taste of great and complete power—two stripes with a star above them...

Dimychka, in the meantime, had met another woman, been intimate with her, and, being an honorable man, decided to marry her. When she learned of this, Mara made a few phone calls, and Dimychka was placed in a mental institution. There they shot him full of all sorts of medicine that made him fat, dazed, and apathetic.

Some friends gave him a Siamese kitten. He called it Mara. After a short time, Mara gave birth to a kitten he called Kuzia. That was Dimychka's family: he, Mara, and Kuzia. He didn't have anyone to leave the cats with, so when he went on a business trip or on vacation, he would put them into a basket and travel with them.

Mara didn't want to give him up to another woman. She had given up enough things and was tired of it. Dimychka didn't rebel. He gave in, just like Kartseva.

But there exists a balance in nature. If winter is severe, then summer will be hot, and vice versa. Retribution came to Mara from an unexpected source; it came in the form of a junior research fellow named Lomeeva, a *limitchik*. *Limitchiks*, i.e., people with only a temporary residence permit in Moscow, are not like the soldiers in Napoleon's army, who came and left. These people are troops of a hardier sort.

Lomeeva came from the Urals. Her abilities were limited, so she had to depend on her butt instead of her head. She had a solid butt and could sit on it for as long as it takes to complete three dissertations. Her mouth could also be counted on for a generous supply of verbal fireballs. When she spat them out, she reduced you to ashes. She didn't need anything from anyone, but she wouldn't give up anything that was hers. The data in her curriculum vitae are as follows: She was born in 1955; her great-grandfather and grandfather died from vodka—one at home, and the other in a ditch; her father is carrying on the glorious tradition; her husband is in the military; her son is a Pioneer. Lomeeva herself is a Party member, morally stable and purposeful.

If Mara was all stars and chasms,[5] then Lomeeva was mediocre and pushy. Mediocrity and pushiness made themselves comfy in scholarship—the Brezhnev era was just the time for them, their moment of stardom.

Intoxicated with her limitless power, Mara made a fatal miscalculation. She unceremoniously ridiculed Lomeeva's dissertation, smearing it on the wall so thickly that you couldn't scrape it off with a spoon. Her dissertation wasn't approved. In turn, Lomeeva exhaled like a fire-breathing dragon, and let loose a dozen fireballs. As a result, Mara's dissertation was also held up in the final exam committee.

In horror, everyone fled for cover, clearing the ground for battle. Mara and Lomeeva came together like the snow leopard and Mtsyri in Lermontov's famous poem. And there "like snakes they became entwined, like friends whom love and passion bind. They fell together in a bound and continued fighting on the ground."[6]

Brezhnev died and was buried on Red Square. The strong guys who lowered his coffin misjudged their movement, and as the coffin hit the ground clumsily, the sound resonated all over the country. That thump was the beginning of a new era.

Andropov aroused people's hope, but that beginning coincided with the end of his life. At his funeral, Chernenko warmed his hands on his ears. Or maybe it was the other way around—he warmed his ears with his hands. It was not clear why they forced him, a sick, old man who gasped for breath and looked like a chief of personnel of the local Party Committee, into such a difficult and responsible position. A year later, they buried him near the same wall, and the camera men tactfully turned their cameras away from the grave, in case the casket should hit the ground again. But by then it was impossible to turn back the wheels of history. A new thaw had begun.

Washnscrub was forced to retire, so the rear of the army was exposed. Lomeeva pinned Mara to the ground. The stars in the sky aligned themselves in a position unfavorable to Mara. Her magnetic storm could no longer sweep away everything around her, as before; not finding an outlet, it moved inward, invading Mara herself. Cancer flared like a torch inside of her. Stress had caused a malignant tumor to explode inside her body. Or perhaps the fact that she had sunbathed topless had something to do with it.

Mara wound up in the hospital. Two surgeons worked on her, one standing beside her chest, the other at her legs, and with their four hands they cut the woman out of Mara.

After the operation, they proceeded to kill the person in Mara. They put her through chemotherapy and radiation treatment. She grew weak. Her hair fell out. But Mara survived. Her hatred and thirst for revenge proved to be stronger than cancer. Mara was like a Pershing missile, speeding towards its target, but temporarily detained for repairs.

A month later, she was released from the hospital half dead, like the pussy willow. She put on a wig and rushed into battle.

Some friends had brought her a prothetic breast back from France. The French make a cult of woman and know how to take care of her in any situation. The prothesis of soft plastic filled with glycerine looked very elegant. It was a perfect imitation of a living body.

Mara tied the depressing objects in a cambric handkerchief and picked up Soms, the dog she'd inherited from her mother. Soms was already old, but, like any little dog, he still looked like a puppy. Lately Mara had been avoiding people and would spend time only with the noble, loving Soms. And so, with the bundle in her hands and Soms on her shoulder, Mara entered the familiar office. It was the same old office, but a new Washnscrub was there. Mara also was not her old self. She couldn't show off her breasts anymore. In place of breasts, she had scars, one running into another, as if the cancer had clenched its jaws.

Mara untied the bundle in front of Washnscrub and said, "This is what my colleagues have done to me."

Washnscrub, naturally, didn't understand, and asked, "What is it?"

Mara briefly told him her story: the fight with Lomeeva, the cancer that had flared up, caused by stress, and, as a result, the loss of her health and possibly her life. Mara had given her life in the fight for justice.

The new Washnscrub, like the previous one, was human, too. He looked with secret horror at Mara, her quivering dog, and her glycerine breast lying separately in front of him. He was struck by the transience of all living things. But the thought about transience was followed by the wish that Mara take her body parts, leave, and not come back again.

But people leave and don't come back only when, to put it in official terms, their case is solved.

Mara's case was solved. In just one month, her dissertation passed all of the official levels of examination. She passed her defense with flying colors.

She stood there during her defense, slender and elegant, like a mannequin, with brightly rouged cheeks, fake hair and artificial breasts. Imitation diamonds hung from her ears like chandeliers. But the sparkle in her eyes was genuine. It never occurred to anyone to see this successful and talented woman as a victim.

After her defense, Mara called me at home. I answered the phone, not suspecting the call would be from her. Apparently her electromagnetic powers had weakened and ceased to be effective from a distance.

"Congratulate me! I got my candidate's degree!"

I already knew about her illness, and I knew what price she had paid for that dissertation. What did she need it for, anyway? She was forty-five years old. That was the age for a doctoral dissertation, not a candidate's. Evidently, Mara had some sort of complex: she hadn't had any children, she didn't have any of her own flesh and blood to leave behind after she was gone, so she wanted to leave behind the ideas contained in her dissertation. She wanted to leave behind a part of herself.

I sighed heavily and said, "Congratulations..."

Mara detected the forced nature of my congratulation and hung up on me. I had probably irritated her.

Having achieved her victory, Mara lost sight of a sense of purpose and came to a halt. The cancer immediately reared its head and crawled along her bones and up her spine. It kept getting harder and harder to get up every day. Mara would lie in her empty apartment and imagine the door bell ringing. She would open the door. Sasha would walk in and say, "I'm tired of living without you. I tried to outwit fate, but fate can't be deceived."

"I'm a cripple now," she would answer.

And he would reply, "You are you, no matter what you're like. I'm a cripple myself with everyone else but you."

But no one rang the doorbell.

Mara would get up and take a taxi to work. She had her own office now, and there was a name plate on the door with an inscription on it reading, "M. P. Alexandrova, Candidate of Education." Lomeeva's office was next to hers, and it had the same sort of name plate. Their fight had ended at a tie of one to one. Lomeeva didn't yield an inch of her territory. Admittedly, she wasn't brilliant. But are scholars really all geniuses? Let's say you take ginseng cream, for example, the kind that is sold in drugstores. How much ginseng is there really in it? One zillionth of a percent. The rest is Vaseline. It's the same thing in scholarship. There's one genius and the rest are Vaseline. There's a whole army of them. Why shouldn't Lomeeva join the army? Is she any worse than the others?

Lomeeva would walk by Mara's office, heels clicking. She was young, whole, and had two large breasts. She would deliberately click her heels loudly as she passed, and each tap would resound in Mara's head. It felt as if nails were being driven into her brain. She would stuff a handkerchief in her mouth to keep from moaning in pain.

I tried to keep in contact with her by phone during that period, but Mara didn't like my calling her.

"What are you calling for?" she would ask. "You think I don't know why? You want to know if I'm dead or not. Well, I'm still alive, just imagine! And I'm working. And in love. And I look wonderful. I'm going to start a new fashion of having only one breast—like the Amazons. But you're ignorant. You haven't even heard of the Amazons..."

I didn't say a word. I really don't know much about the Amazons, except that they galloped about on horseback, shot with bows and arrows, and removed one of their breasts so that it would be easier to shoot.

"You know why else you called?" Mara continued. "Because you're afraid of cancer, and you wonder how people get it, and what it's like for them. Isn't that right? Well, then, why don't you say something."

I don't like it when people think I'm worse than I really am. Each person has an ideal image of himself and when someone puts my ideal down, I get flustered. But right now Mara was worse off than I was, and so if she wanted to walk all over me, then so be it.

"Well, anyway," I said. "Your voice sounds good."

Mara was silent for a minute, then calmly said, "I'm dying, Larisa."

A year passed. Sasha didn't come to see Mara, but Dimychka did. He came with his enigmatic soul, his money, his anesthetic medicinal herb mixture that he had concocted himself, and Mara and Kuzia, his cats, which he carried in a basket. Kuzia had grown up, and she and her mother looked as if they were the same age. Dimychka was proud of Kuzia. She was the only living thing that he had ever raised to adulthood.

Mara needed to be cared for, but she was used to living alone. Having another person around irritated her. It was a living example of dialectics—unity and the clash of opposites. She couldn't live without him, but she couldn't live with him either. She vented her hopelessness on him, but Dimychka closed his eyes: "I don't see you, I don't hear you."

Soms got along well with the cats, which made one wonder whether he was really a dog to begin with.

Whenever Mara's health would show signs of improvement, it would start to seem that everything would turn out just fine. Deep down in her soul Mara knew that she wasn't going to die. Stars explode and continents sink, but she would live on forever.

On such days they went to the theater. One day they went to the Sovremennik. Mara fell asleep from weakness in the middle of the first act. At the intermission, everyone began moving around, and she had to wake up. They went out into the lobby. Mara saw her reflection in a mirror. She saw how cynically and sallowly the cancer glanced at her. It was precisely at this moment that she realized she would die. She would die soon and would be gone forever. That was the only truth she should tell herself. Or maybe she shouldn't, but, just the same, it was the only real truth.

They didn't stay for the second act, but went home instead. When they got home, the livingroom rug had a dark, damp circle in the middle of it.

"Your cats did that!" screamed Mara, and she started hitting the cats with a towel.

"Don't touch my cats. It was your dog." Dimychka came to the defense of his cats and got between them and Mara.

"Get out of here, and take them with you. I don't want even a whiff of you left around here anymore."

"I'll leave on the express," Dimychka said, completely offended.

He put his cats in their basket and left, slamming the door behind him. Soms ran to the door and whimpered forlornly.

Mara went into the bedroom and lay down. Suddenly, for no reason, she recalled the rat from her distant childhood that scrambled about the cage wires, trying to save itself from the inexorably rising water. It is characteristic of all living things to scramble. Someone was standing over Mara with a bucket, and she was up to her chin in water. It was useless to struggle. The only way out was *to love her own death.*

Suddenly Mara saw the sleeping pills that Dimychka had left on the nightstand. He couldn't get to sleep without them. She grabbed the bottle of medicine and ran out of the house. On the way, she realized that she had forgotten to put on her wig and shoes. It was a hot summer day. Her feet and head felt warm. Mara ran barefoot and bareheaded, dressed in her dragon robe. Passers-by turned their heads to look at her, thinking some Japanese was running down the street.

The train station was ten minutes away from her house. The train had already pulled in, but was still empty. Mara ran through all of the cars, not missing a single one. Dimychka was nowhere to be found. She slowly walked along the platform and suddenly saw Dimychka. He was standing across from car number eleven, staring off into space. He never allowed himself to look like that in Mara's presence. When she was around, he always held himself together. But now, alone, he'd weakened and sank to the very bottom of universal loneliness. Grief weighed him down, and he couldn't swim up to the surface. Why should he try, anyway? What was his life without Mara? He needed her, no matter what she was like; even if she betrayed him, was mean to him and was only half-human, he still needed only her. His round-headed cats peeked out of their basket.

Mara wanted to call to him, but her voice was blocked by pity. She fought back the pity and let out a sob.

"Dimychka!" she sobbed.

Dimychka turned around and saw Mara. His eyebrows shot up in surprise, making his face look rather stupid, the way all surprised faces look.

"You forgot your medicine!"

Mara tossed the bottle into the basket with the cats, and hurried off, staggering from her sobs, just as she had when she was little and five kopecks short to buy a movie ticket. Now it was life that she was short of. She hadn't achieved even half of what she'd wanted. The first forty-five years were only a warm-up, the first try before the jump. The main part of her life still lay ahead. She would have only one man, who would be as desirable as Sasha, as faithful as Dimychka, and as all-powerful as Washnscrub. She would have a healthy, beautiful child with that man and raise it to have a bright present and future. It was possible do that now. Times were different. She was different too. But she had to leave. Everything had ended, without ever having gotten started. And what would be—there? What if there's nothing there?...

Mara left no grave behind. She suspected that no one would come to visit it and decided to have the last word herself. It was: "I don't want you to come. I've decided that, not you."

In her will, Mara stated that she wanted Dimychka to scatter her remains in Leningrad. Dimychka didn't know how that was done, though. My husband explained that it was best to do it from a helicopter. But where could he get a helicopter?

Dimychka left with the urn, which looked like a soccer trophy. One beautiful day, he poured her ashes into a plastic bag and boarded a river boat sailing down the Neva.

It was a warm, mild autumn day. The sun was shining without its youthful summertime intensity. A light breeze blew the hair back off Dimychka's forehead. And Dimychka thought that her ashes flew away lightly and gracefully.

Dimychka scattered Mara, her love, talent and electromagnetic storms. But the people standing on the deck thought that he was salting, or, more precisely, peppering the water.

But all of that was later on.

Right then, she walked along the platform, crying, and saying good-bye to me, the pussy willow, Lomeeva, Zhenka Smolin, Myrzik, all her misfortune, because even that was part of life.

Mara emerged from the station. A linden tree was growing in front of it, and its leaves, heavy with dust, looked silvery. Trolley cars were moving along the square, and there was an hour-long line to get a taxi. The linden tree stood surrounded by clanking noise, exhaust fumes and impatient people.

There's the same tree, well, maybe a little different, but still a linden, growing in the forest. Underneath it are grass, little animals and wild strawberries. Above it, the clear blue sky. Beside it are other, similar, trees, whose branches rustle in the free wind. They were talking to each other.

Why is it like that? One's here and the other one's there. Why is that? Why?

"A..."

A clean page. I write: "Alexandrova, Marla Petrovna" and draw a frame around it. She doesn't have a memorial to her. So let it be here. In my address book. Among the living.

Sometimes I dream about her, and then I think about her all day, hold mental conversations with her, and have the strange feeling that we never finished arguing and we are continuing our argument. I have another feeling too—guilt. I am guilty before her. Of what? I don't know. Or maybe I do.

I go on living, but I am always looking back, and it seems to me that I walk around with a twisted neck.

Translated by Kristine Shmakov

From *Novy Mir*, No. 1, 1989

Notes

1. The reference is to the traditional interpretation of medieval horsemen as symbolizing the spirit or mind (the rider), which curbs the passions or body (horse). (See Panofsky.)

2. The reference is to Khrushchev's program for planting limitless corn as a solution to the perennial Soviet dilemma of food shortage.

3. Ernst Neizvestny.

4. The reference is to a children's poem by Kornei Chukovsky called "Moidodyr" (literally, "Wash-until-holes-[appear]), in which the eponymous character marshals cleansing forces to teach a little boy the pleasures of washing.

5. From an ode by Mikhail Lomonosov.

6. In Mikhail Lermontov's narrative poem "Mtsyri" (1839), about the novice who seeks freedom at all costs, the eponymous protagonist Mtsyri battles various forces of nature, including a snow leopard.

Venetian Mirrors

Larisa Vaneeva

The thaw began on Wednesday towards evening; it hadn't occurred to anyone that the children would get soaked. After herding them, wet, into the television room, the teachers went down to the linen room to get boots. Mud flowed through the lobby, and someone said:

"We'll need wheelbarrows to get rid of all this mud."

"Auntie Pasha's sick again."

"Lizanka's the only one who's got it easy. Anufriev will wash the floors for her."

In class Anufriev would crawl under his desk, but he was the one in the group who washed the floors. At boarding school the rules of the game don't apply—and children not bound by rules do as they please. One can't do anything with them: they crawl under their desks in class.

"No one makes him do it," noted Lizanka casually.

She had known since morning, when her temples had started throbbing, that something would happen with the weather. During her coffee break she stood at the window, gazing at the quivering air, at the bulging, crimson road—one and a half kilometers there and back—that ran behind the pine trees and green fence. Noise, aluminum scraping against glass, gray spoons, mayonnaise bottles instead of drinking glasses, so as to cut down on costs, metal plates to eat on, as if they were dogs. It would be five soon. *Good luck, my babies, bye-bye.*[1]

As she walked in the melted snow at dusk, Lizanka recovered slightly, to the point where she felt a ringing lightness. She entered the house, hung the bag of groceries on the door handle, threw off her fur coat, and, instead of preparing dinner, started wandering around the room, hugging her body with her frozen arms. Rhymes struggled to emerge as the rain beat against the tin windowsill: *thaw now—*[2] how long would it go on?

"Just what's going on?" He turned on the light, hung up the fur coats and put the soggy shoes on the radiator.

"So we're fasting for dinner again? Did the thaw get in your way?"

"What?"

"There's such a thing as normalcy, and I want normal relations. A normal woman would have had dinner ready for me when I came home from work. A normal woman wouldn't let me walk around in such shirts." He turns his collar inside out. "A normal woman doesn't keep her apartment like a pigsty!"

"You're right"

"Who do you imagine you are! Give me the tea kettle! You should be doing work, work, and not whining!"

This isn't my house, he isn't my husband, yet he demands his dinner as if he were family. A ficus: why is it standing there, what does it want? A ficus—reviving from its drink of water—look, it'll start talking any moment, and in that portrait beneath the glass the pupils are slightly pierced. In short, there's no home.

No family either, but the next morning, on Thursday, the thaw continued. The children from the forest school crowded together in a dim crack in the Venetian mirror. Weak little necks, knobby, bullet-shaped heads. The headmistress hadn't defended a dissertation entitled "The Ugly as an Aesthetic Category." She liked order: black-and-white portraits of rulers, dark green panelled walls, attendance charts, and report cards. But she'd been too lazy to use up the 800 of the rubles allotted for the month of February—half a ton of apples and oranges—come on, vitamin deficiency in this day and age!, and as for the children, they're only said to be weak, but in fact they're simply abandoned children, unwanted children. It's a children's shelter, not a boarding school. If she had her way, half of them would be in an orphanage, it's too bad formalities won't permit it. As for the parents, if she had her way, she'd lock them all up!

Birch trees reflected the sun's metallic rays. Around the bend a lake has overflowed its banks. Fans of spray shot out from the highway, like artificial irrigation. From the blue woods nearby a moist haze rises. The snowy field is dotted with mirror-like puddles. Something is cheeping. The night ice crackles like cellophane.

At night she dreamed of a starry sky, not war. Cars, airplanes, helicopters, missiles, machines and computers floated through the sky in a circle—like the earthly ring around Saturn; it wasn't war. Someone was taking care of Lizanka—and he broke her neck, so that she wouldn't become a computer too. They hadn't finished breaking her neck when she woke up: is it good to die with your soul preserved, when you haven't become a computer (the pillow lies awkwardly beside a strange man), but on the other hand—should you put your trust in someone else's will like that?

Lizanka grew gloomy. That was something else. To hell with him.

"I'm a bad mother, a bad wife, and a bad homemaker." In the doorway Ania is holding one-year-old Zhenechka in the crook of her arm; he has a white, sleepy face that resembles his mother's. He cries when everyone around him frowns and smiles if you smile at him.

"Just stop tryng to brainwash yourself. You're the embodiment of motherhood. Look at yourself, you're so pale, round, strong. How long did you breastfeed him?"

"For nine months."

"You see. Other women barely last half a year."

"But why does he always go and fall on me? He falls, catches his finger in the door, burns himself, scratches himself, I'm always on edge. I am a bad mother, I let him get away with everything. Why did I just give him that pear?"

In his mother's arms, Zhenechka was shoving a pear-shaped, paper-maché Christmas tree ornament with a green paper leaf and a hook on the end into his mouth. Lizanka was about to lunge for it—a child shouldn't be slobbering over a painted toy—but she kept quiet.

"Where's the leaf? He bit off the leaf and the hook," Ania sticks her finger in his mouth and slaps him on the back, which makes Zhenka howl. Ania turns white, then red. "He swallowed a piece of wire. What's going to happen now!" She makes Lizanka look down his quivering throat,and shoves a spoon there in order to flatten his tongue. With a strange woman trying to look down his throat, Zhenka gets even more hysterical.

"There's nothing there, and his throat isn't scratched."

"And his intestines? Oh, what's going to happen now! He'll have to go to the hospital and have his stomach pumped! It'll get to his heart!"

"Have you gone completely ...? What does his heart have to do with it?"

"Oh, I'm just paranoid, you know. Zhenechka, tell Mama where it hurts. Zhenechka, does your throat hurt? Oh, I'm such a bad mother."

"It hurts because you stuck your finger in his throat and slapped him."

"Did he really start screaming then? Not before?"

"Of course. We'd do better to look for the leaf on the floor."

Ania tries to bite off the wire from the ill-fated pear.

"Look, you can't bite it off!"

"So, you see? And paper isn't harmful."

"That's true, but what will happen to it?"

"It'll digest."

"Really?"

Ania plops Zhenechka onto a chair and gives him some bouillon cubes in a metal container—to play with: "You play a while, Zhenechka. Ah, just look at those cubes! Auntie Liza gave them to you."

Lizanka looks disapprovingly at Zhenechka's new toy. He pulls out the bouillon cubes wrapped in foil and tries to unwrap them. Why ruin food? But, again, she doesn't say anything. Ania grabs a cigarette and exhales smoke into the closed ventilation window.

"Either open the window or don't smoke in front of the baby."

"No, I can't stand it. I need to calm down."

She smokes, exhaling long drifts of smoke into the window, her hand pressed under her breast, looking at Zhenechka now and then, and once again moaning: "What kind of person am I? Why did I give him that pear?"

Zhenechka's hands are covered with something red from the metal container:

"Watch it, he's gone and scratched himself bloody."

Ania stubs out the cigarette, collects the cubes, spits on her finger, and rubs Zhenechka's baby finger.

"You should put iodine on it."

Ania waves her away, takes him on her knees and sits down near the electric burner where the kettle is boiling. Zhenechka waves his hands and brushes against the kettle.

"You see!" Ania jumps up and runs around the kitchen like a hounded animal. "See? Now, what did I tell you? What kind of mother am I!"

She shakes Zhenechka, smears emulsion on the burn, and talks jibberish: "See the flame? Whata flame." She rattles the box of matches.

"What flame?"

"Oh, what am I saying? Oh, why am I giving him matches! It's written all over the place: "Don't let children play with matches!"

"It's mind-boggling that you're a teacher." Lizanka can't restrain herself.

At this Ania gets offended: "I'll have you know, I'm in good standing... I just can't manage my own child, I'm afraid of everything, and he has a knack for getting into trouble even in my arms."

"Why haven't you asked about your husband? Have you left him for good? He misses the baby."

"Oh, I've left him, and that's a fact... And I don't have any feelings for him." She touches her breast, showing where there's nothing. "No tenderness, no kindness. He'll forget us, completely forget us. I'll howl for months if he does."

Lizanka is nervous.

"But when someone invisible does something to you, it's worse," continues Ania, without noticing, "like the Holy Ghost, only how holy can he be, if he flew in, did it, then flew away. What kind of ghost can he be, and invisible at that! He crushed my heart, I couldn't raise a finger to stop it. This, he says, is sacrosanct. I even wrote down the word, I didn't know what it meant, Liz, and looked it up in the dictionary."

"Your wise man spoke to you."

"Oh, I don't know, I just don't know.. I endeavoured to guess from his actions who he was. I asked, Who are you, why, why like this? I, he says, am from the organs of administration. The Party organs, he means! I got so angry I almost cried. I walked around depressed the whole day, the kids kept pulling at my hem, but I wasn't myself."

"Was that something you dreamed, Anka?"

"A dream, a dream," she nods uncertainly.

After singing a paean to the road, Lizanka mindlessly walked around puddles and peered into them, then arrived about three minutes late. There was chaos in the bedroom! Anufriev was methodically banging his head. Shalaputkina was screeching with her legs spread wide. She's in labor, the adolescent midwives explained to her in unison. There was down all over the place, everybody was barefoot and in pyjamas. The night nanny had rushed to leave on the dot, and the simpletons had made good use of their freedom.

The first thing Lizanka did was pull Anufriev away from the wall and clasp his closely cropped head against her. She considered the little fool something of a genius. Sometimes, as they say, he'd "deliver" while washing the floors. An idea would hit him: there's a moon in his stomach. They'd ask him if he wanted some more fried moon. And they'd beat him. Do you want to see Moscow, they'd ask him, and pull him by the ears. He'd fight them off and scream that he'd already seen it, seen and been there, and he'd also been to America, screamed Anufriev in despair, and only Lizanka would listen to him: her road could also take her anywhere.

His favorite pastime was to knock his head against something. What was he trying to bash his way to? Why? Anufriev squirmed under her firm hand. Let's go see what Mashenka's given birth to, she managed to distract him. They asked the neat and timid Svetochka Goryanova for the newborn. Lizanka screamed into Shalaputkina's ear, so she could be heard over the screeching. "Mashenka! It's a boy!" and thrust the newborn at her. Shalaputkina seized the newborn, her sparkling reddish-brown eyes gloating at Svetka. The latter bit her lip, and Lizanka realized that she had committed a pedagogical error. Now Shalaputkina wouldn't relinquish the newborn for anything at all. She had her own score to settle with the gentle, timid Svetka. It was useless for them all to insist that, as a mother, Shalaputkina should take her newborn to the boarding school, to the teacher Goryanova, before the summer (to check it in like an item in the baggage room). She didn't want to. Parents get away with sending parcels and don't appear for the whole school year.

The Venetian mirror in the cloakroom shook from the stamping feet. A lottery schedule from the newspaper was hanging on the wall. Ten tickets each for part of their salary. "It would be ideal if somebody won," announced the director of studies. The plastic garbage can is now full of losing tickets, torn in quarters. The director of studies hates the unlucky group of teachers for being saboteurs.

On the clothesline you can see the school bedsheets and blanket covers that the night nanny, Manefa Vitoldovna, has hung out.

In the summer, shards glitter on the grounds of the estate. Sticks protrude from the undergrowth of nettles. Metallic flies take off quietly. You can smell the rot from the ravine near the dilapidated bridge where the forest school and the locals dump their garbage and ash. Bottle necks, an inner tube, a peeling, punctured gray ball protrude from the pond. One part of the estate is a brownish green, the other ocher; some of the windows are clouded, others shot with blue. In the entrance to the two-story wing where the co-workers live, the Venetian mirrors reflect wash tubs, sinks, hall trunks, cupboards, and worn parquet floors. A newcomer cringes at the cats, pesticides, and rotten wood.

After breakfast, there's a hike to the forest. According to the schedule there should be a gym class, but there's no instructor, nor a music or art teacher. The teachers fill up the hours as best they can.

The golden-violet pine forest overflowed into the field, glowing from happiness, as if it were a proud ocean liner — pine trees have something in common: a closeness, a friendly team spirit. The air stirred over the pine trees.

And it's good they're taking a hike to the forest—the children calm down in the forest and loosen up.

We had just entered the pine forest when we saw a black "Volga" behind the trees. The children shrieked and threw themselves at the wonder. They throw themselves at everything out of boredom. A man got out of the Volga, his tie all askew, and instantly tried to cover up: "Where are you going, you stupid broad? Come to snoop, did you? Get rid of the preemies!"

We returned to the building, the children wilting with disappointment: they didn't see the naked woman, they didn't see anything and don't understand anything... What a disgusting spring this is, even the children; they'll grow up to be just like that guy... It's crazy to have children nowadays. We're not animals, after all... One has to plan first. A house. A cradle. A roof. And there has to be a sky, and not... Someone roars with laughter: It's your first year here, you don't know anything, you take it all to heart, but if you take everything to heart, you won't last long here. As far as the Volgas go, consider yourself lucky—that was the first swallow, the first sign of spring. As soon as it's summer, the Volgas come in droves for hours at lunch time. It's "the usual." Just be more careful—when you go out walking alone, avoid the group. Last spring they found someone who'd been playing blindman's buff in the ravine. This isn't the city, nature herself can lead you astray.

"I'll howl for months. For months, and that'll be it, for good."

"Oh, Ania..."

"My mother-in-law stirred things up," Ania whispers passionately. "She comes over, makes herself comfortable, decides to teach me a thing or two. A real blockhead. She knitted a pair of socks and charged us three rubles for them. It would have been fine if she'd done it to me, but this was for her own son, she counted it down to the last kopeck. She even brags to us that she's saved enough money for two cars. If I wanted to, she said, I could break you up in a jiffy."

"You should pay more attention to her."

"She kept trying to turn him against me. She always nagged that I keep him hungry. Once she came over and decided to do the laundry, it droned on and on and on and on... and it was late, Zhenka couldn't fall asleep. I come out and say: 'I'm giving you ten minutes to get out of here. Ten minutes...' You know, she'll come over, wash her things a second time because we have hot water, she'll wash up, and there's Zhenka's diaper lying next to her — she won't touch it, won't lift a finger! Anyway, she started in on me. I grabbed a basin: 'Get out,' I say, 'or else I'll let you have it!' She got scared, took off, then two weeks later she's back, acting as if nothing happened."

"Do you really use the familiar form of address with her?"

"Why should I address her formally?"

"If I were you. I'd be formal with her. You'd only gain by it. Why sink to her level?"

"At first I was formal with her, called her by her first name and patronymic. She bragged to her neighbors about how her daughter-in-law respected her, and her neighbors were flabbergasted: how could anyone respect a black marketeer like her? And I started being familiar with her."

"No reason to. You have to maintain a distance. Address her only formally, and do it calmly and politely. She gets on your nerves, you explode, and that's what she wants. What business is it of yours what she does? Who is she, if you come down to it, why does she bother you so much?"

"It's fine for you, you're so indifferent.."

"I know what to invest my feelings in and what to ignore without giving it a second thought."

"Did she ever come to see you... even once?"

"Not a chance," grinned Lizanka.

A light burned in the window, but when she entered the room it turned out to be dark.

"Are you asleep?"

A tenderness came over her. Something glowed on the floor behind the cupboard and table. She didn't understand right away what it was, but when she lay down she discovered that there was no one beside her. Why, for Heaven's sake!

"Why!" said Lizanka out loud. She put her hand on the empty place, and thought that it had always been empty beside her.

And she dreamed one of those dreams that become etched in one's memory as if they had really happened. She and her future son, about three years old, were walking through town, and suddenly—though it was calm right then, something, a signal, warned her—that there was clearly going to be an explosion. People started running, and Lizanka grabbed her son in her arms, but there was no bomb shelter, the seconds were ticking away, and she stopped then and there in a public garden, although everybody else was running and screaming. She stopped, lay down on the grass, and made her son lie down. Look, what pretty grass, it smells so good, don't be afraid, don't look at them. The fear in his eyes was fading, something had caught his attention—a bug, crawling along a stalk, which also *didn't know*, but she'd realized—just then—and nestled close to her son, to the grass, to the ground, breathing in their smells for the last time and pressed lightly down on the nape of his neck with the palm of her hand.

Karr! Karrrr... the guardian of the magic kingdom greeted her from the white willows. Greetings, she nodded, without looking up: the hot haze floating over her head seared the eyes. The plantation of blackbearing rowan trees to her left grew velvety with crimson, and the velvety naked branches responded with a ticklish warmth in the palms of the hands. So we've gotten through the winter, winter's behind us, sighed Lizanka, forgetting that it was still February.

To her right floated Nikolskaia Church. Approximately three kilometers away, built on an elevation, the farther away one stood from it, the larger the church appeared, more distinct and grand, while the houses and buildings surrounding it blended in with the scenery. But imagine the surprise of anyone who drove up to it; at about three hundred meters the church began to shrink in size, it became homier, almost tiny, and the belfry was so low, you felt you could touch it.

"So, how are you?" they enquired sympathetically in the teachers' room. "You're terribly pale. We're having our usual nonsense—the telephone isn't working. And your lame brain had another fit during the night. Manefa says she stayed at his side all night."

Someone had moved close to the dim window, putting on lipstick and licking her lips. "Where is he?"

"I just told you, the telephone isn't working, so we didn't call an ambulance, he's lying all swollen in the isolation ward."

Anufriev, completely blue, was submissively studying the ceiling. Sunlight flooded the empty room and the naked beds with nets that resembled coats of mail. The floor had been washed and was drying in spots.

His palm was cold and sweaty.

"Can you hang on a bit longer? Just hang on, all right?"

He grunted indifferently. In the isolation ward, he never hid, never banged his head, never screamed one and the same word for hours; he was an absolutely normal human being. Could he have done it intentionally, to get some rest? Children need to be alone sometimes. Lizanka understood that very well.

"Our Anufriev hung on till his savior came," bleated someone behind her and hugged her by the waist. "We've all been waiting here, expecting Mommy to come any minute, run to the post office, and call an ambulance. She's the youngest, after all, and the quickest on her feet."

The nurse melted into the sweetest smile, like a round snow-white loaf of bread. At the first aid station they brew tea twenty-four hours a day without moving from the spot. She dashed out joyfully, bouncing on her little round feet in fur slippers with fluffy pompoms.

Only tractors or land rovers could plough their way to the post office, churning up the red mud. In the woods the snow was dense, it had settled, but the frozen crust supported one's weight if one walked quickly, barely touching the snow, without pressing down on it. Lizanka hurried, and didn't fall even once, but on the way back she started tripping, and each time she cursed the boarding school: what a dump, a few people there put their hearts in their work, some simply do their job, but the rest, the majority, don't give a damn. They steal from the children like seventh graders. Why did everyone suddenly stop giving a damn? The worst thing is that nothing seems to bother them. They're all like cotton batting. They're good at listening, they think what's correct to think, they support you, but no one cares. It's like a nightmare: everything opens up, all roads are possible, everyone is in solid agreement, but just touch something—and it all vanishes like a mirage.

Not long ago a normal young mother, who was leaving on a long business trip, brought her child, looked at the children in the classroom, and did an about-face: I don't hate my child. It would be better to give up my trip abroad. They're not idiots, they don't have TB, but they've been unwanted since they were born.

Lizanka spent Friday harried and confused. She didn't manage to get done anything that she'd planned with the children because the regular dishwasher had quit, and the teachers had to take turns doing shifts in the kitchen. After washing three sets of three hundred aluminum bowls and three hundred mayonnaise jars, she was so tired that she went home with everyone else by bus. By evening it had clouded over, fog drifted past the windows. After you've done a thousand things, you can barely drag your feet. The road flashed a dull gray at the turn and then disappeared.

He was already home, reading at the table. He only reads at the table. His book was laid open neatly so that the binding wouldn't break:

"It can't go on this way!"

"What can't?"

"You know perfectly well what I mean."

A good punch, a nice one... right to the windpipe. Lizanka sat on the couch, lost in thought. Five minutes of relaxation.

Her suitcase was packed, her books piled and tied together. She lingered at the mirror a bit longer than necessary, still not believing it, then she opened the door and made her way noisily to the corridor with her bundle. So that's that, she repeated, dragging her suitcase along the floor. And, again, she doesn't understand. Something terrible's happening, yet it's as if nothing's happening.

"I'd like to know where you think you're going."

He seizes the suitcase, the books, and quickly takes off with them. She runs after him joyfully, and her face quivers because she doesn't understand where he's going.

"First find a place to live, and then pack your things."

She gets cold feet as she follows him like a little dog, grabbing ineffectually at the strap of the suitcase.

"There's a settlement near the boarding school. I'm going to live there," she informs him, her dignity now fully recovered.

Together they manage the road with difficulty, but quickly, because they hold each other's hands: they slip, but don't fall. An invisible rain is falling, the fog has erased the rowan tree plantation, an electric moss is gradually covering the city behind them—it's barely visible. After wandering around a bit, they come out by a pond where an ice rink spreads out smoothly, shining in the moonlight like another dim mirror.

The landlady has a sweaty face. She constantly wipes her hands on her apron, blocking the entrance. Steam is pouring from her. Steam is pouring out of the house. A damp cloud from the street forces its way into her house. Behind her post-like legs one can see a light coming out of the room where Lizanka would be living.

"I've already rented it. You're too late," the woman says in irritation.

"How would I know who else is renting!" and slams the door.

They pick their way carefully, abashed, their tails between their legs, because they've been insulted, they're humiliated. Being with someone makes life easier. Then you come to terms with yourself. You forgive. It's not good not to forgive someone, so why not forgive yourself too.

They feel insulted with reason. This becomes clear when they move away from the pond and start talking on the road. Or rather, shouting, because the icy wind knocks them off their feet. They slide backwards on the ice, their toes spread wide, with the suitcase and the pile of books; the cord can break any moment, the wind will scatter the books in the mud, and it'll be awful to gather them, to chase—with numb hands—after pages torn to shreds.

They manage to find their balance by holding tightly on to each other. It's as if they're hugging and out of spite Lizanka is annoyed. A lingering spite still annoys her. Holding back, she takes advantage of any small pause to keep her distance from him. In the wind, the air, heavy with drops of water, freezes on his beard and the hood of his sheepskin jacket,covering it with a vizor's ridge. And her fake fur coat crunches with a white layer. The suitcase is iced over with a shining crust. The hair behind her ears makes a scratching metallic sound, as if her ears are blocked. She tries to separate herself from him once again, but it's impossible: the pile on her fur coat adheres to his sheepskin coat.

"Let go, you sausage in cellophane."

"Quiet, you frog in ice."

"You're worried about the furcoat, right? Aren't you?" she managed to say between kisses. "So, will you tell me after all where you were during the summer?!"

Lizanka had made the rounds of all his old haunts, then befriended his first wife, and bought Zhenya some baby's booties—he was, after all, his child. Anka said that he had dropped in, mumbled, "You're all witches," and disappeared.

She didn't believe that he'd spent the summer on a boat in the middle of a lake.

All over Anka's apartment were strewn photographs of toy soldiers, her former suitors, men she'd almost married. Now she'd pensively pick up a photograph: perhaps I should have married this one...

"Yet, when I think that my Zhenya will bring some female home when he grows up, ugh! I have a hard time just breathing."

"You know, I've been wanting to tell you a long time..." Lizanka didn't get to finish because someone burst out into loud, resonant laughter. As they stood in amazement, illuminated, the sky informed the whole district "...is leaving from track number five." The thunderer's resonant laughter rolled over them and away, above the distant forest, where the church stood. A car horn honked in the clouds and suddenly everyone started jabbering and babbling all together. Happy, carefree, free. The low shroud of clouds ripped apart, and from the sunny blue a plump baby's leg, no smaller than a water tower and creased in folds of baby fat, kicked the cloud with its heel. Before they could even gasp, the foot disappeared, and the blue tear closed up. Someone gave a loud giggle of suppressed laughter. "That's enough!" Whoever was above the forest said peremptorily. "Apollonov, you mother fucker, get to the control tower!"

1978

Translated by Valentina Baslyk

From *Chisten'kaia zhizn'*, Moscow, 1990.

Notes

1. In English in original.

2. The Russian original—*ottepel' teper'*—imitates the sound of the rain on the windowsill—something like "pitter patter."

Going After Goat-Antelopes

Svetlana Vasilenko

I'd seen him somewhere, this guy with the long, almost lipless mouth—and just recently, I think. He stared at me as only people with colorless, transparent eyes can stare, for in such eyes the pupils are the most important thing. If you were to put this guy at the bottom of a river and bend over the water, the staring unyielding black ice at the bottom would make you shiver, it would feel as if there were no water, as if you were alone face to face with just those pupils. It's better not to look. And so I didn't look in his direction, but I desperately wanted to turn around and bow to him in jest (and in my mind I repeated this turning around and bowing so many times that my neck muscles actually began to hurt). I couldn't remember at all where I'd seen him (but I *had* seen him before! I'd seen him somewhere! *The Man Who Laughs?*[1] Maybe that's where? No—I'd seen him in person at some time or other—precisely that mouth, that long gash called a mouth, that mouth at once pathetic and mockingly disdainful—you couldn't tell if he was laughing or crying), and my head burned with impatience to remember, and I kept gently shaking my head as if jiggling a kaleidoscope, helping my brain cells shift, so that, wandering around and running into each other, they'd fall happily into place and resurrect not only the light and the smell, but also the tiny pebble in my hand—unneeded, but resurrected, nonetheless. After all, it had existed and made my palm sweat (everything would be resurrected, but now it was eluding resurrection), and then, suddenly,—yes, that was it—the attic, dust that had settled and hardened, in which there were no traces; it dissolved noiselessly under my bare feet; the pigeon nest and two dead fledglings, their unnaturally long blue necks hanging over the edge of the nest, something terrifyingly lilac-colored between the cartilage, the sad long beaky mouths, and their naked deep-blue bodies (the dark color just recently surfaced), and the coldness of those bodies, a coldness unlike anything else, unlike either the coldness of a living being or the coldness of matter forever dead. This was the coldness of death, of something that had been alive and was now dead, but not yet in a state of decomposition, of putrefaction. (Decomposition and putrefaction bring new warmth, as the beginning of a new form of non-life). Yes, I was holding death in my hands: it was defenseless, it had a thin blue skin, and if you pressed down on that skin with your finger, a dent would remain, and this dent would remain just like that, as if it had always been there, and it would be cold—not actually all that cold, but your fingers would fear this coldness, as if they had a premonition, as if they were trying to touch themselves—some number of years from now—when they would die.

There was still a third fledgling in the nest. He was alive. Having hung his neck, like his siblings, over the edge of the nest, he was preparing to die. But he stared at me, opening wide his long beak of a mouth, which was at once pathetic and disdainful; he was almost as cold as his dead siblings, but life kept on throbbing there, under the thin film of his skin, and my life rejoiced in his life and rushed to save it.

I fed the fledgling milk. He slept, wrapped in rabbit fur, yet grew colder and colder: after all, he'd lain for a long time with his dead siblings and had caught their coldness. I tucked him in my armpit and fell asleep. Of course, I wanted to do my best for him, and, to be sure, he did get warm, but when I awoke there was no fledgling. There were only his squeezed-out intestines, his empty, naked skinlet, and his bitterly mocking long beak of a mouth. I'd smothered him.

I remembered all this: unhappily, I found what I'd been looking for: that's where I'd seen that mouth and nowhere else. But there was something, something else in my memory, like that pebble in my sweaty hand, and here's what it was: there, back in the attic, I realized that the fledgling resembled someone, that I had already seen that beaky mouth before. The circle was closing, but couldn't be closed all the way. I got tired. Finally I found the answer: he looked like the fledgling. What else can be said? Finally, we were sitting in a restaurant. And I had calmed down.

Irina and I were sitting in a restaurant, the dining room huge but empty: it was a weeknight. It was the end of a difficult day, a day of solar eclipse; people said there had been a lot of deaths that day. Four small adjoining tables were occupied, everybody seemed to huddle together, trying not to glance at the huge empty space of the dining room, at the patches of light on the empty tables, which suggested that the people who should have been sitting there that day hadn't been able to come because they'd died. We sat in semi-darkness, the fans above us whirring like bats that had gotten tipsy and lost the ability to tune into each other's signals... Turning clumsily, the bat-fans cast the shadow of their hideous wings on the floor.

It was quiet and depressing in the restaurant, and for some reason we all talked in whispers.

The window was closed, and outside, in the stark emptiness of the extinct world, swayed an elm dessicated by the heat. You couldn't hear the noise of the wind and the elm seemed to be swaying on its own in the motionless expanse, shaking itself loose in order to free itself of the now useless earth and to fall down to the ground, to die right then and there without waiting for the dew. The elm swayed rhythmically, the way people sway in grief—a grief that couldn't be cried away through its curled-up black leaves, which were tired of living. In its dull sense of doom, the elm somehow resembled a beached whale.

I looked at the elm for a long time, and it became motionless, and we were the ones who swayed with our small tables, our food, and our drinks, and I had the sensation that all of humankind consisted just of us—ten men and two women—and that we were afraid of losing each other. We had escaped, and we gazed avidly into each other's eyes because we had a long journey ahead of us, yet, try as we might, we couldn't move away from the motionless elm...

But that's not how it really was: four customers paid and left, and another four arrived in their place: three extremely young lieutenants in battle fatigues and a major who was far from old; his little stars were very new and shone happily and proudly in the semi-darkness of his epaulets. These four evidently knew absolutely nothing about our ark, about the Flood and the solar eclipse: during the day they'd slept on the sweaty couchettes of their train compartment, they'd taken turns going to the slimy toilet that reeked strongly and permanently of urine; first singly, then in a group, they'd ganged up to badger the loud-mouthed woman conductor (singing "Oh, conductress, conductress, silken-lashed seductress"[2]); and they'd swigged hard liquor Siberian-style (only swallowing after they'd first swished it around in their mouths). Then they dropped off their suitcases in their hotel room and now they'd come to drink some more, intent on blowing their daily expense account as fast as possible—and in general they hadn't noticed that humanity had become extinct. On the contrary, as far as they were concerned, there were too many humans: railroad carriages and buses were bursting at the seams with humans, the sidewalks were too narrow for them, humanity spilled over into the street, and no one died—they merely prevented the bus from driving on smoothly at a normal speed. Humanity crowded into the hotels, either not finding lodgings—or not wanting to find them in the rest of the empty world. The male half of humanity in our small little town protected the other half of humanity from visitors who arrived on official business. These visitors went to the empty restaurant to drink away their loneliness, hoping to leave the place no longer alone.

And the game for the sake of which we'd come to the restaurant—hiding the fact from each other and from ourselves—was already beginning. Or, rather, the game had begun much earlier when the waitress with the tired, indifferent smile of a professional who knows all the rules of the game, with a glance full of sorrowful omniscience and the disdain of a person aloof from it all—organizing, but not participating in the game— led us to the table under the only lighted chandelier in the dining room. This way everyone had to look at us, whether they wanted to or not. The waitress was like a teacher and I suddenly began feeling embarrassed in her presence, just like a child. I felt embarrassed about my dress, although it was beautiful and suited me. But my feelings were always terribly dependent on my clothes. Low-cut dresses made me tremble: I felt the invisible work of the skin cells, constantly reproducing themselves on my arms, legs, neck, and chest; my arms, legs, neck, and chest seemed separate entities, independent and existing apart from me, having their own thoughts and desires, which didn't coincide with mine. Helplessly and defenselessly exposed, my arms, legs, neck, and chest aroused a confused pity in me for the futility of their life, which wasn't united with mine, and a dim awareness that their life—their irrepressible striving for renewal and beauty, like the striving for renewal and beauty in all of nature—was more important and significant than my life. That's why whenever my arms, legs, neck, and chest were exposed they controlled me and I was afraid of them. And that's why I suppressed my flesh with sweaters that came up to my chin, why I wore pants—and my sheathed flesh remained mute, only rarely crying out. But here I was sitting in my dress, its snakelike green silk now become my skin, and my dress felt like my body, as yet timid and confused, but gradually comprehending and sensing that its day had come, the holiday of the body, the celebration of the body. And, cautiously, with difficulty, I was getting used to this feeling and this thought.

The officers looked us over with painstaking thoroughness, the way experts scrutinize a coin, with the detachment of the ordained. They didn't want to get taken in by a counterfeit product, and, with the impatience of true collectors, they were ready to bite into the coin to test whether it was gold or imitation. Was it worth getting involved or not?

Then we heard the major's order: "The skinny one's yours. I want the chubbier one. Get going!"

And "my" lieutenant, quickly leaning forward and emptying his glass, breathed "Yes, sir!" into the major's face and, all black and elastic, got up (like a bent rubber toy straightening up, suddenly and imperceptibly), and made for our table, his eyes staring into the distance.

He strode as if on parade, pointing the tips of his boots outward, but it didn't seem funny because he had beautiful legs and he knew it and loved them: he knew that he was executing an order and felt sure that this was precisely the way to execute such a gaily-solemn and unusual order—with a gay solemnity, pointing the tips of his boots outward in this unusual fashion. And suddenly I was struck by how inevitably, with the ceremoniousness of a parade, IT was approaching, that IT which the body had been contemplating in its sweater-covered darkness and futility.

He walked past us.

Irina and I expelled our breath simultaneously and—as if we didn't know a thing, as if we'd heard nothing, as if we'd not seen a soul—began talking and laughing without listening to one another. Yet the chaos of empty words and uncalled-for laughter wasn't chaos; it was solid and spherical. At the center of this sphere was a shared feeling of relief, as if an avalanche had been shed, and this feeling attracted words as trifling as iron filings. Irina and I didn't notice anybody now; we were like "things in themselves," like "coins in themselves," and I loved Irina because whenever she laughted she little dimple under her lip kept getting smeared with lipstick and I had to keep watching that dimple constantly and wiping it with her napkin and laughing with her because she was feeling ticklish, and my entire being seemed absorbed in worrying about keeping Irina's chin clean. Yet all the while I was talking and laughing I could hear his steps moving away at a measured pace, I could hear him clattering with the window latch, the windows opening wide, and the wind starting to blow as if it had been turned on, like a radio. I felt the warm air insinuatingly envelop the silk of my dress, the silk growing warm and alive, and it was no longer clear which was sweating, my dress or my body. And with my back I felt him, "my" lieutenant, approaching.

What followed, though, was very natural, possibly because outside, on the street, you could suddenly hear a song by Celentano,[3] and his voice, unrestrained and hoarse, communicated to the three of us a Western ease and lack of restraint, or else because after the discomfort, the awkwardness and the tension, there inevitably had to follow a sense of ease and naturalness, and according to the rules of the game the heavy tension had a purpose, and the greater it had been, the easier and more natural things would be later.

His name was Vladimir, and we changed this name, which was awkward to pronounce, to the easy and natural Vova.[4] He was from Siberia.

"From which town?"

"That's a military secret!"

"Ah, so you're Mal'chish-Kibal'chish!"[5]

"I haven't served long enough. Kibal'chish only had one star, but it was a big one. Our major over there's got one. Want me to get him for you?"

The major had red hair. His name was Piotr. We didn't change it: it was more comical to stay with Piotr.[6] He brought over a carafe of vodka, and we toasted our acquaintance. Everything was already settled. There was no more need to ask or answer, just to laugh. No matter what I said, no matter what Irina said, no matter what Piotr and Vova said—none of it had the slightest significance. That "coin in itself" had got larger, engulfing Piotr and Vova, so as to disintegrate later into two "things in themselves": Vova looked at me, Piotr at Irina—so as to disintegrate later into four parts—this time for good. And this didn't resemble the rules of a game people had thought up, but, rather, an educational film about the life of amoebas: here the amoeba is feeding and growing, here the nucleus is stretching, and here two small halves of a nucleus are separating; there's a pulling apart, the division of the citoplasm, two new amoebas—and the caption: "In the course of twenty-four hours the division may be repeated several times,"—and that's why our conversation had a meaning as ancient as the stretching of the nucleus prior to its division, and that's why the conversation flowed of its own accord.

Vova talked about what people eat in Siberia, namely: venison, bear meat, trout, and other delicacies. I was astonished at how easily and beautifully he spoke. Articulate people have always amazed me, and I could watch them speak for hours on end, rooted to the spot, without analyzing the meaning. This feeling of fascination had to do with my sense of my own lack of eloquence, mixed with admiration. It was with this complex feeling that I looked at beautiful faces, at flashing streetcars, racing swiftly into the night, at the languid flowing movements of cats and the amazing color of negroes' skin. I found speaking difficult, and rehearsed each sentence in my head, honing it inside me, which is why my sentences were slow to emerge and sounded wooden. Yet at times I could speak well, without understanding how it happened, without even knowing exactly what I was saying. I'd hear my own sentences as if they were someone else's, and afterwards I'd repeat to myself the sentences I'd uttered and be surprised at their content, surprised that the thought I'd expressed had never occurred to me, which means it was totally independent of me.

And, spellbound, I observed how easily words flew from Vova's lips, as if he exhaled them instead of air, and how they'd bubble up on his lips and burst. And I laughed when it was appropriate and when it wasn't (something remote and funny would cross my mind), and laughter bubbled on my lips. So we sat there, emitting bubbles. The nucleus kept stretching and would soon divide, and although I was laughing just as before, I suddenly felt that I was looking at Vova in a different way. My eyes grew hot, they were burning, and I placed the backs of my hands up against them and my skin felt a warmth that was greater than its own. Earlier, when my cornea had been cold, no warmer than the rest of my body, and much colder than the stuffy air in the dining room, objects and people had appeared indistinct and blurred to me, haloed with a haze, as if the cornea were glass that had misted over. Now, however, objects and people were in focus, not as on a photograph, but rather as on an X-ray in reverse: the skull appearing black, the flesh white, the frame exposed. Reality had acquired an angular perfection (the perfection of the skeleton); instead of the flesh that fills out and adheres to the frame, there was the emptiness of shining white space. It was as if I'd suddenly stepped out into the frosty air where even the smoke from the chimney stacks gravitated to solid graphic expressiveness, and the houses to a fragile transparency—that's how it was then. My eyes grew hotter and hotter, and the warmth generated in the course of the day by the sun and people felt cold to them. I suddenly saw the cozy dining room, the damply perspiring customers in the frosty bright light (and, as before, I felt the stuffiness and the heat with my skin and my breath, as they did), and the cold spotlighted those things that would remain forever: the chair, its form, will be eternal, the form of the table will be eternal, the cold gleam of knives and forks will be eternal, and the human skeleton will be eternal. So what if thoughts and passions change—the skeleton remains eternal, whereas the warmth enveloping us, the warmth of our flesh, blood, passions, laughter, and thoughts was vanishing into the smoke-stacks of eternity. The coldly sparkling crystal carafe of vodka served as a model for this eternal world, and one shone through the other: through the glass I could see the immured warm liquid, and through the liquid I could see the cold glass. My hot eyes, immured in the cold of the hot world, were also a model of the world and were exhausted by the simplicity and triviality of the world that was revealed to them. I saw the eternal form of the blinding sheen of the major's wiry hair (he had a childlike smile); I saw the lieutenant's dark skull; I saw the guy's lipless, mockingly disdainful grin, and Irina's swaying warm body. Everything was both of this moment and eternal, and their smile, tanned skin, disdain, and swaying flesh—all those crucial things which they possessed at that moment (and many, many crucial things that weren't there then), all that had to vanish into a crystal bottomlessness, into a faceless, concentrated heat, leaving for all eternity things of theirs that weren't crucial: wiry hair, a skull, an exposed skull, and pelvic bones. And this vanishing wasn't a simple disappearance, but a ritual, a dance in which I, despite my visionary powers, inevitably had to participate. My visionary powers were the equivalent of blindness, and my mind was indignant, but my indignation was fruitless, useless, anticipated, woven a long time ago into the overall pattern of the ritual dance. I longed to see nothing and not to feel my mind, and several times I turned my head sharply left and right. As we all know, during a frost the wind burns your eyes and forces out tears, and by turning my head back and forth in this way, I generated wind and began to cry. My tears cooled my eyes, and they no longer saw as they'd seen earlier, and they no longer contained the knowledge and stupid intelligence that can never help anyone preserve what's crucial.

I slowly began my dance, which my lieutenant had doubtless been expecting from me for so long: I began to gaze at him the way whores do, intently, with an inviting tenderness, as though no one else were any longer there and we were alone, only the table was getting in the way, but what's a table for, if not something for us to get around? And my eyes were shining and cold, like freshly washed berries.

"Vova," I said, although there was no longer any need to say anything, and that's precisely why I had to say something.

Something suddenly banged behind me. I turned round.

There, by the window, stood the guy with the lipless mouth, shortish, bony, his loose white shirt and the white blind beside him billowing out like sails and then sagging as the hot wind flapped around in them. The guy's face was flushed and angry: he stared as me as if he were looking into a void, his wide beaky mouth twisted in bitter disdain. He was squeezing the glass necks of the heavy dark champagne bottles with which he took aim at the empty space outdoors. Foam spurted out of the choking bottle necks into his drunken friends' cupped hands.

"Salute!" he shouted to me and his voice was so thin and piercing that it hung in the air, trembling like a cobweb about to break, glittering and stretched tight; his lips twitched as if they wanted to cry. "It's a gun salute!"

"Hurrah!" I said softly, mechanically, and then thought: "That's right. If it's a salute, then it's okay to say 'hurrah.'"

And suddenly I sensed that this guy had understood everything. He understood what I'd discovered, he understood why my eyes had become like wet berries. His mind, lagging behind mine, was indignant and protested against the immemorial dance. But his bitter protest looked so ridiculous that his lips twisted in bitter derision, as if they were keeping abreast and understood everything.

This guy didn't know that there was one thing I felt in myself which my mind, blinded by what it had seen, had never known or felt. He didn't know that besides the icy eternity of forms and the warm eternity that strikes your nose with the strong concentrated sweat of billions of armpits and groins, there's a third eternity. And I felt this eternity in my thoughts and my character, in my face and eyes, in my smile and my gait. Within me I preserved my ancestors, I felt them within me and I carried them inside me cautiously, like an eternal fetus; they lived within me as in a dormitory, each one in his tiny cubbyhole. They were often estranged and hostile to one another, like a mother-in-law with her daughter-in-law, but I felt close to them all, the way a mother-in-law is to her grandmother, or a daughter-in-law to her own mother, and I was in charge of this dormitory, where all the inhabitants were related. I knew all their flaws and weaknesses, and I disapproved of the unruly behavior of one, the craftiness of another, the weakness for alcohol of a third, yet I loved them, not with an administrator's love, but the way one loves close relatives. I loved them without showing it, I loved them the way

I love my son, and I was like a mother to those who had given birth to me, and I was already conceived in my son (no, I loved my son more intensely, after all, since I didn't know whether he and I would meet again in someone else—whether we would meet in my grandson—or whether we would vanish into a common accumulation of warmth. Our love was therefore more intense, as if it were a last love). And whenever I'd emit a cry of rage it wasn't clear whether this cry was mine or that of my Tartar-Mongolian ancestress, and whenever I sang I did so in the voice of my great-aunt (that's a fact, I could hear it myself). And whenever they squeezed my temples with their fingers, the way they squeezed my mother's with an iron band during her imprisonment, I became quiet and apathetic, just as she had. I knew how to speak in a strange, incomprehensible language in which I nonetheless felt at home: in me spoke one of my luckless ancestors, whom none of my other ancestors could understand, and who talked to himself, reciting poetry in his language; and I hated those who were well-fed and I loved the rhythm of a hard fate that coincided with the rhythm of hard work, performed by all my ancestors. I remembered everything, not with my memory but with my whole being and I lived as if I both existed and at the same time didn't exist, and it was unclear what was mine and what wasn't; there wasn't enough of me for me to achieve self-understanding because I didn't exist by myself alone. It was complicated to live like that, but it wasn't lonely and I couldn't understand other people who also carried eternity within themselves, yet didn't understand that fact, and therefore thought of themselves as lonely. They didn't understand that by killing themselves or someone else they were killing at one go thousands of live people who'd been prepared to live forever and whose dying was external. It was a sacrifice to those absurd eternities—to the warm and the cold, to the cold world that gobbled up the warmth yet could never get warm. These people, they didn't understand that death, natural death, was only a ruse devised by everything that was alive so as to deceive absurd dead matter and to preserve the life of what's most crucial. Life pretended to be submissive to fate.

Nor did this guy know that this eternity, pretending to be fatalistic, was fatally unpredictable. This guy didn't know that the person sitting there with the shining moist gaze of a whore wasn't me, but some brazen remote ancestress of mine living in furnished rooms, or my great-grandmother from St. Petersburg playing this brazen creature on the stage, and I was capable of staring just as brazenly, but it was unclear what that would lead to: either everything would go exactly according to the script, either it was fatally predicted, or else the unpredictable would burst into the furnished rooms where everything seemed forecast; an ancestor of mine having nothing to do with rooms designated for a specific purpose, or with theaters, would burst in, brandishing a truncheon or wearing a black skullcap.

"Some guy, huh?" shouted Vova, and I noticed the large whites of his eyes and his gray irises, retreating into the depths of his pupils. His eyes seemed to pant with rapture, like the sweating flanks of a tired gray horse. "I like this guy, don't you?"

And I realized that I liked the guy too. Yes, Vova, I'm very taken with him. And, fatally and unpredictably, the guy was already coming toward our table, shaking the bottles in a ridiculous manner, stopping them up with his thumbs, while a dark-green foam formed inside.

I waited, half-turned to him, and knew all along what he'd say when he reached us. And he said precisely the words I'd been expecting: "Let's have a drink!" he shouted. But he shouted so loudly and shrilly—which none of us had expected—that we all winced. Even he winced and began to shout non-stop, even louder and more shrilly, so that we'd get used to his voice and wouldn't find it strange. "Let's have a drink! Come on, let's do it! There's more where this came from! There's some left! To your being here! After all, you made it here... I'll order more. You did make it, after all. Let's drink to our meeting!" But it was no more possible to get used to his voice than to get used to a squeaky door hinge or look placidly at someone drowning if that person was shrilly calling for help. We seized our glasses feverishly, without noticing that they were vodka glasses, and too small for champagne. We held them out so he'd stop talking and get on with it. We wanted to save those pathetic, panic-stricken pupils, racing as if they were the relatives of the person drowning and shouting shrilly as they raced helplessly along the bank.

His hand shook as he poured the champagne into my glass. Without gauging the size of the glass and the weight of the bottle, he overfilled my glass and the liquid spilled over the edge and ran down my raised arm into my armpit, then along my ribs, separating the silk from my skin. But he kept on pouring.

"That's enough," I said quietly because, after the shrill shout, sounds started emerging again one after another in the resounding, deafening silence, like objects in the dark once you get used to it, and I didn't want my words to destroy the quiet aftermath of that recovered silence, which had taken the form of an indistinct buzz until his shout. "That's enough," I said quietly.

And the guy abruptly righted the bottle, so abruptly that its heavier lower part bumped against my glass. I instantly heard a shrill "Sorry!" and, deafened, almost hating the guy, I rushed to pick up from the floor the shards of glass and silence. He was senselessly trampling around on the shards, and they crunched under his feet, which for some reason were encased in heavy army boots that looked out from under his wide trousers. I picked up the shards with one hand, pressing them into my palm with my thumb, and with the other I waved away the guy, brushing against his face and his hands as I tried to get rid of him. But I couldn't get rid of his shrill voice, which had drilled through my ears. I wanted to hit him on the lips, on his lipless mouth, from which his voice poured non-stop in an unbroken stream: "Leave it, I'll do it... It's my fault, after all... That repulsive bottle... Let me do it..." I straightened up so as to hit him, but found myself looking down right at his head and saw his thin hair, white as ivory, and the bright baby-pink skin from which the hair grew, and my desire to strike him and my pity for his baby-pink skin mingled in my wail-like cry: "Be quiet!"

The guy backed off slowly and sat down at an empty table nearby. He looked on guiltily as I tried to dig out the glass from the parquet floor at the risk of cutting myself. The glass had been ground into the wood by his boots.

Silence wearily reestablished itself once again, recreating itself as it was supposed to, slowly and steadily, the way a photographic image emerges.

Irina's laughing body was swaying serenely, her chin thickly smeared with red. For an instant I felt an involuntary pang of fear for her, connecting the sharp pieces of glass in my hand with the red stain on her chin as cause and effect. Piotr was also laughing, looking at Irina, and wiping his chin on the spot where Irina's chin was smeared, and it wasn't clear whether they saw or heard us.

Vova looked on placidly, as if he were the master of the house, and kept pointing out to me whatever shards of glass caught his eye. He kept tapping his glass against his knee, bending his head, first to one side, then to the other, so that the glittering edges of the shards would be more visible, and each time I found another piece he'd say with satisfaction: "Vova's eyes are as keen as a hawk's. There's another one—no, not there, right in front of you. Maybe we'd better get the waitress to use a broom, it's taking you forever..."

But I knew that he liked the fact that it was precisely me picking up the shards—acting like a housewife, and I, too, liked my lowly housewife role. What's more, it seemed that Vova would have liked to break his glass as well, the way hussars do, but he couldn't make up his mind; it would have looked absurd at that given domestic moment and would have come between us. At last I finished picking up all the shards. There were a lot of them, but they were all tiny and fit into the palm of one hand. I carried them behind the partition that separated the dining room from the serving counter and the kitchen.

There, behind the partition, the waitress sat watching television. The TV was on the gas range, a range which had no burners and had evidently been discarded and replaced by a modern electric range. You could tell that the waitress was bored watching TV, yet she watched it with rapt attention, secretly rejoicing that instead of ticking by in vain, her boring hours on the job were of some use to her and her spiritual development. From here you could hear everything that was going on in the restaurant and you could be sure she'd heard the guy's exclamation, followed by mine, and the sound of breaking glass. Peeved that someone would come now to ask her to remove the broken dishes, she was staring at the TV screen with rapt attention, putting off the moment when she'd have to get up. She winced when I came in, but didn't turn around; instead, she glued her eyes even more peevishly to the screen, absorbing the last few images. Judging by the distressed, restrained way she kept shaking her head, it looked to me as if she wanted to speed up the images in order to increase the amount of time compressed in them—time that she could enjoy free of us.

"Here," I said, holding out my hand with the shards and looking not at her, but at the television: "It was a glass."

"That's all? There was such a racket!" she said, without turning round, and I felt her relax and her sense of time recover its previous slow rhythm.

"Where can I throw this?"

"Over there," she indicated, without taking her eyes off the television. Resentfully I thought that I ought to write a complaint about the waitress and her TV.

As I got rid of the broken glass, a shard stuck to my finger. I tried to brush it off with my other hand, but the piece was deeply embedded in my finger and I stood for a while looking down at it, quietly waiting for a feeling of fear and curiosity to overcome me, knowing and foreseeing what would happen next. Then I shook the piece of glass loose and pulled it out as I would a stinger, quickly and carefully. My finger started to bleed. And the more it bled, the stronger became the feeling of horror I'd had as a child for something I should never have seen, of pity for the finger that was growing numb and had to die because all its blood was pouring out. I felt secretly triumphant that this uncontrollable red life was flowing out of me and not out of someone else, that such beautiful, powerful blood was living in me all on its own. I felt that I should hide it and show it only to my friends, who were crowding around like a herd that has dimly sensed danger; and that I should run away in tears, howling in self-pity and in terror of dying, and that I should call out triumphantly to my mother: "Look! Blood! I'm bleeding!" If I didn't pay close attention to myself, none of this remained in my adult life, except for the words I now uttered with outward calm, but with inward triumph because this minor misfortune would tear the waitress away from her TV, and for a fraction of a moment my bleeding would bring us closer.

"I'm bleeding," I said.

"Cut yourself, did you?" she asked me with perfunctory sympathy. And she didn't turn around.

I began to whimper quietly, licking the blood off my fingers. For some reason it was sour-sweet, like champagne. Why in the world should the woman turn around and look at me? Why in the world should she want to get closer to me because of some dumb finger, when maybe every day she saw smashed and bloody snouts and had to tear herself away from her TV show because of some need to call the police? Maybe the sight of blood made her sick, and if there was no need to call the police, then she wouldn't have to look at someone else's intoxicated blood that was being flaunted; and right now there was no need for the police...

I couldn't tell what made her suddenly tear herself away from the TV and come over to me. She took my hand and said, without looking at me: "Broads really get me! They have their period every month, but just let them cut a finger and they start bawling." These coarse words, probably normal for a waitress, didn't go with her stern school-marm face.

She opened the oven: its maw was unexpectedly white, and she took a bandage out of it and bent over my finger. As if taking the relay baton from her, I stared stupidly over her head at the TV, as if it were impossible to leave without keeping an eye on the images on the screen rushing by with the speed of time.

"*I'll* get them! I'll ask! Champagne glasses! Five of them, there are five of us! Champagne!" We heard the piercing voice and, for the first time, the waitress and I looked at each other. Not that I got any closer to her, my cut was too slight for that, no doubt, yet something gave way, enabling me to ask: "Do you know that guy?"

"No," she said, "I don't, but I've seen him somewhere before."

He came into our sanctuary, muttering and screaming (five tall wine glasses and a bottle), and here, in the neat, almost homelike little room, removed from the excited, lustful dining room, I thought his voice was a disaster. It made you wrinkle your nose, like the smell of unwashed socks, and the guy was drunk, while I was overly sober. Guessing what I was thinking, he started to whisper, his lips twisting painfully as he reined in his recalcitrant voice, hissing sharply where the sounds "s" and "sh" occurred in a word. "Mi-ss, s-some ch-ampagne, plea-s-e, and five tall gla-ss-e-s. Four plu-s one ek-ss-tra, five in all." The waitress left. He suddenly saw my bandaged finger and made a move toward me. He took one step and his body continued to fall forward, as if it hadn't realized that his legs had stopped, and I put my hand behind my back, as if by doing so I could stop his body from falling... and it did stop, and righted itself. His body swayed back and forth, with the abrupt, resilient movement of a spring fastened to the floor.

"Let me ss-ee," he hissed, and I proudly showed him my beautiful snow-white finger. His face froze instantly, imperceptibly, and turned into a mask of grief and horror, and in this frozen mask the gash of his mouth, the protrusion of the nose, the gashes of the eyes and the protrusions of the brows all lost their concrete designation; in the split second of convulsion that transformed his face into a mask, they resembled the dissolving and elusive movement of waves. I felt instinctively sorry for him, instantly experiencing the pain of his cut finger, forgetting that it was my finger that had been cut.

And he stood there, swaying, as if he were crying with his whole body, just as the elm outside had swayed earlier.

"My fault again, it was me. See—it was because of me again..." he muttered in a squeaky rush of words, and I remembered that it was my finger that was hurt.

"It's all right, don't worry," I said, and went over to stand right beside him, so as to curb the angle of his swaying.

"Let's go," he said suddenly. "Let's make a break for it, come on, while they're waiting in there," he glanced around, "for the wine glasses. We'll go to the restrooms. Then we'll run for it. Let them have the champagne..."

"No," I said, and for some reason added, "Later, maybe later."

We followed the waitress into the dining room, and Vova's cynical comment ("Died a hero's death, did it?") regarding my finger, which was swathed like a mummy, for some reason seemed dearer to me than the grimace of pain on the guy's face. I couldn't quite manage the "wet berry" stare, but I knew it was essential for me to do so to put things right. I had one drink and then another, and "my" lieutenant drank with me and gazed at me absently. I saw the caressingly moist whites of his eyes, darkly tinged with blue, like hens' eggs stripped of their shells. And my whole being was completely transformed into body, so shameless and thirsty that it shivered with fever... My brain attempted to resist all this, but it had already become alien to me, and my body, greedily resolving it, as if it were an abscess threatening it with destruction, gradually changed from its state of enervated sensuality to one of dull awareness, like the gaze of a wild beast. My body grew conscious of itself and, because it still did not believe what was happening, it observed intently and with difficulty the desire forming within— a desire that you could touch and smell, that was sweet, tormenting, and obscure. The body dimly remembered that this was precisely how it had felt billions of years earlier when it was a cell that had only just emerged from inanimate matter, in precisely this way the cell had felt exhausted from solitude, and, prepared simultaneously for death and for happiness, it had torn itself in half, remembering that instant forever and making a gift of this memory to my body. But, strangely enough, although my body wanted to stay with Vova (Vova was tanned, while the guy's white skin, which didn't tan, seemed to me—as it would to anyone who grew up on the sandy shore of a big river— somehow indecent and alien), yet I longed to go off with the guy. Maybe it was because with Vova everything seemed obvious and depressing, like jogging in place, whereas with this other one whose name I didn't even know everything was uncertain, including how and where our flight would end. I simply had to run off with him.

(Read on carefully: somewhere around here lies will start cropping up—exactly where, I myself don't know.)

I glanced at him and he understood everything. We understood each other like dumb beasts. I would have to leave my handbag behind. Slowly, so they'd make no noise, I pulled open the zippers of my bag, muffling their rasping voices with my fingers. I had to find out whether my papers were in the bag (Irina had the money). My bag contained a children's book—*Dr. Ouch*—powder, and lipstick. Remembering about my papers and money was automatic and instinctive; my movements were precise, my body was knowing without knowledge. Having sighted the goal, it tensed and braced itself, like the knowing body of a wild animal, and everything was accomplished independently of me, the way it happens in dreams. And as in a dream I noticed that Vova was observing me out of the corner of his eyes, but I didn't acknowledge that. Instead I retreated into myself and started to tug back and forth at the zippers, as if I were doing it for no particular reason. I found myself wishing the zippers would break because it seemed a pity to leave behind a new handbag, whereas if the zippers were broken, it wouldn't be such a pity to lose it for good.

The guy had also noticed Vova's glance and the fact that I'd retreated into myself, but he probably thought that I'd resigned myself and decided to stay. I was moving the zippers altogether too mechanically, which is why everything seemed irrevocable. The zippers produced a rhythmic rumbling sound, like the louder and louder purr of a cat falling asleep. No doubt that was why, alarmed by my yearning and submissive body, he attempted to stem the irrevocable quickening rhythm of my fall, which was inevitable, the way the dance of primitive peoples is inevitable once the rhythm of the tom-toms quickens. So he exclaimed, "Hey! I've some boiled crayfish! A whole case of them! Let's eat them! They're cold, but we can have them like that, they were caught today! Do have some!"

He started tossing them on the table, and they fell with a dry thud, like reddish-orange coffins[7] equipped with claws, so as to bury their own dead within themselves. Their black eyes seemed to have been squeezed out of their sockets. They had a sweetish smell that was made even more loathsome and nauseating by the added smell of spices. They reeked of decomposition and decay, of putrefying flesh boiled with dill. I couldn't watch the others break their red shells into pieces, I couldn't stand it; it was as if they were devouring my stinking flesh with their staring dead pupils. And my ears couldn't stand the choking, hissing, asphyxiating whisper that penetrated the obediently open pores of my body. There was a hissing in the dark pores like the draft in a tunnel caused by an oncoming train, and this hissing reverberated against the bones of my skeleton, then receded, echoing back along the same tunnel into space. My whole being was like a sponge that had absorbed this hissing: "You don't care who you do it with... go on, then, get outside, I'll be there in a minute, wait for me outside... I've still got some more... you don't care who you do it with. I've been waiting all evening, all my life... whereas he... you don't care, he doesn't either, but I... go on, get going..."

I got up and, very quickly and stiffly, afraid of spilling the nausea that had welled up in me, carrying myself like a slop bucket, walked across the parquet floor. I walked across the parquet floor and headed for the stairs, past the carpet on the stairs, past the marble in the lobby, past the metal grill by the entrance (sliding my hands across the wood of the double doors), and went through the doors into the darkness. I turned a corner and went along the asphalt (my burning cheeks brushing against the bristly bark of the elm), turned another corner, and scrambled along the ground up a little hill, my hands and feet clinging to the warm earth, and I grabbed at a wooden pipe because the hill wasn't a hill at all, but a storehouse of earthen goods. As little kids we used to sled downhill from this storehouse, from this hill, which in winter was covered with ice. We used planks yanked off wooden packing crates, and we'd fly on them incredibly far, and as we flew downhill, the boys would squeeze us. While squeezing us, they'd kiss us with foam-covered lips like horses'; their saliva was fresh and clean, as if it were our own, and we'd lick their saliva off our lips and again go stumbling up the hill to do the whole thing over again.

I saw him right away, but I didn't believe my eyes because it was dark. I peered into the darkness for a long time, until my eyes were ready to believe anything. He was standing under the elm, in the light coming from the window, and was whirling around in place, like a white bird that had fallen out of a tree in its sleep.

"Hey!" I said, and he scrambled up the hill, using his hands. His white shirt was dangling loosely down his back like a broken, useless wing, and I felt a vague fear of something until it dawned on me that I was afraid that the crazy evening wind would return and carry him off, lifting him by his drooping wing. He caught hold of the pipe and wanted to say something, but I covered his mouth firmly with my hand because just then three people jumped out of the darkness onto the wide lit path. Clutching their heads with one hand, like caricatures, they ran around the elm, reluctant to cross the boundary between light and darkness, as if the path had glass walls. (One of them had my handbag dangling from his side, like a flat pancake; it banged against his hip and made a sound like a tambourine because it contained copper coins.) Then, having had their fill of light, all three of them plunged as one into the darkness, from which they emerged still clutching their heads with one hand, just as before. I could barely hear the coins rattling in my bag now, the sound growing more and more infrequent and dole-ful, as if the bag were a live creature being forcibly taken away from me, while it tried to draw my attention with its voice. When my bag could no longer be heard, I realized that the officers had been holding onto their caps as they ran, and I started laughing and removed my hand from the guy's lips, as if giving him permission to laugh too. But he didn't laugh, and as I continued laughing, I felt that my hand, which had been cov-ering his mouth, wasn't participating in my laughter either, but seemed to be siding with the guy, and his narrow, half-open beak of a mouth, his front teeth and childlike pointed chin had left an imprint on my palm, on which the lines of fate had been melted by his hot breath, and instead of them there were now traces of his mouth, his teeth, and his chin. I furtively wiped my palm on the rough wooden pipe, just as if I were scraping off a drawing, but it didn't help.

"Well?" I said. I was alarmed, and the fact that he kept silent so long frightened me.

"Let's go," he said.

And we started making our careful way downhill. I held onto his shoulder, trying all the time to put as little weight on it as possible, so that he'd think I was light, and this made my hand suffused with heaviness. As soon as we reached the bottom, he abruptly lurched forward. I almost fell, and grabbed at his arm, hooking it through mine, but it was very awkward; his elbow pushed against my stomach, my elbow knocked against his side, and the skin at the crook of our elbows stuck tightly together. We set off like that, and I asked him:

"Are you from around here?"

And he answered:

"Yes."

We fell silent, walking along like two strangers, and our intertwined arms were alien to us, as if some unknown entity were waddling between us, knocking against us.

The darkness was impenetrable. You seemed to be looking not out of yourself but into yourself, as if you were inhaling and exhaling inside yourself, living and breathing inside yourself, which is why it grew oppressive. I closed my eyes, intending to get some sleep because I didn't feel the space around me or my own movements. My body was motionless, enclosed in the stuffiness of a dark blanket. But as soon as I shut my eyes, I realized where we were going. Smells began to emerge out of the darkness; they seemed to emerge from my memory, and you might have doubted the actual existence of their source, except that one such source was walking right beside me: the guy reeked of overcrowded railroad cars, and to doubt his existence was difficult. The skin at the crook of my elbow was burning, the way bedsores probably burn, and that's why my memory conjured up, out of the smell of damp wood, steam, clean flesh, and bun-dles of birch twigs, the pinkish building of the municipal baths.[8] This ephemeral building constructed in my mind was an exact duplicate of the building we were passing. We went past a boiler-house (the smell of coal dust) and a bakery (that needs no elabora-tion); then memory in its building fever outstripped the smells and, therefore, as I was mentally constructing a shining white building devoid of smells, it promptly was flooded by a hospital smell. And only then did the building become complete, the way an empty room becomes occupied. A real building is merely an abstract sign, but a smell is music more concrete than matter itself. So we went on, breathing in the music of the build-ings, and the farther we went, the quicker, more familiar, and disquieting this music became. I could already name each note: a smell of strawberries (the Kalitins' yard—their whole yard is full of strawberries), the smell of chlorine (the Muraviovs' yard—the back of their outhouse faces the street), the smell of a doghouse (the Gribovs' yard, where Treasure is kept chained), a faint smell of kerosene (the Bobkovs' yard—their house was built on the site of a kerosene store that had been torn down); a rabbity smell mixed with the smell of roses (the yards of the merchants Ivashkin, Nesse, Khalmuratov, Drozdov—they sell roses and gladioluses in the summer, and rabbits in the fall). If we'd walked along this side street, then a symphony of smells from my own street, which I'd known since childhood, would have burst forth. But we stopped; the smell of dried fish—the Sinitsyns' yard (old Boria was a fisherman, a poacher, but a harmless one; he poached black caviar only for his own use, not for sale. As members of "the blue patrols," we children had "waged war" against him).[9]

The guy's skin peeled off mine like a bandaid, and he moved away from me and started fiddling around with the lock on the garage door. I asked: "You live in this house?"

"Yes," he said firmly. But I knew that wasn't true, I knew very well who lived in that house and whose jeep was in the garage, and he smelled too strongly of overcrowded railroad trains for me to trust him.

I went off and stood under the cherry tree. The trunk of the tree was in the yard, but the branches cascaded with their whole weight all over the fence and flowed all the way down to the ground. I stuck my hand through the planks of the fence (it was impossible just to stand there idly when something awful was going on there, near the garage), and my hand touched the tree trunk. For some reason my hand shook as I feverishly explored the cherry tree; its bark felt rough and defenselessly virtuous under my hand, which felt around with maculine boldness. Feeling ashamed of my marauding hand, engaged in something depraved and illicit, I closed my eyes, and the pitch darkness stopped being darkness and was transformed into a pain that my eyes shared with the cherry tree. I tore beads of rosin off its skin and stuffed them into my mouth and furiously chewed and chewed the slippery, sweetish substance, and my mouth filled with saliva. It was as if I were gnawing a thread that I couldn't tear off and gnaw through, the thread that tied me to this guy who was a stranger to me, the thread that wouldn't allow me to run away or cry out. By the way the thread trembled I could feel how his hands were shaking and couldn't turn the key in the lock. And I kept chewing the rosin because I felt awful. As I observed myself from the side, it struck me as deperately funny how my body was posing for someone; my pathetic body was standing there quietly, avoiding unnecessary gestures, always watching me and afraid of superfluous movements, fully aware that they weren't superfluous at all, that they stripped me naked, to my essence. My body was never one with me; in its immobility there was something of Egyptian statues whose outward immobility concealed the fusion of all existing rhythms. Think what you want.

But today my body knew I'd have to become one with it, and all my thoughts and the thoughts of those who could see me inevitably fused with my body's desire and its immobility. I stood under the cherry tree, seemingly independent, on my own, apart from the guy, and seemingly prepared for flight and dazed submissiveness. And it also could look as if it had been raining and I'd run to take shelter under the cherry tree (I knew absolutely nothing about the guy standing a few feet away from me), and also that we were a couple: I was the lady and he, my beau, had moved off to answer nature's call and I was standing to the side, trying not to hear the indecent sound of the stream hitting the ground. Think what you want.

The garage door gave an unexpected creak and the guy unexpectedly started to speak, squeakily, like an ungreased hinge—evidently something was wrong with his vocal cords—I suddenly saw them, rusty, like waterpipes, there in the pink moistness of his throat, and I wanted to clear my throat in his stead.

"Are you there? Get in."

And I obediently trudged over to him and got into the "gazik"[10]—everybody called this make Billy-Goat—an ugly old jeep in which Sinitsyn had returned from the front. The jeep smelled of fish, and it was cold inside, the way it must be in the belly of a fish. As I was crawling past the guy's knees (he was already at the wheel, but hadn't opened the other door), I fell against him accidently-on purpose, and for a second I felt his warm body before I tore myself away from him. I couldn't think about a thing. I began to feel deathly cold after I tore myself away from him, and I started shivering. This wasn't the tremor of desire; I was simply cold, and I had to warm myself against his body, nothing more. But we backed out of the garage; I couldn't fathom why we did, and why I should have to wait, when I had to get warm right away.

Suddenly he honked, and immediately all the dogs in all the yards started barking and the cocks started crowing, and we drove in the barking darkness that rattled its chains and crowed at us, a darkness we bisected with our headlights. We drove past my house, but the smell of fish and the cold made me utterly incapable of remembering, and I just glanced mechanically in the direction of my house. At that moment the guy looked at me; in the faint light his face was yellow and radiated light and warmth, and more than anything I wanted to press my cold lips against his hot yellow ones, to unbutton his silly shirt and to get warm, just to get warm... I was glad he was there, the only human being I'd met in the loathsome fish belly where I was getting frozen to the marrow; and we couldn't possibly part because each of us would have died there alone.

I asked him where we were going; now only words would hide what the body was in no condition to hide. And so words came to the body's aid, clear and simple words, full of falsehood and deceit, however; everything in me was full of falsehood and deceit because I didn't give a damn where we were going and why. Everything within me tried to hide my true self, and I didn't know why I was hiding like that within myself, as if I were hiding God knows what, and not just the simple thought of getting warm, warm, just getting warm.

"After goat-antelopes," said the guy.

I'd been expecting the usual deceitful answer: "down to the creek" or "just driving around a bit," and that's why what he said didn't sink in right away. Staring ahead dully, I thought about those words for a long time. We were driving across the roadless steppe, along the bright corridor (from the headlights) that dead-ended in a black wall. We were racing toward the wall without getting any closer, it kept receding, slowly moving back, yet not disappearing: the dead end remained there, ahead of us. And in the same way the words "after goat-antelopes" kept receding from my consciousness until I got used to them by endlessly repeating them to myself without thinking about their meaning because I was cold and wanted only one thing: to get warm. And my shivering merged with my incessant repetition of the meaningless words, and my longing for warmth took on the form of "going after goat-antelopes." My longing found a name. The words stopped being irrelevant and didn't prevent me from waiting for the moment when I would finally unbutton his shirt and cling to him with my whole body. The anticipation was agonizing because this scene had been spinning around obsessively in my head till I was dizzy, but precisely because of its obsessiveness it had become concrete and the anticipation became joyful: it was as if I'd glimpsed the guy there, in the distance, and we were drawing closer to each other, and the anticipation was realized, just as the fact that the jeep was rushing madly ahead was realized. The road stretched between us, and we rushed toward each other like madmen, our speed shortening the distance and the anticipation.

The jeep stopped as abruptly as if—after walking toward each other—we'd unexpectedly collided in the dark.

We sat without stirring, as distant from each other as before. I waited. Then he turned away from me toward the window and asked in a squeaky voice:

"So what are we going to do next?"

This banal question was familiar to me, and I felt disgusted that we were now going to exchange banalities, that there was no way of avoiding them, and that there was no way of avoiding what he was going to do with me, when all I wanted was to get warm, but it was impossible just to get warm without this embarrassing thing that he was going to do with me.

"Oh, that!" I said. "That's just what we're going to do!"

The more brazen, the better. I crawled into the back of the jeep and brushed my knee against his. He twitched and pulled away, and I felt disgusted again: first he drives off with me, and now he pulls away.

There were dry nets and sacks in the back of the jeep. I sat down on them and said sharply:

"Come over here!" and frowned at my own words. He didn't budge and said nothing.

"Tell me your name, at least," I said.

"Who cares?" he said after a short pause. "It's all the same to you, surely."

"You're crude," I said. I kept frowning, feeling revolted at uttering hypocrisies when I was so very, very cold.

"People are always crude when they talk," he said slowly.

"Talk to me a little, mama,"[11] I said. "Come over here."

"No," he said quietly.

"Why?" I got up and my head touched the roof of the jeep.

"That's how it's going to be," he said, and I could feel him smiling.

"So why in hell, why the hell did you drive off with me?" I shouted.

"Just..." he said. "So they... so they wouldn't..." he stammered.

"So nobody could," I prompted. "Is that it?"

"You've got a son," he said in a whisper. "And a husband."

"Found out, did you? And here I didn't know!" I shouted and sat down again on the sacks. I felt like crying. Damn! I felt deathly cold; I didn't want anything except to get warm. I wanted no more falsehoods and said very softly: "I'm freezing, d'you hear, freezing..." and I was surprised that my breath wasn't visible.

"I know," he said wearily.

"I'm freezing," I said. "Come over here."

"No," he said. "You mustn't."

And suddenly I either saw or recalled his eyes, with their whites and pupils, the eyes of a righteous man.

"A savior," I said, feeling slightly nauseated, as if from hunger. We didn't understand each other and if he'd come to me now, I'd have hit him. "How I hate saviors."

I got up, swaying. I had to get out of the freezing vehicle. I moved past him, leaning against his chest, and my numb fingers didn't feel the warmth of his body. By now I was so cold that he couldn't have warmed me anyway. I opened the door and choked at the dry heat that rushed violently at me. I collapsed as if I'd been shot, as if I'd never learned to stand or walk, as if my frozen feet had suddenly melted. I fell on the steppe and inhaled the burning, bitter scent of wormwood, inhaling it endlessly without exhaling. The void of my body filled with wormwood bitterness, and I slowly began to thaw.

Something hot seared all the way through my back; the crushed wormwood sprang upright again, and shot through me. I writhed in pain and turned my face to the sky—to be blinded; the hot stars blinded me, they burned like the sun, like thousands of white hot shards of sun, which had splintered there in the black sky, and from there—from the sky—along with the heat came a fresh and penetrating scent: the stars smelled of wormwood. And everything turned upside down: I was lying on the black steppe of the sky and stars were shooting through me, and from the earth came the heady scent of wormwood. The whole world was round, huge, black, and hot. The whole world was drenched in the scent of wormwood; the world was destroying me and was sprouting through my useless thawing body, so that my body could merge with it, as snakes, gophers and lizards do, and I protected my eyes, without knowing why yet.

I shielded my eyes with my hand and my yielding body—with fish scales sticking to it—narrowed and lengthened and slowly began to coil into rings, sparing my head—my eyes! my eyes!—and the coils acquired weight and springiness. It was as though I were being born anew out of earth and wormwood, slowly and with difficulty recognizing my ties with the earth and my separateness from it, and my superiority over the unseeing world, for I had eyes. Undulating slowly, my head stretched upward from the coils, but I couldn't tear myself completely away from the earth, I couldn't shoot through the sky, which was swiftly receding from my approaching eyes, while the stars kept getting smaller and smaller. All I could do was pursue the sky the way our jeep had pursued the black wall, which kept slipping away, the way people on ships give pursuit in the void... all the while seeing the black dead end ahead slipping away. And it's possible by turning upside down and distancing yourself from the earth to shoot through the earth and see the black dead end ahead slipping away, and seeing the dead end along the horizontal and the vertical axes and realizing that it can't be reached, yet race ahead anyway. And this optical illusion became the only salvation in this cunning, slippery, unseeing world, and that's why I'd protected my eyes. But I didn't want salvation. There was no salvation. At each and every turn there was only a dead end and I didn't have to race ahead to reach it. I didn't give a damn about the dead end of the stupid, unseeing world, or about eternity—warm, cold, and pulsating eternity. All my reflections were falsehood and deceit; I really didn't give a damn about my ancestors and descendants, whom I'd never seen; I was simply saving myself from myself and the world. But I didn't want salvation. What I wanted was for this guy and me simply to understand each other; if we couldn't do that, what use were eternity and ancestors to me? What's the use of all that to me if the guy's sitting in the jeep, freezing to death, alive, while I'm over here looking at some stars or other.

I got up slowly. My eyes would have been level with the guy's had he been standing there. Now I knew why I needed my eyes. I suddenly longed to see my son and my mother, who were sleeping sprawled on the floor because of the sweltering heat that buzzed over them like a mosquito. There was no forgiving anything in this deadly game. Like all blind creatures, the world had very good hearing and didn't miss a single word, even when it was spoken inwardly.

Since the guy was lying with his chest on the steering wheel and his arms clasped around it, I crawled into the jeep over his back. At that moment I loved him very much, the way I loved my brother, who'd died at birth. My brother was born one month premature. He took one breath... and died without ever exhaling. His name was Vova; they chose the name before he was born. In my mind's eye I'd often see how he took one swallow of air, but couldn't expel it again, it hurt so much. They slapped him on the back, but the air got stuck like a stone in his throat and he couldn't even cry. It wasn't a question of atrophied lungs; something frightened him so terribly that he could neither breathe out nor cry. What did he see? What frightened him? What did he think about in that one minute, that single second? He had blue eyes and black hair. He kept on growing inside me and beside me, and he would have been twenty now. Maybe, just like this guy, he would have dragged me out of the restaurant, would have made me cool off in the steppe, would have reminded me that I had a husband and a son.

"Let's go," I said.

The guy made no sound; you couldn't even hear him breathe. I got scared, and my head started to spin from fear. I hit him on the back, hit him hard, and the jeep responded with an infant's wail, honking weakly and spluttering.

The guy stirred.

"What's wrong with you? Whatever's wrong with you?" I yelled.

"Nothing. Just thinking," said the guy. What could he have been thinking about?

"Let's go," he said. "Want to go home?"

"Yes," I answered.

We were strangers, as before.

And again we raced on, as if standing still, with the steppe before us, nothing but the steppe.

They appeared suddenly. Something changed in the corridor of light along which we were driving. It filled up with golden dust, the dust grew more dense... and suddenly was transformed into the outlines of some absurd golden animals. For a moment we glimpsed their powerful, bob-tailed hindquarters and their lowered heads, which were turned back toward us. They ran very fast, one after another; the noise of the motor had probably startled them quite some time ago. It was strange to see them running so swiftly—faster than our jeep—as if they were golden-reared store models, running one after another in a row. They disappeared immediately.

"Goat-antelopes!" shouted the guy and stepped on the gas.

The beam of the headlights once again picked the antelopes out of the darkness, but this time illuminated all of them together. There were seven. One took a lumbering, clumsy jump toward us, then stopped, and another one collided with it, and they both dropped into the darkness; yet another, which had its head lowered to the ground, like the others, kept looking around blankly as it started moving away slowly and indecisively, as if just then it didn't care whether it ran off or not. It stayed in sight. A fourth leaped up and hung vertically in the night, and for an instant the stars flickered between its lyre-like horns; the rest dashed about as if the end of the world had come, but the last one, its head thrown back, flew like an unseeing mass straight at our jeep.

"Stop!" I yelled and yanked at some lever. The guy hit me in the face with his elbow; with a screech, the jeep jerked to a stop. But it was too late. Leaving the headlights on, we jumped out of the jeep, and saw the goat-antelopes flocked together. They stood there briefly, looking around meekly and timidly, then suddenly started to disappear in complete silence, one after another, as if the darkness were herding them, one by one, through a wicket gate.

It was dying. The goat-antelope was a kid, its muzzle covered with blood. As it inhaled air, the skin on its trunk-like nose wrinkled all the way to its eyes: the air it noisily exhaled was mixed with blood. With its hair still dark and curly, it looked like an ugly humpbacked lamb. Its yellow eyes looked at us trustingly, full of pain, and in fear that we'd go off and leave it alone with that terrible and important thing that was happening to it.

The guy got out his jack-knife. Seeing the blade, the baby kid continued to look at us just as before, trustingly and gratefully, but bleated softly as if asking: "Why?" And far away in the steppe its mother's voice answered. I turned away.

Afterwards we sat, leaning against a tire. He cried with effort, making coughing sounds, spitting up some words:

"Me again... Always me... Why?"

I cried because he was crying, yet I couldn't even touch him or calm him: the dead kid-antelope lay between us. It wasn't hard for me to cry. We were terribly close to each other, yet painfully far apart. As we sat crying in the steppe, the blood of the kid-antelope drew us together and separated us forever ... this was the last time we'd be sitting like that crying. Because the whole thing was my fault. I was guilty of many deaths. That was my fate, that was my cross, but I won't tell anyone about it, I won't confess. I'll bear this myself; I won't unload it onto someone else—I don't want to save myself. He might have become close to me, that guy, if only I'd said a single word, but I didn't want to save myself and that's why he'll be a stranger to me forever. I'll get off quietly with my tears.

We drove along an old road that nobody used anymore.

"We can't go any farther," I said. "There's a gully over there."

He swung round.

We drove back to my house in silence and parted in silence. I stood behind the back door and listened, waiting for him to leave. He didn't leave for a long time. Then I heard his steps, something falling on the porch, steps again, then the sound of a motor. That was it. In the early twilight I saw the blood-covered goat-antelope lying on the porch.

In the morning I dreamed of cutlets. I woke up and the house was filled with the smell of cutlets: mama was frying them before going to work. The smell was odd, as if the cutlets were being fried in rancid butter. But there was no time to think about that. Actually, I didn't wake up of my own accord; someone woke me. It was Liuba. She was retarded, which is why people called her Liuba the Dummy. She was already twenty-five, but her face—dull and vacant—remained forever that of a fifteen-year-old. Her flesh, unwanted by anyone, was ready to explode. As children we used to play together; then we started school and began to make fun of her. She stayed behind with the pre-schoolers and every year she got ready to go to school with some normal little seven-year-old, but that girl went off to grow wiser, while Liuba stayed behind on the bench by her house and waited for next September. She kept waiting to start first grade until she turned twenty. The time came when her girlfriends began to get married and have children, and we would make fun of her by talking in mock seriousness with her about her fiancés. We discovered, to our surprise, that what she dreamed about aloud, excitedly and naively, was what we harbored in our own hearts. Whenever I came home from school I'd notice that her face grew sadder with each year; she'd no doubt realized what her problem was or else someone had explained it to her. She wasn't stupid; it was simply that she stayed exactly as we'd all been in childhood.

"Get up! Get up!" she shouted. "A car wrecked in the dump. The police are there! They came with their sirens howling: ooh! ooh! Like at a fire."

I ran, keeping my eyes fixed on the ground: I was wearing rubber flipflops and it was easy to trip in them. That was why, when we reached the dump, as soon as I raised my eyes I immediately saw him. They were already covering him with a sheet and I only saw his blood-stained shirt, his bitterly smiling long mouth, and his pale eyelashes against his bluish-white face. They covered him with the snow-white sheet, ordering "Move along," "Move along." The jeep was in the gully, its wheels in the air, and Sinitsyn, scarlet-faced, was there with a policeman, Liuba standing next to him, while people reluctantly dispersed.

I turned back. Liuba caught up with me and blurted out:

"It's Sasha Ladoshkin."

The earth tilted. I remembered: the white morning world splintered and whirled about me.

"What?"

"Sasha Ladoshkin. Remember?"

I always remembered him. I loved him and can't think of anyone I ever loved as much later on. I was six. But that didn't matter. I remembered how I went to his house on his birthday; he was four months younger than me. I set out alone in the evening and it got dark quickly. I lost my way in our small town and didn't recognize the club or the movie theater. I was picked up by the woman who delivered milk from house to house in a little handcart, which she does to this day. She knew everybody in our small town. We slowly went around her delivery route, selling milk until we got to Sasha's house, which was next door to Sinitsyn's. Now that there was less milk in the cart, the milkwoman's piercing shout of "Mi-ilk!" had grown fainter in the darkness. I arrived at Sasha's very late. The guests were already leaving. Sasha and my mother sat at the table. On the table was the birthday cake—uncut. Sasha sat with his arms around the cake, guarding it. He'd been sitting like that for a long time. He was waiting for me. I can't recall the expression on his face.

Why did he drive to the gully?

The porch in kindergarten. Sasha and me behind the porch. We're ducking "nap time." Sasha says:

"Want me to teach you how to smoke?"

"Yes," I say.

He lights a match, sticks it in his mouth, and puffs out his cheeks, trying not to breathe. The match goes out in his mouth, and smoke comes out. Then he brings his long, narrow lips close to mine and his lips smell of sulphur. Then it's my turn to "smoke" and we kiss again.

I don't remember anything else. His father went crazy and Sasha and his mother left town. I only remember that I loved him and I'm not sure I ever loved anyone as much later on.

Why did he drive to the gully?

Liuba and I sit on the front stoop, eating cutlets. They have no taste, as if you're chewing rosin.

Liuba's telling me about Sasha. He used to live in Pskov. He studied at the Technological Institute so that he could doctor sick dogs and animals. A veterinarian? Yes, such a long word just to doctor dogs. There are lots of them roaming around, you know, and no one looks after them. He studied a long time to be that word, but they took him into the army. In the army he fought in the war. The war? Yes, the war. He fought and he fought, but they didn't give him a medal, and he got upset and left the war because he liked doctoring dogs and he'd gone to school a long time to be that word. He came back from war the day before yesterday and made Sinitsyn's dog well. Day before yesterday Polkan was limping, but yesterday he stopped. Sasha made his paw well and said he'll make me well and I'll go to school straight to the highest grade. He would have made me well because people and dogs are the same, there's no difference, dogs understand everything and fly through the cosmos like people. He would have made me well because he'd gone to school for a long time to be that word and to make me well. Go on, Liuba, go on... Then he spent the night at the Sinitsyns' and in the morning went to catch crayfish with Sinitsyn because he liked crayfish. Crayfish are healthy, they don't get sick, you don't need to make them well, but among the healthy crayfish there's a terrible one, doctors from all over the world want to make it well, it's very sick and they have to catch it and make it well. Sasha went to catch this sick crayfish, to make it well. I've not been eating crayfish for a long time because I'm afraid of eating the sick one... Go on! Last night Sasha went somewhere. He was supposed to go fishing somewhere that night. Sinitsyn gave him the keys to his jeep. Sinitsyn loved Polkan and Sasha made him well, so Sinitsyn gave Sasha the keys for Polkan's paw, and Sasha went fishing, but he didn't do any fishing 'cause the nets were dry. Sasha makes sick animals well, but fish, you know, don't get sick, so why catch them? The nets were dry, the fish didn't want to be be doctored because they were healthy... Go on. Then he crashed. He crashed close to morning, it was just getting light. He'd taken the old road, the one nobody uses anymore, there's a gully around the bend. The gully wasn't there before, right?

How could Sasha know that?

"See. Besides, he came to get married. He told Uncle Boria he had a fiancée here."

"A fiancée? How come?" I said. "He was six when he left here, wasn't he?"

"Want me to teach you how to smoke?"

"Yes."

"How come?" I said. Nobody knows, of course, that I know the answer.

But Liuba says nothing and I turn around, to see Liuba transformed. Her eyes are full of joy, her face blushing in confusion, like a bride's.

"How come?" I said.

And Liuba starts spouting nonsense: how he'd come in secret every year and promised to marry her and wrote her letters from the war, but she burned them because she thought he was deceiving her. Then he arrived yesterday, but she didn't show herself. She didn't open the door, she'd been real scared, but had stood by the door and he'd told her through the door, through the hole for the key, that he was going to make her well, she'd go to school straight to the highest grade, and then he'd marry her right away, but she didn't show herself because she'd been real scared of getting doctored because they give shots when they doctor you and that really hurts, so she didn't open the door, but hunkered down and looked through the hole for the key and saw his lips and his lips said, "I'll marry you, it's all the same to me now," and there was a smell of smoke and she started coughing; when she'd burned the letters from the war, she'd also coughed, she'd almost suffocated because the letters wouldn't burn and she had to light terribly many matches and there was a fire, but the letters wouldn't burn, the whole house was already on fire, but the letters didn't burn, and she sat there reading them. He wrote that he'd marry her if he didn't get killed and she was to wait, she wasn't to marry anyone else; and she waited and didn't marry anyone else, and her dress had already caught fire, it was a real big fire, and she sat and burned, but the letters wouldn't burn and she read them while the fire engine rode through the town and howled "ooh, ooh," and the letters burst into flame and the words burst into flame, the burning words were ever so terribly hot, and she read them for the last time: "I'll marry you," and she fell asleep, and the fire engine saved her, but they fined her dad because they had to save her.

"Letters? But she doesn't know how to read," I think to myself, and suddenly I start to believe her passionate, lisping account. Now a legend was being born. Tomorrow the whole town would be repeating it. The girls would tell each other how a soldier fell in love with Liuba the Dummy, how he loved her from childhood to the grave. And each of them would blush and secretly believe that Sasha loved *her*, and had come for her and not for Liuba the Dummy, and he was in such a hurry that he wrecked his car.

Is that why you drove to the gully?

I start to feel mad at Sasha, as if he were alive.

"No," I say to Liuba. "You're not telling the truth. I'll tell you what really happened."

And suddenly her face began to cry. Her vacant eyes cried, as did her fat red cheeks, her low forehead, her flat nose, and her big swollen lips. I was struck by how much Liuba looked like me when I cry. It was as if I were seeing myself in a mirror. But however much she looked like me, she had neither a husband nor a son, and never would have. Whereas I had everything, everything! And Sasha as well! Sasha as well!

"I believe you, Liuba, I really do! Liuba!.."

If I were to tell everything that really happened, all the girls in our town would come up to me and one by one would spit in my face. And they'd be right. No one must know everything that really happened, Sasha.

"Want me to teach you how to smoke?"

"You know," says Liuba—she's already smiling. "These are goat-antelope cutlets. I had some once."

I had left the restaurant with Vova.

It was already getting light when someone knocked at the door and asked for me. Mama said I was at a girlfriend's, and didn't open the door. Through the glass panes of the porch she glimpsed a guy in a white shirt. He had a long mouth. Mama had seen him somewhere before. He threw a goat-antelope on the stoop and left.

Everything that happened that morning is true.

1982

Translated by Elisabeth Jezierski

From *Zhenskaia logika*, Moscow, 1989.

Notes

1. Novel by Victor Hugo, *L'Homme qui rit* (1969). Presumably, the reference is to a film version.

2. A popular song.

3. Adriano Celentano (b. in Milan, 1938), prolific Italian singer, composer, actor, and filmmaker, well known in Russia.

4. In informal situations Russians, especially of the younger generations, address each other not by their formal names (which require the use of patronymics), but by a diminutive. Many names have more than one established diminutive. The appropriate one for Vladimir here would be Volodia, not Vova, which denotes a greater degree of intimacy.

5. Mal'chish-Kibal'chish is the name of a youthful revolutionary hero in a children's story by Arkadii Gaidar (1904-41). For refusing to betray military secrets to the enemy, the boy is decorated with a big golden star, which he wears on his chest.

6. To call the major "Piotr" instead of the diminutive "Petia," given the situation, is odd.

7. Red or orange-colored coffin lids are used for official funerals and are propped up next to the church door while the body is on view inside the church.

8. In Russia, birch twigs, with their leaves still attached, are sold on the street outside municipal baths. Customers use these twigs in the sauna or the steamroom to stimulate the circulation by lightly tapping their bodies with the twigs. The birch leaves emit a pungent, pleasant odor.

9. Under the Soviet system, boys and girls about nine to fourteen years of age made up the "blue patrols," a form of junior police watching and reporting on neighbors.

10. A "gazik" or GAZ is a jeep introduced during World War II and subsequently manufactured by the Gorky Motor Works, of which GAZ is an acronym.

11. A line from a popular sixties song, in which a daughter is trying to communicate with her mother, asking her to talk about anything, so long as she speaks to her.

Wicked Girls

Nina Sadur

> Burn up with desire
> Like salt in a fire...[1]
> *Incantation*

As he burst in, his jacket rustled from the wind and rain. His hollow cheeks were a little flushed from the wind and cold. He was a beast. With the face of a beast. Because he was a German; his German mother had him in a camp in 1947. That means that he's fourteen years older than us. You couldn't like a man like that—German hair and the eyes of a besat. A wiry, harsh, wheezy man.

We were drinking; he had raised his eyes and was watching with his pale eyes. I lowered mine and squeezed my knees together. But Emmie says to me, "He's mine." Let him be yours. After all, he's fourteen years older than us. In the second place, there's something of the fascist in him. Apparently it's because he was born in a camp. A babe in arms grew up behind barbed wire and turned into a beast.

We were drinking vodka, and he was watching with limpid eyes. But then rage flashed in them, and I shivered. But Emmie started acting up, she let down her hair, smiled and joked, and they went out on the balcony.

And when they returned, he looked at me with a jeer, and contempt twisted his pale lips. He put his arm on Emmie's shoulder, and his bony, pale hand from time to time sleepily stroked Emmie's blouse. There were light freckles on this hand; I could no longer drink. Emmie rubbed up against him, I squeezed my knees together, and out in the street a blizzard whistled. When they returned from the balcony they were ruddy, very cold, and wretched, the biting snowflakes glittering in his white hair, like salt.

Then we found out that he would be at Gena Galkin's. Emmie says, let's go to Gena's, I say no. But we went—Emmie's crazy. Everything happened all over again, right up to the blizzard, again something gleamed in his hair and didn't want to melt. Of all the people, he was the only one the snow stayed on. And suddenly they separated from us, like a couple, and started to walk just by themselves, without us, in the wet winter twilight. But Emmie likes to mess around, though she says she won't be unfaithful, but that's for about two years. He has three children and a salary of one hundred forty rubles, and Emmie broke up with her boyfriend for him. As a result he says, "I'm throwing away everything for you. My children, my apartment, my way of life. There's nothing for me to lose. If you leave me, I'll kill you." And he's right. What's more, he beats her. Emmie is hot-tempered, she got drunk once and started yelling. And he tells her, "Be quiet. The neighbors will hear." But she yells and stamps her feet. Then he tells her again, "Be quiet. The neighbors can hear." But still she yells. Then he flung himself at her and started to beat her. Emmie fell, shut up, covered her head and just lay there, but he kicks her anyway and howls in German. Until the blood flows. Until she's nearly dead. The beast. They went together half a year, and he beat her three times. Emmie says, "He has pale blood, like water. He cut himself while shaving, and I saw it." She thinks that they will get along. She says, "He won't beat me anymore. We'll get along." But I say, "I know you!" But Emmie: "No, you're wrong. There's something in him that isn't in other men. It always holds me back." And I say, "Come on!"

And there you go. They rented an apartment. They'd already decided everything, officially broken off everywhere, put up with everything and rented an apartment for themselves. Empty. A couch and table.

And a candy box appeared on the table. And in it two chocolate candies.[2] I wanted to take one, but Emmie rushed up to me and wouldn't give me any. I was surprised; I even saw her turn pale. I say, "What is it?" And Emmie says, "Don't eat those." Why's that? I love candy. And this was good candy. Expensive. But Emmie says, "Don't eat them. There's something wrong with them."

Here's what happened: when she and Bern rented this apartment, the box was there on the table, just like this. And all the men got sick from it. We found that out much later. In the box lay exactly two candies. Bern ate one, but Emmie, being diabetic, didn't even try it. Then they began to put the apartment in order, to arrange their things, but after two hours Bern's head began to hurt badly. They went to bed, during the night Bern tossed about in a delirium. In the morning there were again two candies in the box. Each thought that the other had done it. They fought for a while and then figured out that neither of them had sneaked a candy back in. They decided that the landlords had a key, that landlords joke around like that. They changed the lock. Bern ate a candy, his head started to hurt, at night he tossed about and cried. In the morning exactly two candies lay in the box. Now every day the same thing happened. Bern said, "I'll croak, but I'll figure out that candy." They tested the bottom of the box, examined it in every way possible, but didn't find anything. Naturally, any kind of life they'd had ended. Why, Bern was furious. All his strength went to the candy. He abandoned everything. He suffered. He became completely transparent, like a blue flame. He can't do anything. He struggles. He knows his own truth and wants to prove it. He became like the flame over an alcoholic lamp, and everything in him died down.

I went over to this box and opened it, and the stifling smell of chocolate struck my nostrils. The smell was ancient, from far away.[3] The two dark candies lay side by side. Suddenly it hit me. I understood everything. I didn't say anything to Emmie and calmly closed the box.

I looked at Emmie with totally new eyes. She was already pregnant. She stood by the table in her dressing gown, the buttons on the gown already stretched. She looked at me, her face was not made up, but simple, forever simple. I saw that she was no longer my friend. I tried not to walk away from the table. We jabbered, like always, but she suddenly said, "Why are you looking at me like that?" After that I looked down, but Emmie no longer spoke very much, she kept falling silent. However, I didn't leave. I tried not to walk away from the table, and Emmie felt something, she began to breathe quickly, to pull at the buttons on her dressing gown, and her frightened glance ran around the empty room in search of protection.

And then the door slammed, we heard Bern's quick steps. He was literally running. Emmie didn't know what to do, what to be afraid of, her eyes goggled, and tears already stood in them. But until the last instant I didn't make a move, in order not to give myself away. But here he is already running up to the doors, I run up to the table, open the box, grab the candies and gulp them down one after the other, and my throat started to hurt from the big pieces of candy, and I remembered that insult. The sweet taste of chocolate slid down my throat, but I didn't forget that it had hurt, and I will get even. Tears even sprang to my eyes.

He ran into the room, mean, wiry, in his rustling jacket, white, limpid, like an alcohol lamp flame. And he saw two women in tears. And as suddenly as he'd run in, so he stopped. At first he looked furiously with his pale eyes, and we looked back at him through our tears. He looked and looked but suddenly began to understand, to understand. A thin flush suffused his hollow cheeks, and his thin lips parted slightly:

"Oh, what kind of a girl are you...?" he hissed.

And then softly, softly as a whitish little rat, I breathed[4] on him:

"Berrrn..."

Translated by Wendi Fornoff

From "Ne pomniashaia zla," 1990

Notes

1. Salt is a stock image in sorcery. A means of transferring magical power (through consumption), it was also used on at least one occasion as an ingredient in a love potion (Ivanits, Linda J., *Russian Folk Belief* [Armonk, NY: M.E. Sharpe, 1989], p. 114). Salt may furthermore play a key role in "spoiling": the entry into a person by a demon through means of a common substance (such as salt). Spoiling sometimes follows the touch or glance of a sorcerer or witch (Ivanits, 123).

Fire is also mentioned in conjunction with sorcery. Supernatural beings use it to punish humans who fail to display proper deference (Ivanits 34, 61).

2. Magical items often appear in pairs in folklore. For example, in a popular Russian folk tale, the hero offers a Baba-Yaga two golden apples on a silver dish. When she reaches for them, he cuts her head off. In another tale, two apples restore youth to the consumer (Ivanits 172).

3. The description of the smell is a possible allusion to the folklore genre, from which many motifs in this story are taken.

4. More than one meaning is possible here for doxnut'. Stressed on the first syllable, it is "to die (said of animals)." Stressed on the second, it is, as rendered here, "to breathe." A third, slang, definition, is "to achieve orgasm." The meaning is ambiguous because the Russian text, as is typical, does not supply the accent mark.

Sergusha

Alla Kalinina

His name was Sergei Aristarkhovich, but somehow he didn't take his name seriously; he liked everyone to call him Sergusha—that was how he phoned up respectable academic institutions: "Hello, it's Sergusha calling." Nobody was surprised at this. Everyone knew who he was, and they'd long since gotten used to him; they considered it the joke of a genius, since he had a reputation as the new rising star in biophysics, and because of that much was forgiven him. He had introduced himself in this way to Galia, when, after failing to get into a university after graduation, she came to his department to get a job as a lab assistant. She hadn't counted on seeing the famous Pomerantsev himself, that really would have been too much; however, in the research fellows' room, a tall, impudent guy in glasses told her with a chuckle:

"What's with you, don't you know the procedures? Sergusha sees the lab assistants himself. And we still don't know how he'll look at you," he added, thoughtfully looking her over to the accompaniment of friendly laughter from the many people in the room. "On the whole, I think you have some chance! But here's the question—chance at what?"

Galia stepped back in confusion; she understood, of course, that these were all jokes, but she didn't understand the hidden meaning and the point of the jokes.

And then somebody whipped up to her other side.

"So, is it an infatuation with you?" asked a rather old, stocky, sullen fellow.

"How's that? I don't understand." Galia was thoroughly frightened. "What are you asking about?"

"What do you mean 'what about?' About biophysics, of course," blared this newly discovered wit amidst general laughter. "What did you think?"

"I didn't think anything. I've brought an application. Addressed to Pomerantsev." She'd already started getting angry, and stood there, sweaty and flushed, but, knowing that when she was angry everything went even better than usual, she played her anger up a bit. "To whom should I give the application?"

"The fourth floor, to the left, at the end. Don't be offended, miss," said a tall blond in a denim outfit, who for some reason was sitting on a table amidst glass retorts and boxes. "They're joking, it's just that people here like to laugh it up."

But it turned out that all of this was no joke. On the fourth floor to the left was Pomerantsev's office. She realized this immediately because carpet runners started from there and the double doors had a special trim, although there was no name plate on them. She knocked softly. No one answered. Then she opened the door and saw a small room crammed with papers. Everything was a mess. On the desk, a black, withered bouquet of lilac was scrunched up in an expensive vase of Czech glass. It was September. "How long has it been standing here? And why?" thought Galia in amazement. At that moment she heard a high, breathless laugh and a hubbub of several voices speaking at once. Of course, Pomerantsev was there, further off, behind the second door, which was trimmed with oak. She was still wondering whether she could knock when the door was flung open and she saw him. Afterwards, she could never forget her first impression of him, how he stood in front of her with his black, merry eyes rounded, his mouth open. The black, tousled mop of hair swung in ringlets above a large, smooth forehead. The round, effeminate double chin was lowered onto a plump chest. He was young, and might have been attractive had he not been so frankly, so outrageously, fat.

"You were sent to me by God," said Pomerantsev in a high, piercing voice and poked Galia in the side with a fat finger. "Do you see what's going on here?"

"Yes. It's not very tidy," nodded Galia shyly.

"Precisely. Not very. I understand you. Where do you work?"

"Nowhere yet. I brought an application."

"You're a clever girl," he said, already examining her with frank, enthusiastic curiosity. "You really suit me very well—what an instinct! Such a timely occurrence. Come here and I'll quickly explain everything to you. Don't pay attention to them," he gave a funny wave of his fat hand at the three research fellows despondently sitting on the couch, and squeezed his way around an enormous desk.

"You're all free to go," he said to the three. "You can see that someone's come to see me. On business!" he raised his voice. "And what you're talking about isn't business, but hack-work! Is that clear?"

He turned back to Galia, and his face once again beamed in a cordial smile.

"The main thing is answering phone calls," he said joyfully. "Otherwise they'll just drive me crazy, these phones."

On his desk stood three telephones, one of which had already been ringing quietly and annoyingly for a long time. Galia gazed fearfully at Pomerantsev.

"But I really came to you as a lab assistant," she said quietly.

"Nonsense," he smiled carelessly, and the curls on his tousled head shook. "I need a secretary. You think it'll be more interesting to wash the glassware? There's no point in coddling them, let them wash the stuff themselves. You know, so many scientists have bred among us that there's no way to get enough lab assistants for them. Do you know how to type?"

"With two fingers. And slowly," said Galia.

"Wonderful! With me you'll learn how to type like a machine-gun, you simply won't have any other choice. What's your name?"

"Galia," said Galia.

"Very good, it's easy to remember," he said. "And mine is Sergusha, so that you know."

"How's that?" Galia didn't understand.

"Well, here's how. My mother calls me that and that's how I like it: tender and calm, like at home. Otherwise I get very nervous, and everything irritates me, is that clear?"

And suddenly, it was as if a small switch popped inside Galia, and she understood something.

"Clear, Sergei Aristarkhovich," she said happily, and instantly felt that she'd got it just right.

His whole body swayed, his round merry eyes shone and sparkled, his white-toothed, chubby mouth parted, and he again laughed that high, buoyant laugh which suited him so wonderfully.

"You're hired," he said. "The exam in training and appearance has been passed with flying colors. Don't be offended, please—that's a joke. You can dress just a little bit more boldly—I like that. And you start tomorrow, I can't stand red tape."

He again scrambled out from around the desk and gallantly escorted her to the doors. She noticed that his suit was magnificent, but his shirt collar was a little greasy.

"Galochka, I'm really very glad," he suddenly said in a soft, particularly sincere voice that it was impossible not to trust and that could not be ignored; it seemed to bind Galia to friendship and devotion, and she took in this summons with all her heart. He stood in the doorway slightly bent over, his pudgy neck bowed, and all of this somehow turned out not in the least bit funny, but graceful. And also flattering.

And that's how Galia began to work for Sergusha. The work, to her surprise, turned out to be difficult, interesting, and, what was most important—pleasant. She found pleasure in the fact that everyone wanted to get in to see Sergusha in his office, and, moreover, all at the same time, and once they got in, they didn't want to leave because it was very difficult to talk to Sergusha, what with the interminable crush and the endless telephone calls; he was constantly distracted, unfinished sentences hung in the air, new people walked in and were immediately included in conversations that had already started, one meeting imperceptibly drifted into another. Several hours in succession could drag on like this until Sergusha got infuriated and chased everyone out of his office.

"It's a disgrace," he shouted at his colleagues as they left. "Are you ever able to work by yourselves? Why do you have to come running to me with every trifle? If you're incapable of working, then quit, damn it!"

And, dispersing from the office, the research fellows hastily tried to curry favor with Galia.

"Galochka, I beg you, when he comes to himself, call me."

"Galochka, slip these papers onto his desk for him to sign, he asked for them himself, it's terribly urgent."

"What a lovely little outfit you have on, it's so becoming!"

"Galia, find out if he'll be in early tomorrow, so I can call."

After three days of work, everyone already knew her and she knew everyone. She sat in the very center of this small world and drummed on a splendid electric typewriter that hummed quietly and comfortably beneath her hands. The typewriter was especially good because you didn't have to cut your nails to use it, and Galia could use a wonderful, pearly polish on her long, well-groomed nails. The telephone rang continuously, and time and again she interrupted her typing in order to respond into the receiver:

"Sergei Aristarkhovich isn't in now..."

"Sergei Aristarkhovich is in a meeting..."

"Sergei Aristarkhovich left for the academy..."

"Who's calling him? One moment, I'll connect you..."

She was very satisfied and proud of herself, but it was as if Sergusha didn't notice her progress. He had hardly conversed with her after that first time, or, more precisely, he conversed only in passing, giving her hurried, confused assignments, not looking at her, and not inserting anything personal into the conversation, not a drop of his precious charm. For him she was becoming simply a part of the furniture, and, to her great surprise, it turned out that she was very much offended by this.

To tell the truth, she was pretty sure that he liked her, and that maybe he would even try to court her. But nothing of the sort had happened yet; on the contrary, Sergusha kept looking at her more and more sullenly and discontentedly, and she was bothered and at a loss as to what else he wanted.

Once, when he squeezed his bulk by her, angrily mumbling curses and vague threats against someone or other to himself under his breath, she couldn't stand it, dashed after him into his office, and impertinently shouted:

"This is ultimately dishonest, Sergei Aristarkhovich! If you're dissatisfied with me, then say straight out that I don't suit you!" Of course, she expected and hoped that he would be surprised and say that she was working well and would comfort her, but he glanced sullenly at her with hurt, round, dark eyes, the ringlets above his wide forehead shook, and his chin quivered.

"Well, here's yet another one," he said in a capricious voice. "Mutiny on the bounty! And what do you think, that you're working well? Because you break my typewriter with your painted claws? And jabber into the telephone just like a parrot? And do you know what a real secretary's like? A model of perfection! She should be twice as smart as I am, and I'm very smart and cunning. A real secretary should know how to fix what I've messed up, should make apologies for me if I've offended someone, should summon the research scholar I need before it's occurred to me. And should never make a scene in front of me!" he shouted and huffed angrily, shifting from side to side in his armchair. "This is just too funny! A real secretary should answer letters and give them to me just to sign. Should know everyone by voice, by first name and patronymic, and by character. And should toss half of these tormentors out on their ear, shouldn't let them come near me, because they eat up my valuable time. The others also have to be taken in hand so that they won't hang around so much, and our dear research fellows also have to be watched, otherwise they come running to me with every trifle, they come nonstop, they don't want to think or solve anything for themselves! And if I had a real secretary, I might even occasionally be able to do some work in peace..." He exhaled and sat quietly, eyes lowered, with just his plump chest heaving slightly in its sky-blue shirt, as if the last waves of agitation were still running through it.

"So what should I do, resign," asked Galia quietly, "since you're dissatisfied?..."

"Stupidity," answered Sergusha tiredly. "All from the immaturity of the mind. By the way, are you married?"

"What do you mean, Sergei Aristarkhovich! I'm not even eighteen yet."

"So what?... Oh, yes... Well, never mind, you'll get married," he said. "They all do. You'll wise up. You'll settle down to your cares and then you'll be even less suitable. So this still isn't the worst..."

Galia carefully slipped out of the office. She was not at all hurt by any of this, but somehow, on the contrary, interested. It was amazing! He had given her power, half of his kingdom, just like that. She was stunned. And she, fool that she was, had been pleased with herself. Well, just wait, Sergusha, she'd show him what she was capable of, she'd show everyone.

Galia began by going to "Sorceress" and getting a new hairstyle created for herself: she had her ash-blond hair dyed the color of a raven's wing, insisted on bangs down to her eyes, and put hair spray on them so they wouldn't curl.

Her mother, when she saw her, simply clasped her hands together.

"Good God, what have you done with yourself?" she moaned. "Galia, see what you look like!"

"Like Mireille Mathieu... "

"Nonsense, you look like a wildcat, crazed from valerian. It's all your Sergusha, I'm sure he'll bring you to no good. And when are you planning to prepare for exams?"

"Next year, Mom, not sooner."

"You've gone completely mad! What do you want, to be a secretary all your life?"

"And what's so terribly bad about that?" Galia shrugged her shoulders. "Just think! If I go to school at all, it'll only be night school."

"Galia, tell me please, this Sergusha of yours, does he... make passes at you?"

"If only!" said Galia and sighed dreamily. Could she really be in love with him? With such a hulk? Of course not! But she was somewhat captivated, nonetheless, fascinated by his personality. She wondered, if he suddenly went and proposed to her, what would she say?

Like everyone in the department, Galia had long since known all there was to know about Sergusha. He was thirty-two and a bachelor. He had been awarded a doctorate when he was defending his master's dissertation, and he had already once been a candidate for membership in the Academy of Sciences. True, he'd been rejected. Sergusha had a mother who did his housework, a black Scotch terrier, and a six-year-old son who spent Saturdays and Sundays with him. Where a bachelor got a son from was the most difficult thing of all to understand, it was hardly the same thing as an unwed mother. But all the research fellows expounded one and the same thing, with infinite variations. Long ago, in his early youth, he'd had an affair with a childhood friend. She had loved him and had very much wanted to marry him. But Sergusha refused. Sergusha didn't like her voice and she, unfortunately, was a singer. On these grounds, irreconcilable differences arose between them. Sergusha thought that a singer should have the voice of an angel, but she had a voice like a marketwoman selling fish, and if in addition she also had a throat of cast iron, that was no bonus. Anyway, apparently she planned to stop making stage appearances and to sing only for herself, but this frightened Sergusha even more. And so they split up. Nonetheless, the pushy singer continued to love Sergusha and wanted to have his child. Sergusha, after some hesitation, acquiesced.

"I was trapped by my good heart," he supposedly complained to each and every person. "How could I refuse a woman in love? And, of course, she deceived me. She swore that the whole thing would be entirely her business and wouldn't concern me in any way. And what happened? My son happened, so how can it not concern me?"

This legend, obviously elaborated and embellished, was passed by word of mouth, but what actually happened, why he hadn't married this woman and what tragedy lay behind it all—this, of course, nobody knew. And Galia didn't even know whether there was a single drop of truth in the entire story. So she was very surprised when one day a twosome, mother and son, made a personal appearance. The woman turned out to be an elegant, very beautiful blonde whose name was Lidia Alexandrovna, and the boy, Aliosha, was an exact duplicate of his father—the same fatty, with a round, happy, flushed, and very attractive face, but without the curls, his dark hair slicked back precisely with a side part.

It was Friday. Lidia Alexandrovna soon left, proudly swinging her shapely hips, but Aliosha stayed, and Galia gave him tea with candies and led him into the animal lab to show him the dogs, rabbits, and rats.

On this day Sergusha was distracted and taciturn; he'd been about to leave for a meeting scheduled for the following week, and then suddenly he remembered, called Nikolai Pavlovich, the bespectacled young man who had mocked Galia when she first came to the department, and unexpectedly signed three of his articles, which previously he'd put off for half a year.

Walking out of the office, Nikolai Pavlovich winked at Galia and said:

"Wow!"

After this the research fellows began to flock around Sergusha in throngs. The most fashionable woman in the department, Zinaida, asked Sergusha for a business trip to Leningrad, old woman Serafima dragged a mountain of photographs and X-rays over to him; only gloomy Igor Gavrilovich, Sergusha's immediate subordinate, didn't come, although Sergusha summoned him and Galia spoke with him on the phone, but he just muttered incomprehensibly:

"Never mind, he'll manage, I don't like this... you'd think it was universal brotherhood day..."

And for some reason Sergusha let him get away with it. Then he called for a car and left for home with Aliosha. As Aliosha walked out into the hall, he turned and waved to Galia, but Sergusha, on the other hand, forgot to say good-bye.

So time passed. As she got ready for work in the mornings, Galia herself was surprised at how much she had changed; even her face was different, willful, confident, strong, and she had grown up a lot and had learned to deal with things she'd had no idea about before. She now knew that far from everyone in the department supported Sergusha, that he had serious opponents, even enemies, who, while acknowledging his personal talents, nonetheless considered him a slave to routine, relying more on scientific intuition than on objective methods of research. Moreover, this group of research fellows was bothered by his extravagant, unacademic behavior, his caprices and whims, and especially by his manner of breaking things up and yelling at adults, calling them names and teasing them. They considered that, in general, people of his type shouldn't be entrusted with positions of leadership. This group was led by Igor Gavrilovich Artiukhin, who, in case of Sergusha's overthrow, would take his place. Yes, things were far from simple in this collective. And Galia, with all the passion of youth, joined the underground battle. On Sergusha's side, of course. She wasn't very interested in whether Sergusha was right or not, she felt that she was called upon to defend him by the very essence of her position, devotion to him was her job, her moral and ethical duty, and all of her sympathies were on his side. Now she carefully and delicately began to conduct her policy in support of the boss and with a sinking heart thought that very soon she'd become the kind of secretary he wanted, there was just a little more to learn. And at just that time, she almost put her foot in it out of conceit.

One day some bald guy in a jacket and wrinkled pants came to see Sergusha without out a call or any advance warning, and without even a glance in Galia's direction, he sneaked into Sergusha's office. Like a powerful spring, Galia threw herself into the path of this impudent fellow.

"Excuse me, comrade," she said in a frosty voice, "Sergei Aristarkhovich is in a meeting. What is your business?"

"Mine?" said the guy and stared at Galia over the tops of his glasses with frank, insolent curiosity.

"Well, well, not bad," he said, having finished his detailed examination. "And have you been sitting here long?"

"That is none of your concern," hissed Galia, lowering her voice: she was beginning to realize something.

And at that moment Sergusha appeared on the threshold. He looked at Galia with a sad smile.

"Tolia! Come on in, quickly!" he said. "She's still just a stupid little girl. She doesn't know or understand anything."

He walked up to the bald man, embraced him, clasped him to his stomach, and kissed him on the cheek three times with his chubby lips.

It was Anatoly Grigorievich Kolesov, the famous mathematician, Sergusha's only close friend, a personage of no less renown than that legendary singer, Aliosha's mother. Sergusha enveloped him in his arms and, like a spider, led him to his lair, puffing and repeating something in a high, cooing voice.

"She's all right, you know," the mathematician squeaked deafeningly right above Galia's ear. "Why don't you marry her?"

Sergusha gave a shout of laughter:

"Maybe I will. Maybe. I'm still sizing her up."

And only then did Galia guess that their conversation was being broadcast throughout the entire waiting room. Sergusha had forgotten to turn off the switch. Her hand of its own accord stretched out to the call button and froze. "Maybe it's intentional? Maybe he wants me to hear him? I'm sure the switch wasn't turned on before. What does all this mean?" She grew confused. She sat there blushing and scared, and listened to their conversation.

"It's time, it's time, it's time," said Kolesov. "You're not a boy anymore, you have to adjust to real life, you have to have someone close to you at your side. And she's very cute, you know? Such a little vixen... "

"If you only knew what she was like earlier," sighed Sergusha in the same tone of voice, and the sofa springs creaked plaintively beneath him. "Before she dyed her hair that awful color. Why do these girls want to be brunettes, do you understand it?"

"Well, why not?" retorted the mathematician. "They can be brunettes, they can be redheads."

"No, no, no!" insisted Sergusha angrily. "A girl should be fair, pale, and gentle."

"And have the voice of an angel?"

"Stop it."

"Well, how's Zinaida?"

"Ugh, come on, she's a real shrew..."

"And what's this one's name?"

"Her name's Galochka," said Sergusha tenderly, and Galia actually jumped in her chair in surprise.

"Sergei Aristarkhovich," she said into the microphone, stumbling over the words, "Please turn off the switch!"

She felt terrible all day and she couldn't sleep at night. She kept having visions of all kinds of nonsense: of Sergusha stretching his arms out to her, his chubby lips moving, as his round, cheerful, tender eyes shone and the curls above his clear brow stirred. And toward morning she had a dream that she was in love with him and was having a good cry, her face buried in his plump chest. She awoke feeling worn out and like a real fool, not knowing how to act or what to do. She looked with hatred in the mirror at her black locks, which had become matted in her sleep. God, was it really true? Such a man!

But nothing happened at work and the days flowed by calmly as if nothing at all had ever occurred.

At the end of May, a commission came to the department. At first they sat, secluded with Sergusha in his office, and Galia heard his high, offended voice. He would yell something, hurriedly explain to them, and object, harshly and explosively, over the quiet drone of their voices.

Then the commission crawled all over the department, checking out the work. And the indignant, high-strung Nikolai Pavlovich rushed up to Galia.

"Listen," he said in agitation, "This swine, this hack, they've decided to eat him alive. It's funny, really—an elephant and a lapdog. But they'll still give him a lot of trouble. You understand, they're going to question you, too... about deliveries and all of that. So you'd better not screw up, tell then what you should, you know how. You hear, Galka?"

"Oh, yes!"

"No, you're thinking that they're not worth his little finger!" ranted Nikolai Petrovich, his glasses flashing. "So he acts a little odd at times, so what do they care? For all that, he's a genius. For instance, he calls himself Sergusha, but do you know why? Out of pride. He doesn't want anyone calling him a fatty behind his back, or a lump or a hog, so he decided on Sergusha, and Sergusha it is. There's nothing offensive about that. But they mind it. Just let them try and find some mistakes in his work, let them try. We've got such a great experiment going right now—God should grant such a thing to everybody. It's brilliant! A dream come true! All they want is to have equipment handed to them and they'll copy down the figures. Scientists! Trash! Academicians! They're scientists in writing denunciations. Got it?"

After Nikolai Pavlovich left, Zinaida came into the waiting room. She perched on the arm of a chair and silently began smoking a cigarette.

"What do you want, did you come to agitate for my support too?" Galia flew into a rage. "Look, I understand everything just as well as the rest of you do."

"So this means I don't have to agitate with you?" she smiled. "Well, just the same, it's useful to know, for information's sake, that his last work was translated into twelve languages. In general, it's seminal work. Do you understand? He's got to be protected from all that garbage. They just want everything to follow a routine, one thing after another, they're not capable of following his thoughts, so they're furious."

"Zinaida Vasilievna," said Galia suddenly. "Is it true that he went after you earlier?"

"It's true," she said, giving Galia a sly, sidelong glance. "He even proposed to me..."

"And you turned him down?"

"I turned him down." She took a drag on her cigarette and blew smoke up at the ceiling. "Not for any reason, really. He's a nice guy, talented, not like my dummy."

"So what did he do?"

"Nothing," she shrugged. "There wasn't anything between us to fight about. He came to my wedding, he calls me at home sometimes, he chats with Volodka, my husband. He's really very lonely. But why do you ask, do you like him?"

"I don't know," said Galia in fright. "How should I know?"

"What do you mean 'How should you know?' Who else would know? But, basically, if this is a serious talk, we'd all be very glad if he found some happiness. Do you understand?"

"I understand," said Galia, her voice faltering. What had she done and where had it taken her? Everywhere there was only Sergusha, everywhere, she couldn't think about anyone or anything else. But that double chin, that jiggling stomach! What was she to do about all that? She was barely eighteen and she still understood very little, even about herself.

The commission disappeared from the department imperceptibly, somehow, as if it had never been there. Sergusha walked around with a satisfied air, his round eyes sparkling merrily. The gloomy Artiukhin came several times to explain himself, and the last time they walked out of the office with their arms around each other; more accurately, the enormous Sergusha led him out, his pudgy hand on his shoulders, and Artiukhin's face was puckered in a sour smile and he kept shooting nervous glances at Galia. The scene, in truth, was absurd, and Igor Gavrilovich didn't like mockery. But Sergusha! Hadn't he arranged all of this on purpose? He went and showed that Artiukhin was dancing attendance on him. And Galia immediately understood: she was being made responsible for spreading the word throughout the department. She didn't think too long before rushing to see Zinaida. The news was enthusiastically received, and everyone instantly played out the scenario.

"Well, well," laughed the research fellows. "So they've come out of it?"

"Uh-huh."

"Well, Galia, you're a real ace! Let him try and wriggle out of it now, the fighter for justice! Then we'll ask him—did you embrace the tyrant? And that'll do it! That'll shut our Igor up..."

Summer was approaching. Galia was tired. The small reception room was as hot as hell. She walked around as if in a fog, constantly expecting his summons, his smiles, and the appearance of his enormous body in the doorway; she thought about him while she pounded on the typewriter and talked on the telephone and when she looked at herself in the mirror. Her hair had long since grown out and was again ash-blond and light; she gathered it back into a luxurious knot that lay beautifully on her slender neck, which was already a bit tanned.

But Sergusha continued not to notice her, and ploughed by, nodding hurriedly, and giving surly orders.

So, finally, she started planning a vacation.

She put in her request on July 7th—he scribbled his signature on it without reading it. She got a ticket for the 12th, yet was still waiting for something. But nothing happened. On Friday the 11th she went to say good-bye to him. It was an overcast, oppressive, humid day, and stormclouds were gathering. It was nearly dark in the office.

"Sergei Aristarkhovich," said Galia, lowering her eyes and blushing furiously, "Do you remember that I'll be on vacation starting Monday and won't be coming in?"

"What do you mean you won't be coming in?" he asked in surprise, raising his large face framed with shaking curls.

"I mean," she said quietly, "it's my vacation."

"So?"

"So you signed the request yourself!"

"Request? I don't remember. Come here, Galia, sit down," he said.

She obediently sat down next to him in the visitors' chair, and for several extremely long moments they were silent. From time to time there was a rumble of thunder outside, and the room smelled strongly of dust and poplar. The phone rang, but he didn't pick it up.

"So what's going to happen to our friendship?" he suddenly asked quietly.

"What friendship?" she babbled, at a loss. "There really wasn't any friendship..."

"There was," said Sergusha softly. "There really was, wasn't there? Isn't that right?"

"I don't know."

"Well, there you see. And you'd want..." He took her lightly by the hand with his hot, chubby hand. "You would agree for everything to be different, you know, closer, more serious, well... "

"I don't know... yes, probably... of course..." she whispered.

And Sergusha suddenly bent down and kissed her hand. "Galochka," he said in the cooing, tender voice that she found so memorable. "Galochka, do you really have to go on this stupid vacation?"

"Of course I do," she answered in fear, without hearing herself. "I've already got the ticket. For tomorrow."

"For tomorrow," he said, quietly shaking his head. "That's so sad. You won't run away from me for good, will you? You'll come back to me afterwards?"

"I won't run away," she whispered, and to her own surprise, she put her arms around his big, shaggy head.

She felt him sigh and begin to tremble against her chest, and her entire being was filled with happiness and triumph.

"I'll come back to you," she said loudly and boldly, and kissed him on the cheek. Everything was whirling and dancing before her eyes. His round, merry, beaming eyes, the curls over his forehead, his hands.

She flew out of the office and, without asking anyone's permission, left for home. She was as if delirious, got off the bus at the wrong stop, dropped by some shops, stood in front of the store windows without seeing a thing, and waited out the rain in some doorway. What would happen now? What kind of life would begin for her? She would run a bit, and then stop, and sit in some courtyard on a wet bench next to a sandbox. She had no memory of how she got home, and she was surprised to see her mother.

"What's going on? What's with you?" asked her mother in fright. "What's happened to you, can you tell me?"

"I'm getting married to Sergusha," she blurted out to her own amazement. "That's all."

"You've lost your mind," her mother shook her head. "He's a monster!"

"Nothing of the sort!"

"And he's fourteen years older than you."

"So?"

"So you were planning to go on vacation..." Her mother had already reached her last resort.

"And I am going," said Galia drowsily. "I'm going, just like I planned to. But as soon as I get back, I'll get married."

"Galia, is he letting you go? He's not going after you, your Sergusha?"

"Him—after me? What's your problem, mama?" she burst out laughing, and then yawned. "Oh, mom, leave me alone, I'm so tired, I'm dying to sleep."

The following morning she flew to the Crimea, to Simeiz, and by four o'clock she was swimming in the sea. After swimming her fill, she sat on the burning rocks—small, slender, in a multi-colored cotton swimsuit, quite overcome by the sultry air, the sun, the cliffs, and the boundless blue before her eyes. There weren't many people on the beach at this hour, and the sea was totally empty, except for some long-legged guy slowly and carefully wading into the water.

"Hey, you," Galia yelled at him, sweeping by him in a whirl, "Let's swim up to that cliff!"

The guy was silent, but she heard him swimming next to her with a strong, boyish freestroke.

Galia squinted, dived into the cool depth, opened her eyes and saw his long, rhythmically moving legs. He was turning toward the shore.

"Hey, what are you doing?" she shouted, springing to the surface. "And how about the cliffs?"

"I don't swim that far," the guy answered, easily flipping over onto his back, and waved his hand. "Wade out, we'll talk on the shore."

Gayla obediently turned back.

"Why is it you don't swim that far?" she asked immediately, flopping onto the sand next to the guy.

"I gave my word."

"To who?"

"My mother."

"And where's she?"

"At home, in Moscow," the guy laughed.

"So why are you acting like such a fool?" Galia said in surprise.

He shrugged.

"I gave her my word. She said that then she wouldn't worry about me. So now I'm suffering."

"Well, I must say, it's the first time I've ever heard anything like this from a boy."

"No sweat," he said, "That doesn't bother me at all."

"What's your name?" pressed Galia. "Wait a second, let me guess. It's probably something idiotic—Vadia or Edia or Goga."

"My name's Seriozha," the guy said reservedly.

"What?!" Galia sighed, and her heart sank. Of course, it didn't mean anything in particular that this guy's name was also Sergei, it was just a name like any other, but Sergusha was w aiting for her there, and for an instant she felt his heavy, shaggy, hot head on her chest and in her arms.

"So you're Seriozha," she said in a different voice now, and a different tone. "My name's Galia. Have you been here long?"

"Almost a week."

"I just got here today."

"That's obvious," he grinned. "Do you work or go to school?"

"I work. As a secretary," she said quickly, giving him a sidelong glance. He didn't laugh.

"I'm a third-year student..."

"Engineering or med school?"

"Come on! How'd you come up with that? I'm at VGIK,[1] in the theater department."

"You?"

"Me. What's so special about it?"

"You're a C-student, surely? Or are you lying about all this?"

"No," he said very calmly. "I'm not lying. I have talent, you see. It's quite something!"

"I know," she said, but he wasn't listening to her.

"I'm consumed by fantasy," he suddenly burst out ardently, as if he'd been yearning for someone to listen to him. "You understand, I'm always drifting off somewhere. That's why I need a lot of self-discipline. For instance, you can imagine that right now, at this moment, somewhere it's winter, there's a storm and a strong wind, your eyebrows are iced over and your teeth are chattering from cold, and on your shoulders is a heavy, icy fur coat. Or that you're Japanese. And everyone around you is Japanese, and you think in Japanese, and slanting, yellow rain is falling from the sky, and the trees around aren't like the ones here, and you have wooden sandals on your feet. Or... we're in space, and our earth is so small..."

"That's enough," said Galia. "I understand everything. It's even starting to scare me."

They sat on the sand, their shoulders lightly touching. The red sun, attenuating and trembling, was setting into the sea. It was getting cool.

"Where do you live?" Seriozha asked her. "Can I walk you home?"

She nodded.

So that was how everything started, and how everything went. She and Seriozha were hardly ever apart. They hiked in the mountains, lingered in restaurants, took a boat to Yalta, baked side by side on the burning sands, and kissed nonstop. They already knew everything about each other, and the happy Galia even managed to tell him about Sergusha. A hundred stories about the funny fatso Sergusha. She got tanned and even thinner, her lips got chapped, her light hair got sun-bleached and was fluffed up into a golden halo around her head.

That was how she came to the department after her vacation, disheveled, in a too revealing cotton beachdress. She ran through all the rooms, calling out a gay "hello" to the research fellows, and everyone greeted her affably and rejoiced at her return.

And of course along the way she showed up at Zinaida's office. As always, Zinaida was sitting on her desk, her well-groomed feet clad in sumptuous shoes were crossed, and she was smoking.

"Well?" she asked, after examining Galia somewhat strangely and barely smiling at her. "What's the good news, who is he?"

"Oh, Zinaida Vasilievna! It was so great, you can't possibly imagine! He's studying to be an actor. Oh, no, it's not at all what you think .... "

"No, why? Everything's clear, Galia. You don't have to go on." She glanced briefly at the others and turned away.

"So, you turned out to be a real bitch," said Artiukhin suddenly behind Galia. "Just a little bitch."

"Well, that's life," mumbled Nikolai Pavlovich, glancing somewhere to the side. "Listen, don't go see him today. He's preparing a whole banquet, Sergusha is. It's better if I tell him myself...."

"What banquet?" asked Galia helplessly. "What banquet are you talking about? What have I done that's so terrible?"

"Forget it, don't rip yourself apart over it. It happens," said Nikolai Pavlovich. "Just go, go. Don't try to see him now...."

So she stepped across the threshold. And as soon as she did, she suddenly realized very clearly that she would never see him, Sergusha, again. And the bouquet on her desk would again wither away for a long time. Probably roses, there were so many roses in the city now. But what could she do? What?

She sent her letter of resignation through the mail.

Translated by Rebecca Epstein

From *Cheremukhovyi kholod,* Moscow, 1980

Notes

1. VGIK—acronym for the Moscow State Institute of Cinematography.

The Chosen People

Liudmila Ulitskaia

On the seventh of October, on the eve of Sergei of Radonezh,[1] Zinaida dragged her-self to church, her mournful, watery body flowing downward in waves, and she came to a stop on the no man's land that began where the stalls ended and went to the church balustrade, where the beggars formed a herd.

A month had passed since she buried her mother. The funeral money her mother had saved was spent, and the eighteen additional rubles for the funeral meal had to come out of her invalid pension. Zinaida couldn't handle money, Mama had bought everything as long as she'd been well, but when she fell ill, somehow nothing worked out and food became a problem...

Before Mama's death Maria Ignatievna from the second floor had brought down soup, or a little something, but when Mama died, Maria Ignatievna stopped visiting Zinaida because she was offended: she wanted Mama's Chinese jacket, and Zina didn't give it to her. She couldn't spare it. Not because she wanted it for herself. Zina couldn't wear Mama's things; Mama was as small and dry as a beetle while Zinaida was so wide she couldn't get into a tram. Zinaida didn't give her the jacket because it was a memento of Mama—in a Chinese green with covered buttons, and flowers embroidered in wool on the shoulders.

There had been a second jacket, a blue one, but it wasn't there now because Mama had given orders to be buried in the blue one. She was susceptible to chills and had dreaded the coldness of the grave, and she had left orders to be buried in the blue jacket and woollen socks. So Zinaida did as she'd been told and Maria Ignatievna got nothing and was cross.

Furthermore, her mother had ordered Zinaida to place her trust in the Mother of God and when the money ran out she was to go to the cathedral and stand there: "Good people will help you in your poverty for the sake of the Mother of God."

So Zinaida went and stood there. She felt even worse standing than walking; she believed her illness was chiefly in the legs, even though the woman doctor for the dis-trict said it was in the adrenal glands.

Two beggars were sitting on folding stools by the balustrade, right beside the church, but stools like that were no use to Zinaida. They wouldn't support her.

Zinaida had on soft footwear, felt slippers cut out in front, and at home she had galoshes to put over them in wet weather. Mama used to knit socks for her, roomy ones from village wool, and she wore track pants because no stockings would go over her bulging legs. Over this she had put on a new flannel robe in a flaming rust and a good jacket. In her foolishness she had put on her very best things (just as she did when she went to the clinic) because she was going out in public.

So she stood there, while old ladies went by and some younger women, with bags, and a few really young ones, but nobody gave anything to Zinaida. Evidently she was either standing in the wrong place or doing something wrong. Half an hour went by and her legs began to burn fiercely, and she became painfully hungry. She remembered that in the sideboard there was a packet of vermicelli, so she went home quietly, baffled that Mama had deceived her—or been mistaken herself: nobody had given her any-thing to ease her poverty for the sake of the Mother of God.

The next morning it occurred to Zinaida that she hadn't told any of the passers-by that it was for the sake of the Mother of God. She suddenly remembered, but it was too late to go back because the service was already over.

On the next day, however, Zinaida got up earlier and prepared to go to the cathe-dral. Once again it was not an ordinary day, there was an important festival, St. John the Evangelist,[2] and the weather was sunny, unusually warm for the season. Once again Zinaida put on her flaming red robe and her good jacket. Again it didn't occur to her to dress more shabbily. She tied a pink kerchief around her head and set off to wad-dle across the avenue.

There were more people around the cathedral than last time and a whole line of beggars had formed. Zinaida moved a little closer to them, but not too close; she was embarrassed. Now she remembered that she shouldn't just beg but should say it was for the sake of the Mother of God. But none of the people who went by looked in her direction, and she didn't know how to address them.

At last, an extremely unhealthy-looking old woman in glasses with a walking stick walked by, stopped beside Zinaida, and gave her a tarnished kopeck coin.

"For the sake of the Mother of God," said Zinaida belatedly, but the old woman answered promptly:

"The Lord be with you!"

Zinaida was delighted and began to examine her kopeck. It was completely ordi-nary, but all the same it had been given to her.

"Mama had good reason for telling me what she did" thought Zinaida, just as a dark woman with a long nose came up to her. She wore high heels and frightening dark glasses and, putting a twenty-kopeck coin in her hand, asked:

"Pray for the repose of Catherine."

"Thank you very much, I shall," said Zinaida and crossed herself. She didn't know the correct answer, but it didn't look as though the woman in glasses minded.

People kept walking past, not in a dense crowd but in ones and twos, and Zinaida collected a whole handful of coins, though mostly copper. Her legs started to give way and she felt very hungry. She decided to go home, but first to go in the cathedral and thank the Mother of God for her aid.

Zinaida climbed up to the church porch. The steps were difficult. She thought some-one shouted to her, "Hey, you!" but she didn't have any friends here, and she went inside, crossing herself three times near all the doors. She bought a candle for thirty kopeks, which still left her a lot of money—at least a ruble—and placed it next to the Kazan icon (Mama always used to place one there). Then she stumped over to the exit.

Near the box an old woman holding a plate poked her sharply in the side and whispered:

"Stand still, like other people. Where are you off to? They're singing the Cherubim."[3]

But Zinaida didn't understand why the old lady was scolding her and, hunching her back, she shuffled over to the door.

She left the cathedral, her side still aching from the old lady's jab, when all of a sudden—an attack! Yet another old woman in a checked kerchief with a fat mole under her eye, one of those standing in the most advantageous spot right in front of the steps, rushed at her and twisted her hand, so that all the coins she had collected scattered on the ground:

"You come here again and we'll break your legs!" And she started hitting her in the back with a coarse bag.

A lame old man got up from the ground, went round to her other side, and waved his stick, swearing at her:

"Go on, get out of here!"

Zinaida's eyes half closed and she came to a stop. Her legs felt weak and she felt a burning sensation in her thighs and calves.

"Go away, there's nothing for you here, there's enough of us already!" A tiny little old lady in a motheaten fur cap tried to chase her off.

Zinaida would have been happy to run away, but her legs wouldn't hold her. They buckled, and she sat down on the road like a huge bedraggled hen and covered her head with swollen white hands.

Suddenly a furious, hoarse voice rang out over her head:

"Ooh, you pack of jackals, filthy rabble! You're scum, Kotova! You've been standing there for twenty years and it's still not enough for you! You'll take the money with you to the next world! And you, what are you butting in for, you old goat, you Fascist lackey! Come on, get up!"

Zinaida felt an iron hand on her shoulder pulling her up.

"Hey, the woman isn't well, help get her up!" the voice bellowed, and strange hands pulled Zinaida up, half-dragged, half-carried her to the bench and put her down on it. Only then did she open her eyes. In front of her there stood what seemed at first glance a small, broad-shouldered little boy, no, not a boy, a mannish-looking woman in pants with slanting eyebrows and a hard-bitten face. Orange bangs stuck out from her sanctimonious white kerchief. Her widespread nostrils quivered.

"Don't worry, it's okay, I'll twist their tails, the band of scroungers! You go and stand wherever you want, places aren't paid for! Ugh, they've started a Mafia, just like in Sicily! A poor person can't find a corner any more. They're worse than the police!" shouted this strange woman. "Don't you listen to them! If anyone so much as says a word to you, tell them straight away: 'Katia the Redhead said I could!'"

Katia the Redhead stood there, leaning on two stout crutches, then, her anger extinguished, she bent down to Zinaida and asked:

"And where are you from?"

Zinaida wanted to answer, but her tongue wouldn't move.

"Where do you live?," asked Katia again. "Are you deaf?" At that Zinaida shook her head.

"I live here, across the avenue."

"Which apartment block?" Katia inquired matter-of-factly.

"The second," Zinaida answered joyfully.

"Ah," Katia nodded in satisfaction.

"My mama died. I buried her a month ago," Zinaida continued the conversation.

"While mine will never die," noted Katia with regret. "Here's a three-ruble note, take it. Do you drink?"

"No-o," Zinaida was amazed.

"Take it. If you don't drink, it will last you till the festival of the Protection of the Virgin.[4] Don't come tomorrow. Come on the 14th, or you can come on the 13th before the evening service. I'll be here. If there's any trouble, just tell them, 'Katia the Redhead said I could!' What's your name?"

"Zinaida," answered Zinaida shyly.

"They're ignorant, Zinaida, they have no power. They're nasty, like dogs. On second thoughts, they're worse than dogs. You just yell at them and they rub their tails against you. More and more we get scroungers, there are almost no real beggars here. But you go on, keep coming here, don't be afraid!" Katia helped Zinaida to extricate her body from the low garden bench into which she had sunk as though into a trap. And she went home. Her slippers felt damp and the lower part of her body was cold all over.

Chilled and feeling as if her flabby body had shrunk, Zinaida squeezed into the apartment and stopped just inside. She sat down on a stool in the hall, pulled her kerchief off her head, wound it into a knot, a sort of rag doll, started to feel sorry for herself ("You poor, poor thing,") and began to cry.

Zinaida was weak. While Mama was alive she often got mad at Mama for not giving her anything to eat. Zina's appetite never flagged, it was her illness, but Mama stopped her. Then Zinaida, twisting her kerchief into a doll, would sit on the stool near the door and say to Mama: "I'll go away and leave you..."

"Where will you go, you great lump? Where will you go, glutton?" grumbled Mama, unmoved.

And it seemed somehow to Zina as though this cloth dolly were her, Zina, only small, and she whispered:

"We'll go away. Spring will come and we'll go to Anapa."

Zina had been taken to the sanatorium in Anapa when she was ten and the illness was just beginning.

When she had recovered from the fear and the hurt, Zinaida took off her wet pants and went to wash them in the bath. As she bathed her huge, semitransparent hands in the soapy water, she kept sighing—she couldn't do anything right. Before, Mama used to do everything, and now it was all up to her... Her thoughts were large, puffy, clumsy. She thought about her future life of poverty, and about every single piece of food that she was about to eat, and about Katia the Redhead, who had protected her from wicked people...

Zinaida went back on the feast of the Protection of the Virgin. They didn't chase her away any more. She collected a lot of money, almost four rubles. All the time she was there, resting her back against the balustrade, her eyes sought out Katia the Redhead, but she couldn't find her. Three days later, when the money was all gone, she went back, and again collected money, but did not encounter Katia. The old women didn't chase her away, and one even welcomed her, moved over, and said to another one:

"Let the Elephant stand here. Move over to the left."

And Zinaida got back her old nickname—the Elephant. She really was an Elephant, and she'd been called that even at school, but it had hurt then because she was a child, and now it was like her own name...

Zinaida met Katia only when she went to beg for the third time. Katia was walking unsteadily along an asphalt path that led diagonally to the cathedral, limping in one leg and at the same time thrusting the other, fitted with an orthopedic shoe, high to one side. Katia saw Zinaida, nodded, and went into the cathedral.

"She must be in the porch," thought Zinaida. She also wanted to get under cover, but she was afraid that the lady with the mole would chase her away again. So she stood there for almost an hour deep in thought. At first pins and needles ran up and down her legs, and then they went numb. She hadn't been given much, less than anyone else. She had noticed this earlier and privately decided that it was right: you always feel more sorry for someone thin than someone fat.

After hesitating for a little while longer, Zinaida decided to look for Katia in the cathedral. She saw her in the left side-chapel, in the line next to the priest taking confessions. Katia looked stern, her bangs weren't sticking out from beneath her kerchief, which was tied low on the forehead and fell into two deep folds at the temples. She stepped up to the gray-bearded, over-heated priest. He spoke to her for a long time, she shook her head, and then started speaking herself, to Zinaida's great astonishment.

The old man kept shaking his head and then laid a dull-gold stole on her head.[5] She kissed his sallow hand and limped to the Tsar's Doors.[6]

Zinaida intercepted her and tugged at her sleeve, but Katia looked at her with empty amber eyes and said: "Later, later...". Then the cathedral started to thunder with the tremendous sound of singing. They sang "I believe..." and Katia turned away from her and with unexpected delicacy came out with "...in One God, the Father Almighty, Maker of Heaven and earth, and of all things visible and invisible..." Her voice grew soft, rose and fell so firmly that it seemed that Katia alone was leading this large crowd along a slippery mountain path.

Then all the singing stopped, the priest spoke again, the choir sang a little, and again the whole cathedral repeated "Our Father." Zinaida knew it because Mama had taught it to her. But it was very stuffy and crowded, and the people weren't separate individuals; they resembled various trembling drops that had flowed together to form one huge being, and Zinaida felt that everything was turning into a thick mist, yet it was not a damp mist but airy and honey-like. The candle light seemed to dissolve in the air, everything became sweet, soporific, all of life outside, on the street, disappeared like rainbow patterns in a pond, while here everything was golden and kept getting thicker until, in the end, it had the same density as her body, and she broke away and rose and swam between golden pillars, arches, and shimmering aureoles, while the thick air, which she touched with her hand, welcomed and caressed her...

She hadn't noticed that she had been sitting for a long time on the wide, comfortable pew alongside other people. Who had led her there and sat her down she didn't remember. Katia found her there on the bench.

"So they're not chasing you away any more?" asked Katia, bending down.

"No, they're not," Zinaida beamed in response.

"Well, fine," Katia started to move away, then halted and asked, "Did you collect something? Let's go, then, eh?"

And they went out together, swaying as they walked, Zinaida and tiny Katia, like a crooked, withered tree.

"How about going to your place?" suggested Katia and Zinaida was pleased: no one came to visit her except Aunt Pasha, Mama's sister.

On the way home Zinaida bought bread and ice cream, a lot of it. Since Mama had died, she ate to her heart's content and she had developed a passion for ice cream. Her mother had not given her ice cream, saying, "Sweet things are bad for you!" But Zina didn't deny herself sugar.

Katia examined everything in the house with a sharp eye and even sniffed. She noticed the unwashed floor and said:

"I can't bend down normally either, so I wash floors on all fours. I lie on my stomach and slide backwards. I can wash yours, if you like?"

Zinaida was embarrassed by this suggestion: why bother? It was fine as it was. Katia also glanced into the second room, the one off to the side. Zina didn't go in there any more since Mama died; there was nothing for her to do there. While Katia was looking round, Zina prepared them something to eat: she mixed boiled potatoes and soft cheese into a white bowl and poured yogurt on it. She had thought up this dish for herself; first of all, she liked it and, secondly, it didn't need cooking. She only had to mix up everything in turn and it tasted good. Zinaida derived great comfort from eating. She only felt good while she was actually chewing. As soon as she swallowed the food, it was as though a large beast in her stomach began to stir and demand: more, more.

They were about to sit down when Katia jumped up, leaning on one crutch—Zinaida saw then that without support Katia couldn't walk at all, but would fall over right away—she limped into the corridor and brought in a worn cloth bag with a clasp. She snapped the clasp open with a distinct click, pulled out a small bottle of vodka, and put it on the table.

"As it's a holiday, it's not forbidden," she announced didactically, though Zinaida hadn't thought of forbidding anything. She looked for vodka glasses, couldn't find any, and took out some cups. Katia wrinkled her short nose.

"In that case, let's have tumblers."

Zinaida set out two tumblers and dished the mixture onto the dinner plates. Katia took the top off the bottle with a thick nail and poured out a glass each. Zina gasped. She normally didn't drink vodka.

"Too much, is it?" Katia was amazed. "Well, if you don't want it, don't drink it," she allowed condescendingly. She clinked her glass against Zinaida's, and with the words "God be with you, Zina," she crossed herself and tossed the vodka into her open, sparsely-toothed mouth. Zina sniffed her glass and took a small sip. It tasted unpleasant and burnt her throat.

Katia quickly ate the plate of mash and she ate the ice cream too, with moderation and without much enjoyment. She waited until Zinaida had licked the tinfoil wrapper of the ice cream, gathered up the plates from the table and placed them in the sink, and then said significantly:

"Here we are, then."

Zinaida lifted up her face that was somewhat bespattered with ice cream and prepared to listen, open-mouthed.

"Go and wash!" Katia ordered, but Zina didn't move. Instead she wiped her mouth with a rag; that would do well enough. And Katia began:

"Zina, this is what I wanted to say to you." Her voice sounded solemn and full of significance. "Your mother has died, and you're not very bright." Zinaida nodded; it was all true. "What's more, you're sick," added Katia with a note of finality.

"You did the right thing, coming to the cathedral. However, why did you come?" Katia's question didn't need an answer. "You went to beg. And you did the right thing. There's a whole crowd that does that. Most of them are scroungers. It doesn't take a lot of brains. You, Zina, I don't want you to be a scrounger, but a true beggar."

"No, I can never be like Katia," Zinaida thought, in rapture over her new friend. "She has such a voice—booming out when she flew at the old women, then lilting, like a child's, when she sang the liturgy..."

Meanwhile Katia continued her speech:

"Pay no heed to me, I'm a special case, neither this nor that, out of the ordinary. I studied at a technological institute, suffered in so many hospitals, I've been in the kinds of places you wouldn't even dream about. Pay no heed to me. Tell me, first of all, Zina, what do you need?"

Zina frowned, knitted her brows, thought for a moment, and said:

"Today I've got everything I need, Katia."

Katia gave a satisfied smile:

"Right, I guessed right about you! It's a rare person will say: I've got everything I need. Just about everybody feels the need for something. They want all kinds of things, get mad, suffer, hate to the death, and it's all from envy, that someone else has something I don't! Understand?"

"That's so!" Zinaida concurred importantly, flattered by the weightiness of the conversation. She was quite flustered, even blushing slightly.

"I'm not envious, other people's stuff never fits me... I'm so fat!"

"Zinaida, you really are a simpleton," Katia said, somewhat disappointed. "Well, all right, but do you believe in God?"

Zinaida was disconcerted and began fidgeting on her stool.

"Well?" Katia asked sternly.

Zinaida started to twist the rag into a doll.

"Look at you, you're one of God's people, and you don't believe in God," Katia went on, now totally disappointed.

"I... I believe in the Mother of God...," Zinaida lowered her head and recited softly like a schoolgirl with a failing grade for the lesson.

"Well," Katia demanded, sounding like a teacher, "Tell me, whose Mother is she?"

Zinaida pouted, then said softly:

"Mother of her daughter."

At that Katia was stupefied. Her yellow eyes goggled and she threw up her hands, so that the crutch propped up against the windowsill fell down with a loud crash.

"What? Daughter? What daughter? She's the Mother of our Lord Jesus Christ! Why, Zina, you're worse than a Tartar! What will you say next—a daughter!"

Zina sat there, scarlet all over, bells throbbing in her head.

"Jesus Christ, the Son of God, came down from heaven for one thing only—to tell us not to be animals and to love one another, but they seized him and put him to death. They killed him, Zina! Then they had second thoughts, but it was all over! Too late! He rose from the dead, and then disappeared. You'll be whistling in the wind for him!"

Katia moved Zinaida's glass toward her, drank its contents, and, after a moment's silence, shook her head:

"You don't drink, so don't drink it! I'll have it! Everyone, Zin, has either too much or too little of something—good looks, intelligence, all kinds of positive things. Just listen to what happened to me. It was at the time that I got free... got away...." Katia rummaged around in her cloth bag, dragged another quarter-litre bottle out of it, and cast a suspicious sidewise glance at Zinaida, but the latter sat there guilelessly, expressing neither displeasure nor surprise.

Katia again neatly removed the top, poured out half a glass and drank it at a gulp. "I'm from Khimki, the district where I'm officially a resident. I come home and my mother won't register me. My mother's not old, she's good-looking with black eyes and brows, her gypsy blood shows. I can't understand why she won't register me. We never had any special rows... They only told me later, Zin. I had a man, a husband of sorts, Zin, a bit older than me, but that's O.K, it's normal. So when they put me in jail—and it was all because of him, by the way, it all came out—my mummy had taken him for herself. And she had plenty and to spare, even without my Vitka. Why he took up with her I'll never understand. In any case, my mother doesn't register me and with no registration I can't even get my invalid pension, I've got nowhere to go. Then again you can't get a job without a residence permit, even though you're at your last gasp. But she wouldn't, not for anything. My only clothes are what's on me: a padded jacket and torn boots. I had a friend living in Novo-Dachnaia, and I went to see her but she wasn't there—she'd moved. I arrive at Savelovsk station, I don't remember how, I hobble up to Novoslobodskaia.[7] I hear bells ringing. And I think, I'll go in the church. Why not? I was christened, wasn't I? The mood I'm in, I feel like hanging myself. I go in and stand there. I don't even have the money for a little candle. The church was full, it was a festival, I don't remember now which one. I just stand there and think: Lord, why did you bring me into this world? I'm a cripple, and penniless as well, and my own mother chases me away, my man—the hell with him. That my own mother took him away, that's what's unforgivable. I'm thinking this and getting madder and madder at Him. Why are you doing this? Is it fair? Why does my life have to be so miserable while others no better than me have perfectly decent lives? I say to Him, if you're preparing the Heavenly Kingdom for me, then don't bother... I'd rather have it now, this minute... I'm standing there feeling mad, getting more and more carried away. I feel sorry for myself—that I'm a cripple, that God didn't give me good looks or anything else..." Katia sniffed; with a pitiful expression, Zina kept twisting her piece of cloth round in her hands. Katia took hold of the neck of the bottle with her stubby hand, but didn't pour.

"Suddenly I hear a metallic clank behind me, rattle, rattle, I looked around—an old woman behind me was unfolding a cot. She must be out of her mind, I think... And I don't look in her direction any more. After a little while again, I hear tinkle, tinkle... I look around, and see a sight you wouldn't believe, Zina. There are three pillows piled up on the camp-bed, and lying among them, resting on her chin, is neither a mouse nor a frog but a strange little creature. It's a woman, wrapped in a child's blanket that doesn't quite cover her feet, she's swaddled like a baby and tied with strings. A little face peers out of a black kerchief and her eyes burn like fire, just like the boyar's wife Morozova. But, of course, you wouldn't know that lovely picture by the artist Surikov. That's the kind of memory I have, Zina, I just see something once and it stays with me for ever. I remember everything. There she lies, and her eyes are burning, as if they could burn a hole right through me. An old woman picks her up and carries her like a child, and her head droops down over the shoulder, she can't hold her head up, it hangs down. She's just like a seven-year-old child, the blanket isn't quite big enough and her feet stick out in woollen socks, they're tiny, she can't walk on them. The old woman carried her to confession, and, Zina, I walked behind her like a goat on a rope, I couldn't tear myself away. The old woman carries her up to the priest, and he reads these long prayers. At that time I didn't know anything, it was only afterwards I found out everything about what he was reading and why. Now I know the whole service by heart, know it down to the last word, but at that time I didn't know anything about how the church works. He finished reading and then right away went to her and said something. And she answered him like a mouse—squeak, squeak! Zina, inside me—this hasn't happened to me since—I felt such a tickle in my throat and chest and right in my heart, it was as if her hand had simply crawled inside and kept tearing and scratching with her nails. I couldn't take it. That's all I needed! Really! I mean, she'd no legs nor arms nor human voice, she had to be carried around like a sack... at that moment something inside me cracked and started flowing... Zina, I cried torrents! I felt so sorry for her, I can't tell you..." Katia's lips trembled and twitched, she blew her nose and wiped her eyes, then carried on sternly,

"I found out everything about her later, Zina. She's the nun Evdokia, the old woman is her mother, who's also taken vows. Of course, they live in the world—who needs them in the convent? That's someone who's really suffered misfortune! Good Lord, for what? Then it struck me, Zina! You know, everyone who looks at her thinks one and the same thing: her torment is worse than mine, it couldn't get any worse, whereas in my case, whatever happens, I can still get by somehow. She's someone you really have to feel sorry for, and not for yourself. I realized, Zinochka, why the Lord puts people like us, the weak, the freaks, and the cripples on the earth! Do you understand, Zinochka?"

Zinaida sat as if frozen. Mouth open, eyes squinting, she listened to Katia's words without hearing them, but she took in their meaning in some strange way, as if absorbing it through the skin or breathing it in.

"For comparison, as an example, or for consolation. I don't exactly know how to put it," explained Katia. "People are nasty, they find it very comforting to see someone worse off than themselves. Here, look, there are well-known performers, beautiful women, they sell their pictures at stalls, all flowers and roses. You look at them and you feel like throwing up—there's no justice at all. When on the one hand you have an artiste like that, who gets everything, and on the other, sister Evdokia on her cot... Just think! You should stay in the place where God put you! So I think, fine! This is my place, then: I'm a cripple, I stand by the cathedral, people go past and everyone who looks at me says to himself: Praise the Lord I have healthy legs and I'm not the one standing there with my hand out! Someone else will have twinges of conscience and realize that he's ungrateful to God for his blessings. Don't look at the scroungers, Zina, their only concern is to lay hands on some money. But a true beggar, Zina, is one of God's people and serves the Lord! They're a chosen people, the beggars!"

Zina was drifting into a half-sleep. Her eyes were open, but she didn't see Katia or hear her words. She imagined that she was sitting on the ground and her legs were thin and sunburned, and around her were lots of blue and violet flowers, stiff and rather dry, but exceptionally bright. The leaves and stalks were stiff and pricked her bare feet a little, but these pricks were exhilarating, like the gas in lemonade, and she stood up and walked right over the flowers. The ground was rather springy and her legs seemed firmer than the shifting soil on which she walked.

Katia went on talking and talking, but her speech got quieter and quicker and harder to follow:

"But now we praise Him. He sends us sickness, yet we praise Him! He sends us poverty, yet we praise Him! With every breath we praise..." And in mid-word Katia laid her head on the checked oilcloth. Her large masculine-looking right hand lay on the table, while the other dangled loosely, becoming suffused with dark blood.

Meanwhile Zina was still walking through the bright, stiff flowers, and on one side from behind a large stone Mama stepped out, wearing a dark-blue jacket embroidered with woollen flowers on the shoulders,—although Zina knew for a fact that these flowers were on the green Chinese jacket. Mama was walking at an angle but kept getting nearer to Zina, and she kept waving and smiling and was young...

1980s

Translated by Isabel Heaman

From the author's manuscript

Notes

1. The church holiday falls on 8 October, New Style.

2. In the Orthodox calendar, 9 October, New Style.

3. Part of the Russian Orthodox liturgy, sung by the choir.

4. 14 October, New Style.

5 The epitrakhil, translated here as *stole*, is a long band of embroidered silk worn around the neck by the priest.

6 Royal gates or doors in the iconostasis, which is a screen composed of icons separating the sanctuary, where the sacrament of the Eucharist is celebrated, from the nave, i.e., the central section where the congregation stands.

7. Names of Moscow subway stations.

The Phone Call
Tatiana Nabatnikova

He opened the door of the bookcase and reached inside for some old college lecture notes—once in a while they proved useful, and amidst the aging notebooks he felt the hard covers of a photo album. Inside it were the relics of his youth: photographs, his college library card, and some old letters in faded envelopes. Back then, in the sixties, buildings of concrete and glass were still in fashion, and proudly depicted on one of the envelopes was the Novosibirsk Airport, brand new at the time but obsolete almost from the day it was built, owing to its cramped and uncomfortable interior. He remembered that airport—he had flown there to see her a number of times, and always in a state of trepidation. They'd been trying to come to a decision about something, but had never managed to and had given up on it. It was sometime around her junior year that she'd gone off to Novosibirsk. Or *was* it?... How do you like that?! He'd forgotten. He'd already forgotten everything, and here he had always thought of these memories as something precious, something to treasure for life. And now when he reached for this treasure, it half-crumbled in his hands, like some precious artifact ravaged by time and neglect. Ha! So here it was, that stage in life when love itself begins to disintegrate. He sat down with these letters and began to concentrate, to recollect what had happened and when. Oh-oh, he needed to do this more often—the wheels had grown rusty.

He set everything else aside. He was suddenly afraid that the wellspring of his memory had run dry—a sure sign of old age. Old age was when you had used up every last memory and had to live solely off the present. He had read somewhere that the difference between youth and old age was that youth was followed by life, whereas old age was followed by death. Yes, and so it was with him. His past had been completely used up and exhausted, the future that lay ahead of him held nothing in store—he'd come close enough to it to see this—and all that was left to him was the pitiful present.

He'd had a scare. And now he was sitting on the couch, engaged in the serious task of resurrecting the past. He was afraid, really afraid, of growing old! "In the middle of the journey of our life I came to myself in a dark wood..."[1]

At that moment Irka walked in. "What's going on?" she asked, seeing him sitting there in his disheveled state, surrounded by letters and envelopes.

He began to feel ashamed. He really was wasting time on nonsense.

But no, on the contrary, she didn't think it was nonsense at all. She stole quietly out of the room, leaving him alone with his precious nonsense. An understanding wife.

Oh, what a fool he had been! Here she had written: "I don't go to dances here—unlike some people. But I'm glad that you're enjoying yourself and that you're with your friends." Idiot that he was, he had apparently written her a glowing account of the fabulous vacation he and his wild group of friends were having. This vacation had been like a farewell fling to their youth, and "wild" was the word for them. On the eve of their final parting they had been caught up in some sort of hysterical camaraderie. Like a foretaste of winter, an air of finality had permeated everything they did; they had celebrated every day as if it were their last day together, as if once they went their separate ways in the fall, there'd be no more group, no more "us." So they had really gone wild, and he, like a complete jerk, had apparently given her a blow-by-blow description of their exploits. As for the dances, it had seemed to him at the time that he had cleverly omitted the who and what that went with them. But hell, no! He knew now that women see through everything that you cleverly omit and that they instinctively sense any losses they may have sustained in the murky recesses of your heart. But he couldn't have acted otherwise; it had been like a hangover, the "morning after" of their youth. Their youth was over, gone forever—they were now adults—but they kept hastily turning around, eager for one last taste of that which they were leaving behind. They had gulped it down, consuming it quickly, like retreating soldiers burning everything in their wake, leaving nothing for the enemy.

Her letter continued: "But I'm having such a beautiful, such a solitary summer. My God, the mornings here! Granny wakes me every morning at five, so I can milk the cow and drive her out to the rest of the herd. Then I go back to sleep for a while, and the rest of the day I'm on my own—my only companion a thin volume of Gennady Mogilevtsev's poems. His poems are like a drug, an addiction—I feel intoxicated and there's no one to share them with. One night I happened to be leaving the movies with a friend. It was a beautiful night—stars, stillness, a sense of enchantment. I took a chance and begin reciting Mogilevtsev to her:

> Are you sometimes tormented by presentiments?
> Life's sharp corners and the front steps of buildings
> That bring you up short, like a comma in mid-sentence?
> Gloomy and unkempt, the city park cowers behind its bristling iron grillwork.
> But where is that land between sleep and waking?...
> A distant wind ripples the pools of sunlight on the branches
> And a young girl appears from out of nowhere, rises on tiptoe for a kiss
> And then, like a column of heat shimmering upward into the sky,
> She dissolves into the luminous clouds, and I rush after her.
> But on that morning...

"'Ha-ha-ha!' my friend interrupted. I said nothing and once again was alone... "

To tell the truth, his reaction at the time had been the same as her friend's: "Ha-ha-ha!"

No, he had not fully understood her. It had been an effort to keep up with her. He had instinctively feared her, knowing that he wouldn't be able to live up to her expectations. Yes, being with her had been difficult for him. Probably he wasn't worthy of her.

What had it been like? In retrospect, it seemed as if she had been clairvoyant. She had been able to read his thoughts. Not always, of course, but at the height of their love his thoughts had flowed to her with no resistance, as if she were a superconductor.

The local engineering school that they had attended stood next to a forest on the outskirts of town. The edge of the forest bordering the school had been turned into a park. There were tennis courts in the park, and the students would come here to play and hang out. She played too, and it was here that he first saw her. She was from a different department and a year ahead of him. (Yes, there was that too. And back then a year's difference was ridiculously important.) She always smiled when she played, her face glowing and radiant. After seeing her once, then a second and third time, he realized that whenever she wasn't there, he missed her. Then a day came when they were playing against each other in a doubles set. Someone hit the ball out of the court and the other two went to look for it in the grass. An inevitable break in the game. And there they were, standing on opposite sides of the net, and they didn't know each other. Yet, although they were strangers, they knew *only* each other—they didn't even care to know anyone else. And they stood there by the net, and when they finally turned and looked at each other he got up his nerve and said brashly, "You're really good-looking!" "No," she protested right away—heatedly, passionately, in a voice that was only a whisper, "you're the one who's good-looking!" At this point the others returned with the ball and the game started up again. He continued to play, but it was no longer he who played. Some part of him remained on the court and managed to return the ball, but his real self soared upward, floating on high in a state of mindless ecstasy. His body felt absolutely nothing, as if he'd been drugged. Shortly afterward, she left the court. Having lost the set, she and her partner had to yield their place to someone else. After a while he left too. He spent the rest of the day searching for her but couldn't find her anywhere. He had no idea what dorm she lived in or even what her last name was, yet somehow he knew—knew with absolute certainty that he would run into her before the day was over! And a little before midnight, utterly exhausted but with ever increasing agitation, he made his way into the park and sat down on a bench by the tennis court. He sat there like a madman, watching and waiting. Every other minute he would look at his watch. As the minute hand moved closer to midnight, his heart began to pound and his trembling reached a fever pitch. At two minutes before midnight he suddenly heard footsteps—light, echoing footsteps hurrying along the asphalt path leading to the court. He couldn't see anyone but he knew beyond a doubt it was she. Like a hammer pounding on wood, each fateful step left an imprint on his heart. Then suddenly she appeared—he could see her, and she could see him. But she stopped, hesitating, and he stood up from the bench, and he too hesitated. Poor things, they were afraid. They both assumed that their meeting was a matter of chance and didn't dare believe in this miracle of inevitability. He started toward her. Although he had known, known beyond a doubt that it was he who had SUMMONED her (after all, what other explanation could there be for her appearance?), still, fool that he was, he asked in a casual, albeit trembling voice, "Are you taking a walk?" "You too?" she asked by way of reply. And now, side by side, they set out primly along the path. But neither of them was able to TAKE THE NEXT STEP, to summon up the courage to accept the obvious and TAKE THE NEXT STEP. And when he said to her an hour later, "Look up at the stars!" (so that she would lift up her head and he would be able to kiss her unawares), still he was terribly afraid, afraid till the very last second that she would slap his face or push him away. But no, quite the contrary, and at that moment everything broke loose—he let himself go completely, like a sky diver in free fall. She did too, and now they were no longer in the park but in the forest, and the mosquitoes were eating them alive. As anyone who has ever been caught up in a whirlpool knows, the ability to reason simply switches off, and so it was with them...

Expressing the morality of those days, a certain poet had instructed, "Let love begin, but not with the body, not with the body, you hear—with the soul!" Yet what does love care about the preferences of poets? Love despises any order the poet would establish and begins with whatever it feels like. But he, Valerka, trusted the poet more than he trusted love, for the dry rot of such verses was part and parcel of his own inner world. Something inside him rebelled, of course, but the poet's verses continued to exert an influence on him.

Oh, how badly he had behaved!

Then there had been the other thing, the fact that she was a year ahead of him, a year older! This had been a difficult hurdle to get over, a real stumbling block.

Somewhere inside him there was always the reservation that this love of theirs—yes, it was real love, no doubt about that—was not all that permanent, not the sort of love that would mark a fitting close to their youth and result in a good, solid marriage. Rather, it was only one of several, one in a succession of college loves that come and go, one taking the place of the other. In short, not a love to end all others.

He didn't know whether he was her first lover. Yes, she was his first—he had been utterly intoxicated, his mind befogged, anesthetized, remembering nothing, sensing nothing. And he didn't know, he simply couldn't tell. Nor could he sink so low as to come right out and ask her. To this day he didn't know. He had assumed, however, that he was probably not her first; for "the first time" should by all rights have cost him more. There would have been all sorts of fears, conditions, a thousand obstacles—and here she had given herself to him right away, freely, without asking for anything in return. It hadn't cost him even an hour's effort. And that, you understand, shouldn't be, one shouldn't get something precious for nothing! That's wrong. For something precious a person WANTS to pay, and pay dearly.

Now, of course, he understood that she might have given herself freely, from sheer generosity of spirit, because that was the sort of person she was.

But that wasn't right—no, it simply shouldn't be that way.

And thus from the very beginning there had been, and always remained, this chilling and corrosive aftertaste of doubt, of distrust.

But it had been a good summer, a splendid summer. Final exams, his thoughts in a whirl, the park, tennis, the nights, the ever-present mosquitoes, the forest—and Larisa, young and vibrant...

Then came the inevitable parting for summer vacation and a month's separation. A month in one's youth is thirty new lifetimes, and inserted between July and September were thirty other lifetimes that he had spent without her. Other people had come along, other dishes had been prepared with other spices, and it turned out that he didn't have sufficient strength or conviction to resist the temptation to rush off, or be dragged off, in other directions. Like a calf in the springtime, youth likes to kick up its heels and explore all sorts of alternatives. He couldn't yet foresee what losses were hidden behind each seeming gain. And when September came, they returned to each other wistfully and with tears—not of forgiveness but of loss. They would keep coming back to each other not to celebrate their love but to mourn its passing.

She had gone off to Novosibirsk and he had flown to visit her. It was winter and she was ahead of him, walking slowly, pensively, leaving the imprint of her soft reindeer boots in the snow. They still loved each other, but already they each had someone else on their mind and on the tip of their tongue, someone else who half-figured in their calculations. And it was here, on a somewhat bitter note that they half-bid each other farewell.

He was the first to marry. He married reluctantly, not because he wanted to but because he had to, as sometimes happens. As if they had merely been friends, he had sent off a desperate letter to her in Novosibirsk. Abandoning her pride, she had screamed into the post office telephone, "You can't do this, you can't, you've got to reconsider! Let the baby be born, be a father—after all, it's not the baby you marry. This is your whole life you're talking about! Don't go through with it! We'll both regret it! A mistake like this— we'll regret it our whole lives, and I..." She continued to scream incoherently and all he could do was dully shake his head and mumble, "No, no, I can't back out, I can't."

And the result? He had stuck it out for five miserable years and still they had ended up getting divorced. Not even their son could save them.

Thus he could lay claim to having led the statistically average life of the statistically average professional: a degree in engineering, one divorce, a second marriage, one child from each, the rank of senior engineer, a minimal amount of graduate work, a minimal salary, and a two-room apartment that had blended the scents of its three inhabitants into one common scent. And this common scent was happiness as the world defines it, and there was neither time nor need to reflect on it.

But now suddenly, from out of the blue, these old letters.

Irka could sense that something was going on inside him, that he was caught in the grip of his memories, and she didn't pester him with any petty household matters. A normal wife.

When you stopped to think about it, what a love they had wasted! If everything had been as he remembered it, it had indeed been love. But we never appreciate what we have until it's too late.

Suddenly he felt a need to find out where she was and what had become of her. Just as several points are necessary to plot a curve, so he needed her present point in life eighteen years later in order to complete his picture of her. He wanted to understand what had taken place between them, and what she had represented—some sort of miracle or a random dislocation of his everyday life.

It took two days of groping among the shadows of the past to come up with several old acquaintances who were able to put him on her track. And now here he was, staring at the five digits of her telephone number. She was living in a small town in Central Russia.

Unable to suppress his agitation, he explained to Irka, "You see, I didn't realize it back then, but it was she who made a real person of me. She was the one who showed me certain ways of relating to life that would not have been possible for me to learn if I hadn't seen them with my own eyes. Without her I wouldn't have acquired FREEDOM, you see. As people acquired literacy in the past. But at the time, I didn't appreciate the valuable lesson she was teaching me. Sometimes I even thought she was impulsive and naive. Whereas actually, when it comes to morality—genuine morality—she was a shining example, the best you could ask for."

Irka willingly accepted everything he said. She was concerned for him. But she cautioned, "Despite all you've told me, I still think it would be better not to call. You'll be stirring things up, and if she's the sort of person you say she is, she'll drop everything and come rushing here to marry you."

"Come on, don't be silly, I'm simply calling to find out how she is and what's become of her. It'll be enough just to hear her voice. I need to understand WHAT HAPPENED back then. One of these days I'm going to die and I want to understand what happened to me."

Irka understood. "You know," she said, "that's true what you said about hearing her voice. When people tell me at work that some man has called, I always ask, 'Is he handsome?' They give me a funny look. After all, they didn't see him. I give them a funny look too. couldn't they tell from his voice? A handsome man's voice has a certain self-assurance, a certain inflection that's very revealing."

"Yes, that's it—revealing. What I'm hoping is that she won't say anything trite like 'My, how time flies!' Or perhaps that's exactly what she will say. In any case, it'll all be clear."

And so, having gained Irka's tacit consent though not her approval (she's a woman, after all, and can't help but be jealous), he goes ahead and places the call. But the phone is answered by her husband. She's out shopping, naturally. She left only a few minutes ago, you've just missed her.

His voice too is very revealing. In it you can read their whole life together. The mere fact that he doesn't ask suspiciously "Who's calling?" speaks volumes. As does his willingness to help and his regret that this unknown man calling from another city hasn't found his wife at home.

In a word, it's all becoming clear. And actually, it's better this way—talking with her husband gives him a more objective picture.

"I'm an old college friend. It's been eighteen years and I hadn't heard anything. I happened to find out her phone number recently, so I decided I'd call and say hello. Tell me, how is she and what's she doing these days?"

He's happy to talk about her. She has a family, an apartment, and they're all healthy and doing well. No, nobody's been divorced—I'm her first and last.

(A sudden twinge: That's what you think! *I* was her first.)

"She keeps busy with her engineering job, and we have three children."

"What?!"

"Yes, that's right, three children. Is that so unusual? They're sixteen, fourteen and four."

"Well, well!... And you—what do you do if I may ask?"

"I'm an Army officer. A lieutenant colonel and district military commander."

"Ah... then I suppose you have a car and a dacha, right?" Yes, he confirms calmly and good-naturedly, without undue emphasis. "But then, a car and a dacha—is that so unusual? And what message shall I give her?"

"Nothing, just say hello. Tell her that so-and-so called and sends regards. And if you should ever happen to be in our area, my wife and I would be happy to see you both. Here's our address and phone number."

And in the same even tone, now addressing his daughter, "Iulia, give me something to write with, would you?" And along with your greetings he carefully records your full address and phone number.

All this, of course, in Irka's absence—so you won't feel any constraint. But now you have to wait impatiently for her to come home. And you sit here in your disheveled state, trying to assimilate the result of your experiment—this point on the curve—all the while waiting for Irka, so you can discuss with her exactly what this point represents.

"A completely normal, respectable life," said Irka, having returned at long last and heard him out. "The one exceptional thing is the three children. For lack of anything better, I guess that will have to do. Though I must say," and here she paused, secretly delighted but feigning disappointment, "from everything you've told me about her, I would have expected her life to be more interesting. Unhappy perhaps, but colorful in some way, if you understand what I'm getting at."

He understood. He understood very well that it was to Irka's advantage to disparage this Larisa, to blot her completely out of his mind if possible. He also understood the "official" line that she expressed out loud, words to the effect: This is so terribly dull and prosaic. How much better it would have been to have found Larisa at some "colorful" point on the curve, in prison, say... You think that's crazy? Well, I don't know. Just something unusual or dramatic,... something exceptional. A minister of communications, say. Or some sort of technological discovery, an invention whose value no one recognizes, which she's had to struggle to promote, and now they've fired her from her job and declared her insane—or something like that. Or she might actually be in a mental institution... But instead, there's this uninspiring MARITAL happiness and prosperity. Everything so neat and tidy, so respectable... No, no, there's nothing wrong with it, of course; for the average woman it's an ideal fate. For the ordinary, average sort of woman, yes. But not for the exceptional woman you've made her out to be... No, it simply won't do.

And here she sighs in disappointment. Of course, if Larisa had turned up in a mental institution, or if she were an alcoholic, then we'd have the stuff of tragedy. It would be interesting. And more to the point, I'd be overcome by remorse and a sense of obligation and would go rushing off to save her and—who knows—even to marry her...

Or another scenario: Her husband is a drunk, her children are hungry, and she's digging ditches, knocking herself out to feed the children and keep her husband in booze.

But no, nothing of the kind. She has an exemplary husband, every woman's ideal.

Thus they had carried on, and a week later she called. They weren't home, and it was their daughter who told them that so-and-so from such-and-such a town had called.

Well, that's interesting! She's been thinking it over for a week and now she's finally made up her mind. Will she try again? By all rights she SHOULD...

And sure enough, an hour later the phone rang—a frequent, impatient, typically long-distance ring. Clapping her hands in excitement, Irka cried, "That's it, there she is!" He grabbed the receiver. It was she, calling from far away, her voice unrecognizable, cool and polite...

For her it had happened like this. She had come home from shopping and Seriozha had announced, "That old friend of yours called, what's his name?..."

"Well, tell me."

"That friend of yours, from your youth."

"How unprofessional of you, you're beginning to forget names!"

"I'm getting old, you'll have to help me out."

"Uh-uh!" She wanted to, of course. It was on the tip of her tongue, but she didn't dare. What if she said his name and it turned out to be someone else? Where he was concerned, she didn't want to humiliate herself even in her thoughts. For if she wanted it to be HE and it turned out to be someone else, then it would prove all over again that she valued him too highly whereas he valued her not at all. "I don't know who it was, you'll have to think of his name yourself."

"Valera."

Ah!... It was out! His name had been spoken. Her heart stood still.

She made her way into the kitchen and began putting away the groceries. "Well, what did he want?" she called out with the same lighthearted, casual curiosity she reserved for news on the order of: "So-and-so has been fired." "Really?"

"Let's see... he said to give you his best. He wanted to know how you were and what you've been doing. And I filled him in on all the details."

"What sorts of things did he want to know?"

"Even the children's names."

"Oh!" she muttered dismissively, at the same time clattering dishes and slamming the refrigerator door with as much self-control as she could muster. Her heart stopped beating and she stood paralyzed, not daring to ask whether he was going to call back. "Is he going to call back?"

"I got the impression that he wouldn't. He asked me to give you his best and tell you that everything's fine with him."

If he was sending his best that meant... what? That he wouldn't call back? But then why did he call in the first place? If everything's fine, why did he call? He's lying!

"Iulia, please slice the bread!"

"Zhenia, take out the garbage."

"Alik, don't pester me, I'm busy."

"Seriozha, could you read to him for a while—please?"

She had once made a terrible vow. She had made several terrible vows in the course of her life, but this was the most terrible of all. It hadn't even been clothed in words, but was simply a feeling focusing on a target. No, not hatred but an icy composure, the sort of composure with which a sniper focuses his telescopic sight on the heart of his enemy and tracks him relentlessly. And her unspoken vow had been to pull the trigger.

She had never forgotten that evening in the maternity hospital, an old one-story building that had looked more like a log cabin than a hospital. Each morning they would admit nine or ten patients. They would relieve these women of their unwanted burden and release them two days later. Sometimes they even released them the very next morning. It was a humane little hospital, charging only five rubles for the operation. Actually, working women paid nothing and it was only nonworking women who paid the five rubles. As a student, Larisa had been one of the nonworking ones. It was a humane little hospital, and so was the woman doctor; she had understood because she was young herself. "Look at her," she had reproached one woman, "she's just a young girl, and see how she's holding up. And here you are, scared to death!" So Larisa had even received a bonus: the consoling status of heroine. Later, when evening arrived, the women's husbands had gathered by the hospital window, which was open to the warm summer air. They had brought food parcels (Oh, what she would have given for something to eat!) and would smile fondly at their wives as they talked quietly of family matters. But no one in the whole wide world knew about Larisa. No one knew that she was here and what she had endured, and no one would think to come and feed her. Never had she felt so alone! The depressing smell of hospital nightstands—the same smell given off by lonely, hapless old women—would stay with her for life. (And later on, when she stayed in other maternity hospitals as a happy, triumphant mother, even then these nightstands smelled to her of must and decay.)

Nor would she ever forget those witches at the prenatal clinic and what pleasure they had taken in humiliating her with their pointed, suspicious "Are you married?" During her first visit to the clinic she had bandaged the fourth finger of her right hand to hide the fact that she wore no wedding ring. After that, she had borrowed a wedding ring from one of her classmates, which meant, of course, that she'd had to make something up as to why she needed it. "Oh, it's for a practical joke someone's playing," she had fabricated. Oh, the shame, the terrible shame she had felt, and all of it alone. For no one, NO ONE must know. And when it came time to go to the hospital, she had told her roommates that she was spending the night with friends. (What friends—good Lord, it was the middle of final exams! And afterwards, while recuperating in the ward, she had continued to study her lecture notes.)

Evidently that first humiliation in the doctor's office in the prenatal clinic had wounded her deeply. It was a wound that required constant tending, for it never seemed to heal. And each of the three times (Iulia, Zhenia, Alik) that she signed into a maternity hospital later on, she would remember that humiliation, and each time it would seem that she was making up for it. But somehow she could never make up for it completely. The examination, the tests, and the notation on her chart, and finally that strained, cold question: "Do you plan to have the baby or not?" And the marvelous feeling of satisfaction and relief when she replies, "Yes, I plan to have it!" The lady doctor flashes a smile in your direction and suddenly, as if someone has turned on a switch, you're enveloped in radiance, warmth, and sympathetic vibrations. It's a joyous, wonderfully important moment. From now on, you and she will share a common bond, and for the next six months she'll be fussing over you, measuring, weighing, listening, and tapping; she'll come to love you because you make her work meaningful and worthwhile. But that other, cruel and destructive aspect of her work she dislikes, and she feels nothing but disdain for those pleasures purchased at the expense of motherhood.

She had felt the painful aftermath of the surgery as she studied her lecture notes, but what joy it was to know that she had been set free, liberated!

She had left the hospital the next morning, and that afternoon they were out sunbathing, studying for their exams in a clearing in that very same forest. As if nothing had happened. And he without the faintest idea of *where* she had spent the whole previous day and *what* had happened to her. And in this she felt her great superiority over him. They've torn your son from my body and you, my dear boy, don't have a clue. It hasn't even entered your head that you could be a father—you think of yourself only as a SON. You've never once pictured yourself as a father, and even if you did, you'd see that you come up short, that you don't yet measure up to the role in any way, shape or form. And if you were forced into it, like being forced into a strait jacket, you'd measure up even less. You'd be horrified, you'd feel trapped. And what sort of person would I be if I were willing to see fear in your eyes rather than joy, were willing to be tied to you by bonds of necessity rather than those of need? External necessity versus inner need. There is, after all, a difference between them, and I have too much pride to accept one in place of the other.

But everything she had endured was charged to his account: the girl friend's wedding ring; her bandaged wedding-ring finger; that miserable summer evening spent in the maternity ward; the depressing smell of the hospital nightstand; that clearing where they had sunbathed the next day. And a time would come when he would have to pay off his account in kind, with some painful humiliation of his own.

But what prompted this all-consuming desire for revenge?

It was prompted by envy. By the terrible inequality between men and women. One had only to see him playing tennis, for example. Forgetting himself and focusing all his thoughts and desires on the ball, he was completely unaware of how handsome he was. And he was handsome. All he had to do was appear on the court and all heads would turn to admire this perfect work of nature. But he didn't give a damn about his flashing eyes and unruly curls; he valued only his mind and hands because he thought of himself as an instrument which could be used to accomplish something worthwhile. Something like a chisel in the hands of a sculptor. Two things, the sculptor and the chisel, create a third thing: the sculpture. In the same way, two things, nature and man, come together to create a third thing—but what? This was the secret that a woman couldn't fathom. When nature and man joined forces, WHAT WAS IT that they were concocting?

Only a man is able to have a goal outside himself. A woman is a goal in and of herself and wants to be considered as such by all those around her. Imitating the man, she tries, of course, to develop interests outside herself: basket weaving, say, or some sort of scientific research. But these attempts aren't very successful. Larisa, for example, had started playing tennis solely out of envy of the ball. Here was an object, a plaything with no reciprocal power of love, yet look how totally it could rule a man's heart! She, a woman, would be so much more responsive, would meet him more than halfway, yet the man finds it more interesting to be with the ball than with the living, breathing Larisa.

His secret is his obliviousness to self. He yearns to serve something outside himself. A woman, on the other hand, serves only herself, especially if she is a beautiful woman who feels that she is one of nature's perfect creations.

And what does she do in this case? What does a woman do who is competing with a ball for a man? She begins to play ball herself. And she proceeds flawlessly, taking him away from her rival without his even noticing what has happened. In the beginning, he thinks that they've come together in their common love of the ball. But gradually she redirects his love, shifting its focus onto her alone. And now she no longer needs the ball. The man has been taken away from it, won over. But don't assume for a moment that she does any of this consciously. Good Lord, what sort of consciousness does a woman have in such situations?! She's not even aware of what she is doing, and perhaps for that very reason she ends up doing the right thing.

Or take her children, for example. Each new child was a way of calling out to her husband, who had become excessively wrapped up in his work: Hey! Here I am, over here! Three such calls. And perhaps there'll be more. For she wants to remain the center of attraction, that sun around which the planets revolve on their invisible tethers. With one difference, however. For her it is essential not to radiate warmth in her own right but to attract the rays given off by her own planets. What chill and sorrow would ensue if they should suddenly focus their rays in another direction!

But again, one has to keep in mind that inner need and external necessity are two different things. And she had too much pride to accept love that was not freely given. How other women could was beyond her comprehension. So when he wrote to her that he was marrying somebody else out of NECESSITY (and here *she* had been patiently waiting for him to come to her out of NEED—apparently she had waited too long!), at that point something inside her snapped and her pride failed her. You can't go through with this, you mustn't, she had cried into the receiver.

It was so unfair! She hadn't used this dishonorable weapon when it had been in her hands, and now here was this other woman taking advantage of it and, of course, getting her way. She couldn't let it happen! You can't, she had cried, you can't get married like this! It's dishonest!

He would pay for that outburst of hers, for that momentary defeat of her pride.

And her vow was one of terrible vengeance.

"He didn't say anything about himself?" she asks, trying to get more information from Seriozha.

"Mmm... yes. He's an engineer, married for the second time. I think that's about it."

"For the second time. Hmm. So he didn't stay with that first wife...." And she adds to herself: he's not going to stay with this one either. So he hasn't forgotten me.... "Did he leave his address?"

"His address and phone number. Here they are," he says, handing her a piece of paper. Helpful, thoughtful, attentive to detail, as always.

What a treasure he is, what a priceless treasure! How she appreciates him, and he her. Not at all like you, you who didn't appreciate me and were only too willing to give me up. Let me tell you something! We're so used to standing in line for things that when there's no line, we think twice about buying. That's the way we are. We don't trust our own judgment, only that of others. And that's the way it was with you. Once something came your way so easily, you couldn't help wondering whether it was worth the taking. But you should meet my husband! He's a lieutenant colonel, a handsome, intelligent man, a father of three, who adores both his children and me. But *that* you wouldn't want to hear! He would DIE for me. He would die WITHOUT me, just in case you'd like to know!

With each new promotion (first lieutenant, captain, major) she had pictured her happiness ever more brightly, and with each new child this picture had been fleshed out ever more splendidly until all that was needed was a viewer. And HE was that viewer! Weeping, moaning, tearing his hair in remorse, he would say to himself, WHAT A FOOL I'VE BEEN! And sobbing, pitiful, rejected and abandoned, humble and contrite, he would come crawling in the rain to knock at the gate of her kingdom. Please, your majesty, let me in, if only to warm myself at your hearth! And with a show of mercy she would let him in. But *he* had to come crawling to her. Never in this world would she go to him! Not once in all these years had she ever tried to look him up, to find out where he was or what had become of him. Sooner or later, he would come looking for her. And the longer he waited, the worse it would be for him. Let there be more children, even more. For each child was another buttress to the walls of her kingdom, another confirmation of the unassailability of her and the lieutenant colonel's shared happiness.

And now the moment had finally come. He had knocked at the gate.

It can't be that everything's fine with him. He's lying! People don't call when things are going well. "Everything's fine" was not part of the script. What she expected and deserved to hear from him was "everything's gone wrong." She had paid so dearly, and now it was time to wrap up and dispose of this wretched and abandoned, rain-soaked supplicant knocking at her gate.

Each new child had been like an exclamation point confirming her victory. And three exclamation points—what could be more emphatic?!

She would dial his number and ask with utmost humility (How often a sense of superiority disguises itself as humility!), "What's happened, Valer, what's happened to you—has something gone wrong?" Oh, he'd say, oh, Lorka!... What have we done, why did we let love slip through our fingers?

She would sigh along with him and he would go on moaning and groaning about what a fool he had been. We were both fools, she would add modestly. There would be a silence. Then timidly, with a glimmer of hope, he would ask, but perhaps... with your three children, with you to take care of... I could MAKE UP FOR EVERYTHING, for all that I owe you. And she would say, oh, I'd even be willing, but my husband wouldn't survive such a blow, he'd kill himself. And the children—the children are weeping at the very thought, they worship him! The older two found out that you'd called and they're in tears. They realize that their father wouldn't survive this....

And at opposite ends of the line they would both start to weep, to shed tears of regret for this great love that they had let slip through their fingers. And now he would suddenly realize that it was he, and he alone, who had let love slip away, whereas this man, her husband, had been wise enough to hold on to it.

Oh, what bittersweet satisfaction his tears would bring. They would cleanse her as a light rain cleanses the grass. The ultimate put-down, of course, would be not to call him at all. THAT'S HOW LITTLE YOU MEAN TO ME! But he might suspect that Seriozha hadn't relayed his greetings and phone number and that she was simply unaware of his call. No, she had to call, if only to be convinced that he was actually out there in the rain, seeking entrance to her kingdom. And to slam the door in his face—so sorry! She had to receive what was HERS, what she had waited for so long, what she had paid for and deserved. "Seriozha, what do you think, should I call him back?"

"Well, I don't think it's a question of 'should' or 'ought.' If you feel like it, why not go ahead and call?"

"And you're not worried that he may want to take me away from you?" she asked with perhaps inappropriate coyness.

Yes, definitely inappropriate! He immediately burst into laughter, the sort of commiserating laughter reserved for those one feels sorry for.

"Oh, Lorka, spare me, please! As if I had time for such foolishness!"

That hurt. All the more reason to call.

She had to wait a week for Seriozha's next overnight duty assignment. She wanted to be sure of absolute privacy. After all, she would be putting on a performance: in the background, a weeping husband and weeping children; in the foreground, a ruffled mother hen, trying to keep her family out of harm's way.

And now here she was, calling long-distance, her voice unrecognizable, cool and polite.

"With whom am I speaking, please?"

"With me, of course, you're speaking with me!" he shouted joyfully, prompting a smile and even a chuckle from Irka, who couldn't help but be affected by his puppylike enthusiasm. She heard his first few words, then left the room, not wanting to disturb the fragile intimacy of this momentous telephone call.

"It's been ages..." she began.

"Not ages, but eighteen years, a mere eighteen years!" he broke in cheerfully.

"Eighteen years," she pronounced gravely, "is a long time."

"Do you recognize me?" he shouted into the phone.

"No," she answered distractedly. This distractedness of hers, as he realized later, mentally reviewing their conversation for the hundredth time, was a reflection of the fact that she was still laying the groundwork for the important part of the conversation that was yet to come, and hence all her attention was focused on what she was going to say next.

"I didn't recognize you at first either, but now I can tell—it's you!"

"Tell me, how are you?"

"I'm fine!"

"How are things in your personal life?" she asked pointedly.

"Fine!"

"Everything's okay?" she asked again, with a certain note of puzzlement.

"Yes!" he exclaimed, eager to get past these preliminaries to what really mattered, though exactly what this was he wasn't sure.

There was something he expected from this conversation. Was it a sense of shared grief for their long-lost love? Or traces of that love? In any case, it was something poignant; time was running out on them. The loss of their love had been the first death, the first waning of their youth, which had once been as full as a full moon. And now all that remained of it was a crescent, and they should mourn its passing together, like sad accomplices.

"Are you married?"

"Yes! But I already told all that to your husband. didn't he tell you?"

"He did."

"Why haven't you ever gotten in touch all these years?" he broke in, once again knocking her carefully improvised and deliberate speech off course. He didn't detect her agitation.

"I couldn't. It was easy enough for you to track me down, but I couldn't get in touch with you. I would have felt guilty because of my daughter."

"What has your daughter got to do with it?" he asked, somewhat taken aback, like a rider whose galloping horse suddenly slows to a trot.

"She's sixteen, and I would have felt guilty. I have a son too—he's fourteen. And another son—he's four, and today is his birthday," she pronounced sadly and reproachfully.

"Congratulations," he mumbled, his horse now stumbling and slowing to a walk.

So, it seemed that she was passing judgment on him: It was easy enough for you, but I, with my high moral standards and sense of honor, would have felt guilty because of my children...

Robbed of his initial joyful enthusiasm and not knowing what to say next, he began reminiscing about some of their common acquaintances. She listened without any show of interest and when he had finished, she picked up where she had left off.

"My daughter, she knew what you had meant to me... My husband knew too. My daughter was crying... and my husband was upset—not at all his usual self. Your call brought unnecessary confusion into our lives."

"But I talked with your husband... he didn't seem upset to me," he tried to object.

"No, you're wrong. Your call knocked him completely off balance and left him feeling very anxious. All in all, I..." She paused and then uttered her harsh, sad verdict: "Let's not call each other anymore. After all, your wife probably doesn't like this very much either. Is she at home?"

"Yes," he replied, now utterly disconcerted by her reproaches.

"And what—it's fine with her?" she asked in a mocking voice.

"Yes," he replied, now choking and drowning in shame, and at the same time worrying about Irka. If she could hear him, and of course she could, she would guess that he was being reprimanded like a schoolboy. If only for Irka's benefit he had to maintain the same upbeat note on which their conversation had begun. And now he fell completely silent.

"So there's no point to any of this."

"Then why did you call?" he finally lashed out, his voice hostile.

"Why did *I* call?... To find out—I thought something might be the matter... something in your personal life."

"No, thanks anyway, but everything's okay," he replied coldly.

Silence. He felt humiliated, ridiculed, as if he'd been caught in the act, like a little puppy. So great was his shame that he was simply unable to speak. Finally, with a sigh of resignation, he said, "Well okay, Larisa, so long, take care."

"You take care too," she replied. And in farewell: "I wish you all the best, the very best of everything."

"Good-bye." He slammed down the receiver angrily.

He sat there for a good ten minutes, still smarting from the slap in the face she had given him. And how embarrassing it was to have to face Irka. After all, she had warned him that it was an ill-considered call with no clear purpose. What exactly was he trying to accomplish? It'll be taken the wrong way, she had said. You'll be causing trouble for no good reason. YOU'LL MAKE A FOOL OF YOURSELF.

And that's how it had turned out: He had made a fool of himself. With her proud character and out of respect for love, Larisa had no desire to play at friendly relations once love was gone. That would be like disturbing a grave.

And you, gravedigger and defiler, it serves you right! When you decided to dig up love's remains in order to brush off your memories, did you ever think of what it would be like for the deceased to be subjected to your idle, curious gaze? It was wrong, wrong, wrong! You've disgraced yourself. And suddenly he was overwhelmed by an agonizing feeling of shame and disgust, the same feeling he had experienced in childhood upon learning of the nighttime activities of adults. He had wanted to cleanse himself of this sickening knowledge, to excise and expunge it. If memory were a chalk-covered slate, he would have taken a cloth and wiped it clean.

Having come to terms with her rebuff, though still smarting from it, he dragged himself off to find Irka. He gave her a wary account of what had happened—that Larisa had called for the sole purpose of warding off any calls he might make in the future. Calls that would place her in an ambiguous position. That would cast her in the false role of "an old friend," a role she wasn't willing to accept out of respect for her children, for her husband, and for the truth.

What it all added up to was that he had proved unworthy of that which he had so long held dear.

"Good for her!" exclaimed Irka, voicing her warm approval. "She's a wise, brave woman! She did exactly the right thing!"

And a while later, continuing to voice her admiration, she added, "What courage she showed in refusing to rationalize or pretend. Once the break is made, it's made for good. There's no point in trying to put things back together again."

"Yes," he was forced to agree, "yes, she's an extremely moral and resolute person. And she's not one to yield to social niceties."

Still, it was humiliating. The contempt she had shown him and the superior tone she had used in telling him off...

And now Irka once again: she did the right thing, exactly the right thing—it was just what you deserved!

This event continued to preoccupy them for a long time. Finally, they unburdened themselves of its weight, casting it like a stone into the water, where it sank and disappeared from view.

In the home of the lieutenant colonel, Larisa sat by the now silent telephone. She too was digesting their conversation. "Everything's fine with me." Then why the hell did you call, I'd like to know! That had been a terrible disappointment. She had managed to get some things across, but not everything. It had probably been a mistake to worry about his wife's reactions. But never mind, she had really let him have it, right in that smug face of his, a blow he wasn't going to forget! "Let's not call each other anymore"—that had been really clever of her, that had shown what she was made of! It was like handing him the death sentence. Or rather the death sentence of their love. For death, after all, means that from now on there's going to be nothing more, NOTHING. You're cut off from the future and from a part of your own past—from your memories of the past.

Little Alik, in the meantime, was being fed by his older brother and sister in the kitchen. They were forcing him to eat, which was a blow to his self-esteem.

"First eat your spaghetti, then your..."

"Is spaghetti a first or second course?" he inquired as a matter of principle.

"Just eat it and drink it down with milk," they responded without answering his question.

"Is it a first or second course?" he repeated, determined to get an answer.

"Just sit still and eat!"

He came running out to Larisa.

"Mama, is spaghetti a first or second course?"

But his mother, overcome by feelings of bitterness and dismay as she sat by the telephone that had disconnected her forever from her past, could only respond, "Alik, just eat what you feel like!"

Here Alik burst into tears, unable to gain satisfaction from anyone.

Taking him into her arms to comfort him, she too burst into tears, tears that fell directly onto his soft, sweet-smelling hair. "Poor us, Alchenka, you and I have too much pride, much more than is good for us, and we have a hard time of it in this life."

Meanwhile, back in his city, Valera would occasionally give vent to his hurt feelings.

"After all, even for crimes there's a statute of limitations. Oh, I know, I know,... it's because of her noble, superior character, but... just think for a moment! If she weren't so marvelously happy and secure at home, with a husband, children and all sorts of material comforts, would she be able to take such a holier-than-thou attitude? 'I would have felt guilty because of my daughter.' Come on! And isn't it a bit hypocritical for someone who's snug and secure in her own little castle to hoist the banner of unassailable virtue? And lording one's highminded principles over others—isn't that as much a sin as any other form of pride?"

"That's enough! You're just putting her down in order to lessen the moral distance between you. For her to say 'let's not call each other anymore' is, in effect, cutting herself off forever from her own past. And for a woman to cut herself off from her youth or at least from the memory of it—that takes real courage, more than you seem to appreciate! Personally, I'm full of admiration for the woman!"

"Oh, I am too," he mumbled. "It's just that it doesn't come easily after such a put-down."

"Well, you'll just have to rise above that. You should follow her example and learn to value the nobler things in life, like heroism."

Heroism was all well and good, but Valera nonetheless threw out all the letters that he had kept for eighteen years inside the album buried among his old college notebooks. And he wisely resolved that you should let sleeping memories lie if you wish to preserve them.

When Seriozha returned from duty the following morning, Larisa boasted, "Well, I went ahead and called him. I asked him not to bother me anymore. I've no need for this sort of foolishness."

Seriozha suddenly burst out laughing.

"What's so funny?"

"Oh, you two are so silly!" he replied good-naturedly. "You both keep trying to rationalize, and it's all very simple. He called you, which means he still loves you. And you called him, which means the same. Oh, such amateurs! But never mind, it doesn't matter—I'm the same way. I still feel something for all my past loves. But enough of that, old girl, let's have something to eat!"

Translated by Helen Burlingame

From *Iunost'*, No. 2, 1987

Notes

1. The opening lines of the *Inferno* from Dante's *Divine Comedy*.

Rendezvous
Marina Palei

> "The struggle for life is fiercest
> among similar forms."
> Charles Darwin

...Which view from the window should he choose? He'd already smoked half a pack of cigarettes as he'd gone through God knows how many landscapes.

Strictly speaking, he'd have liked something with the freshness of unmediated contact with nature... Say, for example, Pissarro's "Plowed Land."

In the opening of the window there instantly appears a stretch of grayish-brown: on the boundary of the cultivated field, a touch to the right, is a plow or a harrow; to the left, a few thin birches on a knoll.

No, such naiveté may be pretentious; it's not at all what he needs now. He'd always connected the state of being in love with an irresistible desire to combine the object of adoration with the most beautiful exotic landscape, whether it be lofty mountains or a bottomless sea; their quality seemed to intimate the immemorial nature of love, lending that feeling its only faithful tonality... In that sense Monet's temperament was closer to him.

Now an intensely blue sea lapped outside the window, the lilac rocks congealed... ("Rocks at Belle Ile").

So the final touch for the proper setting was found. The background music chosen, flowers on all the flat surfaces. His priceless one, his love—she was to arrive any moment. That enchanting trepidation!

What will she be like today?...

He had to admit that he'd never seen her yet in Eve's garb. And what was particularly important for the effect here, he believed, were the buttocks, of course. Optimally, they're usually as musical as the hidden places of the joints... They say Botticelli was very musical; that's stretching it. Rather, he was constrained and archaic, even somewhat mannered; it was he who started the cult of "relishing" women, but in Botticelli the bottom is somewhat limp, he was more concerned with the line.... Ingres has a much better line, perhaps—you have only to recall "The Eternal Source." True, there's a certain lack of refinement there, a lack of the last refined touch. Most probably the best female buttocks can be found in the cut of Mona Lisa's dress: it gives sufficient intimation—or rather, sense—of the sought for (and calculated) buttocks; it's no wonder Leonardo was so chaste. Now, the neck can be taken from Botticelli. Of course, the neck should be long, but you shouldn't take it from Modigliani, where it smacks of cast iron; that would be the same as taking it from Picasso. In general, the neck shouldn't have any functional sinewiness, otherwise all the emotions are lost. The hair—best from Rubens; there's a lot of everything there, including hair. The hands we'll take from the Japanese. When you imagine fingers like those caressing you—little worms like that— you won't need anything else. Unless it's the breast: it shouldn't be large, there's simply nothing for a gentleman with self-respect to do with it but get distracted. Also of special importance are those hidden parts which more than anything embarrass anyone who's unprepared, for example, a sinewy groin (a ballerina's), the deep hollows of the armpits, that is, all the places where there are natural joints. Incidentally, if all these little cavities behind the knees, at the elbows, and in the ears aren't ugly, then a woman may be considered beautiful. You can take the armpit, again, from Ingres; the knees too. The shoulders will take care of themselves. That's the last touch, the icing on the cake, the eye-catcher. The back's more difficult. There's a lacuna where women's backs are concerned. It's an undiscovered continent, it shouldn't be muscled or fat or bony. What should it be like?.. He doesn't know. But he knows for a fact that that's exactly why Velázquez's "Venus in a Mirror" is so vulnerable—the back doesn't say anything. The feet you should take from a Greek sculpture, most likely of Diana. A self-respecting man starts a woman from her feet. The feet set the tone for the rest. That's why they should be light and chiseled, like Diana the huntress's.

He hears her coming, his beloved! Ah, what's the main thing in a woman?—the first and last are the scent; as the great Sernuda said:

> The scent of a lemon flower...
> Was there that, at least?

Here she is now, his promised one, his sister, his beloved, and he doesn't even need to see her—what's important is the *sensation* of movement; he's prepared to swear that a woman's movement can be so enticing that you cease noticing the rest. The movement should be perfectly free—not constrained, but restrained, not primitively naive, but knowing—while retaining complete freedom.

She sits down in front of him, now, his love... She radiates the fearful arrogance of youth and the scent of wealth... Subtle shades of lilac and gray, the lightest dabs of color—here, warmer tones tending to rose; there, colder ones, tending to pale blue—play like a transparent shadow on her oblong face; here is a moment of life, full of light and peace.

"You don't intend to offer me tea?" the viscous, honeyed streams pour forth.

"Do you take it stronger?"

"Yes, if possible."

"Two sugars or three?"

"Two's enough."

Ah, beloved! What wouldn't he do for her sake! She's precisely what his soul has yearned for. In general, he's certain that a woman—the one and only, of course—shouldn't have anything that's particularly expressive, for that's tiring. Here she is, then, his one and only, and that's because she's wonderfully neither this nor that, neither beautiful nor ugly. He perceives her as he does himself in a mirror, she's his creation, the crowning achievement of his many efforts and experience.

She's his, and he can watch her with pleasure as much as he wants. Now she's sad, she's crying, and on the left side of her neck a graceful little vein is pulsing and you can be driven mad by it, torn between insane pity and sadistic desires. Linger, linger, enchantment[1]; how sweet, tormentingly sweet, it is to see her tears; even sweeter to show in front of his beloved that he too can let fall a tear—miserly... male...

However, he's tired.

Stroking the touching back of her head, he slowly, unobtrusively, moves his hand onto her neck and, locating her seventh vertebra, quickly pushes the power supply button.

The sensory-magnetic joint running along the spinal column instantly appears, the casing showing smooth; he easily removes it, exposing the familiar sight of the internal organs, entangled in the blue-red wiring of the servomechanisms... An efficient order is the basis of harmony: the power supply unit, the computing system, the control unit, the memory unit—he lays it all out into labeled safes.

Phew, is he tired. Say what you will, intercourse saps your energy.... And only compassionate nature gives us authentic repose without demanding anything in return.

He walks over to the window again, breathes in the sea air. No, the Monet, after all—it's overly saturated, and everything that's excessive can't be completely beautiful. Strictly speaking, he's more an advocate of lyrical and leisurely contemplation in the spirit of Sisley: he pushes a button and the sea through the window instantly slips off to the right, followed by a click as "Windy Day in Vienieau" is installed, to fit perfectly in the opening of the window. Oh, no! Not that empty sky and melancholy.... He pushes the button and in the opening Sisley appears again: "La Ville Garenny on the Seine" (a quiet river, a quiet boat, cosy little houses on the opposite bank). Yes, he's always wanted nothing but simplicity and peace. What does he need? A forest, a clearing with a haystack in it... Monet again: now "Haystack in Giverny." Besides, stacks—he agrees with this opinion—are an ideal artistic subject for experiments in tones.

But his weariness doesn't leave him. His state now is the same as if he'd been ordered to divide by zero. His protective relay switches off. The servomechanisms under the casing sag helplessly. His eyes fade.

The view from the window fades automatically.

1991

Translated by Helena Goscilo

From *Otdelenie propashchikh*, Moscow, 1991

Notes

1. The sentence is a line from Fedor Tiutchev's poem "Last Love" (Posledniaia liubov'), written in 1852-54 and inspired by his autumnal love for the much younger E.A. Denis'eva.

Slowly the Old Woman...

Nina Katerli

Today Lidia Matveevna gets up with the radio, exactly at six, as she had her whole life when she worked at her accounting office. The ride by bus and streetcar took more than an hour and, besides, she also had to get Grisha up, feed him and make sure he had his briefcase. How did it go? "Children, get ready for school; the cock quit crowing long ago." Yes... That had been a time of great responsibility.

Lidia Matveevna sits up in bed, lowers her skinny legs down onto the rug and looks for a long time at her son's picture, hanging on the wall between the windows. Grisha was already seventeen then, in the tenth grade! Say what you will, he was a good-looking boy—curls, high forehead, firm lips. Maybe his nose was a little bit... but so what? To make up for it his eyes—everybody admired them—were like two black plums... But he did have one bad habit—he would stoop, and she hadn't been able to cure him of it. She kept telling him, "Grisha, your posture, sit up straight!" And she had taken him to corrective Phys Ed classes, and then enrolled him in a gymnastics class... Poor thing... How is he now, I wonder.

Lidia Matveevna slowly pulls on her stockings and puts on her dress. Does she hurry? Not for anything! The doctor has warned her that hurry is the worst possible thing for her heart. It's going to be a hard day; they've just announced on the radio that the atmospheric air pressure has fallen sharply and she has to find time to do all her shopping because at three o'clock she has an appointment with her neuropathologist. And tomorrow she has to stay home and wait; it's her pension day and the way they do it, you never know what time they'll come. There had even been some items in the newspapers about this, but they couldn't care less!

Yes. Tomorrow Lidia Matveevna will receive her monthly sixty-five rubles. Forty years of service is no joke! It's not much money, but who's complaining? You can live on it; you just have to watch your budget. The first thing, of course, is your rent and utilities. If you don't burn hundred-watt light bulbs, the way some people do, then five rubles will cover everything. So, that leaves sixty. Then comes food. How much do you think an elderly person needs for food? For your information, a ruble and a half is completely sufficient! Again, if you have a head on your shoulders and don't go on eating binges. Extra food at our age, by the way, means extra problems. The most important thing is to get your vitamins, but carbohydrates only in moderation. In the morning it's always a good idea to eat some cottage cheese or some kasha and at dinner have vegetarian soup for the soup course—well, once a week you can boil a chicken without much fat on it, but you shouldn't overdo a good thing! And for the main course, you can eat some stewed vegetables, or some blintzes (fried only with sunflower oil; the butter nowadays is like water—an achievement of our science and technology, and the price is outrageous). But if you are lucky enough to get hold of any kind of edible fish, is that bad? Not at all! Our system needs fish. It's got phosphorus and other minerals. They feed the brain and prevent sclerosis, and sclerosis is the last thing Lidia Matveevna needs right now. She simply mustn't get sick. If Grisha found out, the boy's heart would break from worrying about his mother.

In her letters to her son Lidia Matveevna always tells him that she feels quite well and doesn't need anything. So Grisha won't have to worry and will know that in case, God forbid, anything should happen, there are plenty of good people in the world and she has very solicitous neighbors who are always ready to help her... Ha! *They* would be some help! They wouldn't leave her alone from their help! Only why upset the boy for no reason? Grisha, thank God, doesn't know the neighbors—they moved in just last year. On her left lives Shura, an Asiatic from Tashkent. On her right, in a tiny room, are two newlyweds, Lena and Sergei. Both are short and round, always getting themselves some food and eating it non-stop, and always the same thing—fried eggs. Lidia Matveevna privately calls them "well fed, but ill-bred." Breeding and refinement, of course, is precisely what they lack! And both of them are secondary-school graduates. Nowadays there are lots of people with an education, but no culture! It's true that they, like Shura, are both from other cities, but after all, they're not from the backwoods! We have more people from the provinces here now than real Leningraders. Lidia Matveevna, by the way, has lived in Leningrad since 1930, half a century, that's no short visit! She came from Byelorussia as a girl to work as a cleaning woman, but they talked her out of it and she found herself a technicum student instead of a cleaning woman. That's the kind of time it was! A simple provincial girl and she went to business school and became an accountant. Her sisters and brother, they lived their whole life in the sticks; only Lidia Matveevna got out into the real world. Now, of course, not a single one of her family is left, curse him a thousand times, that Hitler! More than forty years have passed... If her relatives were alive, especially Boris, maybe—who knows?—then things might have worked out with Grisha. And how talented Grisha has always been! He grew up without a father, but he graduated from the Technological Institute! And, as a matter of fact, with honors. Why not—she had lived just for him, she had done whatever she could for him. She never thought of herself, but she never refused the boy anything... Only, it seems, here also moderation was needed: if she had been able to say a firm "no" at the right time, this whole nightmare might not have taken place.

But, just the same, no matter what has happened, Grisha is a decent sort. He has never been afraid of work. He knows how to appreciate a kindness. Young people these days don't appreciate anything. They think that everyone owes them everything, and they don't owe anybody anything. Lena and Sergei don't even know how to say hello. Or maybe they don't want to. And there's never any question of holding a conversation. It's just "Hi!" and then they're gone.

Shura, on the other hand, just chatters and chatters, and she doesn't even care what she's chattering about! Where they're selling what, what rare item is available, what she's managed to buy. She doesn't read the newspapers, doesn't listen to the radio, and on television just watches all sorts of nonsense, comedies and popular music. Of course, that's all right at times, but everything in moderation! I've told her many times: "Shura, why don't you ever turn on your radio? You know, you can sew or clean house, even read a book while listening to the radio. I, for example, can't do anything without my radio. I get up, turn it on right away and it's on until bedtime. You know, there are so many interesting and edifying programs. For example, 'University for the Millions,' or 'International Diary.' And then there's 'What Adults Should Know About Children.' You absolutely must listen to that. You have a son."

She just waves her hands: "To hell with their stupid yapping! In one day at work, even without a radio, I hear such things that I don't know whether to laugh or cry."

Shura works in a psychiatric hospital, with insane people. She's a cleaning lady or something. She had to take the job to get her residence permit. No doubt about it—it's not a nice job, but, after all, somebody has to work there. If you didn't want to go to school and get an education, then go where your country needs a pair of hands. And that somebody might want to go to school and not be able to—that just doesn't happen in our country. Here the only people without an education are lazy bums or really stupid people... And why did she have to come rushing up here to Leningrad? She could have stayed in her own Tashkent! Shura keeps claiming that she's Russian, but that's ridiculous—she's a typical Uzbek. All you have to do is just look at her once. Wide cheekbones and slant eyes. And her bastard kid, Vitalik. A real savage! Of course, in our country everyone is equal, every nation is given equal rights, but if you're an ill-bred slob, there's nothing anyone can do about that. Lidia Matveevna has remarked to her a hundred times, "Shura, when you've finished with the bathtub, you have to wash it carefully with soap and powder, and not just sponge it off. And quit leaving your unwashed pots and pans in the sink overnight. That's not hygienic!" But that one's always got the same answer: "It's my pan. I guess I forgot to ask you when I could wash it!" That's the provinces for you! Lidia Matveevna has to explain, "When you live in a collective, you have to forget about 'mine' and 'I want.' And, incidentally, no one wants flies to start breeding in our communal kitchen because of your filth! Other people cook here too, you're not the only one!" But she'll just wave her arms and walk off. No, with that sort you've got to have patience and more patience! And the boy is growing up disorderly, insensitive, with no self-control. When his elders correct him, he just stomps out. And lately, the final atrocity, he's bought himself a record player and he plays it from morning to night. It wouldn't be so bad if it were really music. Shrieks and yells, no tune, no meaning. And then people are surprised that there's so much crime and vandalism on the streets!

Lidia Matveevna takes her enameled mug and toothbrush, toothpaste, soap and a towel, and trudges into the bathroom to wash up. And after performing her ablutions, back into the kitchen. She puts the teakettle on the burner and goes back to her room. There on the sill between the window and the storm window is a bowl with yesterday's milk and noodles in it. No, don't think that Lidia Matveevna doesn't have a refrigerator. She has a wonderful Saratov refrigerator. But you know what the electric bill is like when you run that refrigerator? Lidia Matveevna does turn it on from time to time in the summer, but right now, in January, that's simply ridiculous!

When she appears again in the kitchen with the bowl in her hands, Lena has already taken over the stove. She's frying eggs so early in the morning. Is that healthy? Eggs every day! And no matter how many times you tell her, she just shrugs her shoulders. In answer to a polite "Good morning" she grunts something unintelligible. What fine manners! Her dressing gown is filthy, barely closes over her belly and her hair is all tousled. And she's a young woman, soon to be a mother! What kind of example will she be later on for her child? And how about her husband? Such "beauty" will soon send him drinking and carousing.

"Would you like some good advice, Lena?" Lidia Matveevna asks gently.

"Nah!" Lena shakes her disheveled head. And if you please, has stuck her nose in her frying pan. And, incidentally, shaking your hair over your food is unsanitary. And Lidia Matveevna bluntly tells Lena so. So she will know next time. And she also adds that if young people won't listen to the opinion of their elders, this never leads to any good result.

"You're going to have a hard time in life, Lena," she concludes in a friendly tone as she lights the burner.

Lena grabs the frying pan with her bare hands, burns herself, jerks away her hand

and holds it up to her mouth.

"And why be so nervous? That's bad for you when you're pregnant. Here, take my rag." Lidia Matveevna offers her the rag that she always uses to pick up hot things. But Lena has already picked up the greasy frying pan with a clean towel and run out of the kitchen. She could at least have said thank you. Ill-bred and vulgar. There are no other words for her!

No, Grisha at her age wasn't like that. One has to be fair. Even now, forty years old, in spite of everything, he's a fine boy. And what an attentive son, you can't imagine! And, by the way, he was always a great one for family. Already for two years now, once a month, a detailed letter to his mother. And that in spite of all his problems! For her last birthday he had somehow managed to send her a package. Lidia Matveevna was simply tired of writing: "Don't deprive yourself. As it is, I'm heartsick worrying about you! Although you write that now everything is fine, I realize what a hard life you have. If there were only some way I could help you..."

The cheerful tone of Grisha's letters does not deceive Lidia Matveevna.

Poor, stupid boy! He got caught; he was tricked into it... It was all because of her, Natasha, her daughter-in-law. It was all her doing. She kept beating her nonsense into his head, and being soft and good-hearted, he could never turn anyone down. And he's still in love with her. It's ridiculous! The main thing, where are his eyes? Really, if there were anything for him to love! The woman has no brains and no looks at all. The only thing she does have is a high opinion of herself. She's a tiny little thing, skinny as a rhesus monkey. Well, all right, that's her business. What's worse is something else: she's got a mean temper. You don't dare say a word to her! And just try and give her some good advice... Right away she says, "Thank you very much, Lidia Matveevna, but we'll make our own decisions." She has to show her independence.

Two years ago, the last birthday of Grisha's that they spent together, Natasha simply spoiled the festivities for everyone. First, for some reason she bought a rich cake with creamy frosting, and that's like killing Grisha: he has liver problems. Lidia Matveevna restrained herself, held her tongue and merely remarked tactfully that Grisha was very thin, didn't look at all well, so maybe somehow he should get a little more nourishment. Well, what was wrong with that? Please tell me. Doesn't a mother have the right to worry about her son's health? "What do you mean? How can you say that?!" Natasha immediately started to pout and sat through the whole dinner like a frozen puppet. And Grisha, of course, was upset... Really, I shouldn't have said that in front of her. They're right: my tongue is my worst enemy.

The noodles are boiling and bubbling. Any minute and they'll start to burn. Lidia Matveevna turns off the burner. And it's already after seven. Shura should have been up long ago; she's overslept again! They're all lazy, don't want to work. All they want to do is sleep.

As she walks past Shura's room, Lidia Matveevna decides she had better knock on her door. No answer. She knocks again. Thank God. Shura hears her; she's awake.

"Who's there? Whadya want?"

"Not 'whadya,' Shura, but *'What do you'* want?" Lidia Matveevna pronounces carefully from the hallway. "And it's way past time for you to be up. You'll be late."

"Go-o-od Lord!" grumbles Shura, "She won't let me get any sleep. And what business is it of yours, anyway? It's my day off, okay? What a meddling busybody! There's no getting away from her!"

Lidia Matveevna purses her lips. Imagine that! "What business is it of mine?!" And she could have said thank you. After all, someone is worried about her, is trying to help her out and, if you please, "What business of yours?" It's only selfish people who don't care about anything. They don't take responsibility for anyone else, but we... are people of a different generation. Everything has always been our business and that's how we fixed it so that people like you can have a happy life!

During breakfast Lidia Matveevna carefully listens to the latest news. She gets upset, shakes her head. Something has to be done; measures have to be taken. That imperialism is running wild, doing whatever comes into its head. They've really gone too far, decided to install their rockets! And they couldn't care less that the whole human race is angry and indignant... And if you please, there are those Israeli bandits again. What are they up to now? What do they want? What are they trying to prove? They're making trouble for everybody! For those poor Arabs (it's not their fault that they're Negroes), and for those brainless souls they have misled with their propaganda... Yes. And... And for us. My God! If only there's no war! If there just won't be any trouble! After all, everything has just barely begun to get straightened out. Everybody has a television set and a refrigerator. Everyone is decently dressed in imported clothing. But, you know, we still have a lot of self-centered people and no matter what you do for them, it's never enough. They don't have that; they need this. So, what does that mean? Work the way you should and you'll have everything you need! Even Shura, who's from Tashkent, still wants to be like everyone else... We still don't carry on enough educational and cultural work with them! And this technical school kid of hers is turning into a real hooligan! Once, just a couple of years ago, when Lidia Matveevna was doing volunteer work with teenagers at the housing office, she would quickly have found a way to handle this Vitalik. She had straightened out worse cases than that! And why don't they give her any teenagers to work with now? Do they think she's a feeble old woman? Or, maybe... No! We don't want any "or maybe's"!

But it's already time to get ready to go shopping. There's still a ruble and a half left until she gets her new pension money tomorrow. That's what it means to know how to live and keep track of everything. As a matter of fact, she can still turn in a kefir bottle and a mayonnaise jar. Today Lidia Matveevna has decided to give herself a treat (a reward for her thriftiness) and buy some apples; right now they have some very nice apples in the stores... No, say what you will, economizing has its benefits. She spends fifty rubles a month on rent and food, and behold: every month Lidia Petrovna is able to put something into savings. In just two years three hundred and sixty rubles have accumulated in her savings book, not counting interest. For Grisha. For that first little while after the boy gets back. He'll have to get settled and there may be problems. But, just the same, Lidia Matveevna is sure that here Grigory will be treated like a human being, with understanding. But now his neighbors and acquaintances—that's a whole other story. You can't keep everybody from talking. There'll be some who will want to rub it in, who'll call him a criminal... Oh, if it weren't for that Natasha!

Lidia Matveevna arranges her coin purse, her glasses, the empty bottle and the mayonnaise jar in her shopping bag, puts on her hat, boots and coat. The coat, of course, is no longer new, but who needs to dress up at her age? As long as it's clean and durable! And the nitroglycerine is in her pocket, as usual. She's ready to go.

It began badly. The saleslady in the dairy store was in a bad mood, you see. She took the bottle, but not the mayonnaise jar.

"We haven't had no mayonnaise for over a month now; so take your container to the recycling station."

"That's very interesting, but what difference does it make whether you are still selling it or not? What's right is right. You have an obligation to take it back, because that's your duty."

"To the recycling station!" That's very nice! Two stops on a streetcar, six kopecks there and back, and then you have to stand on the street in the cold with a bunch of drunks.

"Don't hold up the line!" they say, already pushing impatiently behind her. "She told you they won't take it."

Well, we all know very well that the people in line are always on the side of the sales clerk: they're trying to make a good impression. They're afraid they won't get served.

"You, dearest citizen, please don't shove," Lidia Matveevna says, turning to the woman behind her. "And, incidentally, I wasn't talking to you at all. But here's what I can say to you: it's not at all a matter of a mayonnaise jar. It's a matter of principle. It's dishonest! Let them show me where it's written that they should only accept glass containers for products which are in stock at that particular moment. Let them show me! Right now we are conducting a campaign against lawlessness in commerce. They should read the newspapers!"

"Why don't you drop dead!" the saleslady suddenly yells, all red-faced. "Take your stupid ten kopecks, but just get out of here, for Christ's sake! And take your mayonnaise jar with you!" She pulls a ten-kopeck coin out of the pocket of her (rather dirty, by the way) apron and tosses it on the counter.

"I don't need *your* money!" Lidia Matveevna instantly retorts. "I want *my* money for *my* mayonnaise jar! And I can make you a present of ten kopecks myself. Please show me the complaint book and call your supervisor!"

And the saleslady gives in, the bitch! She grabs the mayonnaise jar, shoves it under the counter and silently hands Lidia Matveevna the triangular token for the cash register clerk. Modestly, but proudly, Lidia Matveevna walks over to get her rightful ten kopecks. And behind her there's a general uproar and shouting. A sizable line has formed and everyone, of course, is in a hurry. The saleslady is yelling loudest of all. "Oo-ooh, the old witch! She keeps coming here... And every day there's some problem. All of them are like that; they'd hang themselves for a kopeck..."

"Well, as far as 'all of them' are concerned, my dear, I could call a policeman about that remark," Lidia Matveevna immediately retorts. "This is not America for you, it's not the Ku-Klus-Klan!"[1]

"Okay, grandma, don't get all wound up!" a fat man in a leather coat says soothingly. "Watch your nerves or you'll have a breakdown!"

Well, there he's absolutely right. And deciding for the time being not to get involved with the insolent sales clerk, Lidia Matveevna leaves the battlefield. And later on we'll see...

Carefully stepping along the uneven, icy sidewalk (before the war they had excellent janitors to keep the walks clear, but now they're nowhere to be found...), she slowly walks toward the fruit and vegetable stand. She's in a cheerful, energetic mood, the way one always feels when one has done the right thing. No, making a scene in front of a long line isn't so sweet, but to let people get away with such scandalous behavior—never, not in any circumstances! All our problems come from people putting up with things they know are wrong. And you just have to try and ignore all kinds of prejudiced outbursts to the effect that "all of them are like that..." We still have remnants of capitalistic behavior. We do; no one denies it. And we do have political excesses in the provinces, but the government is struggling to change this! And, incidentally, no one sits around unemployed and there are lots of people with university degrees. No, here Grisha was completely wrong. In such questions he behaved generally like a madman or a fool, and at the slightest provocation would use his fists. And, as is well known, you don't solve anything with your fists, and you may reap some unpleasant consequences. People have to be reeducated without violence. And how many times have I told him this... But that's Grisha, all right! He always knows better than anyone!.. And all his troubles began right there. Yes, and I do have to admit this, Grisha did have a nasty, mean tongue. He would simply climb up the wall because of some, you know, "injustices." He went looking for them, whether they were there or not... "These people like us Jews; those don't like us." What can that mean? There aren't any "us" and "you" here—we're all the same, live in the same country, speak the same language!

Lidia Matveevna shakes her head. Alright! No one likes an unpleasant truth, and she—what can you do?—has such a character that she must tell people the truth right to their face. If it needs to be said, if it's useful and something they should know, then keeping quiet is a crime. You can't think of yourself and be liked by everyone. You must think about the people who often behave badly and make crude mistakes just because no one ever taught them what is right.

There were about five people in the line in front of the vegetable stand. Lidia Matveevna, with a sigh, went to the back of the line.

"Granny, your bones are tired. You don't have to wait in line."

Who's this? Some very nice woman, quite young, with a baby. No matter what you say, we do have politically conscious young people!

There's a heavy weight in her chest. Her fingers are numb, and it would be very nice not to have to wait in line, especially since she had already done her share of standing during her lifetime; let others do it now... And, nevertheless, Lidia Matveevna refuses. "Never mind. Thank you very much, but I'll just stand here and wait my turn. That's something, thank God, I can still do—stand. I'll wait: we old folks have lots of free time."

Even too much... It'd be nice to know, generally, how much of it—time—she had left. A year? Two? And if it's—one month?.. Well, why not?.. After all, seventy-seven is a good, solid age, and it would be a sin to complain. Only there's Grisha... She absolutely must make arrangements at the savings bank.

Lidia Matveevna thinks about this calmly, as if about tomorrow's pension money. And at the same time she keeps a sharp eye on the line of people. And she notices that some impertinent young girl in a rumpled hat is hanging around near the head of the line. She can't be going to try to break in out of turn? No, she didn't dare. She walked back and got in line right behind Lidia Matveevna.

The apples aren't cheap, a ruble fifty, but everyone is taking two or three kilograms. People have money. There's no doubt about it: we have a good life! But Lidia Matveevna has no use for kilograms. When her turn finally comes, she asks the man to weigh three apples for her, "That nice red one there and the two to the left of it. No, not that one; don't put that one in! Don't you see it's bruised? Better that one, on the end... No, not that one, the next one, if you would be so kind... Have you tried them yourself? How are they, a bit sour?"

"I haven't tried them," the man says rudely. "That'll be eighty-seven kopecks."

A ruble fifty per kilogram, seventy-five kopecks for half a kilogram. On the scales five hundred and eighty grams... No, he didn't seem to be cheating her...

"I think that's a bit more than I can afford, young man. Take off that one, the big one, and give me that smaller one," Lidia Matveevna orders and says to the people in the line, "Eighty-seven kopecks the day before I get my pension, you know, that's my whole fortune." It's a joke, but they don't understand jokes. They're already hot under the collar.

"Stop holding up the line. Take your apples and let somebody else buy something." It was that same girl, in the rumpled hat, trying to be a smart aleck. "Did you come here to buy apples or to gab? People don't have an extra minute and she keeps wagging her tongue, and looks over every apple like she was picking out a husband!"

"Sixty kopecks. Okay?" the man caught on to her game.

"Of course it is! And thank you very, very much, young man. I wish you a good day and hope you have strong nerves—you'll need them with customers like that."

Lidia Matveevna doesn't look at the smart aleck, but she, of course, has realized whose cat swallowed the canary and keeps quiet.

After that everything goes like clockwork. She manages to buy half a kilogram of hake in the little grocery on the corner. It's not perch, you know, but it's a quite decent fish if you know how to prepare it. You can use it for both soup and the main course.

In the fish market they haven't had any fish to sell since morning. The saleslady there is an old woman, uneducated but friendly, and Lidia Matveevna tells her that, you know, tomorrow is pension day, and she won't be able to leave the house. So she needs to stock up on food today, but what can you do if the store has nothing to sell!

"You're lucky," the saleslady responds enviously. "You can afford to stay home. Probably you've got children and grandchildren. But I'm completely alone, and my pension is so small that I can't afford to sit home."

"Yes, I have a granddaughter a year old. A real beauty, no question about it!" Lidia Matveevna says effusively. She pulls Olia's latest picture, wrapped in plastic, out of the side pocket of her purse and shows it to the saleslady. Of course she doesn't let her touch it—the last thing she needed would be to have the child smeared with fish oil!

"A pretty little girl," the saleslady says with a sigh. "You can see right away that she's a healthy thing. Her cheeks are rosy, just like little apples. Do they live with you? I bet she loves her grandma!"

Lidia Matveevna shrugs her shoulders. "One mustn't think about oneself and what one would like, but about the child," she declares didactically, taking the picture and putting it back into her purse. "What does that mean—'loves' or 'doesn't love'? The main thing is for the child to have a good life, to grow and develop properly."

She nods majestically to the saleslady and turns her back on her. No point in arguing with someone like that, who couldn't find the time to have kids of her own, but still has to tell you off!

And now go home, take a short rest, read the newspapers, and then—to the clinic. An appointment with a neuropathologist—that's a real stroke of luck. For a whole week Lidia Matveevna has been going there to try to get to see one. She kept going and going, and finally made it. The neuropathologist was very nice, a young woman, but she seemed to be well trained. Careful and thoughtful. Not like these general practitioners! Their whole physical exam lasts two minutes, simply a disgrace! And if you start to tell them what the problem is, they immediately interrupt you. It's all the same whether you've got the flu or whether you've got cholera. As they say: "It doesn't matter what's wrong with her, just so long as she dies..." But it's true, you have to give them their due. There are lots of us and, so far, not enough of them. But, you know, a neuropathologist finds time for everyone. That means you can, if you really want to. Of course, sometimes you have to wait for hours to get in, but there's always someone in the line with whom you can talk and share experiences. And when you get to see the doctor, then they ask you about everything and listen carefully to everything you say. About the pressure in your chest and how you just generally don't feel well and how you can't get a good night's sleep and haven't received a letter from your son for a month and ten days now. For your information, that's the post office messing up. I should write to the proper authorities. But just the same you worry, my son is my son, and everyone knows what kind of a life he must have there... And now that I have a granddaughter, that's something else to make my heart ache. Poor little girl...

Well, at last! Here's my apartment building. You could break your legs on this ice—nothing serious, just some sort of sabotage! Lidia Matveevna slowly cuts across the courtyard. It's crowded and always has this smell from the garbage cans... And Grisha, when he was little, loved to play here. It used to be that no matter how much I yelled at him, I simply couldn't get him to come into the apartment. I kept telling him, "Grisha? why don't you play in the park across the street? There's greenery and fresh air there. All the nice children play in the park, and you, like some street urchin, always play in the courtyards." But no, he didn't want to play in the park, and this courtyard was driving me out of my mind with worry. And the boys he found to play with here, nothing but trash. Sometimes there would be a fist fight; sometimes they would break a window. But Momma always had to pay. You could go out of your mind, trying to find window glass after the war! But, finally, we got lucky—in the seventh grade he got interested in chemistry, because they had a good teacher. She knew how to get her pupils interested in the subject. He got interested and joined a chemistry group with the Young Pioneers. Then he had less time to get into trouble. That's extremely important, extremely! Keep the child busy, so there's no time to get into trouble... Natasha doesn't understand this. She'll ruin Olia. Oh, God help us all...

It's nearly dark in the entranceway. Lidia Matveevna walks right over to her mailbox. Empty again, what a disappointment! Her legs immediately grow weak and her forehead breaks out in perspiration. She stops, pulls the tube with the nitroglycerine out of her pocket, takes out a tablet and puts it under her tongue. In a minute she feels better and can walk, slowly and carefully, up to the third floor, open the door with her key and turn on the light in the hallway. And then... Well, thank God! There it is, on the hall table, beside the newspaper. So Shura brought it up for her. Now, as quickly as possible, go up to her own room, where she can take off her coat and hat, put on her glasses and slowly, savoring every word, read the letter. But first she has to skim through it quickly to be sure nothing bad has happened.

Everything is fine. He's alive and healthy! That's the main thing—healthy! That's something Grisha wouldn't lie to her about. And the boy is wearing himself out working for them over there in America. But, on the other hand, just try and not work there... "Mother, please forgive me for not having written for so long. I've been nearly killing myself lately, working like a madman, but, at least, I've completely paid off my debts..." That's just inexcusable! Debts! As if no one knows where those debts came from! He's ruined himself, wrecked his health—and for what? It's her fault, all her fault, Natasha's! She's greedy. He's not the one who wanted all that—the car and all the other junk... And see, now he has to... Was Grisha like that when he was younger? We barely made ends meet, because Lidia Matveevna, of course, had refused to accept alimony. (If he didn't want to be a father, we won't let him buy himself out of it with money!) So the boy walked around in sweatpants with patches over the patches and in a homemade hat with ear flaps. Although everything was always clean and pressed. And no debts... And did he ever complain? He went to Young Pioneer club meetings, participated in sports, and read so many books! I even had to stop him: "You'll ruin your eyes..." Now no one will worry about him... No, I must immediately write him a long, stern letter. Now at least he should start to realize that his health is more important than anything else!

And then in the room next door there's a howling and a meowing exactly like a cat's. That retard Vitalik has turned on his "music" again. Lidia Matveevna puts the letter down on the table, stands up and energetically strides over into Shura's room. And she, if you please, is sitting there knitting, her bare legs stretched out on an unmade bed. Ugly, fat legs with untrimmed toenails; no breeding or manners! And her Vitalik is sprawled out on the sofa, listening to jazz.

Without saying a word, Lidia Matveevna cuts across the room and turns off the record player. The howling stops. Vitalik sits up and his eyes bulge indignantly. No, he doesn't greet an elderly person respectfully.

"Why did you...?" he finally asks. "What did... you do that for?"

"In the first place, hello!" Lidia Matveevna declares, addressing both him and Shura. "I want to tell you this: I'm not going to allow any improper behavior in the apartment. I simply have no right to allow it! That isn't music; it's corruption of the morals of minors, and you, Shura, would be wise to think about that! For such things formerly it was possible to reap very, very major unpleasant consequences. I can tell you that! Because it is ideo... ideological subversion! And with your feet on the sofa! A Soviet student should not imitate the vulgar examples of the West! That never leads to anything good. Believe me. I know about that."

"But why? What don't you like about this music?" Vitaly mumbles dully. He looks stupid, like a fool. (He was generally stupid anyway, but now, especially so.) "If this is bad music, what kind is good music?"

"What kind?! You don't know what kind?" Lidia Matveevna throws back her head. "We have lots of good songs. 'Not Even a Rustle Can Be Heard in the Park,' 'This Is the Day of Victory...'"

"I don't believe it!" Vitali looks like a complete idiot now. And Shura's mouth drops open and her eyes are bulging.

"'Wide is my native land; in it are many forests, fields and rivers!'" Lidia Matveevna concludes triumphantly. And stops talking. She gasps for breath; she desperately needs some more nitroglycerine, but she's left it in her room.

"Just listen to her, the old bag!" Vitalik exclaims, almost admiringly. And suddenly he yells in a smart-alecky voice, "And why don't you get out of here? We don't need a kindergarten teacher! 'The-old-woman-slowly-crossed-the-road!' 'Wide is my native land!' A real patriot! And her son ran off to America to get away from her!"

"Shut up, you son of a bitch!" Shura jumps off her bed like a whirlwind. "Shut up, you vermin, or I'll kill you! Don't listen to him, Lidia Matveevna! I'll show him right now, the bastard..."

"Shura... Don't you dare... strike... the child..." Lidia Matveevna articulates barely audibly and clutches at her heart. "And my Grisha... He'll come back... You'll see... He has realized... They tricked him and lied to him... He's definitely coming back, I have... a letter..."

Lidia Matveevna's eyes roll, and, with a brief snort, she drops like a log onto the floor.

Lidia Matveevna doesn't hear Shura's funeral wailing or Vitalik's low bass whimpers, because his mother did slap him across the face. Neither does she hear pregnant Lena come running in to see what all the shouting is about. She doesn't feel Lena and Shura lift her up and carefully lay her on the sofa.

She doesn't regain consciousness until she's given a shot by the doctor from the emergency ambulance, which the terrified Vitalik called. The doctor's young and attractive He reminds her of Grisha and at the same time of Olia's photograph.

"It was a coronary spasm," he explains pretentiously to Shura and Lena. "She needs rest and nursing care. I injected her with a vasodilator."

Shura nods her head as if she understands.

"She probably lives alone?" the doctor asks. "It would be best, of course, to hospitalize her... Except, as you know, for her age. Hospitals don't like to take old people. But if you carry her out on the street, sit her down somewhere, and then call emergency service from a pay phone... Do you understand? Then they have to take her."

"Good Lord!" Lena is horrified. "On the street?"

"So we should just toss someone out on the street, like a dog?!!" echoes provincial Shura.

Lidia Matveevna wants to straighten them out, to say that this is all anti-Soviet propaganda, that hospitals are for everyone, and we mustn't ever forget that medical care in our country is free. Not the way it is in capitalist countries, where some people recover their health in a private room with a color television set at the expense of others, who are starving to death under bridges! And it's disgraceful that a doctor shouldn't know this. After all, he was taught in a Soviet medical institute. Complete lack of culture! And then there's Natasha—just think: she wore a cross on her neck... She has a university degree and she behaves like some superstitious peasant! But why, where is that bright light coming from? After all, it's night outside. Oh-h... it's the candles! So many candles, because today's a holiday. There's an oblong dish on the white tablecloth with stuffed pike. Everyone will get a piece, and Grandpa Hirsch, of course, gets the head. And just look at the different colored decanters of grape vodka! See how they sparkle! Boris, their elder brother, also gets a little vodka, and the girls, Leah, Beylah and Sima, are given a currant liqueur. And they'll all start drinking each other's health and shouting "Lichaim!"... What else is he saying there? Oh, yes, he's writing prescriptions... He's talking about the hospital again... But she's already better. What does she need a hospital for!? O-o-oh, she's still greatly to be envied: she has a wonderful room and a comfortable bed. And her nitroglycerine. And all the food she needs.... She mustn't forget to put the fish outside on the window sill to keep it cool... Tomorrow they'll bring her pension, and right away she'll need to put fifteen rubles in the savings account, for Grisha... And who'll look after her? Never mind... There are people all around. Here everyone is the friend and comrade of everyone else. And who else? And her brother... Her brother asks Grandpa, "How is this night different from other nights?" "Every night we eat both matzo and bread, but tonight, only matzo," Grandpa Hirsch answers.

Shura and Lena, both talking at the same time, thank the doctor and follow him out into the hallway. They leave the door open. Lidia Matveevna can hear the sound of their footsteps, the click of the lock, and their voices.

"I feel sorry for Matveevna," Shura sighs loudly. "After all, she's a decent old lady. She's well read and she understands politics. Her son turned into a bastard. Just think..."

Lena says something but so quietly you can't make out the words.

"If anything," it's Shura's voice again, "if Matveevna... you know, in that case don't you and Sergei just wiggle your ears, okay? Move right into her room that very day. Bring in your things, let them try and prove it later. I mean: she's got fifteen meters of living space just for herself, which will just go back to the government anyway. And you have nine for the two of you, and soon, just think, for the three of you..."

No, she's not at all stupid, that Shura, even if she is an ignorant Asiatic... And there's no reason to feel insulted. Life is life... And why feel insulted? Today is a high holiday, the biggest holiday of the year, and Grandpa Hirsch, sitting at the head of the table, is telling how on this day Moses led the Hebrews out of Egyptian captivity. Leah listens, frightened half to death: Pharaoh with his troops rushed in pursuit, but he couldn't catch them, he couldn't! And he drowned in the Black Sea, along with his horses, soldiers and carts...

Leah laughs and claps her hands. Every year at the first seder Grandpa Hirsch tells this story and at first she's always scared. And Grandpa slowly stands up at the table. He's very big and stern, with a white beard and white hair. But his eyes are black. Like Grisha's.

The light becomes dazzling and noisy, like a ringing in her ears. It's time! With cold fingers Leah scratches the upholstery of Shura's sofa. And, gazing fixedly right into those approaching eyes, she utters through her blue, motionless lips, "Sh'ma, Yisroel! Adonai eloheinu, Adonai echod!"[2]

"Ma!" Vitalik calls. "Ma, quick! Quick! Come here! Look, she... Your old lady has messed herself up!"

Translated by John F. Beebe

From *Vest'*, 1989

Notes

1. The intentional error in the original Russian indicates Lidia Matveevna's ignorance.
2. Hear, O Israel! The Lord, Our God Is One God!

The Way Home

Regina Raevskaia

The fragrance of the mowed hay made her want to cry. The scorching air cloaked her in a shroud. It was probably like this in her mother's womb. Where is her mother? Where is everyone? He is nearby, but that's just by chance. They met on a platform on the way home. It had been the way home a few months before.

That white morning filled them with faith. Their eyes met through the snowflakes and they held each other's gaze until it hurt. They had been separated by miles, years, a war. A war which had just ended, and now they were returning home to each other.

She looked at him, forgot to breathe, and started coughing. She grew numb from coughing. He shoved his way through the crowd and grabbed her in his arms.

"You're—alive?! And," she said in astonishment, "I'm alive, too."

From then on they rode together from station to station. The trains ran short routes, and the main thing was to grab a place, whether sitting or standing. No one asked where they were going. They spent many months like this. Going from south to north, from west to east. But for some reason they never reached their home.

"Do you remember, it's like in that game, Battleship. The one we used to play when we were little: A-10, miss, B-4, miss." His beard barely shook, and he stared fixedly at some point. It was becoming more and more difficult to get food. They'd already sold or bartered all of their things for bread.

"This is the third day we've been sitting on this damn platform, waiting. The train isn't coming. I'm telling you, it's not going to come." He slouched on the bench, and she, for lack of a better place, sat down on the floor, at his feet. "It's not going to come. To hell with it."

She rummaged about, near her breasts, under her torn blouse which at one time had been red. A single button remained and blushed shamelessly against the dirty black wool. The piece of bread that she offered him lit up the eyes of people sitting nearby. He grabbed it quickly and shoved it into his mouth. He kept cramming it into his mouth until he started hiccuping from lack of breath.

The piece of bread vanished. The fire in the strangers' eyes dimmed. Everything quieted down.

After waiting a minute, he asked, "Where did you get it?"

"I traded something for it."

"What? Nothing's left but the rags on us."

The sun rolled over to the other half of the sky as a pregnant woman would—slowly and unwillingly. Flies buzzed, fearlessly drowning out those occasional voices which were expressing their dissatisfaction out of inertia. No one was interested any more in the train.

She shaded her eyes and indistinctly mumbled, to the floor:

"I traded my ring. My wedding ring."

But he didn't hear—he was snoring into his chest.

She stood up abruptly, straightened her skirt, and walked quickly away. When she came back, he looked at her indifferently. She glanced backwards in fright as she squatted down next to him.

"Are you listening? I just met some woman in the restroom. Thank God she didn't see me. I really didn't want to talk to her. She's had such a tragedy. She lost everyone. And what can be done now? I don't want to..."

"Well, don't, if you don't want to! Why are you making all this fuss? Sit still. Sit there like an idiot. Wait for the train that isn't going to come."

She, burning either from the sun or his offensive remarks, had already opened her mouth to say, "I am an idiot. I was so glad when I saw you. My husband! Alive! But what kind of husband are you to me? I've already forgotten what that's about. You're just another mouth to feed." But she bit her lip and moved farther off to a fence, crawling between bodies. She didn't even wrinkle her nose, and she didn't feel the bodies, as if they weren't knocking against her. The only thing that struck her nostrils was the smell of freshly mowed hay, which made her want to cry. She sat, leaning with her back against the fence, lowered her head onto her shoulder, and grew stiff from the cold.

It's impossible to say how much time passed. But unexpectedly everything started to move. She glanced at the black mass. It was like an oil-covered sea raging from some incomprehensible disturbance. The noise swelled with every passing second, and amidst the indistinguishable roar, she suddenly heard, clearly and precisely:

"Liuba! Liubushka, my beloved wife!"

Liuba abruptly turned towards that shout, but the rising mass had already grown into an impenetrable wall, an impassable mountain. For a second she was astounded by the variety of sounds: human voices, stamping, shoving bodies, falling bodies, stamping, trampling, and one more thing—something familiar. A whistle! No, whistles! From two different points, two trains were coming towards each other.

And again: "Liubasha... you're the only one left... I'll come to you..."

Liuba used even her head to shove her way forward, making a path for herself. Seriozha! Where was Seriozha? Which train was he on? Or would he be on... Or was he looking for her?

"Se-rio-zhaaa..."

But the sound of her voice got lost in the din, or maybe she hadn't uttered a sound. Galvanized by hope, she grabbed onto a bar of the departing train. Another shove of her entire body and she was inside, on the platform, her arms behind her back so that they wouldn't get broken. Sweat streamed into her eyes. She didn't see the lonely, decrepit houses flashing by the window, or the trees scorched by embers, or anyone around her on the platform.

She was a bud clinging to a branch. But she was also the tree. And everyone who crushed her from every side belonged to her, and she to them.

So she stood, not seeing anything, with sweat streaming into her eyes, and life struck her nostrils with the fragrance of freshly mowed hay, and it made her want to cry.

Translated by Rebecca Epstein

From the author's manuscript, 1980s

The Blackthorn[1]

Dina Rubina

The boy loved the mother, and she loved him passionately. Yet nothing positive ever came of their love. All in all, it was rough going with the mother, and the boy had already learned to live with the dents and bumps in her character. She was ruled by her moods, and, consequently, the ground rules of their life changed at least five times a day.

Everything changed, even the names of objects. For example, sometimes the mother would call the apartment simply "an apartment," and at others she'd use the lofty and evocative term "cooperative!"

"Cooperative!" The boy liked that—it sounded good, sporty, like "avant garde" and "record." The only trouble was, though, that such words usually came up only when the mother got cranked up on one of her tirades.

"Why do you draw on the wallpaper?! Have you lost your mind?" she would shout in an unnatural, injured tone. "Tell me, are you human? You're not human! I slave away like a run-down mule for this damn cooperative, sitting nights over this idiotic work on the side." When the mother got fired up, she became uncontrollable, and it was better to keep quiet and put up with her inarticulate outbursts. It was better still to look straight into her angry eyes and assume right on cue the same pained facial expression as the mother's.

The boy looked a lot like the mother. She would stumble upon that injured look the way one stumbles upon a mirror in the dark and would calm down immediately. She'd only say feebly, "Are you ever going to act like a human being, eh?" And then everything would be fine; it'd be possible to go on living.

Life with the mother was complicated but interesting. When she happened to be in a good mood, they thought up all sorts of things and gabbed about a lot of nonsense. In general, the mother had so many incredibly interesting things in her head that the boy was content to listen to her endlessly.

"Marina, what did you dream last night?" he'd ask the moment he opened his eyes.

"Are you going to drink your milk?"

"Oh, okay. I'll drink it—only without the skin on top."

"Without the skin it'll be a short dream," she bargained.

"All right. Even with the lousy skin. Now, let's hear."

"Well, what did I dream: about pirates' treasures or how Eskimos found a baby mammoth on an ice-flow?"

"About the treasures," he would choose.

In those rare moments when the mother was in a cheerful mood, he loved her to the point of tears. She never shouted incomprehensible words then and she behaved like any normal girl in their group at kindergarten.

"Let's raise hell!" he'd suggest in wild ecstasy.

The mother would respond by making a ferocious face and come after him, fingers outspread, growling deeply. "Gra, gra! Now I'm gonna crush that human!!" For a second, he would freeze on the spot, screeching in delicious horror. And then cushions would start flying around the room, capsizing chairs, and the mother would chase after him, emitting horrible wails, and finally, they would collapse, exhausted, onto the couch, weak from laughter, and he would writhe as she pinched, poked, and tickled him.

Afterwards she would say in her normal voice:

"That's it... Let's tidy up here. Look at this—it's not an apartment, but God only knows what."

"C'mon, let's crush me some more!" he would plead, just in case, although he knew that the fun was over and that the mother was no longer in the mood to raise hell. He would sigh and begin collecting the cushions and righting the chairs.

But most of the time they'd swear at one another. There were always reasons, train-loads and planeloads of reasons—take your pick. And especially when they both were in a bad mood, then the sparks would really fly. She would grab the belt and lash at him indiscriminately; it didn't hurt, for she had a light hand, but he would howl as if he were being sliced open. Out of rage. They quarrelled in earnest: he'd lock himself in the bathroom and from time to time shout out:

"I'm leaving! I'm gonna get the devil away from you!"

"Go on, leave!" she would scream at him from the kitchen. "Get going!"

"You don't give a darn about me! I'm gonna find myself another woman!"

"Be my guest... But you won't find her locked up in the bathroom..."

What really stood between them like a wall, what spoiled, disrupted and poisoned his life, what robbed him of his mother was Work on the Side.

Where that Work on the Side came from was a mystery. It lay in wait for them like a bandit from behind a corner. It stormed into their life like a one-eyed pirate with a curved knife and immediately seized control over everything. With that knife it hacked away at all their plans—the zoo on Sunday, reading Tom Sawyer in the evenings; everything, absolutely everything was ruined, would go to the dogs and fall apart because of that damned Work on the Side. It was like the third member of their family—and the most important one, because everything depended on it: whether they'd go to the beach in July, whether the mother would buy herself a coat for the winter, or whether they'd pay the rent on time. The boy hated Work on the Side and was terribly jealous of it.

"But why now, why is it On the Side?" he would ask furiously.

"What an idiot! Because I do my regular work all day long at the editorial office. I correct other people's manuscripts and for that they pay me a salary. But today I'll knock off a review for a journal, they'll hand me over 30 rubles for it, and then we'll buy you a pair of boots and a fur cap. WInter's on its way."

On days like that the mother remained in the kitchen, banging on her typewriter well into the night, and it was no use trying to attract her attention—her gaze distracted, her eyes bloodshot, she was all wired-up and strange. She would warm his supper in silence, issue abrupt commands, and fly off the handle at the least little thing.

"Quick! Undress and into bed! And not a peep out of you! I've got an urgent side job!"

"I wish it'd croak," the boy would mutter. He'd undress slowly, climb under the covers and look out the window.

Outside stood an old tree. It was called a blackthorn. It had very large and sharp thorns growing on it. Kids use them to shoot at pigeons with their slingshots. One time his mother went up to the window, pressed her forehead against the pane, and said to the boy:

"That's a blackthorn tree. It's a very old, old tree. Do you see the thorns? People once wove a crown of such thorns and placed it on the head of a man..."

"What for?" he got scared.

"No one knows. Even now, no one knows."

"Did it hurt?" he asked, full of sympathy for the unknown victim.

"Yes, it did," said his mother simply.

"Did he cry?"

"No."

"I get it," concluded the boy. "He was a Soviet partisan."

His mother stared silently out the window at the old blackthorn.

"And what was his name?" he asked.

She gave a sigh and said distinctly:

"Jesus Christ."

The blackthorn extended its crooked arm with outspread fingers right up to the lattice of the window, just like the beggar in front of the store to whom he and his mother always gave a ten kopeck piece. If one looked closely, it was possible to distinguish a large, gnarled letter "I" formed by the entangled branches. It seemed to march along the window transom.

The boy would lie in bed, look at the letter "I," and invent all sorts of travels for it. True, his stories didn't turn out to be as interesting as the mother's. In the kitchen the typewriter would clatter and chatter away energetically, and then fall silent for a few minutes, at which point he would get up and walk to the kitchen. The mother would be sitting stooped over the typewriter, staring intently at the sheet of paper tucked in it. A lock of hair hung over her forehead.

"Well?" she would ask curtly without looking at the boy.

"I'm thirsty."

"Drink, then back to bed on the double!"

"Are you coming to bed soon?"

"No! I'm busy."

"But why does he ask for money?"

"Who?!" she shrieked irritably.

"The beggar near the store."

"Get to bed! I don't have time for this. Later."

"Can't he earn a living?"

"Will you leave me alone now?!" she cried in an exhausted voice. "I've got to turn in the radio program for tomorrow! Back to bed on the double!"

The boy would shuffle off silently and get into bed. But after a minute or two the chair in the kitchen would be shoved back with a clatter, and his mother would run into his room and toss it out in abrupt, nervous tones:

"He can't earn a living! You get it?! It happens. A person just doesn't have the strength, the strength either to earn a living or to go on living. Maybe he had some terrible misfortune, maybe the war or something else... He took to drink, had a breakdown. He doesn't have the strength..."

"And you do have the strength?" he'd ask anxiously.

"Now there's a nice comparison!" she would cry indignantly and hurry back to the kitchen to rap-tap-type her cursed Work on the Side.

His mother had the strength, she had a great deal of strength. And, in general, the boy thought that they were well-off. In the beginning, right after leaving his father, they went to live with the mother's friend, "Aunt" Tamara. It was nice there, but one day his mother quarrelled with "Uncle" Seriozha about some Stalin or other. At first the boy thought that Stalin was a friend of his mother's who had ticked her off royally. Not so. It seems that she had never laid eyes on him. Then why fight with friends over a stranger! At one point, the mother began telling the boy about Stalin as well, but Stalin went in one ear and out the other—it turned out to be a boring story.

...So the mother gave it some thought, and, weighing the options, she decided "to get into a cooperative."

The boy imagined a grandiose spectacle. There it was, waiting for them on the runway—that cooperative, glittering, narrow and light, like a bird! There they were, he and his mother, in their spacesuits, helmets in hand, striding across the field towards it. And look, the hatch is already open, they wave to the crowd below, strap on their helmets and finally get into the latest model of a supersonic cooperative!

But in reality it wasn't like that at all. The mother sold a lot of useless stuff—the yellow chain that beforehand she had never removed from her neck even at night, the earrings with the sparkling pieces of glass, and a ring. Afterwards she stood at the window in the kitchen and cried all evening because the chain and the earrings and the ring had belonged to her grandmother and had been given to her as keepsakes. The boy never left the mother's side; her desolate sense of loss had transmitted itself to him, and he was sorry for his mother. She was weeping so bitterly over such triflings, and he couldn't understand at all what was happening.

Soon, however, they moved into their new apartment, and the mother became more cheerful. The apartment proved to be luxurious: a room, a kitchen, and a bathroom with a shower. There was also a tiny little hallway in which on the very first day they hung up a mirror that was a gift from Aunt Tamara. The room was empty and cheerful. He could drive his truck wherever he wished, from one wall to the next, and never be bored. At first they slept together on a folding bed. They hugged each other tight and it grew warm and the mother told him a long story before going to sleep—every night a new story! How in the world could she remember so many stories all at once!

Then one day he came home from kindergarten and saw a brand new red ottoman in the room. The mother laughed, pulled him over to the ottoman, threw him on it, and began to squeeze and tickle him.

"Well, what do you think?" she asked proudly. "Isn't it gorgeous?" And she bounced up and down on the springy ottoman.

"Sure is," he agreed, and also bounced for a bit.

"It's bad for a person of your age to sleep on a folding bed," explained the mother. "You'll get stoop-shouldered, like a little old man... I haven't been able to stop thinking about that all week long. So this morning, after I dropped you off at kindergarten, I thought to myself, 'Yeah, the hell with it. I have a pair of hands and a brain that works. I'll pay it off with a little work.' So I went to Aunt Tamara and borrowed some money from her."

"You'll be taking Work on the Side, won't you?" he asked, disappointed and upset.

"Uh huh," answered the mother lightly and began to bounce again on the ottoman and to squeeze the boy...

Aunt Tamara often dropped by to see them. A woman from the black market was always bringing all sorts of things to her at work: one time it was a Japanese pullover, another time a Finnish dress. And Aunt Tamara would drop by for a minute to "try them on." She was terribly upset that the mother had "stripped herself naked" and that she had "absolutely nothing to wear." That, of course, was complete nonsense. How could his mother go to work every day if she really had nothing to wear? In fact, she wore a black sweater that the boy liked a lot and a pair of matching jeans that had turned gray from having been washed so often. She'd simply grown deeply attached to these favorite things, and others didn't appeal to her. Not long ago Aunt Tamara had brought by some earrings—after all, the mother had sold hers—and Aunt Tamara was worried that the little holes in her ear lobes would close up and "it would all be over."

Inset with delicate green stones, the earrings turned out to be lovely. With a smile, the mother put them on, and at once you could see just how pretty she was—her eyes were exactly like the earrings, green and oval.

"You've got to buy them!" exclaimed Aunt Tamara in a determined voice. "They really suit you. They're incredibly beautiful."

"Oh, Marina!" gasped the boy. "They're so beautiful!"

"Beautiful," agreed his mother, removing the earrings. "The payment for the cooperative comes due this week..."

Aunt Tamara was cheerful and determined. She did a great deal to help the boy and his mother carry on with life, inspiring them with confidence that everything would be fine.

"So your married life didn't work out—so what!" she said. "Women whose married life has worked out have worn their shoes down to the heels, racing back and forth at a breakneck pace."

He also loved his father, but was afraid that his mother would notice. In general, when the conversation turned to him, the boy kept quiet, knowing the mother's volatile nature. It was easy to get along with his father, things were peaceful. His father never yelled, and you could always predict how he would react to this or that event. In every way the father was different...

He would probably be extremely surprised to learn that the boy kept his eye on him and compared his world to the world in which he and his mother existed.

The father collected him on Saturday afternoons and took him to his place, the very apartment where, earlier, the three of them had lived together and where everything they had previously shared still remained. There remained the boy's tricycle, his sled and scooter. For a fairly long time he pondered why his father hadn't given back even his trike. But he didn't dare ask. Or, rather, he simply knew what the father would answer. He would smile, give him a kiss, and say:

"I simply wanted for your toys to be here and for you to know that this is your home..."

He had already said something once along those lines.

No, his home was where his mother was. The boy felt that most keenly. Even when they hadn't had any sort of home of their own at all and had been cooped up at Aunt Tamara's and Uncle Seriozha's, his home was still wherever she happened to be—her voice, her scent, her black sweater, her gestures and her outbursts.

The boy would not admit even to himself that he loved to visit the father in part because of the presents. The father gave him fun, interesting presents, and this distinguished him favorably from the mother. One time he gave him a pistol with a full clip of deafening cartridges, and, another time, an iron tank with a revolving gun barrel. The father would do all this with an indulgent smile and without any fuss, and he would never pitch a fit if, suddenly, an hour later, the gun barrel fell off or, for whatever reason, the pistol stopped firing.

Yes, the father gave fun presents... The mother's, on the other hand, were boring. Some boots or other for the winter, or a jacket with a hood, or a suit. And she'd be terribly overjoyed with these presents; she'd make him try them on and parade in front of her across the room, insisting that he turn around a hundred times. He'd get tired, feel bored, be at a loss, and ask:

"Isn't that enough, c'mon!"

"Oh, go on and walk a bit more!" ordered the mother, her eyes glowing with happiness.

"Walk slowly over to the wardrobe and turn around towards me. That's it, now back..."

He'd suffer in that heavy winter jacket, but would obediently stamp about as she demanded—from the wardrobe to the ottoman and back.

For some reason he felt sorry for her at such moments.

Heaven forbid that he should soil that jacket or accidentally rip off some unlucky button! Then all hell would break loose!

"Are you human?!" she would cry in a long-suffering voice. "No, tell me—are you human? No, you're not! Because you don't even care whether I sleep nights or stay up to do my work on the side, just in order to earn money for your jacket!"

The desire to educate him would overtake the mother at the most inappropriate moments. For example: the other day when the older guys—even Borka from the second grade was there—invited him to play with them for the first time and from sheer joy he decided to treat them all to candy. Exultant and overflowing with regal generosity, he dashed home from the courtyard and banged on the door with his feet. The mother opened the door, her hands bathed in soap-suds—she must have been doing the wash.

"Marina, give us all candy!" he demanded, breathing loudly.

"Look at what a mess you are!" she screamed with a tormented look on her face. One of her brows quirked. "You only just left! Look at your shirt! How much washing can I do?! Are you human? No, you're not! I don't have any more strength, get it? No more, you get me or not?!"

"I get it, I get it," he uttered hastily, his brow quirked in the same long-suffering fashion. "Give us the candy!"

Yes, the father had one fundamental virtue—he never screamed...

The boy could not understand the mother's passion for acquiring things, especially since he considered the mother to be by nature generous and in this respect even irrational.

Once she brought home two children. It was a rainy Sunday morning, the mother had left early for the store, while the boy, still in bed, lay listening through the haze of morning drowsiness to the rain thrashing in a frenzy against the window sill. His left ear, pressed against the pillow, didn't hear a thing; therefore it was his right ear that took in the incoherent squabbling between the rain and the sill. It got tired, and the boy slid down under the blankets and covered his right ear with the palm of his hand. The steady pounding of the rain against the window sill turned into a drowsy muttering, and there ensued a blissful calm. And in the midst of that calm the boy heard the hall door open and the mother say abruptly:

"Come in, come in!"

The boy threw off the covers and quickly sat up in bed. The rain unleashed its deafening din.

"It's really coming down!" said the mother from the hall. "Go on into the room, children."

And then the boy saw them both. They were unbelievably wet, as if someone had deliberately soaked them for a long time in a tub of water. The elder, a boy, was his own age, about six or seven, and the girl, just a tot, was barely three. Her black eyes, like those of a young jackdaw, stared about, as she stood licking off her lips the drops of rain running down her face from the tangled curls that were plastered to her forehead. Both of them were wearing galoshes on their bare feet.

The boy sat on the bed in his warm pajamas and looked silently at the strangers.

"H-hi," the older of the two managed to squeeze out shyly.

The mother intercepted the boy's bewildered look and explained in a quick patter.

"These are the milkwoman's children... She's delivering milk to the apartments... and they, there they were, standing in the downpour... Watching out for the milkcans, the little idiots... Like wet jackdaws... No proper clothes, no proper shoes... Who needs those cans anyway. Damn that woman!"

"Off with those clothes!" she ordered, and flung open the doors to the wardrobe. She snatched the boy's clothes from the shelves—his tights, shirts, and sweater—and threw them on the ottoman. Then, after a moment's thought, she grabbed last year's waterproof jacket from the rack.

"Here you are," she said. From the bathroom she brought a towel and began drying off the little girl with it. Like a tiny dummy, the tot stood there listlessly, continuing to lick off her lips the raindrops streaming down her face. Her hands and feet were red, rough and covered with goose bumps.

"H-hi..." her brother mumbled once again, barely audible. Apparently, it was the only Russian word he knew.

At the height of this scene with the change of clothing, Granny Shura, a neighbor, appeared. Unlike the boy, she immediately caught on to what was happening, and for a moment she stood there, watching the mother pull the tights onto the girl's still damp legs. Granny Shura was no outsider here; she was very fond of the boy and the mother, and she took their troubles to heart, helping them in numerous ways and taking an active interest in all their affairs. She held her peace about the sweater, but when the mother began to tie up a bundle of the boy's still perfectly decent clothing, including the jacket, Granny Shura couldn't restrain herself.

"What d'you think you're doing, huh?!" she demanded severely. "You want to leave your son barefoot and naked?"

"I'll earn enough to take care of him!" snapped back the mother.

"You fool! That milkwoman's loaded, she's got thousands! Don't be looking at their galoshes. They run around barefoot in their yard all winter, they're used to it."

"All right, Granny Shura," the mother said curtly. "For Christ's sake, what thousands can she have?"

"And how long do you have to slave away to afford those rags, huh? Not long? All night that typewriter clatters away on the other side of my wall. Not long, alright! Go, go ahead, go ahead and take the last clothes right off your child's back!"

"That's enough, Granny Shura!" the mother said forcefully, but calmly.

"Go ahead, go on, you crazy thing... you're not answerable..." and Granny Shura turned and went off to her own room—to spare her nerves.

And the mother said softly to the boy:

"If you don't mind, give them one of your toys."

The boy did mind, but he realized that this was one of those times when he couldn't disobey. Otherwise something horrible and irreparable would transpire between them. At such moments he felt especially the force of her will, felt that it was the magnet and he was the filing.

He shuffled off to the kitchen and from it dragged a cardboard box full of his toys. Without looking at anyone, he said:

"Here... take whatever you want..."

But even then his mother showed him no mercy.

"You choose. Something interesting. That car over there!"

This was deliberate torture—he sensed as much, sensed it with all his heart; he felt the strain of resistance in the back of his neck and in his hands, which stubbornly had no desire to part with his favorite toy. His father had given him the car as a present only recently, and the boy had not yet had the chance to savor fully its green lacquer finish, its elastic tires and its flashing headlights. The car ran backwards and forwards; it would turn in any direction the second he pressed the right button on the control panel. It was a super car!

"Well?" the mother said.

Without saying a word, the boy thrust the automobile at the urchin whom he didn't know. The interloper obediently pressed it to his chest with both hands and once again whispered:

"H-hi..."

"Not 'hello,' but 'thank you!'" the boy corrected him with quiet animosity. He was choking with hurt, jealousy and anger, but he wasn't about to break out crying in front of these bumps on a log.

When the mother left to see the children out, he plunged under the covers and began to weep softly. In the whole wide world there wasn't a single soul who understood him; there was only coercion and indifference around him. She's downstairs right now, most likely hugging those strange children, who clearly don't even know how to say thank you properly. She took care of them alright, but she couldn't care less about her own son—let him lie all alone somewhere, who cares where...

The mother entered the room and lay down next to him. Stroking the back of his quivering head, she said:

"We'll go today and buy that very same car."

At that, he was shaken by sobs. A frenzy of pleasurable pity for himself—destitute, lonely—choked him, and he managed to stammer out in between hiccups:

"Th-they... w-won't... h-have a-any m-more l-like th-that."

"They will," responded his mother tranquilly. "We'll buy all the cars in the store, but I'm going to see to it that you grow into a real human being. And if you don't, I'll kill you with my own hands!"

They hugged each other and lay like that for a long long time until they fell asleep without intending to, and they didn't wake up till noon...

For about three weeks now he had been going to school, to the first grade. He and the mother both had been apprehensive about this change in their lives, but, as it turned out, it wasn't too bad; they could live with it. Back at the beginning of June, they'd really raided the stores and bought up all sorts of things: a strap-on satchel, a uniform for school, and three blue shirts to match his uniform. And then bunches of other stuff to boot: notebooks, a pencil-case, rulers, counting blocks—in a word, the whole kit and caboodle. His mother helped him put on the satchel right in the store, and he sported it all the way home across the whole city. Three times he gave up his seat in the bus. He didn't remember to whom; schoolboys always give up their seats.

As they were walking up the stairs to their apartment, Granny Shura opened the door and stopped dead in her tracks. She put on an idiotic, dumbfounded face, as if a general had just walked through the entrance:

"Wow, who's the pupil?!" she gasped.

"It's me, I'm the pupil!" he said, glowing with happiness.

Then Granny Shura reached out and pulled him towards her by his cheeks and kissed him resoundingly, first on one cheek and then the other, and then on the first again, just as if he had returned from a long trip.

During the first few days at school he felt very isolated. The other children felt at home there right away and they knew all the ropes—where the snackbar was and the assembly hall and the bathroom. But somehow he didn't have a clue about anything; yet, he didn't know how to go about asking anyone else, and on the first day he almost wet his pants. Good thing his mother showed up early. In a doleful whisper he explained his predicament to her, and like a couple of lunatics they dashed out of school and found a place around the corner where there were some private garages.

In the snackbar you had to push and shove. He tried it once, but no dice: he got shoved instead, and his coin flew out of his hand, and some bully from the third grade quickly pounced on it and exclaimed loudly, "Yea! I found me twenty kopecks." The boy didn't make a sound, but walked away and cried for the rest of the recess.

After classes began the "extension," extra-curricular activities for those students, like the boy, whose parents worked. The teacher led them in line to the cafeteria, then in line for a nap, then in line to the assembly hall, where they walked single file in a circle to Shainsky's music. This was called "Rhythmics." The music teacher would stand in the middle of the circle and call out:

"Stamp now! Left foot three times! Right foot three times! Left: one-two-three! Right: one-two-three! Don't move out of the circle!"

> Blue car's a running—shaking away!
> Fast train's picking up lots of steam...

Crocodile Ghena sang in a gentle, cultured voice.

> Ah, why must it come to an end—this day!
> If only the day into a year would stream!

No, the boy had no desire for the day to stream into an entire year. He wished his mother would come pick him up even sooner. Obediently, he would stamp with his right, stamp with his left foot, all the while straining his neck towards the door of the assembly hall.

When at last the mother appeared in the doorway, his stomach would flutter, and the world grew rich with color before his eyes like a glistening, golden fish that surfaces from the deep. He'd continue to mark time to the music, but suddenly in completely different fashion because the end of it all was now in sight, and he wanted to show off in front of his mother as if to say, look at how he's dancing along with everyone else and not a bit worse than anybody. The mother would only nod to him discreetly. She didn't like public displays of moon-eyed affection.

He happened to get a good teacher, Tatiana Vladimirovna, an affectionate young woman whom everyone liked right away. The girls swarmed at her side, arguing who would walk on the right today, who on the left.

The boy also liked the teacher, although she appeared one-dimensional to him, like the number 5, as flat and smooth as a coin. His mother, on the other hand, was multi-dimensional: both round and with angles, rough and smooth, soft and loud—in his mother there were so many layers of all kinds of things.

He believed that he was the worst student in the class. He didn't make do well at all with those lines in his exercise book, nor with those little hooks and crooks that formed the letters. Everything he wrote went in all directions. As regards his studies, the mother reacted with her characteristic inconsistency. When they'd be walking home after school and he'd complain to her about those disobedient hooks and crooks, she'd retort, "Ah, who cares! That's nonsense! You'll get the hang of it." But in the evening when they'd sit down to do his lessons, and he'd open the ill-fated Writing Samples and she pulled up a chair beside him to help, she'd gradually get more and more worked up until she began screaming so loudly that his ears rang.

"Stop!! Where are you going with that line!! I told you already—more to the left! Don't go beyond the margin. Where in the devil are you going with that curl in the letter 'b'? I'll take the belt to you!"

The evenings were stormy. What patience his mother could muster didn't last long. He waited out these cursed sessions with the courage of a stoic, because, after finishing with his lessons, he still had around two hours left before bedtime in which life was worth living.

The moment the dreary Book of ABC'S was slammed shut, the boy's face, along with his mother's, would assume the same look of tired contentment. The heavy daily burden had reached its destination and could be cast off now with relief.

"Do you have anything to do now?" the boy would ask.

"Wash the dishes and make some borscht," the mother would reply in a tired voice.

"OK, then, I'll dry, and you'll tell me some story."

Like a horse bending its neck to the yoke, the mother would put on her apron with reluctance and, at the same time, resignation.

"Well, what story should I tell you?"

"The one about Granny Shura," he asked.

"For the third time?" his mother pointed out without surprise. She respected his passion for hearing over and over again the stories that caught his fancy. After all, she also read and reread her favorite books.

"Well, let's see. When the war started... Pass it to me, please." He rushed to the table and silently passed her the knife—hoping that she wouldn't get distracted again... "When the war started, Granny Shura and her husband lived on the border in a little town called Chernaya Ves, not far from Belostok. Her husband was an officer in the frontier guards and on the very first day of the war, he was killed. So at the age of 21, Granny Shura was left to fend for herself and two-year-old Valya..."

"That's Aunt Valya," the boy would explain to himself under his breath.

"So, as a refugee, she marched across the whole Western front with our army. How many times along the way were they overtaken by bomb attacks! One day some Messerschmitts came swooping down and forced them into a little wood by the roadside. Deafened by the explosions, little Valya grew terrified, tore her hand out of her mother's grasp, and took off running... Granny Shura went after her. Some soldier shouted at them at the top of his voice and pushed the two to the ground; then he hit the dirt himself, right next to them. Shells were exploding all around them, chunks of earth flying about. When it subsided a little, Granny Shura saw the soldier pick himself up, clasping his stomach with both hands. His insides were spilling out of his belly. He stood staring at Granny Shura with insane eyes, holding in his guts with both hands... And then another time after a bomb attack, a soldier beckoned and asked her to bandage him up. Granny Shura takes a look and sees that his whole back is horribly lacerated. He was just a young fellow, very handsome and well-mannered. 'I'm asking you,' he says, 'get a grip on yourself and make me a bandage...' Granny Shura pulled off her slip, tore it into strips, and made him a bandage."

"Did he survive?" the boy would ask hopefully for the umpteenth time, and the mother would answer for the umpteenth time:

"Who knows... They took him off to the hospital, but after that, who knows..."

The boy was afraid to ask about the soldier with his insides spilling out: he knew that the answer would be horrible.

"She saw so much grief that her heart grew heavy, like a stone. She thought nothing could surprise her any more. One day they were driving along the road in their trucks. The Germans had just finished their bomb attack and had flown off. Along the roadside there were dead refugees as far as the eye could see, and there was no one to bury them.

"Then beside the road Granny Shura sees a dead mother lying in the grass, and next to her a child about nine or ten months old. He'd found his mother's breast and was trying to nurse, but there wasn't any milk. So he kept screaming, trying to wake up his mother. But she just lay there, looking into the sky.

"Granny Shura couldn't control herself. She jumped down from the truck, snatched up the baby, and rushed back to the vehicle..."

"That was Uncle Vitaly, wasn't it?"

"That's right, Uncle Vitaly... Hey, you promised to dry the dishes and you aren't drying them! Do you think that's fair?"

Without a word, the boy grabbed the towel and frantically began drying a cup—anything to make her go on with the story.

"...You see, Granny Shura was making her way to her husband's parents, to her in-laws. And when she finally got there, dressed in rags, hungry, with two children, she met with a hostile reception. They said they had no idea who'd fathered the second child, they didn't want to know her, they had nothing to eat themselves and now she'd showed up out of the clear blue.

"So there Granny Shura was, left all on her own in a strange city with no place to go and no shoes and no clothes and two children screaming for food. Shura climbed to the steep bank of the Dnieper and looked down. Her heart stopped beating. She pressed the children close to her and thought. 'We're going to die of hunger anyway! All I need to do is close my eyes and jump down there with them!' But little Vitaly, as if sensing that something was amiss, poked her in the breast with his tiny hands and began to whine: 'Mama... no na na... no na na...'"

"So, she didn't jump?" the boy asked, wide-eyed and full of hope.

"What a dope! Of course she didn't! Use your head: do you think Valya and Vitaly would still be alive today, huh? Do you think Vitaly would keep on bringing you all those stones from his expeditions?"

"You're right," he agreed, and, just to be absolutely sure, he repeated to himself under his breath: "She didn't jump, she didn't..."

"Anyway, she soon settled into a job at a factory; she began receiving her food ration and people she didn't even know gave her shelter. Only, she was hit by a very bad attack of typhus. They took her away to the hospital... Everyone thought she was going to die. When the crisis came, she sat up delirious in bed and undid her braids—back then she had really thick, black hair—and began to sing a song she'd never heard before in her whole life:

> Open the window, open it wide,
> I soon shall be sleeping forever!
> One final time in the freedom outside,
> Allow me to love and to suffer...

She kept tossing in delirium, begging them not to cut her hair—she was afraid she'd look ugly lying in her coffin. Absurd to even think about it. Some hope! They cut it anyway. Later, her hair grew back, but it was never quite as thick as before."

The mother took off her apron. With a clean rag she wiped dry the kitchen table and placed her typewriter on it. That meant that it was now time for the boy to sleep and for her to work...

The boy lay under his warm quilt cover. Outside, the hooked branches of the blackthorn, an accursed tree, loomed ominously. The interweaving branches formed the letter "I" in an endless march; there was no end to its journey... And in a powerful voice the unknown song: Open the window, open it wide, I soon shall be sleeping forever. They showed her no pity, and cut her hair. What does a little hair matter when all over the country insides are spilling out... There on the other side of the wall, Mother's tapping, tapping... Will that many-headed, big-tailed, long-clawed Work on the Side ever end? Open the window, open it wide... Open the window...

On Saturday afternoons around three the father would come by to pick him up. The boy waited for him with secret impatience. The father was a holiday. The father meant the park, swings, bumper cars, small cups of ice cream, as much chewing gum as his heart desired, the merry-go-round, and no scenes of any kind. But he had to hide this joyful anticipation from the mother, just as he did everything else concerning his relationship with the father. Ah, but here the boy was the subtlest of diplomats.

"How 'bout if I get dressed and meet him in the yard?" he would suggest to the mother in an offhand, bored tone. In front of her he never pronounced the father's name or called him "Dad."

"You've got plenty of time," she would retort sullenly, ironing his shirt. And he'd keep quiet, afraid of irritating her. Meeting the father in the yard was incomparably more pleasant than in front of the mother. For a start, it simply didn't pay to have the two of them meet unnecessarily; only unpleasantness came of it. In general the mother was dangerous during such encounters, and even the father, despite his self-control, would suddenly fly off the handle when they were trying to clarify some stupid questions or other. For example, the last time the boy hadn't managed to make it to the yard by the appointed time and the father rang at the door, a disjointed, irritable discussion sprang up between the two of them about the boy's education. One word led to another—the mother tensed, filled with leaden hatred; with quiet enmity, the father gritted through clenched teeth:

"What do you know about education? Have you even read Dr. Spock?"

"No! But I've read a whole lot you haven't—Chekhov and Tolstoy."

Incomprehensible words and an incomprehensible discussion! Two ruthless, hostile worlds with him in the middle—anguished and powerless...

Yes, it was better to meet the father in the yard. Then the meeting would be completely different. He could run towards the father full steam ahead, right into his big, outstretched arms, and fly upward to the father's shoulders and press his cheek against his lips. He never allowed himself to behave this way in front of the mother, for he knew that it would hurt her feelings. All in all, it was a complicated day, Saturday. He had to set things up, to organize everything in such a way so as not to hurt her or offend him. And in the midst of all these intricate relations, he had to manage to seize at least a little fun for himself.

And the fun began as soon as they made it around the corner of the building, right when he and the father turned off for the subway. The fun began with the father's pockets. The boy had been waiting for this minute, and he kept throwing conspiratorial glances at the father. And the father returned his look.

"Well, have a look at what there is hiding in my pocket!" at long last the father would say, slyly screwing up his eyes.

The boy would dip his hand into the father's enormous pocket and with ecstasy would fish out of it: a whistle, chewing gum, an inflatable balloon, and three pieces of candy.

"Hurray!"

It would have been possible to find all these things at home too, if he rummaged around in his cardboard box of toys—but, no, nothing was exactly the same, nothing was quite right. And the carousel of Saturday pleasures would start spinning round. Everything retreated into the background: his home, mother, lessons for Monday, Granny Shura, his friends from the yard... The green carriage with big red polkadots whirled around on top of a circular wooden platform; the father held him tightly by his shoulders, and gaiety wound around them like a variegated ribbon.

They'd make it back to the father's apartment in the evening; the father would make up a bed for the boy on the sofa and undress him, heavy and sleepy as he was. And there, in the soft pillow, the festive, exhilarating Saturday, green with red polka-dots, would sink into oblivion.

Starting Sunday morning, he would already begin to miss his mother. He'd sit at the table drawing and coloring-in with crayons the pictures in a coloring book, but he'd be wondering what his mother was doing at that moment. Maybe she was tapping away at the typewriter, maybe doing the wash, maybe she had gone to the store and met Borka along the way—he was always hanging about on Sundays—and was talking with him? The boy froze for an instant at the thought, feeling jealousy suddenly grip his heart and then recede—but the hurt remained and gnawed at him. What if she started telling Borka some story or other, just the way she did him? About pirates or the baby mammoth. Maybe she even stroked Borka on the head? And here he was, sitting and coloring in this stupid little book?! And what if one of her friends had stopped by, and they were drinking tea and chattering, while he was sitting here without knowing anything?!

"Well, what-a-ya think? Time to get ready?" he'd say in the same off-hand, bored tone. "Or else it'll get dark."

"What do you mean, son?" the father would ask, surprised. "Where are you itching to be off to? It's only after eleven. We see each other so rarely. Now, how can I entertain you? How 'bout I tell you a story? The one about the bear and the hare?"

To keep from offending the father, the boy patiently listened through the age-old tale of the bear and the hare. Afterwards, they played with the train set, watched television, and had lunch—the father would fry up some eggs; and finally, they would begin getting ready to go.

The boy lay on the sofa, his chin propped up on his fists, and watched the father shave in front of the large mirror. He shaved thoroughly and meticulously, the way he did everything. From inside his mouth he'd prop up his cheek with his tongue, stretch out his neck, and draw aside the skin at his temples.

In general, the boy liked the father a lot. He was tall and handsome. He never slouched, and he walked with light, long strides.

"When I grow up, I'll start shaving too," said the boy pensively.

"Mm, hmm..." the father mumbled as he slid the razor under his nose.

"In general, when I grow up, I'll... I'll grow ree-al tall," the boy added confidently, trying to convince himself.

"No doubt about it," the father confirmed. "You'll be ree-al tall. There are no shrimps in our family."

"In our family!" The boy would have given a lot to know once and for all just exactly where it could be found—"our family." Whenever he complained to the mother about the problems he had with his school work, she'd brush it aside: "You'll get the hang of it! There are no dummies in our family." He was curious to know exactly where, in what part of the world, this safe and happy "family" was. It seemed as if his mother and father were not unlike members of the same family, and yet they hadn't got close together; it just hadn't worked out for them.

The father finished knotting his beautiful tie, put on his jacket, and began to look for something on his desk.

"Wow!" he said, bending over the boy's drawing. "You've learned to draw splendidly! What've you got there?"

"It's war," the boy explained.

"Let's see now, those are tanks and airplanes. But what are all those blotches?"

"Bombs dropping."

"Great job... But how come you didn't put in the sun, say—right here in the corner?"

"There isn't any sun during a war," the boy replied.

The father grinned wryly and ruffled his hair:

"You've turned into a philosopher on me... Prematurely..."

Prematurely! There was no pleasing them. The mother kept saying, "Think, think about everything!" He'd asked bewilderedly, "What am I supposed to think about?" "About everything!" she'd insist obstinately. "About everything you see!" And the father had been telling him the same story about the bear and the hare for over two years now...

As they were heading down the steps, the father suddenly slapped the pockets of his overcoat and said:

"Dammit, I forgot my cigarettes! Hey, son, they're in the top drawer of the desk. Be a sport and run get them, O.K.? Here's the key."

The boy darted up the stairs, two steps at a time, breathing heavily, unlocked the door, and ran to the desk. The pack of cigarettes was in the top drawer, lying on top of someone's photograph. The boy grabbed the cigarettes and suddenly saw that it was a picture of his mother. She looked cheerful, with long hair. On the back was written in his father's hand, "Marisha..." In the first flash of recognition, he wanted to take the photo and explain to his father—I took the shot in which Marina looks cheerful, since you no longer need her—but then he thought for a moment, put the photo gently back in place and slid the drawer shut...

"Did you close the door?" the father asked.

"Yes," said the boy blankly.

Exiting the metro, they didn't follow their usual route, but took a detour past the newsstand. For a long time the father had been promising to buy him some badges with dogs. He bought him three badges with various breeds of dogs, and the boy immediately pinned them all on in a row along his jacket. Then, as he looked up, he recognized an old acquaintance near the store—the beggar. He was standing there, as usual, leaning on a stick with one hand and stretching out his cap with the other. As always, he was staring apathetically at the ground. Whenever anyone threw him a coin, he tossed his head like a horse: "Good health to you!" and then he fixed his gaze on the ground once again... The boy grew excited.

"Dad, give me a coin!"

"What for?" his father asked.

"I'll give it to the beggar!"

"Don't be crazy—giving money to drunks!"

"But me and Marina always give him something," said the boy, instantly regretting having said it. He scowled immediately, and his ears turned red. Mother was mother, a whole different world, and he had no business mixing her in the conversation.

"God, that's her to a tee, alright..." the father muttered through his teeth. The boy thought that his mother was probably already sitting on the bench in the yard, waiting for him. She always came out to meet him, most likely worried about how he was and wondering what he was up to... She just couldn't stay in the apartment.

"Let's say good-bye here," he said to the father.

"Why? I'll walk you to the door."

Sure enough, there was the mother sitting on the bench, looking in the direction from which they came. She rose and remained standing where she was.

"Well, let me give you a kiss," said the father. "Take care!"

The boy did not reach out to him in order not to hurt the mother; he merely turned his cheek toward him. The father said:

"Next week, I'll get tickets to the circus. Get going now."

The boy went, trying not to quicken his steps in order not to hurt the father. He even turned and waved to him. The father stood there, following him with his eyes. The mother was also staring at the boy, not at his face, but a little higher, at the tuft of hair protruding from beneath his cap. When at last he reached her, she placed her hands on his shoulders without saying a word, and they headed for the entrance to their building.

She kept silent in the hallway, helping him unwind his scarf with a stony countenance; then she headed for the kitchen.

"What happened?" the boy yelled, following her with his eyes.

"I was at the hairdresser's..." the mother replied quietly from the kitchen. "The hairdresser said half my hair's turned gray. And I realized then and there that my life's over, and I bought myself a Finnish dress."

"Where did you buy it?" asked the boy, wanting her to be more precise, for her muddled manner of expressing herself irritated him. "Not at the hairdresser's?"

"No, at the Central Department Store."

"Oh!..." he said. "Show me. Where is it?"

"Right here, I'm wearing it!"

"Oh!... It's nice... Beautiful."

He embraced her around the waist from behind and pressed his face against her back. He was growing quickly, and this year he already reached her shoulder blades.

"Don't worry, Marina," he said into the green silky fabric. "When I start shaving, I'll marry you."

"Thanks a lot!" she said. "But for the time being, how about eating a little faster, please, and off to bed."

"Work on the Side again?!"

...In his room he undressed slowly, pulling his shirt off over his head and waving its long empty sleeves in the air. He kept glancing sideways at the wall, where the silent shadow of the shirt fluttered furiously like someone possessed. With a sigh, he sat down on the bed. He so badly wanted to tell his mother about his merry-go-round Saturday—and how on the bumper car grounds they kept trying to overtake that blue car with the red-haired boy and the man with a mustache, and how finally they crashed into it with a bang and they all laughed together for a long time. But it was impossible, simply impossible...

He shuffled into the kitchen and sat down on the stool beside the mother.

"What is it?" she asked, correcting something with a pen on the typewritten sheet.

"Do you know just what a bum Sasha Anikeev is?" the boy asked indignantly.

"Umm..."

"He uses awful words. For example, 'bitch.' Now that's really an awful word."

"It's an ordinary word," his mother muttered, "if you use it appropriately."

"But he doesn't! You don't believe me, but he uses real four-letter-words!"

"For crying out loud!" the mother heaved, and began putting the next clean sheet of paper into the typewriter. "Well, any other news?"

"Every recess he makes fun of me and says I've flipped over Oksanka Tishshenko."

"Well, have you?"

"Yes," the boy admitted.

"Then smack him one on the face!" his mother advised.

"I can't, not on the face," he replied.

"Why not?"

"Because the face has eyes, and they look at you..."

"Aha... Then you deal with it the best you can... Is that it?"

"No..." he hesitated... "You know, Sasha says that I'm a Jew," the boy blurted out at last, without taking his eyes off his mother.

"Well, so what?"

"Marina, I don't want to be a Jew...," he admitted.

"Then who do you want to be?" she inquired sullenly.

"I want to be Rinat Xhizmatullin. We share the same desk. He's a great guy."

"I tell you what," his mother said sullenly, "I'll explain all this to you, only tomorrow—got it?"

"Why tomorrow?"

"It's a long talk and it uses up a great deal of strength. Got it? And now, off to bed on the double!"

He sat quietly for a little while longer and listened to the clatter of the typewriter, picking at the hole in his tights with his finger.

"Marina, spend me time."

"Spend some time with me," the mother corrected him mechanically, not looking up from the typewriter.

"Spend some time with me," he repeated obediently.

"Leave me alone," she said in the exact same tone. She suddenly lifted her eyes to look at him, put aside the sheet of paper and said quietly: "Do you want us to go to the beach this summer?"

"You bet!" He perked up.

"For that I have to pound away at the typewriter. I'll earn some money, and in the summer we'll take the train and head for the beach."

"And we'll take our straw hats?" he asked joyfully.

"We'll take them."

"And you'll lie on the beach, and I'll dribble sand on your back in a thin trickle."

"You will..."

"And then I'll sit on your hot back and we'll swim a long-long way?"

"A long-long way," the mother said and turned to the window. The boy realized that she was crying and went into his room so as not to disturb her.

As he dropped off to sleep, he entered the yard again with the father. The mother was there, waiting to meet him, and he walked away from the father towards the mother, as if swimming from one shore to the other. It was difficult, like swimming against the current. The boy felt the father looking at him from behind and the mother looking at the tuft of hair protruding from beneath his cap. What were the two of them thinking about...?

Outside, the darkness had thickened, and it was impossible to see the blackthorn, impossible to see how the independent and courageous letter "I" moved steadily into the distant unknown.

Translated by Brittain Smith

From *Dvoinaia familiia. Povesti. Rasskazy,* Moscow, 1990

Notes

1. In an earlier version published in the 1980s the story shows evidence of censorship. Rubina's original text was restored, however, when the story appeared in her collection *A Double-Barreled Name (Dvoinaia familiia)* in 1990. The differences consist primarily of omissions on puritanical grounds (e.g., the careful elimination of the lines dealing with the boy's uncontrollable submission to the "call of nature" and urinating by some local garages) or ethnic ones (e.g., the boy's comments about his being Jewish). Political reasons motivate the substitution, e.g., of Dostoevsky for Stalin: the section "the mother began telling the boy about Stalin as well, but Stalin went in one ear and out the other" was defanged to an argument his mother had with a friend over Dostoevsky, for we all know that Stalin cannot come in and out of ears or be the protagonist of a boring story. In short, the sanitized version depoliticizes the text and brings it into line with sham decorum or "propriety."

Uncle Khlor and Koriakin

Galina Shcherbakova

If anyone had told Frolov what was going to happen to him, he wouldn't have believed it. Although, of course, you have to assume that a man who decides to marry late in life will run into trouble. After all, he'd lived alone until he was forty and, by the way, lived well. He worked as a newspaper photographer, and the fees—two rubles, sometimes three or even a four-note—piled up. He managed to build a one-room cooperative and pay it off; he bought a sofa and a desk for the apartment, shelves for the kitchen, and also a table with stools. What else does a man need? He made a lucky buy from some soldiers of a good short coat—sheepskin at that. He had a suit and shoes for work and evenings out. A man who doesn't drink has it made, after all; he can arrange his life comfortably for later years. A rarity among photographers, Frolov didn't drink. And he wasn't married and didn't want to be. He was scared. That is, he had been scared off at a young age and was very timid with women. Evidently this stemmed at least partially from the nature of Frolov's work. After all, he saw all sorts of women wearing all sorts of things, and when he looked at them through the lens of his camera, he understood all about them once and forever. What her character was like and how she scratched the back of her head in the morning. Which words she would say and which she kept to herself. Frolov understood a lot. Then women began "appearing" in his bathroom, surfacing as if from the depths of the sea. One minute there was nothing, and suddenly from somewhere an eye appeared. The eye would be so explicit that you could read everything in it and this made Frolov give a minus to the entire female sex and place it outside the parentheses of his life.

Late in life, however, in his forty-fourth year, when a paunch had rounded out the sheepskin coat and a bald spot shone under his rabbitskin cap with flaps, marriage took Frolov by surprise. It happened to him so quickly, so instantly, that before he had a chance to think twice about it a woman was sleeping next to him on his couch, kicking and pulling the blanket off him.

It was all done quite officially. They filed at the registry office and waited three months, but the time passed very fast.

Of course, he had never photographed Valia. He found her, so to speak, at work. The newspaper and the organizations for "Livestock Fattening" and "Office for Combatting Wood Beetles" shared a building. And they shared a toilet. First came the men's and then the women's. The men smoked in the toilet, and the women walked past them. An awkward layout, but what could you do? If you wanted to smoke, you had no choice—either go there or go without.

Frolov noticed that the woman from the beetle office would approach the toilet and, if smokers were standing there, she went farther, pretending she had business in "Livestock Fattening." But she didn't, that was clear. She was just embarrassed. Frolov liked that. He gave that quality a plus, because the other women from the three organizations all rated a minus in that respect.

The holiday orders were coming in. The organizations cooperated in the business.

There weren't enough tangerines to go around, and the women clashed so fiercely that you'd think it was wartime, potatoes and the last bread ration. But not her. She went without tangerines. Just like that, calmly, without yelling. He liked that, too.

And then the electricity in their building was shut off. Well, it became like a real circus and bathhouse, as the general superintendent for the whole building put it. Yelps and squeaks. Candles of some kind, shadows on the walls. Frolov was used to semi-darkness, however—it was in the nature of his work; he walked around calmly and saw everything. For some reason the women from the three organizations began darting out of their rooms and running into the men. The game of tag made Frolov really sick to his stomach. And suddenly he saw Valia creeping along quietly, clinging to the wall to avoid brushing against anyone. That's how she left, in silence, only slamming the door at the main entrance. And it occurred to Frolov that the rest of the women could have gone, too; they'd been told in plain Russian that the electricity wouldn't be turned on. It was as if they'd just been waiting for it—the darkness—so they could cut loose. And they weren't young women, almost all of them were over thirty. Many had children. In short, Frolov got a view of Valentina as a positive person. No more than that. Of all the women working in the building she's the only one without a hardened conscience, he would say.

Valentina was not photogenic. And he liked that, too. Those photogenic women... they were probably the root of all evil.

Then another agreeable detail emerged. Valia lived in the suburbs and came to work by electric train, while Frolov just had to walk across the street to work. Now every time he crossed the street he thought about the hardships she went through, running in the morning to make the train, late and panting from the run, gasping for breath afterward in the car, and hoping somebody would give her a seat...

Frol had a bit of the partisan in him, evidently from his father, who had fought in Belorussia; nobody had any idea that he was making his quiet inquiries. But one day he dropped in on the "beetles," pretending he needed matches, and found out that Valentina had a child, a daughter six years old. She was called Olia. There was no husband as such. Well, what of it? Frolov didn't think much of his own sex, either. He knew that they had become awfully spoiled recently. Both with their drunken binges and with those photogenic women. Men had started permitting themselves a lot of unmanly things: they could cheat and tell lies and get mixed up in squabbles. Modern man had become more petty in caliber. So that even without knowing the circumstances of Valentina's case, Frolov nobly took her side. He assumed that she might have gotten mixed up with a worthless man.

One day they left the building together. It wasn't completely by accident, of course. Frolov had timed Valentina's departure down to the minute. But the handle of Valentina's bag did break by accident that day. Frolov hadn't cut it. The woman started moaning about what she should do. She could leave everything behind, but she'd managed to get some beef liver at the official price, and blood would start to leak out if it wasn't refrigerated overnight. So Frolov said to Valentina, "Come on over to my place. I live across the street. I'll give you my satchel, you can transfer everything, and I'll repair the strap on the handle for you."

"How nice it is here," said Valentina at his place, but with no tone of appropriation. Other women who had "appeared" in Frolov's apartment automatically paced out the kitchen and mentally rearranged the furniture. It was so obvious right away that Frolov made an immediate effort to see those women off on the trolleybus or tram. This one was fine. "It's nice," and that was all. She was happy for Frolov. And she refused his offer of tea—also a plus. In Frolov's opinion a real woman should refuse everything his fellow men offered at least three times. Only on the fourth could she show a little weakness.

Valentina transferred everything to Frolov's bag right there in the hall, and he went along to see her off, because the bag was a healthy load.

Frolov had no intention of getting on the electric train, but he did. And that unexpected bravado (without a ticket!) made him see the situation in a new light. He realized that his intentions were serious.

She continued to startle him up by behaving just the way a woman with high marks for quality should.

"Come on in," she said. "I'll unload everything and give you back your bag."

They went in. An ugly little wooden house with a tilted antenna; her mother, a quiet old woman. "Sit down, please." They stuck a sheet of newspaper under his feet so he wouldn't leave tracks. Olia was a pale, calm little girl.

"Say hello, Olia, this is Uncle Frol."

To tell the truth, everybody in the newspaper office called Frolov "Frol." And over the years he'd gotten used to it. Frol was fine. But now he was just a bit, just slightly aggrieved that she didn't know his name. On the other hand, it was another plus that she hadn't investigated and found out who and what he was. But she should have noticed his byline. Photo by A. Frolov. But maybe she didn't read the newspapers. Why should she? Frolov had long been convinced that newspapers were games played by reporters and the editorial staff. Ordinary people, with their radios and TV sets, had no need for newspapers. And besides, Frolov had noticed that people learned everything they needed to know on their way to work. Who was fired and who was appointed and who was caught stealing and who had turned religious. Therefore, the fact that Valentina didn't read their newspaper was no crime in Frolov's eyes.

Anyway, they handed him his bag—and that meant he should be on his way.

But then Valentina looked up the train schedule—a wise move!—and exclaimed in dismay. It turned out that in those days they were working evenings on the line, and the next train wasn't due for two hours.

They took his coat and sat him down to eat. For supper there were boiled potatoes with homemade sauerkraut and puree of canned fruit from the store. They sliced some salami, too, but Frolov was already so tired of that salami, which was made of bones ground to atoms and colored red, and the potatoes were so perfectly fried and seasoned with garlic that they put the salami back untouched in the Sever-brand refrigerator, and Frolov thought: the family lives more than modestly...

Afterward they talked about all sorts of thing. The women reacted with great sympathy when Frolov told them he had built his own apartment, but again there was no hint at appropriation.

Frolov heard contentment in their pronouncements about their own life. Everything, they said, is just fine. The house will still last a while. Thank God. And if their street was torn up—rumors were going around—then the three of them would get a two-room apartment, which would be simply wonderful. "Anyway," said the old woman, "bread is plentiful, and what else does a person need? We used to live worse..."

Frolov liked that, because in the newspaper office he was surrounded with talk of an opposite kind. Everything was getting worse and worse, they said... He himself, like the old woman, didn't look at it that way. They weren't living in cellars or wearing worn-out shoes, they all had movies right at home—so be content, people! Thank God up there or the Soviet state. But they all told him: You're a fool, Frolov, to consider it a matter of worn-out shoes. You'll try buffalo hides and campfires next. In that case we should be in paradise today.

Frolov wasn't one to argue. He had no ready answer for every outburst from others. But he had his own ideas. He was convinced that a person should keep his list of needs short and be at least a little happy with what he had... And what he didn't have, if it wasn't beyond his powers, he should quietly earn, build, or do whatever else it took. With no grumbling and shouting. Generally, in everything—in life as a whole and at work—with no yelling and shouting. With no initiatives and undertakings and all those slogans of "five years in three" and "three in two" and so on. To tell the truth, the nature of Frolov's work had done him in. He couldn't bear to see those heroes on the front page anymore. Especially because nobody knew better than he what a scam it all was. A load of bull...

Anyway, Frolov liked it at Valentina's house. They lived badly but modestly, and without bearing grudges.

At home he repaired the handle on her bag. When he crossed the street the next day on his way to work, carrying the bag, he felt wonderful somehow, even upbeat. But then he remembered that at that moment Valentina was somewhere out there crushed in the electric train and instantly his good mood faded; he got upset and even started feeling guilty.

And then the flu struck. Frolov was knocked off his feet, and powerfully at that. He stayed home in bed with a temperature of 102 and his bones ached so much he couldn't even get to his feet. Life came to a total halt. There was literally nobody to bring him water. And water was the least of it. He lay there like an idiot, and there wasn't even anybody to cross the street and inform them that he was in no state to photograph the next issue's routine hero. The editor, quick at reprisals, announced a reprimand to Frolov for absence from work. It was two days before somebody posed the human question: could something have happened to the photographer?

But they would have had to go see Frolov at home, and they were all busy with the issue, proofreading and corrections. In short, they didn't get around to it right away. Then the woman from the "beetles" came and told them that Frolov was laid up and in serious condition. The editor at once ordered an around-the-clock watch organized, but the woman said, "There's no need." And they all heaved a sigh of relief.

While Frolov was sick and later, while he was recovering, Valentina kept coming to his place, feeding him and cleaning. He was grateful to her, not so much for that as because she had guessed that he might be sick and had come and rung and rung at the door while he made his way to it, clinging to the wall. He wasn't even strong enough to yell out and say he was coming. He was so weak he could barely turn the key...

Right after his illness they filed at the registry office. Valentina said that she wasn't going to sign out of her house; after all, there were rumors that it would be torn down. Why lose the prospective apartment? Her daughter would live with her mother, near the garden and school. Why uproot the child? Frolov told her firmly that he had nothing against Olenka. But there was something he liked about Valentina's decision. A kind of caution in her perhaps, a kind of tact...

But a month later a calamity took place. The child came down with pneumonia and was put in the hospital. Valentina stayed there for two weeks and came back only after the little girl had begun to recover. She was so tired that she slept like the dead. On Sunday she went out to her mother's place to give the place a thorough cleaning: on Monday Olia would be discharged. Frolov was planning to go with her, but he got an urgent assignment and went to the district headquarters to photograph someone there for the front page.

Valentina and her mother scrubbed and aired the house and then decided to heat it properly so the child would at least come home from the hospital to human conditions. They turned the heat on, went to bed, and were overcome by fumes. Fatally.

The people at the hospital were nice: they let the little girl stay there during the funeral and all the bother...

Frolov could barely remember how things had gone. He had the feeling he had not taken part in anything. It was someone else, a stranger, who walked around and did things. Right at the graveside they started poking him in the back to kiss Valentina. He couldn't figure out why. But he drew closer to the coffin and saw an unfamiliar face, nothing like the woman he knew. It was like burying a stranger. Why should he kiss her? He just couldn't. He stood, looked, and walked away.

The funeral dinner took place in the scrubbed, clean house, which still had a slightly sweetish odor even after all the airing. And at that point Frolov slowly started coming out of his bewildered state. The conversation going on around him was very peculiar. It took great concentration to follow it, and to make a start he had to come to himself.

The relatives, eight or ten people, for some reason were busy demonstrating to each other what distant relatives the deceased women were to all of them without exception, what might be called third cousins twice removed. Some of them just happened to have supplied themselves with documents that confirmed the point, which was a peculiar one to raise, given the occasion. And they kept thrusting the pieces of paper at Frolov as if by chance. "You look here, just look," said the old woman's sister, "we even have different last names... And you say I'm her sister."

But Frolov hadn't said anything about it!

He just sat there as if in a stupor.

"And anyway I'm not from these parts," argued another, younger woman. "And our climate is very damp anyway."

Frolov sat there like a complete fool, but he had begun reviving a bit. Deep in his heart he was an inquisitive person. These relatives who stopped just short of pulling each others' hair to prove that they were the most far-removed began to interest him. Now, quarreling over who was closer would be easy to understand: there were odds and ends the dead women had left. And the house... That was reason enough to make a scene. True, Frolov didn't know for sure whether the house was theirs or the state's. He didn't care. But he'd never in his life seen people fighting to prove they were strangers.

And then it dawned on him. He suddenly realized what these people were afraid of: one of them would have to pick up Olia at the hospital. That was why they'd brought along the documents. "Oh, you dogs!" thought Frolov, quite good-naturedly. "You dogs!" Frolov saw something else as well: from the way they were looking at him, they considered him one of themselves and were protecting him, too.

"What has he got to do with it?" cried one of Valentina's male cousins. "He's been in the family less than a year."

And then the leading actor in this mystery play, an old man exceptionally far-removed from them all, spoke up. He said that the child had a father. That child support came from that father. That the little girl bore his name. So there was nothing to argue about. They should fire off a telegram to... what was his name?

"Koriakin, Koriakin!" the third cousins started shouting.

"Fire it off to Koriakin," repeated the leading actor, "and let him come and collect his daughter. And until then, the crux and matter of the business is that nobody's about to object."

Before the old man finished talking, the rest were all knotting their scarves and piling on coats. "That's right, that's right." "What took us so long? There's Koriakin." And then they were gone with the wind.

Frolov did everything himself. He washed and wiped the dishes and put them in the cupboard. He swept the floor. He shook out the tablecloth on the porch and stuck it in his satchel to take to the laundry. He turned off the electricity, cut off the gas, and went home.

The wide ottoman that he and Valentina had decided to buy instead of a sofa was standing on end alongside the doors to the apartment. He had totally forgotten that delivery had been scheduled for today. On the ottoman lay a note, "Ring at 27." He rang, and a man came out, wearing pajama bottoms and an undershirt with one stretched and dangling shoulder strap.

"You owe me six rubles," he said abruptly. "They made such a fuss I had to pay. Three according to the receipt, and three more besides."

Frolov handed over six rubles. It was hard work dragging the ottoman into the apartment by himself and he sweated over the job for a long time. He was embarrassed to ask the neighbor for help. In any case, hadn't the man seen the ottoman standing on end and that it would have to be put in place? He had, but he didn't come out. Why on earth ask and risk trouble? Frolov finally managed to drag the monstrosity inside. The ottoman turned out to be very wide and gaudy in color; it took up half the room, and now Frolov had absolutely no use for it.

He lay down on his old familiar couch and fell asleep surprisingly soundly; after all, he'd been through a lot these last few days.

He woke up early, and his first thought was of Koriakin, about whom he knew absolutely nothing, but here he was, barely awake, his eyes still shut, and yet he was thinking of Koriakin. The Asiatic-sounding name seemed appropriate; it pierced Frolov's brain to the point of hurting. And right after the hurt came anxiety: he had to pick up Olia at the hospital. They had an agreement with him, Frolov, that once it was all over, they said, they'd discharge her.

Frolov went to the editor and asked for leave. That really shook the man up: how much, he said, can you need? You've already taken three days for the funeral; have a heart now! There's nothing to put on the first page, demands on the press have increased, there's fundamental criticism everywhere, we need optimistic illustrative material as a counterweight, a balance between the one and the other, and here you are, Frolov, all caught up in personal matters!

"I have to get the kid out of the hospital," mumbled Frolov. "I promised...."

"Ask the women from the 'beetles.' They just spend all day knitting anyway," the editor yelled irritably, to which Frolov said firmly, "These are my problems..."

They came to an agreement. From the little factory next door Frolov would quickly slap together an optimistic photoessay and then go about his own business. Some colleagues were near enough to hear the whole thing, and they shook their heads, "You're a fool, Frolov... Why do you need somebody else's grief?... What kind of relative are you to her?"

Frolov didn't say anything. You couldn't start to tell them how the relatives had all crawled off yesterday—across the demarcation line, you might say. If the old man hadn't remembered Koriakin, they might even have declared themselves relatives from a different race, anything to be reckoned as far-removed as possible. But he, Frolov, thank God, was Russian and, due to his grandmother's backwardness, even baptized. So he had no need for any of the "beetle" women; he could manage by himself. He took a taxi and brought Olia back to his place. He set her down on the wide ottoman and said, "You'll live here for now."

The little girl didn't say a word all evening. She refused to eat. Frolov didn't know what to do and rushed around the little kitchen, quite simply in a panic. He remembered himself as a child: what would he have liked in the first years after the war? He couldn't recall. And then suddenly he did. Milk pudding! And he even recalled why he had begun wanting it. His mother read him a fairy tale, and in it were words about "rivers of milk and banks of pudding." He tried hard to imagine it all. The river was all white and flowed in choppy ripples, and the banks were pink and slippery and you could nibble on them. He imagined and imagined it and broke out bawling: "I want milk pudding!" And Mama made it for him. And he couldn't even wait for the pudding to cool, his throat was tight just from the passion of his desire.

"Do you want some milk pudding?" Frol asked Olia just in case.

"Yes," said Olia quietly.

She ate well, and Frolov sat beside her and used a spoon to scrape the remains of the pudding from the bottom and sides of the pot. And for some reason he felt happy, as if he had found grace. "Oh my God, my God!" muttered Frolov.

But that night he couldn't sleep. He lay there and thought about the sad events he'd gone through and how he should write to Koriakin now. The little girl slept and sniffled in her sleep, and that sniffle of hers, weak and pitiful, reminded Frolov of Valentina. She too had sniffled at night. And it was exactly at those moments that he pitied and loved her the most.

In general, to tell the truth, once Valentina had moved in with him, he keenly regretted it. First of all, he was struck by the smell that permeated her clothes—the odor of various chemicals against wood beetles. Her coat hung on the peg and stank up the whole apartment, but Valentina said, "I don't smell it." And her coat was the most repulsive thing. So he came home from work and the first thing he did was to get upset. And although Frolov was by nature a mild-mannered man, at that point fury rolled over him in waves. He wanted to scream bloody murder. But you have to give him credit, he didn't; it was just that everything bothered him already. For instance, Valentina put the hot dishes on the table and then started cutting bread, whereas he was used to having the bread already cut, the salt and mustard-pot on the table, and the glass ready for tea. Then you could eat in peace, in the proper order, without distractions. Then there was doing the dishes. Frolov washed the spoons, knives, and forks first, then the glass, and the plate afterward. But Valentina dumped them all into the dishwater together. In general, Frolov found evenings difficult. But then at night, when the woman began to sniffle, Frolov felt a sudden rush of tenderness from somewhere, and he would dream of buying her a new coat and finding her another job; the poor thing spent all her time with those damn chemicals. And he would wake up the next day feeling happy and, although Valia was no beauty in the morning, with her creased cheeks and swollen eyes, mornings were still easier than evenings. Even the coat didn't stink so much.

But just the same it would have been an exaggeration to say that Frolov had found superhuman happiness in marrying late in life. There wasn't a hint of happiness. It's hard to say how their relations would have shaped up in the future. Anything might have happened...

Now the little girl was asleep on the idiotic ottoman, sniffling gently. Frolov's heart ached, and he couldn't sleep. He got up, went into the kitchen, sat down on a stool, and looked out at the night. Where, he wondered, was Koriakin? And who was he, anyway? Valentina had never told him anything about her first marriage, and he hadn't asked. They were both that kind of people, close-mouthed in regard to their personal life.

The next day Frolov left the little girl alone and dashed off to work to fill out the papers for his leave. One of the third cousins phoned him there and started pestering him with questions. Had he written Koriakin or hadn't he? And just what was he think-ing of, anyway? There was in the third cousin's voice an almost inexpressible something, a nuance or hint that he, Frolov, was on the verge of appropriating something that did-n't belong to him. And even a certain superiority that they, the third cousins, wouldn't take that kind of liberty. Frolov borrowed the editor's car and drove out of town. He unlocked the house and went in. It still had the same sickly sweetish odor. With a mix-ture of timidity and shame he began searching the chest of drawers for traces of Koriakin. And he found them rather quickly. There was a little bag with no handles or lock, bound with underwear elastic. It contained letters and stubs from money orders. And there was a snapshot of a man, with no inscription. Just an ordinary man, looking straight ahead blankly. The face was not photogenic. It was a four-by-six snapshot. He took the whole bag to go through at home. He stopped short by the child's toys: should he take them or not? He was scared that they might suddenly remind the child of her calamity. But he drove to Child's World and bought a stiff-legged doll and a wind-up monkey on a swing. After all, Koriakin wouldn't come tomorrow...

Olia was still sitting on the ottoman. The child's resigned patience was just amazing. But she was delighted with the doll, she could barely gasp, "Thank you, Uncle Khlor."

The child was so happy that he didn't dare correct her. Even Valentina called him Frol and was very surprised to find out that his name was Andrei Ivanovich. Why on earth shouldn't he be Andrei Ivanovich, if that was the name he'd been given? But Frol was all right, too. That wasn't the point. Well, there was no harm in the child calling him Khlor. He'd teach her to get it right before Koriakin arrived.

Frolov didn't want to read the letters. He found it shameful. He tried to determine from the postmarks which was the most recent so he could write Koriakin at the most recent address. There were several addresses, after all. But he couldn't make out a damned thing from the postmarks and was forced to dig into the envelopes. There Koriakin justified his hopes. The man used dates, separating the numbers with a thick dot. Trying to keep from catching sight of the words, Frolov searched for the most recent, the very latest letter. But his eyes betrayed him. They caught not only words, but whole phrases and paragraphs. It was hard not to, because Koriakin's letters were brief, the handwriting round and full, and the words scathing.

"Our short marriage fell short in the fullest sense of the term."

"Perhaps if it had been a son, but a mere girl won't rope a man in."

"I live well and never think of you."

"You sucked me dry before your eighteenth birthday."

"Trying to stagger me with a snapshot? You broads make me laugh."

"For all I care, you can marry the priest and the deacon, too."

Valentina had received that blessing a month and a half ago from the Chelyabinsk district.

The quotations bombarding Frolov gave him a strange feeling. On the one hand, strange as it may seen, he sympathized with Koriakin. He realized how foul it must have been for the man: he couldn't get along with his wife and had to tear up roots from the south and go north. On the other hand, he condemned him for that "you sucked me dry before your eighteenth birthday." That was bad. It wasn't manly. On the third, he didn't know what to make of Valentina, who evidently continued to keep in touch with Koriakin, and that was already unwomanly. There was a fourth hand, too: pity for both of them. You're a fool, Koriakin, a fool, probably still barking away, and she's already in her grave... Oh, Valentina, Valentina. What a luckless end you came to! A real bungler! Over thirty years old, and you never learned to stoke a stove. Anyway, Frolov had such mixed feelings that he decided to wait a while before writing the letter, so he could find the right words.

The little girl gradually settled down. She called him "Uncle Khlor," and he was already embarrassed to correct her. They'd go to the store together, and the girl would wait in line while he went to pay. He took her to see a cartoon show, and on the way back they dropped by the newspaper offices. The kid on contract who was substituting for Frolov had just that day slipped up, and the editor had been called to the regional party committee for explanations. In a caption the kid had called a lathe operator famous throughout the region "a mechanic" and given him the last name of a recently deceased regional-committee instructor. He showed Frolov how it happened. It was simply that all the facts were on the same page of his notebook. Facts about the lathe operator and the mechanic and the instructor, whose photo he had copied from a personnel file for the obituary.

"How can you remember them all?" the kid lamented.

Frolov showed him his system, a foolproof system in which the day, hour, and occasion of the photograph and the number of the roll and the frame were recorded, and never, ever was there more than one name per notebook page.

"Will they fire me?" asked the kid.

"Probably," answered Frolov honestly. "There's no getting around a mix-up with a dead man."

The editor came back. He signed the order and said to Frolov, "I'm calling you back from leave." He caught sight of the little girl. "Your daughter?"

He was a real dope, their editor. He hadn't worked there long and couldn't remember anything. Not about the people or the work. Basically, he was scared. And he also was mad that people didn't understand that—and that everybody was trying to make trouble for him. Now he was mad at Frolov, who'd gotten an itch to go on leave at such a crucial time and hadn't taken time to find a suitable replacement. And, moreover, he drags a child in to work!

Of course, Frolov could have taken the matter to the local party committee and proved that he hadn't been on leave for three years, but Frolov wasn't a man to stand on principle. He was an understanding man, and if the editor was left with no photographer, he would have to go back to work. No two ways about it!

That evening he had to sit down and write the letter to Koriakin. Olenka was asleep, sniffling gently and hugging the stiff-legged doll, and Frolov drew a sheet of paper toward him and brooded over it. This is the letter he finally composed:

> Greetings, Oleg Nikolaevich! (That was Koriakin's name.) This is Frolov writing to you. Your ex-wife Valentina and her mother passed away together and left the little girl Olia. I'm asking your permission to adopt her, since I am your late wife's second husband. I have decent living conditions, don't drink, clear 200-250 rubles a month, and am in a position to provide clothing and shoes and feed the child. Olia is already getting used to me, and with you she'd have to start all over again. That would be a shame for the girl. Answer right away. Frolov.

Koriakin worked as an adjuster at a factory in Chelyabinsk. His photo was on the Honor Board, and he had just won a victory over the dormitory director in a battle for a cunning little cubbyhole in their dormitory. For a single man. When the builders slapped together the dormitory, they forgot about putting a radiator in that room. In the Urals that's no laughing matter. They had to turn it into a storeroom. Then one day it was seized by a family with a child that had been waiting a long time for an apartment. In short, one evening it was still a storeroom, and the next morning three people were living in it. This happened during the summer. Fall came, and the weather turned cold. The enterprising family went and installed a stove with a pipe through the window. One evening there was no stove, and the next morning a real beauty stood there, smoking out the window. There was a scandal, a commission, all sorts of bother... In short, the do-it-yourself occupants lived there for three years, until they produced a second child. After they left, singles started fighting over the room. Heating the installed stove turned out to be not only simple but even a pleasure, if you huddled by it alone. So by way of exception they gave that room to old bachelors, first to a fellow who snored loudly, then to someone who bribed the director...

Now Koriakin was living by the stove, living and keeping a sharp eye on them all. For kicks he hung his favorite stars on the walls—Vysotsky, Celentano, and Irina Alferova. Between the frames stood beer; lard and a jar of marinated sprats cooled in the Morozko-brand refrigerator. Koriakin's socks dried on a line over the stove.

Koriakin found it quiet and peaceful there, and now if somebody, some know-it-all good fairy, were to ask him what he, Koriakin, wanted, he would have answered smartly, "You can go to...." What's surprising about that? Roughly speaking, the man was simply happy.

And then the letter was slipped under his door. Koriakin heard a rustling sound and saw the white square on the floor, but he was in no hurry to get to it. He went on lying there, feeling a profound contentment. There wasn't anybody on earth whose letter could make Koriakin happy or sad. To be more exact, nobody ever wrote to Koriakin anyway, except his latest ex-wife. And he was sure that this square, too, was from her, the cretin. Once again she was informing him of unwanted details about her life and the life of his so-called daughter. What was the idiot after? What did she hope to gain?

Koriakin had lived with Valentina for five months. A real feat! He'd barely lasted a month with his two previous "wives." It was evidently a flaw in Koriakin, but as soon as a woman moved in with him for good, he got the feeling that there was nothing to breathe. Not in the figurative sense, but literally. Maybe it was some kind of allergy or maybe Koriakin just had no luck with the female sex. Both his first wives were northerners, tall, pale, and slow of speech. When he called it quits with the second, he made a firm decision never to get tangled up in that business again. He'd also been lucky he hadn't gotten stuck with a child then. A fortuitous accident, you might say, because there are men who get caught the first time. But then Koriakin began to languish. Nothing went right for him. Everything went wrong. And he went south, where he liked life from the start. He liked having the sea only two hours away. The bazaars were spicy and succulent. And the people, bold, insolent, handsome—in short, people you had to keep a close eye on. In the time it took the guy from Archangel (as Koriakin called all northerners) to turn around, the guy from Krasnodon (his name for southerners) could make a run to Moscow and be back again. In general, the latter were much better adapted to modern times, and Koriakin, a chronic loner who had been reared in an orphanage, appreciated people like that. You had to know how to stand up for yourself. That was the main thing. Friend, comrade, brother—it all sounded fine on May Day, but the rest of the year you were on your own.

Koriakin decided to risk marriage once more. He'd turned thirty and he was tired of washing socks and shirts and getting caught every time on the question of who to marry. Unlike the northern women, Valentina was small, dark, and quick of speech. The external data were suitable. And those five months proved that he hadn't been completely wrong.

And then it all started up again in spades. He couldn't breathe. He had to call it quits again... Only later did he learn that he had a daughter. Big deal, he thought. Unlike his previous wives, who had vanished without a trace, this one went on writing him idiotic letters about chickenpoxes, whooping-coughs, and a tendency to myopia, and it drove him wild. He started running from place to place, but the letters reached him anyway. And every time deep down under his indignation and anger there was something inexpressible—gratification, was that it? Here they were, searching for him and finding him. Or maybe manly pride that he was the sort who got remembered. It was precisely the vagueness of those feelings that suggested answers. Swinish ones, of course, but nevertheless... Koriakin would have flattened anyone who told him that he was keeping up ties with Valentina himself—he would definitely have flattened him, but to tell the truth and nothing but... there was something to it. There was...

Now, lying on the bed, he looked at the square on the floor. At that moment Koriakin was majestic, proud, and independent and, without reading the letter, he was already composing an answer. Like this, for example:

> I've had it with your letters... What should I do, cut my throat? What good would that do you? They don't send child support from the next world... Although police investigation of the matter has produced important results. Maybe Major Pronin is on the prowl over there already? I've got no respect for you, especially now that you're getting married... The fellow didn't break it off, then? Fade in the stretch? I understand the comrade and appreciate his stamina. In his time Koriakin came up short.

It was nice, lying there thinking up letters. Looking at the square on the floor, Koriakin simultaneously thought up a letter to Celentano, too:

> Greetings, pal. Here I am, lounging around, and I decided to drop you a line. I saw your film, *The Taming of Tom Shrew*. I didn't expect it to turn out the way it did. You had a great house there, great broads and negresses, and then you fell for that ninny. Out of character and not true to life. They explained to us in school that your art distorts reality. That I'm convinced of. Especially since that beauty you succumbed to is a real nothing, not the type I like at all. So take more care in choosing where you make your films. You can't rest on your laurels.—Koriakin.

Koriakin jumped lightly out of bed and began playing with the letter, pushing it toward the bed with one foot and hopping on the other. He got tired and finally picked it up. The letter wasn't from Valentina, although it was from those parts. From some Frolov or other. Very interesting, thought Koriakin, what kind of fool would write me?

And then he went crazy...

Maybe he couldn't make a smooth transition from his pal Celentano to the letter or maybe there was some other reason, but he went crazy... That is, his head was empty of everything but a ringing void, and the ringing sound made him even feel hot all over.

Koriakin had nothing of his own. He was a prime example of the individual who dealt only with state property, so to speak, on equal shares with the entire multimillion population. Or maybe the state owned Koriakin, and it was a solid, mutually advantageous marriage? There was much there to debate. And suddenly he finds out that some guy who doesn't drink and has living space wants to grab his daughter, Olga

Koriakina by name. Is he, Koriakin, such a hopeless cripple that people take to passing his daughter around? Giving away his own personal child, on whom he had already spent over three thousand rubles, to a strange stepfather? If you're so clever, Frolov, just go and give birth yourself! Give it a try! His throat was tight with rage; he had to get out a beer and drink it straight from the bottle. He would have tossed the whole thing down, but suddenly—bang! it struck him like a blow to the head—he drank and Frolov didn't. It wasn't like he was a drunk. Of course not. But there was almost always beer standing between the frames. And he had nothing against the other stuff, white and red wine. But he wouldn't touch the hard stuff for anything!

Koriakin slapped the cap back on the bottle and said, "Basta!" And once again he got furious at Frolov, who was trying to trick him out of a ready-made daughter. He dug into his trunk and started rummaging through various papers, searching for the photo of the little girl that Valentina had sent him ages ago. He couldn't find it, and that upset him; it was like he'd lost the child for good. He started thinking that it was close to being grounds for taking Olia away from him. That man Frolov would say, "You don't even have a photo of her!" But where on earth could he have put it? All kinds of references were stowed there, and he had saved snapshots of people he didn't even recognize, but his daughter's wasn't there!

Koriakin barely made it through the night. In the morning he handed in his resignation and created a scandal, yelling that he couldn't wait even one day. He shouted, "My child, they're taking away my child!" It worked. Everybody came to take a look at the man whose child was being brazenly usurped by a stranger.

Then Koriakin made a scene at the airport, and there too they sympathized with him and were amazed at the shameless, insolent act—usurping other people's children, a crime that smacked of capitalism. They'd done that sort of thing for a long time, and now it seems to be starting up here, too.

Miserable and resolved, Koriakin flew through the skies, leaving the sun behind.

At the time Olia was sitting on the ottoman. She and Frolov, both enthralled, were busy making transfers. They were both wet and covered with cotton balls, but rare blossoms were blooming on a piece of drawing paper. Afterward they tacked the paper to the wall and oohed and ahed at its unearthly beauty, and then they ate kasha and milk out of the same bowl. They had long since got in the habit of eating from one bowl. Frolov himself had no idea how the one-bowl business got started, but suddenly there was no greater pleasure at meals than making sure the other got a fair share.

After the little girl fell asleep, Frolov thought uneasily of Koriakin: what would his answer be? Frolov was positive that Koriakin had no need of the child, but he was afraid the man would take his time about replying, and he had to enroll Olia in kindergarten and arrange for her schooling, somehow keeping the bureaucrats from plaguing him because she didn't belong to him. Every time Frolov even thought of that "didn't belong," it kicked up God knows what inside. His whole system protested and rebelled. After all, he would give up his life for the little girl without a second thought.

That night there was a loud and sharp ring in the apartment. Olia yelped. Frolov dashed to the door so fast that there could be no doubt that he was going to flatten whoever had rung.

That was how they came face to face—in character. Frolov and Koriakin.

Climbing the stairs, Koriakin had gotten furious, too. He already pictured himself wrapping his child in a blanket and carrying her away from the fancier of other people's property.

And Frolov—that is, the fancier of other people's property—was fully ready for murder because of Olia's night-time yelp.

You could easily have run the electric network of an underdeveloped country on the voltage that formed at the threshold. It would have worked like a charm.

"I'm Koriakin," said Koriakin.

"So I see," answered Frolov, who had a good professional memory for faces and well remembered that four-by-six snapshot. "Come in."

"Who's that, Uncle Khlor?" asked Olia.

Both men stood on principle, glaring at each other. It was a decisive moment, and a lot depended on it.

"Go to sleep," said Frolov, closing the door into the room. "It's someone on business for me." And he turned to Koriakin, "Go through to the kitchen, and leave your coat and suitcase there..." He pointed to a spot by the door.

They went into the kitchen and sat down on stools. And were silent. Frolov realized that Koriakin's being there was a bad sign. And for his part, although Koriakin knew how old his daughter was, he had been imagining a bawling baby and now all at once he heard what could be called an adult voice. If, of course, it was his daughter...

"Is that her?" he made sure.

Frolov nodded.

"I woke her," said Koriakin in distress. "But I couldn't wait..."

"I understand," answered Frolov. How could he fail to understand the man, running through the night to Olechka? "Well, what's your answer?" he asked, feeling that his death was imminent. "She's had pneumonia, she can't be moved to a new climate...."

"Don't try to pull a fast one on me!" blazed Koriakin immediately. "We'll provide whatever climate she needs."

"What do you mean by that?"

"I mean what I say! Where she's got to be, that's where we'll live. I've got no ties."

"You've never even seen her," said Frolov sadly.

Koriakin didn't like being hit where it hurt. "That doesn't mean a thing," Koriakin snapped. "The child is mine."

And there was the child, standing in the doorway with her hair down, wearing a long nightgown and Frolov's big slippers.

"I wanna pee," said the little girl. And both of them rushed towards her as if peeing was something exceptionally precious that couldn't be left to the whims of fate. And they both stood by the toilet door, both of them waiting, and Frolov saw that Koriakin's chin was quivering, and Koriakin saw that Frolov had turned as white as chalk.

"Here's how things stand," said Frolov afterward, when Olia had given them both a radiant, clear smile and gone back to bed. "Valentina was overcome by fumes. And Olia and I've learned to get along together. I buy her food at the private market..."

"Thanks," said Koriakin. "I'll pay you back."

"Don't be silly!" Frolov threw up his hands. "The main thing is that she be all right. You have an apartment?"

Koriakin remembered his room with the stove and mentally treated himself to a few select curses. Why was he such an idiot? He had had an apartment, that he had! He should have taken leave instead of quitting. What a brainless fool he was! He had given up that beauty of a room, warm and dry—well, true, the toilet was out on the street, but there were chamber pots, thank God; that was no problem. For his child he could put up with that!

"I have everything... And what I don't, I will have," said Koriakin firmly. "I'll do everything for her."

Frolov heaved a deep sigh.

They made a bed for Koriakin on the floor, between the ottoman and the sofa. There was a strong draft from the hall door. Koriakin felt his shoulder blades and back turning cold, but what of it, hadn't he been in fixes like that before? In his life Koriakin had slept in all sorts of places. But now he was scared of getting sick. He couldn't do that now, no way. He spent the whole night trying to keep his back barely arched off the floor.

He heard Olia sniffling gently, just like Valentina. Valentina's sniffles used to drive him wild. "Why do you grunt like that?" he would yell, but she didn't understand. Here and now, however, he liked those vulnerable childish noises in the night, and he thought, "She's dreaming... I wonder what she's dreaming about."

Frolov didn't sleep either. As soon as he saw Koriakin, he realized that the man wasn't one to give in. And what could he do about it? "Oh, woe is me," thought Frolov. For some reason he could see his whole life clearly, a life in essence devoid of joy and filled with nothing but difficulties to be overcome. And if overcoming them had seemed like a mark of valor before, he realized now what nonsense all that was when a person had no joy in life. The little girl had come along, and everything had taken on meaning, but tomorrow Koriakin, her father, would take her away, and why go on living then? Why go on aimlessly? Had he, Frolov, really been born for the sole purpose of taking endless photos of smiling workers and collective-farm women and in this way maintaining the newspaper's balance between criticism and optimism? That kind of life was simply shameful! On the other hand, it wasn't shameful to do all that, knowing that in the evening he and Olia would eat kasha from the same bowl, and she would draw a line through the kasha with her spoon so that he, Frolov, got more, and he would draw his line, and then they would push food at each other and laugh. Nothing could be better than that.

The next morning Frolov got up early. Olia was still sleeping. Koriakin had finally dozed off, curled up in a ball.

Frolov opened and closed the door without a sound.

In the morning the very first thing Koriakin did was wash the floor. To tell the truth, Frolov couldn't do it properly. He was stiff through the small of the back and washed the floor on his knees or, to be more exact, didn't wash it but just sloshed water around. That wasn't Koriakin's style. He scrubbed the floor until it shone. Then he found a piece of foam plastic in Frolov's gear, cut it to the right shape, and nailed it to the underside of the door to keep out the draft. Olia helped him by handing him tacks.

"That's warmed things up," said Koriakin.

"Thank you," said Olia.

Koriakin was embarrassed by that "Thank you." He even caught his breath.

"Yes," he sighed. "Yes...."

"Yes, what?" asked Olia.

Koriakin had no answers. He couldn't put it in words. So he decided to repair the faucets. Frolov let them drip, and the water had left rusty streaks in the toilet bowl and the sink and the bathtub. Koriakin fixed all that. Koriakin made everything shine. Olia simply clapped her hands. "How clean it is!"

Koriakin decided he was on the right track.

He started sorting the laundry, which had been stored in a plastic pail. Olia helped him with that, too. Together they hung it on a line in the kitchen. His conversations with Olia concerned productivity.

"See," said Koriakin, "the hardest spot in a man's shirt is the collar. The damned thing clings to the neck."

"Why are you swearing?" asked Olia.

"Ah! ah! ah!" Koriakin flapped his soapy hands in fright. "Slip of the tongue! I'll have to watch it. My apologies." And Koriakin started talking slowly to keep from inadvertently blurting out a curse.

After that he and Olia went to the store, and Koriakin pushed ahead of an old lady in line and grabbed a nice piece of meat. He and Olia made borshch and ground the meat into cutlets. They were happy together.

"You're a Koriakina and I'm a Koriakin," he said cautiously. "We'll get along fine."

"But why are you a Koriakin?" the girl asked.

"Because... It just worked out that way." Koriakin lost his nerve. "There are lots of us Koriakins."

Then Frolov came home. He saw it all—the cleanliness, the laundry on the line, the dinner, and Olia's contented little face; and he sighed, realizing that he had no choice.

"You live here with her," he said to Koriakin, after Olia had gone to sleep. "I can live anywhere..."

"Nuts," answered Koriakin. "You've gone nuts. I'm the one who can live anywhere. I'm used to it."

"Me, too," sighed Frolov. "It's been two years since I moved in here, and everything's still piled in the corners."

"Two years, and everything's already falling the hell to pieces." Koriakin was outraged. "It's all warped and cracking."

"Well," said Frolov, "in the cooperative things aren't so bad. State housing is much worse."

"As if I didn't know," answered Koriakin. "I lived in a room where they forgot to put in a radiator."

"What sort of people are we!" sighed Koriakin. "Even when it's for us, we just don't try."

They sighed.

The next day Koriakin set about repairing the apartment. Frolov ran in after work and fixed a meal. Olia helped one or the other and ordered them both around.

"Uncle Khlor," she would shout. "I've already salted the potatoes. Don't you dare do it again!"

"Koriakin. You left marks on the ceiling. What's the matter, can't you see?"

Only idiots and greedy people rush from one good thing to another. Koriakin found a job at the little factory next door to the newspaper office. They sold the ottoman to a neighbor and bought two armchair-beds. Olia slept on the sofa, and they slept in the armchairs.

"Who are they to you?" Olia was asked when she entered first grade.

In identical blue suits and snow-white shirts with strangling ties, the two of them stood in the rows of parents. When the bell rang and the women started furtively blowing their noses, they didn't try to hide their tears.

"So, who are they to you?" they pestered Olia.

"Who? Who? Uncle Khlor and Koriakin, can't you see?" the little girl shrugged.

Olia grew up to be a clever girl, resolute, independent, and bold. They say that single fathers are best at raising children. And if in addition there are two of them?

Time will tell how the pedagogical experiment will work out.

In the meantime they have specific problems to solve. The child needs her own room. In the evening Frolov develops copies of an announcement, written in a firm hand, that offers an exchange of apartments, and Koriakin goes around with a jar of glue in his pocket pasting them to utility poles. They've already saved up for the supplemental payment.

"It's a good thing," Frolov thinks at night. "If, God forbid, something should happen to me, there's Koriakin. She's not an orphan anymore."

In the armchair next to him Koriakin is thinking the same thing.

Translated by Mary F. Zirin

From *Ogonēk*, No. 46, 1988

A Bus Driver Named Astap

Tatiana Nabatnikova

"Why *A*-stap?" they asked in surprise.

What was there to be surprised about?

"My father was the commander of a unit that fought against our counterrevolutionaries during the Civil War!"[1]

"That's an explanation?" asked Garik, not understanding.

"Of course," said Zhenia without raising her voice. She cast a quick glance and fleeting smile in Astap's direction. (It wasn't enough—he wanted more.) "What's so difficult to understand, Garik? Astap's heroic father was a unit commander and his military commissar was probably Ostap somebody or other. But the commander didn't know that the name begins with an *o*, so he spelled his son's name with an *a*."[2]

She said all this in an egalitarian spirit, making sure that her voice contained no trace of condescension or derision.

Astap was annoyed and pressed down on the accelerator.

Naturally, they had nicknamed him "Comrade Bender."[3] "They," in this case, were the Republic's all-star field and track team, an imported team,[4] it goes without saying, made up entirely of Russians. He had been their driver during their month-long training session. Every morning he drove them to the stadium—a distance of twenty-five kilometers—then back for dinner, then off to practice once again in the evening. And so it went. The team was staying in a comfortable *pension* outside of town. A comfortable setup for them, but he, Astap, was stuck behind the wheel till ten o'clock every night! And he would curse and complain about his long overtime hours.

"But, Astap, they're going to give you two vacations!"[5]

"Yeah, right," he would respond in the spirit of things. "They'll come after me and give me even more. And if that's not enough, the public prosecutor will add some time of his own!"

He had two small children, a boy and a girl. He had taken their mother back to where he had found her, and the children were being raised by his parents. That left him a free agent, with no need to hurry home every evening. Still, he would protest with a show of bravado, "No, I'm going to quit. Why should I put up with this? Who needs it?!"

And the more he enjoyed the athletes' company, the more stubbornly he would complain.

The team paid no attention to his outbursts. After all, if he left, someone else would be sent to replace him. What did it matter to them? They'd treat the next driver with the same friendly indifference.

"Hey, Astap, let's get going—what d'ya say!"

They were tired of nibbling the fruit from the mulberry tree that stood by the gate of their *pension,* and Astap was taking forever to wash the bus—his "Mustang," as he called it. He stubbornly kept hosing it down and wiping it with a cloth. By now, he had gone over it four times. But the athletes had supple nerves—they weren't the Republic's all-star team for nothing!—and their coach, who was waiting for them at the stadium, was a man with great reserves of patience.

Finally they were ready to leave, and the athletes took their seats inside Mustang. They immediately stretched out and, much to Astap's annoyance, dangled their strong legs, calf muscles bulging, over the armrests of their seats. Except for the two who always sat together—the married couple, Kostia and Zhenia—they all had seats to themselves.

When they reached the railroad crossing, an electric train was passing through and they had to stop. Astap leaned back in his seat and gazed into the rearview mirror. His eyes remained fixed on the passenger section.

"It's a good thing it's not a freight train or there'd be something like 150 to 180 cars!"

"Ha-ha, Garik, very funny."

"What d'ya mean? Well, sixty, then."

"That's more like it."

"But one time there really were 150."

Those two, the couple, smiled but kept silent. They seemed somewhat removed from the rest of the group, as if they knew something special that no one else knew: some secret password to paradise.

But what could they know that was so special? He, Astap, had been married himself and he remembered perfectly well that there was nothing special or mysterious about it.

They would sit there without saying a word, but you could see that they were on the same wavelength. They seemed to be pondering something simultaneously, making a joint effort, as if they wouldn't be able to think it through on their own. They'd work out on the track for a while and then return to the bus, more united than ever and ready to shoulder once again their common, invisible burden. But what exactly this burden was, that was anyone's guess!

"Tomorrow you'll have a chance to relax," the coach had told the team two days before the qualifying meet. Wise man that he was, he was sending them up into the mountains, entrusting them to the care of the aborigine Astap.

The coach had a clear purpose in mind. Up there in the mountains they'd give themselves a good hour's workout. The lack of oxygen at that height would force their bodies to release more hemoglobin into the bloodstream than they would need down below. Afterwards, when they returned to the valley with their newly enriched blood, then they'd really be able to run!

Fired up with the importance of his mission, Astap comported himself like a submarine commander: sternly, silently, and purposefully.

"Astap, what are we waiting for?"

"Just relax, everything's under control."

"But Astap, where are you taking us?"

"You'll know when you get there."

"Our fate is in your hands."

Astap's subsequent behavior only added to the mystery. He drove at breakneck speed into several out-of-the-way villages and, with engine roaring, maneuvered Mustang down back streets and into blind alleys. Then he'd pull to a stop and converse in muffled tones with various shady characters who, with their pointed beards and Asiatic robes, looked like some sort of wise men of old. As Astap spoke to them in the local language they would nod perfunctorily and direct their taciturn gaze at the athletes inside the bus.

"They must be terrorists!"

"Prepare yourselves, they're after our scalps!"

It turned out that Astap had simply been negotiating for the best available shish kebabs, brazier, and charcoal.

At a point just before their mountain destination, the road was blocked off by a padlocked iron gate. There was no way around the gate—only steep rock on one side and a precipitous drop on the other—and already several cars and buses were backed up behind it. Standing nearby were clusters of despondent tourists.

"Astap, let's get a running start and fly over it. It'll be a piece of cake!"

"We could always pole-vault over it."

As Astap got out of the bus to reconnoiter, someone called after him, "Hey, Astap, did you take your revolver?"

There was neither a booth nor a gatekeeper, no relief in sight, but, nursing some forlorn hope, people stood around and waited.

The Republic's all-star team also filed out. They stretched their limbs and began crawling up the rocky incline, only to discover that there was no place to perch.

Zhenia shook the iron rods of the gate. The tourists watched her with interest.

Astap now produced a jack handle from the cab of the bus and positioned it like a lever inside the loop of the padlock. At the very first pry, the loop snapped and the padlock fell to the ground. Ripples of delight reverberated through the captive ranks.

The vehicles at the front of the line passed though the gate and immediately pulled over to the side of the road. There they waited shamelessly, letting others pass them by so that all responsibility for the broken lock would fall on those who had been behind them. Thus it was that Astap eventually found himself at the head of the line. He drove fearlessly ahead, feeling nothing but contempt for these cowardly ingrates who had him to thank for their freedom.

As it turned out, no one stopped them and Astap's heroic deed was forgotten in painfully short order.

"... Poor thing, they enter her in every meet and she always comes in last. She's not going to be able to take it much longer!"

"Oh, I think she'll keep running. She's got a lot of determination."

"One of these days I'm going to be running the 400 meter too."

"You've got to be kidding—you barely get through the 100!"

Astap knew them all by their voices and he listened with rapt attention, but there was never a word about him. He turned around in his seat to remind them.

"Hey, Garik, let me tell you—I always do what I set out to do! If I have to drive through, I drive through!"

"That's for sure," said Garik, not doubting him for a moment.

And once again they returned to their own world of meters, seconds, wins and losses.

But what was Astap to them? He was merely a driver, their transportation.

They had reached their destination.

"Well, what do you think of the spot I've picked out for you?"

A mountain stream flowed sonorously past, creating a special silence of its own. Garik picked up a weather-beaten shoe from the ground.

"Hey, guys, this ground has been trod by a human foot!"

"It's a perfect spot, Astap Ibragimovich,"[6] Kostia reassured him.

He, Astap, was worth his weight in gold. Who else knew how to cook the shish kebab, knew just the right moment to put the skewers on the brazier and the right moment to sprinkle them with water? No one knew but him. But none of them gave the matter a second thought. They seemed to assume that it was his, Astap's, job to cook their shish kebab while they worked out on the road. In their view, he was simply a hired hand!

After their workout they washed up in the mountain stream. Their legs were as taut as springs.

"Hey, are you people out of your minds, lying in the sun before a meet?"

"Oh, I'm not going to qualify anyway."

Astap danced and whirled around the brazier like a shaman performing some priestly rite. At the same time, there was something about him that reminded one of a poodle. He had a lean, wiry body and a luxuriant mane of hair to which, from the look of it, he devoted as much tender, loving care as a housewife to her house plants. He obviously considered himself a handsome fellow, for his personal photo album lay in full view at the front of the bus. In every photograph he gazed out at the viewer—or rather, *past* the viewer—with a look of infinite superiority, and in group pictures he seemed particularly eager to stand out from the crowd.

Zhenia had burst out laughing at one of the pictures. Wounded to the quick, Astap had anxiously surveyed the picture to see what was so funny. It was a full-length shot of him standing in bell-bottom trousers, his feet planted slightly apart. Despite his fiercely obstinate expression, anyone with an open mind would even have found him attractive.

"Well, what's so funny?" he asked in an injured tone. "You probably wore pants like that yourself."

"It's not the pants," Zhenia responded with a smile, barely containing herself, "it's the look on your face!"

"That's enough!" Kostia broke in sternly, pulling her up short. But his attempt to defend Astap wounded the poor man more than the mockery itself.

After their meal they hiked farther up the mountain and visited two local tourist attractions, a cave and a wishing tree. They weren't able to venture very far into the cave because their matches kept sputtering and going out. When they approached the wishing tree, they saw pieces of faded cloth fluttering in the wind. Before making a wish, you were supposed to fasten a piece of your own clothing to the tree. Zhenia tore a strip from her handkerchief and tied it to one of the branches. But what exactly she wished for—that was anyone's guess!

Kostia climbed up a slope and picked some flowers for her—even though they'd been married for a long time and already had a child.

The coach's expectations regarding their high altitude work-out proved to be correct, and at the qualifying meet the next day, the team ran as never before.

Kostia made the team; Zhenia didn't. But it couldn't be helped; she had been prepared for this—such was the nature of their profession. (Yes, for all intents and purposes they were professionals.) Now the team would travel to Moscow and Zhenia would return home to her city in European Russia, no longer a member of the Republic's all-star team. Never mind, the coach reassured her, she had to expect this—after all, she'd been so busy with her procreational activities that she'd missed almost two whole seasons. But next year she'd run for sure, the coach promised. He'd take her back on the team—she just had to keep training and not get discouraged.

Kostia was dismayed. He kept his eyes fixed on the ground, feeling like a traitor.

"It's your own fault. Why did you straighten up just before the finish line?" said Astap, adding his own words of consolation.

This was more than she could take.

"That's all I need—to have you butting in!"

The Republic's all-star team departed for Moscow and Astap's special assignment came to an end. Now he had to return to his regular job driving fifteen-day prisoners[7] to and from their work site. It was a depressing prospect.

On the eve of Zhenia's departure he stopped off at the *pension*. Here, at the *pension*, she was now alone among strangers. He found her sitting by the phone in the lobby, awaiting Kostia's call from Moscow. For a whole hour Astap sat beside her in silent devotion. This time Zhenia treated him like a long-lost friend; he was the only person she knew in the whole area.

"Don't go, Astap, stay a little longer. Today you're like a souvenir from my happy past."

"That's insulting."

"A toy monkey souvenir," she mumbled.

"It's too bad that I can't drive you to the airport," he said, "but that's just when I have to pick up my prisoners."

"Yeah, that *is* too bad," Zhenia agreed, her thoughts elsewhere. "But never mind, I can take the city bus."

"With your suitcase?" he asked, his voice sympathetic.

"It can't be helped."

Kostia's call never came through. Moscow was a long way off.

At six o'clock the next morning Astap woke her with a knock at the door. Still half asleep, she opened the door a crack and peered out. (She sleeps naked, Astap suddenly realized.)

"What are you doing here?" she asked in amazement.

"Let's go!" he whispered, not wanting to wake up anyone else. "I'll take you to the airport and pick up my prisoners afterwards."

He chastely lowered his gaze, not wanting to think about her nakedness there, behind the door.

She shrugged her shoulders in assent and went off to get dressed.

There was still plenty of time and Zhenia wasn't alarmed when they turned off the highway. Undoubtedly Astap had one of his mysterious errands to run along the way. Well, never mind, it was his responsibility to make it to the airport and to pick up his prisoners on time. Her plane departure was still a long way off, not till eleven, and right now it was only seven.

And before long—not long at all, only a few hours!—she would see her little boy again and in the evening Kostia would call from Moscow, and this time he would be calling home.

Only now did she allow herself to feel how much she had missed her son; earlier she had forbidden herself this luxury. Her mother had written that he was sleeping on all fours with his little behind stuck up in the air. And that his toes were identical to her, Zhenia's, toes when she was little. And that he knew and recognized everyone.

The asphalt had come to an end and Astap was now driving along a muddy country road, weaving his way among the low-lying bushes. A stream had overflowed its banks, splitting off into a number of rivulets, and here and there one caught a flash of shallow water and heard the croaking of frogs. A beautiful, clear morning lay ahead, a morning brimming with happiness. But where, she wondered, was Astap's errand taking them? Last night she had lain in bed, listening to the toads' melancholy "errrh-errrh-errrh." And again: "errrh-errrh." She'd been so excited at the prospect of seeing her son that she'd had trouble falling asleep. First she had lain stock still, barely breathing, then she had kneaded her tense stomach, trying to calm her predeparture agitation.

Mustang's engine stalled as they were crossing one of the rivulets. Astap lifted the cover to the engine compartment, which was located inside the cab. Looking down through the spaces between the various engine parts, one could see water gurgling among the pebbles below. Astap's hands were soon covered with grease and he asked Zhenia to pull his shirt off over his head. He took off his trousers himself and was left standing in his swim trunks, a wiry little monkey with a screwdriver.

It seemed to Zhenia that the engine had stalled not quite convincingly. Had that show-off perhaps decided to make her worry about missing her plane just so he could demonstrate later on what a topnotch mechanic he was? Zhenia smiled to herself and once again noticed what a glorious summer morning it was. And right now in her home town, her father, the best dad in the world, was waking up and getting ready to meet her at the airport. Though she was still far away, her city was turning its face in her direction.

Someone on a motorcycle was crossing the stream nearby, a rare traveler in this wilderness. She could probably flag him down and ask for a ride at least as far as the highway. But it would be a betrayal to leave the little monkey Astap here by himself, poking around in the engine. He would feel humiliated.

The motorcyclist disappeared into the dense forest. Zhenia purposely refrained from asking Astap a single question or expressing the slightest concern about their predicament. If he was going to tease her with a breakdown, she'd tease him with her imperturbability.

"Hey, Zhenia, let's just suppose I've kidnapped you," said Astap without looking up from what he was doing. "I sure have brought you to an out-of-the-way spot!"

"Yeah, you've kidnapped me and look where it's gotten you!"

But Mustang finally started up again and they drove out of the water. For some reason Astap didn't put his clothes back on but sat down behind the wheel in his swim trunks.

He pulled into a secluded spot off the road, then got out and walked up to the water to wash his hands. When he returned he didn't get back into the cab but entered the passenger section. Yes, of course, to get dressed; this was where his clothes were.

"But what would happen, Zhenia, if I were really to kidnap you?"

"I'd kill you with the jack handle," she replied, exasperated at her own stupidity. You should never accept favors from people you don't respect. Now she was in his debt and was going to have to put up with his lousy attempts at humor.

Astap was obviously enjoying his little joke. "No, but really, what would happen?"

"Just try it and see!" Zhenia retorted angrily. She was angry at herself, angry at the suspicion that had suddenly crept into her mind regarding this out-of-the-way spot where Mustang had taken cover, his muzzle now buried in the bushes. It was a nasty suspicion and she was ashamed of it. She felt as uncomfortable as if she'd been spattered with dirt.

All the same she pulled an empty Pepsi bottle (a remnant of their mountain picnic) from the pail under her seat. Seizing it by the neck, she showed in savage pantomime how she would break off the end of the bottle, thrust its jagged, razor-sharp edges forward, and advance, teeth bared, upon her enemy.

To act out this silly charade with someone she considered her inferior was very difficult for her. And once again she chided herself for having been lured by calculations of self-interest—the thought that he'd take her directly to the airport. Now you know what it's like to compromise yourself for a possible advantage, and with people you consider beneath you, at that! Whoever pays calls the tune, and now you're going to have to dance to his tune.

She sat down in her seat, the traces of her earlier fierce expression still lingering on her face. She wasn't able to alter her expression, to strike a different note and perhaps instill a different mood in Astap, and the atmosphere between them remained charged and hostile, clouded with suspicion.

Astap took the bottle from her with an unpleasant laugh and sat down on the seat directly opposite her. Thrusting his knees into the aisle, he formed a sort of turnstile from which she had no avenue of escape. And now, that nasty thought that she had tried so hard to ward off suddenly overpowered her, painfully breaching her defenses and penetrating her consciousness with a single rapierlike thrust. And it remained there, hovering above the ruins of her erstwhile faith in human predictability.

Suddenly it was clear to both of them: they weren't pretending, but were in fact confronting that which they hadn't dared even contemplate. A look of horror swept across Zhenia's face, and reflected in Astap's eyes was an intoxicating sense of power. Here she was, this woman—he had her all to himself and *he* was in charge. Whatever he wanted, that's what would be.

"So, now I understand... ," Zhenia said slowly and deliberately, her eyes hardening. "Here it is, your typical Banana Republic. A lousy, brutish country with no higher aspirations! That's Central Asia for you," she grimaced with disgust.

"Why do you say that?" Astap asked mechanically, his thoughts elsewhere.

"Because all you people think about is food—and women! Garka was right when he said that you people aren't fully human—that your whole lives revolve around shish kebabs and bazaars!"

"Yes," Astap confirmed in a pensive voice, and he added sadly, "and your coach said, 'When the first native appears in a ballet on ice, that's when they'll make the field and track team!'" He looked at her intently, as if trying to decide how she was going to pay for this harsh judgment. And he remained immersed in thought: here she was, this snotty white woman who had always looked down on him, had only half-seen him, who could walk right by without even noticing him, as if he were some sort of tree. And look where he had her now—and it was about time she realized it!

Zhenia had decided that she would deliberately wound his pride, that she would say things that were nasty and unfair just so he could prove her wrong by his own magnanimous behavior. But now the minutes were passing—her watch already said eight—and it was high time, more than high time, for him to get on with the magnanimous behavior.

"Well, I guess our coach knows your foul breed through and through!"

"That's insulting," he said indifferently. And he continued to sit there as if stalled. It was as if his emotions had temporarily been put on hold, or perhaps he'd forgotten what was to come next and was in no hurry to remember.

Zhenia gasped, suddenly realizing that the melancholy look on his face, the look of a killer, had been there all along, even when he smiled. But up to now, the realization had never sunk in. Until a person affects you in some tangible way, you don't bother to think about him; and athletes, more than others, tend to be preoccupied with their physical well-being and peace of mind.

She looked around in consternation. What about Mustang—he was almost like a friend. Would he really allow her to perish?

"So that's why we've driven to this godforsaken spot. You had it planned all along!" Astap suddenly came to. "No, we were going to—I really did need to pick someone up."

"So why aren't we picking this person up?!" asked Zhenia, grasping at straws.

"I've changed my mind," he declared coldly.

And afterwards he'll kill me, the thought came to her.

She took stock of her situation. The plane would take off without her—and only last night she'd been so happy and full of anticipation! And this morning she'd carried herself so proudly as she walked out to this damn bus in her windbreaker and track shoes, a bag slung over each shoulder. He had obligingly taken her suitcase out earlier and was already sitting in the driver's seat, ready to go. He had watched her as she approached—his chin resting on the steering wheel, like a dog resting his head on his paws and gazing forlornly at the chain that denies him his freedom. Her rubber soles clinging softly to the pavement, she had moved forward into the early morning light. Feeling his gaze and knowing that she incited his envy, she had sauntered slim-legged and buoyant, all the lines of her body straining upward. (As with most athletes, the most striking thing about her was not her face but her body; her essential being expressed itself most fully in motion—in the lazy, careless gait of a great cat.) Knowing that he was drinking in her every movement and following her every unapproachable step, she had graciously presented herself to his gaze, like a queen presenting herself to the adoring eyes of the crowd. Still feeling a bit groggy as she boarded the bus, she had slumped carelessly into her seat and said, "Let's go!" And now, remembering all this, she suddenly realized that for this moment alone she fully deserved what was happening to her and that this local scum's response was completely justified.

But her recognition of the justness of what was happening didn't make her feel any better. As she sadly contrasted yesterday's extreme joy with her present extreme humiliation, the distance between them was more than she could bear, and she burst into tears.

She wasn't ready to die. If only she'd had a little time to get used to the idea, if only it had happened gradually, but instead, out of the blue like this... And she felt very sorry for herself, bad as she might be.

"What are you crying for?" he asked indifferently. "I'm not even touching you. What have I done to you?"

(This imperceptible dividing line when one moment a person is his usual self and utterly familiar and then suddenly he's a complete stranger, hostile and uncontrollable, like a car without brakes. And his intonation is different, and his logic and the inner laws that he follows are different. This mysterious leap—when does it take place? And what in life can be more terrifying?)

"Oh, so you haven't done anything?!" Zhenia exclaimed indignantly through her tears. "You couldn't do anything worse to me than what you've done already!" she sobbed, secretly hoping that at least her tears might have some effect. "Never in my life have I been so humiliated! But it serves me right! To have misjudged someone so completely!" She shook her head sadly.

He took her by the shoulder. She shook his hand off, exclaiming angrily, "Don't touch me!"

"What have I done to you?" Astap repeated dully, as if in a daze. "I'm just sitting here, talking. I can't see that I've done anything to offend you."

"Oh, no? I've got a plane to catch and he's just sitting here, talking. Terrific!"

"But maybe I feel like talking! I can't see what all the fuss is about."

"And you never will see! You people understand only one thing!"

"That's an insult. As far as I can see, I'm just sitting here and not even touching you."

And now Zhenia began crying in earnest. She took a handkerchief from her bag, and alternately wadding it into a ball and carefully folding it into a narrow strip, she wiped her eyes and nose.

"Come on, don't cry—stop crying!... Have you stopped? Come on, smile." He was trying to shake off his torpor, to behave firmly and decisively.

But firmness was lacking, and sensing this, Zhenia tried to seize the initiative. "Let's go!" she said. She still hoped.

But her words didn't register. Nothing changed.

Once again there were sobs. He took hold of her upper arm and didn't let go. And from his heavy, leaden grip it was evident that nothing stirred inside him, neither consciousness nor feeling. His whole being was stuck in the morass of a single dull desire.

To her it was incomprehensible. How can you desire a woman whom you're tormenting? And suddenly she was struck by nature's indifference and by its ambiguousness. For a particular phenomenon can pass imperceptibly from one side to its opposite, without any demarcation line, as along a Möbius strip. Thus, a warming flame can become a destructive fire; a snake's venom can cure you; and an undeniable source of human pleasure can suddenly turn against you and become a threat and a punishment.

"You're all animals," said Zhenia, still in tears. "You people are simply incapable of understanding what this sort of thing is all about and what it's supposed to be like."

"You're so insulting..."

Again there was a pause, heavy and awkward, like a log blocking a path. For a long time nothing changed. Time stood still. And this was irritating, the sort of irritation you feel when you're standing in line to use a pay phone and the people in front of you are taking their time and can't seem to collect their thoughts. Or as sometimes happens in chess: the game needs to move forward, but the players are nervous and inexperienced, each counting not so much on his own skill as on the weakness of his opponent.

Finally, Astap sighed and hazarded a move.

"What's your view on principles of character?" he asked.

Zhenia looked at him uncomprehendingly.

"Principles of character!" he repeated, pleased at how intelligently he had expressed himself.

Zhenia smiled disdainfully.

"Are you referring to how you always do what you set out to do? At least that's what you boasted when you ripped the padlock from the gate."

Astap felt flattered and smiled. "So you haven't forgotten?"

"There are a lot of things I haven't forgotten! You also boasted that you always keep your word!"

"And I do... What, you don't think so?" he asked anxiously, with obvious concern.

"Yeah, you really keep your word! This morning you told me that you were going to take me to the airport. And now where's that airport, I'd like to know!" She glanced at her watch in despair. It was 8:30. "It's not as if I'd asked you to take me—you came on your own. I thought you were just being nice... And how can you do such a thing, look someone in the eye and then...? What a betrayal!" And, struck by the magnitude of his deception, she once again dissolved in tears. "I've never been treated so despicably in all my life! And here I thought you wanted to do me a favor just to be nice, without any ulterior motive, the sort of thing Russians do all the time. But you, you people here—you don't make a move unless there's something to gain from it! You don't seem to understand that there are other pleasures in life besides the purely animal ones!"

"You're so insulting," he repeated mechanically.

"I'd never have thought that people who were friends, who had looked each other in the eye...!"

A live emotion suddenly animated his face: it was anger. He smiled sarcastically, "We were never friends!"

Zhenia's heart sank. He was right, and she began to cry, whimpering softly.

"You knew exactly what was going to happen," she whispered plaintively.

"No, I didn't," Astap countered, trying to convince himself. "I didn't have anything like this in mind, but now you've said so many insulting things that I'm just not going to let it go!"

This line of reasoning struck him as persuasive and added to his self-confidence. He shifted restlessly in his seat. It was time to stop talking and begin to act.

Disturbing images flashed through Zhenia's mind: the plane would leave without her and he would simply toss her out of the bus and leave her here in the bushes after he had strangled her with his strong, lean hands—hands huge as shovels. What else could one expect from a savage in a frenzy of lust? And there would be no witnesses, no one had seen her leaving with him, and her son was there in...

"God will punish you!!!"

"I don't believe in God."

He stood up. If she'd had the courage, she could have over-powered him with a glance. He was obviously hesitating; it was still possible to dissuade him, to dissipate his still tentative resolve. Just a bit more courage and she would have been able to put him—and everything else—back in their proper places. What was needed was a burst of anger! But her spirit was paralyzed, crushed by the humiliation she had suffered, and all that fluttered to the surface on little bird wings was the plaintive thought: my son an orphan and my poor father waiting there at the airport. He'd be studying the faces of the arriving passengers, and all those faces would be unresponsive, knowing nothing about her. And her father would rush helplessly from one passenger to another, asking after her whereabouts. And they'd only shrug their shoulders and continue on their way, no one would stop...

Once again she was sobbing.

Her sobs goaded him on, excited him as blood excites a shark. How great was his power if it could inspire such terror! And what was the full measure of this power? He felt an urge, a compelling urge to proceed farther, deeper into the abyss—to find out what was waiting there, in the heart of darkness.

He shifted from one foot to the other in one last transitional movement. Apparently his resolve had not yet completely hardened, had not yet reached the point of no return. He took a step, shifting the position of his body. And this step clearly signaled the shift in their relationship. The line had been crossed and there was no turning back. She read this in the glazed expression of his eyes: he had made up his mind.

He heaved a heavy sigh. In a different voice, as if he'd thrown off the remnants of everything human that still restrained him, he said sadly, like a man who had no other choice, "Well, I guess that's it... I'm going to do it."

Zhenia searched feverishly within, but the strength to resist wasn't there.

"What are you going to do?" she asked with a shudder. She looked at him in terror, no longer resisting but simply begging for mercy.

"I've put up with a lot—so many insults! I didn't deserve them and now I'm going to get revenge!" he said, attempting to justify himself. His voice was charged with emotion and kept changing timbre. His agitation was frightful.

"So now you *want* to deserve them. Is that it, you *want* to deserve them?" Zhenia blurted out in desperation, grasping at one last straw.

"I didn't deserve them and now I've got no choice but to take revenge," he repeated more firmly, with a stronger sense of his own rectitude. And he pressed down hard on her shoulders.

She tried to resist, but she was too weak. She, a ranked athlete with national standing, was physically so weak that it was as if all the strength had drained from her body. She felt his seething fury, his cruel passion, and she could picture it all: how he would start to beat her and twist her arms; and what would happen to her clothes in the struggle, not to mention her flesh; and how her face would be bruised and disfigured.

No, from an aesthetic point of view this was simply intolerable. And it would be even more humiliating than if she were simply to give in. But this was not the worst of it: fired up to a fever pitch of hatred and savagery, this male, any male, would not be able, could simply not afford, to leave her alive in the state she'd be in... And now, in utter despair, she begged for mercy.

"Stop, listen to me!"

His sinewy hands were already pressing her against the seat, but he was still able to check himself, and he loosened his grip on her shoulders. But listening was beyond him and he took in nothing more of what she said.

Directing a beseeching glance first at one of his eyes, then at the other—they were so close that she could look at them only one at a time—she nonetheless went on, "Listen to me! You have a son, and I have a son too. He's just a baby, and what is it you want to do to me?" Her gaze shifted from one pupil to the other, feverishly seeking deliverance, but it was nowhere to be found.

And Mustang too had casually betrayed her...

"Don't you understand, a woman has to want it too, then it's a completely different thing. How can you do it this way? You can't," she said, shaking her head.

She had a momentary impulse: she would rise up and, in the words of the song, "defying death by one's willingness to die," she would proudly fling in his face the words: "I hate you!" But then it occurred to her: a person won't put up with hatred that is directed against him. He fears the power of a curse, remembering in his trembling guts and knowing with every fiber of his being that the Word is all-powerful and will be carried out. Feeling does whatever it wants with the same inevitability that once characterized the creation of the world and continues to characterize its tireless evolution. So an evildoer won't allow hatred to be directed against him but will stamp it out the moment he finds it. He'll stamp it out at its source in order to protect himself. And if one tries to resist, at some savage moment he'll see himself for the evildoer he is, and there'll be nothing left for him but to behave like one.

And, fainthearted, she pulled back. She didn't choose a proud death; she wanted to go on living just a little bit longer. She sold herself for this "little bit longer."

Through dim eyes she glanced hastily at her watch. It was nine o'clock. Check-in would start at ten, she calculated, and if things weren't delayed, she might be able to make it.

"Okay," she said in a somewhat harsh, cynical voice and with her eyes half-closed, as if not wanting to see herself or anything around her, "if we do it right now, will you take me to the airport afterwards?"

He didn't answer, but silently, with all his weight, kept pressing her against the seat.

"I've never known such a woman," he uttered unexpectedly, almost in a whisper. Apparently, the words came out in spite of him. While the act of love in this instance was not taking place as nature intended, even the rapist, it seems, cannot totally escape the laws of human nature. "I've never loved anyone," he confided in a whisper. "And no woman has ever loved me.... It seems they're always just after my money." Then he added bitterly, and perhaps sincerely, "And I myself don't know how to love..."

"Poor man," said Zhenia, so taken aback that she forgot about herself. "But this morning, when you came to pick me up, I almost loved you," she said almost truthfully, trying to comfort him. And she too spoke in a whisper.

"And now?" He froze, intently searching her eyes for an answer.

She hesitated.

"I hate you," she admitted feebly, her eyes narrowing.

"Well, so there you are," he smiled in relief.

Her answer left him no option but revenge.

But what did it matter now? Let it happen—she had, in effect, already agreed to it.

"Well, then, you promise to take me to the airport?"

"Turn in your ticket... and stay here!"

(My God, he was actually thinking about love—how awful!)

"That's impossible."

"Then come back later on!"

"I don't know," she equivocated weakly, as if to leave him some shred of hope regarding this love business. Love—my God, what a laugh! If laughter were conceivable in such a situation, then she was laughing bitterly.

"Well then, you'll take me to the airport?"

He gave in.

"I'll take you," he said, his former melancholy torpor returning.

"Let me go, I'll get undressed," she said, pushing him away resolutely.

He yielded.

She would have to hurry. There was enough time, but still it was better to hurry.

"What about the sweater?" he asked.

"The sweater stays on," she replied firmly.

Taking off her sweater would have suggested some level of feeling, something from the realm of love, where the entire surface of one's body in its yearning seeks mutual contact and caresses. He didn't insist. Suddenly he had become shy and obedient. But later on, his hands nonetheless sought a human caress and wandered under her sweater—though this was hardly necessary, for nature had already yielded, surrendered, said the hell with it, and allowed this man to do what he wanted to do. He extended gentle hands for the sake of something human, preserving what was left of his heart, and sought her lips. And Zhenia didn't turn away, for here—Lord, may the good Lord forgive her!—there was an element of calculation: the more yielding and responsive she was, the sooner it would be over. She smiled bitterly and said in a husky voice shaded with velvet, an intimate voice known to only one other person in the world, "This is the first time I've ever been raped."

"I'm not raping you," he whispered in reply, his voice beseeching, "I'm saying goodbye...."

Afterwards they left the bus and, taking turns, walked in silence down to the stream. In silence they made their way back and, with eyes lowered, took their former seats on the bus. Astap started up the engine and they were off.

At a certain moment the bus once again became the old, familiar Mustang.

They turned onto the highway and soon reached the city, where, with Astap's hand pressed firmly on the horn, they raced like a fire engine through one red light after another. Astap drove with the conviction of a man engaged in a rescue operation, experiencing each moment of the ride so intensely that it remained etched in his memory forever. Occasionally, with a fleeting glance of brotherly concern he would look back in Zhenia's direction. Off and on, her eyes would fill with tears. But the tears welled up on their own, without her conscious involvement. She had no strength left for involvement.

Astap had no idea of her emotional state, nor had there been any time for him to reflect on it. All his efforts were concentrated on driving Mustang swiftly and smoothly to the airport. It seemed to him that she should be full of admiration for his skill and audacity.

The police are going to stop us any minute, thought Zhenia apathetically, and I won't make the plane, and it'll all have been for nothing.

But the Devil, gratified by their transgression, was apparently looking after them himself, just as he looks after all his weak and needy subjects, guiding drunks to their doorstep, criminals to their hideout, and the truly deserving to their eternal rest. Thus it was that at precisely ten o'clock Astap slammed on the brakes and brought Mustang to a flying halt directly in front of the main entrance to the passenger terminal. He threw up his arm to look at his watch and stole a backward glance at Zhenia. Had she noticed everything and was she impressed?

Poor fellow...

He opened the bus doors with the press of a button and bounded into the passenger section. He was still fired up from his daring race through town, and the exhilarating sense of his own audacity had blocked out everything else from his narrow, rather circumscribed consciousness, leading him to assume that Zhenia too had nothing else to think about but what a dashing fellow he was. (Astap obviously longed for love.) He grabbed her suitcase and one of her shoulder bags. She didn't object but followed him indifferently into the terminal. Trailing behind him through the main lobby, she made no effort to look for the check-in counter. Let *him* look for it... And, in fact, he rushed around, looking in every direction, and found it.

"Please go now," she begged.

"No, no," he replied in a subdued, apologetic voice full of tenderness and hope.

And he remained doggedly by her side, constantly trying to relieve her of one of her bags and pushing her suitcase forward to keep up with the line. Uttering an occasional sigh, he would survey the lobby, not because it interested him, but for Zhenia's sake: as if to give the airport its due in case it might suddenly feel slighted by her lack of interest. And by his example he hoped to convince her that everything was all right, that nothing had happened. If she'd only look around and see what a magnificent structure this was, she'd have no reason to feel sad.

"Go and buy me a comb. I left mine behind in the room," she said in a lifeless voice, sending him off on an errand so that he would be out of her sight.

He obligingly disappeared, running off before he had figured out where he needed to go. As he looked around, trying to spot a kiosk, his outspread arms flapped first in one direction, then another—a thin, unlikely figure reminiscent of something from a child's drawing, with a sticklike body and sticklike limbs.

He returned very quickly with a fancily carved, blue plastic comb. What else could one expect from him?! She took it without a word and ran it through her boyishly cropped hair. A moment later, when the comb was already in her pants pocket, she burst out angrily, "You bought the wrong kind! Go and get another."

He didn't believe that it was the wrong kind—he had made a point of buying a lady's comb—but he obediently rushed off to carry out her command. He would have carried out a hundred such commands! But all she wanted was for him to be gone, to leave her alone with her tears.

She focused her gaze on the woman in front of her. The woman was carrying a little girl in her arms, a tiny little thing no bigger than Zhenia's own distant son. And Zhenia grieved for her former self, now destroyed, wiped from the face of the earth. But this little girl was so tiny—too tiny to know anything. Yet someday she would grow up, and something like this would happen to her. And since evil couldn't be eradicated from this world, somewhere even now some bastard was growing up to play this role in her life.

Zhenia looked around her, but in the faces of the people passing to and fro through the crowded lobby she could detect no awareness of the existence of evil. Judging by the placid expression on every one of their faces, there was nothing to worry about and one could venture out into the world with carefree abandon. She began to suspect that only she had suffered such misfortune and only she would have to walk through life with her head bowed in shame. These others were pure and innocent.

Once again tears began flowing from her reddened eyes. Why was it that of all these people she alone had had to find out what can happen in this world on a sunlit morning by a sparkling stream?

And now this personification of evil was actually approaching her, with a new comb in his hand and a perplexed, guilty look on his face.

"Why are you crying again?" he asked sadly.

"Do you expect me to be happy?" she asked with a pitiful sob. She wanted his sympathy and made no attempt to hide her tears. Let him who had wronged her take pity and grieve along with her. And why shouldn't he? After all, when you came right down to it, there was no one else she could complain to.

But the little toy monkey Astap had no idea of what was going on in her mind and fell into a chagrined silence. What, he wondered, was all the fuss about? After all, he hadn't killed her, he hadn't injured her, and it wasn't as if she were a virgin. And he hadn't infected her with anything—that he knew for sure.

"It's not your fault," Zhenia said after a moment, having regained her composure. "It's what I deserved for the way I behaved, for the expression on my face.. and for not knowing what sort of person I was dealing with," she added with a momentary flash of anger. But it was only momentary, and she suppressed it. For she no longer felt like offending Astap. They had, after all, shared in that mystery that nature had designed to serve the sacred cause of human renewal. And whatever may have been involved and however it may have come about, they had experienced the sexual union that could have made them kin. Zhenia had been the soil that the poor fellow had sown and instinct dictated that he protect and preserve this soil for the sake of his future offspring. And so here he was, buying her combs and looking after her. And right now he couldn't help loving her, for she held within her a part of himself. Zhenia felt all of this too and could no longer find it in her to hate him.

Hatred came later, in the plane. It spread, permeating to her very marrow: she felt defiled. Out of a need to cleanse herself, she made several trips to the rest room. She kept washing her hands and pressing them to her burning cheeks, but no sense of purification followed. Returning to her seat, she would examine the other passengers with a quizzical eye. Their faces wore the same neutral, unperturbed expression as before, but now she no longer believed that they had no knowledge of the evil that had befallen her. They knew all right, they'd all seen it, but they'd chosen to ignore it and continue about their business as if it had never happened. What beasts they all were! And now she was suddenly convinced that she knew all there was to know about every one of these people. Beneath their peaceful, decorous exterior, each one of them harbored a hidden, shameful truth. For how else but through the favorable environment provided by each of these hosts could the infection—this bacillus of blind, cruel evil—have survived and flourished?

Knowing now the depths to which she herself was capable of sinking, she couldn't help suspecting that the same held true for everyone else. And how much more so for that scoundrel Astap! And yet, she reminded herself, she had no right to think of him that way. For had she behaved differently, he would not have become one.

Feeling utterly exhausted and not knowing how to escape what she had discovered inside herself, she leaned back in her seat and closed her eyes. But this only made matters worse. For no sooner would she close her eyes than Astap's simian face would immediately appear before her in clear, exaggerated detail. And now she wondered in alarm: how was she going to avoid blurting something out in her sleep?

The plane droned on, leaving behind this land where hectarites[8] toiled quietly away, bringing so much profit to themselves and to the collective that one could only throw up one's hands in delight. Under the burning sun of this land, the mulberry tree ripened and shed its fruit, and its green leaves were cut off to provide food for the silkworms that wrapped themselves in gossamer thread. And even this brought profit to those farmers willing to assume the extra burden of cultivating these insatiable creatures. Warmed by a friendly sun, the asphalt road breathed forth heat, and along this road the collective farmers would drive their cars—cars paid for with the fruits of their tireless labor. Next to many of their houses cows with heavy udders grazed at the end of a long tether. Keeping a cow in this land was incomparably easier and more profitable than in Zhenia's homeland, since here one didn't have to stock up on hay for the long winter. And here, in general, the authorities were less resistant to change. It was said that rivers from the poorer Russian areas to the north, where the rivers served no useful purpose, would soon be directed here, where they could do a lot of good. And it was here, precisely here in this rich, abundant land, that Zhenia had left behind her soul—had sold it in order to catch a plane and to save her body from bruises; had forfeited it in order to preserve her father's peace of mind and to return to her tiny son.

As her head rested limply against the back of her seat, the thought came to her that he, that ape, would gradually get used to the idea. He'd begin to think it was possible to behave this way, that this was, in fact, the only way to behave. And he'd keep going on and on. Once a tiger has tasted human flesh it becomes a man-eater forever.

And it was she who had corrupted him; it was she who had made it possible for him to think that he could behave this way.

Should she tell Kostia?... Kostia would drop the national championships in a minute, he'd fly back and track down that ape, he'd fight him—he'd kill him. But that would be the end of everything; it would ruin his whole life. Everything would fall apart—his sports career, his family life. He'd have to go to prison, and there'd be nothing but misery. Or he might come away from their fight with serious injuries. Or perhaps—and this was most likely—he'd vent all his feelings of hatred on the flight back. He'd exhaust himself to the point where he'd have lost all appetite for revenge by the time he arrived. He'd feel confused, burnt out, and empty. He'd suddenly wonder why on earth he had come. He'd reflect for a while and wouldn't be able to remember, but in the meantime he'd have stopped loving her. And all that would be left would be silence and devastation, as after an earthquake.

Or another possibility: his anger would continue unabated; he'd reach his destination and go into battle. But it wouldn't be his territory—it would be Astap's, and Astap would have friends to back him up. And they'd end up killing Kostia, this fair-skinned outsider. Or even worse, they'd humiliate him and leave him permanently maimed. And she wouldn't be at his side to help. After all, he wouldn't take her with him. This was something he'd do on his own, in grim secrecy. No, it was impossible, simply impossible to tell him. He must never know, never!

And to take vengeance on her own, that too was impossible, simply impossible.

Lord, take vengeance for me!

Everything was hopeless, irreparable, awful. But there was something even more awful, something hidden in the darkest recesses of her soul, in the depths of human consciousness where one normally hesitates to look. Most people are afraid to approach the edge of an abyss. But she approached it—she had nothing to lose now—and she peered into it. And what she discovered was that she had been aware from the very first day of the effect she had on Astap. A woman always knows this sort of thing. She had known and it had pleased her.

And if it hadn't been for that, none of the rest would have followed.

Her father stood behind the chain-link fence where people gathered to meet arriving passengers and gazed intently into the distance. He seemed anxious to catch sight of his daughter as quickly as possible. It was as if there were a time limit to their reunion, and the stopwatch had already been set. Before the seconds ran out, their eyes needed to meet and to hold each other in love's field of vision.

But Zhenia, for her part, wanted to hold back, to try to hide behind the other passengers in order to delay the moment when their eyes would meet. She was ashamed, ashamed for herself and for her father, ashamed of what they were both implicated in—guilty accomplices both—ashamed of everything that goes on in this world. But with her tall, athletic build it would be difficult for her to hide. A moment later, it no longer mattered: the feeling had passed. She moved forward, her gaze directed straight ahead.

"How tan you are," said her father, obviously moved.

Yes, the tan was visible, but the other thing wasn't.

A few minutes later, as they were waiting in the baggage area for her suitcase, her father was saying, "Whenever he's upset he starts talking, really belting out his 'words.' Whatever sounds come out, he groups them into clusters. He's trying to make real words. He's always in a rush to get out as many of them as he can. I guess he thinks that the more he says, the better his chances of producing the words that he needs."

Zhenia nodded. Apparently, he was talking about her son.

"... But don't let it get you down," he said suddenly.

She started. What was that about? Oh yes, she hadn't made the team.

"When you were a child, I purposely got you into field and track. It's a demanding sport... but clean and honest. And only people with a sense of integrity flourish in it. And integrity—that, brother, is a matter of courage more than anything else."

Zhenia looked at him long and hard, the hostility in her eyes mounting. For today she was an athlete who had lost those qualities of courage and integrity that her father had put so much faith in. But her father, of course, had something else in mind.

"These are the sort of people I've always been around, people with a strong sense of honor, like the nobility in the old days," said Zhenia with a sigh. "And I'd begun to assume that people were like that everywhere. And now it turns out that they're not."

"Well, what can you do? That's just the way it is," her father conceded.

So, he had known! He had known and hadn't warned her, about life... She was silent, her heart pounding from the realization that he hadn't helped her understand certain things, and now, even though he might want to help, it was too late.

Her father stood beside her, feeling at a loss. He dimly sensed her anguish, as an animal senses danger in the air. But he didn't know what sort of danger it was or what could be done about it. After all, his daughter was standing right beside him, safe and sound, and whom was he to protect her from? After a moment's thought, he took a guess and said, "There's no reason you couldn't become a coach if you're tired of..."

"Sure, Dad,... that's a possibility."

When Zhenia saw her son after their long separation, he seemed small and completely insignificant, not worth what she had sacrificed for his sake. She realized that she didn't love him. There was so little of him compared to the enormous grief inside her.

In the evening, Kostia called. She had dreaded his call and hoped that once again he wouldn't be able to get through. She didn't know whether she could trust her voice.

But living on this earth *after the fact,* living from one hour to the next, she discovered to her surprise that she *could* do it. Taking one step at a time, she could do it. Just as a high jumper, lacking self-confidence and unsure of his own potential, is surprised each time he achieves a new height. And each time the crossbar is raised another notch he wonders what will happen next. Will he be able to clear this one too? So it was with her. But the capabilities of the body are limitless and, as she realized now, so too are those of the soul.

And the soul's limitless capacity for acceptance saddened her.

As Kostia spoke to her over the phone, she did her best to say nothing. He was giving her a careful account of the first days of the championships, trying to protect her self-esteem. Vera, he said, had tripped on level ground and was out of the running. And everyone was getting fed up with that clown Garka. He made the team laugh, of course, but once in a while you did have to run, and not just off at the mouth!

He spoke only of their failures, omitting their successes, so that Zhenia wouldn't feel left out. But what worried her was the possibility that he might suddenly ask her about her trip to the airport. Fortunately, such things as how was your trip, what did you eat, how did you sleep, etc., were not important to them. For them other things were important.

And what about her heroine Carmen, the thought came to her in the middle of the night—Carmen, who valued pride and courage more than life itself?... And what about me, Zhenia reflected sadly? And even in her thoughts her small voice faded and trailed off, as if unworthy to make itself heard in the lofty sphere of human thought, in the realm of the human spirit.

Well, and what would happen next? Kostia would return and she would have nightmares that she wouldn't be able to tell him about. And despite everything she was concealing from him, she'd still have to look him in the eye without flinching. And eventually, she'd begin to rejoice in their quarrels and in his failures, storing them up until there were enough of them to compensate for her betrayal, until it would begin to seem that he somehow even deserved this betrayal. And that would be the end of it, the end of their love.

Either way, it came to the same thing. If she told Kostia, he'd stop loving *her;* if she didn't tell him, she wouldn't be able to love *him.* For goodness is self-generating; it multiplies through simple sharing. And when you've been able to do a good deed for someone, you want to do another. But if you've had to hurt someone, you tend to avoid that person like the plague, not wanting to hurt him any more.

But perhaps she should just go ahead and confess... Right there by the airport fence, she'd stand there and tell him, "Astap's not to blame...." Because the aggressor is never solely to blame. The victim too is always partly to blame, sometimes more, sometimes less. Yes, that's what she'd do, and then Kostia could decide for himself whether or not he wanted to go on living with her. But what would happen to Kostia's face when she told him?... A tank on steel treads, a clanking, grinding sound, and a man is trampled and ground into the earth, blending with it and moistening it with the juices of his former life.

No, not for anything!

And one more thought—about death. But no sooner did the thought come to her than her body instantly recoiled.

Over and over, back and forth—was there any way out?!

And here we'll leave Zhenia, knowing full well that this is one of those situations where there *is* no way out, that in this instance she would find solace only with the passage of time, when her heart had a chance to forget. And eventually, that day would come.

Soon afterwards Astap was involved in a serious accident and his leg had to be amputated from above the knee. He never made any connection between his own misfortune and Zhenia's curse. It was simply fate—blind, deaf, and indifferent. Terrible and unjust. Lord, have mercy!

Translated by Helen Burlingame

From *Kazhdyi okhotnik*, Moscow, 1989

Notes

1. The term *basmachi* used for counterrevolutionaries here makes it clear that the story is set in southern Kazakhstan or in one of the Islamic, Central Asian republics of the Soviet Union.

2. A mistake easily made by the uneducated since the pronunciation of an unstressed *o* in Russian is in most cases identical to that of an unstressed *a*.

3. An appealing con man, Ostap Bender is the protagonist of the two humorous novels *The Twelve Chairs* (1928) and *The Little Golden Calf* (1931) written by Ilia Ilf and Evgeny Petrov, still widely read today.

4. To ensure meaningful competition at the national level, those (largely Central Asian or Islamic) republics lacking a well-developed tradition or adequate training resources for a particular sport have been allowed over the years to hire other (usually Russian) Soviet athletes to represent them.

5. In the context of a certain Soviet witticism, to give someone "two" of something means to give him or her nothing at all.

6. The polite use of the patronymic makes it clear that Astap is somewhat older than the athletes, in his mid-thirties at least.

7. A relatively recent term applied to individuals picked up for public drunkenness. The offender is taken to a sobering-up station administered by the police and is subsequently required to work for fifteen days on a public works project.

8. A term (in Russian: *gektarshchiki*) dating from the Brezhnev era, when in an attempt to boost agricultural production, collective farmers in some areas were allowed to lease a certain number of hectares that had already been sown by the collective. In exchange for tending and harvesting these fields in their spare time, the "hectarites" were allowed to keep a share of the harvest for themselves.

Rush Job

Elena Makarova

At the shore in winter you don't get much business. Who needs a cobbler during the off season?

Yakov put the tea kettle on the electric ring and picked up from the bottom shelf the only pair of boots. A middle-aged man in a sheepskin coat had brought them in the day before. Most likely from the writers' retreat. You can tell the writers in the off season. In summer you can't tell who's a writer and who's a reader, but in winter you can. How? Ask me something easier. Yakov tied on his black apron, brewed the tea and, sipping it from a big mug, inspected the boots. Brand-name, with narrow little soles and slender heels. They'd been worn, frankly speaking, by a less than careful young lady. The leather was peeling on the heels, the toes were scratched, or else she's from the capital, where they all walk on each other's feet...

Yakov set both boots on the counter—where he didn't usually allow customers to place the shoes they unwrapped from the newspapers and dirty plastic bags—took a velvet cloth from his work bench, and wiped the toes. From his window he could see the souvenir store Amber across the street. They didn't make their quota off season either. A Godforsaken time, February. The wind blows from the sea, and the draft can settle in your apartment, too. Only the writers come for the draft. They shut themselves up in their glass and concrete and write.

When Yakov thinks about writers his blood boils. What does he have against them? He has a tooth against them. That's what he has.

Yakov looked in the mirror and bared his teeth, displaying his lower crowns. The top teeth were well preserved, but the lower ones had to be held up by a gold fence. Jail had bleached his fiery red hair, the color had become dull, yolk and white. His hands had gotten rough. Yakov lifted his palms to his face—carved rocks, not cushions. You couldn't shoe a horse with those hands.

He put a boot on the stand and read the receipt attached to the bottom with rubber glue: 12:00.

How many minutes does it take to shoe a flea? Once even a juggler would have envied his agile hands. But even now Yakov worked well, in season he could put out forty heels. And now one pair was standing there, and he didn't feel like getting to work. There was no pressure.

Summer's another thing—the customer says one word, you answer with ten. The writers come like wasps to jam, they eat, but don't give honey.

The door creaked. Yakov buried himself in the boot. He liked customers to find him at work.

"My husband came in here..." a woman's twittering voice resounded right over his ear.

"Your husband's not here," Yakov answered, without raising his head. "Do you think he's hiding behind the workbench?" he added.

"...yesterday, with a pair of boots."

Now Yakov raised his eyes and looked at her from under his brow. She didn't recognize him. Twenty years change a man, what can you do. Count one day in jail as half a life, and how do you count five years? Count or not, jail doesn't beautify a person, get you new teeth, or put a smile on your face...

"There they are!" she said, delighted. "Are they ready?"

"They'll be ready, sit down. Wisdom says there's no truth in the feet, but you don't always find truth higher either, do you?"

She sat down and undid the top button of her red fur coat.

"It's so cozy here..."

"All for the sake of the customer. I can offer you a cup of good tea, it's part of the bill."

"Thank you, I won't say no."

Yakov took off his apron, put the kettle on the burner, and came out from behind the counter.

"Meine aicheleh, meine faigele, meine brechele..."

"Is it really you?!" The woman stood up, but with a gesture Yakov ordered her to sit.

"You're not at a parade; I'm not Marshal Rokossovsky. And was that the same guy I turned you over to on the corner of Krishiany Barona and Tallinskaia? So he's a writer?"

"How did you know?"

"It's written on the soles of your boots, meine aicheleh."

She hadn't changed, she was still a beauty. She'd only replaced her short skirt, the one she'd danced in at the Jewish wedding, with a long one. Short coat and long skirt. That's the fashion now.

"How much sugar?"

"None."

"Are you watching your figure?"

She finally smiled. Yakov placed a steaming mug in front of her. He'd promised her a cup, gave her a mug, what's the good of that. It's not right to offer such a lady tea in a mug.

"Are you in a hurry?"

"No, no, don't worry."

He wasn't worried. Now she was worried. She squirmed in her chair, clasped one knee, then the other, in her hand.

"Is your Mama still alive?"

"Yes. And remembers you often."

"I'd like to see her, if it's possible..."

"Why wouldn't it be possible? Right now if you like. Or if you're here for a long time..."

"No, we're leaving tonight."

"For the capital?"

She nodded. Yakov noticed a few wiry silver hairs among the black. Oh, how her hair had flown when she had danced at the Jewish wedding, how sweet it had smelled, it had smelled so sweet that for a long time after he would still get excited just from the memory of that accursed smell. Her eyebrows were still black, arched high above her eyes, and it seemed to him that she wanted to ask something, but she didn't ask anything.

"I have to be back for dinner by two. Two-thirty at the latest."

"You'll make it," said Yakov. "They'll be ready in a minute."

"How's the goldsmith's shop? I'll never forget your Mama saying: 'You just listen, she has to go to Moscow! What do you need that zoo for? With Yakov you'll be in gold from head to toe. My oldest daughter, Yakov's sister, wears the latest shoes...' "

Yakov silently attached new heels, and his aicheleh, faigele, brechele chirped on:

"I'll never forget how we sat in that jeep, when you stole me from the wedding, remember, and your Mama said: 'My son doesn't look at women, only at gold. I tell him: "son, it's time for you to get married," and he says: "I'm already married to gold." Now you're our gold.'"

"They're finished. Do you want to put them on?"

Yakov gave the boots to Eva. No, she hadn't changed. He bent down and helped her take off a suede boot.

"You have to hold suede over steam, then wipe it with a soft velvet cloth," he said, looking at the removed boot. "That needs fixing too."

"Another time."

"Why? Take off the other one. Service of the highest quality. It will count as a rush job." Yakov took a ruble from his coat pocket.

"Return this to your husband as a redemption fee."

"What do you mean by that? I'm insulted."

Yakov tore up the ruble and threw it at her stockinged foot.

"It's stupid to throw money around."

"Tell that to your grandmother. Or your husband. He'll put it to work, he'll write: 'the cobbler throws money around.'"

"Do you still live in Riga?"

"No, we gave it up for the seashore. Mama can't breathe in the city."

"And why did you change your work?"

"Collecting material for your husband? Or have you caught the writing bug yourself?"

Yakov quickly put the second pair in order, wrapped them in newspaper, and put the bundle in her wine-colored bag, which matched her skirt. Everything matched. He hung up a sign that said "Break."

He didn't live far, rarely traveled to Riga. His friends had all moved away, it was too late to make new ones. Everything was too late for him these days.

In summer they rented out half the house, and during the tourist season he got sick of city children's squeals and crowds in the kitchen, but it was income, and not a bad one; it was all worth putting up with, though it wasn't clear why. He and Mama didn't need much. Give something to the nephews and nieces now and then... There's no such thing as too much money. When you have it you can save it, when you don't...

They walked to the sea. Eva raised the collar of her coat. The wind blew at their backs, prodding them along. She walked with propriety, her hands in her pockets, but when she saw a horizontal bar she ran up to it, jumped, and caught hold of it with her gloved hands. She hung there, swinging her feet with their shiny new heels, and again he thought that she hadn't changed a bit. He couldn't run, jump, and catch hold of a cross bar like that nowadays. Something had died in him, but in her that something still lived, even though her husband was a writer, not a goldsmith.

Eva jumped down and fixed her skirt, pulling the wine-colored folds out from under her coat.

"It's a good place to live," she said.

"Not bad."

"I would like to..."

"I didn't take back my proposal, it was you who ran off to the writer. I'm that kind of person," said Yakov, and thought, "What kind?" "I make a proposal once in my life."

Yakov's wooden house stood among the dunes, surrounded by a pine wood. Squirrel-eaten pine cones lay on the snow.

The television was on. Yakov's mother sat facing it in an armchair. Swollen, fat, like a piece of bread dough.

"Mama, look who's here, do you remember this girl?"

His mother raised her dull eyes to look at Eva. No, she didn't remember.

"Mama, it's my bride!"

His mother only shrugged her shoulders in response, and returned her attention to the television.

"She forgets everything nowadays, it's her age," said Yakov.

To Eva the room looked like a storehouse for pillows and feather beds. It was cold and stuffy.

"You don't smoke?"

"No, I never did. If you want to smoke, let's go to the kitchen."

The tiny kitchen was messy. Yakov didn't even ask Eva to take off her coat. Now he just wanted her to leave as soon as possible. And never to see her again. He didn't need this.

"Is there an ashtray?" Eva settled herself at the windowsill, covered with pots of leftover soup and burnt kasha.

"Such neglect," she thought, remembering the luxurious apartment in the center of town, with the piano on which the bridegroom, head over heels in love, had played "Havva N'Gila," "The 7:40," "Sholom Aleichem," while his dumpy sister with the rows of chins accompanied him in her ringing voice. Then he had gone to his sister's apartment to sleep, and his Mama had kept clucking and trying, after that rich wedding feast, to force bread and red caviar down Eva's throat. "You need to gain weight," she had said. "You have to have a look, a style. Or else you'll buy material for one and it'll be enough for four. Yakov, my Yakov, he never looked at women. He would walk right by, his cap over his eyes...blinded! Oy, meine faigele, meine aicheleh, meine brechele, when you marry him you'll be behind a golden wall."

Yakov scanned the room for something that could serve as an ashtray.

"Use this," he gestured at the garbage pail, full of onion skins. "It's time to take it out anyway."

"Then I'll go," Eva stood up.

"Finish your cigarette in peace and then you'll go. And take care of your boots," he added for some reason.

Eva put out her cigarette on the edge of the garbage pail.

"If there are any problems with the heels or the soles, we're at your service."

They stopped when they got to the shop. Yakov took down the break sign and stood with his back to the door as if to let her know that that was all. He was at his place of work, as it were, on the job.

He saw her leave, heard the new metal reinforcements on her boots clatter down the blocks of closely fitted cobblestones.

"Back then I was a stalk of red hay. If you held a match near me I would have burned to the ground. Tall, red hair, blue eyes, don't look at me, Moishe, turn your eyes the other way and imagine: twenty-eight years old, a young man in his prime, and not a single woman. Everybody said: 'This is no good, Yakov, it's against nature.' But I knew my nature, and I wasn't going to squander it."

Yakov poured himself more vodka.

Lame Moishe, the watchmaker from the next street, didn't drink. He often dropped in on Yakov after work, to talk about this and that. Moishe had been in the watch business now for thirty years. He knew all the artisans inside out, and was friends with none of them. Yakov appealed to him. Yakov's mother had asked him to put a word in for her son, her innocent boy, thrown into jail by evil people. Moishe didn't put much stock in Yakov's mother's words—they don't take people away just like that, 'for no reason at all; gold's not political subversion—but neither did he believe the widespread rumors of acquired millions. Whatever there may have been, nothing remained. Some say that they had one of the richest houses in Riga, but go into that dilapidated hut by the shore and you'll spit on rumors. The artisans said various things—that he'd had his insides damaged by beatings in jail, and that's why he didn't start a family, and that somewhere there was buried a fortune in gold which the investigators had never found, and that's why, enraged, they'd given him such a long sentence... Moishe had seen a lot in his time, and had learned to believe his eyes, not other people's tongues. Yakov was a decent person, took care of his sick mother, didn't rip off the summer people, and if he was solitary and ever more silent, that was his business. After the fine work of a goldsmith, the cobbler's trade was a degradation. But you couldn't find better work on the whole coast.

This was the first time Moishe had ever found Yakov drunk. His eyes were red, his cheeks like beets; he was a roused bull, not a man. In a condition like that a person shouldn't be alone, who knows what... Moishe knew for himself—at eighteen he had been wounded on the front and had wanted to put a bullet through his head. Who needed him now, neither half nor whole; but Izia, God rest his soul, had said: "Moishe, don't betray your line, fear God. You didn't give yourself life, it's not for you to take away." Simple words, spoken in time... and here he is, alive, he's found his place, and when customers come in they don't look at his figure, they look at his work. Why should they stick their noses behind the counter and see what kind of legs Moishe has? They take their watches and say thank you...

"You need some fresh air," Moishe commented meekly to Yakov.

"You remember, twenty years ago, all Riga was ours. And the shore was ours. And they had such weddings, you remember, Moishe, they'd rent a hall, hire musicians... and when your third cousin five times removed got married, the whole clan would come. You could see your grandmother's third cousin and your grandfather's fifth. Everybody found each other.

"If I could only remember whose wedding that was! There were at least a hundred people. A U-shaped table facing the band. Everyone drinking, eating, together with the musicians. When you're all sitting at the table you don't see each other. But when the music started...

"Slow at first, then faster, faster, and you can't keep anybody sitting down, old people, young people—everybody jumped up, put their thumbs under their armpits...

"And then I see that they've all stepped aside, they formed a ring around a little bird, meine faigele, in a short little skirt, so tiny that when she jumped you could see the edge of her white panties, and she was dancing—her hair was black silk, her thin, bare arms... it struck me in the head, not the head, in my heart: that's her. She's the one.

"The music ended, but people didn't wander off. They were waiting for more. They started playing 'The 7:40.' I went up and gave her my hand. How did she get here, who did she come with? I wanted to ask, but I didn't dare. I got shy, Moishe, that had never happened to me before. Her hand was hot, not one ring. Not one piece of jewelry on her. I took the gold chain from my neck and threw it onto her; it lay on her hair. Ah, what hair that was, a net of finest gossamer.

"She looked at me surprised, as if to say: 'What's all this about?' and people were looking at us, but I found my courage, rolled the chain down from her hair, and it hung on her, imagine, Moishe, that chain barely got around my neck, and on her it hung to her blouse. A pink blouse, with buttons, tucked into her skirt, if you could call that a skirt, the old people looked away from shame.

"We danced together, and everybody looked at us. It almost seemed like it was our wedding, and I thought: 'You haven't seen our wedding! I'll invite everybody, and not in this hall, I'll rent two whole floors in the "Perla," but I'll get these musicians, and I'll dress her right.'

"We sat down together at the table. It was summer, hot, she was burned, her nose was peeling, and there were a few big freckles on it. Then I asked her who she came with.

"She looked around the tables and pointed: with him, over there, 'Oh, he's nothing,' I thought. 'I'll take care of him with my little finger.'

"To be honest, I wanted to get her drunk. So she'd be easier to steal. So it could be done without unnecessary words. When the dancing started again I went to my sister and said, 'Send Senya,' that's her husband, you know him, Moishe, 'for a car in half an hour. Tell him to get a van.'

"My sister, may she live a hundred years, never asked me about a thing. Said and done. We dance. I'm steaming, you understand, steam is coming from me, that's how hot I am, but I told myself: 'Stop, Yakov, you've lived and waited twenty-eight years, wait some more, don't touch her, don't put a finger on her shoulder or you'll burn up.'

"When we sat down again I said to her:

"'Meine faigele, meine aicheleh, meine brechele...'

"She said, 'I know what a faigele is, but what's an aicheleh?'

"'An aicheleh is a little hen, but older than a chick.'

"She was almost offended.

"Her name wasn't bad either: Eva. Chavva, to us."

The teapot boiled. Yakov poured a strong infusion into the mug, then added boiling water.

"The car came. A van, like I'd ordered. I collected my whole family: Mama, Papa, Grandmother, my sister with her husband and my two nieces, and we all made a circle around Eva. She got flustered and started beating against us like a bird in a cage.

"Mama said to her: 'Now you're our daughter. Yakov chose you.'

"Mama said that, who couldn't even look at her shameless legs!

"'No, I can't, my father lives in Moscow!'

"So what! Her Papa lives in Moscow! So he'll come to Riga, big deal, Moscow!

"Then she sobbed and said: 'Everything was so good...'

"'It'll be even better,' said Papa. 'You'll wear gold and eat off gold.'

"So, she'd say one word, we'd say ten.

"We finally convinced her, and off we go. It's dark in the car; we sit opposite each other. I see her eyes have dimmed, but I think, 'It's nothing. She'll get used to me, she'll fall in love with me.' Women were always dying over me, but I never gave in. I was waiting, like robbers wait around the corner for their victim. But believe me, Moishe, I didn't want a victim, I wanted love.

"We got to Mama's house. Well, it started. Everybody falling all over each other promising her heaven and earth, but she holds out—she has to go to Moscow. If you don't like it here, you and Yakov will live in Moscow. If it's all a matter of Moscow, then let it be Moscow.

"I saw that Moscow later on. Could you find a link from a gold chain in that circus? You couldn't even find the chain. I rode the metro and thought to myself: it's a beautiful life underground, tons of marble, when will life become beautiful above ground?

Everybody's running, and nobody needs you...

"Drink your tea, Moishe, it'll get cold. So I'm looking at her and burning. I'm angry at my family—if they'd just leave us alone we'd work things out by ourselves. But that's a sin. If they'd left us alone, I wouldn't have vouched for myself. She sits there, her legs together, her knees shaking. To cheer her Up I sat down at the piano. I played 'Havva N'qila,' 'The 7:40'—I 'm sitting there playing, and there's a fiery whirlwind inside me, I'm afraid even to look at her. I play the piano and think: her, or nobody else in the world; her, or I might as well not live. Moscow, Siberia, Vladivostok, anywhere, but with her.

"My sister came to my rescue. Brings out platform shoes, remember, that was the fashion: 'Here, try these on, you'll wear stylish shoes now.'

"She tried them on, and she actually laughed. Two boats. She has small feet, narrow... 'We'll take your measurements and get them custom made,' says my sister.

"She nods, as if to say, 'Fine, fine, just leave me alone.'

"I understood her. Closed the piano, wished her a good night and went out. I don't remember how I waited till morning. My sister said, 'Take a shower, it'll help.' I stood half the night under the shower. I was always able to control my body, Moishe, but that time it refused to listen, and I was ashamed.

"I got dressed somehow, put myself in order, and went to the bazaar. Bought roses and the bucket they were in, and took a taxi to Mama's.

"From behind the door I heard her bird's voice She was talking to Mama. I guess there was a little bit of monkey in her, because she was already talking with our accent.

"'Things are going well,' I thought then.

"I went in and put the bucket of roses at her feet. When I looked up I saw she wasn't wearing the gold chain.

"'Aicheleh, why did you take it off?'

"She didn't answer.

"Mama took me into the other room and said, 'She has a fiancé.'

"'In Moscow?'

"'In Riga,' said Mama, 'I heard her on the phone.'

"I sat on the sofa and couldn't get up for a long time."

"Two-timer," said Moishe. It was his first word since the story had begun.

"No, she wasn't a two-timer," objected Yakov. "I didn't ask her if she had a fiancé. I thought: 'Good. A fiancé's not a husband, a fiancé you can get rid of.' I went to her and gave her my hand: 'Yakov is an honorable man, he won't force you into anything,' that's how I said it, third person, because at that moment I didn't feel myself. I saw everything as if it was a movie. 'Let's go, I'll hand you over. Yakov took you away, Yakov will return you. '

"We went. It was chilly. She kept shaking. And I was shaking. I took her arm. She was so tiny, she barely reached my shoulder.

"'Do you have a warm blouse?' I asked.

"She nodded.

"We walked slowly. For me it was punishment, for her, release. I said, 'Think it over one last time. It's hard to trust a person who had a little too much at a wedding. But trust me.'

"She nodded again. I was a burden to her.

"'Where did you learn to dance?'

"'At my grandfather's house. I had a grandfather, he died in April. That was the first time since his death...' and she burst into tears.

"'Don't cry, faigele, don't cry,' I said to her. 'And will your fiancé love you like I do?'

"She wiped her eyes with her palms and shrugged her shoulders. How many years have passed, it seems like two lives, and I still remember how we stood at the crossing and she wiped her eyes with her palms, licking her wounds like a kitten.

"A man came towards us. 'That can't be her fiancé?!' I thought. I wanted to grab her up in my arms and run to the ends of the earth from such a fiancé. Twenty years older than her, with a pot belly...

"'Is that him?' I asked.

"'Yes.'

"'What do you need him for?'

"'I feel sorry for him.'

"'And me, you don't feel sorry for me?!'

"'I feel sorry for you too,' she said.' But I can't marry two people. I felt sorry for him first.'

"'Go to him,' I pushed her in the back. And she went."

"You shouldn't have let her go," sighed Moishe.

"But I was proud, you understand, if she'd said she was going to a man she loved, then I could have fought. Fought with somebody strong, an equal. But you can't hurt the weak...

"That's what I thought then. What I did was something else.

"I knew a gang, near Porokhovaia Tower. I gave them one grand. And I said: 'Find them.'

"They found them. Then I said: 'I'll give you ten times more to steal her, only do it so he sees, so it happens in front of his eyes. When he rushes in to save her, let him scratch you good... This'll be the picture: She was walking along, you didn't lay a finger on her, and suddenly some kind of maniac, idiot, rushes at you with a knife, wounds you. You defended yourselves, and ai-yai-yai, you lost count of the blows...'"

"You could have turned to murder?!"

"Could have, I could have done anything then. Listen, don't interrupt. Said and done. So my faigele, as if by order, walks away from her husband in broad daylight, they fall on her—I told them to be careful with her, so there wouldn't be a single bruise on her body; if I notice one I'll choke the guy with my own hands—he runs out when he hears her shout, and one, two, the main blow's still coming, from behind, and suddenly she breaks loose and shields him with her body. The car came up, took them all away...

"I wasn't there. The head of Investigation, he and I used to drink together now and then, said she bought two tickets to Moscow. Then I went to Moscow, but who can you find there? What time is it, Moishe?"

"6:30."

"That's all. The train leaves at 18:33."

"What are you talking about, Yakov, you want to go to Moscow again?"

But Yakov was silent. With his head buried in his workbench, he breathed in the odor of the boots he had fixed that noon, and it seemed that through leather and suede he could detect the scent of her hair, the heady, intoxicating smell of his faigele, aicheleh, brechele.

The train began to move.

"Who do you keep looking for?" the husband asked his wife.

"No one," she answered quietly.

He went up to her and put his arms around her shoulders.

"You haven't changed a bit," he said to her. "I'm so happy with you."

She looked at him with her questioning yet trusting expression, carefully freed her shoulders from his embrace, and went into the berth. If her husband hadn't been there, she would have told the whole story to the old man and woman sharing it with them.

"The train just left, and already you have to smoke," sighed her husband, as Eva took cigarettes and matches from her purse. "Should I come with you?"

"No, I'll just take a couple of puffs."

She went out, and the old woman said:

"If I were in your place I wouldn't let my wife smoke. A woman shouldn't smell of tobacco."

Eva leaned back against the door of the car. Holding up her skirt, she studied her boots. She had on the suede ones, they were like new, not a speck. Even the heels still shone. A pot hissed; water was being boiled for the evening tea.

Eva took the package of cigarettes from her pocket, turned it over in her hands, and put it back. She recalled Yakov's hands—coarse, the nails cut short, with black rims. Hands like that can probably hold a mug of boiling water. It was a shame she hadn't even tasted the tea from his mug.

She went back into the berth. The tea was already on the table, four glasses. Eva emptied one, then another.

"Unbelievably thirsty," she said, wiping her mouth with her hand.

"That's from smoking," remarked the old woman.

Eva nodded in agreement. She liked old people's tendency to find a simple reason for everything.

"Why did you bring her here?" his mother was still watching television. "My eyes shouldn't see her, my ears shouldn't hear her!"

"Oh Mama, my faigele," he patted his mother on the cheek. "Don't curse fate. Are we unhappy together?"

"You're drunk, Yakov," she turned away from him.

"Drunk, but cheerful, Mama. Do we have a bad time, you and I, my little one?..."

"No work again?"

"There is. I fixed two pairs of boots."

"Big profits," his mother sighed with her entire body and plunged back into the television.

Yakov lit all the burners—the house had gotten cold during the day—took the garbage pail, and went out.

The moon shone through the pines, the wind was blowing, knocking the cones from the dense, prickly branches. Yakov took the pail to the garbage pile, and turned towards the shore.

He turned over the empty pail and sat on it. He looked at the blue-white distance of the sea, at the edges of ice glittering by the shore. Now his soul felt completely at peace. There, from that crossbar, just a little while ago, his brechele had hung, swinging her repaired boots in the air, how beautiful that had been! He hadn't been mistaken in his choice. And that thought didn't burn him with hellish fire, as it had recently, when he had looked at her in the kitchen and found no better ashtray than this garbage pail.

Yakov scooped up a handful of snow and held it to his mouth. It melted quickly on his tongue. He sat on the pail, pressing his hat to his ears so the wind wouldn't carry it off, and watched his movie: the door creaked, she said one word, he answered with ten, he invited her to sit down, she sat, undid her top button; he saw a few, maybe only two or three, gray hairs, twisted and wiry... oh, how good it had been...

Yakov rose, straightened his shoulders, picked up the pail, and went into the house. It's a bad omen to run across an empty pail. But this time of year, at this hour, nobody would be walking. But something rustled and clattered—no, it had only seemed like it, of course, it had only seemed like it, ha-ha-ha!—and you can imagine anything, especially at night, especially between the pine trunks...

1987

Translated by Lise Brody

From the author's manuscript

Life Insurance

Marina Tsvetaeva

They were sitting, peacefully having supper—or perhaps dinner, it's a question of words, for the salad was the same—and so, fusing Russian supper with French dinner in a Roman salad, they ate: the father, the mother, and the son.

"Mama, how plentiful the French are!" said the son suddenly.

"It's not the French who are plentiful, but the Russians!" the mother replied heatedly. "And, in general, the word is usually applied to countries."

"W-h-y-y?" the boy was astounded. "How can a country be plentiful? It doesn't have hands."

At that second, a knock sounded at the door, and the mother, who hadn't yet figured out her son's latest linguistic half-breed (*habile*/nyi),[1] went to open it. There, in the pitch darkness of the landing, stood someone very tall, hat in hand.

"Excuse me, madam," he said in a youthful voice, "I'm the inspector..."

The mother took a step back, then let him in. The young man strode at her heels into the kitchen, where he stood—between the dinner table, the dish table, the gas, the stove, the sink and the chairs of the diners—as if on the single spot that was dry from the flood and firm between two abysses: on one foot, crossing it with the other, the left one.

"Yes?" inquired the mother with her eyebrows, not raising her eyes, and already seated back at the salad.

"Excuse me for interrupting your dinner, but I am the inspector, and..."

"Taxes!" she said wordlessly to herself. "But we paid them not long ago, or, perhaps, they've remembered that kidnapped general again and they've begun to take a census of all the Russian emigres?"

"Here's my card," the young man continued, raising it to her eyes and immediately—the way they show children tomorrow's "surprise" just for a minute—retrieving an open booklet with some sort of photograph, perhaps really a good likeness if she'd had a chance to look carefully either at it or at the person proffering it.

"But why doesn't he say *sûreté*[2] and show his badge?" she thought, mentally performing for him the gesture of displaying the badge. "And what's he arresting us for, after all?"

"*Assurance*,"[3] his voice rang out above her as if in confirmation.

Hearing at last the fatal word (for she took it for "*sûreté*") she stopped eating and began to wait.

"I'm heading for Nuellement," the voice continued from above, "and I'm inspecting apartments from the standpoint of fire."

("Good Lord!" flashed through her head. "And I have a worn electric cord, all knotted up, which keeps shorting! And what in heaven is Nuellement?")

"You don't seem to understand French?" he inquired, letting those present understand that from the moment of his arrival, in response to everything he had said, they had uttered not only not a single word, but not even a single syllable, so that he could legitimately have asked: "It seems you've lost your power of speech?"

"Oh, no!" exclaimed the mother, wounded to the quick, and as a result growing

186

more spirited. "We understand perfectly. But, pardon me, what do you want from us?"

"You're asking what I want from you?" continued the voice with amusement. "I already told you, I'm on my way to Nuellement!"

"He's unemployed!" she thought. "Evidently, he's on his way home to Nuellement and he's checking stoves on the way. I should give him something." And, at last throwing him a glance:

"We're not very rich," she said timidly, "and all our stoves are clean, but nevertheless..." and she immediately stopped, for she realized that the face she saw standing over her was handsome, young, ruddy, clean-shaven and scrubbed, not at all an unemployed face—even less that of a stove-repairer—a face below which, as her gaze moved back to her plate, it made out both a new cherry-colored tie and a clean gray suit.

"But this is precisely for the poor," the resident of Nuellement became exuberant. "What do the wealthy need it for? Even if their whole family dies off, it won't ruin their lives. This is precisely for those who are hard up, who live by the sweat of their brow."

"But what exactly is 'this'?" she asked, growing bolder.

"Life insurance—but didn't I say that?" And, with new force: "I'm going around to Nuellement (and suddenly she understood that there was no Nuellement at all, that there was *"annuellement,"*[4] the last syllable of which he pronounced "mon") and I'm primarily trying to interest low-income people, those who live by the work of their hands."

(Shifting his eyes to the slender hands of her husband, with their long fingers): "Your husband is an artist?"

"No," forced out the husband.

"No?" he verified with the wife.

"No," confirmed the wife.

"That's curious," he said, pensively, "I was sure he was an artist. I'm primarily going to talk with you, since your husband has the look of someone who doesn't understand French. So, it's important precisely for those who live by the labor of their hands. Imagine you have the misfortune to lose your husband," he said, letting himself go on as if he were speaking not of an obviously present, living and chewing husband, but of some allegorical personage whom she had never laid eyes on and whom for that very reason she had no way of losing, "and you are left alone, with three small children, the youngest still an infant."

"I have no infants," she answered. "The boy you see in front of you is nine."

"But others have them, you can't say that others don't," the inspector corrected her gently (the way they correct a good student who has made a mistake on an exam). "I knew one woman with six small children, and when her husband took a fall at a construction site..."

"Oh!" she exclaimed, trembling at this terrible vision. "How awful! Did he fall far?"

"Yes, from the seventh floor," confirmed the inspector, now standing firmly on his other leg, "And I myself gave her the settlement. You don't think she was happy?"

"How awful!" his listener cried a second time, this time with an entirely different meaning. "How awful to be happy about that kind of money!"

"But she had children," the inspector admonished, "Six small children, and she wasn't happy about their father's death, but about their good fortune. And if you, *madame*, were to have the misfortune of losing your husband..."

"Listen!" she cried. "This is the second time you've mentioned my husband's death. It's offensive. *We* are not accustomed to speaking this way in front of the living. We're foreigners, I'll even tell you we're Russians and (already *en route* to the other room to get her cigarettes) Russians can't stand to hear such things, Russians can only listen to talk of their own death. Yes!"

"*Madame*," sounded the voice of the young man, already in the corridor, "you've misunderstood me, I didn't at all mean to say that you'd surely lose your husband, I only wanted to say that it could happen to you as it could happen to anyone."

"Now that's the third time you've said it!" the young woman interrupted, already smoking and heading straight at him, herding him back into the kitchen. "And I don't want to hear any more. If this is life insurance, then I declare to you that I don't insure other people's lives."

"But *monsieur* would insure his own."

"Neither our own nor anyone else's—it's not in our blood, and besides, we have no money, we have to move to another apartment and..."

"But my proposal is meant just for people who are moving to another apartment. All kinds of accidents can happen during a move: a free-standing wardrobe, for instance, a wardrobe which has been standing for twenty years, a wardrobe with a mirror, you understand me? Suddenly it falls, and..."

("How awful!" and she actually closed her eyes, "Our wardrobe, which was given to us precisely because it was so unstable...")

"We're not afraid of falling wardrobes," she continued in a firm voice. "We, of course, do everything we can to keep the wardrobe from falling, but when a wardrobe falls—that's fate, you understand? That's the way any Russian will answer you."

"Russians always say 'no'," the young man said pensively, rocking his knees back and forth. "In Medon (I live in Medon) there's a whole Russian building, where no one speaks French. You knock on the door, and a gentleman or a lady comes out and says: '*nyet!*' Then I go away immediately, because I know that they won't understand me. Yes, it's not often that they understand me as you do, *madame*. So, to return to the insurance..."

"Better not!" she exclaimed heatedly. "We have no reason in the world to buy insurance: in the first place, we're terribly poor and won't pay in any case, I warn you, as an honest person. You'll keep coming and you won't get any money; you'll write letters, and we'll never answer them. In the second place, and for us this is the most important, my husband and I are sickened by the thought of getting money for the death of either one of us."

"Does *monsieur* agree with you?" asked the inspector. "He doesn't seem to understand French."

"He understands it perfectly, and he thinks just the way I do." (And so as to smooth things over a bit, to distract him): "Perhaps, when my son grows up and gets married... But we're of a different generation, a lyric generation..." (and seeing that this time it was he who failed to understand), "We're 'sentimental,' 'superstitious,' 'fatalistic,' you've probably heard that? About the 'Slavic soul?'"

"Yes, I even saw a film about it with my mother. An old Russian general *dans un bonnet d'astrakhan* is getting married in a huge cathedral, and, noticing that his young wife loves a poor officer, he immediately goes off to Siberia alone, throwing him his purse from his sled. My mother even cried..." And, after long meditation, "Your sentiments do you honor, and let's hope that your son will give you joy. Does he always have such an appetite?"

("I should ask him to sit down," flashed through her head for the umpteenth time. "He's a guest, but where can I fit another chair? Or at least offer him a cigarette...")

"I'm the fifteenth son," continued the inspector in a pensive and totally different voice, as if he were dreaming, "and there were two more after me. I'm twenty-six, and my mother is fifty-two. She's had seventeen children, and two cases of pneumonia, and two operations—in fact, three, because the second time they forgot a piece of sheeting inside her... And she looks as if she were my sister, and she's just as slender as you. She and I always laugh and joke."

"How marvelous—seventeen!" his listener exclaimed, fervently but without conviction. "Are they all alive?"

"No, I'm the only one left. My last brother—he was thirty-four—was killed last year when his car hit a tree."

"And the others?" she asked hesitantly.

"The others? All died in accidents. They drowned, they fell, others were burned alive (*il y en a qui sont brulés vifs*)."

"Joan of Arc," her son muttered, barely audibly.

"You understand that I can't get married? That possibly I'll do that later, possibly later... Mother—she simply couldn't take it... Oh, we were raised very strictly, and if even now I dared contradict my father, I'd get a slap in the face, of course, and I'd accept it. My father is sixty-two, he weighs a hundred and five kilos."

"But your parents probably aren't Parisians?"

"Yes, they are—that is, my mother's a Parisian, my father's from Normandy. Take a look at me, I'm not all that small," he kept towering over her. "But of all of us—them—I'm the least successful. The others were giants! But since it's just me who survived, I shouldn't marry—neither marry nor perish in an accident, for if I were to *pass away*, then there'd be three passing away. My mother is about your height and build, but even such mothers have big sons. Oh, you don't know my mother. Every time, no matter how late I come home from work—accidents happen at all hours, of course!—at ten or eleven, at twelve, at one, she gets up and warms up my dinner. Today, in fact, she's meeting me at Issy-les-Moulineaux. How can I get married? I'm twenty-six, and not once, you understand, not once have I gone to the movies without her or gone for a boat ride. *On prend tous ses plaisirs ensemble.* How could I possibly get married?"

"You're a fantastic son!" she exclaimed with all her heart, involuntarily shifting her gaze to her own, as if in query. "God grant you health, and your mother, and your father!"

"Yes, health is essential to me. I can't pass away. Let's hope your son will bring you joy, too. What would you like to be, little boy?"

"*Service militaire*, and then a pilot."

"No, you can't be a pilot. Your mother would have to look into the sky too often, and there are accidents enough on the ground. Now military service, that's something else. It's a good time, the best time, you'll never be so happy again... And so, *madame*, I wish you happiness in your son. And excuse me if I have somehow offended your feelings... You love your husband, you have a hearth, insurance won't help you, as it does me. Now I understand you.."

And, this time grasping the doorknob, towards which he had already stretched his hand—countless times!—without result, he said, with a deep bow:

"Thank you and good-bye."

"You're out of your mind!" exploded the husband, jumping up from the table like a beast. "I'm going to be late because of you!"

"Why didn't you just leave?" she asked, herself sensing the hypocrisy of the question.

"Why? Because the two of you were blocking the door, I was trapped."

"I accidentally ate the whole tomato, forgive me, mama, I was listening so carefully that I ate your share, too." And, putting the spout of the teapot to his lips, "Oh, I'm thirsty! You know, my throat dried out from listening to him talk."

A knock at the door.

"Excuse me, *madame*, I only wanted to add that today I'm taking my mother to the movies..."

When she had seen off her husband—getting instead of a farewell squeeze of the hand the handle of the door he slammed behind him, and after she had put her son to bed—he fell asleep like a rock—only then, and not even right away, did she come to her senses. The whole episode had the vagueness of a dream, and her heart was beating like that of the worker who fell from the seventh floor. She went over to the table and on the back of the first envelope that came to hand she calculated that at twenty-six, he could have been the fifteenth child of a fifty-two-year old mother only if she had married at fifteen and had her seventeen children one after another, without a break. It does happen... it's not easy, but it's possible. And it's much more plausible if, for instance, there were three sets of twins (who, of course, perished in pairs: two drowned together, two fell at the same time, two burned to a crisp together. Then there would be fewer deaths, too...). But, nevertheless, for all seventeen of them, minus only him, to have died in accidents, all so different, and every possible kind of accident... Taking into account the tone, at once both free-and-easy and official, in which he conveyed the information, as if rattling off a menu by heart... And when she compared that voice with the one in which he spoke about the mother who was meeting him at Issy-les-Moulineaux...

What on earth had that been? She didn't know. But even if he had cooked it all up on the spot in a flood of strange inspiration—nevertheless, wasn't it a touching myth about himself, the mother of seventeen children, and the last surviving, insanely devoted son? wasn't it a kind of daydream about a better self, the real self? wasn't it the wail of a real *profession manquée*? The full potential of filiality?

At twenty-six, tall, handsome—and in his own view, not to mention that of the Paris streets—irresistible, for him to tell an unknown woman, who wasn't so old herself, and looked very young indeed in the dark of the corridor, that to this day he gets slapped by his father and takes it willingly. Could this be the daydream of a modern young man?

"Perhaps," she pursued her thought, "I can't swear to it... Perhaps there were no seventeen children, perhaps, since they didn't exist, there were no seventeen deaths, and perhaps the father from Normandy, who slapped him in the face—each slap weighing one hundred five kilos!—didn't exist either, perhaps—and, it seems, most likely, and this, evidently, was the *key, there was no father at all.*

But there was a mother.

June 1934

Translated by Jane A. Taubman

From *Avrora*, No. 6, 1978

Notes

1. The son has conflated the French "habile" (adroit) with the Russian "obil'nyi" (abundant).
2. Police (Fr.)
3. Insurance (Fr.)
4. The insurance salesman has been saying, "Je passe annuellement," or "Every year I make the rounds."

The Losers' Division

Marina Palei

I

In a quiet spot on a little yellow river there are some floodgates. Opposite them is a two-story hospital; with its usual resemblance to a jail it orphans the naked shore. If you look out the little hospital window from the first floor, you can't see the floodgates themselves, or the sad waterlet, or the worn-away coastal strip that is completely covered by warning signs.

On the other hand, in the middle of a summer's day, there is a moment when right from beneath the earth, from the thick green-black grass of July, something suddenly emerges—something huge, blinding, completely outside of our orbit. It springs up out of the tall grass—slowly, quietly, inevitably, it rises with the ceremonial ease of the sun. It is a ship.

It rises and rises, towering above, and finally freezes at its highest point, as if wondering: should it take off and soar upwards? After a moment's thought, however, it sets off smoothly along the grass and sails off into the distance, beyond the accidental walls of bondage.

On the other side of the window, permeated through and through by the smell of ether and institutional food, is the domain of the director of the gynecological and obstetric divisions, Filipp Arnoldovich Fazmetalsky. He is seeing patients, sitting with his side to the window, in a Chippendale armchair (God knows how such a thing was washed up on the shore of this shallow little river). Opposite him, Daria Petrovna Oglobysheva, a permanent fixture, adorns a sturdy stool; by the door some peasant woman with indistinct features hovers guiltily.

"Well, now, my dear..." Filipp Arnoldovich begins in a bored voice. He stares fixedly at the quick of his nail, paring off the extra flesh with a razor blade. "What do you have to say for yourself?"

The peasant woman stays quiet because Filipp Arnoldovich knows everything anyway. To out-talk him is impossible, but she can out-silence him.

Filipp Arnoldovich doesn't plan to continue his usual monologue, either. For twenty-two long years he has been muttering these words which have no connection to him and go nowhere, and now he doesn't even feel like moving his lips. Daria Petrovna, eyebrows raised high, is writing something in a very business-like way in a notebook that resembles an accountant's ledger. From the monotonously quick movements of her hand, one can surmise that she is filling in dates—probably all the way to the second coming.

"Run along home, dearie." Finally, without tearing himself away from his razor blade, Filipp Arnoldovich announces his bored presence. "And once you're there, do whatever you want. Drink quinine if you want, or take whatever you all poison yourselves with there. Pick up your dear husband if you want. I'm sure he's heavy. Is your husband heavy?"

Outside the window there are no ships, nor water, nor shore. At the entrance to the hospital grounds the yellowing sign announces: "Sunday, July 14 is Memorial Day for deceased workers."

"Did you come to see me two months ago? You did. Did I give you an abortion? I did. Did you have any complaints about me? You didn't." Filipp Arnoldovich turns his head deliberately from side to side in time to the words, thoroughly scrutinizing the quick of his nails, which look like ham rolled in plastic wrap. "And now you want me to make a hole in your uterus? And do you know what will happen to me as a result of this hole?" Without putting down his razor blade, he extends his fingers, lengthened by his profession, and lays the fingers of his other hand across them.

Frozen in her former position, the peasant woman attempts a smile, just to be on the safe side.

Filipp Arnoldovich moves the grid he's made with his fingers closer to his face, and looks at the peasant woman as if she were a target: "I'll be put behind bars, dearie. Is that something I need? Of course it isn't. Run along home, my dear, and quit pestering me."

The peasant woman seems not to really understand about the hole, but she does understand about the bars. More importantly, she sees that Filipp Arnoldovich will not, under any circumstances, give her an abortion. Rumor has it that when Filipp Arnoldovich isn't in a particularly bad mood, he starts lecturing his patients on their health. But the peasant woman is only partly right about this. Filipp Arnoldovich gives lectures in his flat, even voice only when, having laid aside his razor blade, he sits down in the abortion clinic with the expression of a martyr taking up his cross in the form of women's raised legs and Daria Petrovna gently and precisely hands him a washtub, into which he plops the bloody remains. Filipp Arnoldovich seems like the king of kings to the peasant woman, and he, for his part, hasn't lost the ability to be surprised. It surprises him, for example, despite twenty-two long years of practice, that a simple life could so brazenly take root even on worn-away stone. The peasant woman doesn't understand this either, but she isn't surprised by it; she only tries to think of what she can do so that it won't happen.

"Run along, Znobishina," Daria Petrovna opens her mouth a chink. "I'll come visit your Zinka on Friday."

Disappearing behind the doors, the peasant woman still hasn't gotten it through her head that she's saved. As usual, Daria Petrovna takes it upon herself to do the tasks that the doctor is afraid to, and the doctor, without ever showing that he's aware of how things stand, never objects to this.

Outside the window a woman screams, the sound recalling fingernails on a chalkboard.

"How can she even think about keeping it, you tell me," the doctor says to Daria Petrovna, nodding in the direction of the scream. "What's the good of even talking about keeping it when she thrashed around in the bushes with a guy from the surgical ward yesterday? She's six months along, and he rode her at full speed... Is that any way of going about keeping it?"

"Uh-huh..." Daria Petrovna begins for form's sake, knowing that the question is rhetorical.

"What am I supposed to do, lock every damn one of them up in the division, so that not a single floozy can go flouncing around the yard? Now, of course, she's babbling that she's bleeding, of course..."

The door opens, and in comes a pudgy creature, about sixteen—or maybe thirty—years old, with gray hair, sparse, spiky bangs, and glasses on her nose, her huge stomach covered by a black polyester shift.

Filipp Arnoldovich absentmindedly keeps pressing the little white button inset in the side of the standard issue desktop. This was his own improvement—his pride and joy. And in the corridor, the lighted sign keeps flashing "Enter" over the peasant women, who have fallen quiet, just like Pavlov's dogs.

"So, loser, how's it going? What do you have to say for yourself?" Filipp Arnoldovich says dully, putting aside his razor blade. "It's time for you to deliver, and you've done us the favor of deigning to show up for the first time. And what will happen to me if anything goes wrong...?" He makes bars out of his fingers, forming a little window over his eyes, and fixes her with a piercing gaze.

"Well, and what about your man? Are you going to marry him?" Daria Petrovna joins in. She already knows the answer, however, and confidently fills in this section of the passport, not even glancing in the direction of the patient, who is nodding quickly and earnestly.

Meanwhile, the doctor for some reason looks at the sky through a wooden speculum, turning it this way and that, then sighs, takes a tape measure out of the top pocket of his lab coat, and with an expression of mournful patience, stands silently beside the narrow examining table, which is covered by a cold oilcloth.

"Did you pass all your exams?" Daria Petrovna squints. "Take it off, take everything off quickly. Lie down over there."

"All 'C's'..." says the expectant mother, squeezing her hips tightly as she tries to take off the polyester shift. "And I put off the math exam until autumn. I'll already be a junior when I take..."

"When you're a junior, you'll be taking in his lab tests!" Filipp Arnoldovich pokes her in the stomach. "Go on, get a move on, lie down."

The expectant mother uncovers her stomach, which is as firm as a nut and divided by a brown strip down the middle.

His thick brows knitted, the doctor listens to the heartbeat of the fetus, and wonders indifferently who the father could be and what it would take to make you lose your head to the point where you would assault the virginity of this sexless creature.

Heaped together in frightful disorder on a stool near the examining table are a black polyester shift, a green acetate blouse with a pointed collar ("You tell them not to wear synthetics, but it's useless"), a washed-out, piglet-pink girdle with lilac garters and thick brown cloth stockings. On top of the pile, something thick and blue sticks up. For propriety's sake, department stores call them "women's insulated underwear" (looking at them always makes you think of war, destruction, siege), but in real life they are called panties. Naturally, there is no chemise ("stifling in the summer, and in the winter, well, it doesn't keep you warm anyway").

It's not clear why she put on heavy undergarments in such heat. It's not clear why she stuffed herself into suffocating, artificial black fabrics.

To whom isn't it clear? To Filipp Arnoldovich, for example, it's painfully clear; the wench put on her "Sunday best." And you're very wrong if you think that Filipp Arnoldovich didn't know who assaulted her. Actually, he didn't know the pollinator's name, but you don't need the skills of a Maigret to figure out that the voluptuary "acted in a state of alcoholic intoxication." You could assume as a working hypothesis that he was a professional alcoholic, a seasonal worker, a passing truck driver, a gym teacher...What's the difference?

"And it's a good thing they don't show foreign films here," thought Filipp Arnoldovich with his usual malice, not taking his eyes off the blue object that stuck up.

"I'd forbid them under pain of death to show them here in the future, too. And the worst thing is," the doctor moaned inwardly, "what good would it do even if they did show them? It's one damn thing after another, life just keeps replicating itself with the same depressing obscenity, sluggishly and aimlessly...But those at the top," the doctor moans again, "have no right anyway to show foreign films here. It's just refined cruelty, sadism! My God! And they probably think that this place is just one big fetal burial ground!...And, apparently, they're right."

"Come on, tell me honestly—have you been living it up lately or not?"

The doctor addresses this to another patient—a lively-looking, raspberry-cheeked personage with sweaty flaxen ringlets falling over her smooth forehead. Holding her nose as if she were blowing it, the patient giggles and remains stubbornly silent. A week ago, her spouse, an assistant store manager—a man who is no stranger to progress and takes care of his young wife—sent her by private arrangement to the big city, where she had an "American coil" inserted. Checking up on the success of the procedure was part of Filipp Arnoldovich's responsibilities.

"What are you laughing at?" Daria Petrovna chips in. "Just answer him. Remember, doctors and tailors aren't really men."

"But I don't feel it at all," the curly-haired patient deftly changes the subject, unself-consciously hopping up onto the examining table, which all the peasant women hate, "It's just as if it didn't exist at all!"

"Well, you'd better search the bed for it. Maybe you'll find it there," Filipp Arnoldovich grumbles almost good-naturedly as he pulls on his rubber gloves.

On this major chord, the outpatient hours for the day come to an end.

II

In the midst of the muddy autumn hopelessness, Evgeny Igorevich Razduvaev, a young doctor from Leningrad, came to the division. Actually, he had only received his "higher" education in Leningrad, but originally came from distant parts, and, moreover, was a bachelor, which is why, instead of leaving him in Peter, they sent him to the worn-away shores of the yellow river. Evgeny Igorevich had spent a lot of time and effort in the capital running from office to office, trying to get into certain jobs and get out of others, but it was all in vain. He only wasted his strength and arrived at the waterlet more spiteful than ever. In order to ease the sting of defeat, he made it a rule to insist loudly and with a very cheerful expression in front of others that it was much easier to get into a graduate program from the outlying districts and that three years of work here would give him a good shot... Nowadays, the value of practical experience... compared to all those jerks with pull... The way he told it, Evgeny Igorevich had chosen this part of the world of his own free will, following the tried and true principle that "the worse things are, the better they are." From time to time, however, he was subject to illusions—sweet and fleeting, like cheap perfume—that instead of events controlling him, he controlled events.

Filipp Arnoldovich was initially somewhat heartened to see a man "with whom one could talk," but he sourly retreated once he saw through Evgeny Igorevich's simple strategy, which he did even before being given any verbal explanations. The face of his young colleague expressed exaggerated fastidiousness combined with hopeless hypersensitivity; moreover, the second somehow seemed to stem from the first. Filipp Arnoldovich immediately discerned in Evgeny Igorevich his own earlier self of twenty-two years ago, and very quickly developed an acute, nasty, severe antipathy towards him. This antipathy, however, was not caused by envy of Evgeny Igorevich's radiant vision of a graduate program in the capital (a vision, as Filipp Arnoldovich understood, equally remote from both of them) but because his shame at his own former youthful impotence made him conscious of the humiliating similarity of their inglorious, spasmodic efforts.

In the same way, a father with a sense of pained melancholy constantly sees in his son the impossibility of changing fate: he tears off chunks of bread in just the same way, lowers his voice at the end of a phrase the same way, and in sleep he curls his legs up under him the same way... Oh, my God!

On top of all this, the chief of Gyn fell ill. He was seriously ill for a long time, and Filipp Arnoldovich took over for him, appointing Evgeny Igorevich to his own former position, his action increasing the similarity of their paths, collapsing the two tracks into one.

Right from the start, the nurses didn't take to Evgeny Igorevich and they all called him Zhenka behind his back. He was fully aware of this, but, apparently, didn't value the love of the masses at all and soon started a ritual: sneezing histrionically and moaning weakly, he would call one of the nurses into "the doctor's office" (which in a slightly bigger city would have been called a doctor's lounge), where with unshakeable administrative severity he would take off his lab coat, the warm 100% cotton shirt "made in Poland," and the Soviet-made wool striped sailor's vest..."Treating the doctor" became one of the duties of the nursing students; they had to put mustard-poultices on him or leeches, or maybe give him a massage. Who the hell knows what they did in there; the only thing we know for certain is that once, very early in the morning, at the sleepiest time of day, when Zhenka was on his way to the bathroom and passing close by the nurses' station, he heard something clearly referring to him:

"Yeah, well, to hell with him. I wouldn't have let him come sniffing around my bed for anything. There may be no other studs around, but he's no stud either."

A whisper of a different sort reached him, this time from the patients. They were complaining to one another, quietly, timidly, that when Zhenka performed abortions, he scraped carelessly, and that afterwards it bled again ("I woke up in my own home just like a bloody lamb"); if you swelled up a little you would find yourself going a second time to that very same Zhenka. Evgeny Igorevich ignored all of this and didn't deign to explain, but his expression let the peasant women know that the fault lay with their own abnormal organisms, the poor quality of Soviet-made instruments, and the inadequate local conditions.

The voice of the masses reached the ears of Filipp Arnoldovich several times, but there was no substitute for Zhenka on the shores of the shallow little river, and after the voice of the masses began to take the form of stilted written complaints, Filipp Arnoldovich held several revealing political propaganda sessions with the nurses.

Before the November holiday, it suddenly grew nastily cold; the weatherworn, half-dead earth congealed dully in the expectation of protective gauze. During this season, there were three times the usual number of women in Gyn: their female equipment had been cruelly chilled by the cold, despite the insulated women's underwear, or maybe because they disdained it...They inched along sideways, one hand tightly clutching at the throat of their ragged hospital gowns, covered with black inventory marks, the other hand gingerly holding onto aluminum mugs with jello, cautiously pushing their way through the folding beds and institutional cots crammed in on both sides of the grayish-yellow corridor.

The lively cutie with a "coil," the curly-haired little wife of the department store manager, landed on one of these cots, though at least it was in the ward. Every day this manager pestered Zhenka (who was bad-tempered even without this), tearfully repeating that if his wife had "women's cancer," then he should say so right away, for God's sake...we have connections...you won't lose by it...The curly-haired little wife of the department store manager did not have cancer, thank God, but that didn't make it any easier, because Evgeny Igorevich didn't have the most basic medicines for treating the least complicated diseases. When the department store manager understood that the hospital was giving his curly-haired wife only vitamin C in addition to the blue-gray jello, and nothing else, he rushed to persuade Zhenka, heatedly repeating that tomorrow... in the city... his brother-in-law... That's how he got Zhenka to give him a prescription for penicillin.

One result of the prescription was that at the next five-minute doctors' consultation, Filipp Arnoldovich, pointedly keeping his enunciation and tone level, publicly reminded Evgeny Igorevich that medical care in our country happens to be free. So that Evgeny Igorevich would get a clearer sense of this, and would stop trying to obtain medicine for patients at the expense of their relatives, he ordered that the cost of the prescription medicine be taken out of Evgeny Igorevich's salary. (Filipp Arnoldovich had prudently taken the prescription away from the department store manager beforehand.)

Evidently, Zhenka didn't get depressed over this reprimand, especially given that only the official price of the medicine was deducted from his salary, and not the black market price. However, he drew the appropriate conclusions for himself, of course, and at the same time remembered the proverb: "The less we do, the less harm we do." Thus, soon after the consultation, he could be seen in the abortion clinic ingenuously teaching a young intern from the big city the methods of his barbaric science: the frightened med student sat in front of the gaping womb of the unconscious patient, and Zhenka positioned himself like a furtive demon in back of her and with one arm guiding her hand in circular motions in the bloody hole, while she helplessly gripped the long obstetrical curette, with his other hand he squeezed her large breast rhythmically, firmly, leisurely, just as if he were milking her.

...In general, the actions of God's deputy on the shores of the sleepy little river could somehow be understood in connection with Zhenka's prescription: accountability, centralization...what else is there? It's harder to understand the actions of the heavens, free from foolish passions and petty bonds. In other words, the lively, curly-haired young wife of the department store manager, who looked like a little bird and a small monkey, and spent her days in the hospital fussing over her flaxen ringlets and her pink caramel-like nails, died. God took her to himself so quickly that no one even thought of removing the little rubber curlers from her childish bangs.

And, as if out of spite, all of this happened during the pre-holiday chaos. Somewhere beyond the hospital fence an accordion was wheezing and squealing, the sound evoking memories of holiday trimmings: paper flowers, a herring, a quarter liter of vodka, and a ditty, fragmented by the wind, floated in through the window:

> Yeah, she boozed
> Lesbianoozed...

Just as they were bringing the little female body, covered by a white sheet, through the corridor crammed with cots and folding beds, into the washroom, Zhenka decided to order the on-duty nurse to poke around in the "supplies room" (where, all piled in a heap, lay gray surgical shoes without laces, hospital slippers without backs, and a stretcher without wheels, all tangled up in the transparent tubes of the blood transfusion equipment, from which patients and convicts love to make souvenirs). She would certainly find a banner there suitable for the holiday, to put up over the entrance to the division.

After a little while you could hear him yell from the doors of the abortion clinic:

"I told you in plain Russian to put up a banner, and what did you put up?! We call this a flag in Russian! What's the matter with you, can't you tell the difference? A flag is a rag and one stick and a banner is a rag and two sticks!"

Outside, all the way across the barren shore, the dead earth was crucified.

III

Nothing out of the ordinary, however, happened over the course of the winter. The water pipes burst, Filipp Arnoldovich got a seven-ruble raise, Daria Petrovna won an electric samovar, but lost her lottery ticket, and Zhenka removed an indecent tattoo from his left buttock. Of course, one could write that Doctor Evgeny Igorevich, for example, married that seductive little schoolgirl in polyester, with glasses and spiky bangs (it was clear that she'd been fibbing; as if that boozer-seducer would take her to wife...). Evgeny Igorevich, on the contrary, became the president of the temperance society, and so it happened that the former seducer of his wife... and so forth. Why not? However, let's come down to earth, if only to take a look out of curiosity. What is Daria Petrovna staring at with such grim astonishment while brushing soapsuds off her eyebrows from time to time?

Completely naked, she is standing with a basin in her hands, in a long line of equally naked women who, also holding basins, are headed toward the only faucet in the women's side of the bathhouse. The copper faucet is massive and wide, obviously invented in order to pour out generous rivers of cold water as well as—on request—hot. At the moment, however, one lone drop that just can't detach itself is suspended from the faucet.

"Well, I guess Fedka the stoker's been drinking all day, as usual."

"Yeah, could be he's a little drunk."

"Or maybe the water tower doesn't work at all anymore? The pipes are all worn out..."

"Yeah, could be the pipes."

"Girls, what do you bet they'll turn all the water off now?"

"Yeah, could be they will."

Naked and meek, the peasant women, each with basin in hand, chat quietly as they wait determinedly, in single file. A woman's lot is given, like the alternation of day and night, and can be seen in the geography of their well-scrubbed bodies: the scars on their drooping breasts after mastitis, the scars on their stomachs after Caesareans, the flaccid strings of veins on their beaten-up legs, the stretch marks from pregnancy on their sides, and their lumpy stomachs, which had given birth many times, weighed down by aprons and bags...

However, it would be wrong to think that Daria Petrovna was gazing with such grim astonishment at the uselessly sputtering faucet. Finally, it all worked out: the faucet emitted a thin rivulet of cold water, and when her turn came, Daria Petrovna washed off the foam running into her eyes. Now, with her glasses off and the soap washed away, it's clear what is attracting her gaze: a peasant woman, her pregnant belly a trifle pointed (seeing such bellies, people say "it's a boy"), sitting on the bench dyed blue-gray by the soap. The earth is tilted towards the sun again now, but just last summer Daria Petrovna secretly and with her own hands destroyed the unwanted fetus of this Znobishina, when she got knocked-up again like a cat, just two months after the preceding intervention. But if Daria Petrovna's efforts hadn't been crowned with success, then... three... even... nine... no, she would have already given birth. What is this— new stuffing?! Will wonders never cease! If your head doesn't fall off, you'll live to see your beard grow: if we don't see it, we'll surely hear about it!

And by July, they heard. Znobishina gave birth to a jaundiced little boy.

The sun again scorched the faded shores of the little northern river. Whenever Evgeny Igorevich saw an infant of the female sex as he and the pediatrician made their rounds of the obstetric division, he invariably let drop: "Yet another loser is born." And although Znobishina hadn't borne a girl, an expression of eternal guilt froze on her face, never to leave it.

She was already over fifty, and her husband said, "It's embarrassing in front of the neighbors," but God knows, nothing could be done about it. And, to make matters worse, the child apparently had been born defective, because all the other new mothers were given their babies to feed, but not her, and the other women in the ward were eating to make their milk come in, while she swallowed down food to no purpose and took up cot space for no good reason, and was unbearably ashamed of her unexpected idleness.

She was ashamed to bother Evgeny Igorevich with questions, depressed by her parasitism, and upset by the incomprehensible but instinctive sense of carrying contagion within her, but the women told her before any doctor did that she had given birth to a yellow-green little kid that looked like a frog. And now she was learning to lie with her face to the wall.

The women told her the main thing, but certainly not the whole story. They didn't know, for example, that although she had seen everything there was to see (a result of the "home brew" plentiful in these parts), even the midwife Alena Grigorievna was shocked by the bony green freak and once she started the ball rolling, everyone in the unit began calling him "Znobishina's Champion" and then just "Champ." Naturally, they couldn't know either that the middle-level medical personnel in the unit had unreservedly shifted all the responsibility for what had happened onto Zhenka. The fact is that Evgeny Igorevich varied his burdensome nightly duties by dragging the younger nurses into his office (under the guise of applying leeches or poultices). There he got great pleasure from scaring them with stories of unspeakable infant deformities he had supposedly seen when he was still an intern, but which were in fact culled from Caspar Friedrich Wolff's[1] monograph. "And do you know where his male organ is?" he'd draw out the pause, and his bulging eyes goggled. Then, with the gesture of an alcoholic, he'd clap himself sharply on the side of the neck: "Right here!!" Outside the window the gloom became impenetrable, and all this together made the student nurse scream. "He jinxed her, the goggle-eyed froggy!" concluded Alena Grigorievna maliciously, agreeing with the pediatric nurses, none of whom could forgive Zhenka even his frog-like eyes, chock-full of gray-blue aspic.

In short, it was clear to everyone that a "goner" had been born. The only thing that wasn't clear was the length—probably brief in comparison with the norm—of his sojourn in this precarious world.

Towards evening of the third day, when Znobishina was still hoping to see her defective little son at feeding time, Alena Grigorievna entered the ward with a glass jar in her hand and, in a voice which implied that Znobishina already knew all this, she announced that Znobishina's milk was poisonous and that the doctor had given strictest orders for it to be drained off separately, not mixed with the other milk, but poured out in the toilet right away.

Days passed. Champ, meanwhile, had managed to live a whole week, which surprised the staff in a rather disagreeable way. During this time, partly at the request of the pediatrician, Evgeny Igorevich had sent for specialists from the big city: laboratory assistants, consultants, specialists who rightfully shared the burden of responsibility. And they heard the strange, unusual diagnosis: the incompatibility of the mother and fetus was not in any way connected with the Rhesus factor, which would have been comprehensible, but was the result of some other factor, one of those many others which are either not thoroughly researched or else completely unknown...This was all the more strange because Znobishina had borne and raised three completely healthy, normal children.

How is it possible for a child not related to its own mother to come into the world?

It lay, illuminated by the light of the moon, next to the dozing nurse's aide in a tiny cubbyhole that had been a linen closet, from which they had hastily removed the thick, yellow piles of institutional diapers and sheets. It was not sleeping, but lay quietly, wisely not relying on outside sympathy; moreover, its throat was not made for crying, laughter or human speech. Now and then, the creature emitted an incredibly high-pitched sound, quiet and melancholy, that didn't resemble anything human. It was rather the chirr of a grasshopper, the intermittent chirp of a cricket, a sound made by insects without the benefit of a throat. From the beginning, his legs, with their flattened feet twisted inside-out, were not destined to walk this earth; it was clear from the start that his hands—thin latticeworks of twisted bones—were not meant for labor, battle or caresses; and it was not given to his sightless eyes to know the difference between the past and the future. He was doomed to drift, in torment and blindness, from eternity to infinity, a stranger to this outer darkness, a son not related to his own mother.

IV

Far, far away, beyond the hospital walls, beyond the worn-out shores of the little yellow river, sprawls a field. It looks like a bottomless reflection of the sky to which it is attached, and the sky above it sparkles like a dazzling sea. The blue sea and the green sea flow freely into one another, as they kiss sweetly, and, seeing their union, man and beast live in peace. On the borders of this field, beyond the forests and hills, beyond the dark wooden churches, are scattered settlements, Ialosar, Tiasma, Andoma, Pantoga, Megra: the names roll off your tongue harmoniously and pleasurably, like crunchy nuts, and when sung in sequence, they are transformed into ancient spells against sickness, old age, and death. But even if their names are not spoken aloud, their silent sorcery protects the mowers.

Now the hay is being harvested and the flowers at the very edges of the field look with childlike surprise at the five-ton truck. The big-city intern is glad that Zhenka sent her to get some "fresh air" and to help out on the kolkhoz. She quickly feels at home among the locals, who said right off, "We're all family here, so it's OK!" and quickly stripped to their bathing suits, thus breaking down her prejudices about the patriarchal order. True, they didn't take off their boots ("What about the adders?"), and the med student, after thinking a bit, kept her sneakers on, too.

And the world turned—blue, white, yellow, green—steeped in the thick aroma of all kinds of dry grasses, stuffed with the stinging of horseflies, a fleeting puff of wind, of head scarves, hands, a world overflowing with health, happiness, and freedom.

The big-city intern first raked the hay, and then threw it onto the rick with a pitch-fork. Then she ran to the stuffy, dense thickets of the distant forest, where she found a spring and quickly filled her steaming bucket to the top. For this, they finally let her work the hay at the top of the rick. Setting to work eagerly, she began to trample it down savagely, quickly running around the pole in the middle of the rick, not noticing that the earth kept getting farther away, that the dry-grass earth was already becoming firm under her feet, and then, seizing hold of the pole, the girl wound her slim body around it, trampling down in one small place—round and round and round and round—the horizon was fragmented and overturned...

"Well, can you see Leningrad yet?" they bawled from below.

Then hot, light, and sweaty, she slides down the pole, falling straight into the rough paws of an agile peasant, the only male among all the peasant women at the harvest. He inspects the neat rick, then unhurriedly inspects the girl and says seriously and very slowly:

"Picture perfect."

It's not quite certain whether he's referring to the rick or to the girl, but it's clear, happily, peacefully, and completely clear, that we will live forever.

V

"...I like it more on the kolkhoz, because you see results right away and there's fresh air. And the director created a special position and assigned me to a very diseased child, who's going to die anyway because he was born a freak, and his blood is a complete mess. We don't have the right to give the child to his mother, and they won't take him in the specialized clinic because he could die any minute and his mother is taking up cot space for no good reason, and we can't discharge her until the child dies, and only quitters leave..."

That evening, as they were changing shifts, the pediatric nurse said to the girl:

"Don't give Champ anything to drink for the next twenty-four hours. Understand?"

The girl silently nodded. They'd probably arranged tests, the kind of tests where you're not allowed to drink beforehand. And what tests didn't they run on him! The marshy skin which stretched tightly over his prominently ribbed skull was covered with pinpricks, the traces of injections, just like little flea bites. The first week that the nurses fussed over Champ they were bewildered, curious and pitying; the second week, they expressed some irritation ("Why torture the little fellow? Besides, he's already exhausted his mother..."). And when the term of this illegal life spilled over into a third week, though Zhenka kept repeating that it was only a question of hours, the nurses started to gripe both about the stinking green, inhuman urine and about how ridiculous it was to expend so much excellent medical care that was so difficult to get on this creature who was so clearly a goner.

"...At the kolkhoz today, I saw them twist bulls' tails. I thought it was only an expression, but you know what? It turns out they really do it! The bulls are stubborn and don't want to go where they're supposed to, and then, just like that, the cowherd sets to work. It must be really painful. Mom, if you can, please telegraph me about fifteen rubles..."

The intern falls asleep with her face on her school notebook. The overturned horizon dances and strains—round and round and round...In the nearby sky, stacks of fluffy dandelion heads are swaying, while a spring, sparkling in the sunlight, gushes forth toward them. "Don't give him anything to drink today. Understand?" Why? He's so thirsty!...

It's quiet on the division. The only discernible sounds are the barely audible voices, unofficial in tone, coming from the doctor's office: today is Evgeny Igorevich's birthday. Alena Grigorievna capably dilutes grain alcohol in measured beakers. Daria Petrovna is shelling and chopping boiled eggs. She chops them finely, then mixes them with white chicken meat shredded to the consistency of gauze and blends it all together with putrid-looking mayonnaise sent to the doctor from Leningrad. (The treat of a primitive gourmet: mix the mature organism with its own fetus in one dish.)

The creature called Champ lies covered from the head down, its diaper illuminated by the green light of the moon. The creature gazes with its blind eyes through the diaper, through the ceiling, through the roof into the infinite heights, perhaps in the hope of catching a glimpse of its alien father, of attracting his omniscient gaze and, if it's lucky, of finally learning its purpose. Will the infallible one admit his mistake or, having exhausted his patience, will he turn away in contempt from us, eternally mediocre students, as we look at the freak in bewilderment, still not having gotten the hint, not understood the lesson: namely, that the underbelly of life that causes us horror is life's very essence? And does the free field woven with flowers know about this scrap of blind flesh, coexisting with it in one world, whose lot is only pain, nothing but pain? The childlike eyes of the flowers looking with surprise at the truck see no more than do the sightless eyes of the unthinking freak who has fixed them on the naked sky; blindness is their common lot. But the flowers, unconscious of their own beauty, don't torture themselves in the same way as does this accidental sliver of blind life, whose only reason for appearing on earth is boundless, all-consuming suffering, whose only knowledge of the infinite world is unchanging, incessant pain. Devoid of reason, sunk up to its neck in the lava of merciless torment, yet also lacking the ability to compare, is the creature capable of feeling this torment...?

"Nazis! You're going to get it! The exact same thing should happen to you! You bitches! Nazis!"

The midwife, Alena Grigorievna, whose comely face was always placid as a lake, exploded into the linen closet, her face distorted as if she had just been pulled out of the womb with forceps. The intern wakes up, disoriented, lying on her letter. Alena Grigorievna tears off the diaper covering Champ and pushes a bottle of warm water into his dried-out little mouth. The creature, strange as it may seem, unsticks its parched lips and drinks for a long, long time, moaning blissfully from time to time, and now it is audibly grunting just like a human being. Then the creature sighs convulsively and releases a thin rivulet of poisonous green urine.

"What are they doing to the child! What are the bitches doing! A real brainwave: not to give him any water! The same thing should happen to your children..."

Alena Grigorievna, who had christened the freak Champ, tenderly washes his moldy, rotted-out groin with disinfectant, carefully removes the crusts and scabs with oil, soaks up the green pus with gauze, and gently cleans off the scales and film near his caked-up little mouth, and at the edges of his pointed nose. The creature begins to chirp like a cricket again, and that is all it can say for itself.

And so another day goes by.

The next morning, having despaired of waiting for the child to die, they discharge Znobishina and she leaves, growing smaller and smaller until she fades away on the long road.

Towards evening of the same day, her alien son dies.

It's morning again, and life on the worn-away stone has settled back into its familiar routine.

"So, loser, how's it going? What have you got to say to us, my dear?" Evgeny Igorevich Razduvaev, director of the gynecological and obstetric divisions, greets his first outpatient as his office hours begin.

Further on, in the unit, you can see a thin forest of women's raised legs, and as the midwife prepares the newly admitted patients, as usual, she's loudly telling someone off:

"You there! Good God! How did you manage to do that? A tank could get through that hole!"

Further along, in the corridor crammed with cots and folding beds, a line forms of peasant women in stamped hospital gowns, standing single file, with one hand clutching their institutional garb tight at the neck, the other firmly holding a crumpled aluminum mug of gray-blue jello.

Still further along, at the very end of the corridor, there is a window. If you look through it for a long time, then perhaps the grass near the yellow river will flutter, and it's still a long time until fall.

Leningrad, July,1988

Translated by Jehanne Gheith

From the cycle *Poplar Down Days*
(Den' topolinogo pukha) in the author's manuscript.
Published in *Otdelenie propashchikh,* Moscow, 1991

Notes

1. Caspar Friedrich Wolff (1733-94), German anatomist, specializing in embryology.

Worm-eaten Sonny

Nina Sadur

Men are strong. They're tall, dark, and handsome. They have black eyes, burning mouths. A man mesmerizes you and makes you forget yourself. But he can't give you happiness; he's just not made that way. I mulled this over for a long time before I finally understood why things are like that. A man comes and, like a hero, eclipses the world's deformities. When he's around, everything else dims and fades, and all that's left is this brown haze of passion. But he cannot, *cannot* give you happiness—he's just not made that way. He's not what he seems. He's not tall, not dark, not handsome.[1] And he comes along and gobbles everything up. I scrub and scrub, deny myself in everything, and for what? He'll only come along and gobble it all up. Or worse, he won't come at all, and then there's no reason to live, no reason to scrub this lobby, and no one to gobble up your paycheck. But after all the pay is tiny—only seventy rubles, besides another twenty for doing the Ermolov Theater—and you don't get weekends off. There's other profit here, though: little kids at the matinees throw coins around—it comes to about fifty kopecks a month. Besides that there's candy, apples, little pins, rolls. Sometimes even little hankies. With names. "Liuba Vakheta." "Mitia Mishutin." But you won't hook a man with a little hanky. He himself is the tempter. Because *that's* the way he's made. The demon of betrayal has stung him, and he has put on masks. He's sincere in his masks; he thinks they're his real face. But they're only his masks for us. Only the eyes are his, and everything else is all mask. That's why nothing can work out with a man. That's the way he's made, it turns out—he wears masks. And hides his little eyes. But in fact he's a boor. He's a goat. A marauder.[2] A mercenary. He's very greedy. You need to treat him like this—a kick in the noggin and a warning—know your place, servant. Or else he will come along, gobble everything up, gulp everything down. How he bolts things down—the fiery jaws flashing bits of food, wine, silver! And he himself is filled with dark juice. The rebel. But at first he really knows how to act sincere. He breathes into your being. He'll speak softly and touch gently. He'll look at you. And the depths in him! The goat has all kinds of secrets. The tragedian. He calls you to ruin, but croaks on a feather bed, at his wife's side. She puts mustard plaster on him in parting. And he won't even call you before he dies, the old dog.

Men are never old; only old men are old. But all men are traitors, freedom-lovers and tall; wearing masks, they go around gobbling everything up. They gobble us up along with our innocence, our future, our bones. They corrupt us and poison us with death. They drink us down and crumple us up like milk cartons. They're shameless before us—we're not kin to them. But they're ashamed before God. So they say, "I've taken a liking to this woman. Let it turn out well." It won't turn out well. No. And they know that, but thrust themselves on us anyway. And they're not afraid of God. God knows that man has been bitten by the demon of betrayal. Of lust. Of flight. Of free spirit. Of liberty. Of betrayal. As only a demon could sting such a reptile. It would have been better to bite women. So that she could corrupt man, deprive him of *his* innocence and future, drink him down, leave him to grow old alone. So that men would

203

become women, and women men.

Sometimes men have birthmarks. But these are also masks. You can't trust them. Man's good for your health, but he's dangerous. He's a beast. He has swallowed a scorpion. He stings. He tramples woman down, poisons her, teaches her everything, and then hates her for having learned all his dirty games so well. Men covet our underage daughters. They're monstrous and insane and they need to have their heads cut off. Immediately! But even they can make you feel sorry for them, because their masks must have *some* starting point.[3] And they do.

Worms have moved into man's brain, because of all his dangerous life. And they gnaw at his brains in all the convolutions and suck at the gray matter, and they make man even more brutish. And when he is lying down asleep, the worms peep out from his ears: a worm from the left and a worm from the right.

Vanity and cruelty. And the man-mercenary sleeps without a mask, and his face is horrible, and the worm-suckers peep out and cheeeeep, how tasty he is!

Translated by Wendi Fornoff

From "Ne pomniashchaia zla," 1990

Notes

1. In order to retain the grammatical rhyme of Sadur's "nekrasivyi, nevysokii, melkotriaskii," I originally translated this passage as "ugly, stubby, wimpy." But I believe that of greater importance here than the musicality of the text is its purpose of deflating the positive romantic image of man, the stereotypical "tall, dark, and handsome" man of the English-speaking world.

2. Literally "bitt," a post fixed on a ship's deck for securing lines. The slang meaning of *knext* is most likely the one intended here, although the literal definition carries sexual connotations appropriate to the story. Sadur is also capitalizing on the German word *Knecht*, meaning "hired hand" (HG).

3. This rhyming line ("u maski dolzhny byt' zaviazki") puns on the two meanings of *zaviazka*: starting point and string or tie, the combined meanings suggesting that male masks are donned because of some event in the male biography.

Vera Perova
Nadezhda Kozhevnikova

Vera Perova was admired even by women—they enviously recognized what it was about her that men admired. It was natural, they assumed, that anyone who possessed such thick, golden, flowing hair, such eyes—at times steel blue, at times tinged with violet—such a straight little nose, and a mouth which always hid a smile would stand out among other women. Although *others*—but could one really persuade men of this?—tended to be a little wiser, a little more intelligent, on the whole more interesting, and with a richer inner life.

But Vera Perova would appear in her high heels, walking lightly, but somehow unsteadily, somewhat shakily, and the men involuntarily felt a desire to offer her an arm to lean on. The gaze of her limpid eyes seemed utterly confident and, at the same time, evasive and guilty. It was as if she were saying: "Well, really, I've got nothing to do with it..." And her smile said the same thing: "But I just don't understand what the deal is, why everyone's looking at me..."

But she did understand. There was a reason she preferred silvery-gray and sky-blue tones, that she liked having her pale gold hair brushed back onto her crown, revealing her neck and her smooth, sculpted forehead, which could only be called—girlish.

She understood, but she valued completely different qualities in herself: efficiency, energy, tenacity, and what she herself defined as professional qualities—she was a newspaper writer, a journalist.

The newspaper where she was still working now remembered her as a little girl who straight out of school had started as a secretary to one of the deputy chief editors. Then she had switched to the fact-checking division, and later, after finishing night school at Moscow State, she was accepted as a literary contributor; finally, she ended up among the correspondents sent out on assignment—a real star, that is, one of those who weren't in their offices very often and spent the rest of their time on business trips and in the "throes of creation."

This meant progressing from a newspaper item that had three lines left of the five that were in galley proofs, to feature articles which were discussed as major events at "emergency meetings."

It was the kind of life where returning home is connected with a rediscovery of civilization's blessings: hot water, a bath, freshly ground coffee, clean sheets, and a lamp on the bedside table are perceived as a vacation, and the fact that it's already spring at home, while *there* you were accompanied by chronic winter, severe cold, and a blizzard also seems like a vacation. Or, on the contrary, at home deep autumn greets you, while there it was still possible to snatch a bit of summer, and your body, dressed for the local weather, still recalls the other place's warmth and the caressing sun, and your hair even smells of the sea...

In a word, it was a life in which the seasons didn't follow their usual order, one climate and one corner of the globe were replaced by another, and people's faces flashed by kaleidoscopically: those with whom she'd become friends long ago suddenly became distant, whereas the ones with whom she'd been acquainted for only three days seemed close.

But wherever she was, she wanted to go home, where Vera's mother managed the household and took care of Vera's daughter. In Vera's absence everything ran on its own, although, of course, her return was eagerly awaited, and she was respected as the family's breadwinner.

The path from a timid young secretary to a qualified, experienced correspondent for a respectable newspaper might have been considered an enormous rise, but, alas, it had taken years. Vera Perova had turned thirty-five, she'd been divorced from her husband, her daughter was in sixth grade, her mother, thank God, was still in good health—in a word, there was order, and Vera Perova could concentrate fully on herself. On her personal life, as they say.

Nobody had any doubt about Vera's possibilities in that area. With her endowments, her way of smiling, of averting her eyes slyly and shyly, she surely could have gotten anything she'd wished for.

But—and here's the paradox—she didn't wish for it. Even her closest friends didn't understand her in this regard. Why, when she needed only to extend her hand, did she reject what was her due, preferring a manner of existence which required a much greater effort on her part and made it necessary for her to vie with those who had no choice and, therefore, felt they had more rights. Yes, all in all, there really should be some justice! With her flowing golden hair and her sparkling gray-blue eyes, why did Vera try to make it where women who didn't have that kind of hair and eyes struggled?

Why on earth did Vera Perova harness herself to them! She took part in planning and in "emergency meetings." She'd flare up with a blush of indignation, crinkle her forehead angrily, declare that she was not in agreement here, that her position...

Position! Of course, they listened, they nodded–and they couldn't tear their eyes away. She would tap a pencil nervously, she had very slender wrists and fine alabaster-skinned hands, with long, weak fingers, which, however, could probably stroke very gently...

She'd sit down, agitated, disturbed by what had been said, a blue vein twitching, pulsing at her temple—and the back of her head was so wonderful, with its knot of pale gold hair...

She'd burst in on the secretaries' pool: "Did they typeset my material? Where are the galley proofs?" She'd start to read and make some corrections in rapt concentration. Her male colleagues would mill around, smoking. She'd raise her eyes, shimmering, moist: "Yes... the 'tail' is very long. I won't shorten it!"

So room would be made for the "tail." She'd walk out satisfied, and the room would still smell of her perfume for a long time afterwards, and people's heads would spin from the scent.

Vera Perova, Vera Perova, Vera Perova...

She wrote about everything: about industrial topics and under the rubric "Morality and Everyday Life," and sometimes she'd take on an interview if there were worthy candidates.

Well, yes, men again... She'd appear in their offices, which were decorated with wood paneling, and on construction sites, in laboratories, in studios, and in rehearsal halls. She'd look stern, pull out a notepad, and settle herself a little more comfortably, crossing her legs. And a joyous bewilderment would flare in their eyes. Well, of course, she understood them... The human gaze is instinctively drawn to beauty, rests as it dwells on beauty, and expresses gratitude. Vera Perova had gotten used to being thanked in this way, but her ambition demanded other victories, proof of another kind: she was waiting for them to recognize her education, her tact, her mind.

And she tried. She valued that instant when her interlocutor's gaze finally grew serious, even gloomy, and irritated, argumentative tones broke through the voice. Then she mentally told herself: "Yes, well, as long as they don't just think 'look who's turned up.' Say what you want, I know how to get a person to talk."

In fact, the men easily responded to business talk; people usually like to discuss their own concerns. And there's a certain category of men whose personal concerns are embodied precisely in business. Their innermost life is right there, in the laboratory, in the studios, in the factory shop. They stupefied the correspondent Vera Perova with specialized terminology, even while they spoke as if they were revealing their very hearts to her. And she admired and respected these obsessed individuals.

And she'd slam shut her notepad. She'd stand up and thank them. So what were they waiting for, in the end? She was going about her business, too.

She'd say about herself, "I'm a work horse." The corners of her mouth would turn down, and her lilac eyes would narrow, shimmering, shimmering and sparkling like silver. Her appearance was what is called pastel, and one wanted to see her depicted in a portrait in an oval-frame: the pale gold of her hair against a dark background... The delicate blue of her eyelids shades the moist brilliance of her elongated eyes—in old portraits this quicksilver brilliance always casts a spell. And then there's the half-smile lurking at the corners of her stern mouth...

Vera worked out an iron regimen: she'd get up, come rain or shine, at 7:00 a.m., then morning exercises, a shower, and the invariable oatmeal boiled in water. Her day ended with a glass of kefir and a feeling that it hadn't been spent in vain.

"What's the matter with you, don't you see how Fedia Sedykh looks at you?" people would say to her. She'd shrug her narrow shoulders. "And that hero you wrote up in your article came by and asked about you. You were on an assignment then." She'd respond with a barely noticeable smile—yes, fine, the article's already written.

Really, she didn't have the time or energy. Or the desire. And why bother? Hadn't she seen enough? They all said roughly the same things, and it all ended sooner or later. For some reason it ended. Always.

This hadn't happened immediately, of course; she'd built up a defensive layer. Vera remembered mornings when she'd waited for a telephone call, trying to keep busy with something or other, trying to deceive herself: that he hadn't called because he hadn't woken up yet, that he hadn't called because he was afraid of waking her up, that he hadn't called because... because men are different, they get distracted by business and force you to wait; and they themselves don't know the state of expectation, so when they do remember, they dial the phone number without a moment's hesitation.

Which meant that he wasn't reminiscing about her. How humiliating! No matter how much you talk about equal rights, it's all over once a woman starts waiting morning, noon, and night for a call, and the phone doesn't ring.

But maybe it isn't about equal rights, but about the fact that you *don't have to* wait. You can't allow weakness and dependence—the one who wins is the one for whom the previous day is in no way connected with the new day that has dawned. And every word, whisper, and sigh remain as if behind a barrier in the past, for which no one bears responsibility. And it's very important to learn this—don't wait, don't dwell on what happened in the past with bowed head, your face saddened by tenderness, don't try to understand how it's possible, after such absolute trust, to return like a pendulum to your former distance from one another.

That was how Vera Perova had acquired experience. Especially feminine experience. And her conclusion was that you have to act like a man. Men receive the gift of armor at birth, women have to learn to feign invulnerability.

How? Very simple. You respond cheerfully and happily to a telephone call, as if to say, "Everything's fine, nothing happened." Nothing happened! And if you should happen to meet, you don't avert your eyes, you shake hands firmly, in a friendly way, as if to say again, "Don't think that I'm waiting for something, counting on something. No, I'm a modern woman, free and insensitive, don't worry, I don't go in for any kind of sentiment."

Even so—why? It wasn't as if there had been any arguments, no particular differences came up, yet the men would suddenly disappear, she wasn't able to hold on to them, it was as if they were just waiting for a signal to disappear—forever.

Despite her external pastel fragility, Vera Perova had a firm character and in her own home behaved like the head of the household. She provided money for housekeeping and didn't get involved in the petty details of everyday life. Sometimes she'd return very late, but a candle would be burning in the entrance hall, and Vera understood that such a considerate gesture expressed a delicate hint that maybe they'd waited for her and were worried but, of course, no one was infringing on her right to come and go whenever and wherever she pleased.

At one time Vera Perova used to call home without fail if she was detained; she would guiltily listen to all the accusations, and afterwards, even if her mother was angry, she'd come in to wish her goodnight, and perch on the edge of the bed: "You understand, Mama..."

Her mother tried to keep a stern expression on her face, and seemed to understand, to be indulgent, but in fact she was inwardly sighing in relief: well, thank God, thank God...

But now Vera would tiptoe down the hall past the rooms where her daughter and mother were sleeping, close the door behind her, take off her dress, underwear, and stockings, put everything away neatly in the closet, sit down at the vanity and rub her face with cream: the mirror reflected her face, exhausted, apathetic—the face of a grown woman who knows what she can and what she shouldn't tell about herself.

And in the morning she'd do her exercises, eat up her oatmeal boiled in water, brush her golden hair up from the nape, and go about her business.

What Vera had accomplished thus far she'd achieved by herself. That was a fact. And it comforted her, and lent her strength, and marred her character just a little bit, although she herself believed that, on the contrary, it had toughened her. She'd been born into a family that was candidly, artlessly proud to be perfectly ordinary people. Both inside and out they were like everyone else. They had no doubts about how to act or how to react to anything, how to establish a way of life. They bought furniture and arranged it in the same style that could be found in homes similar to theirs. A print appeared on the wall as if at someone's suggestion: a washed-out autumnal landscape so bland that there could be no risk of error, no chance it would stand out. It was destined to be hung there. Just as the unprepossessing ceramic vase was destined to end up on the television set. The television, of course, rested on a stand in the corner, so that the whole family could gather around the screen in the evening after tea.

They had had a good family. Her father worked in an electric lamp factory, her mother was a nurse at a regional polyclinic. When Vera finished school, she at first thought of getting a job at the registration desk in that polyclinic, but she ended up in another job, with a newspaper: the secretary to the assistant chief editor had gone on maternity leave.

Vera worked every other day and had alternate days off: in front of the assistant editor's office, as in front of the chief editor's, there was another cubicle, but a little smaller, where Vera sat in front of five phones. People would come in and indicate the closed door of the assistant editor's office: "Is he in?" She'd say: "Yes," or "No, he's busy." The assistant editor liked very strong tea and drank it without sugar, but with crackers that were kept in a drawer in his desk. He was puny, with thinning hair, and polite, though Vera felt that when he glanced at her it was hard for him to remember her name. But—with an effort—he'd recall it. "Verochka," he'd say, "I'd like some tea..."

The chief editor's secretary was over fifty. She kept shopping bags under her desk, and she'd hang a bag of groceries out the window. People were constantly calling her— first one daughter, then the other, then her son-in-law, who was the husband of her younger, favorite daughter. She'd talk to them for a long time, cupping her hand over the receiver—the visitors waiting in the entrance hall, shrinking under the gaze of her wan, goitered eyes, interfered with her conversation. Her back hurt, too: "Osteochondrosis," she complained to Vera, and because of it she didn't like to get up from behind the desk. Admittedly, whenever the chief called her, she had to. Then she'd fling open the door to his office, standing on the threshold with an expression of attentive readiness, but one could detect censure nonetheless in her goitered eyes.

She didn't have much time left until her retirement, but she didn't concede her power to anyone—she wanted to reign until the very last minute. Sometimes she would allow liberties: she'd run out to the store so she wouldn't have to struggle in a line at the end of the day, and she'd tell Vera: "Stand guard, I'll be back in a second."

And Vera was bored. People would carry damp newspaper galley proofs past her and she'd see their backs huddled around a table when an issue was being planned, yet she'd have to come into the office to shake out the ashtrays and to clear the empty tea-glasses.

It was then she wrote the first blurb in her life, about a book exhibit, and brought it in with her own hands to the secretaries' pool. Once it was printed out on a special list with the newspaper's full title set out in typography, with columns for the editor's caption, the blurb seemed significant to her, serious and worthy of the attention of millions.

The blurb was shortened, marked up with what Vera considered unnecessary corrections, and approved for the fact-checking division's latticed tray. But Vera decided not to throw her brainchild to the whims of fate: she took the blurb and went in person to the fifth floor, so the "girls from fact-checking" would make sure, in her presence, that there were no mistakes in the material and, having secured their John Hancock, she went back down to the secretaries' pool. Modestly, but insistently, she announced that they'd said everything was in order, that it could be sent off for typesetting.

Unfortunately, they set the galley proofs without her supervision, but when she received them—damp, on loose yellowish paper, with boldfaced letters that seemed almost raised to the touch—she sniffed and squinted blissfully.

Then she wrote her next blurb, which she called a review for the sake of respectability; they abridged all her reflections, but published it as an item of information.

Next she started participating in "emergency meetings." It was wonderful to address an audience. The previous orator would give her incentive—his speech revealed a discrepancy, and Vera Perova would throw herself into the fray like a bulldog, noiselessly, without a bark, her jaw clenched in a death grip.

They listened to her. The attention they paid her made her flesh tingle, and she delighted in it, finding the exact words and hanging above a precipice when her thoughts would suddenly scatter in different directions. But she found the strength in herself, during the pauses, not to panic—she was learning to speak and to force others to listen to her.

The newspaper raised a member of the personnel within its own walls. Vera enrolled in night school at Moscow State University, was taken on as a literary contributor, and became a traveling correspondent.

And, as with her first blurb, she kept a close eye on almost all of her material, accompanying it at all stages, from the typist's office to when it was sent to the type-setter's. Even beyond that, she pestered the bosses to ensure that her material not be shelved, that it appear as soon as possible on the newspaper's pages. She wasn't ashamed of appearing pushy, importunate—it was her right, she told herself. After all, she was earning her living.

The newspaper's routine was set up so that you could work without a break or you could do nothing if you wanted, just create an appearance of activity, show up on time, and other than that—do whatever you wanted. You could drop by the section next door, say, and gab there to the point of exhaustion, go with a group to the snackbar to drink coffee, stay on the telephone for hours—and all this could really wear you out by the end of the day. So those who lazed around shamelessly also felt they were part of things.

Such an existence did not suit Vera Perova; she set herself the goal of getting ahead. But perhaps for precisely this reason she encountered difficulties: she'd either leave early—you see, she had to "write up" her material—or she'd race off on an assign-ment without asking permission from her immediate supervisor. She didn't have the patience, and perhaps, the unconsciousness, to keep moving steadily up the ladder.

Here, in fact, her appearance worked against her. Someone else would manage qui-etly to "fade" from a meeting, but her absence was instantly detected. The women were curious: what was she wearing, how did she look? The men also felt her absence. "Ah, Perova didn't show up! I understand..." And it was probably also due to inertia in their thinking—frivolity was attributed to a beautiful woman even if she gave no cause for it. But, really, since she was temptation incarnate, enticing others, couldn't she, as they say, take a back seat?

Vera Perova's reserve, coldness, and businesslike manner were also perceived, alas, as coquetry, as a means of seduction—yes, even her modesty. And the gaze of her icy violet eyes, evasively guilty, supported such an opinion. But she didn't know how else to gaze: was she really guilty? After all, she, Vera Perova, worked so hard and got so upset over her professional setbacks! Work had turned out to be the main, the most important thing for her, and why couldn't they understand that?

They only had to ask her mother and her daughter Tanechka, who could have told them what gloom Vera sank into when things didn't go right at work. Then nothing, nothing could distract her; it was as if mourning had been declared in the home, and her mother and daughter, who were already trained, would tiptoe around the apart-ment so as not to disturb her.

It might seem strange that although Vera had been working at the newspaper for a long time and had come a long way "from" and "to," she hadn't formed close relations with any of her colleagues. She used affectionate nicknames for "the girls" from the fact-checking section and the typing pool and "the boys"—the photo-correspondents, but she spent only as much time with them as was needed, in her opinion, for business. She also didn't stay in the bosses' offices very long, in this case valuing *their* time: she'd perch on the edge of a chair, prepared to stand up instantly, but did so without any ingratiation, just in an emphatically businesslike manner.

This situation suited Vera perfectly. She didn't waste time in idle chatter, she didn't linger over coffee and cigarettes in the snackbar in a close-knit group, none of her female co-workers chose her as a personal confidante, and she didn't share her secrets with anyone. And she assumed that in this way she was avoiding intrigues. That way, she thought, was much safer. And in general, she acted in accordance with her own nature: on assignments and in searching for job-related information she greedily reached out to new people, flung herself upon them, sensing interesting material, but in everyday life she was tired of people, felt oppressed by long conversations, and could barely suppress a yawn or conceal a bored gaze.

At the desk right next to hers, in her section, sat Tonechka Krutova. Sit is exactly what she did: she didn't tear off on assignments, she rarely wrote any independent material—in a word, she wasn't a rival. But Tonechka was known for her painstaking work with authors and her readiness to carry a heavy load of so-called grunt work, because it basically seemed insignificant.

In school Tonechka had definitely been an "A" student, without showing a preference for any one subject and cramming everything out of a sense of duty. But such a quality ceases to be laudable in adult life. Its possessors are incapable of ever doing any kind of hackwork, of economizing their strength somewhere in order to focus on something definite, and in their officious zeal they occasionally remind you of housewives fighting to keep their homes so clean that it finally becomes a mania which makes them suffer.

That's how it was with Tonechka. When she was designated the "reader" for an issue, she studied the paper's type page as if it were a suspect bank note, even though many other people besides her bore responsibility for the issue and it had been checked over many times!

But that was precisely where Tonechka differed from the others, in her heightened sense of duty, her exaggerated diligence in everything. She brushed her hair back very smoothly, so that not a single hair would stick out. And she put on powder—for her this was a sign of agitation—in several layers, covering her face with a rosy, unnaturally bright shade.

She had two children and a drunk of a husband, whom she also kept in tow. Her husband would call her at work, she'd answer him in monosyllables, put down the receiver and immediately start powdering her face, turning away as she covered the traces of her tears with a fresh layer.

She'd cry silently, habitually, and briefly, without interrupting her reading, as she corrected someone's item or article. She'd sniff furtively, stand up, and rush down the hall to clarify something thoroughly, getting to the very bottom of it, so that, God forbid, not a single tiny, infinitesimal blunder might slip through.

And Tonechka's eyes, a dimmed, faded blue, always stared reproachfully, as if she were now blaming herself, now offering others the chance to blame themselves. And her exultant, bell-like, high-pitched little girl's voice didn't accord with that gaze at all.

That tone of incomprehensible, groundless exultation stuck in people's minds as the single vivid trait in Tonechka's image. As for the rest, she seemed like a little gray mouse, and she ran along the wall, through the halls of the editorial office timidly, like a mouse: about to dive into a burrow any minute and disappear.

Tonechka's desk stood next to Vera Perova's, and they shared one phone between the two of them. Fairly often upon picking up the receiver, Tonechka had to answer, "She's not here. She left. She's on an assignment."

But Tonechka never grumbled that the place behind the desk next to hers was, as a rule, vacant, or that their immediate supervisor, a man with fluffy reddish sideburns and a long, pale face was constantly sick, so that she, Tonechka, had a triple workload, even though her salary didn't take that into account, for she continued to receive the same old 150 rubles.

Usually even bosses favor such reliable, inconspicuous workers, and the entourage sympathizes with them, but Tonechka kept herself completely aloof in the editor's office, it was as if she didn't notice that she wouldn't let anyone come close, and kept people at a distance from her. Possibly her reserve sprang from her absorption in countless tasks, difficulties, and family problems. She existed in a state of constant watchfulness, as if something hadn't happened yet, and it was reflected in her look, in her facial expression. And also in the reproachful gaze of her faded eyes.

But, nonetheless, she established the best of relations with Vera Perova. It was as if Tonechka immediately recognized that Vera had special rights which allowed her to enjoy privileges upon which Tonechka didn't even encroach.

She was probably the only woman who sincerely admired Vera: at times Vera sensed her gaze, pensive and contented, upon her—the way people look through a window in sunny weather, or at a picture in a museum, inspired, selflessly rejoicing that this beauty is within reach.

Tonechka's attitude softened even Vera; that habitual readiness for action would temporarily abandon her in Tonechka's presence. Sometimes Vera even allowed herself to be distracted from urgent business, and she'd sit, leaning her elbows on the desk as she conversed leisurely, almost intimately, with Tonechka, who sat across from her. And such a pleasant feeling arose during these conversations, enveloping and relaxing them as they spoke about trifles, about everyday things, but Vera felt a stream of vital warmth exuding from Tonechka and she delighted in it, as if she were luxuriating in a warm bath.

Then they'd go down to the snackbar. Tonechka clutched in her fist a threadbare purse trimmed with beads, but while standing in line at the snackbar counter, they'd stop exchanging remarks and thoughtfully read over the menu, as if the presence of others disrupted the trust that arose between them in private.

Her older son, wearing a tight school jacket and man-sized shoes, would sometimes drop by the editor's office to see her. His two front teeth were noticeably larger than the rest, they stuck out, and when he smiled he looked like a cartoon rabbit.

Tonechka talked about how she was raising him. How? Well, not at all... They had a friendly relationship. Children grow up so fast nowadays. You can't instill respect for parents by force, and it really doesn't have to be reflected in a deferential tone.

The boy-bunny actually did act more patronizing than anything towards his mother, using that sarcasm which, at his age, usually conceals tenderness. And Tonya answered him in about the same way.

Vera, observing Tonya with her son, reflected that this was an example of family troubles not reflecting badly on children, but seeming even to toughen them, making them more stable and resistive—qualities so necessary in life, yet so difficult to teach in a smothering, hothouse environment.

She once expressed her thoughts to Tonechka, who, however, smiled sadly. No, she said, children need to be brought up more in kindness, in warmth, so that what is fragile within them, which later on will certainly be put to the test of pressure, can grow stronger. That's necessary so that it has time to form during their childhood years—and also trustfulness, dreaminess, and mildness. And she was very sorry that things had turned out differently in her family, that her children were sensible beyond their years, and she didn't consider this at all a virtue, and maybe she herself was to blame, since she hadn't managed to protect them till the right time. Their good sense made a lot of things easier for her, their mother, but if you thought about it, at what cost had they obtained it so early?

Vera listened. It's strange, she mused, how sensibly and coherently Tonechka was setting forth her thoughts, whereas around people she completely lacked the ability to speak, she'd break out in dark splotches, her gaze would become tearful, and one would feel really sorry for her, really uncomfortable for her.

Maybe if Vera hadn't spent so much time on assignments, the reproachful gaze of Tonechka's faded eyes and the expression of utmost patience on her plain little face would have started to irritate her, the way the dreary brick building across the way irritated her. But, fortunately, both Tonechka and the brick structure next to the editorial office were intermingled with other, more captivating impressions, so they didn't have time to become thoroughly loathsome to her.

Immediately upon her return, Vera would note the slightest changes in her quiet co-worker's appearance, which certainly escaped the attention of most. Well, who could have found it interesting that Tonechka had put on amber beads or, let's say, had a mosaic brooch below her collar? It didn't embellish her, didn't make her more noticeable. But she'd felt such a need, as she was leaving her troubled home, to pin on the brooch, and this occupied Vera, so to say, on a psychological plane, she paid attention to such details, and Tonechka was so grateful to her for not being indifferent.

So? Well, after all, it's precisely such little things that influence human relations; feelings of sympathy and antipathy are based just on matters like these. "I'm leaving a little early today," Vera would say. "Of course," Tonechka would answer readily. "If anyone asks, what should I say?"

But it so happened that the bosses did become interested in the state of their section. No, Vera's absences were not the cause, but rather the prolonged illness of their immediate supervisor, whose long, pale, flabby face had actually begun to fade from his colleagues' memory. And rumors began to stir in the corridors: they're looking for a replacement, maybe from outside, maybe from within the group itself, but nobody knows yet who's got what chance.

Vera Perova also bestirred herself. Yes, they valued her pen at the newspaper, but her position remained modest in the staff slots, in the sense that she hadn't advanced her career at all in recent years. She suddenly realized how she'd been overlooked. And she herself was to blame. She disdained contacts and was poorly informed about relations within the editorial office: frequent assignments and her preoccupation with her own professional concerns had prevented her from obtaining the necessary information in time.

Now the time was ripe. She felt that besides creative enthusiasm, there had matured within her a need to consolidate her own position. The itch of vanity was suddenly discovered.

Formerly it suited her completely that, say, upon entering a small room where emergency meetings were being held, she'd feel *serious* men staring at her, see smiles in her direction to which she responded cordially as she sat down modestly somewhere in a corner. Emphasizing—indeed, she had a purpose in mind—that she knew her place. But now... her anxiety was roused. Men—their support wasn't worth very much, and weren't they placating her, weren't they lulling her by their politeness, thereby eliminating a possible rival?

And how much of this had escaped her notice earlier! Rather, it wasn't so much that she hadn't seen, but she simply hadn't delved into why certain people came to meetings a little earlier than the scheduled time, and why they didn't leave immediately once the meeting was over, but rather stood around in little groups or whispered tête-à-tête. And it was precisely then that the most important things happened, that business matters were decided, prospects were mapped out, while the naive Vera was rushing back to her desk. Well, now she had to look into things, pay more attention...

The tables in the conference hall were set up in a square, so that all the participants ended up face to face. The conversation was serious: it was about the responsibility of a columnist's work, the obligation to delve into the heart of problems and not be limited to descriptions in minute detail which, despite their skill, dissipated instantly like foam. The presentations were impassioned, and each time the same phenomenon was repeated: the speaker, having gained the floor, lost all awareness of the time limits keenly felt by the audience: "Talk about dragging it out!" some could be heard whispering. "Time's up!" called someone, unable to control his impatience, but as soon as he was granted the opportunity to say his piece, he ended up doing the same thing as the previous speaker.

That's human nature for you—no objectivity whatsoever. As long as you're part of a crowd, with everyone else, it's easy to judge, to evaluate sensibly, but as soon as you step out, separate yourself from the rank and file, you immediately lose your critical instinct, your sense of reality disappears—and you prance and prance until you're hissed off the stage.

These observations occurred to Vera, and she said to herself: "When my turn comes, I'll lay out the crux of the matter in three sentences." She imagined how she'd stand, leaning with her hand on the table, straighten her back, and after calmly glancing around at everyone, so there'd be no silly fuss, how she'd act cool and businesslike—she could do it!

But meanwhile others were speaking, and she looked at them, squinting. Volodka, or, rather, Vladimir Igorevich, had risen, his hands shoved in the pockets of his leather jacket— he was so unconstrained. Well, he could probably take such liberties... His wide, slightly puffy face, with eyes under swollen eyelids and somewhat sharp protruding cheekbones, expressed a practiced benevolence that must be peculiar to tutors who don't allow themselves to get annoyed, no matter how outrageously their charges behave.

Volodya was conducting the meeting. He gave the floor to those who wanted it and, when he considered it necessary, interlaid the presentations with brief summaries which, as a rule, had a tactical function—to stop people from going to extremes and becoming excessively worked up, and to help them stick rather to common sense, as otherwise people might well come to blows from an excess of temperament. Like a ring-side umpire, Volodya was there to enforce order, and he got it. Maintaining an expression of the same tranquillity, he would change his vocal register from baritone to a slightly strained, cautionary bass, as if to say: watch out, I might start snarling.

In general, Volodya handled himself well. But he was really unattractive. He wore his hair short, in a crewcut, as if defiantly emphasizing his unattractiveness on purpose: such a haircut exposed his lumpy skull and made his irregular, rough features jut out. He didn't impress one with his brilliance, either, but there was something about his way of weightily and confidently uttering banalities that inspired respect. He knew how to convince not so much by argument, as by his imposing demeanor. You sensed a hidden strength in him and felt you could trust such a man.

Although sometimes a suspicion would creep in: could it be just a shrewd trick? Maybe Volodya's imposing manner was nothing other than simple pomposity? didn't the darting, persistent gaze of his narrow eyes signal a dread of exposure?

He was lucky! He was incredibly lucky. He'd advanced with such rapidity that there were few left who remembered the origins, the beginning of his rise. But what was there to recall? And why? It simply worked out that way, circumstances arranged themselves accordingly. Luck also, by the way, is a gift, and only obviously envious people are capable of refuting it.

And Volodya sensed the dividing line so marvelously—when a leader's democracy wins people over and when it degenerates into a familiarity that is harmful to authority.

No, it wasn't by chance that Vladimir Igorevich had come to power. His office was lived-in, its owner's character manifested itself in the book collection on the shelves, in the posters signed by the artists, his friends, but even here he observed moderation: yes, it was an office, but it was in no way a den of amassed *goods* and *mementos* which, even without a moss-grown track, would have raised the dangerous suspicion that perhaps the public servant had been in office too long. Volodka had set up his office in such a way that it seemed it would be easy for him to gather up his possessions and move into one more spacious, more boss-like.

But perhaps the most remarkable thing Volodya had achieved was a balance in both his relations with the older generation and the young crowd. The almost imperceptible but obviously respectful bow of his knobby head whenever he dealt with his elders flattered them, gratified their pride, and turned out to be far more effective than the crude, open toadying which already made them squeamish, like fatty foods which are so unnecessary at their age.

On the other hand, when conversing with his contemporaries, Volodya moved just a bit closer, with an expression of approving interest, nodding from time to time—not patronizingly, which could have seemed insulting, but with that degree of both caution and complaisance which especially filled the other person with enthusiasm and the desire to make him think similarly, without fail.

"And just think—where did Volodka's old hustle and bustle disappear to!" Vera exclaimed to herself. The greedy gleam in his eyes; the rapidity of his speech, which came in quick, brief spurts; the confused and bewildered smile, which somehow always appeared out of place on his chubby, swollen lips.

But perhaps that awkwardness of his, which had once been so noticeable, had provided the springboard for his ascent? He'd aroused a need in those around him to somehow smooth over and soften the roughness which seemed inherently characteristic of him; and such a noble impulse was precisely what made people take a liking to him.

They didn't see a rival in him—that's what it was, and he had quietly and unobtrusively rowed up to the finish line, leaving behind those he'd started out with, who had a much brighter potential.

Naturally, he tried to show how much of a hard worker he was. Once he was seated in his armchair, he'd not race off on account of some nonsense, some useless business. He consolidated his reputation as a reliable man good at carrying out orders. His secretary would connect him with a subscriber, while somebody else would try to break in on a direct line. Volodya would answer in a rich, sonorous baritone—yes, what can I do for you—managing not to offend either, to have time for both this one and that one, making each one feel that he was favored over everyone else.

Yes... one must admit Vera also hadn't shown any insight where Volodya was concerned. She poked fun at his advances, which were admittedly not at all daring—he seemed so awkward. But fortunately, even without any particular effort, she found the right tone in her relationship with him—that of platonic friendship, of cooing mockery which made it possible to exaggerate praise and to express approval loudly, a glance from her radiant eyes forcing those who didn't agree to fall silent. It became clear only later how he, Volodya, needed both praise and approval at the time.

He didn't forget. He never forgot anything—that was his nature, equitable and grateful in certain cases, petty and vindictive in others: he repaid good with good, and evil—well, just wait! He didn't display those characteristics of his immediately, of course, and by the time everyone could attest to them it was already too late.

However, it wasn't up to Vera to judge Volodya. He himself didn't aspire to be a model of virtue and it wouldn't have been worth while to make an icon of him. The world's probably set up in such a way that from time to time a forceful person has to step over his less competent fellow human beings.

In a word, on the whole Vera approved of Volodya. Even his reserved tone, which he'd acquired over time, even his unattractiveness, which he himself acknowledged defiantly, impressed her. A man's appearance is a strange thing: even ugliness seems to be distinctive and original, when you know *who* it is who possesses it.

He doesn't have to be a genius, just a public figure with success and good luck. How women hung on Volodya now! But he would never forget anything. He let them entertain hopes up to a certain point, then suddenly, but at a moment he had calculated to a nicety, he'd break everything off.

He seemed to be generous and attentive just for this purpose, just so that, having prolonged their illusions, he could annihilate them in one stroke.

Vera was familiar with some of his victims—cute, all dressed up, no older than twenty-five. Once they grew bolder, they clung to him possessively, poor things... Maybe some of them truly believed they'd fallen for him, but their zealous efforts were striking, nonetheless: Volodya would bring them out and show them to his entourage, but perhaps was actually more interested in the impression he created than in the feelings of his little beauties. In general, he wasn't the most skillful ladies' man.

On the other hand, when the black "Volga" drove up and Volodya opened the door, sat down next to the chauffeur, said "Hi, Petya," and leaned back in self-satisfaction, the immediate result was that all of his gestures, the movement of his stocky figure, acquired an unexpected elegance—that's what power, position, and success mean.

It was nice to ride along with him in the company car, and it did no harm from a practical viewpoint. Volodya's gaze was keen and focused from under his half-closed eyelids. He really was tired, but he also was feigning tiredness, so as to observe more comfortably. A profound, heavy sigh, a limp pose, a sluggish, hollow voice, had a relaxing effect, allaying one's suspicions. At such moments Volodya seemed so accessible that you thought you'd better take advantage of it quickly, get closer to him, enlist his support. So, for a start one had to be candid. Volodya would listen, blinking drowsily, and few could have guessed at the intense work going on inside his head: to extract the prize seed from the husk of endless unimportant things, to conceal it imperceptibly behind his cheek—maybe it'll come in handy—and not to betray his own satisfaction in the slightest—there's no denying it, that requires experience and even refined skill.

The experience of existing in the "lower layers of the atmosphere," in the position of a young guy prepared to oblige everyone and take on anything stood Volodya in good stead. He was trying to get the attention of people who were virtually inaccessible, but who felt the need for precisely such temperaments, with, as it were, a muscular energy, very mobile and not given to annoying you with their own whims. He performed and they used him, but it was a serious school. He came away with the ability to bide his time until the right moment, not to spare any effort, remembering that sooner or later it would pay off, and furthermore, not to let his peers out of his field of vision. The newly fledged boss would have to not only join with the other bosses, but also not forget his own people, to have a retinue, because otherwise he'd end up in a vacuum.

Tact, of course, was also required: to use influence on behalf of worthless friends is one scenario, but it's a completely different one when business interests become first on your agenda, when you're recruiting people who are useful and with whom you have an affinity as well.

This was what Volodya cared about—true, reliable allies. Who were attracted not only by a salary or raise, but first and foremost by a solidarity of thought.

And however much respect his elders elicited, he had to direct his efforts toward his own generation. It's a law of life, and nothing can be done about it. It was already noted long ago in Ecclesiastes that there's a time for every need of the human soul, and there's no point in coercing it, in stubbornly compelling it to peer at the ground, at what is life-sustaining, so to speak, when the gaze is already directed upward and burdened by an excess of vanities.

Needless to say, it took a great deal of energy to introduce a program like Volodya's simultaneously with official duties, taking into account the specific nature of newspaper work, where emergencies are always popping up. But sometimes when Vera glanced at Volodya, it seemed to her that it wasn't work that was exhausting him, but something hidden deep within him that gnawed at him and that he didn't want to admit to anyone.

Can an overly retentive memory really get in a person's way? And what about an armor that has been thickening for years? Can you really turn out to be so invulnerable that you can't get through to yourself? Observing Volodya, who seemed all right, despite all the attributes of success, Vera suddenly felt something like pity for him. He was constantly with people who swamped him in his office and kept calling him at home, but at times his narrow, sharp eyes seemed wrapped in a shroud—was it loneliness, lack of shelter? That's when she wanted to shake him, to convince herself that his inherent spark hadn't been extinguished, but he wouldn't let himself be tempted, and would hide like a tortoise in his shell. "What a drone!"—your temper would start to boil then, but at the same time you'd feel sympathy: thus do people of similar temperaments discover flaws peculiar to their type.

This was what Vera was pondering as she sat in the conference hall at a meeting. But she didn't lose track of the main thing that now occupied her: whom would she be able to rely on if the question of her candidacy for the position of section head came up? More precisely: which of the bosses was capable of announcing her candidacy? And she no longer had any doubts—yes, of course, Volodya. She remembered with relief: how good it was that her relations with him were precisely of a friendly nature.

There was the din of chairs being pulled back and the indistinct hum of chatter; faces softened—the meeting had finally ended. Volodya was surrounded by a dense circle of people, but Vera didn't like to put off business indefinitely, so she decided to wait around and catch Volodya as he left.

She was familiar with that blank, persecuted look on the face of a boss rushing to hide in his office from the supplicants pressing in on all sides, waiting for advice, help, just a minute of attention. Volodya might not even notice her in such an eddy, so she decided to call out to him, and was herself astonished at the unexpected timidity of her voice. He turned around, probably before he had time to wipe the displeasure off his face, and this made her even more tense: so she also ended up in the crowd of supplicants. "Do you have a minute?" she asked the usual. "No!" he responded, but with such cheerful despair that it was clear he hadn't refused her, but was joking. She cheered up. "Let's go," he threw at her without slowing down, and she followed him to his office. "Maria Grigorievna, call for the car, please," he said to the stern, middle-aged secretary, the kind that careful young bosses usually choose. She nodded regally, and Volodya, letting Vera precede him, walked into his office and flopped into an armchair with a look that said—Boy, am I exhausted.

And he smiled, "Well, Verunya, you see what it's like! I can't stand to look at myself. I drudge and drudge. When will it all be over already?!" She was already used to hearing such complaints from him, it's the standard flirtation of over-ambitious people, but she thought the expression on her face should show some sympathy.

"And what kind of problems do you have?" he continued. "You shouldn't be having any!" he declared fervently and both of them burst out in somewhat forced laughter.

Of course, they could be interrupted at any moment, Vera understood that, but she shouldn't rush: there had to be an atmosphere that would allow her to renounce the humiliating role of supplicant and that would divest Volodya of the official aura requiring him to remain strictly within boundaries.

Just then his secretary's voice came in over the intercom: "The car's waiting, Vladimir Igorievich."

He looked at Vera and threw up his hands apologetically: "What can I do? Is it something really urgent?" She lowered her eyes: "Well, no. But I would like to talk to you." "Tomorrow's a crazy day, too," he muttered, rummaging in his notepad. "Things have really come to a sorry pass when there's no time to sit down for a bit like real people. But, listen," he leaned across the desk towards her. "What about leaving together now? I'm needed at the ministry for literally twenty minutes, but it has to be right now, otherwise everyone will go his separate way. And you can sit in the car in the meantime, okay? I'll be quick. And then, if you don't object, we'll have dinner somewhere."

"Okay," she gave a smile that was part flattering, part independent. "Let's go, then," he got up with a jerk. He still retained his earlier jerky movements, an abruptness of motion. "Maria Grigorievna, I won't be back. See you tomorrow."

As they walked out of the anteroom, Vera could feel the secretary's gaze on her back. So what, she thought, let her look. Maybe it's not even bad...

The black "Volga" was waiting for them at the entranceway. Volodya sat down next to the driver, Vera in the back seat. He reached into his briefcase full of papers, while she stared out the window. He was used to traveling in cars, but she wasn't: if she was in a rush and got a taxi, what kind of pleasure could it be when the meter was running? Anyway, she rarely allowed herself to do that, having been raised on her mother's insinuations that all vices begin with riding in a taxi.

It's funny, she thought, how sometimes the prohibitions imposed almost in infancy can still be in effect when your hair is gray. For example, Vera never drank aerated water outside the house, even if she was dying of thirst. She never bought the fried pirozhki sold by street vendors which looked so tasty but in her imagination summoned up the vague "horrors" she'd heard about in childhood. And the same with taxis. She'd drag herself along in the foulest weather, sometimes barely able to move her feet, the green lights of the taxis whizzing by, and she'd look at them as if the devil himself were tempting her, but no, she wouldn't give in.

It was absurd, of course. However, Vera, like most people, in fact, was absurd about some things. Absurdity was what made people different from one another.

And you don't have to go far to find examples. Take Volodya. He was now sitting in front, displaying the shorn back of his head and his sturdy neck, squeezed by a starched collar, and he didn't turn around to face Vera. But he surely felt her gaze, for there had to be a reason that his fleshy earlobes turned beet-red: surely it wasn't that he still remembered that she'd once rejected him?

Her conjectures, however, were now completely irrelevant. But a woman's nature is notable precisely for expecting and demanding that attention be paid to it under all circumstances.

Vera grinned silently: she possessed the ability to see herself from the outside. And then it was easier to find equilibrium. So let Volodya play the imposing boss, she wouldn't start teasing him, testing him with a persistent gaze. Really, why pull such pranks, when she had a definite, serious goal.

Volodya jumped out at the entrance to the ministry. Before slamming the door shut, he thrust his head in the back: "Twenty minutes, I promise. Here, if you want, have a look at this magazine."

"No," she answered, "I have my own light reading. In the meantime I'll sort through the mail."

That was also regarded as her duty—to prepare responses to readers' letters, which were assigned to various sections. Some were addressed personally to her, as the author of material published in the newspaper. It sometimes happened that the topic of a newspaper article turned out to be especially dear to someone, touched upon an innermost concern, and people would write about their personal lives to a journalist they didn't know with a confidentiality that perhaps one can only encounter in diaries.

Sometimes she felt uncomfortable after reading them: she wasn't the person they imagined her to be. The people who turned to her relied on her kindness, her responsiveness, which means that she was perpetrating unintentional fraud if what she wrote didn't reflect her true essence. Vera would often set such letters aside, planning to respond informally, without the superficiality you get in hack-work. But there often wasn't either enough time or the right mood. She'd forget about the letters she'd set aside, and suddenly would stumble upon them unexpectedly and burn with shame, with what we call pangs of conscience.

And the letters piled up in her desk drawers—sheets covered in various handwritings, embarrassing Vera Perova the journalist with their frankness, their conviction that precisely she, Vera, could help by suggesting how to act in the difficult circumstances that had developed.

These letters ruined her mood. And now, too, sitting in Volodya's company car, having arranged the envelopes in piles, she made a face as if she'd suddenly been stung: a familiar handwriting, flowing non-stop, and also very precise. The return address was the village of Krasnogorie. God only knows where it is...

He was writing to her again! He'd decided that his previous letters either hadn't reached her or had gotten lost—in short, she wasn't to blame, she, of course, would have responded... "Judging by your essays, which I read with pleasure, you know how to feel another's pain, how to sympathize with the misfortunes of others, that's why I want to tell you..."

She put aside the sheet of paper and turned toward the window. Yes, she already knew his story, absurd, excruciating, hopeless—and what could she do? One misfortune after another had befallen him: incurable illness, the loss of his beloved job, the gradual loss of his friends—how could she help? With words? She couldn't even find anything to hook newspaper material onto, otherwise she would have set off for Krasnogorie, wherever the hell it is...

As it was, this was the run-of-the-mill cruelty of chance, and you can't make a story out of it that warrants the reader's attention. Alas. Vera's professional instinct, everyone acknowledged, was infallible. For example, she'd unearthed that complicated business near Kazan, had spent a month on it, had gone there twice, that was all she'd lived for. And justice had finally triumphed, and she was so proud...

But not always. She couldn't take off constantly, she didn't have enough strength or time. Although, of course, she should simply write to him to be humanly decent. After all, he wasn't expecting anything else.

The sheet covered with flowing, non-stop handwriting lay on her knees, but she kept looking out the window. She suddenly found the waiting unbearable. And everything ahead seemed unbearable too: Volodya's appearance, his wariness toward her, masked by a friendly tone, and her ostentatious unconcern about seeing her plans through to the end.

She glanced at the sheet and irritably shoved it, together with the envelope, into her bag.

Volodya ran down the steps of the ministry with excessive haste, his coat unbuttoned: "Forgive me, for God's sake," he muttered penitently. "Once you're in, you can't get out. Some guy caught me just as I was leaving, he literally buttonholed me. Some people!"

Vera smiled understandingly. My face could get numb from such a smile, she thought, if this meeting with Volodya continues in the same vein.

"Drop us off at Samotech, Petya," Volodya said to the chauffeur. And when they got out of the car, he said, without looking at Vera: "From here it's three minutes home. Shall we walk?" Vera nodded, inwardly thinking: "Some Mr. Nice!" He'd become cautious to the point of absurdity. And that typical administrative boorishness—he didn't ask whether she agreed to go to his place, he decided himself what was more convenient for him. He probably considered it better not to appear in a restaurant with her. The boy was protecting his reputation...

Vera hadn't been in this apartment of his yet: he moved so often that he didn't have time to give housewarming parties. Now he was living downtown, in a gray cinder-block house, a formerly reliable construction, with "extras"—tasteless, of course, but inspiring respect.

Two rooms, but the entrance hall and corridors were evidence that they weren't economizing on square meters here. Volodya, of course, knew how to get the things that are hard to get—an imported suite of furniture, a crystal and bronze chandelier, a huge stereo "system" with shining nickel—but it didn't seem lived-in. And Volodya himself didn't seem to feel entirely comfortable in his own home.

However, this was understandable, Vera thought. More and more people nowadays don't know how to behave in a domestic setting, don't have normal conversational skills—towards evening, after a working day, they don't feel anything except fatigue, so what can you demand of them? One probably can't blame them either.

Volodya firmly placed a bottle of Armenian cognac on the dull surface of the low coffee table, squatted down in front of one of the door leafs of the wall unit, took out a flat box, and pulled out some new glasses which probably had never been used.

Vera sat in a roomy armchair, wondering whether it was worth offering her help, or whether it was better not to show initiative. If she listened to her inner voice, she'd want—no, not to do it. She thought of how pointlessly people railed against standardization in everyday life, in one's environment, when standardization is simply essential for modern man, it heals his psyche. Standard furniture, standard possessions somehow lead people along, direct their actions and thoughts, construct a program: any moment now Volodya will turn on his stereo "system," sit down opposite her at the table, and take a sip from his glass: furniture *like that* dictates precise poses and gestures *like that*, and even a corresponding facial expression. It's simply marvelous! The nerves rest, one's reasoning faculties become dull—one's really relaxed. And the words come out like a mumble: that's how, he says, things are, he says, that's how we live, say, why don't we have a drink, old buddy-boy?

Vera and Volodya exchanged good-natured, serene glances, without the slightest ulterior motive. Although, Vera privately noted, that friendliness wasn't so much dictated by chastity as it was the result of the exhaustion and overwork that overwhelmed them both. Both now preferred a simple exchange devoid of anything sexual. And the distance between them also suited both of them. Because, Vera realized in a flash of insight, neither of them wanted to reveal their inner resources—or, more precisely, their limitations.

So if one of them were to deviate off course ever so slightly, the other would then have to react some way or other, that is, make some effort. Just imagining it brought on incredible exhaustion! It wasn't interesting, they'd already been through that, they were sick of everything.

It's nice to think that people's understanding draws them closer together. But that's a delusion! She and Volodya were now sitting across from each other, understanding each other perfectly, and for that very reason even the cognac couldn't thaw the chill in them.

"So, what is it, what problems do you have?"

Volodya interrupted her thoughts. And he smiled, as if emphasizing the unofficial nature of the conversation they were about to have.

Vera had been waiting for a signal and she knew from experience that at such a moment vacillation or beating around the bush can annoy the person you're talking to. If it's about business, then be businesslike, come straight to the point.

"You know," she said, "there's a real mess in our section right now. Rumors are going around, and they've even reached me. And, I confess, I'm a little worried." She said the last sentence jokingly. "But nobody's come outright and said anything specific."

He nodded.

"In a word, it's a trying situation," she continued. "I'd been thinking of going on an assignment, but then I thought no, better wait."

He nodded again, encouragingly.

"So I decided to get your advice as a friend," she smiled, "and a colleague who's higher-up. What does all of this bode? For the bosses, maybe, it's God knows what kind of event, but for me, well, you yourself understand... It's my weak feminine nature, I react very uneasily to change."

"Yeah, sure you're weak," he drained his glass. "But I don't know how to reassure you. Nothing's been decided yet about your section. It's obvious that there'll be some changes, but it's not my place to explain them to you, it's not easy with personnel, although it's not as if there aren't more than enough people."

"Of course," she said.

"You're the one better equipped to give help and advice, you know the situation in your section better."

She didn't say anything. This was the moment. And she stretched out, stretched out the pause. Volodya broke the silence.

"By the way, how do you find Krutova? What's your opinion of her?"

Vera straightened up in surprise and pressed her knees against the edge of the table.

"Of Tonechka? You're asking me about Tonechka?! Oh, my God..." she burst into loud, unnatural laughter.

Volodya looked at her expectantly.

"Come on, are your serious? Oh!" she exhaled loudly, the blood rushing to her face; it seemed a long time since she'd felt so indignant. She was actually in danger of losing her self-control. "Hey, you guys up there, forgive me, but do you ever think? Have you seen Tonechka yourself? It's enough to look at her once. Before she gets out a single word, she'll break out in a sweat. And she's not up to newspaper business, she has an alcoholic husband, she's sent him off to a rehab clinic twice, her kids are little. I feel sorry, *really sorry*, for her," she said distinctly. "And you just can't have any other kind of attitude towards her."

"I didn't know," Volodya said quietly. He suddenly grew pensive.

"How incredible!" Vera wouldn't let up, her pride was too wounded. "You don't know, you're not interested, but afterwards it'll be too late to fix it! First they appointed some wimp to run the section, and now they're going one better. It simply leaves one speechless!"

"Vera, you misunderstood me," Volodya was looking somewhere off to the side, studying the pattern on the wallpaper. "I asked you about Krutova for a completely different reason. You've been working together for a long time, and I thought you knew...

"What?"

"Never mind... It's not worth going into it now. It doesn't have anything to do with professional matters." He was silent for a moment. "And as for your section. The question probably won't be settled that quickly. If you feel the situation's distressing, then you really should protect your nerves: you were planning to go on an assignment, and my advice to you is, go."

"You think so?" Vera pricked up her ears. It was a little late, alas. She hadn't shown any savvy, she'd got too choked with emotions, and not of the most noble type—she'd lost perspective. She wasn't exactly sorry, but she cursed herself for her lack of diplomacy. She should have first established clearly what Volodya had in mind, whereas she'd torn into him in typical woman's style, ranting and raving. And now, after all the wailing, she couldn't start talking about herself, she couldn't propose her own candidacy instead of Tonechka's.

"Fool, fool!" she cursed herself mentally. And she knew all too well that Volodya was really something else. It was just his face that was simple, but when it came to various games, he'd got the hang of them. After all, he hadn't refused Vera, he hadn't even let her say her piece, but had simply changed the topic of conversation. He'd slipped in Tonechka Krutova so deftly, and Vera had tripped up.

What now? Sit a little for decency's sake and then leave. Meanwhile Volodya—what a Jesuit!—was inquiring about her daughter and her mother's health in a kind, concerned tone. What could she do? Vera answered absentmindedly. Yes, her daughter was studying English, her mother was sometimes bothered by rheumatism.

"Ah! Forget it!" she said to herself. "So it didn't work out? Well, that's hardly fatal." She summoned up her inner resources to give Volodya an authentically friendly smile.

"So, this means you're advising me to go off on my assignment? And if I need to, can I quote you, say that we talked about it and I'm acting, so to speak, with your blessing?"

"Of course," Volodya assumed his usual dignified manner. "I'm sure you'll bring back excellent material. Oh, if I could only get rid of this red tape, I'd settle down to write, I'd travel around," he said with false dreaminess. "The only thing that remains is what's been written."

Vera stood up.

"Well, thanks, Volodya," she said as she made to leave. "Time for me to go. No, you don't have to see me off. You have to get up early, too."

Volodya didn't start insisting. He readily got up from the armchair and handed Vera her coat—as one of the bosses he'd completely lost his former elementary courtliness.

After exchanging a firm, asexual handshake, they parted. From the elevator Volodya headed for his apartment, and Vera, after going down to the spacious lobby with its "extras," set off for the trolley stop, and was home in half an hour.

She returned from her assignment three weeks later. And it so happened that she came just in time for her vacation: she did the necessary paperwork and collected the signatures she needed without dropping by her office. Why not? Her immediate supervisor was absent, as before.

It was almost April when she showed up at the newspaper. Fresh, cheerful, with a light tan. And with an inner challenge, as if to say: I don't give a damn about your intrigues, I wrote before—and I'll continue to write. In the snackbar, over coffee, I'll find out who my boss is now.

The starched blue top looked good on her, setting off her eyes, the narrow skirt sat nicely, lending an elegant caution to her walk.

"Tap-tap," Vera heard the rhythmic echo of her steps along the resounding halls of the editorial office. As she approached the door to her section she slowed down a little bit: the feeling she experienced reminded her of her school days, when she'd come back to her class after vacation.

"Hello," her clear, sunny voice called out, and she stood on the threshold, looking around.

"Hello," answered an unfamiliar young girl with loose hair and a very bright mouth, slightly swollen, like a child's.

On a wide windowsill, with her back to the window, sat Olya from the fact-checking section. From all appearances, Vera had interrupted their confidential conversation.

"Where's Tonya?" Vera asked much more reservedly, even sternly. She was always disgusted by silly "girls' talk" of this sort, on which many of the women employees spent a lot of their working time, and which for some reason wasn't punished, wasn't considered a breach of discipline.

"Antonina Sergeievna?" the young stranger asked in turn. "What do you mean? You really don't know?" Her face seemed scared and completely childlike. Her lips puckered up as she whispered. "But it's already been a week since they buried her..."

"What?" Vera let go of the door knob.

"She was sick for so long, she was all worn out, the poor dear. We went to see her in the hospital, her son spent entire days with her there." She suddenly gave a slight sniffle. "And she was still young."

Vera walked heavily to her desk, as if her feet weren't her own, and she lowered herself onto a chair. Her desk was empty, smooth—she leaned her elbows on it.

The stranger and Olya from the fact-checking section started talking, interrupting each other, sharing details about how hard it is to get a bed in a good clinic. The chief had personally called the director of the institute, a consultation had been convened, but Antonia Sergeievna could no longer leave her bed. And on, and on.

Vera sat, leaning her elbows on the desk. So that's why Volodya had asked about Tonya that time, she recalled. And she...

She felt a touch on her shoulder: Olya from the fact-checking section was standing over her.

"You were friends, we know that," she said sympathetically.

"Yes," said Vera hollowly. "She had this little purse trimmed with beads..."

Translated by Rebecca Epstein

From *Postoronnie v dome. Povesti,* Moscow, 1983

Albinos

Bella Ulanovskaia

The casement screens still haven't been taken down, the last apples are still dangling, and the garden patch hasn't been dug up, yet we get out our skis and boldly make for the forest.

There's not a thrush to be seen, the rowan tree is dusted with powder, the sky is covered with gray ice. A young white hare has burrowed a hole in the freshly fallen snow. At the clearing I came across a mangy hound. She took some sugar, nearly biting my sleeve in jest, then took off and kept going, searching once more for the trail she'd lost in a ditch full of water.

You can't cross over the swamp yet—there's water under the snow and thin ice.

The hound and the thrush come from conversations I hold aloud with myself. The thrushes, they're from past hunts. They hung on the rowan tree, I held them in my sights for hours—this one, no, that one over there, or should I wait until they come together, then get the two at one go—I slowly raise the barrel, but they've all flown away, the last ones rushing over the pond in fright, and the flock is gone.

Just yesterday the thrushes were still chirping here, frantically attacking the rich clusters of berries. Thin tree trunks swayed under whopping storm clouds, branches cracked, berries poured down; now it's empty and quiet here, on the ground bunches of rowanberries, pecked clean, lie exposed—like dark bird feet dusted with snow—only here and there do a few wrinkled berries remain whole.

The birches haven't shed their leaves yet—what a vivid and exceptional time of year!

It's nice to go out in the morning with a rifle on your shoulder—you not only hear everything around you, but you see yourself from a different perspective. Everything seems fine and in its place, everything's warm and in good shape.

D. E. once recalled Akhmatova's account of a conversation she had with Blok.[1] Blok said: "You write poetry as if you were talking to a man, but one must address God."

Well, I don't think one need address God for just any old reason, even if it's about poetry. Although poetry has more grounds than prose to express the essentials about the soul and about God.

Prose has to feign an interest in reality, to be cluttered with events, at times seemingly trivial or too concrete. In prose there are storerooms, ladders, barns, cellars, bolts, locks, stoves, stacks of firewood, axes, birdhouses, fences, mousetraps, cats, doghouses, even cows are possible, drawing rooms unheated in winter and stuffy bedrooms where the owners lock themselves up when it's cold outside.

What's essential here: the passageway where they keep a barrel of frozen cabbage, or the view from the window of the garden, the river, the dam, the expanses beyond the river? Maybe the arrival of a neighbor with the morning's gossip or Saturday at the bathhouse, where they brought a ninety-year-old woman to be washed when the steam was billowing at top heat, after everyone else; in the sweating window the kerosene lamp was already burning dimly, and the sixty-year-old daughter washed her mama and even poured on more steam.

"That's enough, child," the old woman groaned.

Comparisons between poetry and sculpture, between prose and architecture are well known. They may be right, if you have in mind the multiplicity of constructions and the abundance of auxiliary premises, in which the notion of the author's artistry gets lost (a fair to middling craftsman feels no aversion to the bathhouse)—and does it really make sense to pursue all of this: where are the essential, where the secondary chapters, aren't there too many corridors and entryways—when in the world will we come to the real essence of the story—say, a good stiff drink after a nice hot steam bath.

If it's true about architecture, then how much consistently applied effort is needed; it's not the same as slapping together a bunny from modeling clay.

Towards the end of July, come Ilya's Day, the ice will stay. The water in the lakes has gotten a bit colder, autumn winds have begun to blow, the dogs have started to bark in the darkness of night. The starlings left their birdhouses long ago; gathered in large flocks, they roam the fields and gardens, now arranging themselves along the wires as if imaginary lines had been drawn between them, now churning in the air in unheard-of numbers—each one rushes in confusion, and the flock moves on in an unchanging direction. Madness seizes a young dog—it races through the fields, buries itself in the oats, then leaps out to have a look around and barks impotently. The thrushes, those rowanberry hunters, are already trilling sharply as in autumn, soon the grain will be harvested, great mounds of it will appear in unusual places, forming new landscapes for many, many months, and flocks of thrushes will fly past, tempting the lazy unsuccessful hunter, warming himself on stacks of straw yellowed by the last bit of sunshine.

After clear starry nights the first frosts fall. If you go out beyond the gate at daybreak, you can see the gray grass, shining in the sun, over in the vast expanses of fields which flow smoothly around the forest, like the inlets of a vast lake.

If you walk along the edges of these fields, then go beyond the new promontory made by the forest's central mass, new bays open up and both the thickets and the individual trees, particularly the ones spread out in the wide open spaces ("a couple of shiny white birches"), can be compared to peninsulas and islands of the same vast lake.

For quite some time, almost from the moment we stepped off the porch, we've heard the mating-call of the black grouse. These futile autumn courtships are well known among hunters: deceived by morning frosts reminiscent of early spring, birds begin to murmur in the harvested fields. An endless song pours out and ripples.

Hoarfrost spreads along the fields in strips, suddenly you begin to notice that here and there it's already gone—the grass has dried in the sun and glossy patches of gray have spread out whimsically along the low lands.

In the distance a tractor begins to rattle—and it will go on now for the rest of the day—work begins right at the spot where it was interrupted yesterday, the ploughed darkness grows as the grouse's source of grain shrinks.

A grouse sits on a lone birch and looks at the orange tractor, as it methodically turns over more and more new strips.

Morning is drawing to a close. Time to go back home.

"Well, did you kill any birdies today? Put your boots on the stove and come have tea. The samovar's ready."

An autumn spider. The essence has trickled out, however—drawn from the spider's fat abdomen, it rolled out in a transparent, indistinct substance that congealed as it stretched out; and, as is well known, that which of its own accord turns from a soft state into a defined, quickly thickening one, then congeals, and in spite of its delicacy becomes hard, trickles into its own form—now that is indeed something definite and lasting. Let's run through all these delicate passages and pearly crossings again, let's reread their rambling durability.

And now back again as fast as our little legs can carry us; here's the place where we attached ourselves to the tree, to the branch, to the twig, to the bark, and now, just at the point of attachment—flung to hell knows where by chelicerae—we fly, lifted ever higher and higher, as the southeast wind flows over the forest, over the field, over the river, and playing in the sun is a pearly thread, with a weightless spider dangling on the end.

By the middle of October a snowless Siberian winter has settled in our area. A neighbor's come out to teach his children to skate on the pond that's been frozen since long ago. All day a huge flock of pigeons have been feeding in the harvested oat field, flashing dove-gray as they ascend into the blue and once again gently descend back into the field.

In the mornings I leave the house in time to catch the 8:56 commuter train, making my way down the Rumbolovo hills, and I don't recognize our dreary Finnish locale.

A dry cloudless sky settled long ago in this now unrecognizable village, where all have full stomachs, are rich, live well, wear sable hats, and—even have their own bus stop.

An icy wind carries the dry stinging sand along the naked earth whitened by frost—the "rain of Khakassia," as they say in the Turansk plateau. Some snow remains in the furrows in the fields and in the tractor ruts in the roads, and the bright unshed foliage has frozen to the branches—that's durability, quality, and stability.

Grave mounds of thoroughly frozen earth have turned white from the cold; the leaves on the oak trees tinkle.

A protracted winter prelude. Tomorrow snow will fall and I still haven't gone down to try the ice, haven't peered down into the depths, nor gone racing on skates or on a sled.

A black puppy loses his way, slips, and stumbles on the glossy surface. As the record fades into silence, the wind picks up the tune. And a heavy ungreased cart sets off, gradually gathering speed, from one Sunday to the next.

In the morning I went down for bread, leaving the balcony door open. When I returned I found fresh bluebird droppings right on the table. The first skiers have appeared. It's snowing. The end of October.

I rode around the field on a moonlit night. A dog barked in the direction of the forest. At first I thought there was a squirrel, but then I realized—the neighbors were roaming through the forest, picking out a Christmas tree. I sat by a pile of straw, dozing a while in the frost. It's good to fall asleep before morning, it's not terrifying or cold. When the dog licks his paw, he makes a crunching sound as if he's eating sugar.

Twenty degrees below zero. Consistently clear nights. Strange to fall asleep in this cold room on the edge of icy wide open spaces. Outside there's a field, then a forest, all the way to Lake Ladoga, and even the sky above is frosty cold. The stars shine fiercely with a cold light. And here under a heap of quickening warmth stirs a live ball; it curls up more tightly, tucking in its legs, occupying less and less space as it warms its hands between its knees.

Where does its warmth come from? There's something unnatural in the fact that its temperature contrasts with everything around it. For the sheet and the pillow and the iron and the plate and the chair and the checkered notebook and the field and the tree and the flower in the pot are all cold. You're the only thing that doesn't stiffen from the cold. There'll come a time when you too will become like everything that's frozen stiff.

Am I waiting for visitors? Here's the window with its oft-described view, and here's the dog, and here are mushrooms and roast pork with frosted vodka, and here's a hole in the snow made by yellow grouse droppings—looks like a date pit, and here's the shaggy black mutt zipping along after the skis.

So this is what I'm writing, what I'm eating, where I go and with whom. Here are the letters I've received. How nice. Study them to your heart's content. Just because you didn't come, do you think I'm bored? It's simply a pity that you're wasting your time there. Perhaps it's even for the best that all of you didn't come.

Yesterday afternoon I was walking past the cattle yard. In a hunting cap, pants and felt boots. The dogs tagged along: Mukhtar, Mukha with two of her puppies, and for the first time I let Zorka off the leash. The milkmaids passing by shied away from the pack: "Hey, boy, get your dogs away from us."

The purest voice from their crystal-clear brooks and ice cut from the lake to be saved for summer. When the record ends, the northeast wind, which had arisen as night drew near, picks up the tune.

What can I say about the best evening in the world? Zorka stood motionless in the middle of the room. In the corners it was already murky twilight. Toward night the frost outside increased. The fir trees beyond the field, covered with the morning's fresh snow, were tinted with a special hue at sunset, but a quarter of an hour later I had to turn on the light, everything that had been rosy had turned a deep blue. It hadn't turned completely dark yet, the fields were still white, but the lights of the distant villages of Romanovka, Uglovka, and Kornevo had already lost their mystery.

How nice the old trees in the park looked against a still green sky. The potatoes were boiling, the cabbage soup was heating up, now and then Zorka would run to the door.

Clear February nights, an empty head, and a mutt stretching as it crawled out of its doghouse.

Is it really greediness, a fear of leaving something out? That's what's made me waste away and will destroy me.

I need to get to that turn in the road and stand over there a while—who knows when such a starry night will come again? The dog makes suspicious clumps of unbelievable darkness first here, then there. He roused the watch dogs, ran inside the doorway of someone else's house, jumped out, raced to the forest, veered off toward the pig pen, and disappeared into the field.

The four seasons. That pitiful old woman he—"God"—condescendingly listens to; he holds life in his hands, he doesn't even sit down himself and doesn't offer seats to the whole swarm of miserable wretches buzzing around him, patiently waiting for a pause in the conversation to catch a turn of his head, so as to ask a question. But you were misled by his pause; he's no longer looking at you, he's continuing an interrupted thought. Putting his hands behind him and leaning them against the wall, he seems to be surrounded by a ring of misery.

But how lightly he rests against the wall and looks over everyone's heads—one minute more and he'll shove off and leave, hence the more dense the ring in front of him, the more greedy the gazes fixed upon him, the more tense the wait for pauses—to join in, to step into the empty spot someone just relinquished right in front of him.

Stringbags and satchels have been emptied out into aluminum bowls, but the fruit on the tables doesn't evoke visions of plenitude. Here's one portion: three pears, a bunch of grapes, a loaf of bread—a label with a surname on a bowl, a pitiful catalogue of regulations in an entrybook, an account of poverty permeates everything.

"Acute psychosis, acute psychosis," he says to the old woman. "Come back on Friday, bring a transfer of property form."

"Please let me see you today," she repeats, but he's already parted the ring and set off. She runs a few steps ahead: she's come from out of town, specially—but he's already outside the ring, he's already headed for somewhere on important matters of his own, he's off to wield his scepter, but the old lady is still there, though she's already fallen behind, "Doctor, doctor..." But he, one second looking through the crowd with his indifferent gaze, and the next, seeming to listen with an attentive condescension that appears even sympathetic, harshly snaps, "I SAID THAT'S IMPOSSIBLE," and heads for a group of high ranking guests, whose conversation he's saved for last; now he'll take them into his office, where they'll converse like civilized people.

The hall emptied out.

The parquet floor buffed with red polish, the doors of sections under lock and key, the vaulted ceilings, the standard institutional chairs, the four landscapes on the walls—all the same size, in identical frames—the four seasons. What are they? What are these lifeless vistas for? Gazing at them, it's impossible anyway to imagine either winter or autumn, or the fact that somewhere there exists a real life of wind, cold, and freedom.

More likely than not these pictures, hung here for well-intentioned educational purposes, let you know that what happens here in this former women's prison is not limited to this vaulted hall, this red brick building with its narrow windows rounded at the top, but seeks to spread outside as well, because the text-book representation of winter in this insipid painting is imbued with the same lifelessness, its space is just as finalized, as it is in here. And although the peasant woman going down to the river with her yoke is supposed to personify a healthy picture of village life in the invigorating outdoors, and the hills beyond the river are supposed to beckon you to the fields, you understand all too clearly that what's happening in this building corresponds to this depiction, is kindred to it. And even if you were to assume that the life depicted by this painter really did exist somewhere, then how insulting it would be to acknowledge it!

How dare the radio keep babbling as if nothing had happened, how dare this ostentatious city proceed with life as usual, when here misery humbly asks for assistance, straining to catch every word of its gods, when here an unjust, unthinkable life flows on.

How dare this woman, her cheeks ruddy from the cold, climb down the hill with her buckets, bend over the ice hole, break through the thin crust that has formed overnight, and, pushing the sludge aside, scoop out steaming water with a bucket, then, straining slightly, tensing her behind, shoulder the yoke as usual and smoothly, trying not to spill the full buckets, but nonetheless splashing the heavy water on her boots, cotton skirt, and the hem of her old plush jacket, trudge uphill along the slippery path with difficulty, stepping aside in particularly treacherous spots into the deep, fresh snow, her foot probing for the tracks she made yesterday, now all but swept away by the snow?

How can one believe in all this here, in this hall without windows?

The key in the lock clicked and people came out of the ward, one after another, their warm clothes sewn like quilted jackets, but longer, with intricate quilted hoods. A young nurse let them go ahead, then, after counting them all in her head, relocked the door and shouting something, led them out for a walk.

A veritable complaint book. The most pitiful book of complaints.[2] Quiet complaints about the penetrating wind, damp boots, the mournful landscape of prison walks.

I reread my spider web. Got attached to it and stopped. The flashes have ceased. An image of an escalator with an attendant sitting below—through her flows a volatile, but nonetheless indistinguishable stream of filth. She stares greedily, unable to tear herself away; she follows someone with her gaze, then new figures, like herself, float into her view once again and disappear. Is she seized with horror or has she long since dissolved in that stream?

Now I've floated into her view, stepped onto firm ground, scurried through the door as it slammed shut and disappeared. Does she pause to think about the impersonal existence of the species or does she only register what passes before her eyes: a dress, a hat, an extremely long coat, the long-haired, the dark-skinned, the drunk, those in love?

Every now and then you're stopped dead in your tracks by a cry of recognition from the escalator flowing in the opposite direction: Hey!

There it is, our name, we're always ready to take a step forward, that's why at times we hear some sort of call, but it's only an excess, a surplus of expectation; they'll call our names out one by one—should I take my things?—no, personal belongings aren't allowed.

While one person looks around, also recognizing another, he's removed from the field of vision—a smile, a wave of the hand—they've gone off in different directions, vanished, and once again the faces turn to stone. Withdrawn and recognized, what can he really remember about himself? It seems he just got married. He loves dessert. How he searches for his coat. Only by the checkroom number. He's studying something. Some lakes are very silty, the fish in them are dying in droves; that's the problem he's studying. Somewhere near the lake he found himself a wife. She also studies the respiratory system of fish. Of course they remember the subjects they study. Everybody knows where they're going and by what time they've got to be there, what needs to be done with their version of reality, and where they lay their head at night. Are they happy?

Well-rested, well-fed, not frozen, do they really want to have anything to do with the version of reality assigned to them? Kilometers of cables run in a tunnel outside, numbers of tubing coils flash by, as do windows, on the other side of which are walls of Cambrian thickness and heavy mute faces, God forbid that you make chance contact with anyone's eyes—a greedy, though quite cowardly examination of your species. God forbid that you ride the subway every morning. How can it be that we all still haven't gotten lost? (I can't even remember myself, while you all say—remember us.)

The stupidest thing is that when I appear in front of that immobile female figure (paid for underground and overtime work), I feel superior as a representative of, if not a new life, then at least of movement. She, if I can philosophize a bit, spends her days productively in a grove by a cool brook, watching all of us, rushing senseless ants with useless burdens.

She fetches a velvet sash, throws it on copper supports, and the stream is dammed. For some time the bottom runs empty, then it's stopped and propelled in the opposite direction. Hardly bending their knees, the first adolescents run downstairs.

For the future and the brutal.

Don't disturb my concentration. As dusk was falling and the snow outside had turned deep blue, sharply defining the slopes of the snow drifts, which along with the ski trails and narrow paths suddenly looked white in comparison to the thickening twilight of the snowy surface—come to the window.

As in spring, the shouts of children reach us through the open window, the street lamps are still not lit, and so the lights in the houses burn unnaturally bright.

It was one of those days in mid-February when spring is still far away, when February's hard times, snowstorms, late dawns, wolf matings, and rabbit litters still continue.

"My time's up."

My time's up if it's really true that each of us has a season that's particularly important and significant for us, when what happens in nature at that time most fully corresponds to our essence and hints vaguely at our secret predestination. These significant days in each of our lives come roughly around the month of our birth.

When the heavy frosts began and the strong northeast winds started to blow (it's finally begun), it seemed that it was just the beginning, that the most essential still lay ahead.

But it didn't clear up; spring looked ahead, broke loose, and for three days took us out of the expected blizzard and wolf howls in the impenetrable heart of the forest.

Spring broke loose, needlessly easing the persistent strain of our gloomy expectation of the next gust of wind, stronger than the last. It did away with our sullen concentration on important matters (wait, they'll be here any minute) and with its frivolous blue tones quickened our responsiveness to the earth, indecent in its frankness, since everyone knows how beneficial an effect increased sunlight has on everything that lives. And now it's already begun: the spring sounds of children's voices reach us through the open ventilation window, and all this happiness will start to flow: March's thin crust of ice and the hardened snow below: ta-ta-ta and ta-ta-ta.

And later, there'll follow all of spring's Passion Boulevards and the corresponding sparrows, women's spring finery, and thawing muck—then all those delicate observations of light and color, water and ice, of the road thawing out by day and freezing at night, this game, this intoxicating rapture of perception, will suck us in, will distract us from the most essential, will put this pressing, ponderous question in some dark godforsaken corner for still another year.

The doorbell rang. On the threshold stood a hunchback with a travelling case.

"Do you have rats and mice?" he asked as he came in. "If not, then sign here." And he extended a piece of paper lined by hand.

The second day of the snowstorm. The snow drifts parallel to the earth and rooftops. When the wind blows, its direction is broken. There's also movement above the rooftops—vaporous, most likely—as snow from the roof tops swirls in waves. Right by the windowpane, when you look outside, you can make out each individual snowflake.

All of this is no longer terrifying. The cloud layer is thin, the sun's almost peeking through. You can make out the sparkling tops of snowdrifts far away in the field, which doesn't happen in the dead of winter. More and more birds appear. Fewer haystacks remain by the forest. When it grew dark, the snow was still a deep blue, and such a wind began to blow that all signs of spring were forgotten. Music began to play at the neighbors'.

The third day of the storm. Although there's no less wind than yesterday, it's a typical unabating February storm. The clouds are heavy, dense, and low. The wind is howling for all it's worth.

Does this mild spring depression come from a vitamin deficiency? From the impossibility of finding an expression for the morning's momentum, the deserted morning streets, and the overcrowded forests, ready to accept—if only you can conform—but how, with what? While you languish by the window, the morning gathers strength, coarsens, and ends with nothing special: the streets fill with weary people, the sun shifts around the warm haystacks; grouse have settled on the birches, the ski path that froze last night has dissolved like wet salt; a boring endless day, soon the early birds will come from work, the grouse will bed down in the powdery snow; towards evening, when the edges of the ice holes begin to freeze, a fox will run along the trail it left yesterday on the refrozen ski path. Its trail stretches along the clearing, crosses the lake and speeds off to the field, to the haystacks, where the mice run about, leaving winding trails that resemble two lines of spilt drops.

Meanwhile, sometime after one in the afternoon we managed to load up all the furniture. We decided to carry out the smaller things first: baskets, cardboard boxes, bundles of dishes. Then we attacked the light blue cupboard, the sideboard, and the wardrobe. The neighbor's little girl, dressed in a raspberry jacket, looked greedily at the expensive things as she fixed her dirty kerchief,

Perched on a ladder leaning against a birch, a short-legged fully-grown idiot in an unbuttoned sheepskin jacket swayed together with the tree. Glancing around, he was furiously hacking off branches and parts of the trunk with a short handsaw, according to the yardstick that they were holding for him below.

Sad children's bangs drooped in the windows, a half-dressed woman with a coat thrown over her night shirt shouted on the balcony, and the branches flew, catching in the neighboring trees.

For the third time the airedale was taken out for a walk. A train hauling clay passed by.

Let's cross out this day, so incoherently and senselessly begun. With its drowsiness, tedious lines for milk, gloomy, persistent rise in temperature, and hot benches in the overheated train—had it really existed?

How quickly you can become a bear—roll over heavily in your corner, getting up heavily and dragging your feet in felt boots, for weeks not pick up some necessary little thing that's rolled under the table, quickly glance back (peer) into the corner, drink plain tea ten times a day and go to the window in the evening, after putting out the light in the room, so that the empty street and nearby forest will be more visible.

Abandoned uncracked nuts with sharp teeth marks (sometime later—all of them at one go).

The starlings on their birdhouse perches are like black holes. Yes, indeed, just like black holes.

A small steed, shiny as a chestnut; he and I are galloping somewhere. Some sort of low place, I have to lean down right against his neck, his ears, the reins pulled taut.

"What breed is it?""

"Azbek," answers Papa, who gave me the horse as a present.

The earth carries you, carries you lightly, then suddenly you fall off, the lightness turns out to be illusory, you fall more and more often, your eventless life unravels when it should have been cut off long ago.

Every unit of time has its own fully weighted, self-contained meaning. It's possible to hold your ground, refuse to continue, concentrate on the attainment of just that moment. However, more often than not everything wears out, wanders off the track, wastes time, becomes diluted, and we exist, squandering meanings completely unknown to anyone.

Meanwhile, how much happiness and significance there is here! Everybody just leave me alone. I'll stay here and cry about it all night. Let the snow fall and cover up all the tracks. In the morning the water will freeze in the bucket and, barely dragging my feet, I'll make my way to the well without raising my swollen face. Who knows whether I'll be able to light the damp firewood.

Hunting season opens on May second. Bird-hunting in the cold. There's still snow along the post road and the clearing. From early morning people are busy in their garden plots, no tractors are to be heard, and after their Sunday dinners the neighbors, all dressed up (i.e., without their quilted jackets and rubber boots), stroll around in those spots where it's already dry.

Ah, what a hunt I missed today. The wind suddenly died down and the moon rose. He said: "Put the kettle on, I'll just run down to the river and then we'll eat." The heroine never saw him again. He drowned there and then, before breakfast. That's the fear drummed into us since childhood by the famous play *The Irkutsk Story:* the routine panic of waiting.[3]

(However, let's put out the light and look at the road; no, there's no one there.)

The profligate sons of eminent townsmen didn't call home to say "Don't wait up for me tonight," the soldiers of the Crusades didn't send home picture postcards with scenes of Jerusalem, but every woman always had among her dozen children—those she carried to term, the premature ones, and the others—some "nonresidents" or "goners" who departed this world at different ages.

The entry doors slam, the elevators bang, the shadows of others' husbands sway under the street lights, dogs bark at the edge of the street, and *something's happened* sticks to the window panes and runs to the opposite window at the noise of an approaching car. The light's just gone on inside, the passenger in the back seat leans forward, the cardoor slams, but the taxi light doesn't go on, ah yes, there are still people inside. Run quickly to the switch: somebody without a hat weaves along, takes something out of his pocket, puts it away again, approaches not our building, but the neighbors', and, turning to the wall, stops. Well, we won't pry.

We turn the light on again and see in the windows only ourselves and our wardrobe.

Those stupid nannies, as the domestic help used to say then, who had just gone through sanitary inspection—without it they couldn't be officially registered in the city—would shy away from cars and go to the Palace of Engineering to chat with the soldiers. "What's your name, what's your mama's name?" they'd ask the master's six-year-old daughter and her stupid sixteen-year-old nanny.

Most of all, those big dummies were afraid of crossing the street at the corner of Belinsky and Liteiny, recalling how on that very spot a truck had driven up on the sidewalk, and that's just where they needed to go in order to get to the little garden behind the circus, that's where they said they were going, although in fact they circled the main gates of the Palace of Engineering, where the military school was located.

So, does that mean we have to rail at poor dumb country girls and *The Irkutsk Story*? By the way, so as not to return to them again, our whole apartment, or, rather, the children's contingent, long recalled Nadia and one of her good deeds.

On Sundays Nadia would go to visit her aunt, and one time she requested—not for herself, she was also too young—the novel *Life*.[4] It was a postwar edition, the print set in two columns on paper that bled. We realized that it was precisely that kind of paper only after the book was again settled on top of the wardrobe, a tall wardrobe with a mirror, pullout drawers at the bottom, and a section for linen, in which the dishes were kept.

Now we didn't even have to wait until our parents left the house, it was enough for mother to go to the kitchen for me to pull over a chair, and my neighbor Ania would get the book—she was older, but was also not allowed—and we'd quickly find our favorite places, underlined in ink. Who it was who'd taken the trouble for us, Nadia or her aunt, we didn't know; most likely it was some soldier from the Palace of Engineering skilled at reworking material for political indoctrination lectures.

Hearing steps from the kitchen, we'd throw the terrible book on the wardrobe, fling the door wideopen, help to bring in the pot of boiling water, and then find ourselves for a long time in the power of a strange "as if nothing had happened."

As if nothing had happened, we'd put the pot on the table and get spoons from the wardrobe—this was called helping set the table—but before our eyes were the sickening purple watery lines, which were only written upon later, as it seemed to us at the time.

"Jeanne stood by the window." That's how the novel began. This clever Jeanne—the name's so repulsive—stood at the window as if nothing had happened, no, that will never happen to us.

Sometimes we didn't want to grow up. In general, it should be said that in our girls elementary school, as I noticed only later, we responded with disdain to those kept back who'd already started to mature. I even developed that feeling toward my girl-friend, who surpassed us all in the area of "formation"—as they used to say then; in general, we heard the word "form" or its variants all the time. We were all supposed to wear uniforms; in the evening we were supposed to lay out an ironed uniform; on holidays we were supposed to appear in uniform; little Tsvetkova, who died while still in the first grade, was buried in a uniform; many were promised wool uniforms for an excellent report card; such a uniform was bought for Galia Tsvetkova only after her death—she was an "F" student. At the time someone blurted out, wasn't it all the same to her, but everyone raised their hand in protest, and Valia Ovchinnikova, the daughter of a cook (my mother once called her "cookie") said something like "it was her dream," "her final request."

And so this friend of mine began to grow more and more noticeably out of her uniform, until she was fully formed. On Sundays we'd walk along Nevsky Prospect.[5] We'd set out to get ice cream. She'd talk about her uncle: he sawed away on a violin before evening performances and lately, if no one was at home, he'd taken to making her sit her on his lap, the creep!

She'd interrupt her chatter to whisper: "Look, look at those legs!" And when I admitted that I didn't understand what the difference was, she answered that some are very pretty, like hers, for example—the violinist had told her so—and she'd teach me right now to recognize them.

She and I were just walking out of the movies together and making our way through the crowded courtyard in the rain.

"There, in front, see what's wrong with them?"

"The stockings are splattered?"

"Of course not, you can always wash out stockings, it's that her legs are fat. And those, look over there, though they're not as fat, they're still like an elephant's, the ankles could be somewhat thinner."

That's how she led me along Nevsky, that's how it's remained in my memory—the wide, cleanswept sidewalk from the corner of Maiakovsky to Vosstanie, and us, the discriminating connoisseurs, walking along.

"Oh, look at what you've stepped in."

"What?"

"You walk like a baby. Someone spat here, but you don't see a thing."

For some reason I connected her strange new fastidiousness with her premature growth. It's still too early, I thought, for me to pay attention to this.

"Attention" was also a school word. To call attention to yourself was not nice; sometimes they would say about one of us: "She tries to call attention to herself."

Gawking at everything was also unacceptable.

There's a drunk sprawled over there, they're cursing a blue streak here, but you see nothing, you hear nothing, you don't even raise an eyebrow, don't turn an ear; assembled in pairs, Girls School 193, formerly the Gymnasium where the wife, friend, and true helpmate, Nadezhda Konstantinovna,[6] had studied and received a gold medal, goes on its way; we're going to the puppet theater a block away from school.

Owing to poor health, a certain schoolgirl was let out early for vacation and, contrary to habit, spent the whole spring at home.

In the beginning of May the schoolgirl sat on a log by an abandoned farm; the shingles on the roof stood on end from the wind, the cowshed had long ago been pulled apart for firewood. The schoolgirl grew warm in the hot sun, slid down from the log, and lay down on the still damp, warm earth, squinting at a wagtail that was hopping near her, stealing up closer and closer. What's this sprawled out here?

The wagtail has black wings, a light gray belly and a white head; what's on its neck? A black necktie? A tied napkin? A bib? The wagtail continued to hang around until the schoolgirl shifted her numb arm and sat up.

The wagtail scurried off, but not far. It started to approach again. didn't eat a thing, just walked about.

If a young cow were sprawled out here—so that's what you are, a cow. Look, wagtail: I'm a young cow. You know, I'm here for the first time after a winter in a warm stall, I'm an inexperienced cow, they just let us out.

"Yes, you're just a cow, a big bag of bones, a lot of hair, an untidy chest, there you've gone and sprawled out again."

The wagtail took wing and impudently flew straight over the schoolgirl—that's what you are—and disappeared from the meadow. Who was touched by the cow's inexperience?

The puddles were still cold, life hadn't started swarming in them yet, but the chick's down on the brooms had already turned yellow, snowdrops and yellow foalfoot had started to spring up. Every waterhole, every puddle was still as clear as a cold mountain river. Even the pond by the pigpen—where the hogs lolled about, tossing and turning around in its midst—looked as blue as a mountain lake.

The caretaker's son, a university student, met her in the park and said: "They told me something nasty about you yesterday."

"That doesn't interest me," the schoolgirl answered.

"You'll listen anyway. At five in the morning you supposedly go to watch the grouse mate."

"Yes, I ... Yes, but only to hear them sing, from afar," she said in embarrassment.

"You listen to them sing," the student wouldn't let up, "and dream about love." (As if they were some sort of chickens.)

The light gurgle from the depths of their syrinx is unabating, audible for a couple of miles; the forest makes sounds, the waves on the lake splash, the snow melts, and the puddles dry up, while they call to their mates, murmur, and trill at dawn and dusk, year in and out. What a delicate song! If you don't stop, don't hold your breath, don't lift up the edge of your kerchief, then you won't hear it. Is it a dog's barking in the distance? A ringing in the ears? The gurgling of a stream? If it's neither one nor the other and you're not imagining things, then it's them.

But to the student it's all about mating.

A snipe, the heavenly lamb, sings vibrato in the heavens, the ducks have taken off and flown to the other side of the lake, a woodcock grunts above the birch tops on the forest road, whereas they continue to splash with their moist murmurs. They're everywhere and nowhere. Wherever you go, it won't get any louder or softer.

Some birds cry out from time to time. What are they? Two have perched over there, while behind them rises the sun—a simple red circle—rising in an unexpected spot, absolutely not where you expected. Some others with blurred contours have sat down; what's Olga to do? She froze where she stood—a branch or twig in the forest could... But after sitting a while they looked around and flew away.

At home: Brehm,[7] father's magazines. What were they? Who can say? Like that time with the lamb. First along one side of the swamp, then along the other—not on the ground, but in the sky, over the whole clear meadow—it ascended and fell. Peruse at home: the curlew—similar to the rattle of a cart's wooden wheel; the snipe—the bleating of a lamb.

So that's what it turns out to be; if you had to pick a comparison, of course it would be a lamb, but there by the brook Olga wasn't up to choosing comparisons—it was just a strange bird.

That goes for the fire-bellied toads as well.

The manor pond. The Muravliansk Dam. The country estate. The dark pond. And numerous voices all singing simultaneously in the pond.

After sundown you go off roaming far into the fields. You make your way up the ravine past a certain spot, "Sheep Summit," and you walk past vast old stacks of straw from the steppe; the herded cattle are lowing in the nearby village, you hear individual clanging sounds, the cry of a corn crake; a quail: time to sleep, time to sleep, yet shout after shout comes from the pond, and you can barely make out the park on the periphery of which the pond clangs and resounds.

Frogs? But who in the world can't recognize frogs? Toads? "In the garden resounded the languid cries of toads"? With your permission, ahem ...they're tritons. Who knows? That's really a job for Bazarov.[8]

And at night! Midnight at the Muravliansk Dam! Have you ever been there? (Avenues of dark lindens stood there)[9]—suddenly tearing away, shouting, clinging, breaking off entirely, something terrible leaps down in front of you; you freeze, and discover it's a fledgling rook that fell from its nest in its sleep—you shine a flashlight, the beam runs off along a gnarled tree trunk, and speeds feebly towards the stars; there are lots of stars, possibly a moon, but on the avenues it's dark (it's lighter over the pond)—what dead gnarled trunks, petrified creases, dead bark. And whoever they are in the pond, they keep on shouting, all at the same time, but no one knows what in the world they are.

That's midnight for you. The Muravliansk Dam.

The old gentleman Lykovinov used to walk here often. And the lamb would go "baa, baa."

Is it midnight already? It's passed, moved on. And the nightingales? The nightingales released a flood of song. Especially one cadence: ta-ta, ta-ta.

And Seriozha Prochasov? Lighting the way with a flashlight, he walked beside me, then climbed down to the dam. Now we'll call the frogs. Seriozha Prochasov croaked once. Croaked again. Forgot about everything. Enough, Seriozha, it sounds too real. It's terrifying. No kidding. Seriozha croaks. First like a male, then like a female. He stood ramrod straight over the pond, his dark figure blending with something. It's light over the pond. The best star trembles in the water. Should I go down to him?

"It's answering!" Seriozha cried. "You hear—it's answering."

There it is—a second voice. It comes nearer, a tremulous "wa-a-a-a."

Seriozha keeps bending lower and lower, peering into the pond scum, from which floats out and bubbles forth a wide-mouthed "wa-a-a-a." Gazing at one another, they bellowed their hearts out. Seriozha's a lost cause. Watch out you don't fall into the deep water, Seriozha.

"See how I can do it?," he tore himself away and straightened up. "Now you sing on your own, dummy." We moved away, while the toads went on croaking wildly.

What about the nightingale? The nightingale was rolling its roulades. What was I to do with all of this? Embrace Seriozha Prochasov?

But Prochasov clicks on the flashlight, points his pale light at the stars—his beams get lost, and Prochasov swings the beam down beneath our feet—there's a little bridge, logs, a railing. Olga's dress shows white, you're cold—here's a raincoat, oh, we poor, poor things, there's not a thing we can do with all this.

The end of May. Soon the nightingales and the fire-bellied toads will be gone. Should I go around the whole park once again, this time from the outside, along the fence, the meadows—well, what of it?

At the pond once again. If I were to pull one of them out, how it would shout; let's see, now, what could I compare it to? A mournful sound stretches from the depths, runs upward and breaks on the surface. Here and there, and all around the pond thin pitiful voices go "oonk... oonk..."

Why can't you hear them at the pond in the village nearby, beyond the estate fence? The cattle are driven to a watering hole there, that's why.

After we finished the roast grouse my cheeks stopped burning, and suspicion set in, I imagined a string of days, the coolness gradually increasing. Frantic haste took over— to convince myself, outstrip events, and substantiate my suspicions as soon as possible.

Everything immediately passed as soon as I walked over to the window—my home is my castle, and, moreover, so much of me has spread into my immediate surroundings that this extra reserve was instantly given back to me and once again I have something to dispense. How distinctly that reserve was preserved here!

Our communication here is flawless—if I feel bad, empty, and have nothing—there's not a thing for me to send; but if I have something to say, how gratefully they give themselves back to me, how distinctly they speak of themselves.

How true my expanses are to me!

And yet I was hurt, I cried—as if they didn't exist! The main thing is never to forget them, for they, the dears, remember me!

I often pretend that I've forgotten them—that's when an imitation of the bitter fates of others starts. Is there really something that could harm them?

What could harm them?

They possess a life of their own—every moment they become different. Just try and distract yourself from what belongs to you, and when you turn back to it or even glance at it from the side, everything will have changed. Take right now: it's got darker, the borders between light and dark in the sky have disappeared, new lights have gone on in the villages, yet the fields are light, the roofs of hothouses are visible, no stars yet, and if you look to the north—the sky there is completely light. "I'll look north," said the daughter of a forester of a Vasiliev landowner—she still remembers Bunin[10]—and if Ivan 'Lexeich[11] were to appear here, I'd recognize him immediately. "Farewell, farewell, come visit us, and I'll look north, the sky there's light, you can see your Leningrad white nights."

What can harm a self-contained life—one that flows according to its own laws, that least depends on anything alien or transient?

Yet how easy it is to cause harm, to destroy. First of all, it doesn't take much to block out a view of the sky. Build on the fields, hack down the firs nearby, surround the lake with summer cottages, yet in front of the house—knock on wood—save us from the great transformations of nature.

So, it's easy. Go ahead and change your lighting and turn green at the appropriate time, it doesn't matter that your reserves of pink were senselessly squandered by this dismal light gray wall. At the appropriate hour even its alien plane will be tinted by the sunset, senselessly wasted on these wretched surfaces.

As long as my expanses are alive and not disfigured, I, too, will be like them.

However, I'll remember that invasion is possible, threat exists. What do I care about someone else's iniquitous life? It's about as much use as crying over a train in the distance or the twenty-five-thousand-head pig-breeding factory that's being built on the other side of Romanovka.

I crossed over into someone else's territory, where I felt like a fish out of water. It's time I made for home. The modes of existence imposed upon me, which I patiently tried to endure, have undermined my belief that I have any place to call my own.

This evening I made my usual rounds and confirmed that the long lake was as light as before, the cold sunset from the north gradually dimmed and the light moon was reflected in every puddle. Leaning against a tree trunk, I sat a while by the lake, wondering when our three lakes—the Bottomless, the Long, and the Round, which stretched out in a row—had formed one big body of water.

What am I guilty of? It's impossible to add a familiar suffix to something that has no name. It's metaphysical guilt.

The neighbors put up a scarecrow with a red hat, it still hasn't been faded by the sun, gotten wet in the rain—the clothes on it are still black.

All day a wet spring snow's been falling. The scarecrow's losing its vividness. The milking machines drone. The flowers on the berry bushes are frostbitten. This intoxicating reading is more fitting for an adolescent. Lips sticky with sweet thick cocoa, somnolence, no strength to get up and tear myself away.

An escape in someone else's clothes, a lake at night, a twenty-five-year-old queen galloping on horseback, the outmoded eloquence of an Austrian Freudian. Conquest or downfall, success or utter defeat?

The immediate surroundings brightened somewhat on the threshold of the night frosts. An unpretentious evening. Magpies stroll along the road. Not a soul. A cuckoo cuckoos. Pure peace!

Any utterance is a thousand times more blessed than silence; even if it's inarticulate and betrays itself, it's nonetheless released into the world, it exists. Just a moment ago it didn't, but now it already does—it's defenseless, anyone who keeps silent can ridicule it—yet it exists and some human souls will sigh together; they've been given words, what they'd hidden has been named, they can enter a nonfinalized space of an object, though in fact the object is finalized, limited and complete.

Reality envies the novel's fullness of events, whatever they be. It's essential that something occur and that time be eventful. I realized that reality is happy when it's presented with eventful days. Correspondences, coincidences between them, chance occurrences, and simply as many interwoven relations as possible. If you were to sort out these events, checking their significance, you'd begin to have doubts; however, who'd dare to judge the imaginary activities of a day that's passed? You're involved in life, you're possibly even a part of it, you even braid the threads here and there yourself and are ready to undo the collisions you've created. (Here mosquitoes swooped down and began to buzz, above the meadow the fog descended? ascended? settled? The calves were driven away and the horses were let out in their stead, while with a cry there was a flurry of—was it swallows? Or martins? Eleven p.m.)

In *The Insulted and the Injured*[12] the beginning's wonderful: the city, a mysterious chain of events, a lonely dreamer, what's hidden behind the walls of tenement houses. Then an accumulation of events, turmoil. The villain is happy, as is the author, when he can twist, lead, and provoke reality, divining its possibilities and playing with its consequences. At the same time the villain is a poet, fascinated by the process itself; he's happy that something is occurring and that he's the one responsible for what occurs, the provocateur of events. He's enchanted with the game itself, not only its object. It's not even clear which enchants him more.

The life of a dreamer is a short, tempestuous chain of events and the subsequent reexperiencing, hour by hour, of all that has happened.

Like the heroine of the story "The Tobolsk Bride"[13] (jumping off a wide provincial windowsill and singing): "I've seen him again, now that I've seen him, it'll suffice for May, June, July, August, September."

I wrote and wrote "The Tobolsk Bride," got good and stuck, and went to the kitchen, speared the cabbage with a fork, chewed a bit, and said aloud: none of my stuff will ever come out right, and suddenly bit my tongue so hard that I cried out; I'd drawn blood, it turned out. Which means, don't talk nonsense or just the opposite: it's gospel truth!

What can you do with someone else's consciousness? Either Thomas Mann's polysemy or the rapid rhythm of a travel sketch.

If it's the first, then it's arrogant surprise at someone else's consciousness; if it's the second, then it's a journalist's slap on the shoulder, as if to say, well, we know, we also kept diaries in our salad days, as pimply-faced youths, etc.

Blessed is the place of our first meeting; here's the map, see the cross mark where he stood then.

With the appearance of foliage, the expanses closed in somewhat. The black grouse fell silent long ago. The last streams of melted snow dried up. The roads acquired the usual summer dust. The lapwings' fields were dug up and planted. It got boring. But a cold wind arose and howled, and the space expanded again.

After the rain heavy lilac slugs sway on the fluffy new dill.

One a.m. I'm writing without light, sitting in front of the window. How much strength, how much confidence accrues in the course of such a night. My eyes absorb the pond glimmering between the trees, the fields, the forest, the lights of distant villages, the soft blue hills on the horizon, the sky that's turning green is still rosy in the north, and the pearly clouds.

From sitting so long I've soaked up the expanses, I'm replete, yet can't tear myself away.

The lights of the villages are whoppers—you can count them—six on one side of the road, six on the other, but in Romanovka there's only one. The wind howls, fingering the spidery paws of the nearby firs.

There's a celebration in the club. People are leaving in pairs. It's cold.

The white nights are ending—it's time to take stock of things.

The highest narrative truth (higher than life itself) lies in its ephemeral nature and significance. Sickly virgins die of humiliation, lovers find death in fatal love, villains commit their major act of baseness.

What happens, then, in our case? Life goes on, although by all the laws of plot construction and sense it should have ended long ago. But we're cultivating a good-sized glacier, every winter adding a new thickness, by summer we thaw out a little and crawl in some direction. However, our self-complacent hoarding knows no bounds. Now I know a bit of this and that, it's useful for me to understand you, now I'll have the experience... But for what?

About a rag in a traffic lane, fluttering to meet every bus, and about nothing else.

The envy of the young Dostoevsky—a lonely dreamer—towards life's chain of events, towards life itself, which develops without his knowledge; hence the conglomeration of events in his novels, his dreams of participating in them.

If you stroll around town in nice weather, peek into the basements. Now, more often than not, they're uninhabited, and yet have a life of their own.

Lacking the opportunity to leave the city and finding myself on the street in broad daylight during this hot season, I began to pay particular attention to the characteristic features of various occupations.

Some lightly dressed people have poured out onto the sunny side of the street: several of them shout something into the open windows of the house across the street, others have turned towards the water, leaning on the railing along the embankment. These are the last minutes of the lunch break at a construction bureau.

Daytime strolls reveal a diversity of paradoxical activities. Here's an example of the social division of labor taken to the absurd: the type of job that becomes an extension of one small part of a person's body, not even the part, but just the skin. This skin has the ability to grow faster the more often it's sloughed off. And here's a dozen well-fed women, content with their fate, merrily chattering away, minding their own business, complaining now and then about the quality of skin in particular cases and calculating in how many minutes they'll run home to eat. After an absence, they return, sit down, move more closely together, shake out their napkins, cast a quick glance at a customer and cheerfully set to work, inducing in her as well the feelings of a ripe woman who's just stuffed herself with a roll and cream. There's a young girl in a smock and backless slippers wandering back to her work station, looking at herself in every mirror. Suddenly she seems to notice something, and, without breaking her concentration, draws her face close to the mirror, squints at her nose, moves away, picks up a comb, fixes a curl by her ear and, without turning around, says: "What should I nibble on next?"

Let's get out of there through the doors that open directly onto the street and we won't pity them, they're happy and have no need of pity; let's return from here to Raziezzhaia.

During these hot hours the place is deserted, all the windows are open, and the life flowing behind the thick walls of these old tenements opens a crack and wriggles out a bit.

A window on the first floor. The curtains, drawn back, reveal the backdrop of a poor room: from the cool darkness a housewife's hand with a jar of water stretches out to the flower pots, and her body follows, but we've already moved on, and the scene froze in its distinctness and completeness.

It's hot. Cold rot emanates from the gateways and windows level with the ground. Here's the window of some sort of office. Far below, you can make out the desks crowded up against each other, through the half-opened door to the corridor shines the glass of the Honor plaque,[14] you hear the clack of typewriters.

Whether this flash came immediately from the dark office corridor or took shape in a head overbaked in the sun, I can't say, but the bitterness of the hand outstretched to the pitiful pots, the flash of the Honor plaque (it was probably the silver foil lining the glass that struck my eye so vividly) have given me no peace for quite a long time.

Ah, the story of a raven.
"Well, Fedka, say something. Will we open the museum on time?"
"Caw!"
His crowing rushed up from under the earth as if from the netherworld itself. Passersby stopped, listened, looked around.

A dusty road, down which a herd has just passed. Still early, but already hot. Roads like these happen only in the middle of summer. I'd say it was a hot ripe July summer. The lake's deserted at this time. A school of fish by the bath house. In the afternoon I found out that the striking ripeness of the morning, which suggested the idea of a turning point, really was a turning point: today is indeed a major turning point ("Saints Peter and Paul reduced the days for all...") and is considered the middle of summer.

It's pitiful and painful. Absolutely everything occurs without me. I only manage to catch a hint of a tan...

The complaints of a Turk. Remaining in the basement alone, I locked the door and sat down facing the window. Without the necessary amount of fresh air, my head becomes heavy, my legs are freezing from the cold below, which overflows and rolls into all the nooks and crannies of the spacious basement. The trolleys and buses outside rumble, communicating the vibrations to my writing table, which stands at a level much lower than the roadway.

The surroundings that bent my head and forced me to fling down this book have an unambiguously biological influence here. In this instance the complaint "a prey to one's surroundings" takes on a banal meaning, in the form of particular winged cockroaches nicknamed "blister-makers" running along my bare legs.

The dampness seeping through the walls, the stench, the tickling of the "blister-makers," snatches of conversations from the street, rumbling curses somewhere on the stairway. Well, what can you say—having buried yourself two meters deep, you can only regret your temporarily heavy head.

Sitting behind a desk in front of a window blocked by a grating and glancing outside at the street leaves you with few illusions.

Obvious diversity is reduced to the simplest things. The monotonous tramping of worn boots with iron taps speaks of the proximity of the market, housewives pass by, either alone—their footsteps purposeful, preoccupied—or in pairs, and then the basement is awash in snatches of their conversation, always only a phrase, but inevitably striking in its wretched multiplicity of meanings and surprising typicality.

Listen hard: the clip-clop of broken-in shoes approaching, curls glistening in the sun—the hunter concealed right under the sidewalk, let's scurry to our net, the casement screen, to quickly snag the word that flutters in.

Let's reel in some completely unsuspecting prattle from the stream of speech: it's engraved in our consciousness, it'll be the last word of a reality unaware of its generosity, scattering about its exquisite phenomena generously and, seemingly, without any sense.

Let's separate the last word from the stream; it can be any word, provided it flies into our one and only trap. It's possible to open other windows as well, but I've gotten used to fishing with only one rod.

The trolleys rumble, the windows across the street, which look as though they've just been washed, show deadly black, life rushes on, pulled into a straight line, and in the depths sits a butterfly collector. He's not waiting for an exotic specimen, he's waiting for whatever flies in.

Across the street there's a white sign with "MILK" on it—the symbol of a constantly changing, senseless, rich life. If across the street it's mechanically poured out in toto, in its entirety, into containers and quickly carried off in different directions, then we also absorb, slurp up the straightforward movement occurring right before our eyes, patiently waiting for it to call itself by its own name, under its own power, straight from its own, so to speak, linear nexus.

"I love boiled potatoes..."

Foolish collector, your heart's grown numb, what did you expect from a stagnant, dead stream that loves itself, is proud of itself? That it'll show you immediately where the best young potatoes are for sale? It loves to ride fast, rejoices in the summer day in its washed window and in the dairy store that's in this very building.

"How the sun warms..."

"If you submit an application for..."

"So you tell him that, you know... "

It was August of the year that in the future will go down in history as a time of cholera. This word has become entangled more and more often in our now infected net.

I throw this burdock out with disgust.

August eighth I was wandering on the edge of the forest along the field of oats and suddenly heard myself saying: "Everyone come here." It was an image of death.

The weight of everything that's been written before, of all the unfinished Tobolsk brides, of atrocities in Korea and transparent chapters, chapters, flowing appeals is dragging me down by my feet: how to finish everything once and for all, because one thing's pulling me here, and bubbles are rising to the surface there, and yet elsewhere something that sank is making itself heard. There's a log sticking out here, deep in the silt there are shells from the war, while in the middle an entire pontoon has sunk. Would that I could clean out all of our Bottomless Lake, place a clean sheet in front of me, turn over on my back and drift gently on the surface, rejoicing in my ability to lie on the water. Let it carry us wherever it pleases, nothing under the water threatens us any more.

And what about the crippled body of the girl who drowned that unhappy summer? It's over there on the other side of the narrow bay, where the lake ends,—and we turn over on our stomach and paddle away from that place like mad. It's time to get out of the water, it's cold and soon it's off to work.

The water in this inhabited reservoir is too turbulent.

As I've noticed, the only thing everybody talks and writes about is that unfortunate condition, which still only threatens you, is still only approaching; they talk about it aloud, expecting to interrupt you: "Come *on*, that's not it at all!", "Why should *you* think about that?"

Here's a tale about old age, old-timers at a summer cottage, healthy European break-fasts—what's allowed and what's not, we still love toast with apricot jam, strong jasmine tea from China, a proper regimen. An old man sitting in a chaise longue inspects the obscene apian depths of the flowers obligingly waving by his arm rest. They just seated him there, plumped his pillow, covered him with a lap rug, he was just chatting with us about literature, and here he is, already dozing, mouth open. The guests from Moscow stand up in embarrassment, but at the movement the old man starts, swallows a bit of spittle, and amazes the guests with the accuracy of his judgments.

His energetic middle-aged wife rushes in (a new elegance about her, appropriate for a woman of her age) and invites everyone inside.

After this tale our author ages by ten years, becomes an unquestionably elderly man, in all this time several of his novels get published, but we'll no longer be greeted with coquettish complaints about a new way of life. What will remain and turn into a single short note is surprise: I'm alive, while they died long ago, both my little brother Petia Bachei, and Gavrik, but these will be signs of incipient rigidity in our elderly man, who's crossed some kind of threshold and grown strong, learned to gather the harvest, gained momentum, if you can put it that way, in his old age.

Just as Blok is a poet of youth, and even his aging youths are nevertheless still youths, not men, so Kataev is a prosaist of old age, distilling from it all that it has to give.[15] (Just as our father distills berry wine out of everything that grows in the garden, and when there aren't enough gooseberries, currants, and black rowanberries, jars of ancient preserves suddenly disappear from our house—they can also be distilled.)

In the prose of writers whose literature addresses a certain age group, sometimes, in passing, several gray hairs gleam on the young hero's head and three women sigh: his mother, his wife, and a young girl in a red skirt.

And so, not a word about a truly gray head, only the first glimmers are interesting. The same can be said of solitude. It only wails and complains at first, but that means that it's not the real thing yet. It's only just defined itself: "I've been left all alone in the world." It's possible that it's already searching for a replacement. Complete and long-standing solitude has become rigid, it's become overgrown with habits; just try and put your suitcase there, you've noticed that there's never a place for it, though you still hope that you're protecting and sheltering, are shifting into high gear, bustling about and improving, but suddenly in the middle of your bursts of activity you encounter an unwillingness to change, you already begin to justify yourself—well, it's better this way, smarter, but no, it turns out that it has long been time for you and your belongings to clear out of here.

At V's. What kind of master class was it? I've taken a half-day off. Please come in, yes, ring seven times to get me, sit down where everyone can see you, here's the fifth plate... I was just writing a phrase (how long was it?) "the young wife isn't home, she'll return late." This is how I'll live until they tear the building down.

You say to put them in different envelopes; of course, it's simple that way: why not try it—put them in, send them off, and forget about them. You became engrossed in other things, prose, for example, and suddenly you're getting remarkable honoraria and kind replies from *Working Woman, Peasant Woman, Village Youth, Man and the Law,* and *Good Morning.*

At first we politely declined the offers in the big official envelopes, but the attempts at persuasion grow stronger—and here we are, all together at a table with scissors, glue, and ruler; we lick the stamps, stroke the yellow corners, the cheerful work is in full swing, and the most dedicated of us runs to the post office, hoping to have the time on the way back to buy a bottle before closing time.

And when everyone thought that that's how it would be, for how could it be otherwise, I had to break it off and even explain a few things. At first I explained it to you, then told myself, then told myself again, and unobtrusively cut myself off; I've been drifting for a long time, proclaiming my one and only truth, sensing my displacement—this is it, the essential lesson to be learned—I'm still with the others, yet I'm already alone at my cold? hot? height.[16]

The hour is late, it's time to leave, the guests push back their chairs, but you don't come down, don't condescend—the motors start up properly, roaring steadily—they've already left and that's good, you continue your interrupted (how long is it?) phrase.

Albinos. Once again we dragged the old stuff from the museum from one basement to another, as we'd done seven years ago. Rat droppings in the armchairs (they love anything soft), the seamy side of life, back yards, abandoned residences. You only have to abandon a room to see how quickly it becomes desolate—mold, dry spiders, dampness, stench. Two cats, dirty albinos who'd lost their color, waited on the side until we stopped walking back and forth, carrying the unsettled stuff, with its loose strands of horsehair, from place to place, slamming doors and empty desk drawers, in which rolled about keys and pieces of wooden carvings that had been hurriedly tossed in. Life was turned inside out, its seamy side exposed.

And those kitchens behind the curtains! Old houses are the same as those armchairs where a tired old crone in the smock of a repository worker used to plop herself down.

There are only rears, storerooms, stairways, and kitchens here, but where do the old women who sometimes show themselves in the windows live? Each one has only one window and she peers out of it her whole life; it's most unlikely that they'd manage to give her another. How much strength needs to be spent on driving away desolation, if only into a corner, to clean out just the middle!

And the cupboards, and corners, and baskets, and corridors—how terrifying to delve deep into them! There's nothing more terrifying than deserted residences: those houses abandoned for repair, the furniture removed—I find it repulsive to approach the back of a television or an alarm clock (an incomprehensible seamy side), and there are kilometers of chaos.

There are old women's spheres, consisting of those things that matter to them and interest them, that's their world. Though our truck, from which we unloaded the ramshackle furniture, stood in the way, the passersby waited patiently until the road was clear, only the old women were interested in our pitiful stuff.

Thus at different times in our lives we notice different things. At times dogs, when we're raising our own litter, at others, well-dressed, happy women when we ourselves are depressed and defeated.

Each old woman wipes her window, fearlessly climbing up on the windowsill, bravely stretching upwards, it's not time yet.

"Just look at what they've brought! That junk should have been dumped long ago," they mumble, rhyming their lives with what they see.

Can it be that we see only what we see, and don't see what's still too early?

It's still too early, indeed: early to worry about going by tram without having to transfer, the merits of black rowanberries, and Lotus detergent.

"You're too young to read the novel *Life*," they told Nadia, our sixteen-year-old servant.

Dogs on the street see only cats and other dogs; pay attention to how uneasy and affected little children can be when another child of their age turns up somewhere near them in the subway; a beauty instantly discerns and evaluates another at the opposite end of the car: she'll worry if she finds that the other is better-looking, or will calm down if she remains supreme.

Can it be that we're just beating air with the empty rattling rhymes of our lives?

But it's like that only in unnatural surroundings.

Abandoned dwellings outside the city don't terrify us.

We'll quickly identify erstwhile foundations by the thick birch wood and foalfoot that hide piles of macadam from view; erstwhile flower beds occasionally will peek through in the form of a puny wild daisy; fragments of linden avenues still stand, now shortened, leading from nowhere to nowhere, often partitioned by some brand-new bleachers, and there's a chapel with an underground tunnel dug, for some reason, directly from the manor house. (Ah, you and I once missed each other in this park, I got there late and you hadn't waited.)

But why do we find the daisies so pleasant and the dirty albinos so unpleasant?

Here I am, dragging myself past these walls for the thousandth time, I'll never manage to escape them, nor will the neighbors. Sometimes a clean window will glisten in the sun; so what, seven years have passed and another seven will pass and then yet another and "the traces of pitiful everyday occupations" (a quotation) will still be the same and will rhyme with desolation... and death.

Sometimes there were sunny days, but not many, all in all very few, life even smiled down upon us, even here our expanses shone, but the holidays passed, our joyous excitement jingled off into the distance, and again our surfaces are covered with soot, again our noses have turned red from the cold, dampness, and anemia.

Every little corner on Marat Street rushes out to befriend me, but I don't want, I really don't want to have anything to do with any of you. I'm no longer yours.

And that dear fellow with the wooden snakes at Kuznechny Market whom I run past late every day—you haven't forgotten him, have you? He rhymes with you, every day I run past your rhymes, your abandoned, gray-faced friend. Every morning he sends you greetings with his wrist, diligently working out the stiffness in its joints.

I run past with a sure step—the flowers along the rows keep changing: there were just some lilacs there, and when you next look, chrysanthemums have appeared, we didn't have the time to fry up enough smelt, and now the mushrooms are already gone, all that remains are the frostbitten ones good only for pickling, displayed in heaps along the fence of St. Vladimir's Church—all of this represents my morning conversations with you along an extended metaphor.

We were all supplied with identical flannelette blankets for life on our own. (Taipee, who's been looking at me from her spot for a long time now, just shook her ears threateningly and stood up. I've got to go out, but it's cold, dark, freezing.)

The beginning of October and the pond is frozen solid. Beastly cold, as Remizov[17] loved to say. While we were out walking, it seemed that all my future letters, no matter how many there'll be, will be repetitions of one and the same chain: walls, repositories, the elderly man with the snakes, Taipee, Mardi, Dick—how many of them won't be around then—dogs get replaced fast, their life span isn't long. It's impossible to run back and forth without impunity along a metaphor as long as life.

When the steamship moored in Serdolikov Bay,[18] someone suddenly climbed up on the cliff overhanging the beach: everyone stopped dead in his tracks. He's crazy, stop him, what in the world is he doing! But how light were his movements, how gently he pressed against the cliff; and, having reached the top, he's already coming down. Calmly. His left foot, as it looks for support, sways with much too much spring—the kind of excess that makes you wince; but a gentle jump and, thank God, he's on firm ground.

However, you can't deny the artistry and grace.

Not at all bad to achieve such beauty and lightness in your exercises.

He trained in strange pursuits that no one needs—to conquer the cliffs. And what's the point of these cliffs in general, over there, the majority of people live their lives never suspecting that such misshapen accumulations even exist ("we have it good here, there's nothing of that sort—no earthquakes, no floods. Thank God, we're far from the mountains and the sea, the land's flat," an old woman, a forester's daughter, told me—the central provinces of Russia described in *The Life of Arseniev*).[19]

And here near these grotesque creations the rare art of scaling them takes form. Colonies of such trainees settle on an extinct volcano and perfect their skills far from the eyes of outsiders.

But why does this strange art flourish—it's deserted on top and there's nothing there of interest.

And now one of them, unable to endure the hermetic nature of his pursuits, climbs down into the deserted bay, where a steamship with loudspeakers, a buffet, and radio-broadcasted tours comes daily: waiting until the tourists have bathed, gathered scads of stones, changed into dry things, and are once again gathered on deck waiting to be transported back, he begins to demonstrate his death-defying trick.

So, first take our breath away with your death-defying act (where on earth is he climbing? he's crazy!), then force us to admire the great height of your risky art.

It would be interesting just to find out whether he's a novice who's recently learned a few fundamentals or an experienced mountain climber.

Why does any display of lightness, freshness, sincerity trouble us so, not then in the old days, but now, up close? How beneficial these signs are amidst a lusterless, colorless life, it means that something still might happen, it means that the abandoned lots, trampled and strewn with broken glass, haven't all been exhausted. On the contrary, my peers and contemporaries usually interpose their unsuccessful artistic texts into my life not without indifference. What business is it of mine, what have I got to do with it?

Well, there's a resemblance here; I could conceivably write such filth too, couldn't I? And it already begins to seem that I could; and I can't get up from the sofa, I sleep all day long by a sack of gnawed dry fruit and tomorrow I've got to go to work, and that's how my blessed long-awaited weekend passed.

It's not like that now, hasn't been for a long time. I won't give up my early mornings for anyone now.

And why am I sitting here when this music makes me want to move my feet and knock them all out of their seats (who was it said people, make way, I've just got to dance)?

Here, of course, I could be more circumspect, moving my feet's no big deal.

You perform no great service when you get all fired up by the same good old resources. What you get from pop music you get from a pop book too.

Of course, I should step to the music of my own orchestra (Thoreau) and what good is there in getting fired up by other drummers or the empty country barrelware of a new favorite writer.[20]

However, there's nothing you can do; independence and self-sufficiency, we affirm. But what would we do without these happy supports, the timely omens; however, don't they resemble unstaked peas: poor things, they begin to sway even when there's no wind, their tendrils moving and suddenly catching hold of the succulent plant duckweed, and they crawl behind it on the ground and perish if they don't climb up along something more appropriate.

Life has disintegrated into arguments: everything's lousy, everything's over or it's not so very bad, you can still do something, something fresh and new could appear, which means that I'm not done for yet.

But it's impossible to give in to external events that way, you'll say. Damn the surroundings, it's been proven that your surroundings don't mean a thing, but that's only if we're talking about some petrified dried up vegetable, and not a Vsevolozhsk oak.[21]

Then my own father arrived, noticed the letter from my dear friend on the table, crumpled it up, and threatened to go to her poor parents and say that she shouldn't dare write any more. And now I was no longer in a mood to party, my dear little book lay all by itself, I pitied father and it was absolutely clear—my life was over, over; they'd simply left me in peace for a while, but in the fall they'll start up with me again, everything will go run according to their plan.

Okay. I've known worse. We get up, wipe our faces with a towel and go outside. It's time to cover up the cucumbers for the night. While the instructive example of the peas was being cultivated, a gypsy's cow got into the garden (our patch, on the edge) and ate all the peas growing in the bed. Only a few remained whole.

To make up for it, the curly Kavkaz coriander next to it has grown luxuriantly thick.

The first week after leaving the museum, it was as if I were recovering from a serious illness: I slept several times a day, then, bundled up in my winter clothing, crawled out of the house, weaved my way towards the forest, sat down on the very first stump or fallen tree and warmed myself for hours in the April sun, watched the wrens with sympathy (now I know that wrens are suited for sanitorium windows and avenues), then, sighing, I'd get up and hobble home—what happiness, can it really be all behind me—that's how lonely old women who are content with their life walk home, having remembered that there's still a little something left in their gift box of candy, and later, in prolonged contentment they drink well-brewed tea, always from the same cup.

However, it's time to crawl out of hiding.

In the village of Rumbolovo on Nagorny Street we lift our hoods and look in all four directions.

Yesterday the trash was swept out of the desk at work and the disgraceful arithmetic of "seven and seven again" was finished with—let this one more school remain and produce new recruits. Sometime we'll drop by into this alley again.

Here, in this lane of traffic, a clump of fur was pulled off fat-faced Stalinka's rabbit coat, she raced out of the school doors and rushed across the path of the number six bus towards the house across the street (lucky she, living closer than everyone else), having safely escaped her persecutors, and that's the last we saw of her that day.

Let's turn into this doorway for a minute. I just need to check one thing. So it's true. There's no memorial plaque. What had been written there in golden letters turned out to be a lie.

It's not possible to say that we learned to read from that plaque, but several students, knowing it by heart, managed to hoodwink the adults waiting in the lobby. A blockhead like that had the time, before a lambskin cap with ties under the chin was pulled on him, to turn his head and, as if seeing this enormous plaque for the first time, froze before it and began to read loudly. That's how our Taipee acts when she's called back from the hunt to her lead; though she knows what's up, she suddenly pretends that it's not all over yet in this swamp. Once again she points to a nest we've long known as if she hadn't scared away a snipe at this hillock just half an hour ago.

That was someone's younger brother, Phillipok,[22] but our school wouldn't have accepted him. Our school was for girls.

Wonder what's there now. No, there'd be nothing wondrous about it.

We clear off the desk, take away superfluous books, wipe the dust from the paper, push aside assorted odd objects with our elbow. We clear time, prepare a meadow, and fell a stand of young trees.

Ready. Nothing to disturb us.

A wide swath in fate.

A naked farm wife walks into the water up to her knees and mows a narrow path through the thick weeds near the banks, she's already up to her waist in the water, now you can swim out to the middle of the lake.

Leningrad 1979

Translated by Arlene Forman

From *Ekho*, 1984

Notes

1. Anna Akhmatova (1889-1966) and Alexander Blok (1880-1921), two major poets of the twentieth century.

2. During the Soviet era, institutions and places providing services kept a book of complaints that dissatisfied customers could demand so as to enter their criticisms. Although it is difficult to imagine that anyone actually read these narratives of enraged frustration, requests for the book of complaints, quite inexplicably, often achieved results where pleas, exhortations, threats, and scenes failed.

3. A drama by Alexei Arbuzov (1908-1986), *An Irkutsk Story* (1959) is set in Siberia. The wayward heroine is reformed by the hero, with whom she enjoys a blissful but brief intimacy.

4. Guy de Maupassant's novel titled *Une Vie* (1883) traces a young Frenchwoman's life with a frankness considered daring in its time.

5. The central avenue in St. Petersburg.

6. Nadezhda Konstantinovna Krupskaia (1869-1939), Lenin's wife.

7. Alfred Edmund Brehm (1827-1884), German zoologist, author of a popular compendium entitled *Animal Life* (1863-69).

8. Bazarov is the protagonist of Ivan Turgenev's novel *Fathers and Sons* (1862), where, as a student of the natural sciences, he ritualistically dissects frogs.

9. A quotation from "Dark Avenues" (1938) by Ivan Bunin, who, in turn borrowed the line, albeit imprecisely, from the poem "An Ordinary Story" (1842) by Nikolai Ogariov.

10. Ivan Bunin (1870-1958) emigrated from the Soviet Union in 1920.

11. That is, Bunin (Ivan Alexseevich).

12. A novel by F. Dostoevsky, published in 1861.

13. One of Ulanovskaia's own unpublished works.

14. A board on the wall at most Soviet workplaces that officially honors particularly deserving workers with words of praise, usually accompanied by their photograph.

15. Valentin Kataev's (1897-1986) preoccupation with old age is exemplified in his (semi-autobiographical) works of the 1960s and 1970s, where memory plays a focal role.

16. An embedded reference to Osip Mandelstam's poem "To Bely's Memory."

17. Alexei Remizov (1877-1957) was a prosaist noted for his innovative narrative style and folklore adaptations.

18. Located in Koktebel, a famous resort area in the Crimea associated with many literary figures.

19. Bunin's fictionalized autobiography, published in 1938.

20. The reference is to Vassily Aksyonov's novella *Surplussed Barrelware* (1968).

21. Vsevolozhsk is a rural community approximately 20 kilometers northeast of St. Petersburg, where the author spent much of her adolescence and still resides whenever she leaves the city.

22. "Phillipok" (1863) is the title of a short story by Lev Tolstoi.

The Trap

Anna Mass

I'm lying on a high wooden bed and through a little window I see the nighttime village street and the contours of the forest across the road. I'm a "summer-cottager." What a depressing name! But there's nothing I can do about it. Summer camp has ended, and there's still a whole month of vacation left. My brother and his wife Rita and her mother rented a summer cottage in the country, ten minutes' walk from the summer camp, and I came straight from camp to this new residence. Now, instead of camp, there's a resort.

The owner of our cabin is away visiting her son in the city. We have two small rooms partitioned off by a plywood wall that doesn't reach the ceiling, and a spacious kitchen where Iadviga Vasilievna, Rita's mother, sleeps. We eat on the porch.

Iadviga Vasilievna is dissatisfied with everything. She's annoyed that she's been stuck with me and that we didn't get a voucher to stay at the resort but have to live in the country and go to the resort cafeteria with food containers. But then, it's me who goes to the cafeteria with the food containers. Iadviga Vasilievna regards the vacationers from the resort who come to the village to buy milk and black currants with a certain envious arrogance.

Behind the partition, Aliosha[1] is quietly reciting:

> Shuddering in torment, summer lightning rolled across the earth,
> A shadow from a cloud fell, fused with and disappeared into the grass.
> In the sky the cloud billow stirs, it's harder and harder to breathe,
> A bird swoops low, having flown above my head...[2]

"I've been sitting and working on this article all day long, but something's keeping me from getting it done. I opened a volume of Zabolotsky. Is it ever great stuff!"

Rita brags to her girlfriends that Aliosha gets calls from various editorial offices and that his article was published in the journal *Literary Review,* and they had commissioned another article. And that he's a prominent figure in the department and soon will defend his M.A. dissertation.

Her girlfriends, Vavochka and Tatochka,[3] also summer-cottagers, come to visit Rita and her mother to gab. They can go on for hours and their talk is studded with phrases like "first husband," "second husband," "third wife," "divorced," "got together," "left her the apartment"...

> ... I love this twilight of rapture,
> This short night of inspiration,
> The human rustle of grass, the prophetic cold on a dark hand,
> This lightning flash of thought, and the indolent appearance
> Of the first distant rolls of thunder—the first words in my native tongue...

"'The human rustle of grass'! Just listen to how that's put, Rita, eh?... It simply drives you wild!"

"Listen," it was Rita's business-like voice. "There's a general store in Mikhailovskoe. It's got those same boots."

"Which ones?"

"Those—you know which ones. Remember I ran around looking for them last winter? Austrian fur-lined. One hundred and twenty rubles. They're just sitting there, and nobody's buying them."

"But, kitten, right now we don't have one hundred and twenty rubles."

"What if you borrowed from your relatives?"

"I don't know... it's awkward..."

"But, Lioshk! How can it be awkward to borrow from your own relatives! As soon as you get paid for the article, we'll give it back."

"The article won't be published before December..."

"But, Lioshk! Say it's for my birthday in advance. Let it be their present. And then for my birthday they won't have to bother."

"Kitten, it's really a lot of money. They're planning to go south for their holidays. It's awkward."

Silence. The bed squeaked. Rita's offended voice:

"Get out of here."

"Ritul!"[4]

"Don't kiss up to me!"

"But, kitten!"

"Will you ask or not? For my birthday in advance?"

"I will."

He's a real pushover, my brother, but I partly understand him: he's always been very unsure of himself. He's suffered because of his shortness and his physique, which is hardly heroic, while she is a real beauty!

When Rita walks down the street, people turn around to look at her. I'm sometimes amazed that she could fall in love with my brother. Aliosha's friend Egor courted her, but she preferred Aliosha, although Egor's much better looking.

Having graduated from the technical institute, she works in an architectural studio and, incidentally, works well: her photograph is up on the Board of Achievement.[5] This winter before New Year's, she dressed up as the Snow Maiden and, along with Grandfather Frost, her co-worker, she handed out gifts. That's how it's done at her place of work. The children simply fell madly in love with her and at work she was thanked publicly. When she wants to, she can be both friendly and charming.

And everything is always sparkling clean around her. From the most trivial things—little boxes, bits of board, and pieces of rags—she knows how to make things that people "ooh" and "aah" over. She even knows how to sew and willingly sews for all her girlfriends. For many years we had multi-colored skeins of wool, remnants, lying around not being used. They bothered mother and she even thought about throwing them out; she didn't know how to knit, and the skeins were left from my grandmother. One day, Rita discovered these skeins in a bag with mothballs and knitted such a beautiful sweater for my birthday that when I put it on, everyone notices it.

Yes, of course I can understand Aliosha.

But sometimes I think that Rita doesn't love Aliosha at all. That he's merely a "promising husband" to her. She uses this word "promising" a lot. The promise holds not only the M.A., but also a doctoral, dissertation. The promise holds a cooperative apartment, a car, and the company of academics among whom Rita will shine.

And Aliosha? He works, works as if driven. Once a week he goes into the city, where he's in charge of a literary club in the House of Culture at an automobile factory. He translates abstracts from English for the Institute of Scientific and Technical Information. And, in addition, he has his articles and his dissertation.

He doesn't notice any shortcomings in Rita because he's in love with her; to him, she's everything.

For Rita, he spoiled my ravine. This ravine lay between the resort and the village; it was deep, and had a steep path with alder bushes growing along it. Few people knew about the path; the summer-cottagers took the direct road across the bridge. And I myself was stupid enough to show it to Rita.

Any time it rained, the path would become slippery. Once, during her usual "promenade" to the resort, Rita slipped and almost fell. And just because she had *almost* fallen, Aliosha took a shovel and hacked out wide steps along the entire path. Immediately the ravine lost its former uninhabited look and became somehow slick-looking. I didn't use the steps on principle, but went up and down on the grass along the side even after it rained and the grass was wet. And the shovel with the broken handle which Aliosha had forgotten in the ravine—or had forgotten on purpose to touch-up the steps—I tossed into the bushes.

In general, despite its solitariness, my life at present has some advantages over my former camp life. I can swim where I want. I can swim across the stream—it's not wide, but on the other side the water is just over my head, which is why during camp we were forbidden to swim to the other side. On the other shore is the thickest undergrowth of ripe raspberries. True, it's full of nettles, and I'm in my bathing suit, and some of the stalks of nettles are taller than I am. But only the first two or three stings are painful, and then it's nothing.

When I've eaten my fill of raspberries, I come out of the underbrush and lie down on a warm, sunny knoll, where among the uncut and already slightly faded grass the leaves of the wild strawberries are turning red. A sad berry is drooping under its own overripe weight. I feel sorry for it. Surely it didn't fill with juice just to fall, overripe, on the ground to rot.

The stem joyfully bobbed up and down when I picked the heavy, dark-red strawberry, which left the incomparable taste of an August summer day in my mouth.

Lying on my stomach, I closely examine the blades of grass and the whole tiny and enormous world that we trample with our feet. At this moment, I'd like to become small and weightless because this world suffers under my weight and there's nothing I can do to help it.

I turn over on my back and another world looms above me—huge, blue and white, far, far away. Some words and lines arise in my head: it's not poetry yet, but it's like a presentiment of poetry. And an anxious feeling takes hold of me, as if right now, this very minute, I had stopped before a mystery.

The bite of a mosquito brings me back to reality. I rub my bitten foot and suddenly remember that it's already long past lunchtime and I had forgotten my responsibility—I hadn't brought the food containers from the resort, and that meant that they'd sent Aliosha, and also probably had even turned him against me: here I am wandering around God knows where and they have to worry about me.

With my shift pulled over my damp bathing suit, I run, run across the field, through the ravine in which Aliosha had cut out the steps for his "kitten," and annoyance wells over me at the thought that in a second I'll see Iadviga Vasilievna's sanctimonious mug and Rita's dissatisfied face.

But as I was nearing home, I realized that there wouldn't be any bawling-out. Guests had arrived! It was Aliosha's childhood friend Boria and his wife Katia, whom I'd only heard about and would see now for the first time. I liked her immediately. She was tall—taller than Boris, thin, with a short hair style. She behaved like a boy, brusquely and independently. And Boria, in the time since I had last seen him, had gained a bit of weight and his mustache now turned down at the ends. Boria is an artist who illustrates childrens' books; we already have three books with his drawings and his inscriptions to us. I think the drawings are marvelous. Katia is also an artist, but I haven't seen her drawings yet.

"Look who's here!" yelled Boria, opening his arms wide in a hug to meet me. "Or am I only dreaming?"

He embraced me with one arm, lifted me slightly, and swung me around in a circle. Then he put me down on the ground, took a step back, and, shading his eyes with his hand, looked at me.

"Everything's just right," he informed me. "Everything is right on schedule. When did we see each other last? In the winter? Right, that's when it was. You were neither fish nor fowl then. But now something's hatching. Really. Here, meet my wife Katia."

"Wife Katia" shook my hand and asked: "Is the stream far?"

"It's nearby."

"Shall we go there after lunch?"

"Yes, let's!" I readily agreed.

Iadviga Vasilievna was setting the table with a gracious smile. Rita was helping her.

"How come you're late?" she commented softly. "Aliosha and Egor had to go to get the lunch."

"Egor came too? That's great!"

At that moment I caught sight of Aliosha and Egor. They were coming from the direction of the resort.

"Salute!" Egor said to me.

"Salute!" I answered. "But why aren't you in a military uniform?"

"What's the matter? Don't you like me like this?"

"What do you mean? Sure I do," I said and felt embarrassed.

"Come on, tell me honestly. Give it to me straight, don't be afraid. If I'm not handsome enough for you in civilian clothes, then I'll go and change into parade uniform."

Egor spoke very seriously, even anxiously, which made it even funnier.

How happy I was! Only now did I realize how much I'd missed cheerful company and how dreary it had been spending all of these days in solitude.

By the porch lay a knapsack with Borya's guitar propped against it and a thick orange roll—a rolled-up tent. That meant that in the evening we would light a fire and then the guests would stay overnight and tomorrow I would be with them all day again!

But it looked as if Aliosha was even more pleased than I. I simply don't remember the last time I had seen him so happy.

"Old man, you've lost a bit of weight," said Boria. "Married life isn't doing anything for you. Take me, for example." And he slapped his stomach with self-satisfaction.

"It's because he doesn't listen to me!" said Rita. "I tell him all the time: 'relax,' 'take a rest.' It's like he's gone crazy with his work. He'll be at his wit's end soon."

"Do you hear what your wife is saying?" asked Boria sternly.

I thought: if he had heard the conversation about the boots for one hundred and twenty rubles, he'd have understood what was going on.

"That's it!" said Aliosha decisively. "Complete rest! To hell with it! I'm dog-tired."

Egor untied the knapsack and handed Rita the food supplies they'd brought: cheese, sardines, bunches of onions and fresh radishes, three small yellow melons, loaves of french bread. For the first time, it was really merry at the table and I wanted this lunch to go on for a long time. Although it ended, the festive mood remained. Boria ran to the well for water; all together, quickly and without noticing it somehow, we cleaned everything up, washed the dishes, and set out for the stream. Out of politeness we also invited Iadviga Vasilievna, but she said she wanted to have a nap after lunch and, of course, nobody said anything to talk her out of it.

On the side of the road lay a tire. How many times I had passed it without giving it another thought! But Boria, obviously pleased at having spotted the old tire, rolled it onto the road and it turned out that, with a little imagination, this thing that nobody needed could afford a great deal of pleasure. Boria tried to ride on top of it, even standing, shifting his weight and balancing. It didn't work; he kept falling and Egor and Aliosha cracked a few jokes about Boria's bear-like gracefulness. So they rolled the tire to the stream. And at the stream it turned out to be unbelievably handy. Ceremoniously, they took it down to the water and started to pretend that it was a ship and Egor, an admiral.

"All aboard!" yelled Boria and he and Aliosha tried to push Egor from the tire while the latter resisted. I simply squealed with laughter watching their antics.

Rita sat down on a towel and started watching the swimmers. I've got to know Rita enough to see that she didn't like the fact that no one was paying any attention to her. She was used to being at the center of things, and here it was as if everyone had forgotten about her.

After a while, everyone had fooled around long enough, and came back onto the shore.

Aliosha said, "You know, guys, I really envy you! I'd like to stay in the tent too... We'd reminisce about past times."

"What do you mean you 'envy us'?" said Boria. "Aren't you staying?"

Aliosha looked uncertainly at Rita. "Kitten, how do you feel about it?"

"Well, if it's what everyone wants..." Rita began and glanced expressively at Egor.

"We're not holding anyone by force," said Egor.

Rita gave a laugh and her eyes grew malicious—exactly like Iadviga Vasilievna, only younger.

"Personally, I don't get any pleasure from sleeping in a tent," she said. "There's no reason for Lioshka to stay."

Boria sympathetically slapped Aliosha on the back and jokingly said: "It's OK, it's OK! Sleep at home. You're a family man now."

"And you?" asked Aliosha with annoyance.

"Oh, me. I'd be just as happy to sleep in my own bed, but Katia will drag me out into the open air by force."

"I will," Katka confirmed. "I won't let your fat accumulate."

"That's life!" sighed Boria and threw up his hands.

And it was obvious that he had nothing against such a life and that he really liked it.

And who wouldn't like it? I regretted every passing minute and I didn't want this day ever to end.

Aliosha took Rita aside and heatedly tried to convince her of something, tried to talk her into staying. Then the three of them—Egor joined them—went to the village for the tent and knapsack, while Boria, Katia and I collected brushwood and lit a campfire right on the riverbank on a sandy cape. The sun was setting, the forest on the other shore grew dark, and the flame of our small campfire was reflected in the water. Boria said, "If I could only put this on canvas and then die."

"You'd better stay alive," said Katia. "You'd never be able to transfer it onto canvas anyway."

Egor and Aliosha came back and set about putting up the tent.

"Where's Rita?" asked Katia.

"Oh, she started to feel bad for some reason. didn't feel like coming," answered Aliosha.

I knew it. She'd probably been offended by Egor. Well, that's very good. It's better without her. Only now, Aliosha's spirits dropped and from time to time he looked at his watch, trying to do it so that no one would notice. But I forgot about the time. It was so good to sit around the fire, to sing songs accompanied by Boria's guitar, to roll some thoroughly baked potatoes out of the fire, and burning oneself, eat them.

Aliosha suddenly got up, hesitated a bit, and said: "Know what, guys? I'm going to go. Otherwise Rita will get upset."

"Oh, forget it, old man!" objected Egor. "It's once in a blue moon that we get together."

"I don't want to, but you know, really, she'll..."

"Well, you're just so... So let her get upset for once! Excuse me for saying so, Liokha,[6] but she's got you on too short a leash."

"But you don't understand... That's got nothing to do with it... Anyway, it's time for Valka to go to sleep."

"Wha-a-t?" I blew up. "Don't I have anything to say about that? I'm not going anywhere!"

"We won't let Valka go," Egor supported me. "And we won't let you go either! Borka, grab his legs!"

"Hey, guys, really, they're waiting for me!" Aliosha fought them off. "Without me, they won't go to sleep."

"They can catch up on their sleep during the day!" Boria snapped back and threw him onto the sand, while Egor sat on Aliosha's legs and asked: "Well? Give up?"

"Yes, I do!" Aliosha announced merrily. "I submit to superior strength! Get off me, you hippopotamus, you've crushed my legs."

He was very pleased that they wouldn't let him go.

"And in the future, remember," said Egor, shaking sand off his knees. "We can't allow wives to sit on our backs."

"Did you hear that?" Boria asked Katia loudly.

"You just wait," threatened Aliosha. "You'll get married and start singing another tune."

"I'll only get married to a woman," said Egor, "who'll swear an oath not to interfere in male friendship. I have too many commanders over me to allow my wife to give me orders, too. A wife should be obedient, like a sheep."

"There aren't any like that any more," declared Katia.

"Well then, I don't need to get married," said Egor. "I'll stay single. You'll still envy me. And what are you laughing at?" he asked, turning around to me.

I couldn't answer anything. It was simply that each word of Yegor's sent me into a gale of laughter, why, I don't really know myself. Egor suddenly looked at me attentively, as if assessing me.

"Alexei," he said thoughtfully. "This sister of yours seems to understand humor. How is she regarding obedience?"

"She's just the thing you need!" Aliosha said happily. "Obedient like a sheep. Or, actually, like a wolf in sheep's clothing."

"No kidding! Seriously?" Egor turned to me. "And you wouldn't be afraid to swear an oath of obedience?"

"I wouldn't be afraid!" I could hardly answer through my laughter.

"Here's who I'll marry!" Egor announced with a satisfied air. "That's it. The problem's solved. Come sit down by me and keep the mosquitoes away from me."

I sat down beside him and slapped Egor on the forehead because two mosquitoes were sitting on it.

"Brothers!" wailed Egor, falling back and rolling on the sand as if from my slap. "What tenderness in this touch! Valentina, I love you. Let me kiss you!"

He pulled me over to him and kissed me.

Suddenly, things didn't seem at all funny to me. Maybe if I hadn't liked him I wouldn't have been embarrassed. But I liked him a lot. Even when I was really little and Aliosha and he would come to pick me up at nursery school. Yes, even back then. Now I was almost a grown-up, but for him I was still a child. He didn't stand on ceremony with me.

"I've offended her!" Egor said sorrowfully.

"Don't you get worked up!" said Aliosha.

"Valka!" said Egor. "I was only joking."

Of course, he was joking. I felt that any second I would scream.

I jumped up and ran into the darkness.

The moon was completely round and beneath the moon everything was lit up for a long way around. It was a nocturnal, silvery, mysterious light and the moon shivered and the stars seemed to be slender golden strips because I was looking at them through my tears.

What should I do now? Go to the village? I imagined our cottage, Iadviga Vasilievna's snoring... No, not on your life. Better to wander around by myself all night.

Suddenly I saw Egor coming toward me from the direction of the campfire. He stopped in front of me, turned me to the light, and for several seconds he studied my face carefully. Then he wiped my cheeks with his big hand and said guiltily: "Somehow I'm used to thinking that you're still little. Remember how Lioshka and I dropped you in the puddle?"

I started to laugh. How could I not remember. How, at home, they had hurriedly changed me, covering up the traces of the crime so that mama wouldn't suspect anything. But mama had guessed anyway because they had put my tights on inside out.

We went toward the campfire. I sat down with Katia on the sleeping bag and Egor threw some brushwood onto the fire and sat down on the other side of Katia. Nobody asked us anything. And they didn't make any wisecracks.

The food containers were on the porch railing and from the room Iadviga Vasilievna's irritated voice was audible through the open window:

"She's only got one job to do! And she's late every time, as if out of spite! And what an expression she wears doing it! You'd think that she's doing us all a huge favor!

break! That's what I call a considerate husband..."

I took the containers and set off for the resort. At the pick-up window were several resort employees, among them Vavochka, Rita's girlfriend. I said hello. She asked in a sympathetic tone:

"Well, how is she?"

"Who?"

"Ritochka. Is she feeling better?"

"Better? What's the matter with her?"

"What? You don't know? Yesterday evening Rita was feeling bad. Iadviga Vasilievna and I sat with her until two in the morning waiting for Aliosha. It's really despicable on his part! No sense of responsibility."

"His friends are visiting!" I answered sharply. "Doesn't he have the right to go out? Once in all this time!"

"He has the right, but not when..."

It was her turn in line. She handed her container through the window and stopped talking. And I didn't pursue the conversation. I didn't feel like getting involved with her. I lingered at the cafeteria so we wouldn't have to go back together.

"Why so long?" said Iadviga Vasilievna with dissatisfaction. "You know that we're waiting for you."

I didn't say anything.

At the table there's a gloomy, hostile atmosphere. Rita squeamishly picks at her omelette with a fork. Iadviga Vasilievna, slurping coffee, states:

"The one thing that still has a beneficial effect on my organism is coffee!"

No one reacts to this comment.

"My God, did I get all upset yesterday!" she continues. "I smoked three extra cigarettes."

I can't stand it and I grin.

"Again she's grinning!" suddenly Rita says excitedly. "I can't stand seeing those grins anymore! Why are you putting on airs? What are you making yourself out to be?"

"Valentina," Aliosha says to me with restraint. "Your arrogant behavior is getting on all our nerves."

"I'll smile when I want to," I say to my brother. "I'm not going to toe the line like you!"

"That's none of your business whatsoever!"

"It is my business! Maybe it's revolting for me to see how they've turned you into a slave! And you're glad. Oh, Ritochka! Oh, kitten!"

"What insolence! What gall!" gasps Rita.

"Look who's talking!"

"Apologize right now to Rita!" yelled Aliosha. "You have no right to be rude."

"And what right does she have to insult me and call me insolent?!"

"You've spoiled our whole vacation!"

"It's you who've spoiled my holidays!"

"Be quiet!" says Iadviga Vasilievna. "Stop it right now! People are coming!"

"Good morning!" said Katia, opening the gate. "Bon appetit."

We smile and nod our heads, as if there hadn't been that ugly scene just now. But we smile tensely, awkwardly. Of course, they heard our arguing. Iadviga Vasilievna invites the guests to have some coffee.

"Thank you," answers Katia. "We've already had tea. We dropped by to say good-bye. It's Boria's father's birthday today, so we have to get there a bit earlier to help out."

"Lioshka, can you walk us to the bus?" asks Boris.

"Liosha, I think you were planning to finish off your article today," Rita addresses Aliosha.

"You see, guys, I..."

"Oh, well, if it's that..."

"Really, guys, you see, I'm actually late with this article..."

"OK, OK, we understand," Boria says reassuringly. "Why do you have to see us off, like we don't know the way or something? When are you planning to come into town?"

"On Tuesday."

"Call me."

"Sure thing."

I watched Egor leave and I felt a lump in my throat. I wanted to be alone as soon as possible and think about Egor. I knew that now I would be thinking all the time about him. Before, I had simply liked him, but then there hadn't been what there was now. This feeling had come to me so unexpectedly, had come and had exploded into a multitude of sensations, and now I had to be alone for a while in order to figure out all of these feelings and emotions.

Rita suddenly said in an insulting tone:

"I thought you wouldn't tear yourself away and that you'd go dragging along with them."

"Why should I drag along with them?"

"Well, I don't know why," she said, hinting at something. "Only don't get any high hopes. That place was taken a long time ago and for good!"

"What are you talking about, kitten?" asked Aliosha.

"She and I know what about," she answered.

How I hated her at that moment! How I wanted to take revenge on her somehow! So that she would be as hurt as I was.

"I'm not going to take your food containers anymore!" I announced.

That was stupid. As if it would hurt her. But nothing smarter had occurred to me at that moment.

"Oh, how you've frightened us!" remarked Rita mockingly. "How will we get along without you?"

"I was just going to tell you," announced Iadviga Vasilievna. "We've decided to free you of your responsibility which you carry out so unconscientiously. Rita will go to the cafeteria. Actually, the outings will be very healthy for her."

"Well, let her go," I answered. "It's better for me. I can get alone just fine without your lunches."

"It can only do you some good," said Rita.

I got up and left without saying a word.

"Don't get any high hopes, that place is taken!"

How could she have guessed? But then, she's got a nose for that kind of thing. Could she really be right? Does Egor love her even now and is only hiding it? And why not? After all, I hide it.

It was getting close to lunchtime—a twinge of hunger reminded me of that.

I slowly returned to the village by way of my footpath. Now there was nowhere to hurry; I was only afraid that I would meet Rita with the food containers, and I got angry ahead of time. What right does she have to walk along here? This is my path. But she'll come this way, of course, just to spite me.

I got to the ravine and the sight of the steps cut into the steep slope really enraged me.

An amusing idea came to me. I even burst out laughing. It was quite a cruel idea, but at that moment it seemed ingenious. I searched in the bushes for the shovel with the partly broken-off handle.

In my childhood, there was this game. We would dig a small hole in the ground, cover it with a bit of glass, and drop a fly into it. Through the glass, it was interesting to observe the fly crawling, looking for an opening, and battering against the glass.

But this time, my hole wouldn't be for a fly.

Only, could I do it in time? But then, Rita always dawdles and can't leave home without getting herself all dolled-up.

Why was I so sure that Rita was the one who'd land up in this hole? Few people walked along this path, but, still, there were others who could take it. Of course, there was the risk that my vengeance would fall not on the person it was aimed at, but a risk, I decided, was a noble thing.

Using a shovel with a partly broken handle was not very easy. I dug the hole on my knees. I dug and all the time kept looking up: was she coming? No, she wasn't. If only I could get it done in time. I dug with a kind of joyful inspiration.

Finally the trap was ready. It wasn't very deep, just the kind that you could fall into up to your ankle. O.K., that would do. Now to camouflage it. Laid lengthwise and across, the slender branches formed a lattice. I put grass and leaves on it, so that the earth wouldn't cave in on the inside. And earth went on top of it all. I levelled the ground and dusted off my hands. I stepped back and cast a critical glance at my handiwork. I went back and powdered the too-obviously fresh earth with some dry earth and sprinkled it with leaves. A feeling of joyful malicious pleasure gripped me in anticipation when I imagined Rita ending up in the hole.

I tossed the shovel into the bushes and went to the resort.

I waited for a long time at the cafeteria, but Rita still didn't come. All of the resort employees had already got their lunches. The cook closed the pick-up window.

It was clear that my vengeance had worked and I suddenly became anxious. I had to get back to the village as fast as possible. Was something awaiting me there?

As if in answer to these thoughts, events began to unfold, events which I would really like to forget about, but I know that I never will.

I caught sight of Aliosha running along the grounds of the resort. His run, and especially his shocked face, disrupted the slow, lazy pace and atmosphere of this place with such force of contrast that the vacationers suddenly stopped their leisurely activities and all eyes were turned on Aliosha. He ran up to a group which was sitting on a bench and said something to them. Immediately, this group, as if infected by his excitement, set off with him at a run. Someone was already removing the tarpaulin cover from the bright-red Zhiguli that was parked beyond the volleyball court, and a bald, fat man in pajamas ran into the building and returned dressed in city clothes. He unlocked the car door and got in behind the wheel.

I came up really close, but Aliosha seemed not to notice me. A crowd had gathered by the car. I listened to the conversation.

"It's less than six kilometers."

"Six to Mikhailovskoe and then another two after that."

"It's a small hospital, but they say the doctor there's good."

My heart sank. I really only wanted to...

I pulled at my brother's arm.

"Aliosha..."

His gaze settled on my face.

"Get in, you can help," he said curtly.

The car started off. Aliosha was silent, his lips tightly pressed together, his eyes... I'd never seen him with such eyes before.

"Which cottage?" asked the fat man.

Aliosha's lips parted:

"This one. Right here. By the porch."

On the porch, on the same bench where Rita had chatted with her girlfriends, sat Iadviga Vasilievna, Rita lying with her head on her mother's knees. Rita's face was incredibly white, her eyes wide and frightened. Next to her, sitting on a stool, was Vavochka, holding Rita's hand and saying something as if comforting her.

Rita turned her head and looked indifferently at me, at Aliosha, at the fat man.

"Ritochka, here's a man with a car," said Aliosha. "We'll take you right now. Everything will be fine. They say there's a fabulous doctor there."

Rita suddenly burst into tears. Aliosha picked her up and carried her in his arms to the car. Iadviga Vasilievna started to bustle about; she gathered some of Rita's things and put them in a bag. Vavochka helped her.

Aliosha carefully stepped down from the porch, placed Rita in the back seat, and sat down beside her. Iadviga Vasilievna was sitting beside the driver. The car moved along the village street, carefully negotiating the potholes.

"Oh, why did this have to happen!" said Vavochka.

"What's the matter with her foot?" I dared to ask.

"With her foot? If only it were her foot! She's going to have a baby!"

"Who?"

"What do you mean—who? Rita!"

"A baby?!"

... So that's why...

It was as if the words that explained everything to me suddenly appeared on a clean sheet of paper.

That's why Aliosha was being so considerate! That's why there's such concern in his eyes when he looks at Rita! That's the reason for his guarded phrases: "You know, after all, she's..." "No, you don't understand..."

That's why he had carved out the steps in the ravine!

"Come on! You really didn't know?" Vavochka was amazed. "Why, it's her fifth month, it's already noticeable! Why did this have to happen: she stepped in a burrow."

"A burrow?..."

"Yes, you know, there in the ravine... And now who knows how things will turn out. Whether they'll save the baby. The thing is, she wanted a little girl so much. They predicted it would be a girl. And Aliosha wanted a little girl too."

I put my hand over my mouth. I hadn't wanted to kill a little girl.

The food containers were scattered over the floor of the ravine. I searched for the shovel and filled in the hole, carefully stamping down the earth. Then I sat down on one of the steps and for a long time remained there in a dull stupor.

And I had always thought that a murderer was someone unsavory, heartless, and not a person who saw the world through the same eyes as I do. But maybe this was even more horrible.

To love everything around one, to pity the poor wild strawberry—and to dig a hole for a human being. With my whole being, I realized in these minutes—or hours—that a person is more important than a flower, a bug, or a dog, and that the thread that divides his strength from his weakness is very fine and it's so easy to cut that thread in two with a rusty metal shovel if that shovel falls into someone's vengeful, ruthless hands.

How could I go on living?

In the opening between the trees the road was visible and along this road, a bright-red car passed, heading in the direction of the resort.

I gathered up the food containers and slowly trudged back to the village.

Translated by Teresa Polowy

From *Beloe chudo,* Moscow, 1982

Notes

1. Aliosha is a diminutive form of the name Alexei. Other diminutive and endearing forms for Alexei used in this story are Liosha, Lioshka, Lioshk.

2. "Thunderstorm" (*Groza,* 1946) by Nikolai Alekseevich Zabolotsky (1903-58). Zabolotsky was associated with the "oberiuty" group led by Daniel Kharms in the late 1920s. His poetry contained elements of absurdism, primitivism, grotesque, satire, and futurism. He was arrested in 1938 on the allegation of belonging to a terrorist organization and spent eight years in a hard labor camp.

3. These forms are simpering diminutives of Valeria or Varvara and Tatiana, Tamara or Natalia, respectively. Equally nauseating American equivalents would be Barbie and Tattie, Tammy, or Nattie.

4. Ritul is an affectionate diminutive of Rita, as is Ritochka, used later the story.

5. At most places of work, Soviets typically acknowledged supposedly outstanding employees by placing their names and photographs on a "board of honor" on the wall. The practice was intended to stimulate co-workers to comparable feats.

6. Liokha is a pejorative form of Alexei. Its use here underscores the speaker's disapproval of the control that Rita exerts over Aliosha.

Where Did the Streetcar Go
Irina Polianskaia

We all knew our town was small. It was a small town, but it did have a streetcar—a squeaky red car with an enormous current collector which jutted out of the roof, shooting purple and green sparks. We rode it; we sat on its yellow wooden benches, bragging to each other about our tickets (we didn't get them that often). There were handles hanging from the metal bar that extended the length of the car and the passengers who couldn't reach the bar gripped the handles, swaying with the motions of the streetcar. There we sat, and when you tried to get up and give your seat to an old lady, from all sides you heard cries of, "Sit down, sit down, you're still little."

"You've got tickets, so sit down," said the conductor. "Yes, we've got 'em," we said to everyone and showed our tickets again.

The streetcar ran north to south, from the part of town known as Stropy to the Pogulianka section. There was a cemetery on the Stropy hills and from a distance, if you peered out the window of the streetcar, the graves resembled the steps of a staircase with pine trees towering above them. Sometimes we'd go and walk in the cemetery. We'd read the inscriptions on the gravestones. Actually, I read them to you—you couldn't read then. We'd sigh and put a stem of wormwood or a clover flower on the tombstone and we'd never touch the candy that was left there[1] (frankly, we didn't want to). Once, as we were wandering around, we stumbled upon Yuris's small, fresh grave. It was winter. The inscription was covered with snow, but you could clearly see the little picture of Yuris.[2] "That's Yuris!!" you cried out and covered your face with your hands.

"Yes, it's Yuris," I had to agree. For three months we'd kept the secret from you that poor Yuris, who had such a good heart, had fallen through the thin ice on the river. In order to explain his disappearance to you in a way that you'd understand, we decided to tell you that Yuris had gone away.

"Where'd he go?" you asked.

"Far, far away."

"On the streetcar?"

"Yes," you were told, "on the streetcar, but unfortunately to a place where no streetcar or bus or train or flying carpet can go to now because there are such big snowdrifts there, the likes of which you've never seen before."

"I know why the streetcar doesn't go there," you answered, pursing your lips. "There aren't enough tracks, that's why. If there were more tracks, the streetcar would be able to go farther."

"What a smart little girl," exclaimed our neighbor Barushko. "She can reason like an adult."

Our neighbor Barushko was always dismal and ugly because his wife was always cheerful and pretty. He was dismal because he was ugly, and Taniusha was cheerful because she was pretty, and whenever she stayed late at the factory's drama club rehearsal, where she'd get dressed up in a fancy gown and assume a different voice, Barushko would come over to our place and ask, "What in God's name can you rehearse until ten at night? Tell me! I really want to know!" Our mama didn't know, our papa didn't know, but Grandma, sighing, would say, "Taniusha will be home soon. You can wait for her by the school. There's a dark alley there and she'll be afraid to walk alone."

"I'd better just stay here," Barushko would answer gloomily sipping his tea. "Someone always walks her home, and then she yells at me because I interrupted their conversation. What's on TV?"

We never got to see Taniusha when she'd return home because we always had to go to bed. In the morning, Mama would say, "Who wants a piece of Little Squirrel candy?"[3]

We did.

"But you know what you have to do to get a piece, don't you?"

Unfortunately, we did know. We'd turn our backs on that little squirrel but he'd snap his fingers, whistle and tease us until, unable to hold back, we'd go to Mama with our eyes shut tight and our mouths wide open, knowing we were doomed. In a flash Mama poured spoonfuls of cod liver oil down our throats. We'd quickly chase down the horrible tasting stuff with bread and salt, then take our candies and go out into the yard.

It was more interesting to eat out in the yard. Sometimes we'd share our candies with Stasik and Nonna, sometimes we wouldn't. Stasik didn't care whether it was a Little Squirrel candy or an ordinary toffee, lucky kid, he was indifferent to such things. What he loved most was fire. His little fingers itched to find something to burn, set ablaze, or blow up so that it'd go *kaboom* and *baboom*. All he talked about was where and when he'd make something go kaboom or baboom, and our parents, knowing this, watched him cautiously. At chubby-cheeked Nonna's home, on the other hand, there was always an open box of candies and if she wanted a piece she could just take one and eat it. And she did eat it, though not the way you and I would have eaten a box of candies: we would have devoured it all in the blink of an eye, without drinking it with milk—lemonade would have been better—and, if worse came to worst, we wouldn't have drunk anything with it. We'd just have eaten it, wolfing it all down. Nonna went to ballet classes. Peering through the window while standing on our tippy-toes, we saw how she'd diligently lift her heavy leg, with the toes turned out, her head with the tightly woven braids bowed down. We could do these ballet steps too, real easy, and even without ballet slippers, in felt boots! Stasik came with us too. Sometimes he'd toss a sparkler through the small open window and the flock of little ballerinas would fly to the doors out of fear. Stasik would then take to his heels together with Rain the dog, renamed Raindrop, who had been a colonel's dog but now didn't belong to anyone because the colonel had moved out of town.

I must confess, I didn't like including you in our games or taking you on our jaunts around town. First of all, you were a whole two years younger, and secondly, you were very seriously ill. Your illness, grown-ups would whisper, would sooner or later carry you off to the Stropy hills. Mama called me her "little misery," but she never called you this because you really were her misery. The rest of us, Mama, Papa, myself, and even Grandma, Nonna, and Stasik, were healthy. We were playful and impatient kids, who danced away on the wooden cover of the trash pit, who aimed Stasik's huge slingshot at the huge, dusty crows, who climbed up so high in the trees that we looked like large birds from the ground, who sneaked into the attic and the bombshelter, who walked on the river's thin ice and even stomped on it with our feet, who... There was little we couldn't do! But I couldn't wait for you and you couldn't keep up with us. I wanted to get you off my hands, if only so as not to hear your heavy breathing by my side after we'd run, see your paleness, your pleading look, your weak hands, gripping and pulling at the hem of my dress.

Once we were running behind Stasik towards the river.

"Come on, hurry up," he yelled to me, glancing back over his shoulder. "Hurry up, or the boat will be gone."

"Come on, hurry up," I said, trying to get you to go faster, but you kept falling farther and farther behind. Finally I yelled, "Wait for me right here!" and I dashed off to catch up with the others.

Just then, Yuris came up to you. We knew him—he lived in a house on the edge of town, but his father would come over to play dominoes in the yard. Yuris was the same age as me, but he didn't play with us. He was busy doing his own thing, either building something in the school's workshop or reading while sitting on our swing, waiting for his father.

"So you're bawling, are you?" he asked you.

"I'm not bawling, I'm just crying," you said.

"What's the difference, whether you're bawling or just plain crying? You're whining either way. Blow your nose."

You obediently took a new handkerchief from the pocket of your dress and blew your nose.

"Why'd they leave you here all alone? Are you a tattletale?" he asked.

"No. I'm sick."

"Sick with what?" Yuris asked with interest. "Do you have whooping cough? Or is it a nasal problem?"

"I don't know," you answered. "They say I'm sick. I think I'm sick too because I can't run like the other kids and I can't keep up with anyone."

"Ah, phooey," Yuris countered. "Come on, catch me." And off he ran, his feet in their sneakers taking teeny tiny steps. You took several hesitant steps and reached out for him, but he dodged you, ran ahead, stopped, and beckoned to you. You caught up with him by the maple tree and grabbed him by the sleeve of the wide knit sweater he wore, which hung, dangling on him.

"There, you see?" said Yuris. "And you say you're sick."

And that's how you got to be friends. You became inseparable. And I could go off and do whatever I wanted.

After school Yuris would stand under our window and yell for you. Mama's eyes darkened over with sorrow, but she'd crack a dry smile, saying, "Your admirer's come to see you, darling."

"Your fiancé," prompted Grandma.

Mama then said to Grandma, "This boy comes from a very poor family. Just looking at him your heart goes out to him because he's so thin. Wrap up a pirozhok for him."

You went out to Yuris and said, "Yuris, you're my fiancé. I'll grow up like Taniusha Barushko and we'll get married, okay?"

"No, it's not okay," Yuris objected. "I can't marry you. You see, I've decided to become a sailor. I'll be going out to sea."

Tears filled your eyes.

"What have I done to deserve this?!" he exclaimed. "Oh, all right. You can think of me as your fiancé, just please blow your nose."

Your took out your handkerchief, blew your nose and with the other hand held out the pirozhok to Yuris.

"Ummm, it's really good," said Yuris, taking a bite.

"You eat, Yuris, go ahead. You're from a poor family," you said sympathetically.

Yuris shot you a hard look, then with his gaze shifting towards our window, he drew his arm back, and, with all of his might, hurled the pirozhok on the ground. Then he turned and, shoving his hands deep in his pockets, stalked away.

"A-a-a-a-ah!"

You yelled so loudly that the policeman standing on the corner spun around like a red and gray top.[4] Yuris began to walk slower and slower. Even after you fell silent Yuris could still hear your yell ringing clearly in his ears. Finally he stopped, turned around, and ran to you as fast as his legs would carry him. Trying to anticipate his request, you blew your nose.

"A fine to-do this is," grumbled Yuris, once he'd caught his breath. "Looks like I'm stuck with you whether I want to be or not, my little misery."

"Yes, Yuris," you agreed uneasily.

It seems that Yuris didn't really care for either of his parents, but all the same he showed some preference for his father, even though he drank wine and people called him a good-for-nothing. Sometimes Yuris's mama would beat Yuris's papa with anything she could get her hands on and there were usually people around when she did so. Yuris would turn pale, shake, and throw himself between them. But after a time he got used to it and would simply turn away when he saw his mother sneaking up on the domino players with a ladle in her hand. Yuris's father was very thin, almost as thin as Yuris, but when he would slam a domino down with the palm of his hand, sparks would fly from the table.

Our dear papa, on the other hand, holding his dominoes up before his eyes, would slowly take one piece from his hand and carefully lay it on the table. Our papa was never loud and he never yelled like the other players, particularly Yuris's father.

It was getting colder and the domino players' table stood empty, but you and Yuris stood freezing out on the street. You'd invite him to come to our house, but for some reason he wouldn't come, maybe because he was afraid that Mama and Grandma would sit him down at the table and treat him to pirozhki. So instead he'd invite you to go ride on the streetcar with him. The two of you would get on the streetcar, chattering away excitedly, and ride to Pogulianka, then to Stropy. And you'd ride and ride.

Once on the way between Stropy and Pogulianka it began to snow, and during this snowfall, somewhere on the way between Pogulianka and Stropy, Yuris got off the streetcar. After that day, no matter how much you asked about him, no one would give you a straight answer, so you stopped asking. Once again I had to look after you and now you and I became inseparable. I felt sorry for you and so did Stasik and Nonna. Nonna brought whole boxes of candy out to the yard and we'd eat all of them, washing them down with the snow that kept falling and falling.

For some reason, during this winter Mama began to fight an awful lot with Papa, which broke our hearts. They yelled at each other in horrible voices, which seemed to wilt the geranium and the gloxinia on the windowsill and made the milk turn sour. Mama would bang her fists on the table, insisting that she'd understood everything for some time now. Then she called some Taniusha or other something not very nice. Later I realized that they were talking about Taniusha Barushko and that our Papa was meeting her and walking her home after her drama rehearsals. Papa would answer her in a muffled voice.

"Oh, so it was Mr. Barushko who asked you to meet her?" yelled Mama. "Barushko only asked you to do this once and you still go there every darn day! Ha, ha! It's like asking a fox to guard chickens!"

"What chickens?" you whispered, pressing your ear against the door.

I raised my finger to my lips and listened carefully.

"Idiot!" screamed Papa suddenly. "You're just an idiot! You're spreading gossip about Tatiana because she's not like you..."

"And what's she like, then? You already know, huh?"

"Uh-oh," you said sorrowfully, leaping away from the door. "I don't feel like going home. On top of that, I have this aching feeling, a real ache in my chest. No, I'm not going home."

"All right," I said. "Let's go to Nonna's."

"Oh, no!" you exclaimed. "Nonna's mama will start asking about Mama and Papa, what they're doing, how they've been, and I don't want that. Let's go ride the streetcar. I really feel like riding the streetcar now. Besides, you've got money, I know you do. Stasik gave you a coin."

"Okay, let's go," I said, and we got on the streetcar heading for Stropy. We rode past the house where Yuris lived. You looked back at its windows, but didn't say a word. The sun was setting behind the hills in the snow. The snow turned orange, looking almost warm, and then violet. The trees strode gloomily up the hill, the snow probably reaching to their waists. People kept getting on and off the streetcar. You kept clutching at your chest and breathing heavily (you did that sometimes) and I patted your shoulder. At the stop right before Stropy, Yuris got on the streetcar. You shut your eyes tight and then happily opened them again real wide. Then you sighed and reached out your hands to him.

"But you're already dead, Yuris," I said to him quite sensibly. "Why keep it a secret? He's dead, Sis, you know that, don't you?"

Yuris smiled scornfully. "Naaaw," he said. "Old people die, but I'm still real young. Besides, I'm not here to see you, I'm here to see her."

You sniffled and, wrapping your arms around his neck, pulled him down between us.

"Listen, Yuris," I said, "if you're alive, or if you just think you're alive, you still need to get a ticket. We've still got some money, enough for some ice cream, but if we buy you a ticket we'll only have enough left for a small bit of cocoa mix, but that's fun to munch on too, so I've nothing against buying you a ticket."

Yuris pondered this for a minute. "Well, ice cream is still better than a bit of cocoa," he said. "There's more of it and you'll only get a little bit of cocoa. Don't bother buying a ticket," he decided. "If something happens, I'll just disappear and that's it."

"Why do we keep riding and riding," you suddenly said, "when we've already passed the last stop and the ring. There's Stropy, there's the cemetery, there's the grave of the fat man with the moustache, there's the cross, there's the stone with the dove on it, there's the little grave..." You stumbled. "I'm sorry, Yuris, but that's your grave..."

"Which one? That one? Doesn't look like it at all. Are you sure?" he asked.

"That's it all right," I answered. "I wouldn't want to upset you, Yuris, but that is your grave."

"I don't think so," muttered Yuris. "There's a poplar tree growing overhead, and I never liked these trees, not like maples or pine trees. True, it looks like that's my ball over there beyond the fence,[5] but I must be wrong. That's some other boy's ball."

You burst into tears because you knew that this was indeed Yuris's ball. It was a red, white and green inflatable ball, which had already lost a lot of its air and was losing shape.

"It is your ball, Yuris. I recognize it," you whispered, hugging him and stroking his face.

"If you say so, then it's mine," admitted Yuris with displeasure. "But that's no reason to cry. Here's a handkerchief. Let me wipe your nose."

"Your handkerchief's so clean, Yuris," you said, swallowing your tears. "You never had one this clean before. Actually, you never even had a handkerchief."

"Now I have one," said Yuris, embarrassed.

"And I've never seen this school uniform on you either," you said, sobbing. "Yuris, oh, Yuris, you always wore a knit sweater."

"Where are we going?" I interrupted. "You can't even see the cemetery anymore."

"I don't know," said Yuris happily. "We're just riding. Nothing wrong with that, is there?"

"No, of course there's nothing wrong with it, but we've already gone a long ways and you still don't have a ticket. If we were only going a couple of stops, you could get away with it. But we've ridden pretty far and what if someone asks me 'Where's that boy's ticket?' What can I say?"

"Who's going to ask?" objected Yuris. "Everyone's already got off."

We glanced behind us, and, sure enough, there wasn't anyone on the streetcar besides us. No conductor, no passengers. And the cubicle where the driver had sat shone green, like an aquarium, and seaweed coiled around the driver's seat and a green star was swimming, barely moving its fins.

"Where on earth are we?" I exclaimed. "I don't understand, do you, Sis? We went past Stropy and I don't know what comes after Stropy."

"Past Stropy is Moscow," you explained quite calmly. "Papa brought us these fur coats from there."

"Yuris, aren't you cold without a hat?" you asked. "Yuris, where's your rabbit fur hat?"

Yuris thought for a moment. "Who the hell knows," he said finally. "I've been without a hat for a while now and honestly, I'm not cold."

"And where's your gray coat and your plaid scarf, Yuris?" you persisted.

"What difference does it make?" said Yuris, shrugging his shoulders. "I don't have a coat and I don't have a hat. What does that mean? That I'm not a real person without them? The only bad thing is that the shirt under this uniform is white. It gets dirty real easily and I'll have to wash it a lot. But that's okay, sailors are always nice and neat, so I'll just wash my shirt a lot."

"I'll wash it for you, Yuris," you promised.

"Listen," said Yuris, "don't hug me like that. You're choking me."

"I'm afraid you'll leave again, Yuris," you said with a shudder.

"Well, I probably will leave soon. Sorry, but I've got other things to do," answered Yuris. He motioned with his hand towards the ground, above which we continued to rise higher and higher. "Oh, it's so much fun to tumble into a snowdrift from this height!" he exclaimed. "Look, there's Kraslava. That's where I was born! See?" he said to you triumphantly. "I was born there!"

But you were afraid to take your eyes off him.

Suddenly, something gripped at my heart. The glowing depths of the snow below made me feel so uneasy, so sad. The lights of Kraslava, burning brightly like a Christmas tree, brought tears to my eyes. It seemed to me as if on the slopes of the hills below us people with torches in their hands were moving from all directions, walking one after another, the people held their torches high, trying to see us up in the sky. But our streetcar, flapping its wings, was flying deeper and irrevocably into the sky, while the torches below and the torches around us all became the same size and equally bright. We were floating without touching the stars, and our way was laid out by a milky glow, as the stars called out to one another—we could hear them—they were winking at one another, calling to one another, moving aside, making way for us. Some kind of night bird crashed into the window with her whole body and let out a loud scream, but you still wouldn't take your eyes off Yuris. I got scared and tugged at your sleeve. You kept looking at Yuris.

"Look, don't sit between us," I told him angrily. "Let me sit by my sister."

"I can't," answered Yuris. "She's holding me too tight. If I break loose and go sit somewhere else, she'll start crying for sure."

"That's right, Yuris," you confirmed. "I'll start crying real hard."

"But I'm your sister," I argued. "You should want to sit next to me. Yuris isn't your brother."

"You're right, you're my sister. But Yuris is more important," you said. "He's my fiancé."

"I'm not your fiancé. I'm a sailor," said Yuris.

"Did you hear that?" I said to you. "He says he's a sailor."

"So what? He's still my fiancé," you answered. "Yuris, I'm not going to let go of you ever again. I didn't let them see just how much it hurt to be without you, and they thought that I was just sick, so they kept giving me medicine. They tried to cheer me up, but I can't cheer up when they're trying. I'm sick and tired of them all, especially when they're arguing and yelling at each other."

"Are you sick and tired of me too?" I asked in horror.

"I couldn't stand it either when my mother and father would yell at each other. I wanted to glue my ears shut. And as soon as my father slammed the door, my mother would hug me and start bawling, as if a second ago she hadn't been screaming and stomping her feet at me and at my father. So I left them."

"And where'd you go, Yuris?" I asked him, cautiously.

"Well, here and there," said Yuris, without giving me a direct answer.

"I'm going with you," you said suddenly.

"Okay," he said. "I've probably been missing you all along on my travels too. All right, stay here with me!"

"What do you mean, stay here with you?" I cried. "What about Mama? And Papa? And Grandma? And what about me?"

You finally released your arms, which had been wrapped around Yuris's neck, and for the first time you looked at me.

"Well, you see," you said calmly, like an adult, "a streetcar's not like a plane. It can't carry you, and Mama, and Papa, and Grandma, not counting me and Yuris. Mama would want to bring all of her friends, and Grandma, all of her old lady friends. And Papa would want to bring all of his domino buddies and even the table they play on and the tree above it. And you, of course, would want to bring Stasik, and Stasik's dog Raindrop. No, no way. I'm sorry, but we can't take that many people with us. Find yourselves other streetcars and fly up to visit us. You'll be welcome. Yuris, open the door for her!"

"There you go," said Yuris without moving.

And at that very moment I felt myself being torn away from them, carried through the door by the wind, whisked into the current of the warm snowfall, which fell alternately with red, white, and green balls. I fell along with the snow, down and down, and the snow smelled of medicine and tea with raspberry jam,[6] while the light from a blue lamp was trying to burst some kind of sore open in my ear.

"Have some more tea, little one," whispered Mama, bending over me. "My poor baby."

"She left on the streetcar!" I said, taking a sip.

"Yes, she left on the streetcar," said Mama slowly.

Translated by Julie D. Barnes

From *Predlagaemye obstoiatel'stva*, Moscow, 1988

Notes

1. On the Russian church holiday of Famino Voskresen'e (St. Thomas's Day) relatives commemorate those who have died by going to the cemetery and having a drink and/or food at the grave, where they leave candy, bread or cake. In some areas of Russia this holiday is known as Radonitsa.

2. Most tombstones in Russia contain a small picture of the deceased, mounted in the stone.

3. A type of candy with nuts.

4. Policemen in Russia wear gray coats with red epaulets.

5. Grave plots in Russia are bordered by small fences.

6. Tea with raspberry jam is a common cold remedy.

A Woman in a One-Room Apartment
Liubov Iunina

Daria Pavlovna Laktionova lay still for a few minutes upon awakening without opening her eyes or thinking about anything. She didn't have to look at the clock, for she
knew it was exactly seven. Daria Pavlovna always woke up at exactly seven, though her
sleep was sound and she didn't dream.

Throwing off the blanket, she pulled her right leg up to her stomach, stretching it
abruptly, then the left leg, then both together. Three times. She got up easily, dashed
barefoot into the kitchen, ran hot water from the tap into a mug, returned to her room,
and sat Turkish style on the floor. Nursing the mug between her palms, she began to
drink the water in little sips, looking out the window at the working world. She paid her
dues to fashion by doing yoga exercizes. Who'd taught her this nonsense? Daria
Pavlovna didn't remember and laughed at herself a little for believing in it.

But forty-five is forty-five. The years make you aware of their passing. You may not
notice it right away, but they do. You have to do something about it! Of course, it
would be better to go to a masseuse, but where would she find the time? And yoga
took only five minutes. But she didn't tell anyone about her morning rituals. She didn't
like to reveal her weakness to anyone, not even herself. Maybe it was this trait that
always helped her stand her ground even in the most complicated situations.

Daria Pavlovna couldn't stand showers, but, nevertheless, she'd overcome her aversion and took one every morning. She turned the water not on to hot, not to cold, but
to warm, the temperature which made her feel the best. That kind of shower didn't
invigorate the body; on the contrary, a few minutes afterwards she'd be freezing. But a
shower was somehow necessary, she didn't know why. Not for cleanliness! No! Daria
Pavlovna made time after work, without fail, to spend fifteen enjoyable minutes lying in
a warm bath with a crown of soapsuds. She loved this. Daria Pavlovna was full of vague
prejudices that she herself scarcely understood. She was subject to many "mays,"
"shoulds," and "shouldn'ts" in her life, but she couldn't explain them to herself—she
didn't even try. Somewhere in the depths of her soul she suspected that she was turning into a hypocrite, but she wasn't exactly sure.

Putting on her makeup took up the larger part of the morning. Some women enjoy
putting on their makeup, but Daria Pavlovna wasn't one of them. She hated the length-
iness of this procedure. Quick by nature, she suffered from the need to make dozens of
slow brush strokes on her eyelashes. Curbing her impatience, however, she made herself up carefully. She put on foundation which freshened and slightly darkened her skin,
and meticulously did her hair. She dressed meticulously also. Before she left she stood
in front of the full-length mirror and indulgently gazed at herself. From the mirror, a
woman looked out at her, smiling softly, quite young, quite pretty, fashionable, and
contemporary from head to toe.

Once on the street Daria Pavlovna got her big glasses out of her purse and put them
on. She set off unhurriedly along the street, enjoying the sunny May day. A green haze
hung above the trees and bushes. Sticky little leaves had burst from their buds but not

yet unfolded, this indeterminate condition of theirs seeming to anticipate their beauty. Daria Pavlovna loved this time of year.

She walked through the public garden, not thinking about anything and smiling for no apparent reason. A passerby looked at her lingeringly. She stifled her smile, critically examining herself as if from his point of view and, satisfied, began to smile again. Light gray pants, blue leather jacket, deep blue tight-fitting sweater with a high collar, blue shoes and shoulder bag. Daria Pavlovna was satisfied with herself, with life, and with her status in that life.

Those who had known Daria Pavlovna in her childhood and youth had trouble believing the metamorphosis that had occurred in her. A nice, trusting girl who got carried away easily, she had a rather uneven academic record. Most often she received Cs, but not because she was lazy or obtuse. Rather, her sphere of interests simply lay outside academia. She read a lot, but haphazardly, and every book sent her off on new tangents. For a time, *The Life of Marie Curie* turned Dasha into an "A" student. She decided to be purposeful and studied from morning to night. But then she chanced on Staniukovich's novel *The Indifferent Ones* and understood that one has to lead a wild life.

In the ninth grade Dasha smoked her first cigarette, but she didn't develop any great liking for tobacco, though there were periods when she would smoke. In the tenth grade she went to a restaurant for the first time and liked that very much.

Everyone who knew Dasha in that period of her life thought that she was frivolous and vacuous. Even her closest girlfriends didn't take her seriously. Only Dasha knew that she had another side. She didn't think about how she was then, she dreamed about how she would be. First of all, she would be very famous. Who would she be? That wasn't clear. Maybe an actress (she was an amateur actress), a writer (she wrote very bad poetry), or maybe an important civil servant. What grand dreams Dasha had! In her fantasies she saw herself in a white English suit at the wheel of a convertible. The car is parked, Dasha waits for her husband, while lighting up with a gold lighter. And then He comes. "He" was Lenka Kapustin, who scorned her love and called her an empty fool. What happened next Dasha didn't know. Her fantasy always slowed down somehow when Lenka appeared. She lived in her hazy dreams but didn't do anything to ensure their realization.

No one supposed that Dasha would turn out to be sensible. Only one of her neighbors, a journalist, who herself was a bilious failure, saw something in her. She told Dasha's mother, "That little vixen isn't as simple as she seems. I think she'll become an interesting personality, after all." Dasha's mother was astounded at the neighbor's remark. Dashka? A personality? For a while she paid close attention to her daughter, but found nothing remarkable in her.

Dasha began studying economics. At the time it was a profession without much of a future. Dasha chose it because it was rumored to be the field with the least competition. There was little chance that her "Cs" would get her into a decent university. But at the institute, to her own surprise, she started to study seriously and even to feel some interest in her work.

When Daria Pavlovna remembered her youth she was always surprised: Why had she lived so wastefully? So many years lost for nothing! But they weren't really wasted; she had simply grown up very slowly.

Daria Pavlovna's marriage had failed. However, it was her decision that life with Stepan just wouldn't work out. At that time Daria Pavlovna was a maximalist. She still was, but now she didn't act as rashly as when she was young. Experience had taught her to be more careful. Now she understood that Stepan was not really as bad as he had seemed to her at the time. He was a typical modern man; a little lazy, a little irresponsible. He didn't have a very good character, but it wasn't bad, either. With time everything would have gone smoothly. But at the time it upset her that he let all the family worries fall onto her, that he used his dissertation as an excuse to avoid everything. She had to admit that she herself had pushed him into writing it, but even after he defended it everything remained the same. Daria Pavlovna's patience snapped and they divorced. To this day Stepan worked as a senior researcher in his institute. He wasn't setting the world on fire, and more importantly, he didn't try to. Daria had outstripped him academically long ago, although she defended her dissertation later. She was already a doctor of science, a professor, the deputy director of an institute. If they had stayed together, Daria Pavlovna wouldn't have let him sit for so long, she would have made him move. She thought he had something of a creative streak, but was just very lazy. He was prepared to be satisfied with little if only he didn't have to worry about his valuable self.

Daria Pavlovna had never married again. True, she'd had several suitors, but none of them had been any better than Stepan. It wasn't that Daria Pavlovna regretted parting with her husband. She didn't. But had she been wiser then, she wouldn't have divorced him—she would have been patient and got him to change. He was no great shakes, but he was, after all, the father of her child. She, of course, had got used to her woman's solitude, so used to it that she wondered whether now she could stand having anyone constantly at her side.

Daria Pavlovna crossed the cool vestibule of the old private house where the institute was located. She went up the wide marble stairway to the second floor and greeted her secretary Milochka, who imitated everything she did so that at times Daria Pavlovna felt as if she were looking at herself in the distorting mirror of an amusement park funhouse.

"Hello, Daria Pavlovna," Milochka sang out, looking at her with devotion. "How are you feeling?"

Daria Pavlovna's wince was barely noticeable. Why had Milochka become so interested in her health lately? She wasn't an old woman yet, thank God, and she wasn't sickly. Then she suddenly remembered: a week ago she had noticed that Milochka was pale and asked her how she felt. "Oh, Milochka," thought Daria Pavlovna, "what a little fool you are," Aloud, she said with a smile, "I feel great! I always feel great in the morning, Milochka! But evenings are another story. Toward evening I succumb to decrepitude."

Everything that Daria Pavlovna said seemed witty to Milochka and she laughed. "Oh, really, Daria Pavlovna—'decrepitude'! *You* decrepit?!"

Daria Pavlovna laughed too and proceeded into her office. She was of two minds about her age. On the one hand it bothered her. Forty-five was too close to fifty, the age when they start to call a woman elderly. And Daria Pavlovna had no desire whatever to be elderly because in spirit she didn't feel old at all. But it sickened her to hide her true age. That's why Daria Pavlovna showed off her youthful appearance, health, and fitness—what she called being in good shape—while at the same time always saying that she was, alas, already old. She knew from experience that people believe facts more than words.

As always, the cleaning woman had left a small window open and Daria Pavlovna, who couldn't stand drafts and cold temperatures, closed it angrily.

There was a blooming poplar branch in a narrow ceramic vase on the desk. Daria Pavlovna sniffed it. The slightly bitter scent hit her in the nostrils. She looked at the branch with pleasure. Milochka, who had grown up in Latvia, always kept something green on Daria Pavlovna's desk.

Sitting down in her chair and glancing at her work calendar, Daria Pavlovna gasped. How could she have forgotten that today she had to go to the office of the local executive committee and squeeze an apartment out of them for Maxim Tumanov, who had recently defended his doctoral dissertation? She'd have to meet with the deputy chair Klavdia Agafonovna Agafonova, a somewhat conventional woman who always fought fashion and forbid her employees to come to work in pants. And having forgotten about this meeting, Daria Pavlovna had put on a pantsuit. "How stupid," she thought angrily, "I really have become a feeble-minded old woman." Of course, she didn't care about Agafonova's taste. She didn't think anyone had the right to forbid people from going to the executive committee office in pants. It was just that Klavdia Agafonovna could take this as a challenge and, out of spite, put off the problem of the apartment, especially since the problem was complicated. That's why the director had delegated the negotiations to the diplomatic Daria Pavlovna.

"I'll have to go home and change. An entire hour down the drain," thought Daria Pavlovna. "What a crank this Klavdia is!" She pulled her compact out of her purse, powdered her nose, straightened a lock of her hair, and the businesswoman's business day began.

Somehow Daria Pavlovna always seemed to have more work than she could get through in eight hours. At the institute they shifted a lot of things onto her because she could decide questions quickly and intelligently. She always had a precise sense of what needed to be done in one case or another and how to do it. Because she had extensive professional contacts, where others would have to spend hours and days on a problem, a five-minute telephone conversation was enough for her. She was not only a good organizer but quite prominent in her field. People respected her and listened to her opinions.

Daria Pavlovna liked to work and worked with grace. Although you'd think it would be impossible to work gracefully behind a desk. Yet there was a person who noticed this trait of hers.

The writer Valentin Skudaev had approached the director of the institute and asked him to give him the opportunity "to steep himself in the atmosphere of the research institute," since he was writing a novel, the action of which took place in the same sort of institute. Igor Vasilievich Popov, the director, naturally passed him off onto his assistant. He always passed anything superfluous and unnecessary off onto Daria Pavlovna, since he knew that she was more adroit than he at getting rid of the problem. But for the first time Daria Pavlovna couldn't get rid of Skudaev. Moreover, instead of "steeping himself in the atmosphere of the institute" he preferred to "steep himself" in the atmosphere of Laktionova's office.

At first he annoyed her. He'd come whenever he wanted, often at the most inconvenient time, sit down in the armchair in the corner, smoke, and stare at Daria Pavlovna with his round black eyes. In time she got used to him, at times even forgetting completely that he was sitting in her office. Sometimes, discovering him, she'd say, "Why don't you go look at the laboratories, Valentin Ivanovich? What's so interesting here in my office?"

"I visit the laboratories," Skudaev answered shortly, "But it's more interesting here. In the laboratories, there are only loose threads. You have knots."

"Well, you sit there, then, if there are knots," laughed Daria Pavlovna.

Sometimes, when everything would start quieting down toward the end of the day and Daria Pavlovna found some free moments, they'd talk. Once he asked, "Why aren't you married, Daria Pavlovna?"

Daria Pavlovna didn't like to discuss such topics and she got angry when people brought them up, but this question for some reason didn't bother her now. She shrugged her shoulders, "What a question, Valentin Ivanovich. My answer would change, depending on the year it's asked. So for today I'll answer with a question: What do I need a husband for?"

Skudaev was somewhat confused. "You're pretty, appealing... and you can't live just for your work."

"But I don't live just for my work. Although that's precisely where most of my interests lie. First, I have a son. He's an adult and married even. True, we live separately, because the three of us could hardly get on together. I'm used to giving orders and would order my daughter-in-law about."

"Why are you slandering yourself, Daria Pavlovna! As if you'd order her about! You're so kind."

"Me, kind?" Daria Pavlovna stared curiously at him, then began to laugh. "So, then she'd order me about. But, to be serious for a moment, it's my conviction that young people should live separately from their parents and raise each other. No third party should stand between them. So as soon as my son decided to get married I exchanged my apartment. And now I have a one-room 'bachelor flat' where I can live just as I like."

"You see," said Skudaev with conviction, "You live just for your work. But you work with amazing grace. Until now, the only people I've seen working gracefully have all been machine operators or field hands, who do physical work. I find you simply a delight, Daria Pavlovna!"

"Please," snorted Daria Pavlovna, for she didn't trust praise very much. Her life's experience had convinced her that praise was rarely sincere; a request usually followed it. Although in her heart of hearts Daria Pavlovna had quite a high opinion of herself—maybe even higher than others' of her—she kept that opinion to herself.

Skudaev took offense, "I always speak the truth. And I find you very interesting."

"As a type?"

"As a person! I often think about you. You're a pretty woman. You like to emphasize your looks with clothes and cosmetics, yet you never flirt."

Daria Pavlovna burst out laughing. "Come on, Valentin Ivanovich! Is it really becoming for the assistant director of an institute to flirt?"

"I didn't put it quite the right way. I wanted to say that you behave as if you weren't a woman. By your entire manner you make it clear that to pursue you is taboo."

"I am at work, Valentin Ivanovich."

"I think you're always that way. I doubt that when you leave the institute you hide the little 'taboo' sign in your purse. You strike me as an integrated sort of person. You ask me what you need a husband for. But, then, why try to look pretty? For whom? For your colleagues? They appreciate you for your mind, for your efficiency. Do you do it for yourself?"

"You're making it complicated, whereas it's much simpler. I think that one must be efficient not only on the inside, but also on the outside."

"For that it's enough to wear a severe suit. But look at your elegant dress!"

Daria Pavlovna looked at her dress with pleasure. It was a masterpiece of tailoring. She'd bought it in Paris, spending the last francs of her per diem.

"Looking pretty is my comfort. You know, Chekhov wrote, 'everything in a person should be wonderful.'"

Skudaev looked at her skeptically, while she smiled at him sincerely and openly.

But it wasn't really as simple as Daria Pavlovna had suggested to Skudaev. Like every normal person, she suffered from loneliness, though admittedly not much, since she didn't have time for real suffering. The line, "What do I need a husband for?" was bravado. Theoretically, she'd have liked to have a good, loving and lovable husband, to have someone protect her. She just didn't need a husband in the sense that she didn't need the status of a married woman for the sake of prestige. Therefore, to put it crudely, she wasn't planning to entice anyone with her looks. But a nondescript woman who's alone is one thing, thought Daria Pavlovna. She's alone precisely because she's nothing to look at. A pretty, elegant woman who's alone is another thing entirely. She's alone because she doesn't need a husband. She is happy as she is. In that logical formulation which Daria Pavlovna elaborated there was little logic, as one can see. It was simply that trying to be pretty gave her self-affirmation.

"Daria Pavlovna," asked Skudaev, "Have you really never dreamed about what is banally called 'woman's personal happiness'?"

"Sure I've dreamed about it," laughed Daria Pavlovna. "You know, in my youth I had such a crystal clear dream. I'm sitting behind the wheel of a white convertible (the pernicious influence of foreign films), I'm wearing a white suit and Lenka Kapustin walks by. He sees me and realizes what he's lost."

"And who's Lenka Kapustin?" asked Skudaev curiously.

"An unrealized love. Or rather, an unrequited love. As children we lived in the same apartment building and when he realized that I was in love with him he said that I was an empty fool, moreover, a vacuous one."

Skudaev smiled. "Now your dream's come true. You have a car and a white suit."

"The age isn't right, though!"

"Nonsense! Where's this Lenka now?"

"I don't know. We moved," she sighed. "I've forgotten how to fall in love, Valentin Ivanovich. I don't know if that's good or bad, it just is."

"It's bad. You're robbing yourself."

Daria Pavlovna disagreed.

For some reason today, after returning from the local executive committee, Daria Pavlovna remembered this conversation with Skudaev. Before approaching Agafonova she had gone home to change. She arrayed herself in a modest English suit, and Klavdia Agafonovna was extraordinarily pleased with the way it looked.

"Nice, as always, nice," she said, looking Daria Pavlovna over. Then she intuitively remarked, "I suppose you dressed like this especially on my account."

In appearance and voice Klavdia Agafonovna strongly resembled People's artist Tatiana Peltser. A veteran of the war, she had worked in her present capacity from time immemorial. Except for a few eccentricities, she was an extraordinarily sensible person.

"Of course, I got myself up like this just for you," said Daria Pavlovna. "I can't break the rules of your convent."

"You sly puss! So, what's up?"

Daria Pavlovna stated her business. Maxim Tumanov had just defended his doctoral dissertation. He lived in a fifteen-meter room in a communal apartment. The institute could give him an apartment in its new building, but the space allotment there was a little generous for one person, six extra meters. There were no smaller apartments in the building.

"We can give you a smaller one and you give us that one," Klavdia Agafonovna proposed.

"We'd rather not," Daria Pavlovna twisted her ring on her finger. "He's thirty-seven years old. What if he marries and has a child? Then he would need to change apartments again! You understand, Klavdia Agafonovna, that he's an exceptionally talented person. We have great hopes for him. We beg you to come to an agreement with us."

"Aren't the laws for you too?" muttered Klavdia Agafonovna. "And what if he doesn't get married? Why hasn't he married yet?"

"He's been working like a madman. To be a full professor at thirty-seven isn't exactly a small achievement. Now he'll have a chance to look around, fall in love."

"Good God," Agafonova interrupted Daria Pavlovna. "Any man who hasn't got married by thirty-seven isn't going to. Or is he divorced?"

"Of course not! But we'll marry him off. We'll certainly marry him off! He's our Adonis. And smart too."

"A handsome know-it-all. That's just as bad as a pretty, smart woman, like you. Aren't you also single?"

Daria Pavlovna modestly cast down her eyes.

"I'm an old woman already, Klavdia Agafonovna! That's not for me."

"Don't be silly! You, an old woman? How many meters in the apartment?"

Daria Pavlovna told her. Agafonova shook her head: it was a lot.

"Klavdia Agafonovna," Daria Pavlovna quickly started in, "you don't have to be formal about this. You sometimes give a twenty-meter apartment to a single person, and going by the norm that means giving a few extra meters too. It only seems too much in this case because he has the right, as a doctor of science, to an extra allotment."

Agafonova gave in unexpectedly quickly.

"All right. We'll think about it."

"Thank you!"

Daria Pavlovna stepped briskly through the anteroom and went out into the corridor, where she discovered the lanky Maxim Maximovich Tumanov.

"Hello! What are you doing here?" she said mockingly.

Tumanov became embarrassed. "Don't think that I came to push for that apartment. I just had a question to ask you, and Milochka said that you'd gone home to change, since you had an appointment with Agafonova. I realized that Igor Vasilievich had sent you in his stead to agitate for the apartment for me. I'm uncomfortable when a woman tries to take care of my affairs."

"I'm not a woman!" Daria Pavlovna answered haughtily. "I'm the assistant director of the institute! What's with you, Maxim? What is this medieval chivalry? And does your visit here really change anything at all?"

"I know it's stupid," Maxim said dejectedly. "But please understand that I find it awkward that you're the one who's running around to get me an apartment."

Daria Pavlovna looked at him with interest. What difference did it make to him who saw to his affairs? The result was what was important!

"You may be interested to know that I'm always the one who sees to such matters," she pointed out. "I'm better at it than Igor Vasilievich. He's somewhat awkward," Daria Pavlovna fluttered her fingers vaguely, "and I'll have you know that this time it seems to have worked out too, knock on wood. But let's not crow too soon; I'm superstitious!"

"But I'm not crowing. In fact, I didn't even ask for an apartment. It was Popov who decided that I needed one. I'm perfectly satisfied with my room. The only thing is that there's nowhere to put my books. Otherwise it's great. I have only one neighbor and she's an old woman. She even cooks for me and does my laundry. We live in perfect harmony."

"A neighbor. That's great," Daria Pavlovna said pensively, getting into the car that awaited her. "Are you also going to the institute? But I promised Agafonova that you'd get married. Otherwise I think that she'd have refused. Do you have a fiancée? Are you in love with anybody?" Daria Pavlovna asked casually from the height of her age and position and turned toward Tumanov with a smile, only to encounter a puzzling look on his face that seemed to combine alarm and fear. Experiencing a sensation that was strange for her, Daria Pavlovna hurriedly lowered her eyes and, without waiting for a reply, quickly began to speak. "What an early spring! And it's warm too! I like this time of year most of all!" She mouthed more empty phrases, meaningless words, without understanding what was happening at that moment between Maxim and herself. But something had happened, something strange, she felt it.

At the entrance to the institute he jumped headlong out of the car and opened the door for her. Daria Pavlovna went into the vestibule with the feeling that she was carrying her 'taboo' sign in her purse, not on her chest, where it usually was.

"What was the question you wanted to ask me, Maxim?"

"Question? Oh, yes! I wanted to show you the final theses of my presentation."

"Leave it with Milochka. Right now I'm going to see Igor Vasilievich. On second thought, don't! I'll look at it on the train. I have lots to do before we leave tomorrow."

"And these worries about the apartment on top of all that."

"Take extra money with you. There are many pretty knick-knacks in Riga."

"I'm not any good at that sort of thing."

"We'll look at them together." She nodded at him as she moved off.

In the director's anteroom Daria Pavlovna asked the secretary, "Is he in?"

"Yes."

"Is he alone?"

"Yes."

Daria Pavlovna went into the office. The director was tall, fat, and bald, and wore massive horn-rimmed glasses that made him look like an owl. He was talking on the telephone. When he saw Daria Pavlovna in the doorway he motioned to her with a fat finger, pointing at the chair next to his desk. Daria Pavlovna moved closer and sat down, crossing her legs to reveal pretty, round knees.

There was a pack of cigarettes, Iava brand, on the table and suddenly Daria Pavlovna felt like having a smoke. She reached for the pack and pulled out a cigarette. Popov flicked his lighter and leaned across the desk to give her a light without interrupting his conversation. Daria Pavlovna inhaled with obvious pleasure.

"Well?" asked the director after he'd hung up. "How did it go?"

"Klavdia proved quite obliging today. I did have to promise her that we'd marry Tumanov off soon. But I think that they'll approve the apartment for him."

"That would be good! He's a great mind! He never ceases to delight me! The ideas he gets! The incredible ideas!"

"Ideas, yes! But he's rather strange. You know, Igor Vasilievich, he came tearing along after me to the executive committee office."

"Really?" Igor Vasilievich said with surprise, "That is strange. I thought he was completely uninterested in that apartment—even against it. It almost seemed as if I'd somehow forced it on him. Surely I couldn't have been so wrong!" He got upset and started to run about the office. For his size, he was unexpectedly lightfooted.

Daria Pavlovna blew a smoke ring (she knew how to blow smoke rings and was very proud of it) and watched attentively the way it spread and dissolved.

"I don't think you were mistaken, Igor Vasilievich," she observed unhurriedly, "he was embarrassed for some reason because I was the one who went to see about the apartment instead of you."

"But how did he find that out?" asked Igor Vasilievich, stopping in the middle of the room.

"From Milochka, by accident."

"And so?"

"So nothing!" Daria Pavlovna put out her cigarette in the ashtray and got up.

"Ha," Popov said suddenly. "He's probably in love with you, Daria Pavlovna."

This sort of ridiculous insight was characteristic of him. Daria Pavlovna looked back at him from the doorway.

"Do I really look like the sort of woman, Igor Vasilievich, with whom men fall in love?"

"No!" Popov said sincerely and began to laugh loudly.

Daria Pavlovna shrugged her shoulders and walked out of the office. That's why she remembered now that conversation with Skudaev. So she didn't look like a woman with whom one could fall in love? Was that good or bad? Before it had seemed good to her. But now?

"Tumanov is handsome," Daria Pavlovna thought without any apparent connection. "But what's that to do with me?"

Going into her office, she got her compact out of her purse and glanced in the mirror. The results of this inspection didn't bring her any pleasure. She frowned, put away her compact, and tapped her fingers nervously on the desk. Milochka came in, holding an envelope out to her, "Here's your ticket, Daria Pavlovna."

"Thank you, Milochka. I wonder what the weather's like there."

"I found that out, Daria Pavlovna. The weather's good, warm. Warmer than here in Moscow. People are wearing short sleeves."

Daria Pavlovna shook her head. Milochka really was gradually becoming an ideal secretary.

"And how did you find out?"

"It was very easy. I asked when I made the hotel reservation."

"Milochka, you do stunning work!"

"I try, Daria Pavlovna! I armed myself with an article in *Literaturnaia gazeta.*"

"Clever girl! Thousands of secretaries read that article but didn't draw any conclusions from it. Thank you so much."

"Thank you, Daria Pavlovna. Your son called to remind you that they're dropping by this evening. At seven o'clock."

Daria Pavlovna frowned. She loved her son and missed him, but she preferred to have him visit on Saturday or Sunday.

Daria Pavlovna liked to spend her time after work in solitude. She almost never went out on weekdays and didn't invite anyone over. Worn out from work, tired, she arrived at her one-room apartment in the evenings, drew water for a bath, and drank a glass of milk or juice, or whatever was in the refrigerator, all the while in motion. She undressed on the move, throwing her clothes about on the furniture. An entire day of discipline called for unwinding and Daria Pavlovna unwound in total anarchy. Then she immersed herself in the warm, foamy bath and lay there, not thinking about anything as long as the water stayed warm. Then she wrapped herself in a big terrycloth bathrobe, put on her fluffy fur-trimmed slippers, smeared cream thickly on her face and lay down on her stomach across the ottoman. If she had work, she read and wrote as she lay there. If there was no work she watched television or read something that was currently popular. These evening, night, and morning hours belonged to Daria Pavlovna alone. She valued them highly because at home she didn't need to keep herself together or prove herself. Sometimes Daria Pavlovna talked to herself, especially when something unpleasant had happened. Then she strode about the apartment delivering long monologues. She never cried; never allowed herself to cry. You can cry only when there's someone there to comfort you, and Daria Pavlovna had no one.

She was accustomed to her solitude. She didn't suffer at all from it and with the years had learned to enjoy it. She didn't have to wash the dishes every day, prepare meals, and clean the apartment. She did the housework when she felt like it, or when the disorder got on her nerves, or when someone was coming over.

Her son's visit disturbed Daria Pavlovna's habitual evening routine. She would have to run to the store and make supper. But she herself had asked him to come today because she missed him, and they couldn't have their usual get-together that weekend, since Daria Pavlovna was leaving on a business trip.

Maxim barely made the train. Daria Pavlovna had already started getting nervous and was sharing her worries with her fellow travelers, two middle-aged naval officers, when Maxim appeared in the door of the compartment. He was all disheveled, like a kitten who had fallen under a stream of water and not managed to shake himself off.

"What happened, Maxim?" asked Daria Pavlovna.

"I'm unlucky," he answered gloomily.

The train started and the two sailors got up as if by command.

"What do you think about going for supper?" asked one of them.

"God forbid," Daria Pavlovna said seriously. "I live by that old saying: to stay healthy give your supper to your enemy, dinner to your friend, but eat your breakfast yourself."

The sailors laughed amicably.

"But you, Maxim, go ahead and eat!"

"No, thank you. I don't feel hungry."

The sailors left and Daria Pavlovna, having settled back into her seat, kept darting glances at Maxim with a slight smile.

"Have you recovered your breath? No? What did you do? Run the whole way?"

"I wanted to give you roses, Daria Pavlovna! I thought they sold them at the station. I kept running back and forth! Then I looked at my watch and saw the train was leaving any second! I ran and barely made it."

"What were the roses for?"

"You really don't know?" Maxim asked, surprised. "You give roses to people who are going away."

"But usually it's whoever sees a person off that gives them, so that the person leaving will remember the place he's leaving for a longer time."

"I didn't think about that," Maxim muttered confusedly.

"Give me your presentation, otherwise I won't get a chance to look at it!"

Maxim hurriedly clicked the lock on his small suitcase, took out the folder, and handed it to Daria Pavlovna. She reached for her purse to get her glasses, but hesitated. For some reason she didn't want to use her glasses, since that would reveal that she was not as young as she seemed. Daria Pavlovna glanced at the text: it was legible, clear and she'd be able to read it easily if she moved the manuscript a little farther away. But she immediately got angry with herself, deliberately got out the glasses, and placed them firmly on her nose. Naturally, Daria Pavlovna's glasses were the most fashionble kind, tinted a little; they even suited her.

She began to read but couldn't concentrate right away. What exactly was happening with her? She didn't want to show that she wasn't young? But she never wanted to let her age show. No, that wasn't it. Usually she kept up appearances in general, for everyone, but now it was for one particular person, for Maxim Tumanov. "What stupid thoughts come into my head," Daria Pavlovna sighed, and became absorbed in the text.

Daria Pavlovna had a good command of her field. She loved it and therefore always enjoyed talented work. She forgot about Maxim, sitting across from her, his slender neck stretched out, watching her with fear and rapture. She was delighted with the logic of his supporting evidence, the precision, and the depth of thought.

"It's wonderful, Maxim!" she said. "Although I don't agree with you on one point."

Maxim came to life then. As soon as they began to discuss the problem of his research he changed, became more confident and his eyes and face grew firmer. He argued with her as an equal! He was tough and there was nothing in him of yesterday's absurd knight at the executive committee office or today's no less absurd rose hunter. He forgot about everything, remembering only his research, and it made no difference to him who his opponent was—Professor Popov, Sidorov, Ivanov, or Professor Daria Pavlovna Laktionova, the woman with whom he'd unexpectedly fallen in love.

Daria Pavlovna didn't lose her ability to evaluate everything clear-headedly even in a sharp polemical argument. She remembered everything and took everything into account. She really knew how to think! And it always helped her. But today it was her undoing. Because his maturity and firmness in argumentation didn't hide the confused, tender, absurd Maxim, all the aspects of his character as a whole became unified in her imagination. And for some reason Maxim Tumanov both unnerved her and attracted her precisely because he was this, and that, and the other.

There was a knock at the door and the conductor came in with tea. "You won't give the tea to the enemy, will you, Daria Pavlovna?" Tumanov asked gaily. "I have pirozhki! My neighbor baked them for the road. They're really good!" He got a plastic bag out of his suitcase, and folded the edges down precisely, forming a vaselike container. "Try some!"

Daria Pavlovna liked his precision. Usually men toss everything out on the table without a thought for presentation. She took a pirozhok and bit into it.

"Very good! Your neighbor's an expert."

"Aha! She certainly is! She feeds me non-stop, but I'm always hungry anyway."

"Why didn't you go to the restaurant with the sailors?"

"What for?"

"But you'll still be hungry!"

"It doesn't matter. Anyway, I have more pirozhki." He got another bag out of his suitcase.

Daria Pavlovna burst out laughing, "How many of those bags do you have?"

"One more. For breakfast. But I think that you and I'll eat them all now. I'll get some more tea."

"I have enough."

"Oh, come on! You'll have more!" He took the glasses off the table and went out.

Daria Pavlovna took out her compact and unhurriedly powdered her nose. "Seems as though he's giving me orders!" she mused.

Maxim really did eat all the pirozhki. Observing him wad up the empty bags, Daria Pavlovna said, "You really do need to get married as soon as possible, Maxim. When you move to the new apartment, who'll feed you?"

"What about my neighbor?" Maxim said in surprise. "We already decided that she'll live with me. I'll live in one room and she'll live in the other."

Daria Pavlovna started laughing.

"Why are you laughing?" Maxim became uneasy. Daria Pavlovna laughed harder and harder. "Why are you laughing, Daria Pavlovna? Daria Pavlovna!"

After she had laughed herself out, Daria Pavlovna said, "Oh, Maxim, you're so absurd! The institute gives you an apartment of your own so you can work in peace. And you bring along your neighbor and set up a new communal apartment there! Who on earth does that?"

Maxim frowned, "But I didn't ask for it. I told Igor Vasilievich that I didn't need an apartment. I know how to cook and do laundry and everything else myself, but when I work I don't want any distractions!"

"Well!" Daria Pavlovna shook her head. "I'm at a loss for words!"

"Don't you like me, Daria Pavlovna?" Maxim asked, nervously looking her in the eye.

"Why would you need me to like you, Maxim? You're not a pampered miss!" Daria Pavlovna was rarely cruel, but right now she felt that Maxim was creating a dangerous situation for her with his candidness.

"I'm in love with you," he answered almost impertinently.

Daria Pavlovna laughed lightly, "That's enough nonsense, Maxim! Go out into the hallway so I can get ready for bed."

And he obediently left the compartment.

She got up early in the morning while Maxim and the sailors were still sleeping. She pulled on pants and a blouse, took her cosmetic bag and went off to the bathroom.

For a woman who doesn't appear in public without makeup traveling by train is a real trial. Just try to apply foundation evenly and put on mascara while the car is rocking and bobbing up and down. But Daria Pavlovna coped with the task stoically, fixed her hair, and dabbed Chanel No. 5 on it, on her brows, and behind her ears.

When Maxim and the sailors emerged from the compartment they found Daria Pavlovna standing by the window, smartly dressed, with a fresh, smooth face, a cigarette smoking away in her fingers. Daria Pavlovna rarely smoked, and never in the morning, but today her feelings were in turmoil, and this was already her third cigarette.

At the conference she and Maxim hardly saw each other because for Daria Pavlovna the presentations and communications at these gatherings weren't the only important thing. No less crucial for her were the meetings in lobbies, the conversations with scholars for which it was usually hard to find time from one's regular schedule. And besides, although Maxim was in charge of the laboratory in Daria Pavlovna's institute, as a woman she didn't feel completely comfortable going around constantly hand in hand with a young man. She guarded her reputation as closely as her life. Yet, although she couldn't always see Maxim, she felt his presence somewhere nearby, his gaze always on her.

It had been a long time—fifteen or twenty years—since Kireev, the pilot, had left her. Exactly how long ago that was she could no longer remember. After suffering through this rejection rather intensely, she condemned herself to loneliness thereafter. Since that time she hadn't been close to any man who'd take care of her, protect her, and always remain aware of her existence. Maybe someone was aware, but if so, Daria Pavlovna hadn't felt it.

Kireev was the blackest page in her life. When Daria Pavlovna divorced Stepan, she wasn't thinking of marrying again, of course, but she didn't categorically exclude the possibility. She met Kireev at a health club. He fell madly in love with her and she, apparently, with him. They saw each other for a few months and then he started to call less often, saying he was busy, and finally disappeared altogether. She suffered; her self-esteem suffered in particular because Daria Pavlovna most likely hadn't really loved

Kireev. Then she couldn't understand at all why he had dropped her. She couldn't understand it now either. But now she simply didn't care and only vaguely remembered that romance. How Kireev worried when she sneezed or coughed. How he'd run to the drugstore, bring potatoes, flowers, candy, give her kerchiefs, perfumes—God knows what he gave her, just to make her feel good!

Daria Pavlovna's evenings at the conference were full: she had dinner with colleagues, and this was a continuation of the meetings in the lobby, where they had academic and business conversations. Maxim also attended these meetings. Daria Pavlovna discovered to her surprise that Maxim really knew how to conduct himself, was witty, intelligent, widely educated, and rapidly became the life of any gathering. Sometimes she caught his questioning gaze. "This is the way I am. Do you like me?" she read in his eyes and quickly lowered her eyelashes.

Sometimes after dinner he came by her room for a cup of coffee. There they continued the scientific conversations that interested them both so much. But from time to time, looking at her, Maxim suddenly lost his train of thought and fell silent.

"What's the matter with you?" Daria Pavlovna would ask angrily.

"Nothing," he would answer. "Where did I stop? Oh, yes."

Once, after a telephone conversation she had with her son, he asked, "Are you married, Daria Pavlovna?"

For an instant Daria Pavlovna was speechless. What was he asking her? As if the entire institute didn't know that Daria Pavlovna had divorced long ago and...

"Was that your husband on the phone?" Maxim asked insistently.

Daria Pavlovna shot him a silent, sidelong glance and smiled almost imperceptibly. "It was my son."

"And where's your husband?

"I don't know," said Daria Pavlovna slowly. It had been quite a while since she had been forced to answer such questions. "Don't you think, Maxim, that you're a little too curious?"

"No," he answered. "I simply don't know anything about you."

"But why should you?"

"Well, you know everything about me!"

"That's simply by force of circumstances."

"You're not interested?"

"I'm a curious person, so I'm interested in everything."

"I'm also curious. But you're not just 'everything.' Why don't you want to tell me? Don't you love your husband?"

"You don't let up, do you?" Daria Pavlovna said testily, "I don't love anybody. I divorced my husband so long ago that I don't remember if I loved him or not. And it's not at all nice, Maxim, to pester an old woman."

Maxim didn't answer.

Usually when Daria Pavlovna said that she was an old woman it meant that she didn't really think that about herself at all, otherwise she would never have said such a thing. And the response she always got to her words was, "We should all be as old as you, Daria Pavlovna!" These words of hers were like bait for compliments, of which, if truth be told, she was really very fond. So she was disheartened by Maxim's silence. Did it mean he really thought she was old? No matter how Daria Pavlovna tried to prove to herself that she didn't care what Maxim thought of her, she just couldn't do it. She succumbed more and more to his charm as a person, a man, and finally, as a scholar.

It was not because Maxim thought she was old that he hadn't answered Daria Pavlovna. More likely, he hadn't even heard those words. He didn't care about Daria

Pavlovna's age. He was struck by another phrase of hers, that it's not nice to pester. For him there was something humiliating in that. Could he really have offended Daria Pavlovna? Well, he had asked about her husband. But he knew so little about her, about her life, and he wanted to know everything, so that maybe he could help her with something, be of some service.

Yes, he had fallen in love with her in Moscow at some jubilee or other when, after finally finishing his dissertation, he'd emerged from the closed confines of his laboratory and his monk-like room into the light of day and saw that the world was wonderful.

Of course, he had met Daria Pavlovna, the assistant director of the institute, a beautiful, elegant woman given to sarcasm, earlier. He had run into her at meetings of the academic council and at other meetings. He had read her works, listened to her brilliant presentations, respected her as a scholar.

But then, at the jubilee, an entirely different Daria Pavlovna appeared before him; womanly, festive, gay, witty. He danced with her and suddenly saw her feminine, cunning eyes. He put his arms around her slender, lithe waist, and her hair tickled his cheek. When the dance was finished, she gently touched his nose with the tip of her finger and said, "Thank you, Maxim! It's been a long time since I've enjoyed dancing so much. You are a magnificent partner. All the others are hopeless!"

They danced again and again and it was then that he suddenly realized that he had finally met the woman of his dreams. Of course, he had fallen in love many times in his thirty-seven years. But he'd always become disillusioned quickly because he was too attached to his work and anyone he loved would have to understand the important business to which he had devoted himself.

He didn't count on having his feelings returned. The very fact that Daria Pavlovna existed filled his life with joy. But she'd said it wasn't nice to pester her and that meant that she found him tiresome and repulsive.

Maxim got up and made for the door. Daria Pavlovna, baffled, followed him with her eyes. "Where are you going, Maxim? Wait! What's wrong with you?"

He turned a confused face toward her and Daria Pavlovna saw the suffering in his eyes. She ran up to him, took his hand like a little boy's, led him to an armchair, and sat him down. Oh why, oh why had she thrown out those foolish words "old woman?" Daria Pavlovna was sincerely suffering herself. Like a true woman she believed in the magic of words.

"Daria Pavlovna," Maxim said with difficulty, "Why did you say that I pester you?"

"I said that?" Daria Pavlovna was amazed. "I said that you pester me? When?" She suddenly understood and began to laugh.

She perched on the arm of the chair. Her elbow leaned against Maxim's shoulder and his light brown hair was so close to her palm that she couldn't keep from ruffling it.

"You little fool! You completely misunderstood me!"

Her nearness, the scent of her perfume, intoxicated Maxim. His head spun and he lowered his eyelashes, fluffy like a girl's. Daria Pavlovna lithely bent over him and kissed his closed eyes.

Maxim drew her palm to his lips and whispered, "Daria Pavlovna, drop everything! Marry me!"

She gently freed her hand from his, walked over to the window, and looked out at the square, empty at that hour. Maxim came and stood beside her. They both remained silent.

You couldn't say that men often proposed to Daria Pavlovna. Not often, but three or four times in her life they had. No one, however, had ever proposed with as much ardor as Maxim. She felt her heart overflowing with tenderness for him, and she panicked at that feeling because she understood that if she yielded to it she would cease to be the Daria Pavlovna that she had created for herself, the woman who marched through life so self-assuredly. Who the new Daria Pavlovna would be she didn't know. And she feared that uncertainty.

The sensible Daria Pavlovna, the professor, the assistant director of the institute, should have sent Maxim off to bed now with the warning, "Do drop this nonsense, Maxim!" But in spite of all her efforts Daria Pavlovna's inherent femininity still glimmered inside her. No emancipation, no advanced degrees, no high administrative posts could extinguish it. And that inherent femininity prevented Daria Pavlovna from analyzing logically as it lifted her hand and laid it on Maxim's shoulder and brought her lips closer to his.

Daria Pavlovna whispered, "Now go to sleep, Maxim!" and for the first time without any bravado, she complained, quite simply, "For some reason I just can't think right now."

Daria Pavlovna was leaving on Saturday evening, but Maxim had to stay for a few days, since he also had other business at the Academy of Sciences. Daria Pavlovna had originally intended to leave on Friday, but Maxim reminded her, "You told me to bring extra money and promised to help me buy a few things for my apartment."

"Did I really?" Daria Pavlovna feigned surprise. To tell the truth, Daria Pavlovna would not have wanted Maxim to forget her advice, but since he hadn't said anything about it she had concluded with chagrin that he had forgotten. "And why do you need these things when you're going to fix yourself up a communal apartment anyway?"

"You promised," Maxim repeated stubbornly.

They wandered from shop to shop, looking at vases, paintings, rugs, and candlesticks, but Daria Pavlovna had such highly refined taste that she couldn't find anything she liked. She couldn't just buy things for the sake of it, she had to buy them for some purpose.

"Daria Pavlovna, let's buy something, finally!" begged Maxim. "Even if only this painting!"

"I don't know," Daria Pavlovna answered pensively. "Where will you hang it? You aren't considering the furniture you'll have, or the wallpaper."

"You'll think of somewhere to hang it!"

"No, Maxim, it's rather green. Green's a dangerous color! If the upholstery is another shade they'll clash hideously."

They returned having bought nothing but a small ceramic vase for flowers. Daria Pavlovna found it so bland that it couldn't clash with anything.

Maxim laughed, "Daria Pavlovna! You're amazing! It would never have occurred to me to buy a thing because it was bland!"

"When you've lived to my age," Daria Pavlovna said severely, "many things will occur to you."

Maxim became gloomy.

"And there's no use being gloomy," she continued, still severe, but using the familiar form of address, "Just imagining we're the same age won't make it so."

They went into the hotel room. Daria Pavlovna took off her hat and put it on a chair. Some time ago she had begun to wear hats, since they created a certain imposing air. Daria Pavlovna was gradually getting herself used to an imposing style because she understood that the passing years would not allow her to keep up the sporty style she liked so much.

Maxim still stood by the door.

"Why did you address me familiarly?"

Fixing her hair at the mirror, she half turned toward him. "didn't you propose to me,

Maxim Maximovich?" she said, addressing him formally again.

"You still haven't given me an answer!" He suddenly rushed over to her. "Do you accept?"

"Let's sit down," Daria Pavlovna said sedately. "The train leaves in two hours, and we have a lot to discuss."

But she didn't have the slightest notion of what they should discuss. She knew only one thing, that she loved Maxim, and that he was the last love of her life. She would never love anyone else. She felt that Maxim loved her also, but would she be his last love? Daria Pavlovna didn't know. The difference in their ages was another problem. No matter how she counted, forty-five minus thirty-seven equalled eight. And not one iota less.

Daria Pavlovna could always add well. From odd parts she could create a whole, or harmoniously divide a whole into its factors. But now she couldn't make anything add up, so she remained quiet.

Maxim looked at her, a frightened, questioning expression in his eyes that appeared whenever he began to fear Daria Pavlovna's decision.

"Do you have nothing to say?" Daria Pavlovna suddenly asked angrily.

"Do you love me?" asked Maxim quietly, using the familiar form of address for the first time. And his quiet voice rang in Daria Pavlovna's ears like a bell.

"So what if I do love you?" cried Daria Pavlovna, "In ten years I'll be a pensioner and you'll throw me away because it's not becoming for a forty-seven-year-old man to have a wife who's retired." She flagged suddenly, then quietly added, returning to formal address, "I can't become your lover, Maxim Maximovich, because I am, after all, your supervisor. That would be unethical, again because of the difference in our ages."

And at this point Daria Pavlovna burst into tears for the first time in many years; she sniffed in an unsightly fashion, smearing the mascara from her eyelashes all over her face with her fist. Maxim pulled out a handkerchief and began to dry her tears.

"Don't cry, don't. I love you. The years don't matter. Men die earlier."

Daria Pavlovna began to laugh quietly, "Oh, you're a little fool, such a little fool."

She sat before him, her face wrinkled with tears and laughter, her real domestic self, as few people saw her living alone in her one-room apartment. And he loved her, this tear-stained, middle-aged woman. It so happened that he loved precisely this Daria Pavlovna, and not the other one. What could they do? He'd been late or she'd hurried and appeared early? Was this really grounds, he wondered, not to yield to happiness?

But Daria Pavlovna, glancing at her hand smeared with mascara, looked in the mirror, gasped, and ran into the bathroom. In a few minutes she emerged, calm, with a fresh face, her hair done neatly.

"Well, Maxim," said Daria Pavlovna, "It's not at all simple. It's too hard for me to change my life. There are dozens of pros and dozens of cons."

"You can't judge this like an adding machine," Maxim pointed out.

"But we have to."

"There's one main pro—the fact that we love each other."

"Today love is the main pro, but couldn't it become the main con tomorrow?"

Maxim cautiously kissed her temple.

"It's time to go. I'll stop by my room for a minute on the way."

He came out of his room holding a bouquet of long-stemmed roses awkwardly in his hand. Daria Pavlovna smiled.

"There's nothing to smile about! I've got it right this time. Whoever's seeing someone off gives roses to the one who's leaving."

Daria Pavlovna had a ticket for a two-person compartment in a sleeping car. Maxim looked around jealously: "It would be the last straw if some ladies' man were traveling with you."

"I won't let a ladies' man in," Daria Pavlovna said peacefully.

She hadn't expected Maxim to be jealous. This was another con, since at work Daria Pavlovna dealt most often with men.

But no one came to the compartment.

"Maybe I'll be lucky and end up alone," Daria Pavlovna said dreamily.

"Not likely. I'm unlucky."

But she was lucky. The train pulled away, got up to speed, passed the suburbs of Riga, and Daria Pavlovna was alone with her joys and sorrows. In the morning when she'd arrive, she'd get swamped with work and there would be no time to decide the question that had so strangely and unexpectedly confronted her—to decide Maxim's and her own fate. Above all, her own. But did Maxim's fate really not matter to her?

Someone knocked at the door and the conductor came in.

"Will you be dining?"

Daria Pavlovna sighed.

"Perhaps I will, at that! What do you have?"

He listed the choices.

"Salad, steak, mineral water." After a moment's pause, she added, "And give me a hundred grams of cognac."

"An old woman traveling," Daria Pavlovna thought, laughing, as she looked at the covered table. She took the decanter, splashed the cognac into the glass and drank it. Warmth spread throughout her body, and she closed her eyes, imagining how she'd go into Popov's office and say, "Guess what, Igor Vasilievich, I got married."

"You?" the director would be surprised, "To whom?"

"To Tumanov."

His mouth would open in amazement and Daria Pavlovna would leave the office. Then she would call Skudaev and say, "Just imagine, it turned out that I need a husband, after all."

"Ugh, what nonsense comes into one's head," Daria Pavlovna thought, "It's all because of the cognac." She tried to assess her future realistically. She had lived alone for so long with her habits that it would be difficult for her, no longer young, to change them. Could she change them if Maxim didn't accept them? And what about his habits? For many years she had decided everything to do with her life for herself. Could she reconcile herself to someone correcting her decisions? Hardly! But then Maxim's face appeared before her eyes, firm and decisive one moment and afraid and questioning the next, and she felt her heart swell with tenderness and compassion for him. No, Daria Pavlovna was utterly confused about what was happening to her and was absolutely incapable of making any decision. She just wanted to think about Maxim Maximovich Tumanov.

Daria Pavlovna drank another small glass of cognac and sat back in her seat.

The train carried her home, toward a completely unknown future...

Translated by Robin Bisha

From *Zhenshchina v odnokomnatnoi kvartire,* Moscow, 1985

LIVES IN TRANSIT

Poetry

Elena Shvarts

Imitation of Boileau

for E. L. Linetskaia

I go for poems that are like a tram,
Cruise busily along with clang and wham,

Show pictures in their panes, if but obliquely,
Mansions and yards on which the moon shines weakly,

The sheen of blindness, blur of sleepless times,
The clumsy canter of ungainly rhymes.

The poet loves himself, is greedly for acclaim,
Both gardener and plot of his own name.

His shredded wilderness, home of Dionysus, hangs
As if a cat had raged and snapped in hunger pangs.

The passion of it all, with plain intelligence,
Recalls the man who found the blood's constituents.

Your native language, hound dog tried and true,
Will even let his tail be pulled, if it's by you.

Yet, my young friend, I feel in duty bound
To warn you that the Muse is rather wolf than hound,

And once you've paid the Dread One your address,
Get used to the stale broth of loneliness.

The poet is an eye—you'll learn this in due course—
Connected briefly to a roaring godly force.

Torn out and hanging by a thread, all gory,
It briefly shares the world's ordeal and glory.

1971

* * *

Fate weaves its nets so fine and fair
For children to be caught in there,
But I—I'll tear the meshes and burst free.

I came into the world with palms unlined,
Smooth as a store-doll's, for some reason;
There gypsy soothsayers can find
No prison-house or wicked treason,
They augur me no love or harm:
On the empyreal sapphire floor,
Where cuts are whipped into your palm,
They had no lash free any more.
They did not groove my hand at all,
Or mark out stars on palm and ball;
They could detect no lines to mate,
For me there are not love or hate,
No chance reunions dealt by fate.
Instead, there calls on me at night
The ship of destiny, its hold
Crammed to the deck with fates untold;
It feebly nudges me, then with a whine
Dissolves—a starveling lot unrecognized as mine.

Beast of Blossom

The Judas tree breaks out in violet
blossoms along its trunk.

An augury of life persists right unto death.
A cold flame rides the bones and sears
When a quick shower of luminous rain appears
On Peter's Day, the first of summer breath.
Why, any day now, buds will burgeon out
Along my ribs, my clavicles, my cranial bone.
They'll write "Elena Arborea" on a sprout,
"Found in the ice-bound hyperborean zone,
In brickwork gardens or on turf of stone."
My eyes are by dark clove-pinks overhung,
I am a bush or roses and forget-me-nots in one,
As if a feckless gardener had for fun
Wrapped me about with heavy floral garlands.
I shall be violet and scarlet,
Purple and black and yellow aureoform,

I shall be in a buzzing, perilous swarm,
The sacred watering-place of wasp and bee.
But when I come to wither, woe is me—
What a gnawed-down hunk of ruin will you see,
Stiffened, and with its hide all split and creased,
A wizened, all but lifeless, blossom beast.

July 1976

The Invisible Huntsman

What's precious in me—hopeful sign or not—
May just turn out to be the random plot
Of birthmarks which bestrew my skin and belie
With darkling galaxies their former sky.
It's like a sketch map of the northern sphere—
Andromeda, Swan, Eagle, Charioteer,
Clustering, riveting, and planting rows...
Oh—how those categories frighten me!
What price endowments, character, or voice,
When skin is the criterion of choice,
And the unerring marksman you can't spot
Already lays for it as like as not.
A breed of turtles in the ocean rows
With marks like runes or letters on the hinder shell
(Mutatis mutandis, certain whales as well);
People will hunt them down as curios.
A flutist, let us say, was out of paper
On which to write some music to a mountain sprite;
As he awoke, about his endless night,
He was the first to seize a skein of white
To scribble notes on and then copy them
Upon the cotton-tender skin or an unborn lamb...
He looks for it, perhaps will find and kill it.
Sable, mink, and squirrel—do they know
For how much in dollars their small pelts may go?
May brain disappear and the soul fly off,
But the skin is not there for the bugs to eat,
And there you'll come upon my own skin, pressed
In close safekeeping like a palimpsest
Or like a snapshot of the heavenly child.
How can I hide, how clear myself, where be?
I sense a breathing, piercing glances from behind...
O all those drafts, to nothingness consigned!

March 1975

* * *

You swallow people, earth, o earth,
And bear them in exchange
Castalian spring, carnation turf,
Lilac, and a rocky range.
You, earth, in darkness chew your cud
And grow now slack, now tall,
And ponder in your mind of mud
How you'll outlive us all.
So stand triumphant, then, and pour
Your black milk all among,
You've blended with my blood before
And grate beneath my tongue.
O ancient serpent, you sustain
The grass, the flowering shrub,
And anyone who walks on you—
Bane in his heel you rub.

Two Aspects

I   I never thought I would live to regain
     Those overripe plums in the yeast-yard attain

     The return of that turnabout August-month night
     When not one fruit was spared the blight.

     While no wintry blast has yet been released,
     The tender-skinned fruit is already creased.

     In the froth of ripeness and dissolute zest,
     You go to sleep young, wake with death in your breast

     And whining old age at the tongue-tip, spry;
     She gave a great shout on waking on high.

     We are headed to meet on a common track,
     Changing eye for eye and back for back.

II   Until I shall skim among stars (my kind),
     With a glossy lilac train behind—

Till my mind is cleared by a frosty bloom,
It will burgeon forth with a verbal spume:

Like vines from the rifts of Dionysus' barque,
From me swift dragonfly swarms will arc.

1979

Spire of Cages

A stanza—is like the cage of a bird:
You hear a captive meaning chirp,
It may snarl like an eagle owl,
Wear an empress's fearsome scowl,
Or throb like a nightingale.

They rise, cage on cage, like some cathedral spire
That sings by itself with a spectral choir.
I would give you your freedom, but on high
There glitters a salt-encrusted sky,
And no windows or doors breach that citadel,
That involute spire like a nautilus shell.

But let me open the doors to the cages,
They raise a tempest like heathenish rages
In languages that never were;
Pushing and scrambling, they take the air
And chirrup and cackle,
And cock the ruffs at their throats
And shed rose-colored down
And spatter snow-white droppings,
And peck at each other and crow.

Of my blood they have had their fill,
Neatly tapping my veins,
And I myself—what folly!—have fed
Bits of my brain to each minute head,
Over their eyes fitted shards of mine instead,
And now we sing as the Lord has led,
And we roar and gurgle and shrill;
Cover us up and we fall still.

1972

Translated by Walter Arndt

Tatiana Shcherbina

I can't leave and I shouldn't stay.
Which circle is an orange, sliced,
and I every segment, this operation
lends me centrifugal force.
I shouldn't explode like Chernobyl,
terrorism in the air—shouldn't,
but nightly reflections of a reddening
knife-blade are inside me glittering.
Cut open, I am a holiday orange,
the juice in my veins congealing by nightfall,
and my cross-sections gape wide—
I detonate the airliner I ride!
They order me to land on schedule,
the fuel explodes in mid-air.
I am an orange artwork of the sun:
Write "I'm staying," when I disappear.

* * *

Sappho and Alcaeus

Could a lovely woman, the poet Sappho,
ever love her own rival, Alcaeus?
Suspended on a closet door
she stuck her little mirror before her,
embarrassed, when it showed small faerie lips.
In front of her stretched the glass, paler,
yes, against the pallor, like Zeus with Amalthea.
Under the fast-lane scrutiny of a lens
she started sweating. Where Orpheus went silent,
there Sappho sang, and never missed a beat:
"Reflecting, you admire what you see;
see, we are the fairest of them all!"
It glinted back at her. "Big deal, Alcaeus
was praising me, not you, above all others
with his 'oo la la! What a heavenly silhouette!'"

A mirror's mutiny, a meaningless prick,
but Sappho threw herself off the nearest cliff.
That necrophile, Alcaeus, cried after her, "Sappho!
What do I care about this cupboard door,
and what fun can I find in the armoire?
To mirror you alone, Sappho my own,
see, I've invented these alcaic stanzas."
"Alcaeus, I loved only you, and if
you truly love me—" came from far away—
"master instead my sapphic measures,
make them more popular than yours."

1986-87

The Stepmother

for Volodia Sorokin

Cinderella boiled up borscht,
pickled fish soups and jellies in a pot,
and over the windowstill
of a noisy, sun-drenched culture
saw her bit of landscape—
the tattle-tale of construction dumps—
while Joseph stepped into the bedroom
to his immaculate Mary...
In the clean golden pot
bluebird bouillon stewed,
and only ground black pepper
(like india ink enlivening an eyelash)
saved the little bird from turning green.
Outside the window a policy of turning green
encountered the cool morning, used an alarm clock
to climb in, so that the reaper, the merchant,
the smith of the creto-mycenean charter
saw not a panther at her side
but a known wheat farmer, a party member,
and if he breeds: it'll be a Pioneer.
But what's that smeared on Cinderella's mug?
what about her potty life,
the saucepan unflooded not even with blood,
resembling a funerary urn,
with an engraving of a tsarist gentleman
on the bones of the tenderest of pterodactyls,
already dripping with the adhesive tears
of hookers and golddiggers.

Meanwhile, Mary entertains her husband
and rails against Cinderella, not knowing
that because she is immaculate,
she is wholly unnatural.

1986-87

* * *

Women's Theater

(A play for any number of any kind of female character)

A mustard plaster won't rouse the fallen.
Colored tablets will simply swim in murky schizophrenia
Brains overhung an abyss of stomach like stormclouds
Hoarfrost stuck to tobacco-stained things.

It's fine to be colorful lifeless easy-going inside
the television, in its slightly open cupboard door
—Over there are mustered the old pepperpigs, over there the young peppers,
but the present time, like the Heavenly Kingdom, is incomprehensible
(and like a sheep: whatever its inclination, whether wool or milk—
well, it's incomprehensible and, well, what the fuck).

Watch me turn into a doll with cute nicknames,
let's say, a little match-girl,
a little orphan holding a light,
verily a vital role:
Prometheus of an unheroic time, even without a monicker—
just a little girl. Her light like a little match.

Or Cinderella. A life split in two,
by night in a fine gown dancing from ball to ball,
by day washing out the same gown.
A dual personality—everywhere, they stamp her down.

No, that's not it. Life is gentler now and newer.
I will be a Juliet, in love with my enemy's son.
A Montague, of course, a helpless, banished citizen.
I cross the border. They raise a tower to my love.
With my death I bury my parents' strife,
a political step in the insight of the people.

No, still more recent. Lolita. No *Wunder*. No *Kind*,
but under my ass—Richter's screw won't rise like that.

And it's passed in the senate, congress, parliament:
The children shouldn't be forgotten—
not suddenly put out to pasture.
What's left to Humbert Humberts?
    Interview the little ones.
Clear thoughts spring from secret little sufferings.

(And if they only knew what kind of soil
worldwide sorrow grows in, and quarreling,
then she'd never have given the gray-eyed king
his heroic role.)

Learn the lessons of history:
    if sacrificial pathos and righteous wrath
of dolls is transferred from the floor to the wall,
    from the portal to the nave,
and like a heavenly cloud she looks
    and suddenly sheds a few tears,
know: this is an empress. Catherine. Catherine II.
All alone in the palace
    like a sunbeam in a barn.

Chorus:

An enviable fate: not the madhouse, but with a little panache.
Take on this character; if need be, take another.
History is a play, and you don't stop its being written,
become a chair, a cushion to be lightly touched.
Oh, to be like them all, but reptilian, like them all.
A role transparent as shadow, you pass like a field marshal
    right through sense and style.
Where are the holy fathers? on the screen.
    And over there settlements for the deaf,
islamic piracy and artists with you in the weeding.
As if it were you on the edge—
    no, you yourself in an unknown grave,
this is your ghost here.
Having tried to catch my daydream on a wave,
    they twisted it under.
Alone in the æther it went whistling, unscheduled; and hooked me.
So look how I'm waiting now for these same puppet -masters,
to put me away in a box, tie it up in a ribbon
so I'll be nothing but an invisible presence
    in a box,
            or somewhere.

1986-87

* * *

What does an Apache feel in the other world
once he's survived every mortal venom?
That he's a tough guy from a clan of cripples
with a thinned-out, but still uncurdled brain,
that he is incapable of incantations
in other worldly tongues, that plans
for the planet are like a seahorse among horses,
preserved for parallel Euclidean ends?
Riding his own hobby he kicks up powder
along the waves of an ocean just as dried.
Of course, in that other world he too is dust.
But for him, you know, that might not be so bad.

1990

Translated by Jim Kates

Elena Ignatova

Lot's Wife

"You'll turn around..."
                              "I shan't."
"You'll turn around...
                              "I shan't."
"You'll see the blinding sparks
consume the town you owned.
You'll smell the acrid fume—
Burnt the paternal home!
O woe on Sodom's parks,
Gomorrah's pleasure dome!"

"I shan't turn round. By saints
temptation can be fought;
down rivers of gold
I am borne by the Lord."

"Down golden river streams
he bears you cool and fresh,
while there the smoke-bank screams
incinerated flesh..."
"What song intones the stream?"
"There tar and ashes glare!
High on the angel's gleam
His double pinions flare!"
"They are the guilty."
                              "Yes."
"They are transgressors."
                              "Yes!"
On sinners' flesh by right
is pressed the fiery mark!
A little child in flight
flares like a crimson spark...
"You're crying?"
                              "No... I can't..."
Your body's twist says:
                              "Yes!"

* * *

You read Herodotus, and ages flee
as Scythians battle Persians, these some other set,
and blood will burgeon forth—*your* history
rustles with olives, smells of peasant sweat.

The rugged stock of Greece is being ground;
now into Egypt speeds the trireme flock.
We cannot drain the bitter cup of others,
we have but names, like harvest stubble browned;
the path to yonder lands is carved in rock.

And where are these—the earth of Lydian braves,
the rivers bearing gold, the gilt brocades,
where infant World was still so sound and fair,
where blood from fired cities flowed in heaven,
where man was ruthless, naked, free of care.

* * *

The heavy fields of harvest grain
behind my window dance and sway;
the wheat is smoking, you would say...
Earth groans beneath a wall of rain,
the thunder peals flood half the sky,
the sodden air no bird will fly,
a dead pine bleeds a resin stain.

* * *

By an ice lake, abstracted and tense,
for my life's inscrutable sense
I am sounding its murk with my eyes.
The water turned rosy, flushed,
reflecting a cloud that had touched
on a kingdom beyond the skies.

Translated by Walter Arndt

Zoia Ezrokhi

* * *

I write of a plate or a stick,
or the germ of the common cold.
At times I can't make myself pick
a gorgeous mushroom from its mold.

To kill such a prince—I've a qualm.
To the summer day's melody
I hold a small frog in my palm—
it has no fear of me.

When I lie in my burial chamber,
then from forest mulch and ooze
mushrooms and ants will clamber
to tender their last adieus.

All the beasts I've sung will appear there,
And a mournful bacterium
will shed a clandestine tear there
as it slowly mounts the tomb.

The eyes of lost kittens will stream
and of strays in the canteen mews.
I'll be mourned by moot places and dreams
and barely discernible hues.

The smoke I have left behind
Drifts back for a hug and a kiss:
where else in this dump could it find
a soul that delights in this?

Who'll think smoke is the bushy tail
of a cat never seen before?
Smoke is simple and banal and stale,
and what's simple is a bore.

I'm nobody's wife or mom,
I paddle no big canoe.
And yet I am needed by some,
and I love somebody too.

* * *

In Lieu of an Epic

My husband tells me to write an epic:
Hours and days go by, he says.
You've done a stack of poems, he says,
time now to write and epic.

A new *Onegin* or Lermontov *Novice*,
he says, could really boost my career.
But nothing of any global compass
will arise from my flat, I fear.

How can you lure any epic matter
to a head full of daily trash?
Any pre-dawn imaginings scatter
with an ostrich's scampering dash.

Morning looms like a wall of surf,
half drowning you as you flounder across:
get on the list for the doctor, the nurse,
pick up that slip from the housing boss.

I'm sung dry—my clumsy passes
at the Muse find her mute and irate.
I'm bashful now about climbing Parnassus,
it's been padlocked against me of late.

Ah, poor dumb broads, live demurely,
stay silent and low as the grass.
Yet I, after all, could have surely...
But alas, but alas, but alas.

The Hook

To sow, to knit, to keep your husband sane,
These form a single intertangled skein.

A single hook (plied by a sorceress)
can knit a sock, a dream, or a caress.

A single needle, think of it, is able
to keep both hems and households straight and stable.

Me, I don't know, though, how to sow or knit,
or when to shut my mouth or open it.

I take up tatting, but my fingers seize.
Life's hard to do—but poems are a breeze.

* * *

See Abel and Cain with furious grip
contesting a toy car's ownership.
See Brother's fist raised up to hit
Brother, the toy car crushed in it.

1985

* * *

The Children

One is a scamp, Tom Sawyer fashion,
the other is like Sid, a lamb.
Whenever Tom flies in a passion
he vents it on the other—wham!

All day they're at each others' throat,
a casual touch sets off a bomb,
and every bedtime Mama's hand
is sore from all the butts it smote.

The slightly bigger one will stand
well clobbered in his nook and bawl;
the tyke, alas, I pardon all
just for the dimple in his hand.

Then, all intent upon some game,
their enmity for once suspended,
the two, bright manes completely blended,
will look uncannily the same.

Son

I flip this comical morsel
across my knees like a parcel,
aim the spoon at its muzzle and dig;
it slurps like a suckling pig.

The poor spoon zigzags and wags,
but as soon as the action lags
the kid has a fit, acting tough
like some grand vizier in a huff.

Matt squirms and begins to feel
like a boisterous overstuffed eel—
"bends and unbends with rapid sway
and twirling, trills the spoon away."

This terminates the feeding soon
and liberates the martyred spoon.
6 oz. safe in his insides,
the infant gurgles and subsides.

* * *

Expectant boarders, draped full-length
on couch and sill and chair and lap,
are threatening by now to sap
the last of my remaining strength.

I simply do not have the wealth
to harbor goodness any more;
I ought to kick it out the door
and opt for peace of mind and health.

Those dogs and cats and, loving Christ,
now children also (last, not least);
a throng of bug and bird and beast
wants goodness to be exercised.

Thus addicts curse their lack of spine
but can't resist just two more snorts.
It seems each homeless kitten courts
that truly final fix of mine.

1985

Winter

Like untrodden moss, like a fleece turned about,
without hindrance (forbidden zone),
the deep and glittering snow filled out
the measured dish of the lawn.

The old houses now breathe in such festive ways,
if a wind blew they'd take to the air;
and the trees all melt into downy haze,
like water colors, a blur.

Just stand here and stand, suffused with bliss,
quite lost to the world, to the job—
but I can't, somehow; somehow through all this
a wistful note seems to throb.

Translated by Walter Arndt

Olesia Nikolaeva

Daughter

The little girl that a good family adopted, taken
from the maternity ward when she was seven days old,
is now full of guesses. She's looking for her real
mother and father. She sees someting familiar
about that American woman who's in the magazines,
or the blonde in the limo that just went by.
She studies herself in the mirror. Finds some resemblance.
Presses her eyelashes together for a tragic picture
of terrifying storms descending on a ship:
the passengers survive by hanging on to the wreckage;
or, in overcast weather, a zeppelin is lost and the wind
keels it over: everything's plunged in darkness.
They've crashed on the shores of the Philippines,
or over the Atlantic, or in Siberian forests...
Providence saves them from the deep, from claws and teeth,
but scatters them through the world and forgets them.
—Though her adoptive parents send her to school and escort her
on the subway, what glorious trumpets sound for her in the sky!
The little girl casts sly, furtive glances around her;
she raises her eyebrows and purses her lips.
Something whispers, "That's her, the slender woman
with curly hair!"—an English miniature by an unknown painter.
Something suggests, "That's him, that grand-looking man
with the eagle nose and epaulets; what a princely figure!"
In all its beauty the whole human tribe is gathered before her:
a fluttering of hats and miters and plumes on helmets.
Every one of them has come to this family observance,
right back to Adam, who's still living in Eden.

Sleeplessness

Moscow, I listen as you go to sleep,
as times like those of Pugachev and the Streltsy's execution
rise up, accompanied by childhood diseases, fear of the dark,
hemophilia, hydrophobia.

Fires blaze on bitter, icy shores
and it's time for great schisms and disorder:
gates smeared with tar, houses in flame, earth in snow,
the watchman whacking his frightening clapper as hard as he can.

It's time for Babel-building, table-turning, curses, subversion,
horse-thievery, Tartarism, Babylon, sweat and blood.
From the crowd a voice cries,
       "Hey you, that's enough! It's the middle of the night!"
and gets this in answer:
       "Step up, kind sir, so we can blow your brains out!"

And it is nearly morning by now; in the distance
history's carnival dance, the midnight ball, recedes
and only its refrain,
"Pay for the sins of your Fatherland!"
still knocks on the windows, bangs and breaks in,
roving everywhere,
raving at me.

Translated by Paul Graves and Carol Ueland

Names

Ever since Nina gave birth to a handicapped child,
everybody's been telling her:"Nina,
give that baby up to a home for sick children
or a baby-care center!"
Rita, her mother, tells her: "You can't help her get well anyway!"
Tata, her sister, tells her: "There's no way she'll ever be normal!"
Sveta, her friend, says: "Ninka, Ninka, what good will it do her,
and you'll go and ruin your young life!"

Mama Rita's shacked up with a fellow with sweaty hands,
on meeting people he always apologizes and warns:
"I have sweaty hands."
Tata, the sister, wheezes from her extra weight
and every morning says, "Oh no, I've gained again!"
Sveta, the friend, has terrible relations
with the woman she shares housing with, and says:
"I swear I'm going to get that bitch's resident permit revoked!"

Add to this—endless rain, the elevator out of order,
and, to top it off, the TV had to go on the blink!
Yet with all this, Ninka, as if transfigured, looks, squints,
whispers: "Aglaia, Adelaida" (flipping the saints' calendar),
croons "Anastasia, Angelina, Anna" in various keys and tones.

* * *

At twenty, you manage to live in transports, with gusto and verve,
Charging in all directions, right, left, and ahead;
only later—ah, later—to move circumspectly, sore-footed, unnerved,
careful to keep your distance and balance instead.

Trouble is, once you rely on comfort and sweet talk and glut,
once you approve of yourself, fold your merits like hands on your gut,
that's when the floor will collapse under you
and you'll kick up a Cossack dance on your butt
and croak on the pier-glass of life like a tipsy tart.

The Shade

Behind every scribe, I sense the shade of a monstrous machine.
I crouch, I murmur: "Where, did you say? What days, did you say?"
I am the victim incarnate, my adrenaline
irrigates every lobby and passageway.

I am so sick of my stoop, my expression, and all of this—
I long to slam my fist on the table and hiss:
"Who do you think you are? Who needs your ha'pennysworth?
Love and forgiveness, that's all I want on this earth!"

Simpering wanly, the shadow disperses above,
but while it grows more gaseous, its message is firmly set:
"Yes! You called it! Forgiveness, longsuffering, love...
Granted! Not here, though! And not with this lot! And not yet!

Translated by Walter Arndt

Inna Lisnianskaia

To My Daughter

Why, you would think that nobody would bother
To argue with the plain and simple fact
That I, your ludicrously foolish mother,
Died naturally or of a heart attack.

No need for you to cry! Here's what I say:
What's on the bier, laid out in fine array,
In a small dress with rosebuds stitched in silk,
Is not herself—mere hollow clay you saw;
Yet time was when her nipple, crushed and raw,
Poured into you a scanty thread of milk.

I live in that non-void life used to claim,
When I was part of it, was emptiness;
Weights and velocities are not the same,
Nor even sleep, which by that simple name
Life carried off to everlasting rest.

There is no need for glasses now... You're freckled,
I see your every freckle stand out brown;
Your cheeks are shaded, irises gold-speckled
And you're all radiance, from heels to crown.

There is no need to cry! The little mound
Out where they sleep their dreamless final sleep
Beyond the town, is not my final keep,
It is our secret little meeting-place.
Graced by forget-me-nots in sweet profusion.

Life is a riddle—death is the solution.
How sweet to me these tears are on your face!
Oh, cry some more, bad mother though I've been
By every commonsense criterion.

I won't offend you, be that as it may,
By claiming that I simply lost my way.
That's not the truth. I bear you greater love
Than pampered daughters ever daydreamed of.

* * *

It's clear to the meanest slow-wit
that no common row can be plowed
by the rebel thought of the poet
and the linear mind of the crowd.

Yet what's to be feared even then?
All I own is with me, safe from loss:
Three fingers to hold the pen,
three fingers to sign the cross.

* * *

Above the sanatorium grounds,
above the inmates of the wings,
the sky of not-yet-spring abounds
in bulbous cloudy billowings.

Hunched by the porch steps, every morning
one crazed by anti-Jewish lore
spends hour after hour drawing
pictures of Judas, by the score.

A mass of curls his Judas wore,
his trunk was boneless, serpentine,
one of his hands was red with gore,
the other raked up silver coin.

The artist had prepared his paint
in a much-battered mug of tin;
an inmate, feeling some constraint,
had kept a wary eye on him.

Thus in the township of the sick
the spent and weary winter season
came by degrees to lose its reason
and thrust against the blocks of brick.

* * *

From silence's numb core
the wind sang me a dit:
Who once went off to war
does not come back from it!

Amid Egyptian gloom
a wind from nowhere wailed:
There's no escape from doom
for one who has been jailed!

My ears failed. But the crooner
sang out his fiendish round:
Stop waiting for him. Sooner
a corpse will cleave the ground!

1975

* * *

I always want to leave, go west,
I long for freedom more and more:
my truest urge is to withdraw,
arms humbly laid across my chest.

I've laid some death rehearsals on,
folding my arms across my chest,
no anguish by my face expressed,
lest I look scary when I'm gone.

I once rehearsed it in a tortured
mirage, mind maimed and overpowered:
the pallid sickbed wrappings flowered
like apple blossom in an orchard.

It's seven years since I was sick,
I feel my spirit whole and sane,
but see my life outlined again,
a cobweb strung from twig to twig.

The tiny ladders of its netting
I clamber up and downward, pant,
and freedom, as before, I want,
freedom senseless, all forgetting.

1969

Translated by Walter Arndt

About the Authors

ZOIA EVSEEVNA EZRÓKHI, née Burkova (b. 1946, Leningrad)

In contemporary Russian letters, Ezrokhi has the unique distinction of being a humorous woman poet in whose verses reverberates the major gendered problem publicized by Russian journalism and the "realistic" branch of women's fiction: the "double load" of professional and domestic responsibilities that burden the contemporary "Soviet" woman. In Ezrokhi's lyrics, that burden acquires an added edge, insofar as her calling evokes the image of inspired imagination, while her role as wife and mother necessitates cooking, diapering, cleaning, sewing, and so forth. In many of her poems Ezrokhi wryly and wittily records not only this conflict between elevated creative flights and mundane tasks, e.g., "I sing of the plate and grass" (Vospevaiu tarelku, travu, 1973), but also the discrepancy between female sexual fantasy and empirical everyday existence ("I'd like to live in a harem" [Khotela b ia zhit' v gareme, 1980]), between ideals and reality, hopes and facts.

Ezrokhi's poetry is consistently gynocentric. It focuses on women of all generations—on their appearance, activities, aspirations, obligations, joys and sorrows—and has sustained that focus from such early poems as "Morning in the Country" (Utro v derevne, 1962) and "I'm a Dishwasher" (Ia-posudomoika, 1972) to more recent lyrics, such as "Alone" (Odna, 1987). Whether women's dilemmas are ironically displaced onto animals (e.g., "Murka" [1970], about a pregnant cat and "The Usual Story" [Obyknovennaia istoriia, 1970], about a bitch whose unwanted puppies her owner drowns) or illustrate a more comprehensive human malaise, they imply a bleak vision of the world. What cuts across the desolation of Ezrokhi's worldview is the energy of her rhythm, her facility for rhyme, her tongue-in-cheek use of intertexts, and her manner of closing poems with unexpected *pointes*.

Writings: *Zimnee solntse* (L. 1990).

ELENA ALEXEEVNA IGNÁTOVA (b. 1947, Leningrad)

Although born in Leningrad, owing to a bout of tuberculosis Ignatova spent five of her early childhood years in the countryside. Despite its poverty, that environment vouchsafed her an image of Edenic harmony that she has retained to this day. A teaching assignment at school launched Ignatova on her career as a writer. She wrote fables for her teacher and poetry at the school club. At fourteen, she saw her first poem, "The Hermitage" (Ermitazh), printed in *Smena*.

Financial considerations led Ignatova to work for three years as a guide at the Petropavlovsk Fortress after her graduation from Leningrad University with a specialization in language and literature (1970). Later, she taught at the university, but in 1979 she decided to emigrate with her husband and son, for "it was impossible to breathe in Russia." During that period she wrote a book on Petersburg and its history for a German series on the capitals of Europe.

Her work in film and television dates from 1981, and is primarily devoted to literary figures, e.g., Bely, Blok, and Akhmatova. She had no difficulty gaining acceptance into the Writers' Union and among unofficial circles enjoyed a reputation as a fine poet. Her poems have been published regularly in the Russian émigré press since 1975: e.g., in Baku, Paris, Germany (*Kontinent*). Translations have been made into Swedish, German, French, Czech, and Croatian.

Poetry is Ignatova's major genre, but she has also written fiction, essays, a play, and a hybrid of fable and fairy tale. In 1990 she emigrated with her family to Israel, where she continues to publish in a variety of forms.

Ignatova's poetry unambiguously belongs to the Petersburg culturo-historical tradition. It is solidly grounded in the city and its cultural history. Indeed, numerous identifiable features of Petersburg recur regularly throughout her lyrics, as do references to classical sources. Ignatova also tends to observe traditional metrical and rhyming patterns and to eschew bold imagery or extreme effects. Implicit in her poetry, as if hovering in its margins and occasionally spilling into the verses themselves, is a sense of spiritual tranquility and reconciliation. The search for cultural roots, the impulse toward integration, directs the movement of many Ignatova lyrics. The life she experienced in childhood serves as an inspiration for those poems that pose the quest for harmony. Herodotus, for instance, functions as an image of the tranquil sky, gold as an image of divine peace.

Ignatova subscribes to the conventional Russian notion that man's sphere of activity is broader and more implicated in contemporary issues than that of women, who cleave to a more archaic and solid order of things while simultaneously trying to construct a livable immediate environment. When asked to name her favorites among her own poems, she chose the cycle "To My Son" (K synu), which she conceives of as a talisman, an attempt at a maternal magic spell to ward off potentially harmful forces.

Writings: Poems in *Okno* (Baku, 1974) and *Krug* (L. 1985); *Stikhi o prichastnosti* (Paris, 1976); *Teplaia zemlia* (L. 1989); *Nebesnoe zarevo* (Jerusalem, 1992).

LIUBOV' MIKHAILOVNA IÚNINA (b. 1929, Pochinki, near Moscow)

Despite her early aspirations to become an actress and her amateur attempts at writing plays, Iunina graduated from law school. She worked briefly as a legal consultant at TASS, then as a journalist for a medical newspaper, moved to *Literary Russia* (Literaturnaia Rossiia), and started writing short stories. In 1971 she began working in radio, in the division of literature, where she has remained.

The body of fiction Iunina has produced is slight, and it bears unmistakable traces of journalism. Unmemorable in style, her work treats themes characteristic of the older generation of women writers: love, family problems, maternal dilemmas. The narrative included here holds particular interest because of its dialogic relationship to Baranskaia's brief story "The Kiss." Where Baranskaia's successful middle-aged linguist dismisses the possibility of a liaison with a younger man for a complex of psychological and socially-sanctioned reasons, Iunina's equally successful career woman seems prepared to opt for personal/sexual self-fulfillment through romance. In that sense Iunina's text is unusual for its time, insofar as it conveys without censure a woman's readiness to embrace physical pleasure.

Writings: *Zhenshchina v odnokomnatnoi kvartire* (M. 1985); *Proisshestvie* (M. 1989).

ALLA MIKHAILOVNA KALÍNINA (b. 1935, Moscow)

Trained in engineering and biology, Kalinina worked for almost two decades in a surgical laboratory that conducted experiments on animals. With Vladimir Orlov's encouragement, she made her literary debut with the story "Contact" (Kontakt, 1973), which he helped her place in the journal *Science and Life* (Nauka i zhizn'). Since then she has produced two lengthy novels, approximately a dozen shorter narratives, and a handful of fairy tales for children. Written in a straightforward manner, these works explore the finely webbed processes of self-discovery and self-definition, family bonds and conflicts, the effects of time on personality and relationships, and individual and group psychology.

An admirer of Knut Hamsun, Lion Feuchtwanger, Thomas Mann, and Lev Tolsoi, Kalinina prizes the "monumentalism" and heaviness of German literature as an effective means of drawing the reader leisurely and convincingly into the fictional world. In her own prose she similarly strives for a "thickness" of time, which explains why her novels proceed quite slowly, the temporal flow measured by regular references to seasonal changes. In her recent novel, *In Image and Likeness* (Po obrazu i podobiiu, 1989), the "action" transpires over a month, the days separated into 29 chapters, but Kalinina extends that timespan through extensive reminiscences and ruminations, in addition to an epilogue that places the novel's major events in the perspective of hindsight.

Unlike the majority of contemporary Russian women writers, Kalinina frequently favors a male point of view, as in her first-person novel, *In Image and Likeness*, her novella *Grass under the Snow* (Trava pod snegom), and the stories "The Path through the Field" (Tropinka cherez pole), "Neprukha," and "The Merry Carpenters" (Vesëlye plotniki). That choice doubtless stems from her refusal to include herself and people of her close circle directly in her work in recognizable form. Firmly grounded in the classical tradition of the nineteenth-century novel, Kalinina's prose may strike those readers who privilege modernist techniques as somewhat old-fashioned.

Writings: *Trava pod snegom. Povest' i rasskazy* (Nukus, 1979); *Cheremukhovyi kholod. Povesti i rasskazy* (M. 1980) ; *Kak ty ko mne dobra...* *Roman* (M. 1985) (M. 1990); *Po obrazu i podobiiu.* *Roman* (M. 1989).

NINA SEMENOVNA KATÉRLI (b. 1934, Leningrad)

A native and resident of Leningrad, Katerli graduated from a technical school with an engineering degree. Since her literary debut in 1973, she has published steadily if slowly. The last few years have witnessed her increasing involvement in socio-political causes, much of her activity directed against anti-Semitism.

Most of Katerli's fiction—in the form of stories and novellas—is contained in her three prose collections of 1981, 1986, and 1990. As a prosaist Katerli operates in two basic modes: at her most experimental, she gives free rein to her imagination, incorporating pure fantasy, inexplicable shifts in locale and point of view, radical temporal jumps, unexpected juxtapositions, and modified stream of consciousness into her narrative. In a less venturesome but more consistent vein, she also recreates in concrete detail modern urban settings, against the background of which she explores romantic ties, family problems, communal living, and the inconsistencies and irrational, destructive involutions of the human psyche: e.g. "The Barsukov Triangle" (Treugol'nik Barsukova, wr. 1977), published abroad in 1981, reissued recently in Russia as "Haymarket Square" (Sennaia ploshchad', 1991). The point of departure for Katerli's fiction is human relations—people's failure to make meaningful contact and to understand each other—within the context of Soviet life. Her cast of characters covers the full spectrum of old, middle-aged, young, and adolescent of both sexes.

Unlike the majority of Russian women prosaists, Katerli prefers to survey the world from a male center of consciousness. She favors parallel plot lines and an elliptical style complicated by animal imagery and literary allusions, marked by jagged sentence fragments, and rich in colloquialisms.

From a feminist standpoint, Katerli's novella *Polina* (1984) is a particularly rewarding text, insofar as it envisions an unorthodox alternative to the paradigmatic Soviet ideal of domesticated womanhood. Her most recent and substantial (as yet unpublished) work is a documentary novel entitled *The Lawsuit* (Isk, wr. 1991), which traces the legal and political experiences she underwent in a case of anti-Semitism. If, as Katerli has claimed, the mentality of the typical "Soviet citizen" (sovok) constitutes the mystery that she repeatedly attempts to fathom in her work, in the story included here she focuses on the psychology of a specific and, in Russian literature, rarely portrayed category within that species—the Soviet version of the "Jewish mother" familiar to fans of Woody Allen and Philip Roth.

Writings: *Okno* (L. 1981); "Treugol'nik Barsukova," *Glagol* (1981) 3; *Polina* (1984) 1: 11-60; *Tsvetnye otkrytki* (L. 1986); "Kurzap," *Zvezda* (1986) 11: 88-115; "Zhara na severe. Povest'," *Zvezda* (1988) 4: 3-73; "Solntse za steklom," *Zvezda* (1989) 4: 100-13; *Kurzal. Povesti* (L. 1990); "Sennaia ploshchad'," *Zvezda* (1991) 7: 5-35 (reissue of "Treugol'nik Barsukova"); *Isk* (ms. 1991).

NADEZHDA VADIMOVNA KOZHÉVNIKOVA (b. 1949, Moscow)

As the daughter of Vadim Kozhevnikov, an orthodox Soviet writer who for two decades wielded considerable political power in Moscow's literary world, Kozhevnikova had her access to publishing assured upon graduation from the Gorky Institute of Literature. Since her literary debut in 1967, her fiction has examined the domestic lives of the urban intelligentsia. Its major themes include love, familial ties and pressures, generational conflicts, the obligations and complexities of parenthood, the erosion of romantic illusions, and the uncertainties and misunderstandings—as well as lack of communication—that undermine marital relations. Although several of her works have also analyzed betrayal ("Vera Perova"), loss ("A Toy Store" [Magazin igrushek]) and the impossibility of complete mutual understanding ("Eurydice" [Evridika]), the mere title of one of her novellas, "About Maternal, Filial, Sublime, and Earthly Love" (O liubvi materinskoi, dochernei, vozvyshennoi i zemnoi), accurately points to her chief concern as a writer. Her entire output, in fact, may be seen as a modern gloss of sorts on Tolstoi's "Family Happiness" and *Anna Karenina*, with a touch of Iury Trifonov.

A firm believer in gender distinctions, Kozhevnikova is fascinated by the contrasting roles carved out for men and women by biology, society, and historical precedent. Accordingly, she tends to equate professionalism with male values and "domestic" worries with female psychology. Her narratives often pre-

316 About the Authors

sent women striving to balance those two spheres or to make the transition from one to the other. Those who nurture ambitions frequently resort to "feminine wiles" (e.g., the eponymous protagonist of "Vera Perova"). Whatever their situation, Kozhevnikova's women are acutely aware of just how significantly their psychology and conduct contrast with the culturally entrenched male paradigm.

Like the majority of women writing in Russia today, Kozhevnikova filters her fictional world through her female protagonist, whose voice invariably merges with the omniscient narrator's. That conflation creates a distance between the reader and Kozhevnikova's male characters that often transforms the latter into objects of dispassionate dissection rather than full-fledged humans on a par with their female counterparts. With a few exceptions, Kozhevnikova depicts male characters externally, while leaving the field wide open for her women to reveal their inner world in minute detail.

Possibly because of her training as a journalist, Kozhevnikova faithfully adheres to a conventional, low-key, realistic narrative. Retrospection accounts for the modified time shifts in her fiction, which follows a linear plot, avoids ambiguity and mystification, and favors a language almost wholly devoid of striking imagery and anything redolent of modernism.

Writings: Chelovek, reka i most. Povesti i rasskazy (M. 1976). Okna na dvor (M. 1976). Bremia molodosti (ocherki) (M. 1978). Vorota i novyi gorod. Ocherki (M. 1978). Doma i liudi (M. 1979), O liubvi materinskoi, dochernei, vozvyshennoi i zemnoi. Povesti, rasskazy, ocherki (M. 1979). Elena prekrasnaia (M. 1982). Postoronnie v dome. Povesti (M. 1983). Vnutrennii dvor (M. 1986). Posle prazdnika (M. 1988).

INNA LVOVNA LISNIÁNSKAIA (b. 1924, Baku)

Lisnianskaia started writing poems at an early age. By 1948 she was being published in prestigious Moscow journals, and in 1957 she joined the Soviet Writers' Union. Collections of her verses appeared regularly during the 1950s, 1960s, and 1970s, until her career came to an abrupt halt with the Metropole affair of 1979. After the scandal over the unofficial publication under Vassily Aksyonov's leadership, Lisnianskaia and her husband, fellow-poet Simeon Lipkin, resigned from the Writers' Union in protest against the organization's exclusion of the two youngest participants, Evgeny Popov and Viktor Erofeyev. After a protracted period of harassment, during which Lisnianskaia and Lipkin underwent severe material hardships and were published exclusively abroad, the Writers' Union reinstated both in 1987.

Gifted especially in the short lyric, Lisnianskaia shows a penchant for intensity, relative simplicity of rhyme, traditional meter, and, on occasion, extraordinarily powerful images—often of sickness, psychic violence, and disintegration. Pain, suffering, profound loss, unappeasable yearning, inner turmoil, psychological conflict, and a general preoccupation with inner personal experience characterize Lisnianskaia's verses. In a paradox typical of the history of Soviet culture, Lisnianskaia, the most apolitical of poets, became an internal émigré on moral-political grounds. Since her "rehabilitation," Lisnianskaia's recent poems, as well as those from the late 1970s and early 1980s, have appeared in most of the mainstream journals.

Writings: Eto bylo so mnoi (1975); Vernost' (1958); Ne prosto liubov (1963); Iz pervykh ust (1966); Vinogradnyi svet (1978); Dozhdi i zerkala (1983); Stihotvoreniia: na opushke sna (1984); Vozdushnyi plast (1990); Stupeni (1990).

ELENA GRIGORIEVNA MAKÁROVA (b. 1951, Baku)

Prose writer, essayist, pedagogue, and exhibit organizer, Makarova is the daughter of the famous Muscovite lyric poet Inna Lisnianskaia. Emerging from a psychologically beleaguered childhood, Makarova briefly studied at the Surikov Art Institute (an experience that informs her story "Uncle Pasha" [Diadia Pasha]) before joining the Gorky Institute of Literature. Although she began writing relatively early, her primary occupation has been teaching art and sculpture at an experimental school to psychologically disturbed children of kindergarten age (evoked in her volume of essays "Free the Elephant" ("Osvobodite slona," 1985). Her involvement with handicapped children led her to Friedl Dicker-Brandeis, an art teacher at the Terezin concentration camp during World War II, who struggled to help the doomed children cope with their terrors through art. After a research trip to Prague, Makarova succeeded in mounting an exhibit in Moscow of Brandeis's and her pupils' work. Subsequent official harassment, among other motivations, spurred Makarova to emigrate to Israel in 1990 with her husband and two children, where she continues writing and arranging talks and shows of Brandeis's materials.

Makarova's fiction addresses issues of perception, understanding, and maturation, primarily among adolescents, in a prose receptive to modernist influences. Her two illustrated collections of stories and novellas, largely from the 1970s, (*Spool* [Katushka, 1978] and *Overfull Days* [Perepolnennye dni, 1982]) draw heavily on her biography. Although some are set in Baku, most portray primarily Moscow intelligentsia, and combine subtle psychological insight, originality of subject matter and perspective, and a vivid language in which slang and colloquialisms consort with philosophical aphorisms and numerous literary references.

The majority of Makarova's protagonists are adolescents trapped in situations they are ill-equipped to handle. Their vulnerabilities, sense of inadequacy, or naiveté provides the focal point of many Makarova stories (e.g., "Bonjour, Papa... and a Curtsey" [Bonzhur, Papa... i kniksen, 1977], "Fish-Needle" [Ryba-igla, 1978]).

Makarova's fiction depicts marital relations in somber hues and presupposes that melancholy, frustration, and restlessness are humanity's common lot. Her youthful protagonists, nonetheless, seek some form of permanence, and although their search dissolves in disappointment, it usually provides an education.

Owing to the elliptical nature of Makarova's style, with logical links frequently omitted amidst temporal leaps and shifts in locale, her narratives proceed in spurts and bounds. The terseness, uneven pacing, and highly introspective nature of these narratives lend a vitality to Makarova's prose. She never underestimates her readers' abilities, preferring to stimulate their curiosity and imagination with cryptic allusions rather than engage in protracted explanations. The texture of her predominantly first-person narratives is enriched by linguistic diversity, brimming with slang, foreign phrases, jargon comprehensible only to a specific circle, poems, and songs.

Makarova's first two collections reveal psychological acuity, narrative flair, and a secure command of language. The same traits mark Makarova's most recent anthology of five novellas, *An Open Final* (Otkrytyi final, 1989). Several of these portray Jewish life and explore isolation and the inability to ease others' suffering, while "Preserving" (Na sokhranenii, 1976) offers a dry-eyed, grim picture of diverse women preparing for both birth and abortion in a maternity ward.

Writings: *Katushka: povesti* (M. 1978). *Perepolnennye dni: rasskazy i povesti* (M. 1982). *"Osvobodite slona"* (M. 1985). *Leto na kryshe* (M. 1987). *Otkrytyi final* (M. 1989). "Poslezavtra v San-Frantsisko," *Daugava* 9: 1989, 11-36. *V nachale bylo detstvo* (1990).

ANNA VLADIMIROVNA MASS (b. 1935, Moscow)

The daughter of a well-known actress and a highly successful dramatist, Mass developed an interest in folklore and experienced *Wanderlust* while still a student at Moscow State University. Her first foray into literature (1959) took the form of an essay on her travels. Upon marrying a geologist (1961) whom she met on one of her expeditions, Mass trained as a geophysicist and combined a career in geology with that of writer. Accepted into the Writers' Union in 1972 after the publication of her story "Liubka's Wedding" (1965), Mass has half a dozen volumes to her credit and has regularly worked for radio and published in journals, yet remains relatively unknown among her fellow literati.

The psychological maturation of youth and the difficulties of attaining selfhood form the thematic core of Mass's fiction.

Since she explicitly bases her fiction on real events, much of it treats women geologists in the field or returning home for brief visits, frequently divided by the conflicting claims of personal obligations and professional advancement. Equally central to her oeuvre is the moment of access to self-knowledge on the part of young, developing personalities. At the heart of her narratives, which often unfold in the midst of familial or group gatherings, lies the complex problem that lends weight and meaning to the plot line: the question of individual identity and how to realize that sense of self in decisions and actions, especially under powerful social pressures.

Mass's straightforward, unadorned style presents few complications for the reader beyond the occasional use of technical geological terms. Her favored device of juxtaposition enables her to make her point and to create dramatic effects with eloquence and succinctness.

Writings: *Zhestokoe solntse: Povest' v deviati novellakh* (M. 1967). *Raznotsvetnye cherepki: Povest' i rasskazy* (M. 1970). *Dereviannyi tiulen'* (M. 1972). *Beloe chudo: Rasskazy i povesti* (M. 1982). *Na Kolodozere: Rasskazy Iriny Konstantinovny Bogdanovoi* (M. 1982). *Mal'chik i sneg: Rasskazy i povest'* (M. 1984). *Krugovaia lapta* (M. 1990).

TATIANA ALEXEEVNA NABÁTNIKOVA (b. 1948 in the Altai region)

Descended from Ukrainian and Russian peasant stock and raised in the countryside, Nabatnikova lacked a solid home atmosphere throughout her childhood and adolescence. She claims that her two marriages, which produced two children, failed because she herself possesses no familial skills. After graduating from the Novosibirsk Electrochemical Institute (1971), where she also avidly pursued the bicycling that taught her the value of tireless effort, Nabatnikova briefly worked as an engineer at a plant. She subsequently attended the Gorky Institute of Literature (1975-81) and launched her career with a series of short stories while still living in Cheliabinsk. Several of her anthologies won prizes, her popularity grew, and in 1989 she moved to Moscow, where she currently resides.

As Nabatnikova herself acknowledges, the problematic relations between the sexes dominate her fiction, which explores behavioral patterns and their motivation within and outside marriage. Her narratives of romantic and familial relationships present sobering pictures, most often, of deeply flawed or disintegrating unions. Few illusions color Nabatnikova's worldview, which assumes that egotism, self-delusion, and infinite psychological censoring mechanisms guide human behavior. Her novel *Every Hunter* (Kazhdyi okhotnik, 1987) caused a stir largely because of the seemingly dispassionate bleakness with which it records the calculation of the "huntress" Rita's maneuvers to advance her husband's career, and, more generally, its unsparing dissection of destructive and compromised modes of life. A basic conviction that people dwell in existential solitude informs the majority of Nabatnikova's narratives. It is especially visible in such stories as "In Memoriam" (Na pamiat'), where a dying cancer patient abandoned by her son leaves a diary only her doctor bothers to peruse, or in "The Bus Driver Astap," included in this collection.

However tangled the psychology of Nabatnikova's personae, her plots tend toward simplicity. She favors a clean, rhetoric-free prose, sometimes relying on the artless device of italicizing words to underscore key concepts.

Writings: Fiction: *Rasskazy* (Novosibirsk, 1982). *Domashnee vospitanie. Rasskazy, povest'* (M. 1984). "Kazhdyi okhotnik. Roman," *Sibirskie ogni* 1987 1-3. *Na zolotom kryl'tse sideli. Rasskazy, povest'* (Cheliabinsk, 1987). *Kazhdyi okhotnik. Roman. Rasskazy* (M. 1989). *Zagadai zhelanie* (M. 1990). *Dar Izory* (M. 1991).

OLESIA (OLGA) ALEXANDROVNA NIKOLÁEVA (b. 1955, Moscow).

One of the most widely published poets among the younger generation, Nikolaeva does not fit into any recognizable group, such as the lyricists who write primarily of love in a traditional meter (e.g., Rimma Kazakova), the avantgardists who experiment or play with postmodernist techniques (e.g., Tatiana Shcherbina), or the "modern" poets who nonetheless have strong ties with classical Russian verse (e.g., Elena Shvarts). Nikolaeva's verses differ from those of her contemporaries in their synthesis of fragmented syntax, irregular lines, approximate or absent rhymes, bold images, the judicious use of a deliberately prosaic lexicon, and a markedly spiritual orientation.

Although Nikolaeva began writing poetry at eleven, she claims to have realized her calling at an even younger age. In like fashion, she felt religious stirrings as an adolescent, yet was only christened at 24. After turning to religion, she became a Church activist and learned ancient Greek.

Educated at the Gorky Institute of Literature, Nikolaeva has read widely in philosophy, religion, and Western literature (including Jung). Her worldview shows her affinities with the Russian philosophical tradition constituted by Florensky, Rozanov, Leontiev, Berdiaev, Sergei Bulgakov, and Averintsev. The Bible, however, is her Ur-text, the sole volume she keeps rereading, and it serves as the source of multiple allusions in her poetry.

She made her literary debut in 1972 (with poems published in *Smena*) and has translated poetry from Georgian, Polish, Moldavian, Slovenian, and Hungarian. With three verse collections to her credit, Nikolaeva in the last three years has also taken up prose. Nowadays her works regularly appear in mainstream journals.

Nikolaeva tends to perceive the world through binary oppositions (dark and light, sin and saint-liness, heaven and earth, male and female, etc.). Her poetry reflects her preoccupation with meta-physical issues, though some of her lyrics address social questions. Her themes include the primacy of spirit over matter, the joys of transcendance, human frailty, and cultural continuity (sometimes formulated as maternity). Technically, her poetic line is dynamic and full of tension, its lyric flow abruptly halted both by an unexpectedly inserted prosaism and a shift in rhythm. The title of her prose collection, *Keys to Peace/the World* (Kliuchi ot mira), points to the "global" or metaphysical cast of her thought, while the narratives explore the "pros and cons" of two worlds pitted against each other: everyday society, with its material concerns, and the ascetic retreat of a monastery, where the soul and its salvation reign supreme. The novella "Childhood Invalid" (Invalid detstva, first pd. in *Iunost'*) is structured most clearly on that juxtaposition.

Nikolaeva belongs to that sizable majority of Russian women writers who conceive of gender as inherent and preordained. In her own words, "the Bible demonstrates [men's and women's] onto-logical heterogeneity, the difference of their rank and mission and in the long run the metaphysical subordination of woman to man" (*SovLit*). That conviction informs many of her poems, including "All-Girls' Shower" (Devichnik), "Girlfriends" (Podrugi), "Familial Passions" (Semeinye strasti), and "Seven Beginnings" (Sem' nachal). Gender issues, however, do not figure prominently in Nikolaeva's oeuvre, of which the true "heroine" is the soul.

Writings: Over fifty poems published in *Novyi mir, Druzhba narodov, Ogonёk,* etc., collected in her anthologies: *Sad chudes* (M. 1980); *Na korable zimy* (M. 1986); *Smokovnitsa* (Tbilisi, 1990); "Invalid detstva. Povest'," *Iunost'* (1990) 2: 34-61; *Zdes'* (M. 1990); *Kliuchi ot mira* (M. 1990); "Proshchanie s imperiei," *Znamia* (1992) 7: 3-6.

MARINA ANATOLIEVNA PALÉI (b. 1955, Leningrad)

With both parents engineers, Palei herself pursued a medical training. She graduated from a medical college, but, with her illusions about the chances of a genuine medical profession shattered, Palei held a series of menial jobs to support herself, including those of orderly and nurse, cleaner, watchwoman, stoker, and model, before turning seriously to writing. Starting as a poet, she entered the Gorky Literary Institute as a critic, and graduated in 1990 as a prosaist. Her fiction began appearing steadily in various journals, and, surprisingly quickly for a "beginning author," she has produced a substantial corpus of prose. She is currently at work on a novel.

Palei's stint in medicine seeps into her stories in a number of ways: in the settings she selects and the physiological details she supplies, as well as in her knowledge of biological and medical facts and her focus on the body. Like other writers of the young generation (e.g., Vasilenko, Vaneeva), Palei creates a gynocentric fictional world. Women's physical, spiritual, and emotional experience, their sufferings and joys as mothers, lovers, and dedicated workers/professionals, their understand-ing of the world and their own place in it seem to be what, for the most part, concerns Palei. Yet her overarching preoccupation is with existential issues (perhaps most transparently in the story titled "Elevator" [Lift]) and with the aesthetics of composition, especially language.

The two stories included here highlight two aspects of Palei's writing. In "The Losers' Division" we find the uneasy balance between brutal, indifferent reality (anchored in and metaphorized by the physical body) and the magical, ideal world conjured up by the imagination's flight, symbolized by the ever receding distant ship (Emma Bovary). "Rendezvous" exemplifies Palei's ironic manner, which not infrequently targets men and their foibles as the object of sardonic scrutiny.

Writings: "Evgesha i Annushka," *Znamia* 7 (1990): 10-45; *Otdelenie propashchikh* (M. Moskovskii rabochii, 1991); "Kabiriia s Obvodnogo Kanala," *Novyi mir* 3 (1991): 47-81.; "Reis," *Novyi mir* 3 (1993): 82-95.

IRINA NIKOLAEVNA POLIÁNSKAIA (b. 1952, Kasli, the Urals)

Polianskaia's parents were scientists, her father a noted chemistry professor who studied with the famous M. Zelinsky. Imprisoned in a German camp during World War II, upon his return to Russia he was sentenced to Kolyma. Owing to his work on the construction of the atomic station in Obminsk, he was exposed to large doses of radiation, as a consequence of which Polianskaia's brother was born with Down syndrome. During her childhood Polianskaia felt distanced from her strict, remote father and her long-suffering mother, but found a haven in the nurturing presence of her affectionate, religious grandmother.

After finishing school in 1969, Polianskaia briefly studied music, then, from 1971, theater, in Rostov on the Don. Although her studies were complicated by a bout of tuberculosis, she graduated in 1975, by which time she had begun writing verses and irregularly working as a journalist.

Upon moving to Moscow, she joined the prose section of the Gorky Institute of Literature. Since her graduation in 1980 she has devoted all of her time to prose. Married to the editor Vladimir Kravchenko since 1976, she has one daughter, spends much of her time at home, and tends to avoid contacts.

Polianskaia's fiction draws heavily on her biography. Her longest and most complex work, the novella *Mitigating Circumstances* (Predlagaemye obstoiatel'stva, 1984), as well as several of her stories (e.g., "Clear Zone" [Chistaia zona, 1990]), openly recreates her early family experience. Like Makarova and Rubina, Polianskaia makes no effort to smooth over the psychological depravations (and deprivations) of children raised in the atmosphere of emotional tension and volatility that usually stems from parental incompatibility. Yet she captures all of the lyric nuances and poignant joys that may be salvaged from the ruins of a once intimate relationship contracted in a spirit of optimism. Her prose shows a special sensitivity to the significance of a given moment or gesture, customarily conveyed via metaphor.

Naming Andrei Voznesensky, Andrei Bitov, Liudmila Petrushevskaia, and Sasha Sokolov as writers crucial to her creative and spiritual development, Polianskaia credits Sokolov with providing the immediate stylistic impulse for her mature prose. From him, she maintains, she learned the primacy of intonation and the importance of writing "beautifully" even about horrors. Like Tolstaia, Polianskaia often finds inspiration in music for her creative activity. And, like Vaneeva, she is profoundly concerned about ecological issues.

Recurrent motifs in Polianskaia's fiction include family scenes, music, cemeteries, and symbolic use of color, sound, temperature, and space. According to her, the story included here is her personal favorite among her fiction.

Writings: *Predlagaemye obstoiatel'stva* (M. 1988); *Poslannik* (M. 1990?), "Chistaia zona," *Znamia* 1 (1990): 64-73; "Bednoe serdtse Mani," *Literaturnaia gazeta* 5 Sept. 1990: 6; "Mama," *Literaturnoe obozrenie* 11 (1990): 36-38; *Chistaia zona* (M. 1991).

REGINA RAÉVSKAIA (b. Moscow)

A graduate of Moscow's Musical-Pedagogical College (1967) and the Maurice Thorez Institute of Foreign Languages (1974), Raevskaia emigrated to the United States in 1978. She has worked as an interpreter in both Russia and the States. The story included in the collection is her second publication.

DINA ILINICHNA RÚBINA (b. 1953, Tashkent)

Born into a cultured household (her father was a painter, her mother a history teacher), at her parents' insistence Rubina studied music at the Tashkent Conservatory, although she had already decided on a writer's profession. Recognition came early. Her first story, "A Restless Nature" (Bespokoinaia natura), written in her late teens, launched her lengthy relationship with *Iunost'*, where it appeared. The publication there of her longer narrative "So, When Will It Start Snowing?" (Kogda zhe poidët sneg?...) in 1973 elicited a flood of correspondence. Turned into a play and broadcast on the radio, the story brought Rubina to the public's attention. Translations of her works soon appeared in Eastern and Central Europe. In 1984 she moved to Moscow, where she lived with her second husband (a painter) and two children until emigrating to Israel in 1988.

Written primarily for and about adolescents, Rubina's humorous, readable, unpretentious short stories deal largely with family issues and the process of maturation. Her youthful protagonists typically attempt to define themselves and their needs in an adult environment that operates by rules they do not fully comprehend. All too often the children of divorced or incompatible parents, they experience insecurity, bewilderment, and a division of loyalties. In struggling to cope with their inner conflicts, they mature and attain a measure of understanding that promises future integration into the adult world. Stories that exemplify this process include "The House Behind the Green Gate" (Dom za zelënoi kalitkoi, 1980) and "The Blackthorn" (Ternovnik), included in this collection. In other texts, Rubina examines the trials and joys of parenthood, most notably in the poignant story of a husband who grows to love his wife's son by another man ("The Double-Barreled Name" [Dvoinaia familiia, 1989]). Elsewhere Rubina offers a backward glance at relationships that seem inimical or unequal at the time, but in retrospect reveal unrealized potential for intimacy ("That Strange Man Altukhov" [Etot chudnoi Altukhov] and "Recapitulation" [Vozvrat k proidennomu]).

Rubina's profound sensitivity to the shaping powers of time and to the intrinsically subjective nature of perception informs her skillful handling of perspective. She has a penchant for presenting a problem or a relationship from two contrasting viewpoints without favoring either. Those perspectives may reside in two separate beings or may characterize a single individual at different stages of her or his development. In either case, partly by strongly subjectivizing particular points of view and not subsuming them under an omniscient authorial position, Rubina creates a fictional world permeated by a sense of human tolerance and sympathy in the face of inevitable error, frailty, and conflict.

An admirer of Chekhov and Salinger, Rubina believes that women's writing reveals a greater capacity for fine shading, for capturing psychological gradations, than does male fiction. Style, she claims, unavoidably reflects all aspects of a writer's lived experience.

Writings: *Kogda zhe poidët sneg?...* (Tashkent, 1980); *Zavtra, kak obychno...* (Plovdiv, 1985); *Otvorite okno* (Tashkent, 1987); *Dvoinaia familiia* (M. 1990).

NINA NIKOLAEVNA SADÚR (b. 1950, Novosibirsk)

Born into the intelligentsia (her mother was a teacher of Russian literature, her father a poet), Sadur nonetheless grew up in a working class neighborhood in Siberia from which she felt alienated, just as she now finds the urban intelligentsia arid and tedious. Her interest, she claims, lies in the common people, especially in their rich language and superstitious beliefs.

At twenty-seven (1978) Sadur moved to Moscow and completed five years at the Institute of Literature. Although she started out as a prosaist (she began writing stories in her childhood), Sadur turned to drama after attending Viktor Rozov's drama seminar. Acceptance among playwrights came early, and on the basis of her plays she unproblematically gained membership in the Union of Writers (1989).

Known primarily for her plays, which were collected in the anthology *The Wondrous Old Woman* (Chudnaia baba, 1989), Sadur has also authored a half-dozen narratives, a cycle of stories (*Touched* [Pronikshie, 1980s]), and a collection of narratives titled *Immortals* (Bessmertniki, 1992) that still await publication. Probably her best-known play is "Pannochka," staged in a number of theaters with considerable success in recent years. As her "teachers" she cites Rozov and the late Evgeny Kharitonov, to whom her marvelously original one-act play "The Strength of Hair" (Sila volos, 1984) is dedicated. At first glance, however, her works suggest Gogol as a potential stylistic predecessor.

Sadur's technique consists of focusing on the mundane and everyday, then infusing seemingly commonplace events and actions with magic. That infusion draws on a folkoric dimension that Sadur creates with extraordinary skill and conviction, most particularly in *Pronikshie*, a cycle of gnomic narratives she wrote rapidly in a flash of inspiration, and to which the two stories included here belong.

Spiritual isolation as the defining, inescapable fact of human life is Sadur's major concern, thematized in her drama and fiction alike. That tragic sense of cosmic desolation allies some of her works with the Existentialists—a link most evident, perhaps, in the plays "Red Paradise" (Krasnyi paradiz) and "Go!" (Ekhai, 1983). The world portrayed by Sadur is a fundamentally inimical sphere of uncontrollable powers and incessant desires, frequently manifested in extreme and enigmatic acts that shade into the grotesque. The grotesque strain in Sadur derives in part from her powerful use of language: lexical synthesis of colloquial, poetic, and substandard forms; exploitation of such rhetorical devices as paronomasia, tautology, repetition, and omission; and syntactic contrasts, whereby short, fragmented clauses alternate with complex, heavily freighted sentences.

In *Pronikshie* the majority of conflicts and struggles play themselves out along gendered lines. Within the animistic, mysterious world of externalized psyches that Sadur constructs, relations between the sexes acquire the status of cosmic battles that recast a variety of cultural myths.

Writings: "Devochka noch'iu," *Vstrechnyi khod* (M. 1989): 85-102; *Chudnaia baba* (M. 1989), "Pronikshie," *Ne pomniashaia zla* (M. 1990): 217-50; "Krasnyi paradiz," *Novye Amazonki* (M. 1991): 255-74; "Chto-to otkroetsia," *Vidimost' nas* (M. 1991): 44-55; "Iug," *Znamia* 10 (1992): 9-40; "Cherti, suki, komunnal'nye kozly...," *Teatr* 6 (1992): 177-91; "Milen'kii, ryzhen'kii," *Teatr* 8 (1992): 171-77; *Bessmertniki* (1992, ms.).

GALINA NIKOLAEVNA SHCHERBAKÓVA, née Rezhabek (b. 1932, Dzerzhinsk)

A graduate from the languages and literatures department at Rostov University, Shcherbakova taught school before turning to journalism—a job that required constant travel all over the Soviet Union. She took up fiction in the 1970s, and during the 1980s wrote film scenarios to augment her family's finances. Married to the journalist AlexandEr Shcherbakov (on the staff of *Ogonek*), with two adult children and a grandchild, Shcherbakova now resides in Moscow.

Shcherbakova's narratives examine moral choices, the psychology of love, and the effects of time's passage on the postwar generation in a modern (mostly urban) setting. One of her best-known novellas, *You wouldn't Dream of It* (Vam i ne snilos'), adapted into a popular film by the same name, as well as her play entitled *Roman and Julie* (Roman i Iul'ka), portrays the self-sacrificing life of two tenth-graders. Other pieces, such as "The Wall" (Stena) and "The Kuzmenko Incident" (Sluchai s Kuz'menko), explore the dynamics of marriage, tracing the disillusionments, betrayals, and dissatisfactions that accumulate over the years. These works also unflinchingly acknowledge the price paid in human values by self-deluded careerists motivated solely by utilitarian principles.

Like most contemporary women writers in Russia, Shcherbakova has the habit of retrospection, seeking clues to characters' current dilemmas in experiences and decisions of the past. As part of that movement backward, she allows her characters to reveal themselves in interior monologues and mental free associations that provide highly suggestive links and explanations. Her longest work, a diptych called *Anatomy of Divorce* (Anatomiia razvoda, 1990), consisting of an "ideal version" (*The Year of Tangerines* [Mandarinovyi god]) and an "ironic version" (*Alena's Year* [God Alëny]) of romantic-sexual-domestic entanglements that Shcherbakova handles in a sobering, down-to-earth manner, contains some of her best writing. Two somewhat lighter recent narratives, "Uncle Khlor and Koriakin" (Diadia Khlor i Koriakin, 1988)—included in this collection—and "Daughters, Mothers, Birds, and Islands" (Dochki, materi, ptitsy i ostrova, 1991) offer a tongue-in-cheek study of a reconstituted family and uninhibited female sexuality, respectively. Both overturn gender stereotypes with humor and a certain zest.

Shcherbakova's favorite genre, which showcases her strengths, is the novella (*povest'*). Possibly because of her training as a journalist, her writing has the concise, spare preciseness of reportage. It also reflects a keen eye for the eloquent gesture and an ear sensitive to individual speech patterns.

Writings: *Sprava ostavalsia gorodok* (M. 1979); *Roman i Iul'ka: P'esa-razmyshleniia* (M. 1982); *Vam i ne snilos'* (M. 1983); *Otchaiannaia osen': Povesti* (M. 1985); "Krushenie," *Zhurnalist* (1987) 1 & 2: 61-70 & 72-80; *Dver' v chuzhuiu zhizn'* (M. 1985); *Sneg k dobru* (M. 1988); *Krushenie* (M. 1990); *Anatomiia razvoda* (M. 1990); "Emigratsiia po-russku...," *Ogonëk* (1991) 9: 18-21; "Dochki, materi, ptitsy i ostrova," *Soglasie* (1991) 6: 82-89; *Ubikvisty, Soglasie* (1992) 2: 11-88; "Puteshestviia," *Ogonëk* (1992) 20-21: 16-18.

TATIANA SHCHERBÍNA (b. 1954, Moscow)

Born into an educated and well-to-do family, Shcherbina attended Moscow University (1971-76), where she studied in the department of languages and literatures and enrolled in classes on journalism.

She launched a career in poetry in 1975, and shortly thereafter started giving readings on an unofficial basis, e.g., at *Club* (1977-78). None of the mainstream literary journals recognized her work, however, until 1985 (*Literaturnaia ucheba*). While continuing to write poetry, from 1989 to 1992 she also broadcast for "Radio Liberty" in Munich, where she currently resides.

A volume of her poetry (*Nothing-Nothing* [Nol'-Nol']) has been translated into French (1992), and other translations into English and German have appeared in the last few years. In addition, Shcherbina has written a "novel," *Private Residence* (Osobniak, 1989), and a number of essays and articles. Since 1991, when her previously underground volume *Nothing-Nothing* was reissued by a regular Moscow publishing house, she has gained official acceptance in Russia.

Although Shcherbina speaks of her poetry as erasing the culture of binary oppositions and synthesizing all traditions on an international scale, her verses may be described as "traditionally avant-garde," inasmuch as they rely on techniques normally associated with modernism: downplaying of structure and linear development; fragmentation on all fronts, coupled with an effort to reglue some of the pieces in unexpected combinations; ironic, subversive use of rhyme or absence of rhyme altogether; an addiction to paradoxes; flauntedly "inappropriate" or unconventional juxtapositions—of thoughts, objects, names, etc.; a universal irreverence; and paronomasia.

Writings: *Lebedinaia pesnia* (nd., np.) *Novyi Panteon* (M. 1983), *Natiurmort s prevrashcheniami* (M. "Abrakhas," 1985), *00 [Nol'-Nol']* (1986-87; M. 1991), *Ispoved' shpiona, osobniak* (wr. 1980-85), *Osobniak, Mitin zhurnal* (1988), 21.

ELENA ANDREEVNA SHVARTS (b. 1948, Leningrad)

An only child raised in a household of women, Shvarts never knew her father (a professor at Kiev University), and uses the surname of her mother, who works in the Gorky Theater in today's St. Petersburg. Herself a graduate of the Theater Institute, Shvarts never pursued the theater professionally. She began writing poetry at the age of seven, turned to prose at thirteen, and, in adulthood, to make ends meet, translated from various of the six languages she has studied: German, French, Italian, Polish, English, and Latin.

Although until glasnost Shvarts had practically no publications in Russia, throughout the 1980s she enjoyed the deserved reputation of one of Leningrad's finest young poets. Her verses first appeared in the Tartu University newspaper in 1973 and in the anthology *Circle* (Krug, 1985). Others followed only a decade later. In the meantime, three volumes of her works were printed in the West. With the lifting of censorship and the dramatic changes in publishing practices ushered in under Gorbachev, two slim collections of her poems have been issued in Russia during the last few years.

Shvarts's art derives inspiration from spiritual values and cultural traditions. With sophistication, elegance, subtle fervor, and stylish irony, it treats such questions as the role of the Word, mortality and mutability, the connection between flesh and soul, passion and discipline *cum* denial, and the rich mystery of visions and dreams. To be initiated into Shvarts's poetic world requires a broad knowledge of culture, for the multiple references and resonances range widely throughout literature, myth, and religion. A blend of classical and modern imagery, bold juxtapositions, irregular lines, traditional rhymes, and understated sardonic humor are the hallmark of her style. Perhaps her best—and certainly her most complex and original—works are cycles of poems that form a kind of *poema*, exemplified in the narrative-diary that comprises *The Works and Days of Lavinia, Nun of the Order of the Circumcision of the Heart* (1987).

Shvarts's own tastes in literature suggest the range of her interests and allegiances. While it is unsurprising that she claims Tsvetaeva as her favorite Russian poet, the same cannot be said of love for Baratynsky, Khlebnikov, and Coleridge (for his visionary capacities) among poets and Makanin in prose. Her heterodox tastes as a reader match her self-assured originality as a poet.

Writings: *Tantsuiushchii David* (1984); *Trudy i dni Lavinii, monakhini iz orden obrezaniia serdtsa* (Ardis 1987); *Stikhi* (L./Paris/Munich, 1987); *Storona Sveta* (L. 1989); *Stikhi* (L. 1990)

VIKTORIA SAMOILOVNA TÓKAREVA (b. 1937, Leningrad)

A graduate of the Leningrad Music School who dreamed of becoming an actress, Tokareva enrolled in the Moscow State Institute of Cinematography (VGIK) in 1963, and a year later published her first story. After graduating from VGIK's scriptwriting department in 1967, Tokareva continued to write both fiction and scripts for film and television. In addition to receiving several film awards, she also has enjoyed enormous success as the author of several volumes of stories and short novellas (povesti) published throughout the two decades of "stagnation."

Tokareva's talent has defined itself primarily in ironic stories reminiscent of the satirical sketches of earlier writers such as Nadezhda Teffi and Mikhail Zoshchenko. Brevity, lightness of touch, and inconclusiveness characterize the majority of her laconic narratives, which are peppered with pseudosyllogisms and mocking literary references. Their humor is underlaid with a profound seriousness that has surfaced increasingly since glasnost.

Tokareva's overriding concern is the quest for a meaningful and authentic existence, a quest undertaken in the teeth of human fallibility and discouraging empirical circumstances. Although it often takes the form of a receptivity to romantic love, in her most recent narratives Tokareva has located a more realistic potential for self-realization in familial commitment and professional excellence, which often present an alternative to romance or compensation for its failure.

Success and happiness for the most part recede into the inaccessible distance, for Tokareva's fictional world rests on the philosophical premise (and stylistic device) of discrepancy—between individuals, between aims and means, desires and actual possibilities, expectations and execution, style and essence, etc.

In countless stories (e.g., "Nothing Special" [Nichego osobennogo]) the breezy irony of Tokareva's narrative voice serves a deflective function. It distances her ostensibly ingenuous protagonists, as well as readers, from experiences that otherwise would seem unbearably painful, for the events Tokareva records convey a gloomy picture of human relations (especially marital ties) and social institutions (especially schools, hospitals, and orphanages).

If Tokareva's prose until the mid-1980s wittily explored universal issues and perennial human problems, her most recent works (e.g., "I Am. You Are. He Is" (Ia est'. Ty est'. On est', 1991) have acquired a topical flavor and moralistic overtones. In that respect the story included here exemplifies her glasnost- and post-glasnost fiction.

Writings: O tom, chego ne bylo. Rasskazy (M. 1969); Kogda stalo nemnozhko teplee (M. 1972); Zanuda. Rasskazy (Tallin, 1977); Letaiushchie kacheli. Rasskazy, povest' (M. 1978) (Tallin, 1982); Nichego osobennogo. Povesti i rasskazy (M. 1983); "Druzhba prevyshe vsego," Avrora 3 (1986): 101-22; Letaiushchie kacheli. Nichego osobennogo (M. 1987); "Piat' figur na postamente," Oktiabr' 9 (1987); (Kirka i ofitser," Ogonek 10 (March 1991): 14-16; "Kak ia ob''iavil voinu iaponii," Krokodil 12 (April 1991): 8-9. Skazat'—ne skazat' (M. 1991), Korrida (M. 1993).

MARINA IVANOVNA TSVETÁEVA (1892-1941, Moscow)

One of Russia's most renowned 20th-century poets, Tsvetaeva belongs to that minuscule group of Russian women whose talent has received full recognition, if only posthumously. The grim facts of her personal and professional life (marked by poverty, isolation, a chain of tragic losses) and the chilling circumstances of her suicide by hanging have tinged her biography with the aura of martyrdom that infused her own self-perception.

Known principally as a poet, Tsvetaeva also turned her hand to criticism and a series of prose works that reside on the border of several genres: essay, memoir, character sketch, and autobiography. Belonging to the "prose decade" (1928-1939) of her emigration, these pieces ruminate on culture, ethics, and art while simultaneously attempting to capture a now-vanished moment in Russia's cultural history. They are marked by a precision of factual detail, multiple viewpoints, jagged syntax, an alternation of close-up with a cosmic perspective, a penchant for hyperbole, vivid images, and irony.

The "story" included in this collection was written in 1934 outside of Paris. Unlike Tsvetaeva's other narratives authored during this period, which focus on Russia, "Life Insurance" reveals a rare glimpse of French life as experienced by Tsvetaeva. What the narrative conveys, with scant fictionalization, is Tsvetaeva's profound sense of her "Russianness," her tense anxiety and constant expectation of disaster under conditions of acute material want, as well as her participation in the national myth of Russians' unique generosity and capacity for human empathy. The laconicism, word play, use of colloquialisms, and rapid transfers from dialogue to "inner speech" are characteristic features of Tsvetaeva's prose style. For readers interested in issues of gender, Tsvetaeva's narrative valorization of maternity and her strong contrasting of responses to a tragic fate (however illusory) by the female and male listeners offers rich material for analysis.

Prose Writings in Translation: Marina Tsvetaeva, *A Captive Spirit: Selected Prose*, ed. and trans. J. Marin King (Ardis, 1994; London: Virago, 1983; Ardis, 1980, 1994).

IZABELLA (BELLA) IURIEVNA ULANÓVSKAIA (b. 1943, Irbit in the Urals)

The backgrounds and occupations of Ulanovskaia's parents widely diverged: her mother was a piano teacher, who thrived in an urban environment, her father a specialist in animal breeding, whose profession demanded a rural setting. Ulanovskaia herself, who claims a greater closeness to her father, has retained an affection for the wilds of the far north, from where the family moved to Leningrad in 1946. Her admiration for its inhabitants' strong physicality and her own experiences in hunting emerge in stories that reproduce aspects of the region's topography, customs, and mores.

A graduate of the languages and literatures department at Leningrad State University (1967), after a brief stint at a newspaper, Ulanovskaia became an (unpaid) correspondent for the journal *Neva* and subsequently a member of the group that organized the Dostoevsky Museum (1969-71). At various stages of her life, Ulanovskaia's literary idols have been Iurii Kazakov, Ivan Bunin, and Iury Nagibin, as well as Melville and Thoreau—all of whom possessed a profound knowledge of nature, which figures so prominently in Ulanovskaia's life and fiction.

The vivid detail in which she perceives the natural world marks all of her narratives, of which "Albinos" (Al'binosy, 1979) is the most substantial and ambitious to date. A network of vignettes from her own experiences—presented in a mélange of philosophical reflections, superb descriptions of landscape and mood, and occasional snatches of speech—the text ruminates on the waning or "discolorization" of culture to which the metaphorical title adverts. Her predilection for fragments, for juxtaposing concrete objects and other externally disparate phenomena linked only through psychological association, manifests itself not only in "Albinos," but also in her few shorter publications, as, for example, "A Trip to Kashgar" (Puteshestvie v Kashgar) and "The Frogs' Autumn Excursion" (Osennii pokhod liagushek, 1987).

Writings: "Al'binosy," *Echo* (Paris, 1984) 13: 117-43; "Al'binosy," *Krug*, B.I. Ivanov & Iu. B. Novikov, comp. (L. 1985): 215-44; "Osennii pokhod liagushek," *Neva* (1987) 12: 129-36; "Boevye koty," *Znamia* (1992) 2: 112-22; *Osennii pokhod liagushek* (St. Petersburg: Sovetskii pisatel', 1992).

LIUDMILA EVGENIEVNA ULÍTSKAIA (b. 1943, Bashkiria)

The only child of a biochemist and an agricultural engineer, Ulitskaia grew up in an intellectual household in a communal Moscow apartment. Still a schoolgirl when her parents divorced, she enjoyed close ties with her grandparents. Graduating as a geneticist from Moscow State University (1967), Ulitskaia married a physicist, then a fellow-geneticist, from whom she had two children. After leaving the laboratory where she worked in research, Ulitskaia joined the staff of a theater, and since then has worked as a filmscript writer and a prosaist.

A devotee of Nabokov, Tsvetaeva, Platonov, and Bunin, Ulitskaia may be considered a proponent of "art for art," and protests against the inclusion of ideology and morality in literature. If, as she claims, her major theme is love, then her fiction explores the diversity of its manifestations, whether sexual, domestic, familial, philosophical, or Christian. Ulitskaia's work boasts an unusually rich cast of characters, often Jewish, sometimes on the fringe of society, often vulnerable to disasters that they learn to live with in a spirit of quiet reconciliation (e.g., the loss of their child by an old couple in "Lucky" [Schastlivye]). A matter-of-fact acceptance of sexuality as a "natural" human drive informs Ulitskaia's fictional universe, which sometimes documents extreme or anomalous acts of congress (e.g., rape in "Bron'ka" and a one-night stand between a middle-aged man and his mother's closest friend, also her age, in "Gulia," included in this collection).

Humor occasionally inflects Ulitskaia's narratives, which move rapidly, register precisely rendered settings with economic conciseness, focus on character, and are decidedly gynocentric. She skillfully balances poignancy and an understated intimation of life's seamier, more brutal aspects. Her compact prose, refreshingly free of bathos and purple patches, has a precision that creates the illusion of simplicity. In Russia, however, where her works have started appearing in the last two years, critics such as Mikhail Zolotonosov perceive her as a representative of the "sentimentalist" tradition.

Writings: "Bron'ka," *Ogonëk* (1989) 52: 20-23; "Za kapustoi," *Krest'ianka* (1989) 2:32-33; "Schastlivyi sluchai" and "Bumazhnaia pobeda," *Krest'ianka* (1990) 3: 332-35; "Doch' Bukhary," *Russkaia Mysl'* (1990), also in *Ogonëk* (1991) 2; "Genele-Sumochnitsa," *Novoe Russkoe Slovo* (20 April 1990); "Vtorogo marta togo goda," *Russkaia Mysl'* (July 26 & August 9, 1991); "Narod izbrannyi," *Kontinent* (1990) 65, also in *Piatyi ugol*, Sergei Kaledin, ed. (M. 1991): 126-36.

LARISA LVOVNA VANÉEVA (b. 1953, Novosibirsk)

Born into a family of teachers, Vaneeva received a solid education in the humanities. After graduation she briefly worked as a journalist with a youth newspaper in Novosibirsk before enrolling in Moscow's Institute of Literature, where she studied with Iury Trifonov and Alexander Rekemchuk. She also held a job as a janitor. For over a decade virtually no journal would publish her work. With the dramatic changes in Russian publishing practices of the 1990s, however, Vaneeva's prose appears semi-regularly in collections and anthologies. A passion for nature and an interest in environmental issues, which her fiction conveys, partly account for her having taken up residence outside of Moscow.

A representative of the "new women's prose," Vaneeva combines a matter-of-fact acceptance of the physical side of life with a preference for the modernist devices of abrupt, unexplained temporal and spatial shifts, an elliptical style, a blurring of boundaries between mental and empirical phenomena, and a penchant for omissions that lead to mystification or, sometimes, outright confusion. Much of her technique—especially the treatment of space and relational categories—derives from modernist painting (to which the title of her collection *Out of the Cube* [Iz Kuba] adverts). Violence, degradation, and physical dissolution interplay with lyric nature descriptions and philosophical ruminations in her texts. Her female protagonists undergo such ordeals as rape (e.g., in "Antisin" [Antigrekh] and "Venetian Mirrors" [Venetsianskie zerkala], included in this collection), drug addiction and alcoholism (e.g., in "Parade of the Planets" [Parada planet, wr. 1981]), even as they muse on life in a cosmic and ultimately transcendent vein.

A gynocentric writer who favors a female center of consciousness communicated through quasi-direct discourse, Vaneeva tends to depict men who appear weak, indecisive, or brutal—invariably the objects of gendered subjectivity. What poetry and idealism infiltrate Vaneeva's fictional world are reserved for the sphere of nature, whose grandeur, beauty, and self-perpetuating restorative powers contrast with the frailties of humankind.

Vaneeva's language unconstrainedly mixes slang, vulgarisms, and poetic lexicon, interspersed with references to high and popular culture, both Russian and foreign (e.g., Chardin, the Beatles).

Writings: "Priznak odnogo tallintsa, ili Gibel' Odessy" and "Razvenenie rybok," *Zhenskaia logika*, L. V. Stepanenko and A. V. Fomenko, comp. (M. 1989): 48-65 and 65-99; "Venetsianskie zerkala," *Chisten'kaia zhizn'*, Anatolii Shavkuta, comp. (M. 1990): 159-70; *Iz Kuba. Rasskazy, povest'* (M. 1990); *Skorb' po ploti. Kubichestkii traktat i rasskazy* (M. 1990); "Mezhdu Saturnom i Uranom," *Ne pomniashchaia zla*, Larisa Vaneeva, comp. (M. 1990): 251-314; *Igra tuchi s dozhdëm* (M. 1991); "Antigrekh," *Novye Amazonki*, S, V, Vasilenko, comp. (M. 1991): 224-52.

SVETLANA VASILIEVNA VASILÉNKO (b. 1956, Kapustin Iar)

Vasilenko is acutely aware of her identity as a child of the atomic age. Born in the Russian equivalent of America's Cape Canaveral to a Ukrainian technician and a professional military man who spec ialized in rocketry, Vasilenko spent her first years in the security zone surrounded by a wire fence, which she ironically calls "a garden." In recalling that period, she refers to her "cosmic childhood"—one of remoteness from her perennially absent father but emotional closeness to her mother, whose surname Vasilenko bears. Like countless other Russian children, Vasilenko harbors a special affection for her paternal grandmother in Leningrad, whom she visited annually during her childhood and adolescence.

After moving to Moscow, Vasilenko worked as a fruit hauler, then as a postwoman to support herself. In 1977 Vasilenko married the considerably older engineer whose child she was already carrying (her teenage son now writes short stories). Although Vasilenko had composed poetry since her childhood, she enrolled as a prosaist in the Gorky Literary Institute, where she studied under Baklanov, graduating in 1983. Six years later she completed her training in film directing and the following year began work with Andrei Konchalovsky on a film of Tristan and Isolde.

The story included here was Vasilenko's first publication, in 1982. It created a stir among *literati*, who hailed her as a significant new talent, but to this day remains virtually unknown to the broad reading public. Her second publication came six years later, a time lapse that prompted her shift to writing film scenarios. The majority of her publications since glasnost have appeared in women's collections.

Vasilenko's stories evidence her hypersensitivity to the sound, color, and connotations of language. A rich blend of heightened lyricism, poetic images, and dense network of suggestive motifs, on the one hand, and pungent vulgarisms, minutely observed realia, and elliptical structures, on the other, constitutes her authorial signature. An aura of fatality, of a world irremediably tainted by radiation and a "cosmic rape," hovers over her narratives. Yet they also open up to stunning spiritual revelations and moments of uninhibited physical pleasure that Vasilenko conveys with verbal zest and conviction.

The eponymous heroine of "Shamara," one of Vasilenko's boldest and most colorful narratives, represents a rare instance in recent women's fiction of a female subjectivity that is non-intellectual, sensual, complex, and ultimately inaccessible. The absurdist humor, often whacky and visual, of Vasilenko's "Silly Stories" (Duratskie rasskazy) is similarly unusual for women's prose. The combination of matter-of-factness and wildness that coexist in Vasilenko's world may be found in the anthology of contemporary women's writing she assembled, entitled *The New Amazons* (Novye Amazonki, 1991) and filled with zanily expressive cartoon-like illustrations.

Writings: "Gen smerti," *Vstrechnyi khod* (M. "Stil'," 1989); "Suslik," "Za saigakami," "Zvonkoe imia," "Schast'e," "Kto ikh poliubit?", "Tsaritsa Tamara," *Zhenskaia logika* (M. Sovremennik, 1989): 100-204; "Zvonkoe imia," *Chisten'kaia zhizn'* (M. "Molodaia gvardiia, 1990); "Shamara," *Ne pomniashchaia zla* (M. Moskovskii rabochii, 1990); "Duratskie rasskazy," *Novye Amazonki* (M. Moskovskii rabochii, 1991): 311-22.